Computer Science

A Structured Programming Approach in C

Fourth Edition

Hassan Afyouni, Ed.D.

Behrouz A. Forouzan

Australia • Brazil • Canada • Mexico • Singapore • United Kingdom • United States

Computer Science: A Structured Programming Approach in C, **Fourth Edition**

Hassan Afyouni/Behrouz A. Forouzan

SVP, Product: Cheryl Costantini

VP, Product: Thais Alencar

Portfolio Product Director: Mark Santee

Portfolio Product Manager: Tran Pham

Product Assistant: Ethan Wheel

Learning Designer: Mary Convertino

Senior Content Manager: Michelle Ruelos Cannistraci

Associate Digital Project Manager: John Smigielski

Technical Editor: Danielle Shaw/Nicole Spoto

Developmental Editor: Ann Shaffer/ Mary Pat Shaffer

VP, Product Marketing: Jason Sakos

Director, Product Marketing: Danae April

Product Marketing Manager: Mackenzie Paine

Content Acquisition Analyst: Ashley Maynard

Production Service: Straive

Designer: Erin Griffin

Cover Image Source: iStockPhoto.com/ Ajwad Creative

For product information and technology assistance, contact us at **Cengage Customer & Sales Support, 1-800-354-9706 or support.cengage.com.**

For permission to use material from this text or product, submit all requests online at **www.copyright.com.**

Library of Congress Control Number: 2023901242
ISBN: 978-0-357-50613-4

Cengage
200 Pier 4 Boulevard
Boston, MA 02210
USA

Cengage is a leading provider of customized learning solutions. Our employees reside in nearly 40 different countries and serve digital learners in 165 countries around the world. Find your local representative at **www.cengage.com.**

To learn more about Cengage platforms and services, register or access your online learning solution, or purchase materials for your course, visit **www.cengage.com.**

Notice to the Reader

Printed in the United States of America
Print Number: 01   Print Year: 2023

BRIEF CONTENTS

CONTENTS

Computer programming is the basis of computer science, which is primarily focused on developing and forming logic to solve a specific problem. Over time, many computer programming languages have been created and developed; hence, there are several types of programming structures, and each language falls into a specific category. C is a general-purpose, structured programming language designed and developed to enable programmers to create applications that are machine hardware and operating system independent.

Computer Science: A Structured Programming Approach In C, Fourth Edition, teaches students using the C language. The book offers comprehensive instructions on how to use C constructs along with detailed explanations and examples. Throughout this book, programming best practices are presented with full analysis explaining the use of each C construct.

The Approach

This text has three primary objectives as described here:

> Teach the basic principles of programming as outlined in the ACM (Association for Computing Machinery) curriculum for a foundational computer science class

> Teach the basic constructs of the C language

> Introduce software engineering concepts and coding best practices based on decades of proven experience in industry and academia

The following instructional and programming approaches serve as foundations for this text.

Principle Before Practice: Whenever possible, we develop the principles of a subject before we introduce the language implementation. For example, in Chapter 5 ("Selection — Making Decisions"), we first introduce the concept of logical data and selection, and then we introduce the `if. . . else` and `switch` statements. This approach gives the student an understanding of selection before introducing the nuances of the language.

Coding Techniques: Drawn from industry and classroom experience, coding techniques are demonstrated throughout the text. These demonstrations provide specific suggestions and best practices to help students develop programs that are more efficient and easier to read. Most importantly, students can transfer these lessons to future coding challenges and strengthen their ability to think critically.

Structure and Style: One of our basic tenets is that good habits are formed early. The corollary is that bad habits are hard to break. Therefore, we consistently emphasize the principles of structured programming and software engineering. Throughout each chapter, short code snippets and programs are used to demonstrate techniques. Complete programs are written in a well-documented, consistent style. As programs are analyzed, style and standards are further explained. While we acknowledge that there are many good styles, our experience has shown that if students are exposed to one good style and adopt it, they will be better able to adapt to other good styles. Our experience working with programs that have functioned for 10 to 20 years in real-world environments convinced us that readable and understandable programs are easier to work with than programs written in a terse, cryptic manner. For that reason, and to emphasize the structure of the language, we label the sections in a function with comments. We consistently follow a style that places only one declaration, definition, or statement on a line.

Visual Approach: A brief scan of the book will demonstrate that our approach is visual. There are more than 400 figures, along with more than 80 tables and 250 program examples. This visual approach makes it easy for students to follow the material.

Course Overview

The examples and exercises in this book will help you achieve the following objectives:

> › Use C constructs and syntax
>
> › Understand and work with C Programming structures
>
> › Use logical constructs, such as loops and `if-else` statements
>
> › Read input and display output interactively
>
> › Read and write from text and binary files
>
> › Apply practical use of one-dimensional and multidimensional arrays
>
> › Handle string structures
>
> › Understand the uses and programming of pointers and memory allocation
>
> › Define and use enumerated type, structures, and union types
>
> › Learn how to use bitwise operators and create encoding and decoding programs
>
> › Write and call recursive functions
>
> › Identify the uses and programming of linked lists using pointers

What's New in This Edition?

This edition continues the previous edition's focus on computer programming in a software engineering context. The text conforms to the standards of C18, the latest version of the C language at the time of authoring this book. The order of some chapters was changed in this edition to enhance the logical continuity of the topics covered. A major content change in this edition is the addition of a new chapter on pointers (Chapter 9: "Pointers"), as this topic, which is at the core of the C language, deserves to be explained in detail. Also, the new chapter on recursion (Chapter 14: "Recursion") provides a comprehensive introduction to recursion concepts explained in a simple way and reinforced with real-life scenario examples, exercises, and projects. In addition, throughout the book, the end-of-chapter exercises, problems, and projects have been updated. The following list highlights the updates and changes for each chapter:

> › **Chapter 1: "Introduction to Computers"**
> - ▪ The evolution of computer languages
> - ▪ Computing environments, specifically cloud computing
> - ▪ Waterfall and Agile system development life cycles
> - ▪ Updated end-of-chapter review questions, exercises, problems, and projects
>
> › **Chapter 2: "Introduction to the C Language"**
> - ▪ Updated end-of-chapter review questions, exercises, problems, and projects
>
> › **Chapter 3: "Structure of a C Program"**
> - ▪ Updated end-of-chapter review questions, exercises, problems, and projects
>
> › **Chapter 4: "Functions"**
> - ▪ Updated end-of-chapter review questions, exercises, problems, and projects
>
> › **Chapter 5: "Selection — Making Decisions"**
> - ▪ Updated end-of-chapter review questions, exercises, problems, and projects
>
> › **Chapter 6: "Repetition"**
> - ▪ Updated end-of-chapter review questions, exercises, problems, and projects
>
> › **Chapter 7: "Text Input/Output"**
> - ▪ Updated end-of-chapter review questions, exercises, problems, and projects
>
> › **Chapter 8: "Arrays"**
> - ▪ Updated end-of-chapter review questions, exercises, problems, and projects

> **Chapter 9: "Pointers"**
  - Detailed coverage of the use of pointers, providing beginners with the fundamentals necessary to develop efficient programs
  - Updated end-of-chapter review questions, exercises, problems, and projects

> **Chapter 10: "Strings"**
  - Updated end-of-chapter review questions, exercises, problems, and projects

> **Chapter 11: "Enumerated, Structure, and Union Types"**
  - Updated end-of-chapter review questions, exercises, problems, and projects

> **Chapter 12: "Binary Input/Output"**
  - Updated end-of-chapter review questions, exercises, problems, and projects

> **Chapter 13: "Bitwise Operators"**
  - Updated end-of-chapter review questions, exercises, problems, and projects

> **Chapter 14: "Recursion"**
  - A comprehensive introduction to recursion, covered in a simple way, with full analysis, visuals, and explanations
  - Numerous program examples showing various practical uses of recursion
  - Updated end-of-chapter review questions, exercises, problems, and projects

> **Chapter 15: "Lists"**
  - Various programming techniques that tie in concepts covered throughout the book
  - Updated end-of-chapter review questions, exercises, problems, and projects

Features of the Text

Several features of this book are intended to make it easy for beginning students to understand the concepts presented and ensure a successful learning experience.

Learning Objectives: Each chapter begins with a list of objectives that orient the student to the main topics covered in the chapter.

Color: Color-coding is used to help students decipher program statements. The following colors are used in the program examples and code snippets throughout each chapter:

> `Green`: Comments

> `Brown`: Preprocess directives

> `Purple`: Data types

> `Navy Blue`: C operators

> `Blue`: C keywords

> `Black`: User coding and statements

Figures and Tables: Figures help illustrate a variety of programming concepts throughout the chapters, and many include flowcharts demonstrating step-by-step program logic, as well as short program examples and output. Tables are used to present specific information pertaining to syntax, codes, and other data.

Notes: These blue-shaded elements appear throughout the chapters to provide additional helpful information on specific techniques and concepts.

Algorithms: This feature highlights instances where pseudocode is provided to illustrate a programming concept or describe the necessary steps for a program that students must develop as part of an end-of-chapter problem or project.

Programs: Complete programs presented throughout the chapters provide students with the opportunity to interact with code that has been optimized to show well-documented and consistent style. These programs are analyzed and explained so that students can learn and adopt good programming.

Programming Examples: The "Programming Examples" section contains content and programs intended to emphasize ideas and concepts presented in the chapter and to allow students to further study programming technique and style.

Software Engineering: A discussion of software engineering principles concludes most chapters. The intent is not to replace a separate course in software engineering. Rather, the belief is that by incorporating basic software engineering principles early in their studies, students will be better prepared for a formal treatment of the subject. In general, the software engineering sections directly or indirectly pertain to the chapter material. Where they don't, they discuss general software engineering subjects, such as cohesion, coupling, and quality.

Review Material: The following end-of-chapter material meets two pedagogical objectives: First, it helps the students to review or summarize what they have learned, and second, it tests the students' mastery of the chapter material.

> **Tips and Common Programming Errors:** This resource points out helpful hints and possible problem areas students should pay attention to.

> **Summary:** The chapter summary section contains a concise overview of the key points in the chapter students should understand.

> **Key Terms:** A list of the important terms introduced in the chapter appears after the chapter summary. Definitions of the key terms appear in the glossary.

> **Review Questions:** This section includes a set of multiple-choice questions intended to reinforce the main concepts covered in the chapter.

> **Exercises:** The questions included in this section include both multiple-choice and short-answer questions that ask students to apply concepts presented in the chapter.

> **Problems:** This end-of-chapter section includes short coding problems, generally intended to be run on a computer. They can usually be developed in two to three hours.

> **Projects:** The final section in each chapter includes longer assignments that may take the average student six to nine hours to develop.

> **Appendices:** The appendices are intended to provide quick reference material or to provide a review of material, such as numbering systems, usually covered in a general computer class.

> **Glossary:** A glossary contains definitions for all key terms in the book.

Ancillary Package

Additional instructor resources for this product are available online. Instructor assets include an Instructor's Manual, Educator's Guide, PowerPoint® presentations, a Solution and Answer Guide, Solution files, a test bank powered by Cognero®, and a Transition Guide for the Fourth Edition. Sign up or sign in at *www.cengage.com* to search for and access this product and its online resources.

Instructor's Manual: The Instructor's Manual includes additional instructional material to assist in class preparation, including sections such as "Chapter Objectives," "What's New in This Chapter," and "Chapter Outline."

Educator's Guide: The Educator's Guide contains a detailed outline of the course.

PowerPoint Presentations: The PowerPoint slides can be used to guide classroom presentations, to make available to students for chapter review, or to print as classroom handouts.

Solution and Answer Guide: Solutions to all end-of-chapter assignments are provided along with feedback.

Solutions: Solutions to all programming exercises are available.

Test Bank: Cengage Testing Powered by Cognero® is a flexible, online system that allows you to:

> Author, edit, and manage test bank content from multiple Cengage solutions.

> Create multiple test versions in an instant.

> Deliver tests from your LMS, your classroom, or wherever you want.

Transition Guide: The Transition Guide outlines information on what has changed from the Third Edition.

About the Authors

Hassan Afyouni, Chief Executive Officer, ConServ Gulf (conservgulf.com)
Dr. Hassan Afyouni has been working in the information technology field for more than thirty years. He is a computer scientist specializing in software engineering and database architecture. He is a certified Oracle® RAC Expert, an enterprise architect, and an information technology expert and educator. Dr. Afyouni has been an instructor for several colleges and universities in Canada, the United States, and Lebanon, and he is a respected author of several leading books in the database field. Hassan Afyouni can be reached at *sam@afyouni.net*.

Behrouz A. Forouzan has more than 38 years of electronics and computer science experience in industry and academia. His industry experience includes designing electronic systems. After leaving the industry, he joined De Anza College as a professor of computer science. In addition to this text, he has authored and co-authored nine other textbooks including: *Computer Science: A Structured Approach Using C++*, and *Data Structures: A Pseudocode Approach with C++*, as well as titles on data communication and networking, and TCP/IP protocols.

Acknowledgments

No book of this scope can be developed without the support of many people. Creating the Fourth Edition of this text has truly been a team effort. Special thanks to the Cengage team, Michelle Ruelos Cannistraci, Mary Convertino, and Tran Pham, to Developmental Editors, Ann Shaffer and Mary Pat Shaffer, and to Quality Assurance and Technical Editors, Danielle Shaw and Nicole Spoto. Thanks also to the production team of copyeditors, proofreaders, and compositors at Straive. And many thanks to the reviewers who provided valuable feedback: Dr. John E. Carroll (Tennessee Wesleyan University) and Pranshu Gupta, Ph.D. (DeSales University).

Finally, I dedicate this book to my precious children Aya, Wissam, Sammy, and Luna. Special dedication to a special person in my life, Afaf.

CHAPTER 1

Introduction to Computers

Learning Objectives

When you complete this chapter, you will be able to:

1.1 Describe basic computer system concepts

1.2 Identify the different computing environments and their components

1.3 List and describe the classifications of computer languages

1.4 Identify the steps in the development of a computer program

1.5 Describe the system development life cycle (SDLC)

1.1 Computer Systems

Welcome to computer science! You are about to explore a wonderful and exciting world—a world that offers many challenging and exciting careers. This chapter introduces basic computer science concepts, with a focus on how these concepts pertain to computer programming. You will learn about the hardware and software components of a computer system. You will also learn about the evolution of computer programming languages and how the C language fits into the picture. Finally, you will be introduced to the tools and steps involved in writing a computer program, and review the system development methodology.

Computer systems are found everywhere. They are an essential part of daily life, facilitating interactions with family and friends, governments, and small and large businesses. But what is a computer? A computer is a system made of two major components: hardware and software. The computer hardware is the physical equipment. The software is the collection of programs (instructions) that allow the hardware to do a specific job. **Figure 1-1** represents a computer system.

Computer Hardware

The **hardware** component of a computer system consists of five parts: input devices, central processing unit (CPU), primary storage, output devices, and secondary storage devices such as internal and external hard drives, USB (Universal Serial Bus) devices, and external backup tapes (**Figure 1-2**).

Figure 1-1 A computer system

Computer system

Hardware

Software

Figure 1-2 Basic hardware components

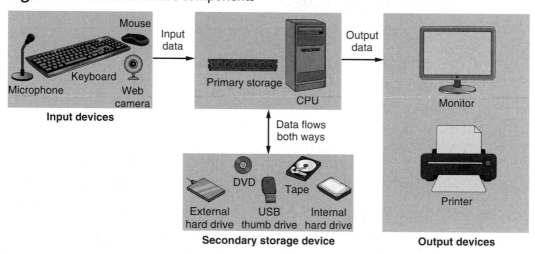

Input devices

Microphone
Keyboard
Mouse
Web camera

Input data

Primary storage
CPU

Data flows both ways

Secondary storage device

External hard drive
DVD
USB thumb drive
Tape
Internal hard drive

Output data

Monitor

Printer

Output devices

The most common **input device** is a keyboard, where programs and data are entered into the computer. Examples of other input devices include a mouse, a pen or stylus, a touch screen, a camera, and a microphone or other audio input unit. The term **input** refers to data flowing into the computer system.

The **central processing unit (CPU)** is responsible for executing instructions such as arithmetic calculations, comparisons among data, and movement of data inside the system. Today's computers may have one, two, or more CPUs. **Primary storage**, also known as **main memory**, is composed of Read Only Memory (ROM) and Random Access Memory (RAM). Programs and data are stored temporarily in main memory during processing. The data in primary storage are erased when the personal computer is turned off or when a user is logged off from a time-sharing computer.

The **output device**, usually a monitor or a printer, allows the user to see the results, or output, of a computer program. If the output is shown on the monitor, it is referred to as a **soft copy**. If it is printed on the printer, it is referred to as a **hard copy**.

Secondary storage, is used for both input and output. It is the place where the programs and data are stored permanently. In a PC, a hard drive is typically used as secondary storage. When the computer is turned off, programs and data remain in the secondary storage, ready for the next use.

Computer Software

Computer software is divided into two broad categories: system software and application software. System software manages the computer resources. Application software, on the other hand, is directly responsible for helping users solve their problems. **Figure 1-3** shows this breakdown of computer software.

Figure 1-3   Types of software

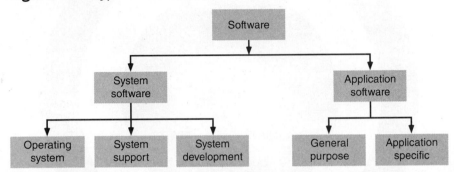

System Software

System software consists of programs that manage a computer's hardware resources and perform information-processing tasks. These programs are divided into three classes: the operating system, system support, and system development.

The operating system provides a user interface (that is the screen the user interacts with, including dialog boxes, buttons to click, and textboxes in which to enter information), as well as access to files and databases. The operating system also interacts with communication systems such as Internet protocols. The primary purpose of this software is to keep the system operating in an efficient manner while allowing the users access to the system.

System support software provides system utilities and other operating services. Examples of system utilities are sort programs and disk format programs. Operating services consist of programs that provide performance diagnosis and statistics.

The last system software category, development software, includes the language translators that convert programs into machine language for execution, debugging tools to ensure that the programs are error-free, and computer-assisted software engineering (CASE) systems that are beyond the scope of this book.

Application Software

We divide application software into two classes: general-purpose software and application-specific software. The first, general-purpose software is purchased from a software developer and can be used for more than one application. Examples of general-purpose software include word processors, database management systems, and computer-aided design systems. They are labeled general purpose because they can solve a variety of user computing problems.

The second type, application-specific software, can be used only for its intended purpose. A general ledger system used by accountants and a material requirements planning system used by a manufacturing organization are examples of application-specific software. They can be used only for the task for which they were designed; they cannot be used for other generalized tasks.

The relationship between system and application software is shown in **Figure 1-4**. In this figure, each circle represents an interface point. The inner core is the hardware. The user is represented by the outer layer. To work with the system, the typical user uses some form of application software. The application software in turn interacts with the operating system, which is a part of the system software layer. The system software provides the direct interaction with the hardware.

If users cannot buy software that supports their needs, then a custom-developed application must be built. In today's computing environment, one of the tools used to develop software is the C language that you will be studying in this text.

Figure 1-4   Relationship between system and application software

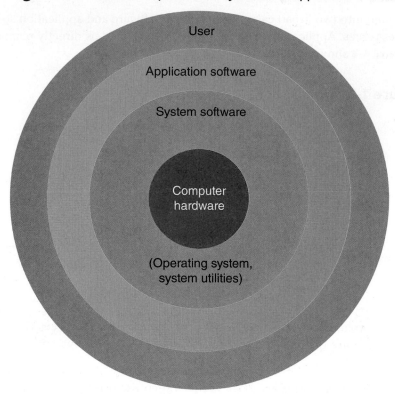

1.2 Computing Environments

In the early days of computers, there was only one environment: the mainframe computer hidden in a central computing department. With the advent of minicomputers and personal computers, the environment changed, resulting in computers on virtually every desktop. In this section we describe several different environments.

Personal Computing Environment

In 1971, Marcian E. Hoff, working for Intel, combined the basic elements of the central processing unit into the microprocessor. This first computer on a chip was the Intel 4004 and was the grandparent many times removed of the chips now used in computers around the world. The rapid development of computer chips ultimately led to the transition from large main frame computers to a smaller, self-contained device known as a personal computer in the 1970s. The market soon diverged into two main types of personal computers. The first type ran the Microsoft DOS operating system and then, later, Microsoft Windows, and were manufactured by many different companies. The term PC (short for "personal computer") is now used to refer primarily to computers that run Microsoft operating systems. The second type were computers manufactured exclusively by Apple. The early versions of these computers were designed to sit on a desktop. Now, personal computing devices take several forms, including smart phones, tablets, laptops, desktops setups with monitors and towers, and all-in-one desktop computers, which combine the CPU and the monitor into one device. **Figure 1-5** shows an array of modern personal computing devices.

Time-Sharing Environment

Although, it is not as common as it used to be, some organizations still employ what is known as a time-sharing environment. In the time-sharing environment, many users are connected to one or more computers. These computers may be minicomputers (nowadays known as servers) or central mainframes. The terminals they use are often nonprogrammable, although today we see more and more microcomputers being used to simulate terminals. Also, in the time-sharing environment, the output devices (such as printers) and secondary storage devices (such as disks) are shared by all of the users. A typical college lab in which a minicomputer is shared by many students is shown in **Figure 1-6**.

Figure 1-5 Modern personal computing devices

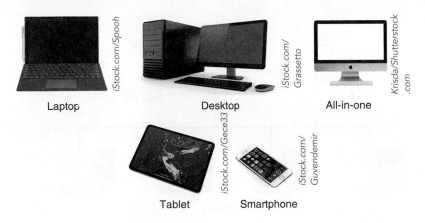

Laptop   Desktop   All-in-one

Tablet   Smartphone

Figure 1-6 Time-sharing environment

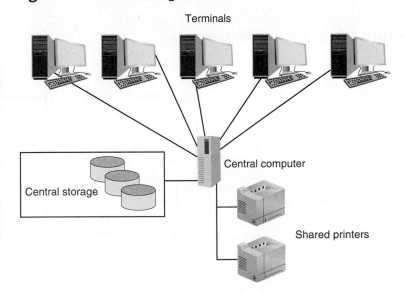

Terminals

Central computer

Central storage

Shared printers

In a time-sharing environment, all computing must be done by the central computer. In other words, the central computer has many duties: It must control the shared resources; it must manage the shared data and printing; and it must do the computing. All of this work tends to keep the computer busy. In fact, it is sometimes so busy that the user becomes frustrated by the computer's slow responses.

Client/Server Environment

A client/server computing environment splits the computing function between a central computer and users' computers. The users are given personal computers or workstations so that some of the computation responsibility can be moved from the central computer and assigned to the workstations. In the client/server environment, the users' workstations are called the client. The central computer, which may be a powerful computer, minicomputer, or central mainframe system, is known as the server. Because the work is now shared between the users' computers and the central computer, response time and monitor display are faster and the users are more productive. **Figure 1-7** shows a typical client/server environment.

Distributed Computing

A distributed computing environment, introduced in the 1990s, is a large network of servers and clients scattered geographically to provide a seamless integration of computing functions. In a distributed computing environment (illustrated in **Figure 1-8**), all resources of the servers, such as CPU and memory, are pooled together to provide

Figure 1-7   The client/server environment

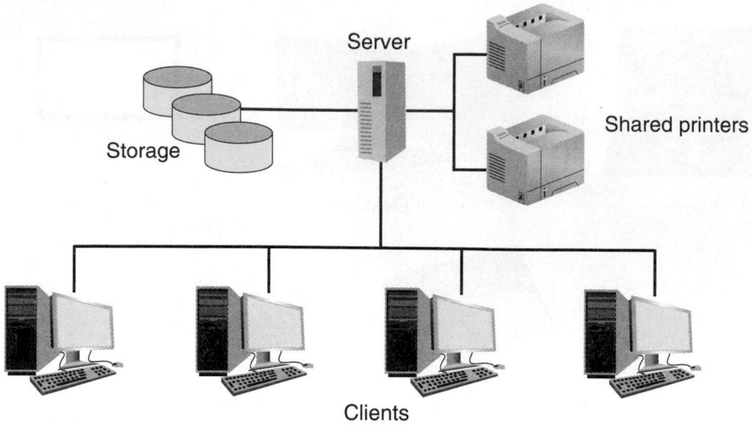

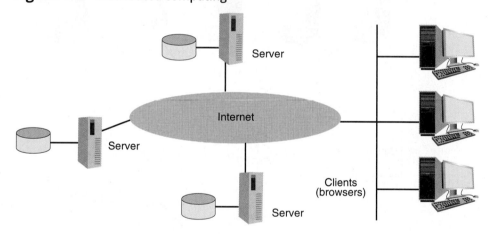

Figure 1-8   Distributed computing

high processing power for applications. This environment provides a reliable, scalable, and highly available network. Large organizations like Amazon use many servers housed in many data centers to provide its shopping services for online consumers.

Cloud Computing

In the early 2000s, cloud computing (illustrated in **Figure 1-9**) started to take shape, eventually becoming an essential computing technology. In a cloud computing environment, servers and storage devices are spread out across multiple geographic areas and connected via the Internet. Cloud computing environments provide services such as Software as a Service (SaaS), Platform as a Service (PaaS), and Infrastructure as a Service (IaaS). For example, Microsoft offers Office 365 software as SaaS, which means users can use the software without having to download it and install it on their own computers. Many high-tech companies, such as Amazon, IBM, Google, Microsoft, and Oracle, offer cloud services.

1.3 Computer Languages

To write a program for a computer, you must use a computer language. Over the years, computer languages have evolved from machine languages to natural languages. A summary of computer languages is provided in **Figure 1-10**.

Figure 1-9 Cloud computing

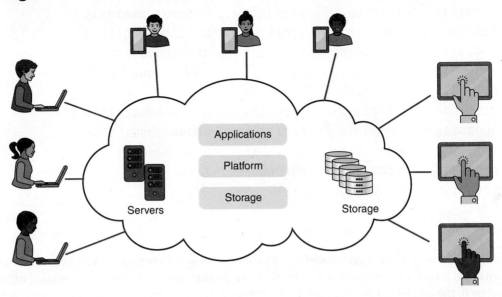

Figure 1-10 Computer language evolution

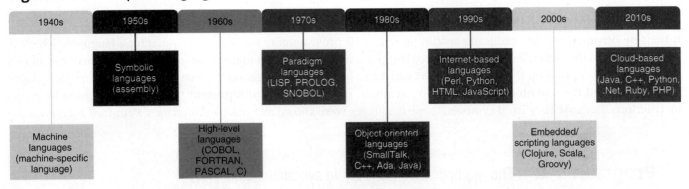

Machine Languages

In the earliest days of computers, the only programming languages available were machine languages. Each computer has its own **machine language**, which is made of streams of 0s and 1s. **Program 1-1** shows an example of a machine language. This program multiplies two numbers and prints the results.

Program 1-1 | Multiplication program in machine language

```
1    00000000    00000100    0000000000000000
2    01011110    00001100    11000010    0000000000000010
3    11101111    00010110    0000000000000101
4    11101111    10011110    0000000000001011
5    11111000    10101101    11011111    0000000000010010
6    01100010    11011111    0000000000010101
```

(continue)

Program 1-1   Multiplication program in machine language *(continued)*

7	11101111	00000010	11111011	0000000000010111
8	11110100	10101101	11011111	0000000000011110
9	00000011	10100010	11011111	0000000000100001
10	11101111	00000010	11111011	0000000000100100
11	01111110	11110100	10101101	
12	11111000	10101110	11000101	0000000000101011
13	00000110	10100010	11111011	0000000000110001
14	11101111	00000010	11111011	0000000000110100
15	01010000	11010100	0000000000111011	
16	00000100	0000000000111101		

The instructions in machine language consist of streams of 0s and 1s because the internal circuits of a computer are made of switches, transistors, and other electronic devices that can be in one of two states: off or on. The off state is represented by 0; the on state is represented by 1. Although more advanced computer languages have been developed since the early days of computing, the hardware of any computer can still only understand machine language. So to actually cause a computer to do something, all programs must ultimately be translated into machine language.

Symbolic Languages

It became obvious that few programs would be written if programmers had to work in machine language, which is very difficult. In the early 1950s, Admiral Grace Hopper, a mathematician and naval officer, developed the concept of a special computer program that would convert programs into machine language. These early programming languages simply mirrored the machine languages using symbols, or mnemonics, to represent the various machine language instructions. Because they used symbols, these languages were known as symbolic languages. **Program 1-2** shows the

Program 1-2 | The multiplication program in symbolic language

```
1       entry   main,<r2>
2       subl2   #12, sp
3       jsb     C$MAIN_ARGS
4       movab   $CHAR_STRING_CON
5       pushal  -8(fp)
6       pushal  (r2)
7       calls   #2,SCANF
8       pushal  -12(fp)
9       pushal  3(r2)
10      calls   #2,SCANF
11      mull3   -8(fp),-12(fp),-
12      pushal  6(r2)
13      calls   #2,PRINTF
14      clrl    r0
15      ret
```

multiplication program in a symbolic language. Note that symbolic language code is usually laid out in three columns, one containing labels, one operators, and one operands. For the sake of simplicity, the code in Program 1-2 contains only operators and operands. The numbers on the left are line numbers included to make the code easier to discuss.

Because a computer does not understand symbolic language, programs written in symbolic languages must be translated to machine language. A special program called an assembler translates symbolic code into machine language. Because symbolic languages had to be assembled into machine language, these languages became known as **assembly languages**. Assembly languages use symbols, or mnemonics, to represent the various machine language instructions. This name is still used today for symbolic languages that closely represent the machine language of a computer's hardware platform.

High-Level Languages

Although symbolic languages greatly improved programming efficiency, they still required programmers to write code specifically designed for the hardware of a particular computer. Working with symbolic languages was also very tedious because each machine instruction had to be individually coded. The desire to improve programmer efficiency and to change the focus from the computer to the problem being solved led to the development of **high-level languages**.

High-level languages are portable to many different computers, allowing the programmer to concentrate on the application problem at hand rather than the intricacies of the computer. High-level languages are designed to relieve the programmer from the details of the assembly language. High-level languages share one thing with symbolic languages, however: They must be converted to machine language. The process of converting them is known as **compilation**.

The first widely used high-level language, FORTRAN, was created by John Backus and an IBM team in 1957; it is still widely used today in scientific and engineering applications. (FORTRAN is an acronym for FORmula TRANslation.) Following soon after FORTRAN was the language COBOL. (COBOL is an acronym for COmmon Business-Oriented Language.) Admiral Hopper was again a key figure in the development of the COBOL business language.

C is a high-level language used for system software and new application code. **Program 1-3** shows the multiplication program as it would appear in the C language. In this program, colors are used to indicate different parts of the code.

Program 1-3 | The multiplication program in C

```
 1   /* This program reads two integers from the keyboard
 2       and prints their product.
 3       Written by:
 4       Date:
 5   */
 6   #include <stdio.h>
 7
 8   int main (void)
 9   {
10   // Local Definitions
11       int number1;
12       int number2;
13       int result;
14
15   // Statements
```

(continue)

Program 1-3   The multiplication program in C *(continued)*

```
16    scanf ("%d", &number1);
17    scanf ("%d", &number2);
18    result = number1 * number2;
19    printf ("%d", result);
20    return 0;
21 } // main
```

Depending on what program you use to write C code, you might see different colors, or you might see your code in simple black and white. You'll learn more about the meaning of the colors used for C code as you become a more experienced programmer. As in Program 1-2, the numbers on the left are line numbers included to make the code easier to discuss.

1.4 Creating and Running Programs

As you learned in the previous section, computer hardware can only understand machine language. In this section, we explain the procedure for turning a program written in C into machine language. The process is presented in a straightforward, linear fashion, but you should recognize that these steps are repeated many times during development to correct errors and make improvements to the code.

It is the job of the programmer to write and test the program. There are four steps in this process: (1) writing and editing the program, (2) compiling the program, (3) linking the program with the required library modules, and (4) executing the program. These steps are shown in **Figure 1-11**.

Writing and Editing Programs

The software used to write programs is known as a **text editor**. In a text editor, you can enter, change, and store character data. It's also possible to use a word processor program, which you would normally use to write letters or reports. But typically, programmers use text editors, included with the compiler, which are specially designed for writing programs. These text editors include features designed to make writing code easier, including applying colors to specific parts of a program.

Some of the features you should look for in a text editor are search commands for locating and replacing statements, copy and paste commands for copying or moving statements from one part of a program to another, and formatting commands that allow you to set tabs to align statements.

After completing a program, you need to save the file so it can be input to the compiler. This saved file is known as a **source file**.

Compiling Programs

The code in a source file must be translated into machine language. This is the job of the **compiler**. The C compiler is actually two separate programs: the **preprocessor** and the **translator**.

The preprocessor reads the source code and prepares it for the translator. While preparing the code, it scans for special instructions known as **preprocessor commands**. These commands tell the preprocessor to look for special code libraries, make substitutions in the code, and in other ways prepare the code for translation into machine language. The result of preprocessing is called the **translation unit**.

After the preprocessor has prepared the code for compilation, the translator does the actual work of converting the program into machine language. The translator reads the translation unit and writes the resulting **object module** to a

Figure 1-11 Building a C program

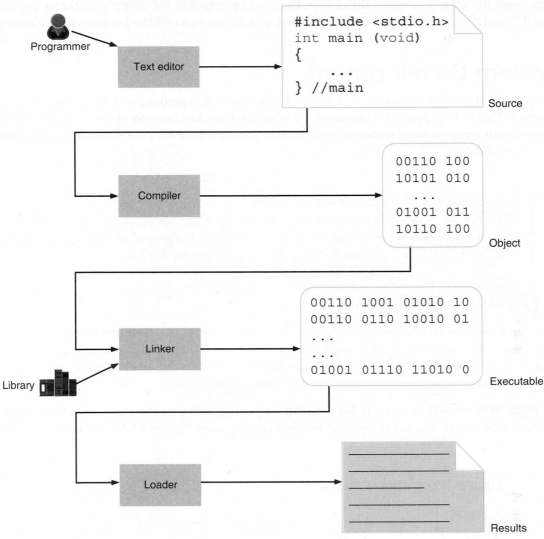

file that can then be combined with other precompiled units to form the final program. An object module is the code in machine language. Even though the output of the compiler is machine language code, it is not yet ready to run; that is, it is not yet executable because it does not have the required C and other functions included.

Linking Programs

As you become a more experienced programmer, you will see that a C program is made up of many functions. When you write a C program, you might actually write some of the functions yourself. However, some functions, such as input/output processes and mathematical library functions, exist elsewhere and must be attached to the program. The **linker** assembles all of these functions, as well as the system's, into a final **executable program**.

Executing Programs

After your program has been linked, it is ready for execution. To execute a program, you use an operating system command, such as run, to load the program into primary memory and execute it. Getting the program into memory is the function of an operating system program known as the **loader**. It locates the executable program and reads it into memory. When everything is loaded, the program takes control and begins execution. In today's integrated development environments, these steps are combined under one mouse click or pull-down window.

In a typical program execution, the program reads data for processing, either from the user or from a file. After the program processes the data, it prepares the output. Data can be output to the user's monitor or to a file. When the program has finished its job, it tells the operating system, which then removes the program from memory.

1.5 System Development

You've now seen the steps that are necessary to build a program. In this section, we discuss *how* we go about developing a program. This critical process determines the overall quality and success of the completed program. If you carefully design each program using well-structured development techniques, your programs will be efficient, error-free, and easy to maintain.

> **Note**
>
> Many computer scientists believe that all programs contain at least one bug—an undetected error—that is just waiting to cause problems, given the right set of circumstances. Programs have run for years without problems only to fail when an unusual situation occurs. Perhaps the most famous bug was the one known as Y2K because it caused programs to fail on January 1, 2000.

System Development Life Cycle

Today's large-scale, modern programming projects are built using a series of interrelated phases commonly referred to as the **system development life cycle**. Although the exact number and names of the phases differ depending on the environment, there is general agreement as to the steps that must be followed. Whatever the methodology, however, today's software engineering concepts require a rigorous and systematic approach to software development.

One very popular development life cycle is the **waterfall model**. Depending on the company and the type of software being developed, this model consists of between five and seven phases. **Figure 1-12** is one possible variation on the model.

Figure 1-12   Waterfall model

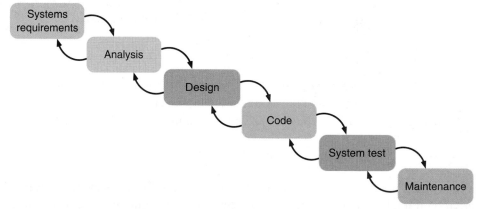

The waterfall model starts with the **systems requirements phase**. In this phase, the systems analyst defines requirements that specify what the proposed system is to accomplish. The requirements are usually stated in terms that the user understands. In the **analysis phase**, the systems analyst looks at different alternatives from a system's point of view. In the **design phase**, the systems analyst determines how the system will be built. This includes determining the functions of the individual programs that will make up the system and designing the required files and the databases. Finally, in the fourth phase, **code phase**, the program is written. This is the phase that is explained in this book. After the programs have been written and tested to the programmer's satisfaction, the project proceeds to **system test**. All of the programs are tested together to make sure the system works as a whole. The final phase, **maintenance phase**, involves keeping the system working after it has been put into production.

Although the implication of the waterfall approach is that the phases flow in a continuous stream from the first to the last, this is not really the case. Note the iteration as indicated by the backward-flowing arrows in Figure 1-12. As each phase is developed, errors and omissions will often be found in the previous work. When this happens, it is necessary to go back to the previous phase to rework it for consistency and to analyze the impact caused by the changes. Hopefully, this is a short rework. However, it often happens that, just as a project reaches the code and test phases, it becomes clear that it actually cannot be implemented and is therefore canceled. Depending on the scope of the project, this can result in losses of millions of dollars and years of development.

Agile, a widely used software development methodology, takes an adaptive, iterative approach to software development, with the goal of expediting the development life cycle and involving the user early in the development process. Customer feedback is solicited regularly and incorporated into program development. Agile advocates speedy development iterations, continuing until the full product is completed and deployed. Agile methodology has gained popularity due to four major advantages: fast development, adaptivity, collaboration of development members, and customer interaction in the development process. **Figure 1-13** illustrates the Agile development model. As you can see, development starts with collecting customer requirements, which the analyst and developer use to begin planning the program. In the design phase, the team creates a design document and product prototype. Coding begins in the development phase. Iterative cycles of customer feedback and development, known as sprints, continue until the product is finally deployed.

Figure 1-13 Agile takes an adaptive, iterative approach to software development

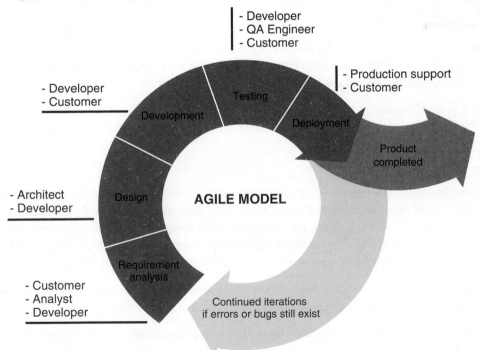

Program Development

Program Development involves these major steps: understanding the problem, developing a solution, writing the program, and then testing it. When you are assigned a program to develop, you will be given a program requirements statement and the design of any program interfaces. You should also receive an overview of the complete project so that you can understand how your part fits into the whole. Your job is to determine how to take the inputs you are given and convert them into the specified outputs. The entire process of creating the program is known as program design. To give you an idea of how this process works, let's look at a simple problem: calculating the square footage of a house. How do we go about doing this?

Understand the Problem

The first step in solving any problem is to make sure you understand it. Start by reading the requirements statement carefully. Then, review your understanding of the problem with the user and the systems analyst. Often this involves asking questions to confirm your understanding.

For example, after reading the requirements statement for the square footage program, you should ask clarifying questions such as:

> What is the definition of square footage?

> How is the square footage going to be used?

- For calculating a quote for home insurance?

- For calculating the amount of paint required to paint the inside of the house? Or the outside?

- For calculating the amount of carpet required to carpet all or part of the house?

> Is the garage included?

> Are closets and hallways included?

Each of the potential uses requires a different measure. If we don't clarify the exact purpose—that is, if we make assumptions about how the output is going to be used—the answer supplied by the program might be wrong.

As this example shows, even the simplest problem statements need clarification. Imagine how many questions must be asked for a programmer to write a program that will contain hundreds or thousands of detailed statements.

Develop the Solution

After you fully understand the problem and have clarified any questions you may have, the next step is to develop the solution. Three tools will help in this task: (1) structure charts, (2) pseudocode, and (3) flowcharts. Generally, you will use only two of them—a structure chart and either pseudocode or a flowchart.

The structure chart is used to design the whole program. Pseudocode and flowcharts, on the other hand, are used to design the individual parts of the program. These parts are known as modules in pseudocode or functions in the C language.

Structure Chart

A structure chart, also known as a hierarchy chart, shows the functional flow of the program. Large programs are complex structures consisting of many interrelated parts; thus, they must be carefully laid out. This task is similar to that used by a design engineer who is responsible for the operational design of any complex item. The major difference between the design built by a programmer and the design built by an engineer is that the programmer's product is software that exists only inside the computer, whereas the engineer's product is something that can be seen and touched.

The structure chart shows how the program will be broken into logical steps; each step will be a separate module. The structure chart shows the interaction between all the parts (modules) of the program.

It is important to realize that the design, as represented by the structure chart, is done before the program is written. In this respect, it is like the architect's blueprint. You would not start to build a house without a detailed set of plans. Yet one of the most common errors of both experienced and new programmers alike is to start coding a program before the design is complete and fully documented.

This rush to start is due in part to programmers thinking they fully understand the problem, when in fact some parts of the problem might not be so obvious, or still require clarification. By taking the time to design the program, programmers will continue to ask questions about the problem, and therefore will gain a better understanding of exactly what kind of program they need to write.

Note | An old programming proverb: Resist the temptation to code.

The second reason programmers code before completing the design is just human nature. Programming is a tremendously exciting task. To see your design begin to take shape, to see your program creation working for the first time, brings a form of personal satisfaction that is a natural high. So often programmers jump in and start writing program code before they are actually ready.

In the business world, the completed structure design is reviewed by a committee, which conducts a structured walk-through of the program to determine whether it satisfies the requirements. The committee usually consists of a representative from the user community, one or two peer programmers, the systems/business analyst, and possibly a representative from the testing organization. The committee then offers constructive suggestions as to how to improve the design.

The primary intent of this review is to increase quality and save time. The earlier a mistake is detected, the easier and less expensive it is to fix it. So even if the walk-through eliminates only one or two problems, the time will be well spent. Naturally, in a programming class, you will not be able to convene a full committee and conduct a formal walk-through. What you can do, however, is review your design with some of your classmates and your professor.

Let's return to the problem at hand: calculating the square footage of a house. Let's assume the following answers to the questions raised in the previous section.

1. The purpose of calculating the square footage is to install linoleum and carpeting.

2. The garage and closets will not be considered.

3. The kitchen and bathrooms will be covered with linoleum; the rest of the house is to be carpeted.

With this understanding, you decide to write separate modules for the kitchen, bathroom(s), bedrooms, family room, and living room. You use separate modules because the various rooms may require a different quality of linoleum and carpeting. The structure chart for the design is shown in **Figure 1-14**.

Figure 1-14   Structure chart for calculating square footage

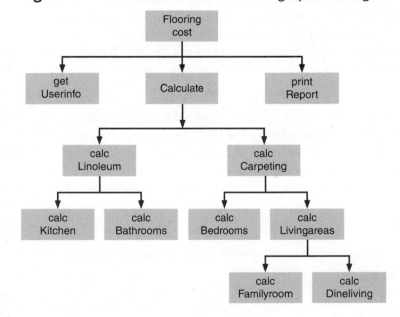

Whether you use a flowchart or pseudocode to complete the design of your program will depend on your experience, the difficulty of the program you are designing, and the culture and standards of the organization where you work. It's helpful for new programmers to first learn program design by flowcharting because a flowchart is a visual tool that is easier to create than pseudocode. On the other hand, pseudocode is more common among professional programmers.

Pseudocode

Pseudocode is part English, part program logic. Its purpose is to describe, in precise algorithmic detail, what the program is being designed to do. This requires defining the steps to accomplish the task in sufficient detail so that they can be converted into a computer program. Pseudocode excels at this type of precise logic. The pseudocode for determining the total amount of linoleum required for the bathroom is shown in **Algorithm 1-1**.

Algorithm 1-1 | Pseudocode for Calculate BathRooms

1 prompt user to enter (input) linoleum price
2 prompt user and read number of bathrooms
3 set total bath area and baths processed to zero
4 while (baths processed < number of bathrooms)
   4.1 prompt user and read bath length and width
   4.2 total bath area = total bath area + bath length * bath width
   4.3 add 1 to baths processed
5 bath cost = total bath area * linoleum price
6 return bath cost
end Algorithm Calculate BathRooms

Most of the statements in pseudocode are easy to understand. A prompt is simply a displayed message telling the user what data are to be entered. The `while` statement is a loop that repeats the three statements that follow it and uses the number of bathrooms read in statement 2 to specify when to stop. Looping is a programming concept that allows us to repeat a block of code. In this case, it allows us to process the information for one or more bathrooms. You will learn more about loops as you become a more experienced programmer.

Flowchart

A flowchart is a program design tool in which standard graphical symbols are used to represent the logical flow of data through a function. The flowchart in **Figure 1-15** shows the design for calculating the area and cost for the bathrooms. A few points merit comment here. This flowchart is basically the same as the pseudocode. It begins with prompts for the price of the linoleum and the number of bathrooms and reads these two pieces of data. The loop reads the dimensions for each bathroom. Finally, when the total area is known, the price is calculated and results are returned to `calcLinoleum`.

Write the Program

Now it's time to write the program! But first, let's review the steps that we've used.

1. Understand the problem.
2. Develop a solution.
   a. Design the program—create the structure chart.
   b. Design the algorithms for the program using either flowcharting or pseudocode or both.
3. Write the program.

When you write a program, you start with the top box on the structure chart and work your way to the bottom. This is known as top-down implementation. You will find that it is a very easy and natural way to write programs, especially if you have done a solid job on your design.

Figure 1-15   Flowchart for calculating bathrooms

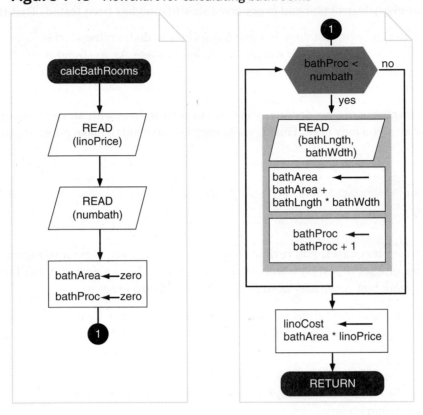

As you begin learning C, your early programs will be so simple that they will require only one module, represented by the top box of the structure chart. Later, however, as you begin to write functions, the structure charts will get larger. At that time you will learn more techniques for writing structured programs. For now, concentrate on writing good pseudocode or flowcharts for the main part of your programs.

Test the Program

After you write a program, you must test it. Program testing can be a very tedious and time-consuming part of program development. As the programmer, you are responsible for completely testing your program. In large development projects, there are often specialists known as quality assurance engineers who are responsible for testing the system as a whole—that is, for testing to make sure all the programs work together.

There are two types of testing: blackbox and whitebox. Blackbox testing is done by the system test engineer and the user. Whitebox testing is the responsibility of the programmer.

Blackbox Testing

Blackbox testing gets its name from the concept of testing the program without knowing what is inside it—that is, without knowing how it works. In other words, the program is like a black box that conceals the code inside it.

Blackbox test plans are developed by looking only at the requirements statement. (This is only one reason why it is so important to have a good set of requirements.) The test engineer uses these requirements and his or her knowledge of systems development and the user's working environment to create a test plan that will then be used when the system is tested as a whole. You should always ask to see this test plan before writing the program. The test engineer's plan will help you make sure you fully understand the requirements and also help you create a solid test plan.

Whitebox Testing

Whereas blackbox testing assumes that the tester knows nothing about the program, whitebox testing assumes that the tester knows everything about the program. In this case, the program is like a glass house in which everything is visible.

Whitebox testing is your responsibility. As the programmer, you know exactly what is going on inside the program. You must make sure that every instruction and every possible situation has been tested. That is not a simple task!

Experience will help you design good test data, but one thing you can do from the start is to get in the habit of writing test plans. You should start the test plan when you are in the design stage. As you build your structure chart, ask yourself what situations, especially unusual situations, you need to test for and make a note of them immediately because you won't remember them an hour later.

When you are writing flowcharts or pseudocode, you need to review them with an eye toward test cases and make additional notes of the cases you may need. Finally, while coding, you need to make notes about test cases that might be needed.

Note	Except for the simplest program, one set of test data will not ensure that the program is error- and bug-free.

When it is time to construct test cases, you review your notes and organize them into logical sets. Except for very simple student programs, one set of test data will never completely validate a program. For large-scale development projects, 20, 30, or even more test cases may need to be run to validate a program.

Finally, while you are testing, you must think of more test cases. Again, write them down and incorporate them into your test plan. After your program is finished and in production, you will need the test plan again when you make modifications to the program.

How do you know when a program is completely tested? In reality, there is no way to know for sure. But there are a few things you can do to help the odds. While some of these concepts will not be clear until you have read other chapters, they are included here for completeness.

1. Verify that every line of code has been executed at least once. Fortunately, there are programming tools on the market today that will do this monotonous task.

2. Verify that every conditional statement in your program has executed both the true and false branches, even if one of them is null.

3. For every condition that has a range, make sure the tests include the first and last items in the range, as well as items below the first and above the last—the most common mistakes in array range tests occur at the extremes of the range.

4. If error conditions are being checked, make sure all error logic is tested. This may entail making temporary modifications to the program to force the errors. (For instance, an input/output error usually cannot be created—it must be simulated.)

Software Engineering

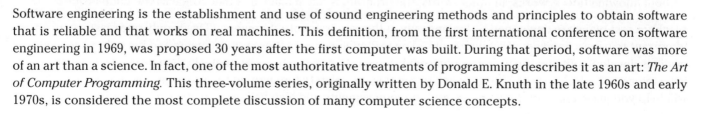

Software engineering is the establishment and use of sound engineering methods and principles to obtain software that is reliable and that works on real machines. This definition, from the first international conference on software engineering in 1969, was proposed 30 years after the first computer was built. During that period, software was more of an art than a science. In fact, one of the most authoritative treatments of programming describes it as an art: *The Art of Computer Programming*. This three-volume series, originally written by Donald E. Knuth in the late 1960s and early 1970s, is considered the most complete discussion of many computer science concepts.

Because the science and engineering base for building reliable software did not yet exist, programs written in the 1950s and 1960s were a maze of complexity known as "spaghetti code." It was not until Edsger Dijkstra wrote a letter to the editor of the *Communications of the ACM* (Association of Computing Machinery) in 1968 that the concept of structured programming began to emerge.

Dijkstra was working to develop algorithms that would mathematically prove program accuracy. He proposed that any program could be written with only three constructs or types of instructions: (1) sequences, (2) the if...else selection statement, and (3) the while loop. As you will see, language developers have added constructs, such as the for loop and the switch in C. These additional statements are simply enhancements to Dijkstra's basic constructs that make programming easier. Today, virtually all programming languages offer structured programming capabilities.

Throughout this text you will learn about the concepts of good software engineering. Chief among them is the concept of structured programming and a sound programming style. The "Software Engineering" section in each chapter will include a discussion of these concepts, with specific emphasis on the application of the material in the chapter.

The tools of programming design have also changed over the years. In the first generation of programming, one primary tool was a block diagram. This tool provided boxes, diamonds, and other flowchart symbols to represent different instructions in a program. Each instruction was contained in a separate symbol. This concept allowed programmers to write a program on paper and check its logic flow before they entered it in the computer.

With the advance of symbolic programming, the block diagram gave way to the flowchart. Although the block diagram and flowchart look similar, the flowchart does not contain the detail of the block diagram. Many instructions are implied by the descriptive names put into the boxes; for example, the read statements in **Figure 1-15** imply the prompt. Flowcharts have largely given way to other techniques in program design, but they are still used today by many programmers for working on a difficult logic problem.

Today's programmers are most likely to use a high-level design tool such as tight English or pseudocode. We will use pseudocode throughout the text to describe many of the algorithms you will be developing.

Finally, the last several years have seen the automation of programming through the use of computer-assisted software engineering (CASE) tools. These tools make it possible to determine requirements, design software, and develop and test software in an automated environment using programming workstations. The discussion of the CASE environment is beyond the scope of this text and is left for courses in systems engineering.

 # Tips and Common Programming Errors

1. Become familiar with the text editor in your system so you will be able to create and edit your programs efficiently. The time spent learning different techniques and shortcuts in a text editor will save time in the future.

2. Also, become familiar with the compiler commands and keyboard shortcuts. On most computers, a variety of options are available to be used with the compiler. Make yourself familiar with all of these options.

3. Read the compiler's error messages. Becoming familiar with the types of error messages and their meanings will be a big help as you learn C.

4. Remember to save and compile your program each time you make changes or corrections in your source file. When your program has been saved, you won't lose your changes if a program error causes the system to fail during testing.

5. Run your program many times with different sets of data to be sure it does what you want.

6. The most common programming error is not following the old proverb to "resist the urge to code." Make sure you understand the requirements and take the time to design a solution before you start writing code.

Summary

> A computer system consists of hardware and software.

> Computer hardware consists of a central processing unit (CPU), primary memory, input devices, output devices, and secondary storage.

> Software consists of two broad categories: system software and application software.

> The components of system software are the operating system, system support, and system development.

> Application software is divided into general-purpose applications and application-specific software.

> Over the years, programming languages have evolved from machine language, to symbolic language, to high-level languages.

> The C language is a high-level language.

> The software used to write programs is known as a text editor.

> The file created by a text editor is known as a source file.

> The code in a source file must be translated into machine language using the C compiler, which is made of two separate programs: the preprocessor and the translator.

> The file created by the compiler is known as an object module.

> An object module is linked to the standard functions necessary for running the program by the linker.

> A linked program is run using a loader.

> The system development life cycle is a series of interrelated steps that provide a rigorous and systematic approach to software development.

> To develop a program, a programmer must complete the following steps:

1. Understand the problem
2. Develop a solution using structure charts and either flowcharts or pseudocode
3. Write the program
4. Test the program

> The development of a test plan starts with the design of the program and continues through all steps in program development.

> Blackbox testing consists primarily of testing based on user requirements.

> Whitebox testing, executed by the programmer, tests the program with full knowledge of its operational weaknesses.

> Testing is one of the most important parts of your programming task. You are responsible for whitebox testing; the systems analyst and user are responsible for blackbox testing.

> Software engineering is the application of sound engineering methods and principles to the design and development of application programs.

Key Terms

Agile

analysis phase

application software

application-specific software

assembly languages

blackbox testing

central processing unit (CPU)

client

client/server

code phase

compilation

compiler

computer language

computer system

design phase

development software

distributed computing environment

executable program

flowchart

general-purpose software

hard copy

hardware

high-level languages

input

input device

linker

loader

machine language

main memory

maintenance phase

object module

operating system

output device

PC

personal computer

preprocessor

preprocessor commands

primary storage

program development

pseudocode

secondary storage

server

soft copy

software

source file

structure chart

symbolic languages

system development life cycle

system software

system support software

systems requirements phase

system test

text editor

time-sharing environment

translation unit

translator

waterfall model

whitebox testing

Review Questions

1. Computer software is divided into two broad categories: system software and operational software.
   a. True   b. False

2. The operating system provides services such as a user interface, file and database access, and interfaces to communications systems.
   a. True   b. False

3. The first step in system development is to create a source program.
   a. True   b. False

4. The programmer design tool used to design the whole program is the flowchart.
   a. True   b. False

5. Blackbox testing gets its name from the concept that the program is being tested without knowing how it works.
   a. True   b. False

6. Which of the following is a component(s) of a computer system?
   a. Hardware
   b. Software
   c. Both hardware and software
   d. Pseudocode
   e. System test

7. Which of the following is not an example of application software?
   a. Database management system
   b. Language translator
   c. Operating system
   d. Accounting system
   e. Virus detection

8. Which of the following is not a computer language?
   a. Assembly/symbolic language
   b. Binary language
   c. High-level languages
   d. Machine language
   e. Natural language

9. The computer language that most closely resembles machine language is _____.
   a. assembly/symbolic
   b. COBOL
   c. FORTRAN
   d. high level

10. The tool used by a programmer to convert a source program to a machine language object module is a _____.
    a. compiler
    b. language translator
    c. linker
    d. preprocessor
    e. text editor

11. The _____ contains the programmer's original program code.
    a. application file
    b. executable file
    c. object file
    d. source file
    e. text file

12. The series of interrelated phases that is used to develop computer software is known as _____.
    a. program development
    b. software engineering
    c. system development life cycle
    d. system analysis
    e. system design

13. The _____ is a program design tool that is a visual representation of the logic in a function within a program.
    a. flowchart
    b. program map
    c. pseudocode
    d. structure chart
    e. waterfall model

14. The test that validates a program by ensuring that all of its statements have been executed—that is, by knowing exactly how the program is written—is _____.
    a. blackbox testing
    b. destructive testing
    c. nondestructive testing
    d. system testing
    e. whitebox testing

15. Which of the following is not an advantage of an Agile software development model?
    a. Rapid development
    b. Customer involvement
    c. Very structured
    d. Adaptive
    e. Team collaboration

Exercises

16. Describe the two major components of a computer system.

17. Computer hardware is made up of five parts. List and describe them.

18. Describe the major differences between a time-sharing and a client/server environment.

19. Describe the two major categories of software.

20. What is the purpose of an operating system?

21. Identify at least two types of system software that you will use when you write programs.

22. Give at least one example of general-purpose and one example of application-specific software.

23. List the levels of computer languages discussed in the text.

24. What are the primary differences between symbolic and high-level languages?

25. What is the difference between a source program and an object module?

26. Describe the basic steps in the system development life cycle.

27. What documentation should a programmer receive to be able to write a program?

28. List and explain the steps that a programmer follows in writing a program.

29. Describe the three tools that a programmer may use to develop a program solution.

30. What is meant by the old programming proverb, "Resist the temptation to code"?

31. What is the difference between blackbox and whitebox testing?

32. What is software engineering?

Problems

33. Write pseudocode for `calcLivingAreas`, based on the structure chart shown in Figure 1-14.

34. Create a flowchart for a routine task, such as calling a friend, that you do on a regular basis.

35. Write pseudocode for the flowchart you created in Problem 34.

36. Create a flowchart to convert Fahrenheit temperature to Celsius and then write pseudocode for the flowchart.

CHAPTER 2

Introduction to the C Language

Learning Objectives

When you complete this chapter, you will be able to:

2.1   Describe the development of the C language

2.2   Describe the structure of a C-language program

2.3   Create good identifiers for objects in a program

2.4   List, describe, and use the C basic data types

2.5   Create and use variables in a program

2.6   Create and use constants in a program

2.7   Use simple input and output statements

2.1 Background

In this chapter you will learn about the basics of the C language. You will write your first program, which is traditionally known in C as the "Hello World," or "Greeting," program. Along the way you will learn about the concepts of data types, constants, and variables. Finally, you will learn about two C library functions that read and write data. Because this chapter is just an introduction to C, most of these topics are covered only in sufficient detail to enable you to write your first program. They will be fully developed in future chapters.

We'll start with the evolution of the C language. Computer languages evolved from machine languages to high-level languages like C. Because you are going to spend considerable time working with C, you should have some idea of its origins and evolution.

C is a structured programming language. It is considered a high-level language because it allows the programmer to concentrate on the problem at hand and not worry about the machine the program will be using. While many languages claim to be machine-independent, C is one of the closest to achieving that goal. That is another reason why it is used by software developers whose applications have to run on many different hardware platforms.

C, like most modern languages, is derived from ALGOL, the first language to use a block structure made up of sequence of code statements. ALGOL never gained wide acceptance in the United States, but it was widely used in Europe.

ALGOL's introduction in the early 1960s paved the way for the development of structured programming concepts. Some of the first work was done by two computer scientists, Corrado Bohm and Giuseppe Jacopini, who published a paper in 1966 that defined the concept of structured programming. Another computer scientist, Edsger Dijkstra, popularized this concept. His letter to the editors of the *Communications of the ACM* (Association of Computing Machinery) brought the structured programming concept to the attention of the computer science community.

Several obscure languages preceded the development of C. In 1967, Martin Richards developed a language he called Basic Combined Programming Language, or BCPL. Ken Thompson followed in 1970 with a similar language he simply called B. B was used to develop the first version of UNIX, one of the popular network operating systems in use today. Finally, in 1972, Dennis Ritchie developed C, which took many concepts from ALGOL and BCPL. This path, along with several others, is shown in **Figure 2-1**.

Figure 2-1   Taxonomy of the C language

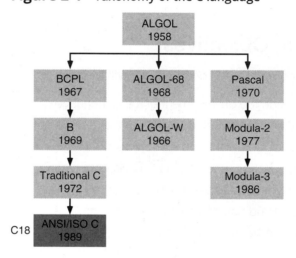

What is known as traditional C is this 1972 version of the language, as documented and popularized in a 1978 book, *The C Programming Language,* by Brian W. Kernighan and Dennis Ritchie. In 1983, the American National Standards Institute (ANSI) began the definition of a standard for C. It was approved in December 1989. In 1990, the International Standards Organization (ISO) adopted the ANSI standard. This version of C is known as C89.

In 1995, minor changes were made to the standard. This version is known as C95. A much more significant update was made in 1999. The changes incorporated into the standard, now known as C99, are summarized in the following list.

1. Extensions to the character type to support non-English characters

2. A Boolean type

3. Extensions to the integer type

4. Inclusion of type definitions in the `for` statement

5. Addition of imaginary and complex types

In 2011 the C standards known as C11 incorporated the C++ style line comment (//). In addition, C11 included new features like multithreading and bounds-checking, and other improvements that allowed for better compatibility with C++. In 2018, a new version of C, known as C18, was published. It contains technical corrections but no new features. This text is based on C18 standards.

2.2 C Programs

It's time to write your first C program! This section will present and demonstrate the basic parts of a C program.

Structure of a C Program

Every C program is made of one or more preprocessor commands, a global declaration section, and one or more functions. The global declaration section comes at the beginning of the program. This will be discussed more later, but the basic idea of global declarations is that they are visible to all parts of the program.

The work of the program is carried out by its **functions**, blocks of code that accomplish a task within a program. One, and only one, of the functions must be named `main`. The `main` function is the starting point for the program. All functions in a program, including `main`, are divided into two sections: the declaration section and the statement section. The declaration section is at the beginning of the function. It describes the data that you will be using in the function. Declarations in a function are known as local declarations because they are visible only to the function that contains them. (By contrast, global declarations, which you will learn about later, are visible to every function in the program.)

The statement section follows the declaration section. It contains the instructions that cause the computer to do something, such as add two numbers. In C, these instructions are written in the form of **statements**, which gives the name for the section.

Figure 2-2 shows the parts of a simple C program. Everything in this program is explained except for the preprocessor commands. They are special instructions to the preprocessor that tell it how to prepare the program for compilation. One of the most important of the preprocessor commands, and one that is used in virtually all programs, is include. The include command tells the preprocessor that the information from selected libraries known as **header files** is needed. In today's complex programming environments, it is almost impossible to write even the smallest of programs without at least one library function. In your first program, you will use one include command to tell C that you need the input/output library to write data to the monitor.

Figure 2-2 Structure of a C program

```
Preprocessor directives
Global declarations
int main (void)
{
       Local declarations
       Statements
} // main
Other functions as required.
```

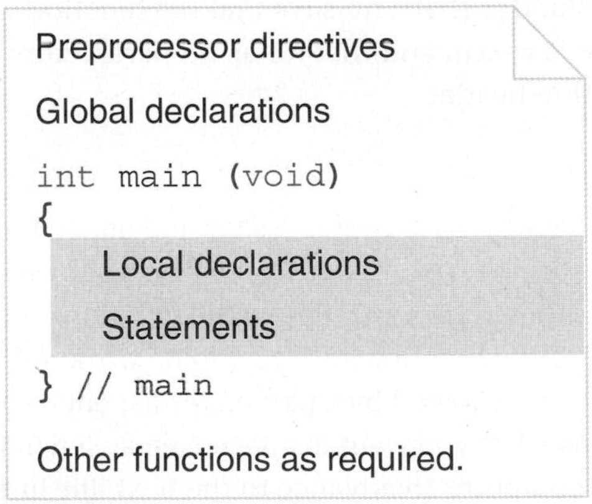

Your First C Program

Your first C program will be very simple (see **Figure 2-3**). It will have only one preprocessor command, no global declarations, and no local definitions. Its purpose will be simply to print a greeting to the user. Therefore, its statement section will have only two statements: one that prints a greeting and one that stops the program.

Figure 2-3 The greeting program

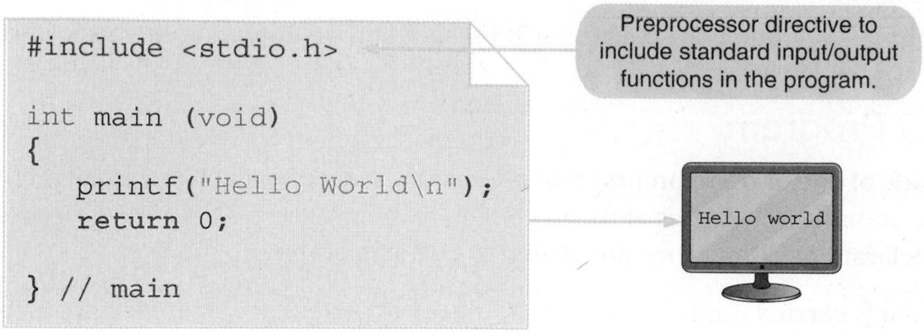

```
#include <stdio.h>

int main (void)
{
    printf("Hello World\n");
    return 0;

} // main
```

Preprocessor directive to include standard input/output functions in the program.

Hello world

Preprocessor Commands

The preprocessor commands come at the beginning of the program. All preprocessor commands start with a pound sign (#); this is just one of the rules of C known as its syntax. Preprocessor commands can start in any column, but they traditionally start in column 1.

The preprocessor command tells the compiler to include the standard input/output library file in the program. You need this library file to print a message to the terminal. Printing is one of the input/output processes identified in this library. The complete syntax for this command is shown below.

```
#include <stdio.h>
```

The syntax of this command must be exact. Because it is a preprocessor command, it starts with the pound sign. There can be no space between the pound sign and the keyword, include. Include means just what you would think it does. It tells the preprocessor that you want the library file in the pointed brackets (< >) included in your program. The name of the header file is stdio.h. This is an abbreviation for "standard input/output header file."

main

The executable part of the program begins with the function main, which is identified by the function header shown below. For now, all you need to understand is that int says that the function will return an integer value to the operating system, that the function's name is main, and that it has no parameters (the parameter list is void). Note that there is no punctuation after the function header.

```
int main (void)
```

Within main there are two statements: one to print your message and one to terminate the program. The print statement uses a library function to do the actual writing to the monitor. To invoke or execute this print function, you **call** it—that is, you include a statement that explicitly refers to the function and specifies any parameters may require, which are values the program must pass the function so it can do its work. All function call statements consist of the name of the function, in this case printf, followed by a parameter list enclosed in parentheses. For your simple program, the parameter list simply contains what you want displayed, enclosed in two double quote marks (" . . . "). The \n at the end of the message tells the computer to advance to the next line in the output.

The last statement in your program, return 0, terminates the program and returns control to the operating system. One last thing: The function main starts with an open brace ({) and terminates with a close brace (}).

Comments

Although it is reasonable to expect that a good programmer should be able to read code, sometimes the meaning of a section of code is not entirely clear. This is especially true in C. Thus, it is helpful if the person who writes the code places some explanations, known as **comments**, in the code to help the reader. Such comments are merely internal program documentation. The compiler ignores these comments when it translates the program into executable code. To identify a comment, C uses two different formats: block comments and line comments.

Block Comment

A **block comment** is used when the comment will span several lines. This comment is called a format block comment. It uses opening and closing comment tokens. A **token** is one or more symbols understood by the compiler to indicate code. Each comment token is made of two characters that, taken together, form the token; there can be no space between them. The opening token is /* and the closing token is */. Everything between the opening and closing comment tokens is ignored by the compiler. The tokens can start in any column and they do not have to be on the same line. The only requirement is that the opening token must precede the closing token. **Figure 2-4** shows two examples of block comments.

Figure 2-4 Examples of block comments

```
/*   This is a block comment that
     covers two lines.                */
/*
**   It is a very common style to put the opening token
**   on a line by itself, followed by the documentation
**   and then the closing token on a separate line. Some
**   programmers also like to put asterisks at the beginning
**   of each line to clearly mark the comment.
*/
```

Line Comment

The second format, the **line comment**, uses two slashes (//) to identify a comment. This format does not require an end-of-comment token; the end of the line automatically ends the comment. Programmers generally use this format for short comments. The line-comment token can start anywhere on the line. **Figure 2-5** contains two examples of line comments.

Figure 2-5 Examples of line comments

```
// This is a whole line comment
a = 5; // This is a partial line comment
```

Although they can appear anywhere, comments cannot be nested. In other words, comments inside comments are not allowed. After the compiler sees an opening block-comment token, it ignores everything it sees until it finds the closing token. Therefore, the opening token of the nested comment is not recognized, and the ending token that matches the first opening token is left standing on its own. This error is shown in **Figure 2-6**.

Figure 2-6   Nested block comments are invalid

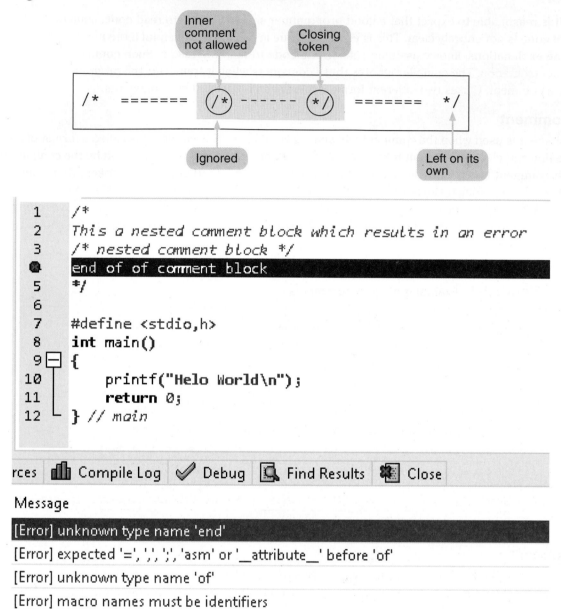

The Greeting Program

Program 2-1 shows the greeting with comments at the beginning explaining what the program is going to do. It should be emphasized here that each program begins with documentation explaining the purpose of the program. This is considered a best practice according to professional programming style. Program 2-1 also includes comments identifying the declaration and statement sections. The numbers on the left in Program 2-1, and in other programs in the text, are line numbers that you can use as references when discussing the code. They are not part of the program.

Program 2-1 | The greeting program

```
1   /* The greeting program. This program demonstrates
2      some of the components of a simple C program.
3      Written by: your name here
4      Date:  date program written
5   */
6   #include <stdio.h>
7
8   int main (void)
9   {
10  // Local Declarations
11
12  // Statements
13
14      printf("Hello World!\n");
15
16      return 0;
17  } // main
```

2.3 Identifiers

One feature present in all high-level computer languages is the identifier. Identifiers allow the programmer to name data and other objects in the program. Each identified object in the computer is stored at a unique address. The main purpose of the identifiers is to symbolically represent data locations. Otherwise, we would have to know and use each object's address, which would make programming very difficult. Rather than using specific memory addresses, it's simpler to assign identifiers to data and let the compiler keep track of where the data are physically located.

Different programming languages use different syntactical rules to form identifiers. In C, the rules for identifiers are very simple. The only valid name symbols are the capital letters A through Z, the lowercase letters a through z, the digits 0 through 9, and the underscore. The first character of the identifier cannot be a digit.

To avoid confusion, make sure your names do not duplicate system names. For example, do not begin an application program with an underscore, because many of the identifiers in the C system libraries start with an underscore. Also, keep in mind that names cannot be keywords. Keywords, also known as reserved words, include syntactical words, such as if and while.

Good identifier names are descriptive but short and often contain abbreviations. One way to abbreviate an identifier is to remove any vowels in the middle of the word. For example, student could be abbreviated stdnt. C allows names to be up to 63 characters long. If the names are longer than 63 characters, then only the first 63 are used. **Table 2-1** summarizes the rules for identifiers.

Table 2-1   Rules for Identifiers

1. First character must be alphabetic character or underscore.
2. Must consist only of alphabetic characters, digits, or underscores.
3. First 63 characters of an identifier are significant.
4. Cannot duplicate a keyword.

You might be curious as to why the underscore is included among the possible characters that can be used for an identifier. It is there so that you can separate different parts of an identifier. To make identifiers descriptive, you may combine two or more words. When the names contain multiple words, the underscore makes it easier to read the name. As indicated earlier, an identifier must start with a letter or underscore; it may not include a space or a hyphen.

Another way to separate the words in a name is to capitalize the first letter in each word. The traditional method of separation in C uses the underscore. A growing group of programmers, however, prefer to capitalize the first letter of each word. **Table 2-2** contains examples of valid and invalid names.

Two more comments about identifiers. Note that some of the identifiers in Table 2-2 are capitalized—that is, they start with uppercase letters. Typically, capitalized names are reserved for preprocessor-defined names. The second comment is that C is case sensitive. This means that even though two identifiers are spelled the same, if the case of each corresponding letter doesn't match, C thinks of them as different names. Under this rule, num, Num, and NUM are three different identifiers.

Table 2-2   Examples of valid and invalid names

VALID NAMES		INVALID NAMES	
`a`	`// Valid but poor style`	`$sum`	`// $ is illegal`
`student_name`		`2names`	`// First char digit`
`_aSystemName`		`sum-salary`	`// Contains hyphen`
`_Bool`	`// Boolean System id`	`stdnt Nmbr`	`// Contains spaces`
`INT.MIN`	`// System Defined Value`	`int`	`// Keyword`

2.4 Types

A **type** defines a set of values and a set of operations that can be applied on those values. For example, a light switch can be compared to a computer type. It has a set of two values, on and off. Only two operations can be applied to a light switch: turn on and turn off.

The C language has defined a set of types that can be divided into four general categories: void, integral, floating-point, and derived, as shown in **Figure 2-7**.

Figure 2-7   Data types

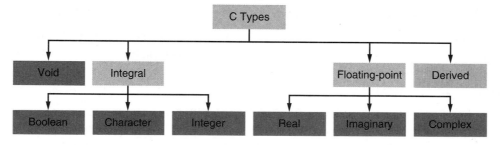

This chapter focuses on only the first three types (void, Integral, and Floating-point). You will learn more about the derived type as you gain more experience as a programmer.

Void Type

The void type, designated by the keyword `void`, has no values and no operations, Although having no values and operations might seem unusual, the `void` type is a very useful data type. For example, it is used to designate that a function has no parameters as we saw in the `main` function. It can also be used to specify that a function has no return value. It can also be used to define a pointer to generic data as you will learn as you become a more experienced programmer.

Integral Type

The C language has three integral types: Boolean, character, and integer. Integral types cannot contain a fraction part; they are whole numbers.

Boolean

With the release of C99, the C language incorporated a Boolean type. Named after the French mathematician/philosopher George Boole, a Boolean type can represent only two values: `true` or `false`. Prior to C99, C used integers to represent the Boolean values: a nonzero number (positive or negative) was used to represent true, and zero was used to represent false. For backward compatibility, integers can still be used to represent Boolean values; however, it is recommended that new programs use the Boolean type. The Boolean type, which is referred to by the keyword `bool`, is stored in memory as 0 (`false`) or 1 (`true`).

Character

The third type is character. Although characters are thought of as the letters of the alphabet, a computer has another definition. To a computer, a character is any value that can be represented in the computer's alphabet, or as it is better known, its character set. As illustrated in **Figure 2-8**, C standard provides two character types: `char` and `wchar_t`. The latter, `wchar_t`, is a wide character data type used to represent characters that require more memory than standard `char` data type.

Figure 2-8   Character types

Most computers use the American Standard Code for Information Interchange (ASCII—pronounced "ask-key") alphabet. You do not need to memorize this alphabet as you did when you learned your natural languages; however, you will learn many of the special values by using them.

Most of the personal, mini-, and mainframe computers use 1 byte to store the `char` data types. A byte is 8 bits. With 8 bits, there are 256 different values in the `char` set. Although the size of `char` is machine dependent and varies from computer to computer, normally it is 1 byte, or 8 bits.

If you examine the ASCII code carefully, you will notice that there is a pattern to its alphabet that corresponds to the English alphabet. The first 32 ASCII characters and the last ASCII character are control characters. They are used to control physical devices, such as monitors and printers, and in telecommunication systems. The rest are characters that are used to compose words and sentences.

All the lowercase letters are grouped together, as are all the uppercase letters and the digits. Many of the special characters, such as the shift characters on the top row of the keyboard, are grouped together, but some are found spread throughout the alphabet.

What makes the letter *a* different from the letter *x*? In English, it is the visual formation of the graphic associated with the letter. In the computer, it is the underlying value of the bit configuration for the letter. The letter *a* is binary `0110 0001`. The letter *x* is `0111 1000`. The decimal values of these two binary numbers are 97 and 120, respectively.

To support non-English languages and languages that don't use the Roman alphabet, the C99 standard created the wide character type (`wchar_t`). Without going into all of the complexities, C supports two international standards, one for four-type characters and one for two-byte characters. Both of these standards support the traditional characters found in ASCII; that is, all extensions occur above the last ASCII character. The original ASCII characters are now known as the basic Latin character set. Generally speaking, the wide-character set is beyond the scope of an introductory programming text and is not covered in this text.

Integer

An integer type is a number without a fraction part. C supports four different sizes of the integer data type: `short int`, `int`, `long int`, and `long long int`. A `short int` can also be referred to as `short`, `long int` can be referred to as `long`, and `long long int` can be referred to as `long long`. C defines these data types so that they can be organized from the smallest to the largest, as shown in **Figure 2-9**. The type also defines the size of the field in which data can be stored. In C, this is true even though the size is machine dependent and varies from computer to computer.

Figure 2-9   Integer types

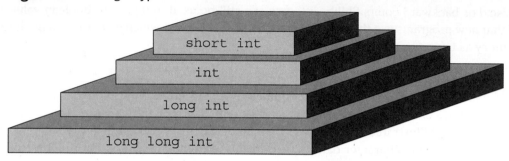

If you need to know the size of any data type, C provides an operator, `sizeof`, that will tell you the exact size in bytes. Although the size is machine-dependent, C requires that the following relationship always be true:

> `sizeof (short) ≤ sizeof (int) ≤ sizeof (long) ≤ sizeof (long long)`

Each integer size can be a signed or an unsigned integer. If the integer is `signed`, then one bit must be used for a signed (0 is plus, 1 is minus). The unsigned integer can store a positive number that is twice as large as the signed integer of the same size. For a complete discussion, see Appendix B, "Numbering Systems." **Table 2-3** contains typical values for the integer types. Recognize, however, that the actual sizes are dependent on the physical hardware.

Table 2-3   Typical integer sizes and values for signed integers

TYPE	BYTE SIZE	MINIMUM VALUE	MAXIMUM VALUE
`short int`	2	–32,768	32,767
`int`	4	–2,147,483,648	2,147,483,647
`long int`	4	–2,147,483,648	2,147,483,647
`long long int`	8	–9,223,372,036,854,775,807	9,223,372,036,854,775,806

To provide flexibility across different hardware platforms, C has a library, `limits.h`, that contains size information about integers. For example, the minimum integer value for the computer is defined as `INT_MIN`, and the maximum value is defined as `INT_MAX`.

Floating-Point Types

The C standard recognizes three floating-point types: real, imaginary, and complex. Like the limits library for integer values, there is a standard library, `float.h`, for the floating-point values. Unlike the integral type, real type values are always signed.

Real

The real type holds values that consist of an integral and a fractional part, such as 43.32. The C language supports three different sizes of real types: `float`, `double`, and `long double`. As was the case for the integer type, real numbers are defined so that they can be organized from smallest to largest. The relationship among the real types is seen in **Figure 2-10**.

Figure 2-10 Floating-point types

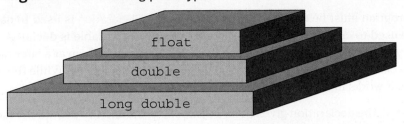

Regardless of machine size, C requires that the following relationship must be true:

> **sizeof** (float) **≤ sizeof** (double) **≤ sizeof** (long double)

Imaginary Type

C defines an imaginary type. An imaginary number is used extensively in mathematics and engineering. An imaginary number is a real number multiplied by the square root of –1 ($\sqrt{-1}$). The imaginary type, like the real type, can be of three different sizes: float imaginary, double imaginary, and long double imaginary.

Most C implementations do not support the imaginary type yet and the functions to handle them are not part of the standard. They are mentioned here because the imaginary type is one of the components of the complex type.

Complex

C defines a complex type, which is implemented by most compilers. A complex number is a combination of a real and an imaginary number. The complex type, like the real type, can be of three different sizes: float complex, double complex, and long long complex. The size needs to be the same in both the real and the imaginary part. The following provide two program examples that use complex numbers at the end of this chapter.

Type Summary

Table 2-4 provides a summary of the four standard data type categories.

Table 2-4 Type summary

CATEGORY	TYPE	C IMPLEMENTATION
Void	Void	`void`
Integral	Boolean	`bool`
	Character	`char, wchar_t`
	Integer	`short int, int, long int, long long int`
Floating-Point	Real	`float, double, long double`
	Imaginary	`float imaginary, double imaginary, long double imaginary`
	Complex	`float complex, double complex, long double complex`

2.5 Variables

Variables are named memory locations that have a type, such as integer or character, which is inherited from their type. The type determines the values that a variable may contain and the operations that may be used with its values.

Variable Declaration

Each variable in your program must be declared and defined. In C, a declaration is used to name an object, such as a variable. Definitions are used to create the object. With one exception, a variable is declared and defined at the same time. The exception, as you will see later, declares them first and then defines them at a later time. For variables, definition assumes that the declaration has been done or is being done at the same time. While this distinction is somewhat of an oversimplification, it works in most situations.

When variables are created, the declaration gives them a symbolic name and the definition reserves memory for them. Once defined, variables are used to hold the data that are required by the program for its operation. Generally speaking, where the variable is located in memory is not a programmer's concern; it is a concern only of the compiler. From the programmer's perspective, the main concern is being able to access the data through their symbolic names, their identifiers. The concept of variables in memory is illustrated in **Figure 2-11**.

Figure 2-11　Variables

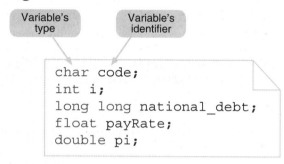

A variable's type can be any of the data types, such as character, integer, or real. The one exception to this rule is the type void; a variable cannot be type void.

To create a variable, we first specify the type, which automatically specifies its size (precision), and then its identifier, as shown below in the definition of a real variable named price of type float.

```
float price;
```

Table 2-5 shows some examples of variable declarations and definitions. As you study the variable identifiers, note the different styles used to make them readable. You should select a style and use it consistently. Most programmers prefer to use an uppercase letter to identify the beginning of each word after the first one.

Table 2-5　Examples of variable declarations and definitions

DECLARATION	DEFINITION	DESCRIPTION
bool	fact;	
short	maxItems;	// Word separator: Capital
long	Long_national_debt;	// Word separator: underscore
float	payRate;	// Word separator: Capital
double	tax;	
float	complex voltage;	
char	code, kind;	// Poor style. It's better to define // each in its own statement.
int	a, b;	// Poor style. See text. It's better // to define each in its own statement.

C allows multiple variables of the same type to be defined in one statement. The last two entries in Table 2-5 use this format. Even though many professional programmers use it, this is considered poor programming style. It is much easier to find and work with variables if they are defined on separate lines. This makes the compiler work a little harder, but the resulting code is no different. This is one situation in which ease of reading the program and programmer efficiency are more important than the convenience of coding multiple declarations on the same line.

Variable Initialization

We can initialize a variable at the same time we declare it by including an initializer. When present, the initializer establishes the first value that the variable will contain. To initialize a variable when it is defined, the identifier is followed by an equals sign (=), which is known as the assignment operator, and then the initializer, which is the variable's starting value when the function starts. This simple initialization format is shown below.

```
int count = 0;
```

Every time the function containing count is entered, count is set to zero. Now, what will be the result of the following initialization? Are both count and sum initialized or is only sum initialized?

```
int count, sum = 0;
```

The answer is that the initializer applies only to the variable defined immediately before it. Therefore, only sum is initialized! If you wanted both variables initialized, you would have to provide two initializers.

```
int count = 0, sum = 0;
```

Again, to avoid confusion and error, it is preferred to use only one variable definition per line. The preferred code in this case would be

```
int count = 0;
int sum = 0;
```

Figure 2-12 repeats Figure 2-11, initializing the values in each of the variables.

Figure 2-12   Variable initialization

```
char       code      = 'B';                        B  code
int        i         = 14;                         14  i
long long  natl_debt = 1000000000000;              1000000000000  natl_debt
float      payRate   = 14.25;                      14.25  payRate
double     pi        = 3.1415926536;               3.1415926536  pi
```
              Program   Memory

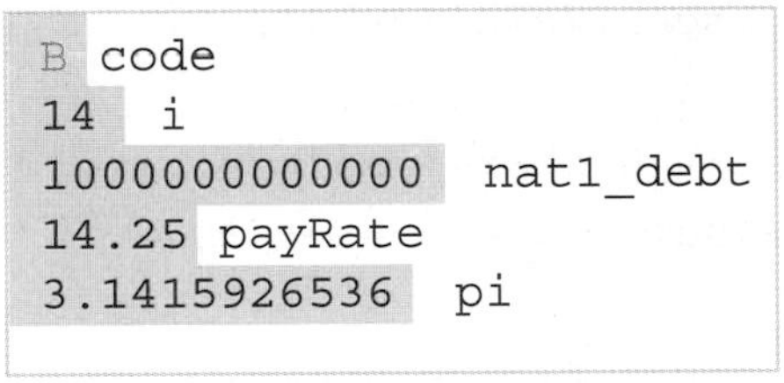

It is important to remember that, with a few exceptions that we will see later, variables are not initialized automatically. When variables are defined, they usually contain garbage (meaningless values left over from a previous use), so we need to initialize them or store data in them (using run-time statements) before accessing their values. Many compilers display a warning message when a variable is accessed before it is initialized.

Note | When a variable is defined, it is not initialized. It is best practice to initialize any variable requiring prescribed data when the function starts.

One final point about initializing variables when they are defined: Although the practice is convenient and saves you a line of code, it also can lead to errors. It is better, therefore, to initialize the variable with an assignment statement at the proper place in the body of the code. This may take another statement, but the efficiency of the resulting program is exactly the same, and you will make fewer errors in your code.

At this point you might like to see what a more complex program looks like. As you read **Program 2-2**, note the blank lines that separate different groups of code. This is a good technique for making programs more readable. You should use blank lines in your programs the same way you use them to separate the paragraphs in a report.

Program 2-2 | Print sum of three numbers

```c
 1  /* This program calculates and prints the sum of three numbers
 2      input by the user at the keyboard.
 3      Written by:
 4      Date:
 5  */
 6  #include <stdio.h>
 7
 8  int main (void)
 9  {
10  // Local Declarations
11     int a;
12     int b;
13     int c;
14     int sum;
15
16  // Statements
17     printf("\nWelcome. This program adds\n");
18     printf("three numbers. Enter three numbers\n");
19     printf("in the form: nnn nnn nnn <return>\n");
20     scanf("%d %d %d", &a, &b, &c);
21
22     // Numbers are now in a, b, and c. Add them.
23     sum = a + b + c;
24
25     printf("The total is: %d\n\n", sum);
26
27     printf("Thank you. Have a good day.\n");
28     return 0;
29  } // main
```

(continue)

Program 2-2   Print sum of three numbers *(continued)*

Output
```
Welcome. This program adds
three numbers. Enter three numbers
in the form: nnn nnn nnn <return>
11 22 33
The total is: 66
Thank you. Have a good day.
```

Study the style of this program carefully. First, note how it starts with a welcome message that tells the user exactly what needs to be entered. Similarly, at the end of the program, an ending message is printed. It is a good style to print a start and end message.

This program contains three different processes. First it reads three numbers. The code to read the numbers includes the printed instructions and a read (scanf) statement. The second process adds the three numbers. While this process consists of only a comment and one statement, it is separated from the read process. This makes it easier for the reader to follow the program. Finally, the results are printed. Again, the print process is separated from the calculate process by a blank line.

2.6 Constants

A constant is a data value that cannot be changed during the execution of a program. Like variables, constants have a type. In this section, Boolean, character, integer, real, complex, and string constants are discussed.

Constant Representation

In this section, we show how to use symbols to represent constants. In the next section, you'll learn how to code constants.

Boolean Constants

A Boolean data type can take only two values: true and false. So it makes sense that only two symbols are used to represent a Boolean type: 0 (false) and 1 (true). Because we use the constant true or false in our program, we need to include the Boolean library, stdbool.h.

Character Constants

A character constant is enclosed between two single quotes (apostrophes). In addition to the character, a backslash (\) before the character is used. The backslash is known as the escape character. It is used when the character we need to represent does not have any graphic associated with it—that is, when it cannot be printed or when it cannot be entered from the keyboard. The escape character says that what follows is not the normal character but something else. For example, '\n' represents the newline character (line feed). So, even though there may be multiple symbols in the character constant, they always represent only one character.

Wide-character constants are coded by prefixing the constant with an L, as shown in the following example.

```
L'x'
```

The character in the character constant comes from the character set supplied by the hardware manufacturer. Most computers use the ASCII character set, or as it is sometimes called, the ASCII alphabet.

C has named the critical character values so we can refer to them symbolically. Note that these control characters use the escape character followed by a symbolic character. They are shown in **Table 2-6**.

Table 2-6 Symbolic names for control characters

ASCII CHARACTER	SYMBOLIC NAME
null character	`'\0'`
alert (bell)	`'\a'`
backspace	`'\b'`
horizontal tab	`'\t'`
newline	`'\n'`
vertical tab	`'\v'`
form feed	`'\f'`
carriage return	`'\r'`
single quote	`'\''`
double quote	`'\"'`
backslash	`'\\'`

Integer Constants

Although integers are always stored in their binary form, they are simply coded as they would be used in everyday life. Thus, the value 15 is simply coded as 15.

When you need to code the number as a series of digits, use the type signed integer, or signed long integer if the number is large. You can change this default signed by specifying unsigned (u or U), and long (l or L) or long long (ll or LL), after the number. The codes may be combined and may be coded in any order. Note that there is no way to specify a short int constant. When the suffix on a literal is omitted, it defaults to int. While both upper- and lowercase codes are allowed, it's best to use uppercase to avoid confusion (especially with the lowercase letter *l*, which often looks like the number 1). **Table 2-7** shows several examples of integer constants. The default types are typical for a personal computer.

Table 2-7 Examples of integer constants

REPRESENTATION	VALUE	DEFAULT TYPE
+ 123	123	int
−378	−378	int
−32271L	−32,271	long int
76542LU	76,542	unsigned long int
12789845LL	12,789,845	long long int

Real Constants

The default form for real constants is double. If you need the resulting data type to be float or long double, you must explicitly specify that in your code. As you might anticipate, f and F are used for float and l and L are used for long double. Again, do not use the lowercase l for long double; it is too easily confused with the number 1.

Table 2-8 shows several examples of real constants.

Table 2-8   Examples of real constants

REPRESENTATION	VALUE	TYPE
0.	0.0	double
.0	0.0	double
2.0	2.0	double
3.1416	3.1416	double
–2.0f	–2.0	float
3.1415926536L	3.1415926536	long double

Complex Constants

Complex constants are widely used in engineering. They are coded as two parts: the real part and the imaginary part, separated by a plus sign. The real part is coded using the real format rules. The imaginary part is coded as a real number times (*) the imaginary constant (`_Complex_I`). If the complex library (`complex.h`) is included, the imaginary constant can be abbreviated as `I`. **Table 2-9** shows several examples of complex constants. Note that programmers usually use the abbreviated form for the imaginary part.

Table 2-9   Examples of complex constants

REPRESENTATION	VALUE	TYPE
12.3 + 14.4 * I	$12.3 + 14.4 * (-1)^{1/2}$	double complex
14F + 16F * I	$14 + 16 * (-1)^{1/2}$	float complex
1.4736L + 4.567561 * I	$1.4736 + 4.56756 * (-1)^{1/2}$	long double complex

The default form for complex constants is `double`. If you need the resulting data type to be `float` or `long double`, you must specify that explicitly in your code. As you might anticipate, f and F are used for `float` and l and L are used for `long double`. Again, do not use the lowercase letter *l* for `long double`; it is too easily confused with the number *1*.

> **Note** | The two components of a complex constant must be of the same precision. That is, if the real part is type `double`, then the imaginary part must also be type `double`.

String Constants

A string constant is a sequence of zero or more characters enclosed in double quotes. You used a string in your first program without even knowing that it was a string! Look at Program 2-1 to see if you can identify the string.

Listed in **Figure 2-13** are several strings, including the one from Program 2-1. The first example, an empty string, is simply two double quotes in succession. The second example, a string containing only the letter h, differs from a character constant in that it is enclosed in double quotes. In C, strings are treated differently. This means there's a big difference between storing h as a character and as a string. The last example in Figure 2-13 is a string that uses wide characters.

Figure 2-13   Some strings

```
""                      // A null string
"h"
"Hello World\n"
"HOW ARE YOU"
"Good Morning!"
L"This string contains wide characters."
```

It is important to understand the difference between the null character (see Table 2-6) and an empty string. The null character represents no value. As a character, it is 8 zero bits. An empty string, on the other hand, is a string containing nothing. **Figure 2-14** shows the difference between these two constant types.

Figure 2-14   Null characters and null strings

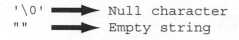

```
'\0'  ───▶   Null character
""    ───▶   Empty string
```

At this point, this is all you need to know about strings. As you become a more experienced programmer, you will learn how they are stored in a computer.

> **Note** | Use single quotes for character constants. Use double quotes for string constants.

Coding Constants

This section presents three different ways to code constants in programs: literal constants, defined constants, and memory constants.

Literal Constants

A literal is an unnamed constant used to specify data. If we know that the data cannot be changed, then we can simply code the data value itself in a statement.

Literals are coded as part of a statement using the constant formats described in the previous section. For example, the literal 5 is used in the following statement.

```
a = b + 5;
```

Defined Constants

Another way to designate a constant is to use the preprocessor command define. Like all preprocessor commands, it is prefaced with the pound sign (#). The define directive is usually placed at the beginning of the program, although it is legal anywhere. Placing them at the beginning of the program makes them easy to find and change. A typical define command might be

```
#define SALES_TAX_RATE  .0825
```

Note that the preceding example contains a sales tax rate, which can change often. It's a good idea to place constants that are likely to change at the beginning of the program, so you can easily find them when you need to change them.

As the preprocessor reformats the program for the language translator, it replaces each defined name, SALES_TAX_RATE in the previous example with its value (.0825) wherever it is found in the source program. This action is just like the search-and-replace command found in a text editor. The preprocessor does not evaluate the code in any way—it just blindly makes the substitution. For a complete discussion of defined constants, see Appendix C, "Preprocessor Commands."

Memory Constants

The third way to use a constant is with memory constants. A memory constant uses a C type qualifier, const, to indicate that the data cannot be changed. Its format is:

```
const type identifier = value;
```

As you have seen, a variable definition does nothing more than give a type and size to a named object in memory. Now assume that you want to fix the contents of this memory location so that they cannot be changed. This is the same concept as a literal, only now you give it a name. The following code creates a memory constant, cPi. To help you remember that it is a constant, you preface the identifier name with c.

```
const float cPi = 3.14159;
```

Three points merit discussion: (1) The type qualifier comes first. (2) Then there must be an initializer. If the constant is not initialized, then it would take whatever happened to be in memory at cPi's location when the program starts. (3) Finally, since cPi is a constant, it cannot be changed.

Program 2-3 demonstrates the three different ways to code PI as a constant.

Program 2-3 | Memory constants

```
 1  /* This program demonstrates three ways to use constants.
 2
 3     Written by:
 4     Date:
 5  */
 6  #include <stdio.h>
 7  #define PI 3.1415926536
 8
 9  int main (void)
10  {
11  // Local Declarations
12     const double cPi = PI;
13
14  // Statements
15     printf("Defined constant PI: %f\n", PI);
16     printf("Memory constant cPi: %f\n", cPi);
17     printf("Literal constant: %f\n", 3.1415926536);
18     return 0;
19  } // main
```

Output
```
Defined constant PI: 3.141593
Memory constant cPi: 3.141593
Literal constant:  3.141593
```

2.7 Input/Output

Although previous programs have implicitly shown how to print messages, they have not formally discussed how to use C facilities to input and output data. As you become a more experienced programmer, you will learn more about C input/output facilities and how to use them. In this section, we describe simple input and output formatting.

Streams

In C, data is input to and output from a stream. A stream is a source of, or destination for, data. It is associated with a physical device, such as a terminal, or with a file stored in auxiliary memory.

C uses two forms of streams: text and binary. A text stream consists of a sequence of characters divided into lines with each line terminated by a new-line (\n). A binary stream consists of a sequence of data values such as integer, real, or complex using their memory representation.

A terminal can be associated only with a text stream because a keyboard can only send a stream of characters into a program and a monitor can only display a sequence of characters. A file, on the other hand, can be associated with a text or binary stream. Data is stored in a file and later retrieved as a sequence of characters (text stream) or as a sequence of data values (binary stream).

In this chapter, it is assumed that the source of data is the keyboard and the destination of data is the monitor. In other words, the terminal devices produce or consume text streams. In C, the keyboard is known as standard input and the monitor is known as standard output.

> **Note** | A terminal keyboard and monitor can be associated only with a text stream. A keyboard is a source for a text stream; a monitor is a destination for a text stream.

Figure 2-15 illustrates the concept of streams and the two physical devices associated with input and output text streams.

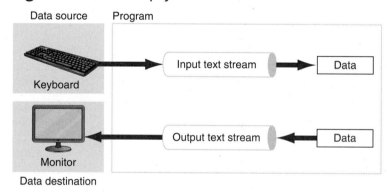

Figure 2-15 Stream physical devices

Formatting Input/Output

The previous section discussed the terminal as a text stream source and destination. The program can only receive text streams from a terminal (keyboard) and send text streams to a terminal (monitor). However, these text streams often represent different data types, such as integer, real, and Boolean. The C language provides two formatting functions: printf for output formatting and scanf for input formatting. The printf function converts data stored in the program into a text stream for output to the monitor; the scanf function converts the text stream coming from the keyboard to data values and stores them in program variables. In other words, the printf and scanf functions are data to text stream and text stream to data converters.

Output Formatting: printf

The output formatting function is printf. The printf function takes a set of data values, converts them to a text stream using formatting instructions contained in a format control string, and sends the resulting text stream to the standard output (monitor). For example, an integer 234 stored in the program is converted to a text stream of three numeric ASCII characters (2, 3, and 4) and then is sent to the monitor. What is seen on the monitor is these three characters, not the integer 234. However, we interpret the three characters together as an integer value. **Figure 2-16** illustrates this concept.

Figure 2-16 Output formatting concept

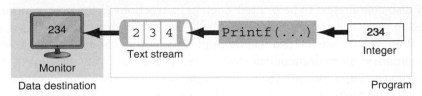

Basic Concept

The `printf` function uses an interesting design to convert data into text streams. Here we describe how the text stream should be formatted using a **format control string** containing zero or more **conversion specifications**. In addition to the conversion specifications, the control string may contain textual data and control characters to be displayed.

Each data value to be formatted into the text stream is described as a separate conversion specification in the control string. The specifications describe the data values' type, size, and specific format information, such as how wide the display width should be. The location of the conversion specification within the format control string determines its position within the text stream.

The control string and data values are passed to the print function (`printf`) as parameters, the control string as the first parameter and one parameter for each value to be printed. In other words, the following information is supplied to the `print` function:

1. The format control string, including any textual data to be inserted into the text stream.

2. A set of zero or more data values to be formatted.

Figure 2-17 is a conceptional representation of the format control string and two conversion specifications.

Figure 2-17 Output stream formatting example

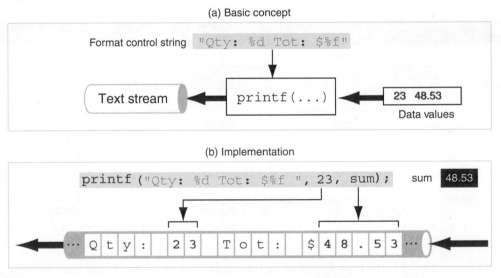

Figure 2-17(a) shows the format string and the data values as parameters for the print function. Within the control string quantity (`Qty:`) and total (`Tot:`) are specified as textual data and two conversion specifications (`%d` and `%f`). The first specification requires an integer type value; the second requires a real type value. The conversion specifications are discussed in detail in the following section.

Figure 2-17(b) shows the formatting operation and the resulting text stream. The first data value is a literal integer; the second data value is the contents of a variable named `tot`. This part of Figure 2-17 shows how the `printf` function expands the control stream and inserts the data values and text characters.

Format Control String Text

The control string may also contain text to be printed, such as instructions to the user, captions or other identifiers, and other text intended to make the output more readable. In fact, as you have already seen, the format string may contain nothing but text, in which case the text will be printed exactly as shown. You employed this concept in the greeting program. In addition, you can printcontrol characters, such as tabs (\t), newlines (\n), and alerts (\a), by including them in the format string. Tabs are used to format the output into columns. Newlines terminate the current line and continue formatting on the next line. Alerts sound an audio signal, usually to alert the user to a condition that needs attention. These control characters were listed earlier in Table 2-6.

Conversion Specification

To insert data into the stream, we use a conversion specification that contains a start token (%), a conversion code, and up to four optional modifiers as shown in **Figure 2-18**. Only the field-specification token (%) and the conversion code are required.

Figure 2-18   Conversion specification

%	Flag	Minimum width	Precision	Size	Code

Approximately 30 different conversion codes are used to describe data types. For now, however, we are concerned with only three: character (c), integer (d), and floating point (f). These codes, with some examples, are shown in **Table 2-10**. Note that one item in this table, Size, is discussed in the next section.

Table 2-10   Format codes for output

TYPE	SIZE	CODE	EXAMPLE
Char	None	c	%c
short int	h	d	%hd
Int	None	d	%d
long int	None	d	%ld
long long int	ll	d	%lld
Float	None	f	%f
Double	None	f	%f
long double	L	f	%Lf

The size modifier is used to modify the type specified by the conversion code. There are four different sizes: h, l (el), ll (el el), and L. The h, used with the integer codes to indicate a short integer value, is a carry-over from assembler language where it meant "half word." The l is used to indicate a long integer value; the ll is used to indicate a long long integer value; and the L is used with floating-point numbers to indicate a long double value.

A width modifier may be used to specify the minimum number of positions in the output. (If the data require using more space than allowed, then printf overrides the width.) It is very useful to align output in columns, such as when we need to print a column of numbers. If a width modifier is not used, each output value will take just enough room for the data.

If a floating-point number is being printed, then the number of decimal places to be printed with the precision modifier must be specified. The precision modifier has the format

.m

where m is the number of decimal digits. If no precision is specified, printf prints six decimal positions. These six decimal positions are often more than is necessary.

When both width and precision are used, the width must be large enough to contain the integral value of the number, the decimal point, and the number of digits in the decimal position. Thus, a conversion specification of %7.2f is designed to print a maximum value of 9999.99. Some examples of width specifications and precision are shown below.

```
%2hd    // short integer—2 print positions
%4d     // integer—4 print positions
%8ld    // long int—8 (not 81) positions
%7.2f   // float—7 print positions: nnnn.dd
%10.3Lf // long double—10 positions: nnnnnn.ddd
```

The flag modifier is used for four print modifications: justification, padding, sign, and numeric conversion variants. The first three are discussed here. You'll learn about the conversion variants as you gain more experience as a programmer.

Justification controls the placement of a value when it is shorter than the specified width. Justification can be left or right. If there is no flag and the defined width is larger than required, the value is right-justified. The default is right justification. To left justify a value, the flag is set to minus (-).

Padding defines the character that fills the unused space when the value is smaller than the print width. It can be a space, the default, or zero. If there is no flag defined for padding, the unused width is filled with spaces; if the flag is 0, the unused width is filled with zeroes. Note that the zero flag is ignored if it is used with left justification because adding zeros after a number changes its value.

The sign flag defines the use or absence of a sign in a numeric value. Three formats can be specified: default formatting, print signed values, or prefix positive values with a leading space. Default formatting inserts a sign only when the value is negative. Positive values are formatted without a sign. When the flag is set to a plus (+), signs are printed for both positive and negative values. If the flag is a space, then positive numbers are printed with a leading space and negative numbers with a minus sign.

Table 2-11 documents three of the more common flag options.

Table 2-11   Flag formatting options

FLAG TYPE	FLAG CODE	FORMATTING
Justification	None	right justified
	–	left justified
Padding	None	space padding
	0	zero padding
Sign	None	positive value: no sign
		negative value: −
	+	positive value: +
		negative value: −
	None	positive value: space
		negative value: −

Output Examples

This section contains several output examples. Here are the `printf` statements, followed by what would be printed. Cover up the solution and try to predict the results.

Example: `printf` output 1

```
printf ("%d%c%f", 23, 'z', 4.1);
```

Output

```
23z4.100000
```

Note that because there are no spaces between the conversion specifications, the data are formatted without spaces between the values.

Example: `printf` output 2

```
printf("%d %c %f", 23, 'z', 4.1);
```

Output

```
23 z 4.100000
```

This is a repeat of `printf` output 1 with spaces between the conversion specifications.

Example: `printf` output 3

```
int num1 = 23;
char zee = 'z';
float num2 = 4.1;
printf("%d %c %f", num1, zee, num2);
```

Output

```
23 z 4.100000
```

Again, the same example, this time using variables.

Example: `printf` output 4

```
printf("%d\t%c\t%5.1f\n", 23, 'Z', 14.2);
printf("%d\t%c\t%5.1f\n", 107, 'A', 53.6);
printf("%d\t%c\t%5.1f\n", 1754, 'F', 122.0);
printf("%d\t%c\t%5.1f\n", 3, 'P', 0.1);
```

Output

```
23      Z       14.2
107     A       53.6
1754    F       122.0
3       P        0.1
```

In addition to the conversion specifications, note the tab character (\t) between the first and second, and second and third conversion specifications. Because the data are to be printed in separate lines, each format string ends with a newline (\n).

Example: `printf` output 5

```
printf("The number%dis my favorite number.", 23);
```

Output

```
The number23is my favorite number.
```

Since there are no spaces before and after the format code (`%d`), the number 23 is run together with the text before and after.

Example: `printf` output 6

```
printf("The number%7d my favorite number.", 23);
```

Output

```
The number is       23
```

If you count the spaces carefully, you will note that five spaces follow the word is. The first space comes from the space after `is` and before the `%` in the format string. The other four come from the width in the conversion specification.

Example: `printf` output 7

```
printf("The tax is %6.2f this year.", 233.12);
```

Output

```
The tax is 233.12 this year.
```

In this example, the width is six and the precision two. Because the number of digits printed totals five (three for the integral portion and two for the decimal portion), and the decimal point takes one print position, the full width is filled with data. The only spaces are the spaces before and after the conversion code in the format string.

Example: `printf` output 8

```
printf("The tax is %8.2f this year.", 233.12);
```

Output

```
The tax is 233.12 this year.
```

Example: `printf` output 9

```
printf("The tax is %08.2f this year.", 233.12);
```

Output

```
The tax is 00233.12 this year.
```

This example uses the zero flag to print leading zeros. Note that the width is eight positions. Three of these positions are taken up by the precision of two digits and the decimal point. This leaves five positions for the integral portion of the number. Because there are only three digits (233), `printf` inserts two leading zeros.

> **Example:** printf output 10

```
printf("\"%8c %d\"", "            h 23", 23);
```

Output

```
"                h           23"
```

In this example, we want to print the data within quotes. Because quotes are used to identify the format string, we can't use them as print characters. To print them, therefore, we must use the escape character with the quote (\"), which tells printf that what follows is not the end of the string but a character to be printed, in this case, a quote mark.

> **Example:** printf output 11

```
printf ("This line disappears.\r...A new line\n");
printf ("This is the bell character \a\n");
printf ("A null character\0kills the rest of the line\n");
printf ("\nThis is \'it\' in single quotes\n");
printf ("This is \"it\" in double quotes\n");
printf ("This is \\ the escape character itself\n");
```

Output

```
...A new line
This is the bell character
A null character
This is 'it' in single quotes
This is "it" in double quotes
This is \ the escape character itself
```

These examples use some of the control character names found in Table 2-6. Two of them give unexpected results. In example 11, the return character (\r) repositions the output at the beginning of the current line without advancing the line. Therefore, all data that were placed in the output stream are erased.

The null character effectively kills the rest of the line. If a newline character (\n) was not used at the beginning of the next line, it would have started immediately after character.

> **Example:** printf output 12

New example with multiple flags.

```
printf("|%-+8.2f| |%0+8.2f| |%-0+8.2f|", 1.2, 2.3, 3.4);
```

Output

```
|+1.20   | |+0002.30| |+3.40   |
```

This example uses multiple flags. As shown in the output, each value is enclosed in vertical bars. The first value is printed left justified with the positive flag set. The second example uses zero fill with a space for the sign. Note that there is a leading space in the output. This represents the plus value. It is then followed by the leading zeros. The last example demonstrates that the zero fill is ignored when a numeric value is printed with left justification.

Common Output Errors

Each of the following examples has at least one error. Try to find each one before you look at the output. Your results may vary depending on your compiler and hardware.

Example: `printf` output error 1

```
printf ("%d %d %d\n", 44, 55);
```

Output

```
44 55 0
```

This example has three conversion specifications but only two values.

Example: `printf` output error 2

```
printf ("%d %d\n", 44, 55, 66);
```

Output

```
44 55
```

This example has two conversion specifications with three values. In this case, `printf` ignores the third value.

Example: `printf` output error 3

```
float x = 123.45;
printf("The data are: %d\n", x);
```

Output

```
The data are: 1079958732
```

This is a very common error in which the format specification (integer) does not match the data type (real).

Input Formatting: `scanf`

The standard input formatting function in C is `scanf` (scan formatting). This function takes a text stream from the keyboard, extracts and formats data from the stream according to a format control string, and then stores the data in specified program variables. For example, the stream of 5 characters `'2'`, `'3'`, `'4'`, `'.'`, and `'2'` are extracted as the real `234.2`. **Figure 2-19** shows the concept.

Figure 2-19   Formatting text from an input stream

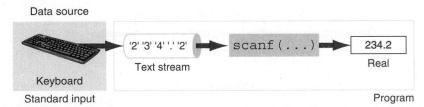

The `scanf` function is the reverse of the `printf` function. The following is a list of guidelines for using `scanf` function.

1. A format control string describes the data to be extracted from the stream and reformatted.

2. Rather than data values as in the `printf` function, `scanf` requires the variable addresses where the pieces of data are to be stored. Unlike the `printf` function, the destination of the data items cannot be literal values, they must store in the variables.

3. With the exception of the character specification, leading whitespaces are discarded.

4. Any nonconversion specification characters in the format string must be exactly matched by the next characters in the input stream.

We must be careful about extra characters in the control stream. Extra characters in the control string can be divided into two categories: nonwhitespace and whitespace.

Nonwhitespace characters in the control string must exactly match characters entered by the user and are discarded by the scanf after they are read. If they don't match, then scanf goes into an error state and the program must be manually terminated.

It is recommended that you don't use nonwhitespace characters in the format string, at least until you learn how to recover from errors. However, there are some uses for them. For example, if the users want to enter dates with slashes, such as 5/10/06, the slashes must either be read and discarded using the character format specification (see the discussion of the assignment suppression flag in the later section, "Conversion Specification") or coded as nonwhitespace in the format specification. Reading and discarding them is preferred.

Whitespace characters in the format string are matched by zero or more whitespace characters in the input stream and discarded. There are two exceptions to this rule: the character conversion code and the scan set (see Chapter 11) do not discard whitespace. It is easy, however, to manually discard whitespace characters when necessary to read a character. Simply code a space before the conversion specification, or between the two parts of the conversion specification, as shown below. Either one works.

```
" %c" or "% c"
```

Remember that whenever you read data from the keyboard, there is a return character from a previous read. If you don't flush the whitespace characters when you read a character, therefore, you will get the whitespace from the previous read. To read a character, you should always code at least one whitespace character in the conversion specification. Otherwise the whitespace remaining in the input stream is read as the input character. For example, to read three characters, you should code the following format string. Note the spaces before each conversion specification.

```
scanf(" %c %c %d", &cl, &c2, &c3);
```

Figure 2-20 demonstrates the input format string concept with a control string having two fields (%d and %f). The first one defines that a character will be inserted here; the second defines that a real will be inserted there. We will discuss these place holders, or format specifiers, later in the chapter.

Figure 2-20   Input stream formatting example

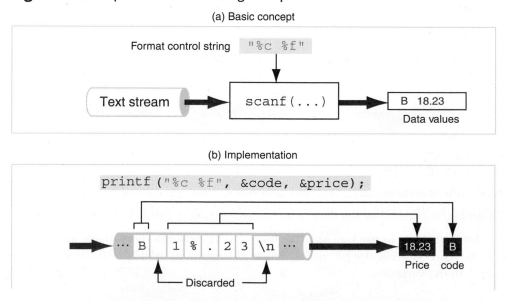

Format Control String

Like the control string for `printf`, the control string for `scanf` is enclosed in a set of quotation marks and contains one or more conversion specifications that describe the data types and indicate any special formatting rules and/or characters.

Conversion Specification

To format data from the input stream, we use a conversion specification that contains a start token (%), a conversion code, and up to three optional modifiers as shown in **Figure 2-21**. Only the field-specification token (%) and the conversion code are required.

Figure 2-21   Conversion specification

There are only three differences between the conversion codes for input formatting and output formatting. First, there is no precision in an input conversion specification. It is an error to include a precision; if `scanf` finds a precision it stops processing and the input stream is in the error state.

There is only one flag for input formatting, the assignment suppression flag (*). More commonly associated with text files, the assignment suppression flag tells `scanf` that the next input field is to be read but not stored. It is discarded. The following `scanf` statement reads an integer, a character, and a floating-point number from the input stream. The character is read and discarded. The other fields are read, formatted, and stored. Note that there is no matching address parameter for the data to be discarded.

```
scanf ("%d %*c %f", &x, &y);
```

The third difference is the width specification; with input formatting it is a maximum, not a minimum, width. The width modifier specifies the maximum number of characters that are to be read for one format code. When a width specification is included, therefore, `scanf` reads until the maximum number of characters have been processed or until `scanf` finds a whitespace character. If `scanf` finds a whitespace character before the maximum is reached, it stops.

Input Parameters

For every conversion specification there must be a matching variable in the address list. The address list contains the address of the matching variable. How do we specify an address? It's quite simple: Addresses are indicated by prefixing the variable name with an ampersand (&). In C, the ampersand is known as the address operator. Using the address operator, if the variable name is price, then the address is &price. Forgetting the ampersand is one of the most common errors for beginning C programmers, so you will have to concentrate on it when you use the `scanf` function. Note that `scanf` requires variable addresses in the address list.

Remember that the first conversion specification matches the first variable address, the second conversion specification matches the second variable address, and so on. This correspondence is very important. It is also very important that the variable's type match the conversion specification type. The C compiler does not verify that they match. If they don't, the input data will not be properly formatted when they are stored in the variable.

End of File and Errors

In addition to whitespace and width specifications, two other events stop the `scanf` function. If the user signals that there is no more input by keying end of file (EOF), then `scanf` terminates the input process. While there is no EOF on the keyboard, it can be simulated in most systems. For example, Windows uses the `<ctrl + z>` key combination to signal EOF. Unix and Apple Macintosh use `<ctrl + d>` for EOF. The C user's manual for your system should specify the key sequence for EOF.

Second, if `scanf` encounters an invalid character when it is trying to convert the input to the stored data type, it stops. The most common error is finding a nonnumeric character when it is trying to read a number. The valid characters are leading plus or minus, digits, and one decimal point. Any other combination, including any alphabetic characters, will cause an error. Although it is possible to detect this error and ask the user to re-input the data, you won't learn about the logic for detecting errors until you become a more experienced programmer. Until then, full caution should be taken when entering data into your program.

Input Formatting Summary

The following list summarizes the rules for using scanf.

1. The conversion operation processes until:

    a. End of file is reached.

    b. The maximum number of characters has been processed.

    c. A whitespace character is found after a digit in a numeric specification.

    d. An error is detected.

2. There must be a conversion specification for each variable to be read.

3. There must be a variable address of the proper type for each conversion specification.

4. Any character in the format string other than whitespace or a conversion specification must be exactly matched by the user during input. If the input stream does not match the character specified, an error is signaled and scanf stops.

5. It is a fatal error to end the format string with a whitespace character. Your program will not run correctly if you do.

Input Examples

This section contains several examples. We list the data that will be input first. This allows you to cover up the function and try to formulate your own scanf statement.

1. `214 156 14Z`

    ```
    scanf("%d%d%d%c", &a, &b, &c, &d);
    ```

    Note that if there were a space between the 14 and the Z, it would create an error because %c does not skip whitespace! To prevent this problem, put a space before the %c code as shown below. This will cause it to skip leading whitespace.

    ```
    scanf("%d%d%d %c", &a, &b, &c, &d);
    ```

2. `2314 15 2.14`

    ```
    scanf("%d %d %f", &a, &b, &c);
    ```

    Note the whitespace between the conversion specifications. These spaces are not necessary with numeric input, but it is a good idea to include them.

3. `14/26 25/66`

    ```
    scanf("%2d/%2d %2d/%2d", &num1, &den1, &num2, &den2);
    ```

    Note the slashes (/) in the format string. Because they are not a part of the conversion specification, the user must enter them exactly as shown or scanf will stop reading.

4. `11-25-56`

    ```
    scanf ("%d-%d-%d", &a, &b, &c);
    ```

    Again, we see some required user input, this time dashes between the month, day, and year. While this is a common date format, it can cause problems. A better solution would be to prompt the user separately for the month, the day, and the year.

Common Input Errors

Each of the following examples has at least one error. Try to find it before you look at the solution. Your results may vary depending on your compiler and hardware.

1.
```
int a = 0;
scanf ("%d", a);
printf("%d\n", a);
```

Input: 234
Output: 0

This example has no address token on the variable (&a). If the program runs at all, the data are read into an unidentified area in memory. What is printed is the original contents of the variable, in this case 0.

2.
```
float a = 2.1;
scanf ("%5.2f", &a);
printf ("%5.2f", a);
```

Input: 74.35
Output: 2.10

This example has no precision in the input conversion specification. When scanf finds a precision, it stops processing and returns to the function that called it. The input variable is unchanged.

3.
```
int a;
int b;
scanf ("%d%d%d", &a, &b);
printf ("%d %d\n", a, b);
```

Input: 5 10
Output: 5 10

This example has three conversion specifications but only two addresses. Therefore, scanf reads the first two values and quits because no third address if found.

4.
```
int a = 1;
int b = 2;
int c = 3;
scanf ("%d%d", &a, &b, &c);
printf ("%d %d %d\n", a, b, c);
```

Input: 5 10 15
Output: 5 10 3

This example has only two conversion specifications, but it has three addresses. Therefore, scanf reads the first two values and ignores the third address. The value 15 is still in the input stream waiting to be read.

Programming Example: Working with Input and Output

In this section, we show some programming examples to emphasize the ideas and concepts we have discussed about input/output.

Program 2-4 is a very simple program that prints "Nothing!"

Program 2-4 | A Program that prints "nothing!"

```
1   /* Prints the message "Nothing!".
2      Written by:
3      Date:
4   */
5   #include <stdio.h>
6
7   int main (void)
8   {
9   // Statements
10     printf("This program prints\n\n\t\"Nothing!\"");
11     return 0;
12  } // main
```

Output
```
This program prints

     "Nothing !"
```

Program 2-5 demonstrates printing Boolean values. As the program shows, however, while a Boolean literal contains either `true` or `false`, when it is printed, it is printed as 0 or 1. This is because there is no conversion code for Boolean. To print it, you must use the integer type, which prints its stored value, 0 or 1.

Program 2-5 | Demonstrate printing Boolean constants

```
1   /* Demonstrate printing Boolean constants.
2      Written by:
3      Date:
4   */
5   #include <stdio.h>
6   #include <stdbool.h>
7
8   int main (void)
9   {
10  // Local Declarations
11     bool x = true;
12     bool y = false;
13
```

(continue)

Program 2-5   Demonstrate printing Boolean constants *(continued)*

```
14 // Statements
15   printf ("The Boolean values are: %d %d\n", x, y);
16   return 0;
17 } // main
```

Output

```
The Boolean values are: 1 0
```

Program 2-6 demonstrates that all characters are stored in the computer as integers. We define some character variables and initialize them with values, and then we print them as integers. As you study the output, note that the ASCII values of the characters are printed. The program also shows the value of some nonprintable characters.

Program 2-6 | Print value of selected characters

```
1   /* Display the decimal value of selected characters,
2      Written by:
3      Date:
4   */
5   #include <stdio.h>
6
7   int main (void)
8   {
9   // Local Declarations
10     char A   = 'A';
11     char a   = 'a';
12     char B   = 'B';
13     char b   = 'b';
14     char Zed    = 'Z';
15     char zed    = 'z';
16     char zero   = '0';
17     char eight  = '8';
18     char NL = '\n'; // newline
19     char HT = '\t'; // horizontal tab
20     char VT = '\v'; // vertical tab
21     char SP = ' ';  // blank or space
22     char BEL     = '\a';    // alert (bell)
23     char dblQuote   = '"';       // double quote
24     char backslash  = '\\'; // backslash itself
25     char oneQuote   = '\'';      // single quote itself
```

(continue)

Program 2-6   Print value of selected characters *(continued)*

```
26
27 // Statements
28    printf("ASCII for char 'A' is: %d\n", A);
29    printf("ASCII for char 'a' is: %d\n", a);
30    printf("ASCII for char 'B' is: %d\n", B);
31    printf("ASCII for char 'b' is: %d\n", b);
32    printf("ASCII for char 'Z' is: %d\n", Zed);
33    printf("ASCII for char 'z' is: %d\n", zed);
34    printf("ASCII for char '0' is: %d\n", zero);
35    printf("ASCII for char '8' is: %d\n", eight);
36    printf("ASCII for char '\\n' is: %d\n", NL);
37    printf("ASCII for char '\\t' is: %d\n", HT);
38    printf("ASCII for char '\\v' is: %d\n", VT);
39    printf("ASCII for char ' ' is: %d\n", SP);
40    printf("ASCII for char '\\a' is: %d\n", BEL);
41    printf("ASCII for char '\"' is: %d\n", dblQuote);
42    printf("ASCII for char '\\' is: %d\n", backslash);
43    printf("ASCII for char '\' ' is: %d\n", oneQuote);
44
45    return 0;
46 } // main
```

Output
```
ASCII for character 'A' is: 65
ASCII for character 'a' is: 97
ASCII for character 'B' is: 66
ASCII for character 'b' is: 98
ASCII for character 'Z' is: 90
ASCII for character 'z' is: 122
ASCII for character '0' is: 48
ASCII for character '8' is: 56
ASCII for character '\n' is: 10
ASCII for character '\t' is: 9
ASCII for is: 11
ASCII for character ' ' is: 32
ASCII for character '\a' is: 7
ASCII for character '"' is: 34
ASCII for character '\' is: 92
ASCII for character ' ' ' is: 39
```

The following is a program that calculates the area and circumference of a circle using a preprocessor-defined constant for π. Although we haven't shown you how to make calculations in C, if you know algebra you will have no problem reading the code in **Program 2-7**.

Program 2-7 | Calculate a circle's area and circumference

```
1   /* This program calculates the area and circumference of a
2       circle using PI as a defined constant.
3       Written by:
4       Date:
5   */
6   #include <stdio.h>
7   #define PI 3.1416
8
9   int main (void)
10  {
11  // Local Declarations
12      float circ;
13      float area;
14      float radius;
15
16  // Statements
17      printf("\nPlease enter the value of the radius: ");
18      scanf("%f", &radius);
19
20      circ = 2 * PI  * radius;
21      area = PI * radius * radius;
22
23      printf("\nRadius is :  %10.2f", radius);
24      printf("\nCircumference is : %10.2f", circ);
25      printf("\nArea is :   %10.2f", area);
26
27      return 0;
28  } // main
```

Output
```
Please enter the value of the radius: 23
Radius is :   23.00
Circumference is :  144.51
Area is :   1661.91
```

You are assigned to a new project that is currently being designed. To give the customer an idea of what a proposed report might look like, the project leader has asked you to write a small program to print a sample. The specifications for the report are shown in **Figure 2-22**, and the code is shown in **Program 2-8**.

Figure 2-22 Output specifications for inventory report

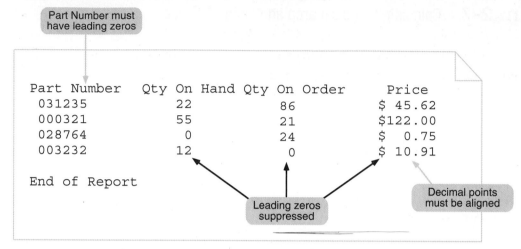

The report contains four fields: a part number, which must be printed with leading zeros; the current quantity on hand; the current quantity on order; and the price of the item, printed to two decimal points. All data should be aligned in columns with captions indicating the type of data in each column. The report should be closed with an "End of Report" message.

Program 2-8 | A Sample inventory report

```
1   /* This program will print four lines of inventory data on an
2       inventory report to give the user an idea of what a new report
3       will look like. Because this is not a real report, no input is
4       required. The data are all specified as constants
5
6       Written by:
7       Date:
8   */
9   #include <stdio.h>
10
11  int main (void)
12  {
13  // Statements
14      // Print captions
15      printf("\tPart Number\tQty On Hand");
16      printf("\tQty On Order\tPrice\n");
17
```

(continue)

Program 2-8   A Sample inventory report *(continued)*

```
18      // Print data
19      printf("\t %06d\t\t%7d\t\t%7d\t\t $%7.2f\n",
20              31235, 22, 86, 45.62);
21      printf("\t %06d\t\t%7d\t\t%7d\t\t $%7.2f\n",
22              321, 55, 21, 122.);
23      printf("\t %06d\t\t%7d\t\t%7d\t\t $%7.2f\n",
24              28764, 0, 24, .75);
25      printf("\t %06d\t\t%7d\t\t%7d\t\t $%7.2f\n",
26              3232, 12, 0, 10.91);
27
28      // Print end message
29      printf("\n\tEnd of Report\n");
30      return 0;
31 } // main
```

There are a few things about Program 2-8 that you should note. First, it is fully documented. Professional programmers often ignore documentation on "one-time-only" programs, thinking they will throw them away, only to find that they end up using them over and over. It only takes a few minutes to document a program, and it is always time well spent. If nothing else, it helps clarify the program in your mind.

Next, look carefully at the formatting for the print statements. Spacing is controlled by a combination of tabs and format code widths. The double spacing for the end of report message is controlled by placing a newline command (\n) at the beginning of the message in Statement 29.

Finally, note that the program concludes with a return statement that informs the operating system that it concluded successfully. Attention to details, even in small programs, is the sign of a good programmer.

A complex number is made of two components: a real part and an imaginary part. In mathematics, it can be represented as a vector with two components. The real part is the projection of the vector on the horizontal axis (x) and the imaginary part is the projection of the vector on the vertical axis (y). In C, we use a complex number and a predefined library function to print the real and imaginary values. We can also find the length of the vector, which is the absolute value of the complex number and the angle of the vector, which is the argument of the vector. These four attributes are shown in **Figure 2-23**.

Figure 2-23   Complex 0

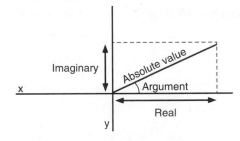

As the figure shows, the absolute value of the complex a + b * I can be found as $(a + b)^{1/2}$. The argument can be found as arctan (b/a). The conjugate of a complex number is another complex number defined as a — b * I.

Program 2-9 shows how to print the different attributes of a complex number using the predefined functions creal, cimag, cabs, and carg.

Program 2-9 | Print complex number attributes

```c
1   /* Print attributes of a complex number.
2       Written by:
3       Date
4   */
5   #include <stdio.h>
6   #include <math.h>
7   #include <complex.h>
8
9   int main (void)
10  {
11  // Local Declarations
12      double complex x = 4 + 4 * I;
13      double complex xc;
14
15      // Statements
16      xc = conj (x);
17      printf("%f %f %f %f\n", creal(x), cimag(x),
18              cabs(x), carg(x));
19
20      printf("%f %f %f %f\n", creal(xc), cimag(xc),
21              cabs(xc), carg(xc));
22      return 0;
23  } // main
```

Output
```
4.000000 4.000000 5.656854 0.785398
4.000000 -4.000000 5.656854 -0.785398
```

In C you can add, subtract, multiply, and divide two complex numbers using the same operators (+, -, *, /) that are used for real numbers. **Program 2-10** demonstrates the arithmetic use of operators with complex numbers.

Program 2-10 | Complex number arithmetic

```c
1   /* Demonstrate complex number arithmetic.
2      Written by:
3      Date:
4   */
5   #include <stdio.h>
6   #include <math.h>
7   #include <complex.h>
8
9   int main (void)
10  {
11  // Local Declarations
12     double complex x = 3 + 4 * I;
13     double complex y = 3 - 4 * I;
14     double complex sum;
15     double complex dif;
16     double complex mul;
17     double complex div;
18
19  // Statements
20     sum = x + y;
21     dif = x - y;
22     mul = x * y;
23     div = x / y;
24
25     printf("%f %f %f %f\n", creal(sum), cimag(sum),
26     cabs(sum), carg(sum));
27     printf("%f %f %f %f\n", creal(dif), cimag(dif),
28     cabs(dif), carg(dif));
29     printf("%f %f %f %f\n", creal(mul), cimag(mul),
30     cabs(mul), carg(mul));
31     printf("%f %f %f %f\n", creal(div), cimag(div),
32     cabs(div), carg(div));
33     return 0;
34  } // main
```

Output
```
6.000000 0.000000 6.000000 0.000000
0.000000 8.000000 8.000000 1.570796
25.000000 0.000000 25.000000 0.000000
-0.280000 0.960000 1.000000 1.854590
```

Software Engineering

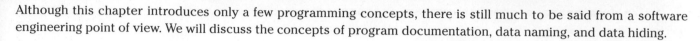

Although this chapter introduces only a few programming concepts, there is still much to be said from a software engineering point of view. We will discuss the concepts of program documentation, data naming, and data hiding.

Program Documentation

There are two levels of program documentation. The first is the general documentation at the start of the program. The second level is found within each function.

General Documentation

Program 2-11 illustrates recommended program documentation. Each program should start with a general description of the program. Following the general description is the name of the author and the date the program was written. Following the date is the program's change history, which documents the reason and authority for all changes. For a production program, whose use spans several years, the change history can become extensive.

> **Program 2-11** | Sample of general program documentation

```
 1   /* A sample of program documentation. Each program starts
 2       with a general description of the program.
 3       Often, this description
 4       can be taken from the requirements specification
 5       given to the programmer.
 6       Written by: original author
 7       Date:  Date first released to production
 8       Change History:
 9          <date> Included in this documentation is a short
10          description of each change.
11  */
```

Module Documentation

Whenever necessary, a brief comment for blocks of code should be included. A block of code is much like a paragraph in a report. It contains one thought—that is, one set of statements that accomplish a specific task. Blocks of code in a program are separated by blank program lines, just as we skip blank lines between paragraphs in reports.

If the block of code is difficult, or if the logic is especially significant, then a short—one- or two-line—description of the block's purpose and/or operation should be provided.

Some programming experts recommend documenting each variable in a program. We disagree with this approach. First, the proper location for variable documentation is in a data dictionary. A data dictionary is a system documentation tool that contains standard names, descriptions, and other information about data used in a system.

Second, good data names eliminate the need for variable comments. In fact, if you think you need to document the purpose of a variable, check your variable name. You will usually find that improving the name eliminates the need for the comment.

Data Names

Another principle of good structured programming is the use of **intelligent data names**. This means that the variable name itself should give the reader a good idea about what data it contains and maybe even an idea about how the data are used.

Although there are obvious advantages to keeping names short, the advantage is quickly lost if the names become so cryptic that they are unintelligible. Programmers often struggle for hours to find a bug, only to discover that the problem was an incorrect variable. The time saved keying short, cryptic names is often lost ten- or a hundredfold in debugging time.

Here are some guidelines to help you construct good, intelligent data names:

1. The name should match the terminology of the user as closely as possible.

   Let's suppose that you are writing a program to calculate the area of a rectangle. Mathematicians often label the sides of a rectangle *a* and *b,* but their real names are length and width. Therefore, your program should call the sides of the rectangle length and width. These names are commonly used by anyone describing a rectangle.

2. When necessary for readability, and to separate similar variables from each other, combine terms to form a variable name.

   Suppose that you are working on a project to compute a payroll. There are many different types of taxes. Each of the different taxes should be clearly distinguished from the others by good data names. **Table 2-12** shows both good and bad names for this programming situation. Most of the poor names are either too abbreviated to be meaningful (such as ftr) or are generic names (such as rate) that could apply to many different pieces of data.

Table 2-12 Examples of good and poor data names

GOOD NAMES		POOR NAMES
`ficaTaxRate`	`fica_tax_rate`	`rate ftr frate fica`
`ficaWitholding`	`fica_witholding`	`fwh ficaw wh`
`ficaWthldng`	`fica_wthldng`	`fcwthldng wthldng`
`ficaMax`	`ficaDlrMax`	`max fmax`

Note the two different concepts for separating the words in a variable's name demonstrated in Table 2-12. In the first example, the first letter of each word is capitalized. In the second example, the words are separated with an underscore. Both are good techniques for making a compound name readable. If you use capitalization, keep in mind that C is case sensitive, so you must be careful to use the same cases for the name each time you use it.

3. Do not create variable names that are different by only one or two letters, especially if the differences are at the end of the word. Names that are too similar create confusion. On the other hand, a naming pattern makes it easier to recall the names. This is especially true when user terminology is being used. Thus, all the good names in Table 2-12 start with `fica`.

4. Abbreviations, when used, should clearly indicate the word being abbreviated.

   Table 2-12 also contains several examples of good abbreviations. Whenever possible, use abbreviations created by the users. They will often have a glossary of abbreviations and acronyms that they use.

   Short words are usually not abbreviated. If they are short in the first place, they don't need to be made shorter.

5. Avoid the use of generic names.

   Generic names are programming or user jargon. For example, `count` and `sum` are both generic names. They tell you their purpose but don't give you any clue as to the type of data they are associated with. Better names would be `emplyCnt` and `ficaSum`. Programmers are especially fond of using generic names, but they tend to make the program confusing. Several of the poor names in Table 2-12 are generic.

6. Use memory constants or defined constants rather than literals for values that are hard to read or that might change from system to system.

Some constants are nearly impossible to read. We pointed out the space earlier. If you need a space often, create a defined constant for it. **Table 2-13** contains several examples of constants that are better when coded as defined constants.

Table 2-13   Examples of defined constants

`#define SPACE ' '`	`#define BANG '!'`
`#define DBL_QTE ""`	`#define QUOTE '\"'`
`#define COMMA ','`	`#define COLON ':'`

Data Hiding

In "Structure of a C Program" in Section 2.2, you read about the concept of global and local variables. We pointed out that anything placed before `main` was said to be in the global part of the program. With the exception of data that must be visible to other programs, no variables should be placed in this section.

One of the principles of structured programming states that the data structure should be hidden from view. The two terms you usually hear in connection with this concept are data hiding and data encapsulation. Both of these principles have as their objective protecting data from accidental destruction by parts of your program that don't require access to the data. In other words, if a part of your program doesn't require data to do its job, it shouldn't be able to see or modify the data. Until you learn to use functions, however, you will not be able to provide this data-hiding capability.

Nevertheless, you should start your programming with good practices. And since your ultimate objective is good structured programming, we now formulate our first programming standard: Any variables placed in the global area of your program—that is, before `main`—can be used and changed by every part of your program. This is undesirable and is in direct conflict with the structured programming principles of data hiding and data encapsulation. Thus, you should never place a variable in the global area of a program.

Tips and Common Programming Errors

1. Well-structured programs use global (defined) constants but do not use global variables.

2. The function header for `main` should be complete. The following format is recommended:

   ```
   int main (void)
   ```

   a. If you forget the parentheses after `main`, you will get a compile error.
   b. If you put a semicolon after the parentheses, you will get a compile error.
   c. If you misspell `main` you will not get a compile error, but you will get an error when you try to link the program. All programs must have a function named `main`.

3. If you forget to close the format string in the `scanf` or `printf` statement, you will get a compile error.

4. Using an incorrect conversion code for the data type being read or written is a run-time error. You can't read an integer with a `float` conversion code. Your program will compile with this error, but it won't run correctly.

5. Not separating read and write parameters with commas is a compile error.

6. Forgetting the comma after the format string in a read or write statement is a compile error.

7. Not terminating a block comment with a close token (*/) is a compile error.

8. Not including required libraries, such as `stdio.h`, at the beginning of your program is an error. Your program may compile, but the linker cannot find the required functions in the system library.

9. If you misspell the name of a function, you will get an error when you link the program. For example, if you misspell `scanf` or `printf`, your program will compile without errors, but you will get a linker error. Using the wrong case is a form of spelling error. For example, each of the following function names are different:

```
scanf, Scanf, SCANF printf, Printf, PRINTF
```

10. Forgetting the address operator (&) on a `scanf` parameter is a logic (runtime) error.

11. Do not use commas or other characters in the format string for a `scanf` statement. This will most likely lead to a run-time error when the user does not enter matching commas or characters. For example, the comma in the following statement will create a run-time problem if the user doesn't enter it exactly as coded.

```
scanf ("%d, %d", &a, &b);
```

12. Unless you specifically want to read a whitespace character, put a space before the character conversion specification in a `scanf` statement.

13. Using an address operator (&) with a variable in the `printf` statement is usually a run-time error.

14. Do not put a trailing whitespace at the end of a format string in `scanf`. This is a fatal run-time error.

Summary

> In 1972, Dennis Ritchie designed C at Bell Laboratories.

> In 1989, the American National Standards Institute (ANSI) approved ANSI C; in 1990, the ISO standard was approved.

> The basic component of a C program is the function.

> Every C function is made of declarations, definitions, and one or more statements.

> One and only one of the functions in a C program must be called `main`.

> To make a program more readable, use comments. A comment is a sequence of characters ignored by the compiler. C uses two types of comments: block and line. A block comment starts with the token /* and ends with the token */. A line comment starts with the // token; the rest of the line is ignored.

> Identifiers are used in a language to name objects.

> C types include `void`, integral, floating point, and derived.

> A `void` type is used when C needs to define a lack of data.

> An integral type in C is further divided into Boolean, character, and integer.

  ■ A Boolean data type takes only two values: `true` and `false`. It is designated by the keyword `bool`.

  ■ A character data type uses values from the standard alphabet of the language, such as ASCII or Unicode. There are two character type sizes, `char` and `w_char`.

  ■ An integer data type is a number without a fraction. C uses four different integer sizes: `short int`, `int`, `long int`, and `long long int`.

> The floating-point type is further divided into real, imaginary, and complex.

  ■ A real number is a number with a fraction. It has three sizes: `float`, `double`, and `long double`.

  ■ The imaginary type represents the imaginary part of a complex number. It has three sizes, `float imaginary`, `double imaginary`, and `long double imaginary`.

  ■ The complex type contains a real and an imaginary part. C uses three complex sizes: `float complex`, `double complex`, and `long double complex`.

> A constant is data whose value cannot be changed.

> Constants can be coded in three different ways: as literals, as define commands, and as memory constants.

> Variables are named areas of memory used to hold data.

> Variables must be declared and defined before being used in C.

> To input data through the keyboard and to output data through the monitor, use the standard formatted input/output functions.

> `scanf` is a standard input function for inputting formatted data through the keyboard.

> `printf` is a standard output function for outputting formatted data to the monitor.

> As necessary, programs should contain comments that provide the reader with in-line documentation for blocks of code.

Programs that use "intelligent" names are easier to read and understand.

Key Terms

address list	floating-point types	parameter list
address operator	format control string	precision modifier
ASCII	functions	program documentation
binary stream	global declaration section	real type
block comment	header files	reserved words
Boolean	identifier	sign flag
character constant	imaginary type	size modifier
character set	include	statements
comments	initializer	statement section
complex type	integral types	stream
constant	intelligent data names	string
conversion code	justification	string constant
conversion specifications	keywords	syntax
declaration	Latin character set	token
declaration section	line comment	type
definitions	literal	type qualifier
end of file	memory constant	variable
escape character	padding	width modifier
flag modifier	parameter	

Review Questions

1. The purpose of a header file, such as `stdio.h`, is to store a program's source code.
   a. True
   b. False

2. Any valid printable ASCII character can be used in an identifier.
   a. True
   b. False

3. The C standard function that receives data from the keyboard is `printf`.
   a. True
   b. False

4. Which of the following statements about the structure of a C program is false?
   a. A C program starts with a global declaration section.

b. Declaration sections contain instructions to the computer.

c. Every program must have at least one function.

d. One and only one function may be named `main`.

e. Within each function there is a local declaration section.

5. Which of the following statements about block comments is false?

   a. Comments are internal documentation for programmers.

   b. Comments are used by the preprocessor to help format the program.

   c. Comments begin with a /* token.

   d. Comments cannot be nested.

   e. Comments end with a */ token.

6. Which of the following identifiers is not valid?

   a. `_option`

   b. `amount`

   c. `sales_amount`

   d. `salesAmount`

   e. `$salesAmount`

7. Which of the following is not a data type?

   a. `char`

   b. `float`

   c. `int`

   d. `logical`

   e. `void`

8. The code that establishes the original value for a variable is known as a(n) _____.

   a. assignment

   b. constant

   c. initializer

   d. originator

   e. value

9. Which of the following statements about a constant is true?

   a. Character constants are coded using double quotes (").

   b. It is impossible to tell the computer that a constant should be a `float` or a `long double`.

   c. Like variables, constants have a type and may be named.

   d. Only integer values can be used in a constant.

   e. The value of a constant may be changed during a program's execution.

10. The _____ conversion specification is used to read or write a short integer.

    a. `%c`

    b. `%d`

    c. `%f`

    d. `%hd`

    e. `%lf`

11. To print data left justified, you would use a _____ in the conversion specification.

    a. flag

    b. precision

    c. size

    d. width

    e. width and precision

12. The _____ function reads data from the keyboard.

    a. `displayf`

    b. `printf`

    c. `read`

    d. `scanf`

    e. `write`

13. One of the most common errors for new programmers is forgetting to use the address operator for variables in a `scanf` statement. What is the address operator?

    a. The address modifier (@) in the conversion specification

    b. The ampersand (&)

    c. The caret (^)

    d. The percent (%)

    e. The pound sign (#)

Exercises

14. Which of the following is *not* a character constant in C?

    a. `'C'`

    b. `'bb'`

    c. `"C"`

    d. `'?'`

    e. `' '`

15. Which of the following is *not* an integer constant in C?

    a. -320

    b. +45

    c. -31.80

    d. 1456

    e. 2,456

16. Which of the following is *not* a floating-point constant in C?

    a. 45.6

    b. -14.05

    c. 'a'

    d. pi

    e. 40

17. What is the type of each of the following constants?

    a. 15

    b. -14.24

    c. 'b'

    d. "I"

    e. "16"

18. Which of the following is *not* a valid identifier in C?

    a. A3

    b. 4A

    c. if

    d. IF

    e. tax-rate

19. What is the type of each of the following constants?

    a. "7"

    b. 3

    c. "3.14159"

    d. '2'

    e. 5.1

20. What is the type of each of the following constants?

    a. "Hello"

    b. 15L

    c. 8.5L

    d. 8.5f

    e. '\a'

21. Which of the following identifiers are valid and which are invalid? Explain your answer.

    a. num

    b. num2

    c. 2dNum

    d. 2d_num

    e. num#2

22. Which of the following identifiers are valid and which are invalid? Explain your answer.

    a. num-2

    b. num 2

    c. num_2

    d. _num2

    e. _num_2

23. What is output from the following program fragment? To show your output, draw a grid of C at least 8 lines with at least 15 characters per line.

```
// Local Declarations
int x = 10;
char w = 'Y';
float z = 5.1234;
// Statements
printf("\nFirst\nExample\n:");
printf("%5d\n, w is %c\n", x, w);
printf("\nz is %8.2f\n", z);
```

24. Find any errors in the following program.

```
// This program does nothing
int main
{
    return 0;
}
```

25. Find any errors in the following program.

```
#include (stdio.h)
int main (void)
{
    print ("Hello World");
    return 0;
}
```

26. Find any errors in the following program.

```
include <stdio>
int main (void)
{
    printf('We are to learn correct');
    printf('C language here');
    return 0;
} // main
```

27. Find any errors in the following program.

```
/* This is a program with some errors
   in it to be corrected.
*/
int main (void)
{
// Local Declarations
    integer a;
    floating-point b;
    character c;
// Statements
    printf("The end of the program.");
    return 0;
} // main
```

28. Find any errors in the following program.

```c
/* This is another program with some errors in it to be
corrected.
*/
int main (void)
{
// Local Declarations
    a int;
    b float, double;
    c, d char;
// Statements
    printf("The end of the program.");
    return 0;
} // main
```

29. Find any errors in the following program.

```c
/* This is the last program to be
corrected in these exercises.
*/
int main (void)
{
// Local Declarations
    a int;
    b: c : d char;
    d , e, f double float;
// Statements
    printf("The end of the program.");
    return 0;
} // main
```

Problems

30. Code the variable declarations for each of the following:
   a. a character variable named `option`
   b. an integer variable, sum, initialized to 0
   c. a floating-point variable, `product`, initialized to 1

31. Code the variable declarations for each of the following:
   a. a short integer variable named code
   b. a constant named `salesTax` initialized to .0825
   c. a floating-point named sum of size double initialized to 0

32. Write a statement to print the following line. Assume the total value is contained in a variable named cost.

```
The sales total is: $ 172.53
```

33. Write a program that uses four print statements to print the pattern of asterisks shown below.

```
* * * * * *
* * * * * *
* * * * * *
* * * * * *
```

34. Write a program that uses four print statements to print the pattern of asterisks shown below.

```
*
* *
* * *
* * * *
```

35. Write a program that uses defined constants for the vowels in the alphabet and memory constants for the even decimal digits (0, 2, 4, 6, 8). It then prints the following three lines using literal constants for the odd digits.

```
a e i o u
0 2 4 6 8
1 3 5 7 9
```

36. Write a program that defines five integer variables and initializes them to 1, 10, 100, 1000, and 10000. It then prints them on a single line separated by space characters using the decimal conversion code (%d), and on the next line with the float conversion code (%f). Note the differences between the results. How do you explain them?

37. Write a program that prompts the user to enter a quantity and a cost. The values are to be read into an integer named `quantity` and a float named `unitPrice`. Define the variables and use only one statement to read the values. After reading the values, skip one line and print each value, with an appropriate name, on a separate line.

38. Write a program that prompts the user to enter an integer and then prints the integer first as a character, then as a decimal, and finally as a float. Use separate print statements. A sample run is shown below.

```
The number as a character: K
The number as a decimal: 75
The number as a float: 0.000000
```

Projects

39. Write a C program using `printf` statements to print the three first letters of your first name in big blocks. This program does not read anything from the keyboard. Each letter is formed using seven rows and five columns using the letter itself. For example, the letter B is formed using 17 b's, as shown below as part of the initials BEF.

```
BBBB      EEEEE    FFFFF
B   B     E        F
B   B     E        F
BBBB      EEE      FFF
B   B     E        F
B   B     E        F
BBBB      EEEEE    F
```

This is just an example. Your program must print the first three letters of your first name. Design your `printf` statements carefully to create enough blank lines at the beginning and end to make your initials readable. Use comments in your program to enhance readability as shown in this chapter.

40. Write a program that reads a character, an integer, and a floating-point number. It then prints the character, first using a character format specification (`%c`) and then using an integer specification (`%d`). After printing the character, it prints the integer and floating-point numbers on separate lines. Be sure to provide complete instructions (prompts) for the user.

41. Write a program that prompts the user to enter three numbers and then prints them vertically (each on one line), first forward and then reversed (the last one first), as shown in the following design.

```
Please enter three numbers: 15 35 72 Your numbers forward:
        15
        35
        72
Your numbers reversed:
        72
        35
        15
```

42. Write a program that reads 10 integers and prints the first and the last on one line, the second and the ninth on the next line, the third and the eighth on the next line, and so forth. Sample input and the results are shown below.

```
Please enter 10 numbers:
10 31 2 73 24 65 6 87 18 9
Your numbers are:
        10      9
        31      18
        2       87
        73      6
        24      65
```

43. Write a program that reads nine integers and prints them three in a line separated by commas as shown below.

Input

```
10 31 2 73 24 65 6 87 18
```

Output

```
10, 31, 2
73, 24, 65
6, 87, 18
```

CHAPTER 3

Structure of a
C Program

Learning Objectives

When you complete this chapter, you will be able to:

3.1 List and describe the six expression categories

3.2 Explain the rules of precedence and associativity in evaluating expressions

3.3 Describe the result of side effects in expression evaluation

3.4 Predict the output when an expression is evaluated

3.5 Define implicit and explicit type conversion

3.6 Identify and use the first four statement types: null, expression, return, and compound

3.1 Expressions

Two features set the C language apart from many other languages: expressions and pointers. Both of these concepts lie at the very heart of the language, giving C its unique look and feel. This chapter explores the first of these concepts: expressions. Expressions are not new to you; you have used them in mathematics. However, C's use of expressions is unique to the C language. Closely tied to the concept of expressions are operators, precedence and associativity, and statements, all of which are discussed later in this chapter.

An **expression** is a sequence of operands and operators that reduces to a single value. Expressions can be simple or complex. An operator is a syntactical token that requires an action be taken. An operand is an object on which an operation is performed; it receives an operator's action.

A **simple expression** contains only one operator. For example 2 + 5 is a simple expression whose value is 7; similarly, -a is a simple expression. A **complex expression** contains more than one operator. An example of a complex expression is 2 + 5 * 7. To evaluate a complex expression, we reduce it to a series of simple expressions. In the previous example, we first evaluate the simple expression 5 * 7 (35) and then the expression 2 + 35, giving a result of 37.

Every language has operators whose actions are clearly specified in the language syntax. The order in which the operators in a complex expression are evaluated is determined by a set of priorities known as precedence; the higher the precedence, the earlier the expression containing the operator is evaluated. **Table 3-1** shows the precedence of each operator.

As you can see in Table 3-1, in the expression 2 + 5 * 7, multiplication has a higher priority than addition so the multiply expression is evaluated first. We discuss precedence in more detail in the next section.

Table 3-1 Precedence

OPERATOR	DESCRIPTION	EXAMPLE	SIDE EFFECTS	ASSOC	PR
	Identifiers	`amount`	N	N/A	16
	Constants	`3.14159`			
	Parenthetical Expressions	`(a + b)`			
`[ ]`	Array Index	`ary[i]`	N	Left-Right	16
`f(...)`	Function Call	`doIt(x, y)`	Y		
`.`	Direct Member Selection	`str.mem`	N		
`->`	Indirect Member Selection	`ptr->mem`	N		
`++  --`	Postfix Increment • Decrement	`a++`	Y		
`++  --`	Prefix Increment • Decrement	`++a`	Y	Right-Left	15
`sizeof`	Size in Bytes	`sizeof(int)`	N		
`~`	Ones Complement	`-a`	N		
`!`	Not	`!a`	N		
`+  -`	Plus • Minus	`+a`	N		
`&`	Address	`&a`	N		
`*`	Dereference/Indirection	`*ptr`	N		
`( )`	Type Cast	`(int)ptr`	N	Right-Left	14
`*  /  %`	Multiply • Divide • Modulus	`a * b`	N	Left-Right	13
`+  -`	Addition • Subtraction	`a + b`	N	Left-Right	12
`<<  >>`	Bit Shift Left • Bit Shift Right	`a << 3`	N	Left-Right	11
`<  <=  >  >=`	Comparison	`a < 5`	N	Left-Right	10
`==  !=`	Equal • Not Equal	`a == b`	N	Left-Right	9
`&`	Bitwise And	`a & b`	N	Left-Right	8
`^`	Bitwise Exclusive Or	`a ^ b`	N	Left-Right	7
`|`	Bitwise Or	`a	b`	N	Left-Right	6
`&&`	Logical And	`a && b`	N	Left-Right	5
`||`	Logical Or	`a || b`	N	Left-Right	4
`?  :`	Conditional	`a ? x : y`	N	Right-Left	3

`=  +=  -=`
`*=  /=  %=`
`>>=  <<=`
`&=  ^=  |=`
	Assignment	`a = 5`
		`a %= b`
		`a &= c`
		`a |= d`
			Y	Right-Left	2

`,`	Comma	`a, b, c`	N	Left-Right	1

If two operators with the same precedence occur in a complex expression, another attribute of an operator, its associativity, takes control. **Associativity** is the parsing direction used to evaluate an expression. It can be either left-to-right or right-to-left. When two operators with the same precedence occur in an expression and their associativity is left-to-right, the left operator is evaluated first. For example, in the expression 3*4/6, there are two operators, multiplication and division, with the same precedence and left-to-right associativity. Therefore, the multiplication is evaluated before the division. We also discuss associativity in more detail in the next section. It should be noted that an expression always reduces to a single value.

We can divide simple expressions into six categories based on the number of operands, relative positions of the operand and operator, and the precedence of operator. **Figure 3-1** shows the categories.

Figure 3-1   Expression categories

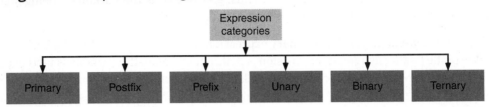

Primary Expressions

The most elementary type of expression is a primary expression. A **primary expression** consists of only one operand with no operator. In C, the operand in the primary expression can be a name, a constant, or a parenthesized expression. Although a primary expression has no operator, the null operator in this expression has the precedence of 16 according to the table of precedence. In other words, a primary expression is evaluated first in a complex expression.

Names

A name is any identifier for a variable, a function, or any other object in the language. The following are examples of some names used as primary expressions:

```
A      b12 price      calc     INT_MAX SIZE
```

Literal Constants

The second type of primary expression is the literal constant. As you already know, a constant is a piece of data whose value can't change during the execution of the program. The following are examples of literal constants used as primary expressions:

```
5      123.98     'A' "Welcome"
```

Parenthetical Expressions

The third type of primary expression is the parenthetical expression. Any value enclosed in parentheses must be reducible to a single value and is therefore a primary expression. This includes any of the complex expressions when they are enclosed in parentheses. Thus, a complex expression can be enclosed in parentheses to make it a primary expression. The following are primary expressions:

```
(2 * 3 + 4)   (a = 23 + b * 6)
```

Postfix Expressions

The postfix expression consists of one operand followed by one operator. Its category is shown in **Figure 3-2**. There are several operators that create a postfix expression as you can see in the precedence table. We discuss only three of them here: function call, postfix increment, and postfix decrement.

Figure 3-2   Postfix expressions

Function Call

We have already used a postfix expression. In the hello world program, we wrote a message on the monitor using the `printf` function. Function calls are postfix expressions. The function name is the operand and the operator is the parentheses that follow the name. The parentheses may contain arguments or be empty. When present, the arguments are part of the operator.

Postfix Increment/Decrement

The postfix increment and postfix decrement are also postfix operators. Virtually all programs require somewhere in their code that the value 1 be added to a variable. In early languages, this additive operation could only be represented as a binary expression. C provides the same functionality in two expressions: postfix and prefix.

In the postfix increment, the variable is increased by 1. Thus, `a++` output is the variable a being increased by 1. The effect of `a++` is the same as `a = a + 1`.

Although both the postfix increment (`a++`) and binary expression (`a = a + 1`) add 1 to the variable, there is a major difference. The value of the postfix increment expression is determined *before* the variable is increased. For instance, if the variable a contains 4 before the expression is evaluated, the value of the expression `a++` is 4. As a result of evaluating the expression and its side effect, a contains 5. The value and side effect of the postfix increment are graphically shown in **Figure 3-3**.

Figure 3-3   Result of postfix a++

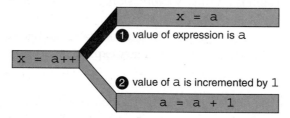

The postfix decrement (`a--`) also has a value and a side effect. As with the increment, the value of the expression is the value of a before the decrement; the side effect is the variable is decremented by 1.

Program 3-1 demonstrates the effect of the postfix increment expression.

> **Program 3-1** | Demonstrate postfix increment

```
 1   /* Example of postfix increment.
 2      Written by:
 3      Date:
 4   */
 5   #include <stdio.h>
 6   int main (void)
 7   {
 8   // Local Declarations
 9      int a;
10
11   // Statements
12      a = 4;
13      printf("value of a: %2d\n", a);
```

(continue)

Program 3-1 Demonstrate postfix increment *(continued)*

```
14    printf("value of a++: %2d\n", a++);
15    printf("new value of a: %2d\n\n", a);
16    return 0;
17 } // main
```

Output
```
value of a: 4
value of a++: 4
new value of a: 5
```

Prefix Expressions

In prefix expressions, the operator comes before the operand as seen in **Figure 3-4**.

Figure 3-4 Prefix expression

Variable

Prefix Increment/Decrement

In C, we have only two prefix operators that form prefix expressions: prefix increment and prefix decrement. Just like the postfix increment and postfix decrement operators, the prefix increment and prefix decrement operators are shorthand notations for adding or subtracting 1 from a variable.

Note | The operand in a postfix expression must be a variable while the operand of a prefix expression must be a variable.

There is one major difference between the postfix and prefix operators, however: with the prefix operators, the effect takes place *before* the expression that contains the operator is evaluated. Note that this is the reverse of the postfix operation. **Figure 3-5** shows the operation graphically.

Figure 3-5 Result of prefix ++a

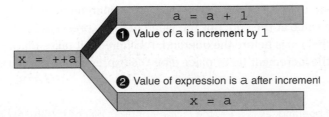

The effect of both the postfix and prefix increment is the same: The variable is incremented by 1. If we don't need the value of the expression—that is, if all we need is the effect of incrementing the value of a variable by 1— then it makes no difference which one we use. You will find that programmers use the postfix increment and decrement more often, if for no other reason than that the variable is shown first and is therefore easier to read. It should be noted here that (++a) has the same effect as (a = a + 1).

On the other hand, if we require both the value and the effect, then our application determines which one we need to use. When we need the value of the expression to be the current value of the variable, we use the postfix operator;

when we need the value to be the new value of the variable (after it has been incremented or decremented), we use the prefix operator. **Program 3-2** demonstrates the prefix increment expression. Study it carefully, and compare it to the output from Program 3-1.

Program 3-2 | Demonstrate prefix increment

```
 1   /* Example of prefix increment.
 2      Written by:
 3      Date:
 4   */
 5   #include <stdio.h>
 6   int main (void)
 7   {
 8   // Local Declarations
 9      int a;
10
11   // Statements
12      a = 4;
13      printf("value of a : %2d\n", a);
14      printf("value of ++a : %2d\n", ++a);
15      printf("new value of a : %2d\n", a);
16      return 0;
17   } // main
```

Output
```
value of a : 4
value of ++a : 5
new value of a : 5
```

The only difference in the output of Program 3-1 and Program 3-2 is the use of the increment operators. The first program uses the postfix increment; the second uses the unary prefix increment. In both cases, we start with the same value for a and it has the same value at the end. But the value of the expression itself is different. To help remember the difference, use this rule: If the ++ is before the operand, the increment takes place before the expression is evaluated; if it is *after* the operand, the increment takes place *after* the expression is evaluated.

Note | If ++ is after the operand, as in a++, the *increment* takes place after the expression is evaluated. If ++ is before the operand, as in ++a, the increment takes place before the expression is evaluated.

Unary Expressions

A unary expression, like a prefix expression, consists of one operator and one operand. Also like the prefix expression, the operator comes before the operand. Although prefix expressions and unary expressions look the same, they belong to different expression categories because the prefix expression needs a variable as the operand while the unary expression can have an expression or a variable as the operand. Many of the unary expressions are also familiar to you from mathematics and will require little explanation. In this chapter we discuss the `sizeof` operator, the plus/minus operators, and the cast operator. You'll learn about others as you become a more experienced programmer. The format of the unary expressions is demonstrated in **Figure 3-6**.

Figure 3-6 Unary expressions

sizeof

The `sizeof` operator tells us the size, in bytes, of a type or a primary expression. By specifying the size of an object during execution, we make our program more portable to other hardware. A simple example will illustrate the point. On some personal computers, the size of the integer type is 2 bytes. On some mainframe computers, it is 4 bytes. On the very large supercomputers, it can be as large as 16 bytes. If it is important to know the exact size (in bytes) of an integer, we can use the `sizeof` operator with the integer type as shown below.

```
sizeof (int)
```

It is also possible to find the size of a primary expression. Here are two examples.

```
sizeof -345.23   sizeof x
```

Unary Plus/Minus

The unary plus and unary minus operators are what we think of as simply the plus and minus signs. In C, however, they are actually operators. Because they are operators, they can be used to compute the arithmetic value of an operand.

The plus operator does not change the value of the expression. If the expression's value is negative, it remains negative; if the expression's value is positive, it remains positive.

The minus operator changes the sign of a value algebraically—that is, to change it from plus to minus or minus to plus. Note, however, that the value of the stored variable is unchanged. The operation of these operators is seen in **Table 3-2**.

Table 3-2 Examples of unary plus and minus expressions

EXPRESSION	CONTENTS OF A BEFORE *AND* AFTER EXPRESSION	EXPRESSION VALUE
+a	3	+3
−a	3	−3
+a	−5	−5
−a	−5	+5

Cast Operator

The third unary operator we discuss in this chapter is cast. The cast operator converts one expression type to another. For example, to convert an integer to a real number, we would use the following unary expression.

```
(float) x
```

It is important to note that, as with all of the unary operators, only the expression value is changed. The integer variable, x, is unchanged. We discuss the cast operator in detail in "Explicit Type Conversion (Cast)" in Section 3.5.

Binary Expressions

Binary expressions are formed by an operand-operator-operand combination. They are perhaps the most common expression category. Any two numbers added, subtracted, multiplied, or divided are usually formed in algebraic notation, which is a binary expression. There are many binary expressions. We cover the first two in this chapter. **Figure 3-7** shows the format of a binary expression.

Figure 3-7   Binary expressions

Multiplicative Expressions

The first binary expression we study, multiplicative expressions, which takes its name from the first operator, includes the multiply, divide, and modulus operators. These operators have the highest priority (13) among the binary operators and are, therefore, evaluated first among them.

The result of a multiply operator (*) is the product of the two operands. The operands can be any arithmetic type (integral or floating-point). The type of the result depends on the conversion rule that we discuss later in this chapter.

```
10 * 3    // evaluates to 30
true * 4  // evaluates to 4
'A' * 2   // evaluates to 130
22.3 * 2  // evaluates to 44.6
```

The result of a divide operator (/) depends on the type of the operands. If one or both operands is a floating-point type, the result is a floating-point quotient. If both operands are integral type, the result is the integral part of the quotient. The following shows some examples of the division operator.

```
10 / 3    // evaluates to 3
true / 4  // evaluates to 0
'A' / 2   // evaluates to 32
22.3 / 2  // evaluates to 11.15
```

Multiply and divide are well known, but you may not be familiar with the modulus operator (%), more commonly known as modulo. This operator divides the first operand by the second and returns the remainder rather than the quotient. Both operands must be integral types and the operator returns the remainder as an integer type. The following examples demonstrate the modulo operator.

```
10 % 3    // evaluates to 1
true % 4  // evaluates to 1
'A' % 10  // evaluates to 5
22.3 % 2  // Error: Modulo cannot be floating-point
```

Because the division and modulus operators are related, they are often confused. Remember: The value of an expression with the division operator is the quotient; the value of a modulus operator is the remainder. Study the effect of these two operators in the following expressions:

```
3 / 5    // evaluates to 0
3 % 5    // evaluates to 3
```

Another important point to remember: if the first integral operand is smaller than the second integral operand, and the result of division is 0, the result of the modulo operator is the first operand as shown below:

```
3 / 7    // evaluates to 0
3 % 7    // evaluates to 3
```

Additive Expressions

In additive expressions, the second operand is added to or subtracted from the first operand, depending on the operator used. The operands in an additive expression can be any arithmetic type (integral or floating-point). Additive operators have lower precedence (12) than multiplicative operators (13); therefore, they are evaluated after multiplicative expressions. Two simple examples are shown below:

```
3 + 7    // evaluates to 10
3 - 7    // evaluates to -4
```

Now let's look at a short program that uses some of these expressions. **Program 3-3** contains several binary expressions.

Program 3-3 | Binary expressions

```
 1  /* This program demonstrates binary expressions.
 2     Written by:
 3     Date:
 4  */
 5  #include <stdio.h>
 6  int main (void)
 7  {
 8  // Local Declarations
 9     int a = 17;
10     int b = 5;
11     float x = 17.67;
12     float y = 5.1;
13
14  // Statements
15     printf("Integral calculations\n");
16     printf("%d + %d = %d\n", a, b, a + b);
17     printf("%d - %d = %d\n", a, b, a - b);
18     printf("%d * %d = %d\n", a, b, a * b);
19     printf("%d / %d = %d\n", a, b, a / b);
20     printf("%d %% %d = %d\n", a, b, a % b);
21     printf("\n");
22
23     printf("Floating-point calculations\n");
24     printf("%f + %f = %f\n", x, y, x + y);
25     printf("%f - %f = %f\n", x, y, x - y);
26     printf("%f * %f = %f\n", x, y, x * y);
27     printf("%f / %f = %f\n", x, y, x / y);
28     return 0;
29  } // main
```

(continue)

Program 3-3   Binary expressions *(continued)*

```
Output
Integral calculations
17 + 5 = 22
17 - 5 = 12
17 * 5 = 85
17 / 5 = 3
17 % 5 = 2

Floating-point calculations
17.670000 + 5.100000 = 22.770000
17.670000 - 5.100000 = 12.570000
17.670000 * 5.100000 = 90.116997
17.670000 / 5.100000 = 3.464706
```

This simple program requires only three explanatory comments: (1) Note that even for a simple program we include all of the standard documentation comments. (2) We do not recommend that you include calculations in print statements as we have done in this program—it is not a good structured programming technique. We include them in this program because you haven't yet learned how to save the output of a calculation. (3) Study the format string in statement 20. To print a percent sign as text in the format string, we need to code two percent signs.

Assignment Expressions

The assignment expression evaluates the operand on the right side of the operator (=) and places its value in the variable on the left. The assignment expression has a value and a side effect.

> The value of the total expression is the value of the expression on the right of the assignment operator (=).

> The side effect places the expression value in the variable on the left of the assignment operator.

> The left operand in an assignment expression must be a single variable.

There are two forms of assignment: simple and compound.

Simple Assignment

Simple assignment is found in algebraic expressions. Three examples of simple assignments are shown below.

```
a = 5    b = x + 1    i = i + 1
```

Of course, for the effect to take place, the left variable must be able to receive it; that is, it must be a variable, not a constant. If the left operand cannot receive a value and we assign one to it, we get a compile error.

Compound Assignment

A compound assignment is a shorthand notation for a simple assignment. It requires that the left operand be repeated as a part of the right expression. Five compound assignment operators are discussed in this chapter: *=, /=, %=, +=, and -=.

To evaluate a compound assignment expression, first change it to a simple assignment, as shown in **Table 3-3**. Then perform the operation to determine the value of the expression.

Table 3-3 Expansion of compound expressions

COMPOUND EXPRESSION	EQUIVALENT SIMPLE EXPRESSION
x *= expression	x = x * expression
x /= expression	x = x / expression
x %= expression	x = x % expression
x += expression	x = x + expression
x -= expression	x = x - expression

When a compound assignment is used with an expression, the expression is evaluated first. Thus, the expression

    x *= y + 3

is evaluated as

    x = x * (y + 3)

which, given the values x is 10 and y is 5, evaluates to 80.

Program 3-4 demonstrates the first three compound expressions.

Program 3-4 | Demonstration of compound assignments

```
 1   /* Demonstrate examples of compound assignments.
 2      Written by:
 3      Date:
 4   */
 5   #include <stdio.h>
 6
 7   int main (void)
 8   {
 9   // Local Declarations
10      int x;
11      int y;
12
13   // Statements
14      x = 10;
15      y = 5;
16
17      printf("x: %2d | y: %2d ", x, y);
18      printf(" | x *= y + 2: %2d ", x *= y + 2);
19      printf("  x is now: %2d\n", x);
20
21      x = 10;
```

(continue)

Program 3-4   Demonstration of compound assignments *(continued)*

```
22      printf("x: %2d | y: %2d ", x, y);
23      printf(" | x /= y + 1: %2d ", x /= y + 1);
24      printf("  x is now: %2d\n", x);
25
26      x = 10;
27      printf("x: %2d | y: %2d ",  x, y);
28      printf(" | x %%= y - 3: %2d ", x %= y - 3);
29      printf("  x is now: %2d\n", x);
30
31      return 0;
32 }    // main
```

Output
```
x: 10 | y:  5  | x *= y + 2: 70    x is now: 70
x: 10 | y:  5  | x /= y + 1:  1    x is now:  1
x: 10 | y:  5  | x %= y - 3:  0    x is now:  0
```

Note that we have used an assignment statement in the `printf` statements to demonstrate that an assignment expression has a value. As we said before, this is not good programming style, but we use it here to match the format used in Program 3-3. Also, since we are changing the value of x with each assignment, even though it is in a printf statement, we need to reset it to 10 for each of the print series.

Note | Do not hide calculations in `print` statements.

3.2 Precedence and Associativity

Precedence determines the order in which different operators in a complex expression are evaluated. Associativity is used to determine the order in which operators with the same precedence are evaluated in a complex expression. Another way of stating this is that associativity determines how operators with the same precedence are grouped together to form complex expressions. Precedence is applied before associativity to determine the order in which expressions are evaluated. Associativity is then applied, if necessary.

Precedence

The concept of precedence is well-founded in mathematics. For example, in algebra, multiplication and division are performed before addition and subtraction. C extends the concept to 16 levels, as shown in Table 3-1.

The following is a simple example of precedence:

```
2 + 3 * 4
```

This expression is actually two binary expressions, with one addition and one multiplication operator. Addition has a precedence of 12. Multiplication has a precedence of 13. This output in the multiplication being done first, followed by the addition, as shown below in the same expression with the default parentheses added. The value of the complete expression is 14.

```
(2 + (3 * 4)) → 14
```

As another example consider the following expression:

```
-b++
```

Two different operators are in this expression. The first is the unary minus, the second is the postfix increment. The postfix increment has the higher precedence (16), so it is evaluated first. Then the unary minus, with a precedence of 15, is evaluated. To reflect the precedence, we have recoded the expression using parentheses.

```
- (b++)
```

Assuming that the value of b is 5 initially, the expression is evaluated to –5. What is the value of b after the expression is complete? It is 6 because the operator has an effect that is separate from the value of the expression.

Program 3-5 demonstrates precedence by printing the same expression, once without parentheses and once with parentheses to change the precedence. Because the parentheses create a primary expression that must be evaluated before the binary multiply, the answer is different.

Program 3-5 | Precedence

```
 1   /* Examine the effect of precedence on an expression.
 2      Written by:
 3      Date:
 4   */
 5   #include <stdio.h>
 6
 7   int main (void)
 8   {
 9   // Local Declarations
10      int a = 10;
11      int b = 20;
12      int c = 30;
13
14   // Statements
15      printf ("a * b + c is: %d\n", a * b + c);
16      printf ("a * (b + c) is: %d\n", a * (b + c));
17      return 0;
18   } // main
```

Output
```
a * b + c is: 230
a * (b + c) is: 500
```

Associativity

Associativity can be left-to-right or right-to-left. **Left-to-right associativity** evaluates the expression by starting on the left and moving to the right. Conversely, **right-to-left associativity** evaluates the expression by proceeding from the right to the left. Remember, however, that associativity is used only when the operators all have the same precedence.

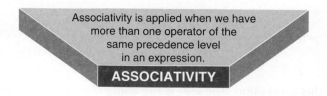

Note	**Associativity**
	Associativity is applied when there is more than one operator of the same precedence level in an expression.

Left-to-right Associativity

The following shows an example of left-to-right associativity. Here we have four operators of the same precedence (* / % *).

```
3 * 8 / 4 % 4 * 5
```

Associativity determines how the subexpressions are grouped together. All of these operators have the same precedence (13). Their associativity is from left to right. So they are grouped as follows:

```
((((3 * 8) / 4) % 4) * 5)
```

The value of this expression is 10. A graphical representation of this expression is shown in **Figure 3-8**.

Figure 3-8   Left-to-right associativity

Right-to-left Associativity

Several operators have right-to-left associativity, as shown in the precedence table. For example, when more than one assignment operator occurs in an assignment expression, the assignment operators must be interpreted from right to left. This means that the rightmost expression will be evaluated first; then its value will be assigned to the operand on the left of the assignment operator and the next expression will be evaluated. Under these rules, the expression

```
a += b *= c -= 5
```

is evaluated as

```
(a += (b *= (c -= 5)))
```

which is expanded to

```
(a = a + (b = b * (c = c - 5)))
```

If a has an initial value of 3, b has an initial value of 5, and c has an initial value of 8, these expressions become

```
(a = 3 + (b = (5 * (c = 8 - 5))))
```

which output in c being assigned a value of 3, b being assigned a value of 15, and a being assigned a value of 18. The value of the complete expression is also 18. A diagram of this expression is shown in **Figure 3-9**.

Figure 3-9   Right-to-left associativity

A simple but common form of assignment is shown below. Suppose we have several variables that all need to be initialized to zero. Rather than initializing each separately, we can use a complex statement to do it.

```
a = b = c = d = 0;
```

3.3 Side Effects

A side effect is an action that output from the evaluation of an expression. For example, in an assignment, C first evaluates the expression on the right of the assignment operator and then places the value in the left variable. Changing the value of the left variable is a side effect. Consider the following expression:

```
x = 4;
```

This simple expression has three parts. First, on the right of the assignment operator is a primary expression that has the value 4. Second, the whole expression (x = 4) also has a value of 4. And third, as a side effect, x receives the value 4.

Let's modify the expression slightly and see the same three parts.

```
x = x + 4;
```

Assuming that x has an initial value of 3, the value of the expression on the right of the assignment operator has a value of 7. The whole expression also has a value of 7. And as a side effect, x receives the value of 7. To prove these three steps to yourself, write and run the following code fragment:

```
int x = 3;
printf("Step 1--Value of x: %d\n", x);
printf("Step 2--Value of x = x + 4: %d\n", x = x + 4);
printf("Step 3--Value of x now: %d\n", x);
```

Now, let's consider the side effect in the postfix increment expression. This expression is typically coded as shown below.

```
a++
```

As we saw earlier, the value of this expression is the value of a before the expression is evaluated. As a side effect, however, the value of a is incremented by 1.

In C, six operators generate side effects: prefix increment and decrement, postfix increment and decrement, assignment, and function call.

3.4 Evaluating Expressions

Now that we have introduced the concepts of precedence, associativity, and side effects, let's work through some examples.

Example: Expression without Side Effects

The first expression is shown below. It has no side effects, so the values of all of its variables are unchanged.

```
a * 4 + b / 2 - c * b
```

For this example, assume that the values of the variables are

3	4	5
a	b	c

To evaluate an expression *without side effects,* follow the simple rules shown below.

1. Replace the variables with their values. This gives us the following expression:

```
3 * 4 + 4 / 2 - 5 * 4
```

2. Evaluate the highest precedence operators, and replace them with the resulting value. In the above expression, the operators with the highest precedence are the multiply and divide (13). We therefore evaluate them first from the left and replace them with the resulting values. The expression is now

```
(3 * 4) + (4 / 2) - (5 * 4) → 12 + 2 - 20
```

3. Repeat step 2 until the result is a single value.

In this example, there is only one more precedence, binary addition and subtraction. After they are evaluated, the final value is –6. Because this expression had no side effects, all of the variables have the same values after the expression has been evaluated that they had at the beginning.

Example: Expression with side effects

Now let's look at the rules for an expression that has side effects and parenthesized expressions. For this example, consider the expression

```
--a * (3 + b) / 2 - c++ * b
```

Assume that the variables have the values used above, a is 3, b is 4, c is 5. To evaluate this expression, use the following rules:

1. Calculate the value of the parenthesized expression (3 + b) first (precedence 16). The expression now reads

```
--a * 7 / 2 - c++ * b
```

2. Evaluate the postfix expression (c++) next (precedence 16). Remember that as a postfix expression, the value of c++ is the same as the value of c; the increment takes place after the evaluation. The expression is now

```
--a * 7 / 2 - 5 * b
```

3. Evaluate the prefix expression (--a) next (priority 15). Remember that as a prefix expression, the value of --a is the value after the side effect, which means that we first decrement a and then use its decremented value. The expression is now

```
2 * 7 / 2 - 5 * b
```

4. The multiply and division are now evaluated using their associativity rule, left to right, as shown below.

```
14 / 2 - 5 * b → 7 - 5 * 4 → 7 - 20
```

5. The last step is to evaluate the subtraction. The final expression value is -13 as shown in the final example.

```
7 - 20 → -13
```

After the side effects, the variables have the values shown below.

2	4	6
a	b	c

Program 3-6 evaluates the two expressions in this section.

Program 3-6 | Evaluating expressions

```
1  /* Evaluate two complex expressions.
2     Written by:
3     Date:
4  */
5  #include <stdio.h>
6  int main (void)
7  {
8  // Local Declarations
9     int a = 3;
10    int b = 4;
11    int c = 5;
12    int x;
13    int y;
14
15 // Statements
16    printf("Initial values of the variables: \n");
17    printf("a = %d\tb = %d\tc = %d\n\n", a, b, c);
18
19    x = a*4 + b/ 2- c*b;
20    printf("Value of a* 4+b /2-c *b: %d\n", x);
21
22    y = -a * (3 + b) / 2 - c++ * b;
23    printf("Value of -a * (3 + b) / 2 - c++ * b: %d\n", y);
24    printf("\nValues of the variables are now: \n");
25    printf("a = %d   b = %d   c = %d\n\n", a, b, c);
26
27    return 0;
28 } // main
```

(continue)

Program 3-6 Evaluating expressions *(continued)*

Output
```
Initial values of the variables:
a = 3 b = 4 c = 5

Value of a* 4+b /2-c *b: -6
Value of -a * (3 + b) / 2 - c++ * b: -13

Values of the variables are now:
a = 2 b = 4 c = 6
```

> **Note**
>
> **Warning**
>
> A warning is in order: In C, if an expression variable is modified more than once during its evaluation, the result is undefined. C has no specific rule to cover when the side effect takes place, and compiler writers can implement the side effect in different ways. The result is that different compilers will give different expression output.

3.5 Type Conversion

Up to this point, we have assumed that all of our expressions involved data of the same type. But, what happens when we write an expression that involves two different data types, such as multiplying an integer and a floating-point number? To perform these evaluations, one of the types must be converted.

Implicit Type Conversion

When the types of the two operands in a binary expression are different, C automatically converts one type to another. This is known as implicit type conversion. For implicit type conversion, C has several complicated rules that we gradually introduce throughout the book. We mention some of the simple conversions in this section.

Conversion Rank

Before we discuss how conversions are handled, we need to discuss the concept of conversion rank. In C, we can assign a rank to the integral and floating-point arithmetic types. **Figure 3-10** shows the ranks as we use them for conversion in this chapter. While the 1 to 9 scale we use is conceptually correct, the actual implementation is much more complex.

As shown in Figure 3-10, a long double real has a higher rank than a long integer and a short integer has a higher rank than a character.

Figure 3-10 Conversion rank

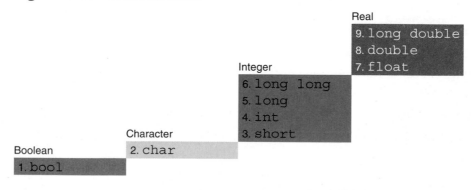

Conversions in Assignment Expressions

A simple assignment involves an assignment operator and two operands. Depending on the difference in the rank, C tries to either promote or demote the right expression to make it the same rank as the left variable. Promotion occurs if the right expression has lower rank; demotion occurs if the right expression has a higher rank.

Promotion

There is normally no problem with promotion. The rank of the right expression is elevated to the rank of the left variable. The value of the expression is the value of the right expression after the promotion. The following examples demonstrate some simple promotions.

```
bool        b = true;
char        c = 'A';
int         i = 1234;
long double d = 3458.0004;
c = b;  // value of c is SOH (ASCII 1)
i = c;  // value of i is 65
d = b;  // value of d is 1.0
d = i;  // value of d is 1234.0
```

Demotion

Demotion may or may not create problems. If the size of the variable at the left side can accommodate the value of the expression, there is no problem; however, some of the output may surprise you.

Any integral or real value can be assigned to a Boolean type. If the value of the expression on the right is zero, false (0) is stored; if the result is not zero, either positive or negative, true (1) is stored.

When an integer or a real is assigned to a variable of type character, the least significant byte of the number is converted to a character and stored. When a real is stored in an integer, the fraction part is dropped. However, if the integral part is larger than the maximum value that can be stored, the output are invalid and unpredictable. Similarly, when we try to store a `long double` in a variable of type `float`, the output are valid if the value fits or invalid if it is too large.

The following examples demonstrate demotion.

```
bool    b = false;
char    c = "A";
short   s = 78;
int     j = INT_MAX;
int k
... k = 65;
b = c;       // value of b is 1 (true)
s = j;       // value of s is unpredictable
c = k + 1;   // demotion: value of c is 'B'
```

Conversion in Other Binary Expressions

Conversion has a different set of rules for the other binary expressions. The rules are sometimes very complicated, but we can summarize them in three steps, which cover most cases:

1. The operand with the higher rank is determined using the ranking in Figure 3-10.

2. The lower-ranked operand is promoted to the rank defined in step 1. After the promotion, both expressions have the same rank.

3. The operation is performed with the expression value having the type of the promoted rank.

The following examples demonstrate some common conversions.

```
bool        b = true;
char        c = 'A';
int         i = 3650;
short       s = 78;
long double d = 3458.0004;
b + c   // b promoted; result is "B" ('A' + 1)
i * s;  // result is an int
d * c;  // result is long double
```

Let's look at a small program to see the effect of implicit conversions. In **Program 3-7** we add a character, an integer, and a float. We can add characters to integers and floating-point values because all characters have an ASCII value that can be promoted.

Program 3-7 | Implicit type conversion

```
 1  /* Demonstrate automatic promotion of numeric types.
 2     Written by:
 3     Date:
 4  */
 5  #include <stdio.h>
 6  #include <stdbool.h>
 7
 8  int main (void)
 9  {
10  // Local Declarations
11     bool b = true;
12     char c = 'A';
13     float d = 245.3;
14     int i = 3650;
15     short s =78;
16
17  // Statements
18     printf("bool + char is char: %c\n", b + c);
19     printf("int * short is int: %d\n", i * s);
20     printf("float * char is float: %f\n", d * c);
21
22     c = c + b;  // bool promoted to char
23     d = d + c;  // char promoted to float
24     b = false;
25     b = -d; // float demoted to bool
26
```

(continue)

Program 3-7   Implicit type conversion *(continued)*

```
27      printf("\nAfter execution...\n");
28      printf("char + true: %c\n", c);
29      printf("float + char: %f\n", d);
30      printf("bool = -float: %f\n", b);
31
32      return 0;
33 } // main
```

Output
```
bool + char is char: B
int * short is int: 284700
float * char is float: 15944.500000

After execution...
char + true: B
float + char: 311.299988
bool = -float: 1
```

Several points in this program require explanation. First, as we stated before, it is not a good programming practice to code an expression in a print statement. We do it in this program, however, to demonstrate the promotion or demotion of the expression.

The first print series displays the value of mixed type expressions. As you examine each result, note that the value printed is in the form of the higher ranked variable. For example, in statement 18 the Boolean in the expression (b) is promoted to a character and then added to the value of the character expression (c). The result is the character B, which is then passed to the `printf` function where it is printed using the format specification %c.

The second print series displays the output of assignments. In the first one, we add true (1) to the letter A. The result is B as you would expect. In the second assignment, we add the letter B from the previous assignment to a real number. The new value of the real number is almost 66 greater than the original value. The difference occurs because real numbers are not exact. Rather than storing 245.3, the value stored was 245.299988.

Finally, note what happens when we assign a negative, real number to a boolean. The result is *true*.

Explicit Type Conversion (Cast)

Rather than let the compiler implicitly convert data, we can convert data from one type to another ourself using explicit type conversion. Explicit type conversion uses the unary cast operator, which has a precedence of 14. To cast data from one type to another, we specify the new type in parentheses before the value we want converted. For example, to convert an integer, a, to a `float`, we code the expression shown below.

```
(float) a
```

Note that in this operation, like any other unary operation, the value stored in a is still of type `int`, but the value of the expression is promoted to `float`.

One use of the cast is to ensure that the result of a divide is a real number. For example, if we calculated the average of a series of integer test scores without a cast, the result would be an integer. To force a real result, we cast the calculation as shown below.

```
average = (float) totalScores / numScores;
```

In this statement, there is an explicit conversion of `totalScores` to `float`, and then an implicit conversion of `numScores` so that it will match. The result of the divide is then a floating-point number to be assigned to average.

But beware! What would be the result of the following expression when a is 3?

```
(float) (a / 10)
```

Are you surprised to find that the result is 0.0? Because no conversions are required to divide integer 3 by integer 10, C simply divides with an integer result, 0. The integer 0 is then explicitly converted to the floating-point 0.0. To get a *float* result, we must cast one of the numbers as shown below.

```
(float) a / 10
```

One final thought about casts: Even when the compiler can correctly cast for you, it is sometimes better to code the cast explicitly as a reminder that the cast is taking place.

Program 3-8 demonstrates the use of explicit casts. In this program, we divide several mixed types. While the output are nonsense, they demonstrate the effect of casting.

Program 3-8 | Explicit casts

```
 1   /* Demonstrate casting of numeric types.
 2      Written by:
 3      Date:
 4   */
 5   #include <stdio.h>
 6
 7   int main (void)
 8   {
 9   // Local Declarations
10      char aChar = '\0';
11      int intNum1 = 100;
12      int intNum2 = 45;
13      double fltNum1 = 100.0;
14      double fltNum2 = 45.0;
15      double fltNum3;
16
17   // Statements
18      printf("aChar numeric: %3d\n", aChar);
19      printf("intNum1 contains: %3d\n", intNum1);
20      printf("intNum2 contains: %3d\n", intNum2);
21      printf("fltNum1 contains: %6.2f\n", fltNum1);
22      printf("fltNum2 contains: %6.2f\n", fltNum2);
23
24      fltNum3 = (double)(intNum1 / intNum2);
25      printf
26          ("\n(double)(intNum1 / intNum2): %6.2f\n",
27              fltNum3);
```

(continue)

Program 3-8 Explicit casts *(continued)*

```
28
29     fltNum3 = (double)intNum1 / intNum2;
30     printf("(double) intNum1 / intNum2: %6.2f\n",
31             fltNum3);
32
33     aChar = (char)(fltNum1 / fltNum2);
34     printf("(char)(fltNum1 / fltNum2): %3d\n", aChar);
35
36     return 0;
37 } // main
```

Output
```
aChar numeric: 0
intNum1 contains: 100
intNum2 contains: 45
fltNum1 contains: 100.00
fltNum2 contains: 45.00

(double)(intNum1 / intNum2): 2.00
(double) intNum1 / intNum2 : 2.22
(char)(fltNum1 / fltNum2): 2
```

Study the casts carefully. The only difference between statements 24 and 29 is the use of parentheses around the calculation. In statement 24, both operands are integers so the result of the division is integer, which is then cast to a `double`. In statement 29, `intNum1` is cast to a `double`. The compiler automatically casts intNum2 to a `double` before the division. The result is therefore a `double`. Finally, in statement 33, we cast the result of the integer division into a character.

3.6 Statements

A statement causes an action to be performed by the program. It translates directly into one or more executable computer instructions.

You may have noticed that we have used a semicolon at the end of the statements in our programs. Most statements need a semicolon at the end; some do not. When we discuss statements, we identify those that do.

Statement Type

C defines eleven types of statements, which are shown in **Figure 3-11**. In this chapter, we will discuss the first four. You will learn about other types as you become a more experienced programmer.

Null Statement

The null statement is just a semicolon (the terminator) as shown below:

```
;    // null statement
```

Figure 3-11 Types of statements

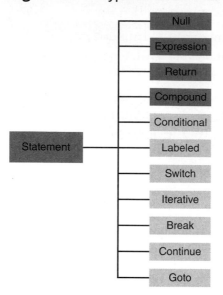

Although they do not arise often, there are syntactical situations where we must have a statement but no action is required. In these situations, we use the null statement.

Expression Statement

An expression is turned into an expression statement by placing a semicolon (;) after it.

```
expression;  // expression statement
```

When C sees the semicolon, it completes any pending side effects and discards the expression value before continuing with the next statement. An expression without side effects does not cause an action. Its value exists and it can be used, but unless a statement has a side effect, it does nothing.

Let us look at some expression statements. First, consider the expression statement

```
a = 2;
```

The effect of the expression statement is to store the value, 2, in the variable a. The value of the expression is 2. After the value has been stored, the expression is terminated (because there is a semicolon), and the value is discarded. C then continues with the next statement.

The next expression statement is a little more complex.

```
a = b = 3;
```

This statement actually has two expressions. If we put parentheses around them, you will be able to see them clearly.

```
a = (b = 3);
```

The parenthesized expression (b = 3) has a side effect of assigning the value 3 to the variable b. The value of this expression is 3. The expression statement now output in the expression value 3 being assigned to the variable a. Because the expression is terminated by the semicolon, its value, 3, is discarded. The effect of the expression statement, therefore, is that 3 has been stored in both a and b.

You are already familiar with the scanf and printf functions. These statements present interesting insights into the concepts of expressions and side effects. Consider the following scanf function call:

```
ioResult = scanf("%d", &x);
```

This statement has two side effects. The first is found in the `scanf` function. Reading an integer value from the keyboard and placing it into the variable x (note the address operator before the variable) is a side effect. The second side effect is storing the value returned by `scanf`, which represents the number of values that were converted correctly. In this case, the return value could be EOF, 0, or 1. Assuming that the user correctly keys the integer, the value will be 1. The assignment operator stores the return value in `ioResult`. The expression then terminates, and the `scanf` value is discarded.

In a similar fashion, `printf` has the effect of displaying data on the monitor and returning a value, the number of characters displayed. This is seen in the statement below.

```
numDisplayed = printf ("x contains %d, y contains %d\n", x, y);
```

As a general rule, however, the number of characters displayed is discarded without being stored. Therefore, we normally code the above statement as shown below.

```
printf("x contains %d, y contains %d\n", x, y);
```

Now consider the following expression statement. Assume that a has a value of 5 before the expression is evaluated.

```
a++;
```

In this postfix expression, the value of the expression is 5, the value of the variable, a, before it is changed by the side effect. Upon completion of the expression statement, a is incremented to 6. The value of the expression, which is still 5, is discarded because the expression is now complete.

Although they are useless, the following are also expression statements. They are useless because they have no side effect and their values are not assigned to a variable. We usually don't use them, but it is important to know they are syntactically correct expression statements. C will evaluate them, determine their value, and then discard the value. (In an optimized compiler, the translator determines that there is no effect and generates no code.)

```
b;   3;   ;
```

Return Statement

A return statement terminates a function. All functions, including `main`, must have a return statement. When there is no return statement at the end of the function, the system inserts one with a `void` return value.

```
return expression;   // return statement
```

In addition, the `return` statement can return a value to the calling function. For example, while we have not talked about it or used it, the `scanf` function returns the number of variables successfully read. In the case of `main`, it returns a value to the operating system rather than to another function. In all of our programs, `main` returns 0 to the operating system. A return value of zero tells the operating system that the program executed successfully.

Compound Statements

A compound statement is a unit of code consisting of zero or more statements. It is also known as a block. The compound statement allows a group of statements to become one single entity. You used a compound statement in your first program when you formed the body of the function `main`. All C functions contain a compound statement known as the function body.

A compound statement consists of an opening brace, an optional declaration and definition section, and an optional statement section, followed by a closing brace. Although both the declaration section and the statement sections are optional, one should be present. If neither is present, then we have a null statement, which doesn't make much sense. **Figure 3-12** shows the makeup of a compound statement.

Figure 3-12   Compound statement

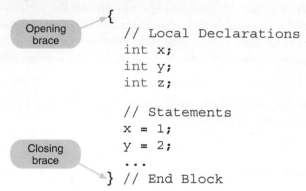

One important point to remember is that a compound statement does not need a semicolon. The opening and closing parentheses are simply delimiters for the compound statement. If we put a semicolon after the closing brace, the compiler thinks that we have put an extra null statement after the compound statement. This is poor style, but it does not generate any code or generate a compile error, although it may generate a warning message.

C requires that the declaration section be included before any statements within a compound statement block. (The one exception to this rule is in the `for` statement, which you will learn about as you become a more experienced programmer.) The code in the declaration section and statement section cannot be intermixed. The compound statement does not need a semicolon.

The Role of the Semicolon

The semicolon plays an important role in the syntax of the C language. It is used in two different auscultations.

> Every declaration in C is terminated by a semicolon.

> Most statements in C are terminated by a semicolon.

On the other hand, we must be careful not to use a semicolon when it is not needed. A semicolon should not be used with a preprocessor directive such as the include and define. In particular, a semicolon at the end of a define statement can create a problem as discussed in the next section.

Statements and Defined Constants

When we use preprocessor-defined commands, we must be very careful to make sure that we do not create an error. Remember that the defined constant is an automatic substitution. This can cause subtle problems. One common mistake is to place a semicolon at the end of the definition. Since the preprocessor uses a simple text replacement of the name with whatever expression follows, the compiler will generate a compile error if it finds a semicolon at the end of the definition. This problem is seen in the following example:

```
#define SALES_TAX_RATE 0.825;
salesTax = SALES_TAX_RATE * salesAmount;
```

After the substitution, the following erroneous code occurs because we coded a semicolon after the constant value:

```
salesTax = 0.0825; * salesAmount;
```

This can be an extremely difficult compile error to figure out because we see the original statement and not the erroneous substitution error. One of the reasons programmers use uppercase for defined constant identifiers is to provide an automatic warning to readers that they are not looking at the real code.

Programming Example: Programming Technique and Style

This section contains several programs that you should study for programming technique and style.

Let's write a program that calculates and prints the quotient and remainder of two integer numbers. The code is shown in **Program 3-9**.

Program 3-9 | Calculate quotient and remainder

```
 1  /* Calculate and print quotient and remainder of two
 2     numbers.
 3     Written by:
 4     Date:
 5  */
 6  #include <stdio.h>
 7
 8  int main (void)
 9  {
10  // Local Declarations
11     int intNum1;
12     int intNum2;
13     int intCalc;
14
15  // Statements
16     printf("Enter two integral numbers: ");
17     scanf ("%d %d", &intNum1, &intNum2);
18
19     intCalc = intNum1 / intNum2;
20     printf("%d / %d is %d", intNum1, intNum2, intCalc);
21
22     intCalc = intNum1 % intNum2;
23     printf(" with a remainder of: %d\n", intCalc);
24
25     return 0;
26  } // main
```

Output
```
Enter two integral numbers: 13 2
13 / 2 is 6 with a remainder of: 1
```

Using good programming style, the program begins with documentation about what it does, who created it, and when it was created.

Program 3-9 has no global variable declarations, so after including the standard input/output library, we start immediately with `main`. Following `main` is the opening brace. The matching closing brace is found on line 26.

The most difficult part of this program is figuring out how to get the remainder. Fortunately, C has a modulo operator (%) that does the job for us. The rest of the problem is straightforward.

Another problem that requires the use of the modulo operator is to print a digit contained in an integer. **Program 3-10** prints the least significant (rightmost) digit of an integer.

Program 3-10 | Print right digit of integer

```
1   /* Print rightmost digit of an integer.
2      Written by:
3      Date:
4   */
5   #include <stdio.h>
6
7   int main (void)
8   {
9   // Local Declarations
10     int intNum;
11     int oneDigit;
12
13  // Statements
14     printf("Enter an integral number: ");
15     scanf ("%d", &intNum);
16
17     oneDigit = intNum % 10;
18     printf("\nThe right digit is: %d", oneDigit);
19
20     return 0;
21  } // main
```

Output
```
Enter an integral number: 185
The right digit is: 5
```

Program 3-11 reads four integers from the keyboard, calculates their average, and then prints the numbers with their average and the deviation (not the standard deviation, just the difference plus or minus) from the average.

Program 3-11 | Calculate average of four numbers

```c
1   /* Calculate the average of four integers and print
2      the numbers and their deviation from the average.
3      Written by:
4      Date:
5   */
6   #include <stdio.h>
7   int main (void)
8   {
9   // Local Declarations
10      int num1;
11      int num2;
12      int num3;
13      int num4;
14      int sum;
15      float average;
16
17  // Statements
18      printf("\nEnter the first number: ");
19      scanf("%d", &num1);
20      printf("Enter the second number: ");
21      scanf("%d", &num2);
22      printf("Enter the third number: ");
23      scanf("%d", &num3);
24      printf("Enter the fourth number: ");
25      scanf("%d", &num4);
26
27      sum = num1 + num2 + num3 + num4;
28      average = sum / 4.0;
29
30      printf("\n ******** average is %6.2f ******** ", average);
31
32      printf("\n");
33
34      printf("\nfirst number: %6d -- deviation: %8.2f",
35             num1, num1 - average);
36      printf("\nsecond number: %6d -- deviation: %8.2f",
37             num2, num2 - average);
38      printf("\nthird number: %6d -- deviation: %8.2f",
39             num3, num3 - average);
40      printf("\nfourth number: %6d -- deviation: %8.2f",
41             num4, num4 - average);
```

(continue)

Program 3-11   Calculate average of four numbers *(continued)*

```
42
43    return 0;
44 } // main
```

Output
```
Enter the first number: 23
Enter the second number: 12
Enter the third number: 45
Enter the fourth number: 23

******** average is 25.75 ********
first number:    23 -- deviation:     -2.75
second number:   12 -- deviation:    -13.75
third number:    45 -- deviation:     19.25
fourth number:   23 -- deviation:     -2.75
```

Program 3-11 is a little more complex than the previous ones. At the beginning of `main` are several variable declarations, five integers, and a floating-point number. The first four are for the variables read from the keyboard, the fifth is for the sum, and the floating-point number is for the average.

The statements section starts by reading the data. Each read is preceded by a display so the user will know what to do. The specific instructions about what to input are known as user prompts. You should always tell the user what input is expected from the keyboard. After the user has keyed the data, the program continues by adding the numbers, placing the total in `sum`, and computing `average`. It then displays the output. Notice that the program displays the output in a format that allows the user to easily verify that the program ran correctly. The program not only prints the average but also repeats each input with its deviation from the average. After completing its work, the program concludes by returning to the operating system.

Look at the output carefully. Note how each series of numbers is aligned so that they can be easily read. Taking the time to align output is one of the things that distinguishes a good programmer from an average programmer. Always pay attention to how your program presents its output to the user. Paying attention to these little details pays off in the long run.

One way to measure an angle in a circle is in degrees. For example, the angle formed by a clock at 3 o'clock is 90°. Another way to measure the angle is in radians. One radian is equal to 57.295779 degrees—or, more precisely, 180 / π. In **Program 3-12** we ask the user to input an angle in radians, and we convert it to degrees.

Program 3-12 | Convert radians to degrees

```
1   /* This program prompts the user to enter an angle
2      measured in radians and converts it into degrees.
3      Written by:
```

(continue)

Program 3-12   Convert radians to degrees *(continued)*

```
 4      Date:
 5  */
 6  #include <stdio.h>
 7
 8  #define DEGREE_FACTOR 57.295779
 9
10  int main (void)
11  {
12  // Local Declarations
13     double radians;
14     double degrees;
15
16  // Statements
17     printf("Enter the angle in radians: ");
18     scanf("%lf", &radians);
19
20     degrees = radians * DEGREE_FACTOR;
21
22     printf("%6.3f radians is %6.3f degrees\n",
23             radians, degrees);
24     return 0;
25  } // main
```

Output
```
Enter the angle in radians: 1.57080
1.571 radians is 90.000 degrees
```

In this short program we introduce the defined constant. Defined constants are an excellent way to document factors in a program. We could have just as easily used a memory constant. Factors are usually placed at the beginning of the program where they can easily be found and changed as necessary. Remember that the area before main is global and that it should be used only for declarations and constants—not variables.

Program 3-13 calculates a sale given the unit price, quantity, discount rate, and sales tax rate.

Program 3-13 │ Calculate sales total

```
1  /* Calculates the total sale given the unit price,
2     quantity, discount, and tax rate.
3     Written by:
```

(continue)

Program 3-13   Calculate sales total *(continued)*

```
 4      Date:
 5   */
 6   #include <stdio.h>
 7
 8   #define TAX_RATE 8.50
 9
10   int main (void)
11   {
12   // Local Declarations
13      int quantity;
14
15      float discountRate;
16      float discountAm;
17      float unitPrice;
18      float subTotal;
19      float subTaxable;
20      float taxAm;
21      float total;
22
23   // Statements
24      printf("\nEnter number of items sold:   ");
25      scanf("%d", &quantity);
26
27      printf("Enter the unit price:     ");
28      scanf("%f", &unitPrice);
29
30      printf("Enter the discount rate (per cent): ");
31      scanf("%f", &discountRate);
32
33      subTotal = quantity * unitPrice;
34      discountAm = subTotal * discountRate / 100.0;
35      subTaxable = subTotal - discountAm;
36      taxAm = subTaxable * TAX_RATE / 100.00;
37      total = subTaxable + taxAm;
38
39      printf("\nQuantity sold:   %6d\n", quantity);
40      printf("Unit Price of items: %9.2f\n", unitPrice);
41      printf("----------------------------\n");
42
43      printf("Subtotal:   %9.2f\n", subTotal);
44      printf("Discount:    -%9.2f\n", discountAm);
45      printf("Discounted total:   %9.2f\n", subTaxable);
```

(continue)

Program 3-13   Calculate sales total *(continued)*

```
46      printf("Sales tax:   +%9.2f\n", taxAm);
47      printf("Total sale: %9.2f\n", total);
48
49      return 0;
50 } // main
```

Output
```
Enter number of items sold: 34
Enter the unit price:   12.89
Enter the discount rate (per cent): 7

Quantity sold:  34
Unit Price of items:    12.89
------------------------
Subtotal:  438.26
Discount:   - 30.68
Discounted total:   407.58
Sales tax:  +   34.64
Total sale: 442.23
```

Look at the output of this program carefully. Do you see any problems? Just because a program runs doesn't mean that it is running correctly. In this case, the total is incorrect (407.58 + 34.64 is not equal to 442.23). The problem is created by the floating-point arithmetic and rounding errors. If we wanted absolute accuracy, we would have to do the arithmetic in integer (cents) and then divide by 100 to print the report.

Program 3-14 calculates the average score for a student. The class has four quizzes (30%), two midterms (40%), and a final (30%). The maximum score for all quizzes and exams is 100 points.

Program 3-14 | Calculate student score

```
1  /* Calculate a student's average score for a course
2      with 4 quizzes, 2 midterms, and a final. The quizzes
3      are weighted 30%, the midterms 40%, & the final 30%.
4      Written by:
5      Date:
6  */
7  #include <stdio.h>
8
9  #define QUIZ_WEIGHT  30
10 #define MIDTERM_WEIGHT 40
11 #define FINAL_WEIGHT 30
```

(continue)

Program 3-14   Calculate student score *(continued)*

```
12 #define QUIZ_MAX    400.00
13 #define MIDTERM_MAX 200.00
14 #define FINAL_MAX   100.00
15
16 int main (void)
17 {
18 // Local Declarations
19    int quiz1;
20    int quiz2;
21    int quiz3;
22    int quiz4;
23    int totalQuiz;
24    int midterm1;
25    int midterm2;
26    int totalMidterm;
27    int final;
28
29    float quizPercent;
30    float midtermPercent;
31    float finalPercent;
32    float totalPercent;
33
34 // Statements
35    printf ("=========== QUIZES ==================\n");
36    printf("Enter the score for the first quiz: ");
37    scanf("%d", &quiz1);
38    printf("Enter the score for the second quiz: ");
39    scanf("%d", &quiz2);
40    printf("Enter the score for the third quiz: ");
41    scanf("%d", &quiz3);
42    printf("Enter the score for the fourth quiz: ");
43    scanf("%d", &quiz4);
44
45    printf ("========== MIDTERM ========\n");
46    printf("Enter the score for the first midterm: ");
47    scanf("%d", &midterm1);
48    printf("Enter the score for the second midterm: ");
49    scanf("%d", &midterm2);
50
51    printf("=============== FINAL ==============\n");
52    printf("Enter the score for the final: ");
53    scanf("%d", &final);
54    printf("\n");
```

(continue)

Program 3-14   Calculate student score *(continued)*

```
55
56    totalQuiz = quiz1 + quiz2 + quiz3 + quiz4;
57    totalMidterm = midterm1 + midterm2;
58
59    quizPercent =
60        (float)totalQuiz * QUIZ_WEIGHT / QUIZ_MAX;
61    midtermPercent =
62        (float)totalMidterm * MIDTERM_WEIGHT / MIDTERM_MAX;
63    finalPercent =
64        (float)final * FINAL_WEIGHT / FINAL_MAX;
65
66    totalPercent =
67        quizPercent + midtermPercent + finalPercent;
68
69    printf("First Quiz %4d\n", quiz1);
70    printf("Second Quiz %4d\n", quiz2);
71    printf("Third Quiz %4d\n", quiz3);
72    printf("Fourth Quiz %4d\n", quiz4);
73    printf("Quiz Total %4d\n\n", totalQuiz);
74
75    printf("First Midterm %4d\n", midterm1);
76    printf("Second Midterm %4d\n", midterm2);
77    printf("Total Midterms %4d\n\n", totalMidterm);
78
79    printf("Final   %4d\n\n", final);
80
81    printf("Quiz %6.1f%%\n" , quizPercent);
82    printf("Midterm %6.1f%%\n" , midtermPercent);
83    printf("Final %6.1f%%\n" , finalPercent);
84    printf ( "--------------\n" );
85    printf("Total %6.1f%%\n" , totalPercent);
86
87    return 0;
88 } // main
```

Output

```
Enter the score for the second quiz: 89
Enter the score for the third quiz: 78
Enter the score for the fourth quiz: 79
========= MIDTERM ========
Enter the score for the first midterm: 90
Enter the score for the second midterm: 100
============== FINAL ==============
```

(continue)

Program 3-14   Calculate student score *(continued)*

```
Enter the score for the final: 92

First Quiz   98
Second Quiz  89
Third Quiz   78
Fourth Quiz  90
Quiz Total   355

First Midterm    90
Second Midterm   100
Total Midterms   190

Final    92

Quiz     26.6%
Midterm  38.0%
Final    27.6%
-------------
Total    92.2%
```

This rather long program contains several points to consider. First, note how the program starts with a series of defined constants. Putting the definitions of constant values at the beginning of the program does two things: (1) It gives them names that we can use in the program, and (2) it makes them easy to change.

Now study the statements. Notice how they are grouped? By putting a blank line between a group of related statements, we separate them, much as we would separate paragraphs in a report. This makes it easy for the user to follow the program.

Finally, study the input and output. Notice that the user was prompted for all input with clear instructions. We even divided the input with headings. The output is also divided, making it easy to read. It would be even easier to read if we aligned all the amounts. You will learn how to implement that as you become a more experienced programmer.

Software Engineering

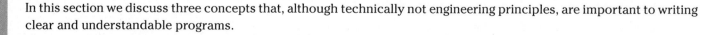

In this section we discuss three concepts that, although technically not engineering principles, are important to writing clear and understandable programs.

KISS

Keep It Simple and Short (KISS) is an old programming principle. Unfortunately, many programmers tend to forget it, especially the simple part. They seem to feel that just because they are working on a complex problem, the solution must be complex, too. That is simply not true. Good programmers solve the problem in the simplest possible way; they do not contribute to a complex situation by writing obscure and complex code.

A trivial example will make the point. If you were writing a program that reads floating-point numbers from the keyboard, you would not program it so that the user had to enter the integral portion of the number first and then the fractional part. Although this would work, it is unnecessarily complex, even though it might be a fun way to solve the problem.

Unfortunately, C provides many operators and expression rules that make it easy for a programmer to write obscure and difficult to follow code. Your job as a programmer is to make sure that your code is always easy to read. Your code should be unambiguous: It should not be written so that it is easy to misread it.

Another old structured programming principle is that a function should not be larger than one page of code. Now, for online programming in a workstation environment, a function should be no longer than one screen—about 20 lines of code. By breaking a problem down into small, easily understood parts, we simplify it. Then we reassemble the simple components into a simple solution to a complex problem.

One element of the C language that tends to complicate programs, especially for new programmers, is side effects. We explained in Section 3.4, "Evaluating Expressions," that side effects can lead to confusing and different output depending on the code. You need to fully understand the effects when you write C code. If you are unsure of the effects, then simplify your logic until you are sure.

Parentheses

One programming technique to simplify code is to use parentheses, even when unnecessary. While this may lead to a few extra keystrokes, it can save hours of debugging time created by a misunderstanding of the precedence and associativity rules. Whenever a statement contains multiple expressions, use parentheses to ensure that the compiler will interpret it as you intended. Computers do what you tell them to do, not what you intended to tell them to do. Make sure your code is as clear and simple as possible.

User Communication

You should always make sure you communicate with your user from the very first statement in your program to the very last. As mentioned previously, we recommend that you start your program with a message that identifies the program and end with a display that says the program is done.

When you give your user instructions, make sure that they are clear and understandable. In Program 3-13, we used three statements to give the user complete and detailed instructions on what we wanted entered. We could have simply said

```
"Enter data"
```

but that would have been vague and subject to interpretation. How would the user know what specific data were required? For each input in Program 3-13, we told the users exactly what data we needed in terms that they understand. If you don't tell users exactly what data to input, they may do anything they feel like, which is usually not what you wanted or expected.

One common mistake made by new programmers is to forget to tell the user anything. What do you think would be the user's response to **Program 3-15** when confronted with a blank screen and a computer that is doing nothing?

Program 3-15 | Program that will confuse the user

```
1   #include <stdio.h>
2   int main (void)
3   {
4       int i;
```

(continue)

Program 3-15   Program that will confuse the user *(continued)*

```
5       int j;
6       int sum;
7
8       scanf("%d%d" , &i, &j);
9       sum = i + j;
10      printf("The sum of %d & %d is %d\n", i, j, sum);
11      return 0;
12 } // main
```

We now rewrite the program in **Program 3-16** with clear user communication. With the addition of one print state-ment, the user knows exactly what is to be done.

Program 3-16 | Program that will not confuse the user

```
1   #include <stdio.h>
2   int main (void)
3   {
4       int i;
5       int j;
6       int sum;
7
8       printf("Enter two integers and key <return>\n");
9       scanf("%d%d", &i, &j);
10      sum = i + j;
11      printf("The sum of %d & %d is %d\n", i, j, sum);
12      return 0;
13 } // main
```

Output
```
Enter two integers and key <return>
4 5
The sum of 4 & 5 is 9
```

We will return to these three concepts from time to time when we introduce new structures that tend to be confusing or misunderstood.

Tips and Common Programming Errors

1. Be aware of expression side effects. They are one of the main sources of confusion and logical errors in a program.

2. Use decrement/increment operators wisely. Understand the difference between postfix and prefix decrement/increment operators before using them.

3. Add parentheses whenever you feel they will help to make an expression clearer.

4. It is a compile error to use a variable that has not been defined.

5. It is a compile error to forget the semicolon at the end of an expression statement.

6. It is a compile error to code a variable declaration or definition after you have started the statement section. To help yourself remember this rule, use comments to separate these two sections within a function.

7. It is most likely a compile error to terminate a defined constant (#define) with a semicolon. This is an especially difficult error to decipher because you will not see it in your code—you see the code you wrote, not the code that the preprocessor substituted.

8. It is a compile error when the operand on the left of the assignment operator is not a variable. For example, a + 3 is not a variable and cannot receive the value of b * c.

   ```
   (a + 3) = b * c;
   ```

9. It is a compile error to use the increment or decrement operators with any expression other than a variable identifier. For example, the following code is an error:

   ```
   (a + 3)++
   ```

10. It is a compile error to use the modulus operator (%) with anything other than integers.

11. It is a logic error to use a variable before it has been assigned a value.

12. It is a logic error to modify a variable in an expression when the variable appears more than once.

Summary

> An expression is a sequence of operators and operands that reduces to a single value.

> An operator is a language-specific token that requires an action to be taken.

> An operand is the recipient of the action.

> C has six kinds of expressions: primary, postfix, prefix, unary, binary, and ternary.

> The most elementary type of expression is a primary expression. A primary expression is an expression made up of only one operand. It can be a name, a constant, or a parenthesized expression.

> A postfix expression is an expression made up of an operand followed by an operator. You studied function call and postfix increment/decrement expressions in this chapter.

> A unary expression is an expression made up of an operator followed by an operand. You studied six in this chapter: prefix increment/decrement, sizeof, plus/minus, and cast expressions.

> A binary expression is an expression made up of two operands with an operator between them. You studied multiplicative, additive, and assignment expressions in this chapter.

> Precedence is a concept that determines the order in which different operators in a complex expression act on their operands.

> Associativity defines the order of evaluation when operators have the same precedence.

> The side effect of an expression is one of the unique phenomena in C. An expression can have a side effect in addition to a value.

> To evaluate an expression, we must follow the rules of precedence and associativity.

> A statement causes an action to be performed by the program.

> Although C has eleven different types of statements, you studied only four types in this chapter:

  ▪ A null statement is just a semicolon.

  ▪ An expression statement is an expression converted to a statement by keeping the side effect and discarding the value.

  ▪ A return statement terminates a function.

  ▪ A compound statement is a combination of statements enclosed in two braces.

> KISS means "Keep It Simple and Short."

> One of the important recommendations in software engineering is the use of parentheses when they can help clarify your code.

> Another recommendation in software engineering is to communicate clearly with the user.

Key Terms

additive expressions	explicit type conversion	operator
assignment expression	expression	postfix expression
associativity	expression statement	precedence
binary expressions	implicit type conversion	primary expression
block	KISS	promotion
cast	left-to-right associativity	right-to-left associativity
complex expression	multiplicative expressions	side effect
compound statement	name	simple expression
conversion rank	null statement	unary expression
demotion	operand	user prompts

Review Questions

1. A unary expression consists of only one operand with no operator.
   a. True
   b. False

2. The left operand in an assignment expression must be a single variable.
   a. True
   b. False

3. Associativity is used to determine which of several different expressions is evaluated first.
   a. True
   b. False

4. Side effect is an action that output from the evaluation of an expression.
   a. True
   b. False

5. An expression statement is terminated with a period.
 a. True
 a. False

6. A(n) _____ is a sequence of operands and operators that reduces to a single value.
 a. expression
 b. category
 c. formula
 d. function
 e. value

7. Which of the following is a unary expression?
 a. `i + j`
 b. `+a`
 c. `c++`
 d. `scanf (...)`
 e. `x *= 5`

8. The _____ expression evaluates the operand on the right side of the operator and places its value in the variable on the left side of the operator.
 a. additive
 b. assignment
 c. multiplicative
 d. postfix
 e. primary

9. _____ is used to determine the order in which different operators in a complex expression are evaluated.
 a. Associativity
 b. Evaluation
 c. Category

 d. Precedence
 e. Side effect

10. _____ is an action that output from the evaluation of an expression.
 a. Associativity
 b. Evaluation
 c. Category
 d. Precedence
 e. Side effect

11. Which of the following statements about mixed expressions is false?
 a. A cast cannot be used to change an assigned value.
 b. An explicit cast can be used to change the expression type.
 c. An explicit cast on a variable changes its type in memory.
 d. An implicit cast is generated by the compiler automatically when necessary.
 e. Constant casting is done by the compiler automatically.

12. Which of the following statements about compound statements is false?
 a. A compound statement is also known as a block.
 b. A compound statement is enclosed in a set of braces.
 c. A compound statement must be terminated by a semicolon.
 d. The declaration and definition section in a compound statement is optional.
 e. The statement section in a compound statement is optional.

Exercises

13. Which of the following expressions are not postfix expressions?
 a. `x++`
 b. `--x`
 c. `scanf (...)`
 d. `x * y`
 e. `++x`

14. Which of the following are not unary expressions?
 a. `++x`
 b. `--x`
 c. `sizeof (x)`
 d. `+5`
 e. `x = 4`

15. Which of the following is not a binary expression?

    a. 3 * 5

    b. x += 6

    c. y = 5 + 2

    d. z - 2

    e. y % z

16. Which of the following is not a valid assignment expression?

    a. x = 23

    b. 4 = x

    c. y % = 5

    d. x = 8 = 3

    e. x = r = 5

17. If originally x = 4, what is the value of x after the evaluation of the following expression?

    a. x = 2

    b. x += 4

    c. x += x +3

    d. x *= 2

    e. x /= x +2

18. If originally x = 3 and y = 5, what is the value of x and y after each of the following expressions?

    a. x++ + y

    b. ++x

    c. x++ + y++

    d. ++x + 2

    e. x-- - y--

19. What is the value of each of the following expressions?

    a. 24 - 6 * 2

    b. -15 * 2 + 3 C. 72 / 5

    c. 72 % 5

    d. 5 * 2 / 6 + 15 % 4

20. What is the value of each of the following expressions?

    a. 6.2 + 5.1 * 3.2

    b. 2.0 + 3.0 / 1.2

    c. 4.0 * (3.0 + 2.0 / 6.0)

    d. 6.0 / (2.0 + 4.0 * 1.2)

    e. 2.7 + 3.2 - 5.3 * 1.1

21. Given the following definitions, which of the following statements are valid assignments?

    ```
    #define NUM10 10
    int x; int y = 15;
    ```

    a. x = 5;

    b. y = 5;

    c. x = y = 50;

    d. x = 50 = y;

    e. x = x + 1;

    f. y = 1 + NUM10;

    g. 5 = y;

22. If originally x = 2, y = 3, and z = 2, what is the value of each of the following expressions?

    a. x++ + y++

    b. ++x - --z

    c. --x + y++

    d. x-- + x-- - y--

    e. x + y-- - x + x++ - --y

23. If originally x = 2, y = 3, and z = 1, what is the value of each of the following expressions?

    a. `x + 2/6 + y`

    b. `y - 3 * z + 2`

    c. `z - (x + z)% 2 + 4`

    d. `x - 2*(3 + z) + y`

    e. `y++ + z-- + x++`

24. If x = 2945, what is the value of each of the following expressions?

    a. `x % 10`

    b. `x / 10`

    c. `(x / 10) % 10`

    d. `x / 100`

    e. `(x / 100) % 10`

25. What is the output from the following code fragment?

```
int a;
int b;
a = b = 50;
printf ("%4d %4d", a, b);
a = a * 2; b = b / 2;
printf ("%4d %4d", a, b);
```

Problems

26. Given the following pseudocode, write a program that executes it. Use floating-point types for all values.

    1. read x

    2. read y

    3. compute p = x * y

    4. compute s = x + y

    5. total = s2 +p* (s − x) * (p + y)

    6. print total

27. Write a program that reads two integers from the keyboard, multiplies them, and then prints the two numbers and their product.

28. Write a program that extracts and prints the rightmost digit of the integral portion of a `float`.

29. Write a program that extracts and prints the second rightmost digit of the integral portion of a `float`.

30. Write a program that calculates the area and perimeter of a rectangle from a user-supplied (`scanf`) length and width.

31. We are all familiar with the fact that angles are measured in degrees, minutes, and seconds. Another measure of an angle is a radian. A radian is the angle formed by two radii forming an arc that is equal to the radius of their circle. One radian equals 57.295779 degrees. Write a program that converts degrees into radians. Provide good user prompts. Include the following test data in your run:

    90° is 1.57080 radians

32. The formula for converting centigrade temperatures to Fahrenheit is:

$$F = 32 + \left(C \times \left(\frac{180.0}{100.00} \right) \right)$$

Write a program that asks the user to enter a temperature reading in centigrade and then prints the equivalent Fahrenheit value. Be sure to include at least one negative centigrade number in your test cases.

33. Write a program that changes a temperature reading from Fahrenheit to Celsius using the following formula:

$$Celsius = \left(\frac{100.0}{180.0}\right) \times (Fahrenheit - 32)$$

Your program should prompt the user to enter a Fahrenheit temperature. It then calculates the equivalent Celsius temperature and displays the output as shown below.

> Enter the temperature in Fahrenheit: 98.6
> Fahrenheit temperature is: 98.6
> Celsius temperature is: 37.0

34. Write the C code for each of the following formulas. Assume that all variables are defined as *double*.

   a. $KinEn = mv^2/2$

   b. $res = b + c/2b$

35. Write the C code to calculate and print the next two numbers in each of the following series. You may use only one variable in each problem.

   a. `0,  5,  10,  15,  20,  25,  ?,  ?`
   b. `0,  2,  4,  6,  8,  10,  ?,  ?`
   c. `1,  2,  4,  8,  16,  32,  ?,  ?`

Projects

36. Write a program that converts and prints a user-supplied measurement in inches into
   a. foot (12 inches)
   b. yard (36 inches)
   c. centimeter (2.54/inch)
   d. meter (39.37 inches)

37. A Fibonacci number is a member of a set in which each number is the sum of the previous two numbers. (The Fibonacci series describes a form of a spiral.) The series begins

0, 1, 1, 2, 3, 5, 8, 13, 21, ...

Write a program that calculates and prints the next three numbers in the Fibonacci series. You are to use only three variables, `fib1`, `fib2`, and `fib3`.

38. Write a program that prompts a user for an integer value in the range 0 to 32,767 and then prints the individual digits of the numbers on a line with three spaces between the digits. The first line is to start with the leftmost digit and print all five digits; the second line is to start with the second digit from the left and print four digits, and so forth. For example, if the user enters 1234, your program should print

```
0   1   2   3   4
1   2   3   4
2   3   4
3   4
4
```

39. Write a program to create a customer's bill for a company. The company sells only five different products: TV, VCR, Remote Controller, CD Player, and Tape Recorder. The unit prices are $400.00, $220, $35.20, $300.00, and $150.00, respectively. The program must read the quantity of each piece of equipment purchased from the keyboard. It then calculates the cost of each item, the subtotal, and the total cost after an 8.25% sales tax.

The input data consist of a set of integers representing the quantities of each item sold. These integers must be input into the program in a user-friendly way; that is, the program must prompt the user for each quantity as shown below. The numbers in boldface show the user's answers.

How Many TVs Were Sold? **3**

How Many VCRs Were Sold? **5**

How Many Remote Controllers Were Sold? **1**

How Many CDs Were Sold? **2**

How Many Tape Recorders Were Sold? **4**

The format for the output is shown in **Figure 3-13**.

Figure 3-13   Output format for project 39

```
QTY              DESCRIPTION          UNIT PRICE      TOTAL PRICE
- - - - - - - - - - - - - - - - - - - - - - - - - - - - - - - - - - -
XX               TV                     400.00          XXXX.XX
XX               VCR                    220.00          XXXX.XX
XX               REMOTE  CTRLR           35.20          XXXX.XX
XX               CD  PLAYER             300.00          XXXX.XX
XX               TAPE  RECORDER         150.00          XXXX.XX
                                                      - - - - - - - - - - -
                                      SUBTOTAL         XXXXX.XX
                                      TAX               XXXX.XX
                                      TOTAL            XXXXX.XX
```

Use either defined constants or memory constants for the unit prices and the tax rate. Use integer variables to store the quantities for each item. Use floating-point variables to store the total price for each item, the bill subtotal, the tax amount, and the total amount of the bill. Run your program twice with the following data:

SET 1 → 2 1 4 1 2

SET 2 → 3 0 2 0 21

CHAPTER 4

Functions

Learning Objectives

When you complete this chapter, you will be able to:

4.1 Design multifunction programs using structure charts

4.2 Design and implement programs with more than one function

4.3 Describe the purpose of the function declaration, call, and definition

4.4 Discuss how two functions communicate through parameters

4.5 List the four basic function designs

4.6 Recognize the differences between global and local scope

4.1 Designing Structured Programs

So far you have used only the three nonderived types, void, integral, and floating-point. Although these types are very useful, they can solve only a limited number of problems. There are six derived types in C, as shown in **Figure 4-1**.

Figure 4-1 Derived types structure chart

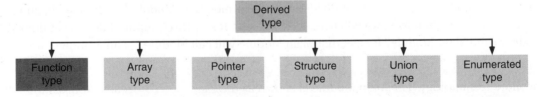

In this chapter we introduce the first derived type, the function type. The function type is derived from its return type. The return type can be any type except an array, which you will learn more about as you become a more experienced programmer.

The programs we have presented so far have been very simple. They solved problems that could be understood without too much effort. As we consider larger and larger programs, however, you will discover that it is not possible to understand all aspects of such programs without somehow reducing them to more elementary parts.

Breaking a complex problem into smaller parts is a common practice. For example, suppose that for your vacation this year you decide to drive in a circular route that will allow you to visit as many national parks as possible in two weeks. Your requirements for this problem are very simple: Visit as many parks as possible in two weeks. But how will you do it? You might first gather some data about national parks and then calculate the distance between each of them to figure out the travel time. Next, you would estimate how much time it would take to visit each park. Finally, you would put all your data together to plan your itinerary. Then you would make your motel and camp reservations and any other arrangements that had to be in place in advance.

The planning for large programs is similar. First, you must understand the problem as a whole; then you must break it into simpler, understandable parts. We call each of these parts of a program a module and the process of subdividing a problem into manageable parts top-down design.

The principles of top-down design and structured programming dictate that a program should be divided into a main module and its related modules. Each module should also be divided into submodules according to software engineering principles that we discuss in the "Software Engineering" section later in this chapter. The division of modules proceeds until the module consists only of elementary processes that are intrinsically understood and cannot be further subdivided. This process is known as factoring.

Top-down design is usually done using a visual representation of the modules known as a structure chart. The structure chart shows the relation between each module and its submodules. The rules for reading and creating structure charts are also covered in the "Software Engineering" section later in this chapter, but at this point, we only need a few simple rules. Reading the structure chart in **Figure 4-2** top-down, left-right, we first come to Main Module, which represents the entire set of code required to solve the problem.

Figure 4-2   Structure chart

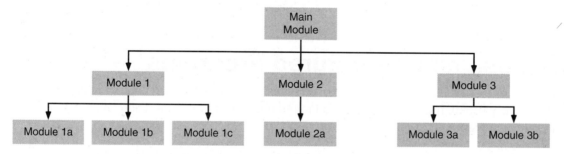

The Main Module consists of three submodules. Thus, moving down and left, we come to Module 1, which will be our focus. As you can see, Module 1 is further subdivided into three modules: Module 1a, Module 1b, and Module 1c. To write the code for Module 1, therefore, we will need to write code for its three submodules. What does this say about writing the code for the Main Module? It says that Main Module will call Module 1, and Module 1 will call Module 1a, 1b, and 1c.

Now for some more terminology. The Main Module is known as a calling module because it has submodules. Each of the submodules is known as a called module. But, because Modules 1, 2, and 3 also have submodules, they are also calling modules; they are both called and calling modules.

Communication between modules in a structure chart is allowed only through a calling module. If Module 1 needs to send data to Module 2, the data must be passed through the calling module, Main Module. No communication can take place directly between modules that do not have a calling-called relationship.

With this understanding, how can Module 1a send data to Module 3b? It first sends the data to Module 1, which in turn sends it to the Main Module, which passes it to Module 3, and then on to Module 3b.

Although passing data to a function sounds complex, it is easily done using a technique known as parameter passing. The parameters are contained in a list that is a definition of the data passed to the function by the caller. The list serves as the formal declaration of the data types and names.

4.2 Functions in C

In C, top-down design is implemented using one or more modules. As you may have inferred, a module is actually known as a function in programming languages. A C program is made of one or more functions, one and only one of which must be named `main`. The execution of the program always starts and ends with `main`, but it can call other functions to do special tasks. **Figure 4-3** shows a C program structure chart.

Figure 4-3   Structure chart for a C program

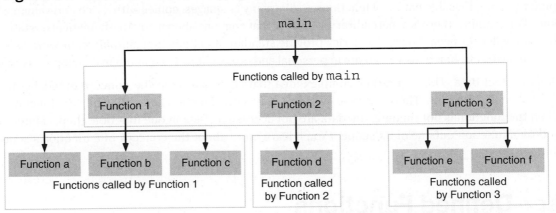

A function in C (including `main`) is an independent module that will be called to do a specific task. A called function receives control from a calling function. When the called function completes its task, it returns control to the calling function. It may or may not return a value to the caller. The function `main` is called by the operating system; `main` in turn calls other functions. When `main` is complete, control returns to the operating system.

In general, the purpose of a function is to receive zero or more pieces of data, operate on them, and return at most one piece of data. At the same time, a function can have a side effect. A function side effect is an action that results in a change in the state of the program. If a side effect occurs, it occurs while the function is executing and before the function returns. The side effect can involve accepting data from outside the program, sending data out of the program to the monitor or a file, or changing the value of a variable in the calling function. **Figure 4-4** illustrates how a function does its work.

Figure 4-4   How a function works

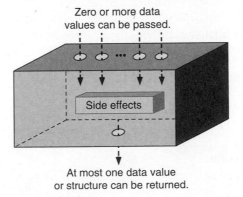

Why use functions? They provide several benefits in C or any other language. The major advantages are:

1. As already described, functions allow us to factor problems into understandable and manageable steps.

2. Functions provide a way to reuse code that is required in more than one place in a program. Assume, for instance, that a program requires that we compute the average of a series of numbers in five different parts of the program. Each time the data are different. We could write the code to compute the average five times, but this would take a lot of effort. Also, if we needed to change the calculation, we would have to find all five places that use it to

change each of them. It is much easier to write the code once as a function and then call it whenever we need to compute the average.

> **Note** | A function in C can have a return value, a side effect, or both. The side effect occurs before the value is returned. The function's value is the value in the expression of the return statement. A function can be called for its value, its side effect, or both.

3. To capitalize on the reusable-nature of functions, C, like many languages, comes with a rich and valuable library of functions. For example, there is a math library, math.h, that contains almost any mathematical or statistical function that you will ever need. These C libraries provide standard functions that simplify your work as a programmer. You can also save functions you create in personal and project libraries that make developing systems easier.

4. Functions protect data. This is a rather complex idea that centers around the concept of local data, which is data described in a function. These data are available only to the function and only while the function is executing. When the function is not running, the data are not accessible. Data in one function, then, cannot be seen or changed by a function outside of its scope. (You'll learn more about the concept of a function's scope later in this chapter.)

4.3 User-Defined Functions

We have already used several functions, such as scanf and printf, in our programs. These functions, however, were written by the creator of the C environment. Now you will learn how to write your own functions. Before getting into the details, look at **Program 4-1**, which demonstrates how to write and call a function.

> **Program 4-1** | Sample program with subfunction

```
1   /* This program demonstrates function calls by calling
2      a small function to multiply two numbers.
3      Written by:
4      Date:
5   */
6   #include <stdio.h>
7
8   // Function Declarations
9   int multiply (int num1, int num2);
10
11  int main (void)
12  {
13   // Local Declarations
14      int multiplier;
15      int multiplicand;
16      int product;
17
18  // Statements
19      printf("Enter two integers: ");
20      scanf("%d%d", &multiplier, &multiplicand);
21
```

(continue)

Program 4-1   Sample program with subfunction *(continued)*

```
22      product = multiply (multiplier, multiplicand) ;
23
24      printf("Product of %d & %d is %d\n",
25      multiplier, multiplicand, product);
26      return 0;
27 } // main
28
29 /*===========multiply============
30    This function will Multiply two numbers and returns product.
31    Pre num1 & num2 are values to be multiplied
32    Post product returned
33 */
34 int multiply (int num1, int num2)
35 {
36 // Statements
37    return (num1 * num2);
38 } // multiply
```

Output

```
Enter two integers: 17 21
Product of 17 & 21 is 357
```

Like every other object in C, functions must be both declared and defined. The function declaration (line 9 in Program 4-1), which needs to be done before the function call, gives the whole picture of the function that needs to be defined later. The declaration mentions the name of the function, the return type, and the type and order of formal parameters (line 9 in Program 4-1). In other words, the declaration uses only the header of the function definition ended in a semicolon. The function definition, which is traditionally coded after the function that makes the call, contains the code needed to complete the task. Note that a function name is used three times: in the declaration, the call, and the definition.

Figure 4-5 shows the interrelationships among these function components. As you study Figure 4-5, note that the function name is used three times: when the function is declared, when it is called, and when it is defined. In the following sections you'll learn more about the various parts of Figure 4-5.

Figure 4-5   Declaring, calling, and defining a function named `greeting`

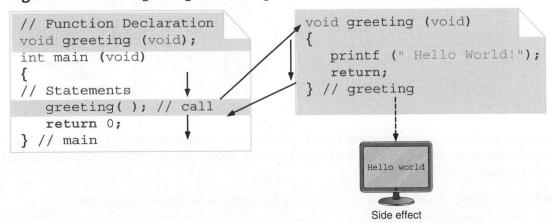

Side effect

Basic Function Designs

We classify the basic function designs by their return values and their parameter lists. Functions either return a value or they don't. Functions that don't return a value are known as void functions. Some functions have parameters and some don't. Combining return types and parameter lists results in four basic designs: void functions with no parameters, void functions with parameters, functions that return a value but have no parameters, and functions that return a value and have parameters. We discuss these four designs in the sections that follow.

void Functions without Parameters

A void function can be written with no parameters. The greeting function in Figure 4-5 receives nothing and returns nothing. It has only a side effect, displaying the message, and is called only for that side effect.

The call still requires parentheses, however, even when no parameters are present. When we make a call to a function with no parameters, it is tempting to leave the parentheses off the call. Although this is valid syntax, it is not what we intended. Without the parentheses, it is not a function call.

Because a void function does not have a value, it can be used only as a statement; it cannot be used in an expression. Examine the call to the greeting function in Figure 4-5. This call stands alone as a statement. Including this call in an expression, as shown in the following, would be an error.

```
result = greeting();    // Error. Void function
```

void Functions with Parameters

Now let's call a function that has parameters but still returns void. The function printOne, as seen in **Figure 4-6**, receives an integer parameter. Because this function returns nothing to the calling function, main, its return type is void. As with the greeting function discussed previously, this function must be coded as a stand-alone call because it does not return a value; it cannot be included as part of another expression. Note, however, that while printOne returns no values, it does have a side effect: The parameter value is printed to the monitor.

Figure 4-6 void function with parameter

```
// Function Declaration
void printOne (int X);
int main (void )
{
// Local Declarations
    int a = 5;
// Statements
    printOne (a); // call
    return 0;
} // main
```

```
void printOne (int x)
{
    printf ("%d\n", x);
    return ;
} // printone
```

a
5

5
x

Side effect

As you study Figure 4-6, note that the name of the variable in main (a) and the name of parameter in printOne (x) do not have to be the same. On the other hand, there is no reason why they can't be the same if that makes it easier to understand the code.

In **Program 4-2**, printOne is used to demonstrate that a function can be called multiple times.

Program 4-2 | `void` function with a parameter

```c
1   /* This program demonstrates that one function can be
2      called multiple times.
3      Written by:
4      Date:
5   */
6   #include <stdio.h>
7
8   // Function Declarations
9   void printOne (int x);
10
11  int main (void)
12  {
13  // Local Declarations
14     int a;
15
16  // Statements
17     a = 5;      // First call
18     printOne (a);
19
20     a = 33;
21     printOne (a);     // Second call
22
23     // Done. Return to operating system.
24     return 0;
25  } // main
26
27  /*==============printOne===============
28     Print one integer value.
29     Pre x contains number to be printed
30     Post value in x printed
31  */
32  void printOne (int x)
33  {
34  // Statements
35     printf ("%d\n", x);
36     return;
37  } // printOne
```

Output

```
5
33
```

Non-void Functions without Parameters

Some functions return a value but don't have any parameters. The most common use for this design reads data from the keyboard or a file and returns the data to the calling program. We show this design in **Figure 4-7**. Note that the called function contains all of the code required to read the data. In this simple example, only a prompt and a read are required. Later we introduce concepts that require much more code.

Figure 4-7 Non-void function without parameters

```
// Function Declaration
int getQuantity (void);
int main (void)
{
// Local Declarations
   int amt;
// Statements
   amt = getQuantity ( );
   return 0;
} // main
```

```
int getQuantity (void )
{
// Local Declarations
   int qty;
// Statements
   printf ("Enter Quantity");
   scanf ("%d" , &qty);
   return qty;
} // getQuantity
```

Non-void Functions with Parameters

Figure 4-8 contains a function that passes parameters and returns a value—in this case, the square of the parameter. Note how the returned value, b, is placed in the variable. This is not done by the call; it is a result of expression evaluation. Because the call is a postfix expression, it has a value—whatever is returned from the function. After the function has been executed and the value returned, the value on the right side of the assignment expression is the returned value, which is then assigned to b. Thus, again we see the power of expressions in the C language. Note that the function, sqr, has no side effect.

Figure 4-8 Calling a function that returns a value

```
// Function Declaration
int sqr ( int x);
int main (void )
{
// Local Declarations
   int a;
   int b;
// Statements
   scanf ("%d", &a);
   b = sqr (a);
   printf ("%d squared: %d\n", a, b);
   return 0;
} // main
```

Returned stored here

a   b

```
int sqr (int x)
{
// Statements
   return (x * x);
} // sqr
```

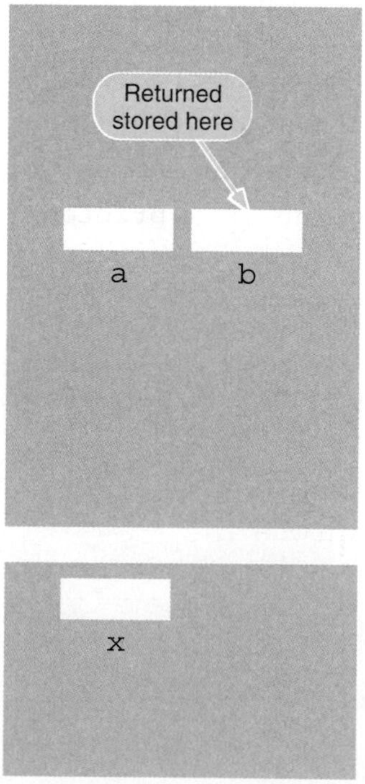

x

In main, the function call is evaluated first because it is a postfix expression, which has a higher precedence than the assignment expression. To evaluate it, the function call is executed. Its value is the value returned by the called function. The expression value is then used in the binary expression (assignment). The side effect of the binary expression stores the returned value in the variable.

As you have learned, an expression becomes an expression statement when it is terminated by a semicolon. The function call, which is a postfix expression and is terminated by a semicolon, is an expression statement. Functions that do not return a value (void functions) can only be used in an expression statement as shown in the following example.

```
printOne (); //
```

Functions that return a value can be used either in an expression statement or as an expression. When it is used as an expression statement, the return value is discarded. When it is used as an expression, as in Figure 4-8, its value is the value returned from the function. The following example demonstrates calling sqr as an expression statement and as an expression. Note that the expression statement is useless because neither the function call nor the statement has a side effect.

```
sqr (a);      // Expression Statement. No side effect
b = sqr(a);     // Return value is stored in b
```

In large programs, main is written with only function calls. To demonstrate how this would be done with our simple example, we combine our square and print functions into **Program 4-3**.

Program 4-3 | Read a number and square it

```
1   /* This program reads a number and prints its square.
2      Written by:
3      Date:
4   */
5   #include <stdio.h>
6
7   // Function Declarations
8   int getNum (void);
9   int sqr  (int x);
10  void printOne (int x);
11
12  int main (void)
13  {
14  // Local Declarations
15     int a;
16     int b;
17
18  // Statements
19     // Get number and square it
20     a = getNum ();
21
22     // Square the number just read
```

(continue)

Program 4-3   Read a number and square it *(continued)*

```
23      b = sqr (a);
24
25      // Now print it
26      printOne (b);
27
28      return 0;
29 } // main
30
31 /*===============getNum==============
32    Read number from keyboard and return it.
33    Pre nothing
34    Post number read and returned
35 */
36 int getNum (void)
37 {
38 // Local Declarations
39    int numIn;
40
41 // Statements
42    printf("Enter a number to be squared:");
43    scanf("%d", &numIn);
44    return numIn;
45 } // getNum
46
47 /*===================Sqr====================
48    Return the square of the parameter.
49    Pre x contains number to be squared
50    Post squared value returned
51 */
52 int sqr (int x)
53 {
54 // Statements
55    return (x * x);
56 } // sqr
57
58 /*=================printOne==================
59    Print one integer value.
60    Pre x contains number to be printed
61    Post value in x printed
62 */
63 void printOne (int x)
64 {
```

(continue)

Program 4-3   Read a number and square it *(continued)*

```
65 // Statements
66    printf("The value is: %d\n", x);
67    return;
68 } // printOne
```

Output
```
Enter a number to be squared: 81
The value is: 6561
```

This simple program has grown to four functions, including `main`. This is an example of decomposition, the process of breaking a complex problem into simple parts. While this example is not really complex, it still demonstrates the concept.

We made one slight modification to `printOne` in this program. To make the output a little more meaningful, we added `The value is:` to the print statement. As a general principle, the person at the monitor should not have to guess what the output is.

Function Definition

Now that you have reviewed the basic function formats, let's look at functions in more detail. We begin with the function definition.

The function definition contains the code for a function. It is made up of two parts: the function header and the function body, which is a compound statement. Remember that a compound statement must have opening and closing braces, and it has declaration and statement sections. The function definition format is shown in **Figure 4-9**.

Figure 4-9   Function definition

Function Header
```
return_type function_name (formal parameter list)
```

```
{
// Local Declarations
    ...
// Statements
    ...
} // function_name
```

Function Header

A function header consists of three parts: the return type, the function name, and the formal parameter list. A semicolon is not used at the end of the function definition header.

With the implementation of the C99 standard, the return type became a required element of the syntax. When nothing is to be returned, the return type is `void`.

Function Body

The function body contains the local declarations and the function statements. The body starts with local definitions that specify the variables needed by the function. After the local definitions, the function statements, terminating with a `return` statement, are coded. If a function `return` type is `void`, it can be written without a `return` statement.

For the sake of clarity, it's important to explicitly code default statements. So, every function, even `void` functions, should have a `return` statement.

Figure 4-10 shows two functions, `first` and `second`. The function `first` has been declared to return an integer value. Its `return` statement therefore contains the expression x + 2. When the `return` statement is executed, the expression is evaluated and the resulting value is returned. The function `second` returns nothing; its `return` type is `void`. It therefore needs no `return` statement—the end of the function acts as a `void` return. Again, we strongly recommend that you include a `return` statement even for `void` functions. In this case, the `return` statement has no expression; it is just completed with a semicolon.

Figure 4-10 Function `return` statements

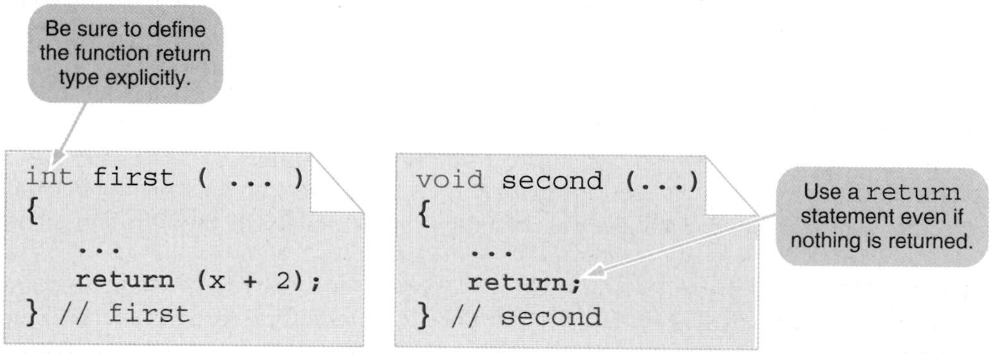

Formal Parameter List

In the definition of a function, the parameters are contained in the formal parameter list. This list defines and declares the variables that will contain the data received by the function. The parameter list is always required. If the function has no parameters—that is, if it does not receive any data from the calling function—then the fact that the parameter list is empty is declared with the keyword `void`.

In C, you must define and declare each variable fully with multiple parameters separated by commas. To make the parameter list easier to read when there are multiple lines, you should align the parameter types and their names with tabs. Attention to these little details makes the code much easier to read and understand.

In **Figure 4-11**, the variables x and y are formal parameters that receive data from the calling function's parameters. Because they are value parameters, copies of the values being passed are stored in the called function's memory area. If the function changes either of these values, only the copies will be changed. The original values in the calling function remain unchanged.

Figure 4-11 Function local variables

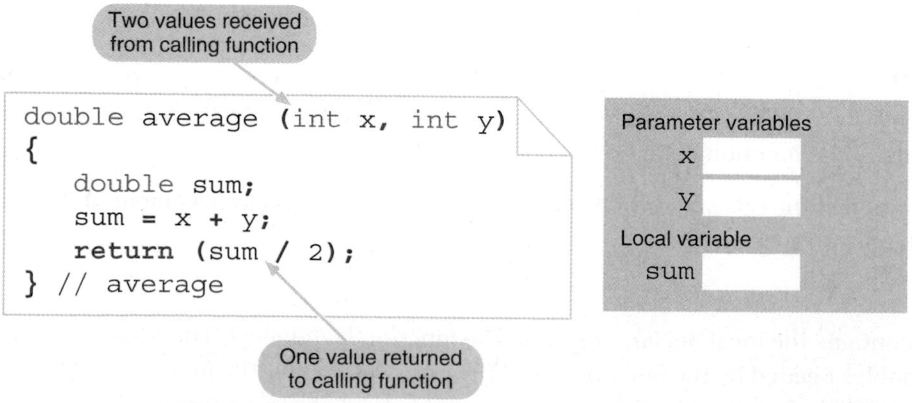

Local Variables

A local variable is a variable that is defined inside a function and used without having any role in the communication between functions. Figure 4-11 shows an example of a function with both formal parameters and a local variable, sum.

> **Note** | Formal parameters are variables that are declared in the header of the function definition. Actual parameters are the expressions in the calling statement. Formal and actual parameters must match exactly in type, order, and number. Their names, however, do not need to match.

Function Declaration

Function declarations consist only of a function header; they contain no code. Like function definition headers, function declaration headers consist of three parts: the return type, the function name, and the formal parameter list. Unlike the header for the function definition, function declarations are terminated with a semicolon.

The return type and the parameter list are required entries. If the program has no parameters, we code void in parentheses. If the program has multiple parameters, we separate each type-identifier set with commas.

The C standard does not require identifier names for the function declaration's formal parameters. But to make your code easier to read and understand, you should use identifier names. One point to note, however, is that the names do not need to be the same in the function declaration and the function definition. However, to prevent a compiler error, the types *do* have to be the same. The compiler checks the types in the function statements with the types in the call to ensure that they are the same or at least compatible. The major reason to include the identifiers in the function declaration is documentation, but this is only helpful if the names are meaningful. Don't use generic identifiers such as a or x.

Declarations are placed in the global declaration section before main. Grouping all function declarations at the beginning of the program makes them available whenever they are needed. Function declarations also provide an excellent quick reference for functions used in the program, making them excellent documentation.

Figure 4-12 illustrates several of these concepts. The function declaration tells the program that a function named multiply, which accepts two integers and returns one integer, will be called. That is all the compiler needs; it does not need to know anything else to evaluate the call.

Figure 4-12 Parts of a function call

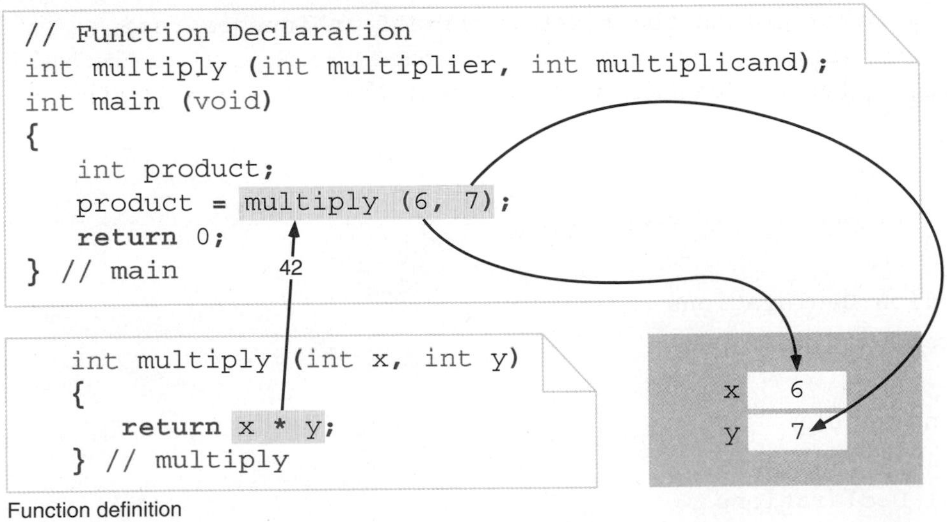

```
// Function Declaration
int multiply (int multiplier, int multiplicand);
int main (void)
{
    int product;
    product = multiply (6, 7);
    return 0;
} // main              42
```

```
int multiply (int x, int y)
{
    return x * y;
} // multiply
```

| x | 6 |
| y | 7 |

Function definition

Figure 4-12 also shows that the formal parameter names in the declaration do not need to be the same as the actual parameter names. In this case, the names in the function declarations are much more meaningful and therefore should have been used in the function definition.

The Function Call

A function call is a postfix expression with precedence 16. The operand in a function call is the function name; the operator is the parentheses set, (. . .), which contains the actual parameters. The actual parameters identify the values that are to be sent to the called function. They match the function's formal parameters in type and order in the parameter list. If the program has multiple actual parameters, they are separated by commas.

There are many different ways to call a function. In **Figure 4-13**, multiply is called six different ways. The first three show calls with primary expressions. The fourth uses a binary expression, a + 6, as the first parameter value, and the fifth shows the function multiply (a, b) as its own first parameter. The last example sums it all up: Any expression that reduces to a single value can be passed as a parameter.

Figure 4-13 Examples of function calls

```
multiply (6, 7)                   multiply (a, 7)
multiply (6, b)                   multiply (a + 6, 7)
multiply (multiply (a, b), 7)     multiply (... , ...)
```

Expression   Expression

Functions can be classified by the presence or absence of a return value. Functions that cannot return a value have a return type of void. Because these types of functions do not have a value, they can be used only as a stand-alone statement; that is, they cannot be included as part of an expression. All other functions return a value and can be used either as part of an expression or as a stand-alone statement, in which case the value is simply discarded.

Function Examples

This section contains four examples of programs in which functions call functions. Look for the points they demonstrate.

Program 4-4 prints the least significant (rightmost) digit of any integer read from the keyboard.

Program 4-4 | Print least significant digit

```
1   /* This program prints the first digits of an integer read
2       from the keyboard
3       Written by:
4       Date:
5   */
6   #include <stdio.h>
7
8   // Function Declarations
9   int firstDigit (int num);
10
11  int main (void)
12  {
13  // Local Declarations
14      int number;
15      int digit;
16
```

(continue)

Program 4-4   Print least significant digit *(continued)*

```
17 // Statements
18    printf("Enter an integer: ");
19    scanf("%d", &number);
20
21    digit = firstDigit (number);
22    printf("Least significant digit is: %d\n", digit);
23
24    return 0;
25 } // main
26
27 /*===========firstDigit===========
28
29    This function extracts the least significant
30    digit of an integer.
31    Pre num contains an integer
32    Post Returns least significant digit.
33 */
34 int firstDigit (int num)
35 {
36 // Statements
37    return (num % 10);
38 } // firstDigit
```

Output
```
Enter an integer: 27
Least significant digit is: 7
```

This extremely simple program demonstrates how to call a function from main. Note that even though `firstDigit` is used only in `main`, its function declaration is at the global level. In the sample run, when `firstDigit` was executed, it returned 7, which was then put into `digit` and printed.

This next example shows a function that extracts and adds the two least significant digits of any integer number. The design is shown in **Figure 4-14**. It consists of four functions: `main`, `addTwoDigits`, `firstDigit`, and `second-Digit`. The function `addTwoDigits` is called by `main`; `addTwoDigits` calls `firstDigit` and `secondDigit`. (See the "Software Engineering" section later in this chapter if you have trouble understanding the structure charts.)

Figure 4-14   Design for add two digits

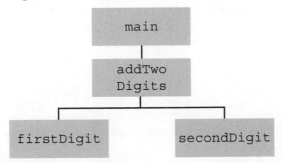

The code is shown in **Program 4-5**.

Program 4-5 | Add two digits

```
 1   /* This program extracts and adds the two least significant
 2      digits of an integer.
 3      Written by:
 4      Date:
 5   */
 6   #include <stdio.h>
 7
 8   // Function Declarations
 9   int addTwoDigits (int num);
10   int firstDigit (int num);
11   int secondDigit (int num);
12
13   int main (void)
14   {
15   // Local Declarations
16      int number;
17      int sum;
18
19   // Statements
20      printf("Enter an integer: ");
21      scanf ("%d", &number);
22
23      sum = addTwoDigits (number);
24      printf ("Sum of last two digits is: %d", sum);
25
26   return 0;
27   } // main
28
29   /* ================= addTwoDigits =================
30      Adds the first two digits of an integer.
31      Pre num contains an integer
32      Post returns sum of least significant digits
33   */
34   int addTwoDigits (int number)
35   {
36   // Local Declarations
37      int result;
38
39   // Statements
40      result = firstDigit(number) + secondDigit(number);
```

(continue)

Program 4-5   Add two digits *(continued)*

```
41     return result;
42 } // addTwoDigits
43
44 /*=================firstDigit =================
45    Extract the least significant digit of an integer.
46    Pre num contains an integer
47    Post Returns least significant digit.
48 */
49 int firstDigit (int num)
50 {
51 // Statements
52    return (num % 10);
53 } // firstDigit
54
55 /* ================= secondDigit =================
56    Extract second least significant (10s) digit
57    Pre num is an integer
58    Post Returns digit in 10s position
59 */
60 int secondDigit (int num)
61 {
62 // Local Declarations
63    int result;
64
65 // Statements
66    result = (num / 10) % 10;
67    return result;
68 } // secondDigit
```

Output
```
Run 1
Enter an integer: 23
Sum of last two digits is: 5
Run 2
Enter an integer: 8
Sum of last two digits is: 8
```

A natural question asked by students when they first read this program is, "Why not put firstDigit and second-Digit as in-line code in addTwoDigits?" This may seem to be an obvious way to code the problem. And after all, each of the called functions is only one statement.

The answer is that, although each function is only one statement, it does a job that can be used in other places. One of the principles of structured programming is that processes should appear in a program in only one place. For example, we have used the same code for firstDigit that we used in the first program. If a function is to be reusable in this way, it must do only one thing. The short answer, then, is that it is better structured programming. It is the nature of the task to be performed, not the amount of code, that determines if a function should be used.

An interesting point to note is the way these two different digits were calculated. To get the least significant digit, we took the 10s modulus of the number. But to get the second digit, we had to divide by 10. Can you figure out how to sum the digits in a three-digit number? We will give you a chance to do this in the problems at the end of the chapter.

Note that we tested the program with two different numbers, one containing only one digit. It is often necessary to run the program with more than one test case. Another test case that should be run is a negative number. What do you think would happen? As a programmer, you should not only run several tests but you should also predict the results before you run the program.

Program 4-6 reads a long integer and prints it with a comma after the first three digits, such as 123,456. The number is printed with leading zeros (see field specification %03d in Statement 40) in case the value is less than 100,000.

Program 4-6 | Print six digits with comma

```
1   /* This program reads long integers from the keyboard and
2       prints them with leading zeros in the form 123,456 with a
3       comma between 3rd & 4th digit.
4       Written by:
5       Date:
6   */
7   #include <stdio.h>
8   // Function Declarations
9   void printWithComma (long num);
10
11  int main (void)
12  {
13  // Local Declarations
14      long number;
15
16  // Statements
17      printf ("\nEnter a number with up to 6 digits: ");
18      scanf ("%ld", &number);
19      printWithComma (number);
20
21      return 0;
22  } // main
23
24  /* ================= printWithComma =================
25      This function divides num into two three-digit numbers and
26      prints them with a comma inserted.
```

(continue)

Program 4-6   Print six digits with comma *(continued)*

```
27     Pre num is a six digit number
28     Post num has been printed with a comma inserted
29 */
30 void printWithComma (long num)
31 {
32 // Local Declarations
33     int thousands;
34     int hundreds;
35
36 // Statements
37     thousands = num / 1000;
38     hundreds = num % 1000;
39
40     printf("The number you entered is \t%03d,%03d",
41     thousands, hundreds);
42     return;
43 } // printWithComma
```

Output
```
Run 1
Enter a number with up to 6 digits: 123456
The number you entered is  123,456
Run 2
Enter a number with up to 6 digits: 12
The number you entered is 000,012
```

Once again, we have a simple program that has the makings of a very useful function. C has no built-in functions that will provide number formatting such as commas and dollar signs. We have to program these details. And because this logic will be used over and over again, it must be in its own function. Note, however, that more work is needed to print numbers less than 100,000 correctly. However, we have not yet introduced the tools to do the complete job.

Again, we have used two test cases to show that more work must be done. An even bigger problem occurs if we try to format a small negative number. Can you see what the problem is? If not, code the problem and run it to see. You will learn how to handle these problems as you become a more experienced programmer.

Our next example calculates and prints the annual tuition for a student enrolled in Acme College. In this college, students can take an unlimited number of units each term. (This is, of course, not realistic, but it is useful for demonstration purposes.) Each term, the students are charged $10 per unit plus a $10 registration fee. To discourage students from overloading, the college charges $50 extra for each 12 units, or fraction thereof, a student takes after the first 12 units. For example, if a student takes 13 units, the tuition is $190 ($10 for registration, plus 13 times $10 for units, plus a $50 penalty for the one extra unit). If a student takes 25 units, the tuition is $360 ($10 for registration, plus 25 times $10 for units, plus $100 for two penalty fees). The design for this problem is shown in **Figure 4-15**.

Figure 4-15 Design for Acme College fees

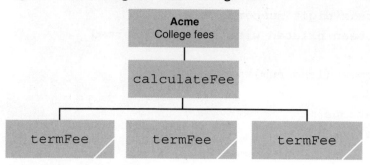

The code for Acme College is shown in **Program 4-7**.

Program 4-7 | Acme college fees

```
1   /* This program prints the tuition at Acme College.
2      Acme charges $10 for registration, plus $10 per unit and a
3      penalty of $50 for each 12 units, or
4      fraction of 12, over 12.
5      Written by:
6      Date:
7   */
8   #include <stdio.h>
9
10  #define REG_FEE 10
11  #define UNIT_FEE 10
12  #define EXCESS_FEE 50
13
14  // Function Declarations
15  int calculateFee (int firstTerm, int secondTerm,
16                    int thirdTerm);
17  int termFee (int units);
18
19  int main (void)
20  {
21  // Local Declarations
22     int firstTerm;
23     int secondTerm;
24     int thirdTerm;
25     int totalFee;
26
27  // Statements
28     printf("Enter units for first term: ");
29     scanf ("%d", &firstTerm);
30
```

(continue)

Program 4-7   Acme college fees *(continued)*

```
31    printf("Enter units for second term: ");
32    scanf ("%d", &secondTerm);
33
34    printf("Enter units for third term: ");
35    scanf ("%d", &thirdTerm);
36
37    totalFee = calculateFee
38                  (firstTerm, secondTerm, thirdTerm);
39    printf("The total tuition is: %8d\n", totalFee);
40
41    return 0;
42 } // main
43
44 /* ================= calculateFee =================
45    Calculate the total fees for the year.
46    Pre The number of units to be taken each term.
47    Post Returns the annual fees.
48 */
49 int calculateFee (int firstTerm, int secondTerm,
50                   int thirdTerm)
51 {
52 // Local Declarations
53    int fee;
54
55 // Statements
56    fee = termFee (firstTerm)
57            + termFee (secondTerm)
58            + termFee (thirdTerm);
59    return fee;
60 } // calculateFee
61
62 /*================= termFee =================
63   Calculate the tuition for one term
64   Pre units contains units for the term
65   Post The fee is calculated and returned
66 */
67 int termFee (int units)
68 {
69 // Local Declarations
70    int totalFees;
71
72 // Statements
73    totalFees = REG_FEE
```

(continue)

Program 4.7   Acme college fees *(continued)*

```
74                       + ((units - 1)/12 * EXCESS_FEE)
75                       + (units * UNIT_FEE);
76     return (totalFees);
77 } // termFee
```

> **Output**
>
> Enter units for first term: 10
>
> Enter units for second term: 20
>
> Enter units for third term: 30
>
> The total tuition is: 780

The most interesting aspect of Program 4-7 is how we call `termFee` three different times in one function. Let's look at how it works. The key statement follows.

```
fee =   termFee (firstTerm)
      + termFee (secondTerm)
      + termFee (thirdTerm);
```

A function call is a postfix expression. Therefore, it evaluates from the left. To evaluate the expression (three function calls) on the right of the assignment operator, we first evaluate the first expression, the call to `termFee` with the number of units for the first term. When `termFee` completes the first time, the return value (110) replaces the call. At this point, we have the expression shown in the following example.

```
110 + termFee (secondTerm) + termFee (thirdTerm)
```

When `termFee` is executed a second time, its return value (260) becomes the value of the second expression and we have

```
110 + 260 + termFee (thirdTerm)
```

After the third call to `termFee`, the expression on the right of the assignment operator is ready for evaluation. Its value is 780, which is assigned to `fee`.

At least two more tests are needed to completely evaluate this program. We would run it with all three terms having 0 units and then do another test of 11, 12, and 13 units.

4.4 Inter-Function Communication

Although the calling and called function are two separate entities, they need to communicate to exchange data. Data flows between the calling and called functions in three different ways: a downward flow from the calling to the called function, an upward flow from the called to the calling function, and a bidirectional flow in both directions. **Figure 4-16** illustrates all three forms of data flow.

Figure 4-16   Data flow strategies

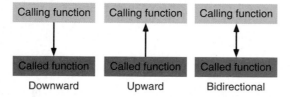

Basic Concept

Let us first discuss the general concept before we discuss how they are done in C.

Downward Flow

In downward communication, the calling function sends data to the called function. No data flows in the opposite direction. In this strategy, copies of the data items are passed from the calling function to the called function. The called function may change the values passed, but the original values in the calling function remain untouched. An example of this type of communication is passing data to a print function.

Upward Flow

Upward communication occurs when the called function sends data back to the called function without receiving any data from it. A good example of this type of communication is when the called function reads data from the keyboard that needs to be passed back to the called function.

Bidirectional Flow

Bidirectional communication occurs when the calling function sends data down to the called function. During or at the end of its processing, the called function then sends data up to the calling function. For example, the calling function may send data to the called function, which it manipulates and sends up to the calling function.

C Implementation

Now let us examine how these three types of communication are implemented in C. In the discussion that follows, it is important to remember that the flow refers to the data. The data flows down to the called function. The data flows from the called function back to the calling function.

> **Note**   Most programming languages have three strategies for interfunction communication: pass by value, pass by reference, and return. The C language, unfortunately, uses only the first and last strategies; there is no pass by reference in C. The C language uses only pass by value and return to achieve three types of communications between a calling and a called function.

Downward Communication

The pass-by-value mechanism in C is a perfect solution for the communication in the downward direction. A variable is declared and defined in the called function for each value to be received from the calling function. The calling function sends a copy of each value to the called function; no data flows upward.

Figure 4-17 illustrates downward communication. Two data items are passed from `main` to the `downFun` function. One data value is a literal, the other is the value of a variable.

Figure 4-17 Downward communication in C

```
int main (void)
{
    int a;
    ...
    downFun (a, 15);
    ...
} // main
```

```
void downFun (int x, int y)
{
    ...
    return ;
} // downFun
```

Downward communication is one-way communication. The calling function can send data to the called function, but the called function cannot send any data to the calling function. **Figure 4-18** illustrates downward and upward communication.

Figure 4-18 Downward and upward communication in C

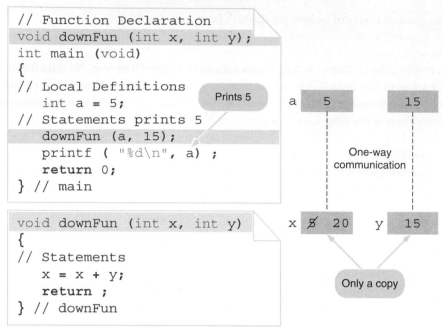

Upward Communication

C provides only one upward direction flow, the `return` statement. While it works well, only one data item can be returned. The only way that a called function can pass multiple data items up to the calling function is to access variables in the calling function and deposit the data there. However, C does not allow us to directly reference a variable in the calling function; in other words, we cannot access a variable in the calling function by its identifier. Therefore, we need another strategy to solve the problem.

The solution is for the calling function to pass the address of the variable to the called function. Given the variable's address, the called function can then put the data in the calling function. The calling function needs to declare a data variable to receive the data. The called function needs to declare a variable to store the address that it receives from the calling function.

In C, a variable that can store data is different from the variable that can store an address. So the called function needs a special type of variable, an address variable, or as it is called in C, a pointer variable, that points to the variable in the called function.

The calling function needs to pass the address of a variable to receive the data from the called function. This action is a pass-by-value mechanism although what is passed is not data, it is an address.

To get the address of a variable, we use the address operator (`&`). If the name of the variable in the calling function is x, we extract its address using the address operator (`&x`) and pass it as a parameter in the function call. The following example passes the addresses of a and b to a function named `upFun`.

```
upFun (&a, &b);
```

The called function needs to declare that the parameter is to receive an address; in other words, it needs to create an address variable. To declare an address variable, we use an asterisk (`*`) after the type. In other words, if x in the calling function is of type `int`, we need to declare and define a variable in the called function of type `int*`. This is done in the header of the called function. For example, to define our `upFun` function, we use the following function header.

```
void upFun (int* ax, int* ay)
```

The asterisk signifies that the variables ax and ay are not data variables but address variables holding the address of int variables. Note that the asterisk as used in the declaration belongs to the type, not to the variables (ax and ay).

To change the data in the calling function, we need to use the variable's address parameter. Changing data through an address variable is known as indirect access; that is, we access the variable indirectly through its address stored in the parameter list and then change the data. For this reason, the asterisk is known as the indirection operator. To change the data, we again use an asterisk. This time, the asterisk is put immediately in front of the address variable's name. For example, to change the variable in the calling function to 23, we would use the following statement.

```
*ax = 23;
```

It is important to remember that these two uses of the asterisk, declaring an address variable and indirectly accessing the data, play completely different roles. The first asterisk, in the declaration, belongs to the type; the second asterisk is an expression that indirectly accesses the variable in the called program as shown in **Figure 4-19**.

Figure 4-19 Upward communication in C

```
int main (void)
{
    int a;
    int b;
    ...
    upFun (&a , &b);
    ...
} // main
```

```
void upFun (int* as: , int * ay)
{
    *ax = 23;
    *ay = 8;
    return;
} // upFun
```

We need to emphasize that when only one data item needs to be returned, we use the standard return statement. Only use upward communication when multiple items need to be returned. **Figure 4-20** shows the techniques for upward communication.

Figure 4-20 Upward communication

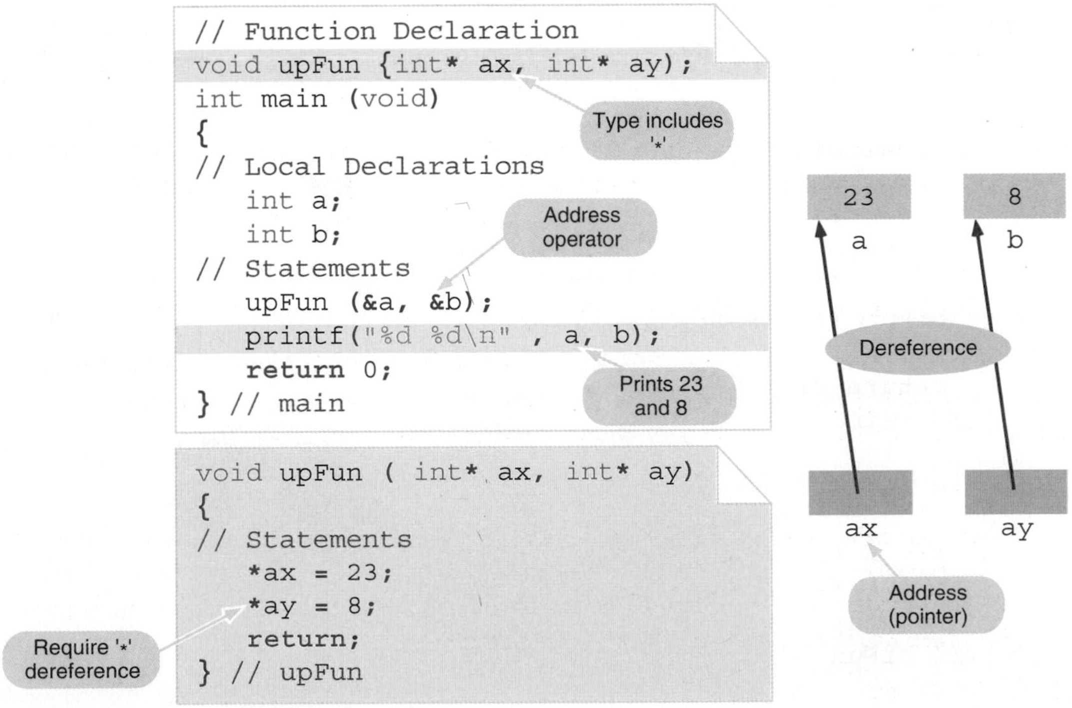

> **Note**
>
> To send data from the called function to the calling function:
>
> 1. We need to use the & symbol in front of the data variable when we call the function.
> 2. We need to use the * symbol after the data type when we declare the address variable.
> 3. We need to use the * in front of the variable when we store data indirectly.

Bidirectional Communication

The strategy described for the upward direction can easily be augmented to allow the communication in both directions. The only difference is that the indirect reference must be used in both sides of the assignment statement. The variable in the called function first is accessed for retrieving using the address variable in the right-hand side. The same parameter is accessed again to store a value in the left-hand side. We demonstrate bidirectional access in **Figure 4-21**.

Figure 4-21   Bidirectional communication in C

```c
int main (void)
{
    int a;
    int b;
    ...
    biFun (&a , &b);
    ...
} // main
```

```c
void biFun(int* ax, int* ay)
{
    *ax = *ax + 2;
    *ay = *ay / *ax;
    return;
} // biFun
```

Figure 4-22 illustrates bidirectional communication flow.

Figure 4-22   Bidirectional communication

```c
// Function Declaration
void biFun (int* ax, int* ay);
int main (void)
{
// Local Definitions
    int a = 2;
    int b = 6;
// Statements
    ...
    biFun (&a, &b);
    ...
    return 0;
} // main
```

```c
void biFun (int* ax , int* ay)
{
    *ax = *ax + 2;
    *ay = *ay / *ax;
    return;
} // biFun
```

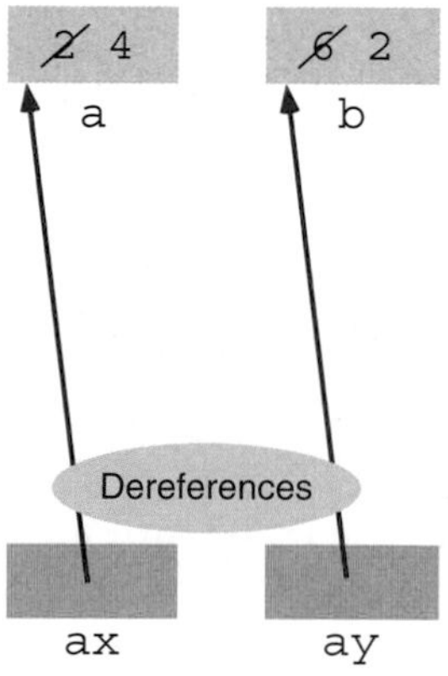

Communication Summary

Let's summarize the rules for interfunction communication. Like many aspects of learning a language, they must be memorized.

1. Rules for downward communication

   a. Use values in the function call to pass data.

   b. Use appropriate data types in the function parameter list to receive the data values.

   c. Use the parameter identifiers in the called function to access the local copies of the data.

2. Rules for upward and bidirectional communication

   a. Use `&variableName` in the function call to pass a reference to the variable.

   b. Use `type*` in the function parameter list to receive the variable's address.

   c. Use `*parameterName` in the function to reference the original variable.

Communication Examples

In this section we write some short programs to demonstrate function communication.

Let's look at a program that uses the indirection operator to dereference data. One common process that occurs often in programming is exchanging two pieces of data. Let's write a function that, given two integer variables, exchanges them. Because two variables are being changed, we cannot use the `return` statement. Instead we pass addresses to make the changes.

First, make sure you understand how to exchange two variables: We cannot simply assign variables to each other, as shown in the following example.

```
x = y;   // This won't work
y = x;   // Result is y in both
```

If you carefully trace these two statements, you will see that the original value of y ends up in both variables. Therefore, to exchange variables, we need to create a temporary variable to hold the first value while the exchange is being made. The correct logic is shown in the following example.

```
hold    = y;    // value of y saved
y    = x;    // x now in y
x    = hold; // original y now in x
```

The `exchange` function and its data flow are shown in **Figure 4-23**. First, examine the function declarations in Figure 4-23 carefully. Note the asterisk in the declaration of num1 and num2. The asterisk is used with the type declaration to specify that the type is an address—in this case, the address of an integer. Now, look at the call statement in `main`. Because we will change the values of a and b in `main`, we need to pass their addresses. The address operators (`&`) tell the compiler that we want their addresses passed, not their values.

Figure 4-23 Exchange function

```
// Function Declarations
void exchange ( int* num1, int* num2);
int main (void)
{
// Local Definitions
    int a;
    int b;
// Statements
    ...
    exchange (&a, &b);
    ...
    return 0;
} // main
```

Note that the type includes an asterisk.

Address operators

```
void exchange (int* num1, int* num2)
{
// Local Definitions
    int hold;
// Statements
    hold  = *num1;
    *num1 = *num2;
    *num2 = hold;
    return;
} // exchange
```

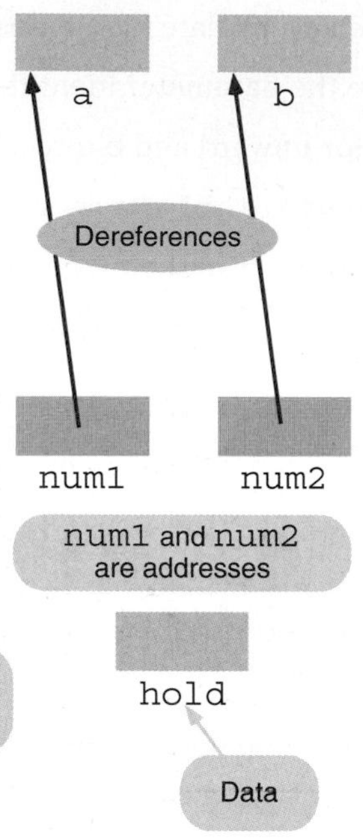

Note the indirection operator is used for dereferencing.

a

b

Dereferences

num1   num2

num1 and num2 are addresses

hold

Data

Now, look at the statements in exchange. First, we copy num1's value to hold. Because hold is a local variable, it is treated the same as any local variable—no special operators are required. However, num1 contains the address of the data we want, not the data itself. To get the value it is referring to, we must dereference it. This is done with the indirection operator, the asterisk (*). The statement is shown in the following example.

```
hold = *num1;
```

In the same manner, we can now dereference num2 and copy it to num1 and then complete the exchange by copying hold to num2. These statements are seen in the following example.

```
*num1= *num2;
*num2 = hold;
```

Note that with the exception of hold, all of the data movement is done in the calling program's area. This is the power of the indirection operator.

Here is another simple example, one that uses both pass-by-value and pass-by-address parameters. We need to write a function that, given two numbers, calculates both the quotient and the remainder. Because we can't return two values, we will pass the addresses where we want the quotient and remainder stored. This problem is shown in **Figure 4-24**.

Let's examine divide first. Note that the first two parameters are pass by value. You can tell this because their types are just int ; there are no asterisks indicating that they are addresses. The last two parameters are addresses. Their types are int*; therefore, any references to them in the function must use the indirection operator.

Figure 4-24   Calculate quotient and remainder

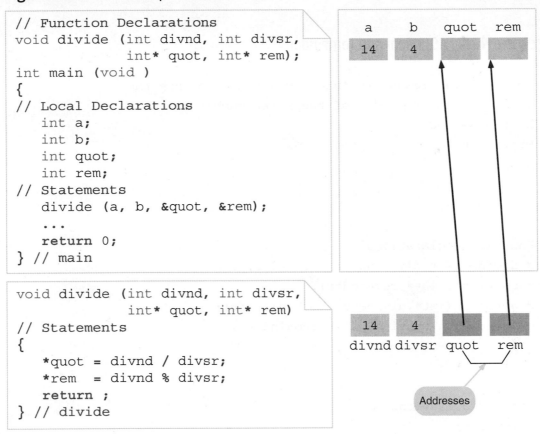

```
// Function Declarations
void divide (int divnd, int divsr,
             int* quot, int* rem);
int main (void )
{
// Local Declarations
    int a;
    int b;
    int quot;
    int rem;
// Statements
    divide (a, b, &quot, &rem);
    ...
    return 0;
} // main
```

```
void divide (int divnd, int divsr,
             int* quot, int* rem)
// Statements
{
    *quot = divnd / divsr;
    *rem  = divnd % divsr;
    return ;
} // divide
```

Now look at the call in main. Note that a and b are simply passed by using their identifiers. They are primary expressions whose value is the contents of the variable. On the other hand, quot and rem are passed as addresses by using the address operator. In this case, the value of the primary expression created by the address operator and the identifier is the address of the variable. Therefore, we pass an address value rather than a data value.

As the programmer, it is your job to know what needs to be passed, a value or an address, when you write a call. Similarly, when you use the parameters in the called program, you must remember to use the indirection operator when you have an address.

Let's use divide in a program that reads two integers, divides them, and then prints the quotient and the remainder. The design for this program is shown in **Figure 4-25**.

Figure 4-25   Quotient and remainder design

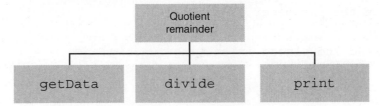

The code is shown in **Program 4-8**.

Program 4-8 | Quotient and remainder

```
1   /* This program reads two integers and then prints the
2      quotient and remainder of the first number divided
3      by the second.
4      Written by:
5      Date:
6   */
7   #include <stdio.h>
8
9   // Function Declarations
10  void divide (int dividend, int divisor,
11  int* quotient, int* remainder);
12  void getData (int* dividend, int* divisor);
13  void print (int quotient, int remainder);
14
15  int main (void)
16  {
17  // Local Declarations
18  int dividend;
19  int divisor;
20  int quot;
21  int rem;
22
23  // Statements
24     getData (&dividend, &divisor);
25     divide (dividend, divisor, &quot, &rem);
26     print (quot, rem);
27
28     return 0;
29  } // main
30
31  /*================= getData =================
32    This function reads two numbers into variables
33    specified in the parameter list.
34    Pre Nothing.
35    Post Data read and placed in calling function.
36  */
37  void getData (int* dividend, int* divisor)
```

(continue)

Program 4-8   Quotient and remainder *(continued)*

```c
38 {
39 // Statements
40    printf("Enter two integers and return: ");
41    scanf ("%d%d", dividend, divisor);
42    return;
43 } // getData
44
45 /*================= divide ==================
46   This function divides two integers and places the
47   quotient/remainder in calling program variables
48   Pre dividend & divisor contain integer values
49   Post quotient & remainder calc'd
50 */
51 void divide (int dividend, int divisor,
52 int* quotient, int* remainder)
53 {
54 // Statements
55    *quotient = dividend / divisor;
56    *remainder = dividend % divisor;
57    return;
58 } // divide
59
60 /*================= print ==================
61   This function prints the quotient and the remainder
62   Pre quot contains the quotient
63   rem contains the remainder
64   Post Quotient and remainder printed
65 */
66 void print (int quot, int rem)
67 {
68 // Statements
69    printf ("Quotient : %3d\n", quot);
70    printf ("Remainder: %3d\n", rem);
71    return;
72 } // print
```

Output
```
Enter two integers and return: 130 23
Quotient :   5
Remainder:  15
```

First, look at the design of this program. Note how main contains only calls to subfunctions. It does no work itself; like a good manager, it delegates all work to lower levels in the program. This is how you should design your programs.

Study the getData function carefully. First note that the parameters identify the variables as addresses. Verify that they contain an asterisk as a part of their type. Now look at the scanf statement carefully. What is missing? There are no address operators for the variables! We don't need the address operators because the parameters are already addresses. We have used the address operator (&) up to this example to tell the compiler that we want the address of the variable, not its contents. Because the parameters were passed as addresses (see line 24 in Program 4-8), we don't need the address operator.

Now study the way we use quotient and remainder in divide. We pass them as addresses by using the address operator. Because we are passing addresses, we can change their values in main. In the function definition, the formal parameters show these two parameters to be addresses to integers by showing the type as int* (see statement 52). To change the value back in main, we use the indirection operator when we assign the results of the divide and modulo operations.

4.5 Standard Functions

C provides a rich collection of standard functions whose definitions have been written and are ready to be used in our programs. To use these functions, we must include their function declarations. The function declarations for these functions are grouped together and collected in several header files. Instead of adding the individual declarations of each function, therefore, we simply include the headers at the top of our programs.

Figure 4-26 shows how two of the C standard functions that we have used several times are brought into our program. The include statement causes the library header file for standard input and output (stdio.h) to be copied into our program. It contains the declarations for printf and scanf. Then, when the program is linked, the object code for these functions is combined with our code to build the complete program.

Figure 4-26   Library functions and the linker

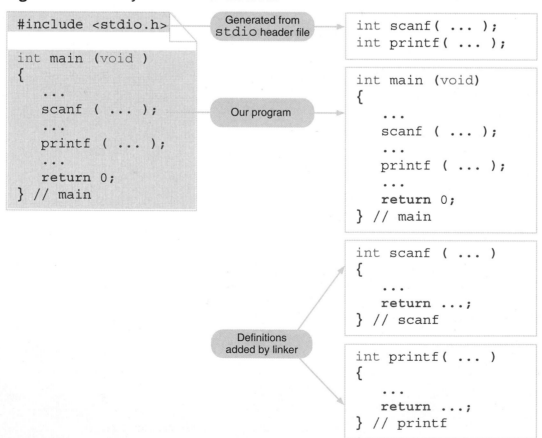

Math Functions

Many important library functions are available for mathematical calculations. Most of the function declarations for these functions are in either the math header file (`math.h`) or standard library (`stdlib.h`). In general, the integer functions are found in `stdlib.h`.

Absolute Value Functions

The functions described in this section return the absolute value of a number. An absolute value is the positive rendering of the value regardless of its sign. There are three integer functions and three real functions.

The integer functions are `abs`, `labs`, and `llabs`. For `abs` the parameter must be an `int` and it returns an `int`. For `labs` the parameter must be a `long int`, and it returns a `long int`. For `llabs` the parameter must be a `long long int`, and it returns a `long long int`.

```
int   abs  (int     number);     // stdlib.h
long      labs    (long   number);     // stdlib.h
long long   llabs   (long long  number);     // stdlib.h
```

The real functions are `fobs`, `fabsf`, and `fabsl`. For `fobs` the parameter is a `double`, and it returns a `double`. The `float` version is named `fabsf` and the `long double` version is named `fabsl`.

```
double  fabs   (double number);     // math.h
float    fabsf  (float   number);     // math.h
long double fabsl   (long double   number);     // math .h
```

> **Example:** Absolute Numbers

```
abs (3) returns 3
fabs (-3.4) returns 3.4
```

Complex Number Functions

The functions for manipulating complex numbers are collected in the `complex.h` header file. Some of the complex number functions are shown in **Table 4-1**.

Table 4-1 Complex number functions

DATA TYPE	FUNCTION NAME	FUNCTION PARAMETER	COMMENT
double	cabs	(double complex number);	// absolute
float	cabsf	(float complex number);	
long double	cabsl	(long double complex number);	
double	carg	(double complex number);	
float	cargf	(float complex number);	// argument
long double	cabsl	(long double complex number);	
double	creal	(double complex number);	// real
float	crealf	(float complex number);	
long double	creall	(long double complex number);	
double	cimag	(double complex number);	// imaginary
float	cimagf	(float complex number);	
long double	cimagl	(long double complex number);	

Ceiling Functions

A ceiling is the smallest integral value greater than or equal to a number. For example, the ceiling of 3.0000001 is 4. If we consider all numbers as a continuous range from minus infinity to plus infinity (**Figure 4-27**), this function moves the number right to an integral value.

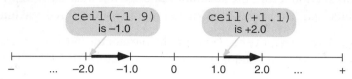

Figure 4-27 Ceiling function

Although the ceiling functions determine an integral value, the return type is defined as a real value that corresponds to the argument. The ceiling function declarations are

```
double    ceil     (double number);
float     ceilf    (float   number);
long double ceill    (long double    number);
```

> **Example:** Ceiling Function

```
ceil    (-1.9)   returns -1.0
ceil    ( 1.1)   returns 2.0
```

Floor Functions

A floor is the largest integral value that is equal to or less than a number (see **Figure 4-28**). For example, the floor of 3.99999 is 3.0. Again, looking at numbers as a continuum, this function moves the number left to an integral value.

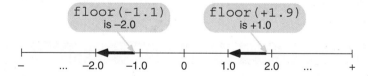

Figure 4-28 Floor function

The floor function declarations are

```
double    floor    (double number);
float     floorf   (float   number);
long double floorl   (long double    number);
```

> **Example:** Floor Function

```
floor    (-1.1)   returns -2.0
floor    ( 1.9)   returns 1.0
```

Truncate Functions

The truncate functions return the integral in the direction of 0. They are the same as floor function for positive numbers and the same as ceiling function for negative numbers. Their function declarations are

```
double    trunc    (double number);
float     truncf   (float  number);
long double truncl  (long double    number);
```

Example: Truncate Function

```
trunc    (-1.1)   returns -1.0
trunc    ( 1.9)   returns 1.0
```

Round Functions

The round functions return the nearest integral value. Their function declarations are

```
double        round    (double        number);
float         roundf   (float         number);
long double roundl  (long double number);
```

In addition to the real round functions, C provides two sets that return a `long int` or a `long long int`. Note that no round function returns an `int`. Their function declarations are

```
long int        lround    (double        number);
long int        lroundf   (float         number);
long int        lroundl   (long double number);
long long int llround   (double        number);
long long int llroundf  (float         number);
long long int llroundl  (long double number);
```

Example: Round Function

```
round    (-1.1)     returns -1.0
round    ( 1.9)     returns 2.0
round    (-1.5)     returns -2.0
```

Power Functions

The power (`pow`) function returns the value of the x raised to the power y– that is, x^y. An error occurs if the base (x) is negative and the exponent (y) is not an integer, or if the base is zero and the exponent is not positive. The power function declarations are

```
double        pow  (double n1, double n2);
float         powf (float n1, float n2);
long double powl (long double n1, long double n2);
```

Example: Power Function

```
pow (3.0, 4.0)   returns 81.0
pow (3.4, 2.3)   returns 16.687893
```

Square Root Functions

The square root functions return the nonnegative square root of a number. An error occurs if the number is negative. The square root function declarations are

```
double       sqrt  (double n1);
float        sqrtf (float n1);
long double sqrtl (long double n1);
```

Example: Square Root Function

```
sqrt (25) returns 5.0
```

Random Numbers

A random number is a number selected from a set in which all members have the same probability of being selected. Random numbers are useful in many areas of computer science. Two examples are application testing and gaming.

Random Number Generation

Because of their usefulness, most languages provide functions to generate random numbers. Each time the function is called, it generates another number. The function that generates random numbers uses a formula that has been mathematically designed to ensure that each number in the set in fact has the same probability of being selected; in other words, to ensure that each number is truly random. As a part of the formula, the function uses the previous random number. The design is shown in **Figure 4-29**.

Figure 4-29   Random number generation

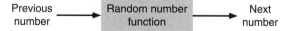

Now that we understand the basic design of a random number generator, a logical question is "How is the first random number generated?" The answer is from a seed. In C, we can use the default seed provided by the system (1) or we can specify our own seed, this is known as random number seed.

Because C uses only one algorithm to generate random numbers, the series it produces is a pseudorandom number series. Only by using different seeds can we generate different random series. Calling the random function several times generates a series of random numbers as shown in **Figure 4-30**.

Figure 4-30 Generating a random number series

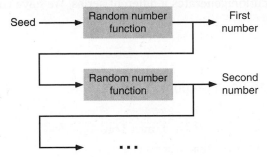

We can create the same series or a different series of random numbers each time we run our program. Some programs require that the series be the same each time the program runs; others require that the series be different each time. We control the type of series by our choice of seeds.

Random Numbers in C

C provides two functions to build a random number series, seed random (`srand` and random (`rand`). These functions are found in `stdlib.h`.

Seed Random Number Function

The seed random function, (`srand`), creates the starting seed for a number series. Its function declaration is

```
void srand (unsigned int seed);
```

Example: Generate the Same Series in Each Run

To generate the same number series in each run, we can either omit `srand` or we can provide a constant seed random, preferably a prime number, such as 997.

```
srand (997);
```

Example: Generate a Different Series in Each Run

To generate different series in each run, we use the time of day as the seed. The C call for the time, which requires the `time.h` library, is used in the following example.

```
srand(time (NULL));
```

Whichever series we need, `srand` should be called only once for each random number series, usually only once in a program. It should be noted here that `srand` must be called only once for each random number series.

Random Number Function

The random number function, (`rand`) returns a pseudorandom integer between 0 and `RAND_MAX`, which is defined in the standard library as the largest number that `rand` can generate. The C standard requires that it be at least 32,767. Each call generates the next number in a random number series. The random number function declaration is

```
int rand (void);
```

Program 4-9 is a simple program that prints three random numbers. Because we seed the random number generator with the time of day, each program execution generates a different series. We have run it twice to demonstrate that the random numbers are different.

Program 4-9 | Creating temporal random numbers

```
1   /* Demonstrate the use of the time function
2      to generate a temporal random number series.
3      Written by:
4      Date:
5   */
6   #include <stdio.h>
7   #include <stdlib.h>
8   #include <time.h>
9
10  int main (void)
11  {
12  // Statements
13      srand(time(NULL));   // Seed temporally
14
15      printf("%d\n", rand());
16      printf("%d\n", rand());
17      printf("%d\n", rand());
18
19      return 0;
20  } // main
```

```
Output
First Run
9641
16041
6350
Second Run
31390
31457
21438
```

Program 4-10 is a simple program that prints three random numbers. Because we seed the random number generator with a constant, each program execution generates the same series. We would have also generated the same series if we didn't use srand. We have run it twice to demonstrate that the random numbers are the same.

Program 4-10 | Creating pseudorandom numbers

```
1   /* Demonstrate the use of the srand function to generate
2      a pseudorandom number series.
3      Written by:
4      Date:
5   */
6   #include <stdio.h>
7   #include <stdlib.h>
8
9   int main (void)
10  {
11  // Statements
12     srand(997);
13
14     printf("%d\n", rand());
15     printf("%d\n", rand());
16     printf("%d\n", rand());
17
18     return 0;
19  } // main
```

Output
First Run
10575
22303
4276
Second Run
10575
22303
4276

Using Random Numbers

The numbers returned by the random number generator are in a large range. The C standard specifies that it must be at least 0 to 32,767. When we need a random number in a different range, we must map the standard range into the required range. Two common ranges are a real-number series, usually 0.0 to 1.0, and an integral range, such as 0 to 25 or 11 to 20. Note that 0.0 is included in the range but 1.0 is not. The maximum number is 0.99999999.

Generating Random Integrals

To generate a random integral in a range x to y, we must first scale the number and then, if x is greater than 0, shift the number within the range. We scale the number using the modulus operator. For example, to produce a random number in the range 0 ... 50, we simply scale the random number as shown in the following example. Note that the scaling factor must be one greater than the highest random number needed.

```
rand ( ) % 51
```

Modulus works well when our range starts at 0. But what if we need a different range? In that case, we must shift the result. For example, suppose we want a random number between 3 and 7 (**Figure 4-31**). If we call rand and then use modulus 8, our range will be 0 through 7. To convert to the correct range, we first determine our modulus factor by subtracting the starting point (3) from the modulus divisor (8) and then adding the starting point to the resulting number. Thus, for our example, we subtract 3 from 8, which makes the modulus divisor 5.

Figure 4-31 Random number scaling for 3–7

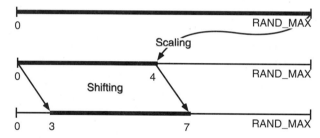

Generalizing the algorithm, we get

```
rand () % range + minimum
```

where range is (maximum − minimum) + 1, minimum is the minimum number and maximum is the maximum number in the desired range. For example, to create a random number in the range 10–20, we would use the following expression:

```
range = (20 - 10) + 1;    //11
randNo = rand() % range + 10;
```

Program 4-11 generates a random number series in the range 10 to 20.

> # Program 4-11 | Generating random numbers in the range 10 to 20

```
1   /* Generate a random series in the range 10 to 20.
2       Written by:
3       Date:
4   */
```

(continue)

Program 4-11   Generating random numbers in the range 10 to 20 *(continued)*

```c
5   #include <stdio.h>
6   #include <stdlib.h>
7   #include <time.h>
8
9   int main (void)
10  {
11  // Local Declarations
12  int range;
13
14  // Statements
15      srand(time(NULL));
16      range = (20 - 10) + 1;
17
18      printf("%d", rand() % range +10);
19      printf(" %d", rand() % range + 10);
20      printf(" %d\n", rand() % range +10);
21
22      return 0;
23  } // main
```

Output
```
10 11 16
```

Generating a Real Random Number Series

To generate a real random number series between 0.0 and 1.0 we divide the number returned by the random number generator by the maximum random number (RAND_MAX), which is found in `stdlib.h`, and then store it in a real number type. **Program 4-12** illustrates the generation of a real random number series in the range of 0 to 1.

Program 4-12 | Generating random real numbers

```c
1   /* Generate a real random series in the range 0 to 1.
2      Written by:
3      Date:
4   */
5   #include <stdio.h>
6   #include <stdlib.h>
7   #include <time.h>
8
```

(continue)

Program 4-12 Generating random real numbers *(continued)*

```
 9  int main (void)
10  {
11  // Local Declarations
12      float x;
13
14  // Statements
15      srand(time(NULL));
16
17      x = (float)rand() / RAND_MAX;
18      printf("%f", x);
19      x = (float)rand() / RAND_MAX;
20      printf(" %f", x);
21      x = (float)rand() / RAND_MAX;
22      printf(" %f\n", x);
23
24      return 0;
25  } // main
```

Output
```
0.782006 0.264260 0.348460
```

To scale a random real number into a range other than 0.0 to 1.0 (exclusive), we first generate the random number as we did in Program 4-12. Then we re-scale it to the new range. For example, to generate random real numbers in the range 100.0 to 300.0 (exclusive), we multiply the random number by the range (200.0) and then add the minimum (100.0). Using the results from Program 4-12, our random real numbers would be 256.4012, 152.852, and 169.692.

4.6 Scope

Scope determines the region of the program in which a defined object is visible—that is, the part of the program in which we can use the object's name. Scope pertains to any object that can be declared, such as a variable or a function declaration. It does not pertain directly to precompiler directives, such as define statements; they have separate rules. Scope is a source program concept: It has no direct bearing on the run-time program.

To discuss the concept of scope, we need to review two concepts. First, a block is zero or more statements enclosed in a set of braces. Recall that a function's body is enclosed in a set of braces; thus, a body is also a block. A block has a declarations section and a statement section. This concept gives us the ability to nest blocks within the body of a function and allows each block to be an independent group of statements with its own isolated definitions. Second, the global area of our program consists of all statements that are outside functions. **Figure 4-32** is a graphical representation of the concept of global area and blocks.

An object's scope extends from its declaration until the end of its block. A variable is in scope if it is visible to the statement being examined. Variables are in scope from their point of declaration until the end of their block.

Figure 4-32 Scope (or global and block areas)

```
/* This is a sample to demonstrate scope. The techniques
   used in this program should never be used in practice.
*/
#include <stdio.h>
int fun (int a, int b);
                                                   Global area

int main (void )
{
   int a;
   int b;                                          main's area
   float y;
   ...

      {
        // Beginning of nested block
          float a = y / 2;
          float y;
          float z;                                 Nested block
          ...                                         area
          z = a* b;
          ...
      } // End of nested block

   ...
} // End of main

int fun (int i, int j)
{
   int a;
   int y;                                          fun's area
   ...
} // fun
```

Global Scope

The global scope is easily defined. Any object defined in the global area of a program is visible from its definition until the end of the program. Referring to Figure 4-32, the function declaration for fun is a global definition. It is visible everywhere in the program.

Local Scope

Variables defined within a block have local scope. They exist only from the point of their declaration until the end of the block (usually a function) in which they are declared. Outside the block they are invisible.

In Figure 4-32, we see two blocks in main. The first block is all of main. Since the second block is nested within main, all definitions in main are visible to the block unless local variables with an identical name are defined. In the inner block, a local version of a has been defined; its type is float. Under these circumstances, the integer variable a in main is visible from its declaration until the declaration of the floating-point variable a in the nested block. At that point, the local variable a in main can no longer be referenced in the nested block. Any statement in the block that references a will get the float version. After we reach the end of the nested block, the float a is no longer in scope and the integer a becomes visible again.

We have also defined a new variable y. Note, however, that before we can define the local variable y in main we need to set the initial value for a. Although this is flagrant disregard for structured programming principles and should never be used in practice, it demonstrates that a variable is in scope until it is redefined. Immediately after using y, we defined the local version, so y in main is no longer available. Because the variable b is not redeclared in the block, it is in scope throughout the entire block. It is poor programming style to reuse identifiers within the same scope.

Although local variables in main are visible inside the nested block, the reverse is not true. The variables defined in the block, a, y, and z, exist only for the duration of the block and are no longer visible after the end of the block.

Within the function fun, which is coded after main, only its variables and any global objects are visible. Thus, we are free to use any names we want. In Figure 4-32, we chose to use the names a and y even though they had been used in main. This is an acceptable practice; there is nothing wrong with it.

Programming Example: Incremental Development

In the "Software Engineering" section, later in this chapter, we discuss a concept known as top-down design and development. Top-down design, a concept inherent to modular programming, allows us to develop programs incrementally. By writing and debugging each function separately, we are able to solve the program in smaller steps, making the whole process easier. To demonstrate the concept, we begin the development of a calculator program in this section. In later chapters we add functionality.

The calculator program asks the user to input two numbers. The program then calls a function that adds the numbers. It concludes by displaying the sum of the two numbers.

The design is shown in **Figure 4-33**. It consists of a calculator function (main), and three subfunctions, getData, add, and printRes.

Figure 4-33   Calculator program design

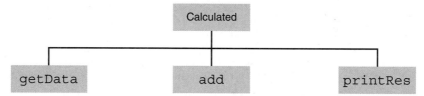

First Increment: `main` and `getData`

When we develop programs incrementally, we begin by writing an abbreviated main function and one subfunction. Our first program also contains the necessary include statements and any global declarations that are required. It is shown in **Program 4-13**. Note that the program includes documentary comments as we understand them at this point in the development.

Program 4-13 | Calculator program—first increment

```
1  /* This program adds two integers read from
2     the keyboard and prints the results.
3     Written by:
4     Date:
5  */
6  #include <stdio.h>
7
8  // Function Declarations
9  void getData (int* a, int* b);
10
11 int main (void)
12 {
13 // Local Declarations
14    int a;
15    int b;
16
17 // Statements
18    getData (&a, &b);
19
20    printf("**main: a = %d; b = %d\n", a, b);
21
22    return 0;
23 } // main
24
25 /*===========getData===========
26   This function reads two integers from the keyboard.
27   Pre Parameters a and b are addresses
28   Post Data read into parameter addresses
29 */
30 void getData (int* a, int* b)
31 {
32    printf("Please enter two integer numbers: ");
33    scanf("%d %d", a, b);
34
35    printf("**getData: a = %d; b = %d\n", *a, *b);
36    return;
37 } // getData
```

Output
```
Please enter two integer numbers: 8 13
**getData: a = 8; b = 13
**main: a = 8; b = 13
```

It's common to make syntactical errors when writing even the simplest programs. But you can easily correct minor errors by compiling a program in its simplest slate. Compiling a program also verifies that the communication between functions is valid. That is, compiling the program verifies that the variable types match the parameter types and that the data are being properly passed down and back up.

In this first incremental program, we pass the addresses of the two input variables to the get data function. It then reads and prints the input to verify that the data are correctly read. When we are back in `main`, we again print the input data to verify that it was properly passed up to `main`. Because we were careful to align the print formatting, we can easily check that the values are the same.

One point to note in the program is that we prefix temporary `print` statements with two asterisks. This allows us to tell the difference between permanent output and debugging output. As we move to the next increment, we remove the temporary statements from the debugged functions.

Second Increment: `add`

After the first compile has been run and verified, we are ready to write the next function. While it is sometimes better to work in a different order, normally we select the next function in the program flow as shown in the structure chart, in this case the `add` function. This incremental version of the program is seen in **Program 4-14**.

> **Program 4-14** | Calculator program—second increment

```
1   /* This program adds two integers read
2      from the keyboard and prints the results.
3      Written by:
4      Date:
5   */
6   #include <stdio.h>
7
8   // Function Declarations
9   void getData (int* a, int* b);
10  int add   (int a, int b);
11
12  int main (void)
13  {
14  // Local Declarations
15     int a;
16     int b;
17     int sum;
18
19  // Statements
20     getData (&a, &b);
21
22     sum = add (a, b);
23     printf("**main: %d + %d = %d\n", a, b, sum);
24     return 0;
```

(continue)

Program 4-14   Calculator program—second increment *(continued)*

```
25 } // main
26
27 /*===========getData===========
28    This function reads two integers from the keyboard.
29    Pre Parameters a and b are addresses
30    Post Data read into parameter addresses
31 */
32 void getData (int* a, int* b)
33 {
34    printf("Please enter two integer numbers: ");
35    scanf("%d %d", a, b);
36    return;
37 } // getData
38
39 /*===========add===========
40    This function adds two numbers and returns the sum.
41    Pre a and b contain values to be added
42    Post Returns a + b
43 */
44 int add (int a, int b)
45 {
46 // Local Definitions
47    int sum;
48
49 // Statements
50    sum = a + b;
51    printf("**add: %d + %d = %d\n", a, b, sum);
52
53    return sum;
54 } // add
```

Output
```
Please enter two integer numbers: 8 13
**add: 8 + 13 = 21
**main: 8 + 13 = 21
```

Once again, we include `print` statements to verify that the `add` function received the correct data and properly returned it to `main`.

Final Increment: `print results`

The third and final increment includes the `print results` function. We do not need any debugging statements, however, because the `print results` function prints everything as a part of its requirements. The final program is shown in **Program 4-15**.

Program 4-15 | Calculator program—final increment

```
1   /* This program adds two integers read
2      from the keyboard and prints the results.
3      Written by:
4      Date:
5   */
6   #include <stdio.h>
7
8   // Function Declarations
9   void getData (int* a, int* b);
10  int add  (int a, int b);
11  void printRes (int a, int b, int sum);
12
13  int main (void)
14  {
15  // Local Declarations
16     int a;
17     int b;
18     int sum = 0;
19
20  // Statements
21     getData (&a, &b);
22
23     sum = add (a, b);
24
25     printRes (a, b, sum);
26     return 0;
27  } // main
28
29  /*===========getData===========
30     This function reads two integers from the keyboard.
31     Pre Parameters a and b
32     Post Returns a + b
33  */
34  void getData (int* a, int* b)
35  {
36    printf("Please enter two integer numbers: ");
37    scanf("%d %d", a, b);
38    return;
39  } // getData
40
41  /*=========== add ===========
```

(continue)

Program 4-15   Calculator program—final increment *(continued)*

```
42     This function adds two integers and returns the sum.
43     Pre Parameters a and b
44     Post Returns a + b
45  */
46  int add (int a, int b)
47  {
48  // Local Definitions
49     int sum;
50
51  // Statements
52     sum = a + b;
53     return sum;
54  } // add
55
56  /*===========printRes===========
57     Prints the calculated results.
58     Pre a and b contain input; sum the results
59     Post Data printed
60  */
61  void printRes (int a, int b, int sum)
62  {
63     printf("%4d + %4d = %4d\n", a, b, sum);
64     return;
65  } // printRes
```

Output
```
Please enter two integer numbers: 8 13
   8 + 13 = 21
```

Software Engineering

In this section we discuss three different but related aspects of software engineering design: the structure chart, functional cohesion, and top-down design.

Structure Charts

The structure chart is the primary design tool for a program. Therefore, you should create it before you start writing your program. An analogy will help you understand the importance of designing before you start coding.

Assume that you have decided to build a house. You will spend a lot of time thinking about exactly what you want. How many rooms will it need? Do you want a family room or a great room? Should the laundry be inside the house or in the garage? To make sure everyone understands what you want, you will prepare formal blueprints that describe everything in detail. Even if you are building something small, like a dollhouse for a child or a toolshed for your back yard, you will make some sketches or plans.

Figuring out what you want in your house is comparable to determining the requirements for a large system. Drawing up a set of blueprints parallels the structure chart in the design of a program. All require advance planning; only the level of detail changes.

Professional programmers use the structure chart for another purpose. In a project team environment, before programmers start writing a program, they must have its design reviewed. This review process is called a structured walkthrough. The review team consists of the systems analyst responsible for the area of the project, a representative of the user community, a system test engineer, and one or two programmers from the project.

The design walk-through serves three purposes: First, it ensures that you understand how your program fits into the system by communicating your design to the team. If the design has any omissions or communication errors, the team should detect them now. If you invite programmers who must interface with your program, you will also ensure that the interprogram communication linkages are correct.

Second, the walk-through validates your design. In creating your design, you will have considered several alternative approaches to writing your program. The review team will expect to see and understand the different designs you considered and hear why you chose the design you are proposing. They will challenge aspects of the design and suggest approaches you may not have considered. The result of the review will be the best possible design.

Finally, the walk-through gives the test engineer the opportunity to assess your program's testability. This in turn ensures that the final program will be robust and as error-free as possible.

Structure Chart Rules and Symbols

Figure 4-34 shows the various symbols that we use to write a structure chart. Although we include all symbols here for completeness, in this chapter we will discuss only the two colored symbols. In addition to the symbols, we will discuss several rules that we follow in designing our structure chart.

Figure 4-34   Structure chart symbols

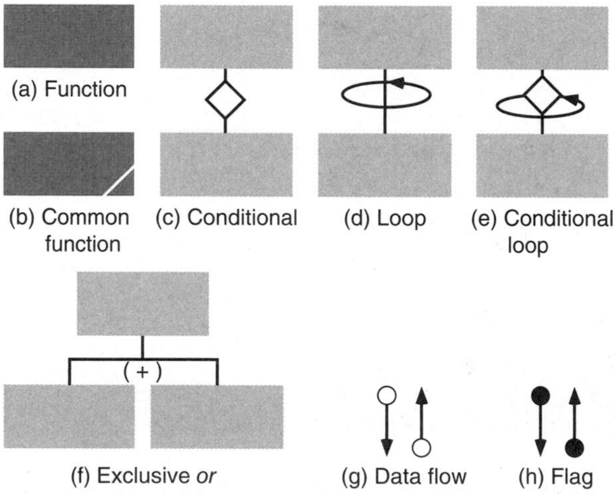

(a) Function

(b) Common function   (c) Conditional   (d) Loop   (e) Conditional loop

(f) Exclusive *or*   (g) Data flow   (h) Flag

Function Symbol

Each rectangle in a structure chart (see Figure 4-34) represents a function that we write. Functions found in the standard C libraries are not shown. The name in the rectangle is the name we will give to the function when we write the program. It should be meaningful. The software engineering principle known as intelligent names states that the names used in a program should be self-documenting; that is, they should convey their intended usage to the reader. In general, we use intelligent names for both functions and for data names within our program.

Now that we have explained that all names should be descriptive, we will break our own rule because we want to concentrate on the format of a structure chart rather than a particular program. The names in **Figure 4-35** identify the various modules for discussion.

Figure 4-35 Structure chart design

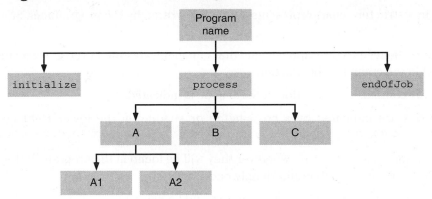

Reading Structure Charts

Structure charts are read top-down, left-right. In Figure 4-35, `ProgramName (main)` consists of three subfunctions: `initialize`, `process`, and `endOfJob`. According to the left-right rule, the first call in the program is to `initialize`.

After `initialize` is complete, the program calls process. When process is complete, the program calls `endOfJob`. The functions on the same level of a structure chart are called in order from the left to the right.

The concept of top-down is demonstrated by process. When a process is called, it calls A, B, and C in turn. Function B does not start running, however, until A is finished. While A is running, it calls A1 and A2 in turn. In other words, all functions in a line from process to A2 must be called before Function B can start.

No code is contained in a structure chart. A structure chart shows only the function flow through the program. It is not a block diagram or a flowchart. As a map of our program, the structure chart shows only the logical flow of the functions. Exactly how each function does its job is shown by algorithm design (flowchart or pseudocode). A structure chart shows the big picture; the details are left to algorithm design. Structure charts show only function flow; they contain no code.

Often a program contains several calls to a common function (see Figure 4-34b). These calls are usually scattered throughout the program. The structure chart shows the call wherever it logically occurs in the program. To identify common structures, the lower right corner of the rectangle contains a cross-hatch or is shaded. If the common function is complex and contains subfunctions, these subfunctions must be shown only once. An indication that the incomplete references contain additional structure should be shown. This is usually done with a line below the function rectangle and a cut (~) symbol. This concept is shown in **Figure 4-36**, which uses a common function, `average`, in two different places in the program. Note, however, that we never graphically show a function connected to two calling functions.

Figure 4-36 Common functions in a structure chart

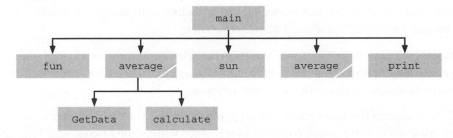

It is not necessary to show data flows (Figure 4-34g) and flags (see Figure 4-34h), both of which represent parameters, although it may be helpful in certain circumstances. If they are shown, inputs are on the left of the vertical line and outputs are on the right. When they are included, the name of the data or flag should also be indicated.

The structure chart rules described in this section are summarized in the following list:

1. Each rectangle in a structure chart represents a function written by the programmer. Standard C functions are not included.

2. The name in the rectangle is a descriptive name that communicates the purpose of the function. It is the name that will be used in the coding of the function.

3. The function chart contains only function flow. No code is indicated.

4. Common functions are indicated by a cross-hatch or shading in the lower right corner of the function rectangle.

5. Common calls are shown in a structure wherever they will be found in the program. If they contain subfunction calls, the complete structure need be shown only once.

6. Data flows and flags are optional. When used, they should be named.

7. Input flows and flags are shown on the left of the vertical line; output flows and flags are shown on the right.

Functional Cohesion

One of the most difficult structured programming concepts for new programmers is knowing when and how to create a function.

Functional cohesion is a measure of how closely the processes in a function are related. A function that does one and only one process is functionally cohesive. A function that contains totally unrelated processes is coincidentally cohesive. We provide a few rules here to help you write cohesive functions.

Before we discuss the rules, however, you should understand why the concept is important. Following are the three primary reasons for using structurally cohesive functions:

1. **Correctness:** By concentrating on only one thing as you write a function, you will be less apt to make an error. It is much easier to get a simple task right than a complex task.

2. **Maintainability:** Production programs can live for years. The better structured a program, the easier it is to change. When programs are not well structured, making a change in one part of the program often leads to errors in other parts.

3. **Reusability:** Some processes are so common that they are found in many programs. Good programmers build libraries of these functions so that they don't have to reinvent the function each time it is needed. This not only leads to quicker program development but also reduces debugging time, because the library functions have already been debugged.

Only One Thing

Each function should do only one thing. Furthermore, all of the statements in the function should contribute only to that one thing. For example, assume that we are writing a program that requires the statistical measures of average and standard deviation. The two statistical measures are obviously related, if for no other reason than they are both measures of the same series of numbers. But we would not calculate both measures in one function. That would be calculating two things, and each function should do only one thing.

One way to determine if our function is doing more than one thing is to count the number of objects that it handles. An object in this sense is anything that exists separately from the other elements of the function. In the previous example, the average and the standard deviation are two different objects.

As another example, to compute the taxes for a payroll program in the state of California, we would deal with FICA taxes, state disability insurance, state unemployment taxes, state withholding taxes, and federal withholding taxes. Each of these is a different object. Our design should group all of these taxes together in a function to calculate taxes, and it should call subfunctions to calculate each individual tax. This design is seen in **Figure 4-37**.

Figure 4-37 Calculate taxes design

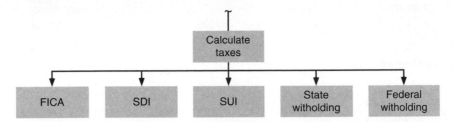

In One Place

The corollary rule is that the one thing a function does should be done in only one place. If the code for a process is scattered in several different and unrelated parts of the program, it is very difficult to change. Therefore, all the processing for a task should be placed in one function and, if necessary, its subfunctions. This is the reason we created the function `calculateTaxes` in Figure 4-37.

An example of scattered code common among programmers is found in printing reports. Suppose that we needed to write a program that, among other things, prints a report that includes a heading, some data with a total, and then an end-of-report message. A well-structured solution is seen in **Figure 4-38**. It is quite common, however, to find the statements for each of these subtasks scattered in `main` and other parts of the program.

Figure 4-38 Design for print report

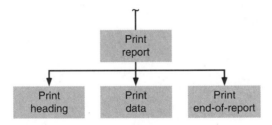

Testability

As a final measure of a program's structure, we should be able to test its functions independently. We will discuss a technique for this in the next section. Let us simply say here that **testability** is an attribute of a well-designed and well-structured program that allows each section of the program to be tested separately from the rest of the program.

Top-Down Design Implementation

If we have designed our program using structured programming concepts and a structure chart, we can then proceed to implement it in a top-down fashion.

Referring again to Figure 4-35, a top-down implementation starts with the code for `main` only, shown in the structure chart as `ProgramName`. The code for the first compile and test is shown in **Program 4-16**.

> ## Program 4-16 | Top-down design implementation example

```
1   /*Sample of top-down design example using stubs.
2     Written by:
3     Date:
```

(continue)

Program 4-16   Top-down design implementation example *(continued)*

```c
4   */
5   #include <stdio.h>
6
7   // Function Declarations
8       int initialize (void);
9       int process (void);
10      int endOfJob (void);
11
12  int main (void)
13  {
14  // Statements
15      printf("Begin program \n\n");
16
17      initialize ();
18      process ();
19      endOfJob ();
20      return 0;
21  } // main
22
23  /* -----------------initialize------------------
24      Stub for initialize.
25  */
26  int initialize (void)
27  {
28  // Statements
29      printf("In initialize: \n");
30      return 0;
31  } // initialize
32  /*=========process=========
33      Stub for process
34  */
35  int process (void)
36  {
37  // Statements
38      printf("In process: \n");
39      return 0 ;
40  } // process
41  /* ===========endOfJob=========
42      Stub for endOfJob
43  */
44  int endOfJob (void)
45  {
46  // Statements
47      printf("In endOfJob: \n");
48      return 0 ;
49  } // endOfJob
```

(continue)

Program 4-16 Top-down design implementation example *(continued)*

Output
```
Begin program
In initialize:
In process:
In endOfJob:
```

Note that this program has only the first four boxes from the structure chart: ProgramName (`main`), initialize, process, and endOfJob. For each of `main`'s subfunctions, all that is included is a stub. A stub is the skeleton of a function that is called and immediately returns. Although it is a complete function, it does nothing other than to establish and verify the linkage between the caller and itself. But this is a very important part of testing and verifying a program. At this point the program should be compiled, linked, and run. Chances are that you will find some minor problems, such as missing semicolons or errors between the function declarations and the function definitions. Before you continue with the program, you should correct these problems.

The top-down design implementation then continues with the coding of `initialize`, `process`, or `endOfJob`. Normally, you develop the functions left to right, but it is not necessary to do so. To develop process, you again stub its subfunctions, A, B, and C, and then test the program. This top-down design implementation continues until the complete program has been coded and tested.

Tips and Common Programming Errors

1. Several possible errors are related to passing parameters.
   a. It is a compile error if the types in the function declaration and function definition are incompatible. For example, the types in the following statements are incompatible:

   ```
   double divide (int dividend, int divisor);

      ...

   double divide (float dividend, float divisor)
   {
      ...
   }   // divide
   ```

   b. It is a compile error to have a different number of actual parameters in the function call than there are in the function declaration.
   c. It is a logic error if you code the parameters in the wrong order. Their meaning will be inconsistent in the called program. For example, in the following statements, the types are the same but the meaning of the variables is reversed:

   ```
   double divide (float dividend, float divisor);

      ...

   double divide (float divisor, float dividend)
   {
      ...
   }   // divide
   ```

2. It is a compile error to define local variables with the same identifiers as formal parameters, as shown in the following example.

```
double divide (float dividend, float divisor)
{
// Local Declarations
   float dividend;

   ...

}   // divide
```

3. Using a `void` return with a function that expects a return value or using a return value with a function that expects a `void` return is a compile error.

4. Each parameter's type must be individually specified; you cannot use multiple definitions like you can in variables. For example, the following is a compile error because `y` does not have a type:

```
double fun (float x, y);
```

5. Forgetting the semicolon at the end of a function declaration is a compile error. Similarly, using a semicolon at the end of the header in a function definition is a compile error.

6. It is most likely a logic error to call a function from within itself or one of its called functions.

7. It is a compile error to attempt to define a function within the body of another function.

8. It is a run-time error to code a function call without the parentheses, even when the function has no parameters.

```
printHello; // Not a call
printHello ( ); // A valid call
```

9. It is a compile error if the type of data in the return statement does not match the function return type.

10. It is a logic error to call `srand` every time you call `rand`.

Summary

> In structured programming, a program is divided into modules.

  ■ Each module is designed to do a specific task.

  ■ Modules in C are written as functions.

> Each C program must have one and only one function called `main`.

> A function can return only one value.

> A function can be called for its returned value or for its side effect.

> The function call includes the function name and the values of the actual parameters to provide the called function with the data it needs to perform its job.

> Each actual parameter of the function is an expression. The expression must have a value that can be evaluated at the time the function is called.

> A local variable is known only in a function definition. The local variables do not take part in communication between the calling and the called functions.

> The general format for a function definition is

```
return_type function_name (parameter list)
{
// Local Declarations
// Statements
} // function_name
```

> If a function returns no value, the return type must be declared as `void`.

> If a function has no parameters, the parameter list must be declared `void`.

> The actual parameters passed to a function must match in number, type, and order with the formal parameters in the function definition.

> When a function is called, control is passed to the called function. The calling function "rests" until the called function finishes its job.

> It's highly recommended that every function have a `return` statement. A `return` statement is required if the return type is anything other than `void`.

> Control returns to the caller when the `return` statement is encountered.

> A function declaration requires only the return type of the function, the function name, and the number, types, and order of the formal parameters. Parameter identifiers may be added for documentation but are not required.

> The scope of a parameter is the block following the header.

> A local variable is a variable declared inside a block. The scope of a local variable is the block in which it is declared.

> Structure charts are used to design a program.

> Structure charts contain no code.

> Functional cohesion is a measure of how closely the processes in a function are related.

> Programs should be written using a top-down implementation with stubs for functions not yet coded.

Key Terms

absolute value	floor	pass by reference
actual parameters	formal parameter list	pass by value
bidirectional communication	function body	pointer variable
called function	function call	pseudorandom number series
called module	function declaration	random number series
calling function	function definition	return
calling module	function header	scope
ceiling	functional cohesion	random number seed
data flow	indirection operator	stub
decomposition	local variables	testability
downward communication	module	top-down design
factoring	parameter	upward communication
flags	parameter passing	

Review Questions

1. The principles of top-down design and structured programming dictate that a program should be divided into a main module and its related modules.
   a. True
   b. False

2. The function definition contains the code for a function.
   a. True
   b. False

3. Function calls that return `void` may not be used as a part of an expression.
   a. True
   b. False

4. The address operator (`&`) is used to tell the compiler to store data at an address.
   a. True
   b. False

5. Variables defined within a block have global scope.
   a. True
   b. False

6. The process of dividing a program into functions—which in turn are divided into functions until they consist of only elementary processing that is intrinsically understood and cannot be further subdivided—is known as _____.
   a. charting
   b. flow charting
   c. factoring
   d. programming
   e. structuring

7. Which of the following statements about function declaration and definition is truer?
   a. The function call is found in the called function.
   b. The function declaration requires that the parameters be named.
   c. The function definition is done with a function declaration.
   d. The function definition contains executable statements that perform the function's task.
   e. The function definition header concludes with a semicolon (;).

8. Which of the following is not a part of a function header?
   a. Name
   b. Parameter list
   c. Return type
   d. Title

9. Which of the following statements about function parameters is true?
   a. Empty parameter lists are declared with the keyword `void`.
   b. If there is only one parameter, the function list parentheses are not required.
   c. In the definition of a function, the parameters are known as actual parameters.
   d. Parameters are separated by semicolons.
   e. The parameters in a function definition are defined in the function's body (local declaration section).

10. Which of the following statements about local variables is false?
    a. A local variable's value may be returned through a `return` statement.
    b. Local variables are defined inside a function.
    c. Local variables cannot be referenced through their identifiers outside the function.
    d. Local variables may be initialized with an initializer.
    e. Local variables' names can be the same as the function's parameter names.

11. To tell the compiler to store data at an address, use the _____.
    a. address operator (`&`)
    b. array operator (`[ ]`)
    c. dereference operator (`#`)
    d. indirection operator (`*`)
    e. pointer operator (`*`)

12. The function that returns the absolute value of a long integer is _____.
    a. `abs`
    b. `dabs`
    c. `fabs`
    d. `labs`
    e. `tabs`

13. Which of the following statements will generate a random number in the range 30–50?
    a. `rand (33 )`
    b. `(rand () % 20) + 1`
    c. `(rand () % 21) +20`
    d. `(rand () % 21) +30`
    e. `(rand () % 51) + 1`

14. Which of the following statements about structure charts is false?

  a. Structure charts are a replacement for flowcharts.

  b. Structure charts are the primary design tool for a program.

  c. Structure charts are used in a structured walk-through to validate the design.

  d. Structure charts can be used to assess the testability of a program.

  e. Structure charts should be created before you start writing a program.

Exercises

15. Find any errors in the following function definition:

```
void fun (int x, int y)
{
    int z;

    ...

    return z;
} // fun
```

16. Find any errors in the following function definition:

```
int fun (int x, y)
{
    int z;

    ...

    return z;
 } // fun
```

17. Find any errors in the following function definition:

```
int fun (int x, int y)
{
    ...

    int sun (int t)

    ...

    {

    ...

    return (t + 3);
    }

    ...

    return z;
} // fun
```

18. Find any errors in the following function definition:

```
void fun (int, x)
{
    ...

    return;
} // fun
```

19. Find any errors in the following function declarations:

   a. `int sun (int x, y);`

   b. `int sun (int x, int y)`

   c. `void sun (void, void);`

   d. `void sun (x int, y float);`

20. Find any errors in the following function calls:

   a. `void fun ( );`

   b. `fun (void);`

   c. `void fun (int x, int y);`

   d. `fun ( );`

21. Evaluate the value of the following expressions:

   a. `fabs (9.5)`

   b. `fabs (-2.4)`

   c. `fabs (-3.4)`

   d. `fabs (-7)`

   e. `fabs (7)`

22. Evaluate the value of the following expressions:

   a. `floor ( 9.5 )`

   b. `floor ( -2.4 )`

   c. `floor ( -3.4 )`

   d. `ceil ( 9.5 )`

   e. `ceil ( -2.4 )`

   f. `ceil ( -3.4 )`

23. Evaluate the value of the following expressions when x is 3.5, 3.45, 3.76, 3.234, and 3.4567:

   a. `floor (x * 10+0.5) / 10`

   b. `floor (x * 100 + 0.5) / 100`

   c. `floor (x * 1000 + 0.5) / 1000`

24. Define the range of the random numbers generated by the following expressions:

   a. `rand( ) % 10`

   b. `rand( ) % 4`

   c. `rand( ) % 10 + 1`

   d. `rand( ) % 52`

   e. `rand( ) % 2 + 1`

   f. `rand( ) % 52 - 5`

25. What would be printed from **Program 4-17** when run using 3 5 as data?

Program 4-17 | Program for Exercise 25

```
1    #include <stdio.h>
2
3    // Function Declarations
4    int acme (int x, int y);
5
6    int main (void)
7    {
8    // Local Declarations
```

(continue)

Program 4-17   Program for Exercise 25 *(continued)*

```
 9      int a;
10      int b;
11      int r;
12      int s;
13
14  // Statements
15      scanf("%d %d", &a, &b);
16      r = strange (a, b);
17      s = strange (b, a);
18      printf("%d %d", r, s);
19      return 0;
20  } // main
21  //=========strange=========
22  int acme (int x, int y)
23  {
24  // Statements
25      return (x - y);
26  } // strange
```

26. What would be printed from **Program 4-18** when run using 3   5   4   6 as data?

Program 4-18 | Program for Exercise 26

```
 1      #include <stdio.h>
 2
 3      // Function Declarations
 4      int strange (int x, int y);
 5
 6      int main (void)
 7      {
 8      // Local Declarations
 9        int a;
10        int b;
11        int c;
12        int d;
13        int r;
14        int s;
15        int t;
16        int u;
17        int v;
18
```

(continue)

Program 4-18   Program for Exercise 26 *(continued)*

```
19   // Statements
20     scanf ("%d %d %d id", &a, &b, &c, &d);
21
22     r = strange (a, b);
23     s = strange (r, c);
24     t = strange (strange (s, d), strange (4, 2));
25     u = strange (t + 3, s + 2);
26     v = strange (strange (strange (u, a), b), c);
27
28     printf ("%d %d %d %d %d", r, s, t, u, v);
29     return 0;
30   } // main
31   //-----------------strange-----------------
32   int strange (int x, int y)
33   {
34   // Local Declarations
35     int t;
36     int z;
37
38   // Statements
39     t = x + y;
40     z = x * y;
41     return (t + z);
42   } // strange
```

27. Draw the structure chart for **Program 4-19**. What output does it produce?

Program 4-19 | Program for Exercise 27

```
1    #include <stdio.h>
2
3    // Function Declarations
4    int funA (int x);
5    void funB (int x);
6
7    int main (void)
8    {
9    // Local Declarations
10     int a;
11     int b;
12     int c;
13
```

(continue)

Program 4-19 Program for Exercise 27 *(continued)*

```
14  // Statements
15     a = 10;
16     funB (a);
17     b = 5;
18     c = funA (b);
19     funB(c);
20     printf("%3d %3d %3d", a, b, c);
21     return 0;
22  } // main
23
24  int funA (int x)
25  {
26  // Statements
27     return x * x;
28  } // funA
29
30  void funB (int x)
31  {
32  // Local Declarations
33     int y;
34
35  // Statements
36     y = x % 2;
37     x /= 2;
38     printf ("\n%3d %3d\n", x, y);
39     return;
40  } // funB
```

Problems

28. Write a function to print your name. Write a call as it would be coded in a calling function, such as `main`. The output should look like the following.

```
******************************
*                            *
*        Your Name Here      *
*                            *
******************************
```

29. Write a program that generates a random number from the following set:

```
1, 2, 3, 4, 5, 6
```

30. Write a program that generates a random number from the following set:

```
1, 4, 7, 10, 13, 16
```

31. Explain what is meant by the statement "a function should do only one thing."

32. Code and run Program 4-16, "Top-down design implementation example," to demonstrate how stubs work.

33. Write a function to convert inches into centimeters. (One inch is 2.54 centimeters.) Then write a program that prompts the user to input a measure in inches, calls the conversion function, and prints out the measurement in centimeters.

34. Write a program that reads three integers and then prints them in the order read and reversed. Use four functions: `main`, one to read the data, one to print them in the order read, and one to print them reversed.

35. Expand the calculator program, Program 4-15, to calculate the difference, product, quotient, and modulus of the numbers. Calculate the quotient and modulus in one function.

36. Modify Program 4-5, "Add two digits," to add the least significant three digits (hundreds, tens, and ones).

37. Write a function that receives a positive floating-point number and rounds it to two decimal places. For example, 127.565031 rounds to 127.570000. Hint: To round, you must convert the floating-point number to an integer and then back to a floating-point number. Print the rounded numbers to six decimal places. Test the function with the following data:

```
123.456789 123.499999 123.500001
```

38. Write a program that reads a floating-point number and prints the ceiling, floor, and rounded value. Use the function in Problem 37 for the average and test it with the same values as Problem 37.

39. Write a function to compute the perimeter and area of a right triangle (**Figure 4-39**) when given the length of the two sides (a and b).

Figure 4-39   Triangle for Problem 39

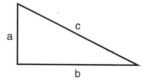

The following formulas may be helpful:
```
c² = a² + b²
area = .5 * (a * b)
```

Projects

40. Prepare a payroll earnings statement for the sales force at the Arctic Ice Company. All of Arctic's employees are on a straight commission basis of 12.5% of sales. Each month, they also receive a bonus that varies depending on the profit for the month and their length of service. The sales manager calculates the bonus separately and enters it with the salesperson's total sales for the month. Your program must also calculate the withholding taxes and retirement for the month based on the following rates:
  a. 25% Federal withholding
  b. 10% State withholding
  c. 8% Retirement plan

Use the test data in **Table 4-2** to test the program.

Table 4-2   Test data for Project 40

SALESPERSON	SALES	BONUS
1	53,500	425
2	41,300	300
3	56,800	350
4	36,200	175

41. Write a program that, given a beginning balance in your savings account, calculates the balance at the end of 1 year. The interest is 3.5% compounded quarterly. Show the interest earned and balance at the end of each quarter. Present the data in tabular columns with appropriate headings. Use separate functions to compute the interest and print the balance.

42. The formula for converting centigrade temperatures to Fahrenheit is $F = 32 + C\frac{180.0}{100.0}$. Create a program that asks the user to enter a temperature reading in centigrade and then prints the equivalent Fahrenheit value. It then asks the user to enter a Fahrenheit value and prints out the equivalent centigrade value. Run the program several times. Be sure to include at least one negative temperature reading in your test cases. Provide separate functions as needed by your design. One possible design is shown in **Figure 4-40**. (Your `main` function should have only function calls.)

Figure 4-40 Possible design for Project 41

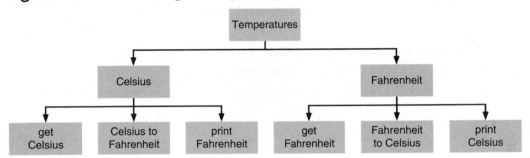

43. Write a program that uses standard functions. The program may be written entirely in `main` and must follow the pseudocode shown in **Algorithm 4-1**. Give the output appropriate captions and align the data.

Algorithm 4-1 | Pseudocode for Project 43

1. Prompt the user to enter a number
2. Read number
3. Display number
4. Get a random number and scale to range 3...37
5. Display random number
6. Set product to number * random number
7. Display product
8. Display ceiling of random number
9. Display floor of product
10. Display number raised to power of random number
11. Display square root of random number

44. Write a C program that creates customers' bills for a carpet company when the following information is given:
a. the length and the width of the carpet in feet
b. the carpet price per square foot
c. the percent of discount for each customer

The labor cost is fixed at $0.35 per square foot. It is to be defined as a constant. The tax rate is 8.5% applied after the discount. It is also to be defined as a constant. The input data consist of a set of three integers representing the length and width of the room to be carpeted, the percentage of the discount the owner gives to a customer, and a real number representing the unit price of the carpet. The program is to prompt the user for this input as shown here. (Colored numbers are typical responses.)

```
Length of room (feet)?                30
Width of room (feet)?                 18
Customer discount (percent)?          9
Cost per square foot (xxx.xx)?        8.23
```

The output is shown here. Be careful to align the decimal points.

```
              MEASUREMENT
Length                      XXX ft
Width                       XXX ft
Area                        XXX square ft
              CHARGES
DESCRIPTION      COST/SQ.FT.   CHARGE
----------------------------------------
Carpet           XXX.XX        $xxxx.xx
Labor            0.35          XXXX.XX
                               ----------
INSTALLED PRICE                $xxxx.xx
Discount         XX %          XXXX.XX
SUBTOTAL                       $XXXX.XX
                               ----------
Tax                            XXXX.XX
TOTAL                          $XXXX.XX
```

The program's design should use `main` and at least the six functions described as follows:

a. Read data from the keyboard. This function is to use addresses to read all data and place them in the calling function's variables.

b. Calculate values. This function calls three subfunctions. Each function is to use addresses to store their results.

- Calculate the installed price. This function calculates area, carpet cost, labor cost, and installed price. The installed price is the cost of the carpet and the cost of the labor.

- Calculate the subtotal. This function calculates the discount and subtotal.

- Calculate the total price with discount and tax. This function calculates the tax and the total price.

c. Print the result. Use two subfunctions to print the results: one to print the measurements, and one to print the charges.

Test your program with the test data shown in **Table 4-3**.

Table 4-3   Test data for Project 44

TEST	LENGTH	WIDTH	DISCOUNT	COST
1	23	13	12	$14.20
2	35	8	0	$ 8.00
3	14	11	10	$22.25

CHAPTER 5

Selection—Making Decisions

Learning Objectives

When you complete this chapter, you will be able to:

5.1 Explain how the logical operators *and*, *or*, and *not* are used by computers to make decisions

5.2 Use two-way selection (`if … else` statements) in your program

5.3 Use multiway selection (`switch` and `else … if`) in your program

5.4 Write programs using logical and comparative operators

5.1 Logical Data and Operators

As you have learned, any program can be written with three constructs: sequence, selection, and loop. You are already familiar with the C language implementation of the first construct, sequence. In this chapter, we turn our attention to the second construct, selection. A **selection statement** allows us to choose between two or more alternatives. In other words, it allows us to make decisions.

What a dull world it would be if we didn't have any choices. Vanilla ice cream for everybody! Uniforms all around! And no debates or arguments to keep things interesting. Fortunately, our world is filled with choices. And because our programs must reflect the world in which they are designed to operate, they, too, are filled with choices and opportunities for decision making.

In this chapter, you will learn how a computer makes a decision. One of the main points to keep in mind is that the decisions made by a computer must be very simple, because everything in the computer ultimately reduces to either true or false. If complex decisions are required, it is the programmer's job to reduce them to a series of simple decisions that the computer can handle.

A piece of data is called logical if it conveys the idea of true or false. We need logical data in real life as well as in programming. In real life, logical data (true or false) are created in answer to a question that needs a yes or no answer. For example, we ask if an item is on sale or not. We ask if a business is open or not. The answer to these questions is a piece of data that is usually yes or no. We can also ask questions such as "Is x greater than y?" The answer is again yes or no. In computer science, we use true or false instead of yes or no.

Logical Data in C

Traditionally, C had no logical data type. C programmers used other data types, such as `int`, to represent logical data. If a data value is zero, it is considered false. If it is nonzero, it is considered true. This concept of true and false on a numeric scale is seen in **Figure 5-1**.

Figure 5-1   True and false on the arithmetic scale

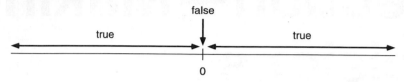

The C99 standard introduced the Boolean data type, `_bool`, which is declared as an unsigned integer in the `stdbool.h` header file. Also defined in the header files are the identifiers `bool`, `true`, and `false`. Although the standard still supports the traditional use of integers for logical data, we recommend that the Boolean type, `bool`, be used.

Logical Operators

C has three logical operators for combining logical values and creating new logical values: *not, and,* and *or.* A common way to show logical relationships is in truth tables. Truth tables list the values that each operand can assume and the resulting value. The truth tables for logical operators are shown in **Figure 5-2**.

Figure 5-2   Logical operators truth table

not

x	!x
false	true
true	false

and

x	y	x && y
false	false	false
false	true	false
true	true	false
true	true	true

or

x	y	x ‖ y
false	false	false
false	true	true
true	false	true
true	true	true

not **Operator**

The *not* operator (`!`) is a unary operator with precedence 15, as shown in **Table 5-1**. It changes a true value to false and a false value to true.

Table 5-1   Precedence table

OPERATOR	DESCRIPTION	EXAMPLE	SIDE EFFECTS	ASSOC	PR
	Identifiers	`amount`	N	N/A	16
	Constants	`3.14159`			
	Parenthetical Expressions	`(a + b)`			
`[ ]`	Array Index	`ary [i]`	N	Left-Right	16
`f (...)`	Function Call	`doIt (x, y)`	Y		
`.`	Direct Member Selection	`str.mem`	N		
`->`	Indirect Member Selection	`ptr->mem`	N		
`++   --`	Postfix Increment • Decrement	`a++`	Y		

OPERATOR	DESCRIPTION	EXAMPLE	SIDE EFFECTS	ASSOC	PR
++ --	Prefix Increment • Decrement	`++a`	Y	Right-Left	15
sizeof	Size in Bytes	`sizeof(int)`	N		
~	Ones Complement	`-a`	N		
!	Not	`!a`	N		
+ -	Plus • Minus	`+a`	N		
&	Address	`&a`	N		
*	Dereference/Indirection	`*ptr`	N		
( )	Type Cast	`(int)ptr`	N	Right-Left	14
* / %	Multiply • Divide • Modulus	`a * b`	N	Left-Right	13
+ -	Addition • Subtraction	`a + b`	N	Left-Right	12
<< >>	Bit Shift Left • Bit Shift Right	`a << 3`	N	Left-Right	11
< <= > >=	Comparison	`a < 5`	N	Left-Right	10
== !=	Equal • Not Equal	`a == b`	N	Left-Right	9
&	Bitwise And	`a & b`	N	Left-Right	8
^	Bitwise Exclusive Or	`a ^ b`	N	Left-Right	7
|	Bitwise Or	`a | b`	N	Left-Right	6
&&	Logical And	`a && b`	N	Left-Right	5
||	Logical Or	`a || b`	N	Left-Right	4
? :	Conditional	`a ? x : y`	N	Right-Left	3

= += -=
*= /= %=
>>= <<=
&= ^= |=
	Assignment	`a = 5`
		`a %= b`
		`a &= c`
		`a |= d`
			Y	Right-Left	2

,	Comma	`a, b, c`	N	Left-Right	1

and Operator

The *and* operator (`&&`) is a binary operator with a precedence of 5. Because *and* is a binary operator, four distinct combinations of values in its operands are possible. The result is true only when both operands are true; it is false in all other cases.

or Operator

The *or* operator (`||`) is a binary operator with a precedence of 4. Again, because it is a binary operator, four distinct combinations of values in its operands are possible. The result is false if both operands are false; it is true in all other cases.

Evaluating Logical Expressions

Computer languages can use two methods to evaluate the binary logical relationships. In the first method, the expression must be completely evaluated before the result is determined. This means that the *and* expression must be completely evaluated, even when the first operand is false and it is therefore known that the result must *be* false. Likewise, in the *or* expression, the whole expression must be evaluated even when the first operand is true and the obvious result of the expression must be true.

The second method sets the resulting value as soon as it is known. It does not need to complete the evaluation. In other words, it operates in a short-circuit fashion and stops the evaluation when it knows for sure what the final result will be. Under this method, if the first operand of a logical *and* expression is false, the second half of the expression is not evaluated because it is apparent that the result must be false. Again, with the *or* expression, if the first operand is true, there is no need to evaluate the second half of the expression, so the resulting value is set true immediately. C uses this short-circuit method, which is illustrated in **Figure 5-3**.

Figure 5-3 Short-circuit methods for *and/or* expressions

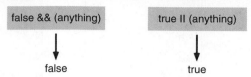

Although the C method is more efficient, it can cause problems when the second operand contains side effects, which is poor programming practice. Consider for example, the following expression in which a programmer wants to find the value of the logical expression and at the same time wants to increment the value of the second operand:

```
x && y++
```

Everything works fine when the first operand is true. But if the first operand is false, the second operand will never be evaluated and therefore will never be incremented. It is the same with the following *or* example. If the first operand is true, the second operand will never be incremented.

```
x || y++
```

Program 5-1 demonstrates the use of logical data in expressions.

Program 5-1 | Logical expressions

```
 1   /* Demonstrate the results of logical operators.
 2      Written by:
 3      Date:
 4   */
 5   #include <stdio.h>
 6   #include <stdbool.h>
 7   int main (void)
 8
 9   {
10   // Local Declarations
11      bool a = true;
12      bool b = true;
13      bool c = false;
14
15   // Statements
16      printf ("    %2d AND %2d:%2d\n", a, b, a && b);
17      printf ("    %2d AND %2d: %2d\n", a, c, a && c);
18      printf ("    %2d AND %2d: %2d\n", c, a, c && a);
19      printf ("    %2d OR  %2d: %2d\n", a, c, a || c);
20      printf ("    %2d OR  %2d: %2d\n", c, a, c || a);
21      printf ("    %2d OR  %2d: %2d\n", c, c, c || c);
22      printf ("NOT %2d AND NOT %2d: %2d\n", a, c, !a && !c);
```

(continue)

Program 5-1   Logical expressions *(continued)*

```
23      printf("NOT %2d AND %2d: %2d\n", a, c, !a && c);
24      printf("    %2d AND NOT %2d: %2d\n", f a, c, a && !c);
25 return 0;
26 } // main
```

Output

```
    1   AND     1:  1
    1   AND     0:  0
    0   AND     1:  0
    1   OR      0:  1
    0   OR      1:  1
    0   OR      0:  0
NOT 1   AND NOT 0:  0
NOT 1   AND     0:  0
    1   AND NOT 0:  1
```

Each print statement in Program 5-1 contains a logical expression that evaluates either to true or false. Make sure you understand why each of the expressions evaluates as shown in the results. Note that even though the results are of type Boolean, they must be printed as integer (%d). This is because while the expressions evaluate to true or false, there is no conversion code for Boolean. Therefore, when we print them, we must use the integer field specification.

Comparative Operators

In addition to logical operators, C provides six comparative operators. Comparative operators are divided into two categories, relational and equality. They are all binary operators that accept two operands and compare them. The result is a Boolean type—that is, the result is always true or false. The operators are shown in **Table 5-2**.

Table 5-2   Relational and equality operators

TYPE	OPERATOR	MEANING	PRECEDENCE
Relational	<	less than	10
	<=	less than or equal	
	>	greater than	
	>=	greater than or equal	
Equality	==	equal	
	!=	not equal	9

As you can see in Table 5-2, relational operators (less than, less than or equal, greater than, greater than or equal) have a higher priority (10) than the equality and not equal operators (9). This means that relational operators are evaluated before the equality operators when they appear together in the same expression.

It is important to recognize that each operator is a complement (counterpart or similar comparative operator expression) of another operator in the group. But, surprisingly, the complement is not the one that you might expect. **Figure 5-4** shows each operator and its complement.

Figure 5-4 Comparative operator complements

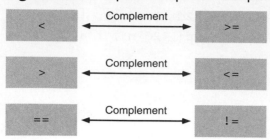

If we want to simplify an expression involving the *not* and the *less than* operators, we use the *greater than or equal* operator. This concept is important for simplifying expressions and coding expressions in good, clear style. **Table 5-3** shows an example of each expression and its simplified version.

Table 5-3 Examples of simplifying operator complements

ORIGINAL EXPRESSION	SIMPLIFIED EXPRESSION
! (x < y)	x >= y
! (x > y)	x <= y
! (x != y)	x == y
! (x <= y)	x > y
! (x >= y)	x < y
! (x == y)	x != y

Program 5-2 demonstrates the use of the comparative operators.

Program 5-2 | Comparative operators

```
1   /* Demonstrates the results of relational operators.
2      Written by:
3      Date:
4   */
5   #include <stdio.h>
6
7   int main (void)
8   {
9   // Local Declarations
10     int a = 5;
11     int b = -3;
12
13 // Statements *
```

(continue)

Program 5-2   Comparative operators *(continued)*

```
14     printf("%2d < %2d is %2d\n", a, b, a < b);
15     printf("%2d == %2d is %2d\n", a, b, a == b);
16     printf("%2d != %2d is %2d\n", a, b, a != b);
17     printf("%2d > %2d is %2d\n", a, b, a > b);
18     printf("%2d <= %2d is %2d\n", a, b, a <= b);
19     printf("%2d >= %2d is %2d\n", a, b, a >= b);
20     return 0;
21 } // main
```

Output
```
5 < -3 is 0
5 == -3 is 0
5 != -3 is 1
5 > -3 is 1
5 <= -3 is 0
5 >= -3 is 1
```

Program 5-2 follows the same patterns we saw in Program 5-1. Once again, make sure that you understand why each of the representations in the results evaluates to true or false.

5.2 Two-Way Selection

The basic decision statement in programming is the two-way selection statement, which a computer processes as a conditional statement that can be answered either true or false. If the answer is true, one or more action statements are executed. If the answer is false, then a different action or set of actions is executed. Regardless of which set of actions is executed, the program continues with the next statement after the selection. The flowchart for two-way decision logic is shown in **Figure 5-5**.

Figure 5-5   Two-way decision logic

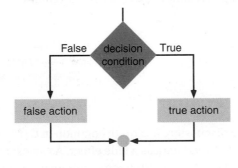

`if ... else`

C implements two-way selection with the `if ... else` statement. An `if ... else` statement is a composite statement used to make a decision between two alternatives. **Figure 5-6** shows the logic flow for an `if ... else` statement. The expression can be any C expression. After it has been evaluated, if its value is true, `statement1` is executed: otherwise, `statement2` is executed. It is impossible for both statements to be executed in the same evaluation.

Figure 5-6 `if ... else` logic flow

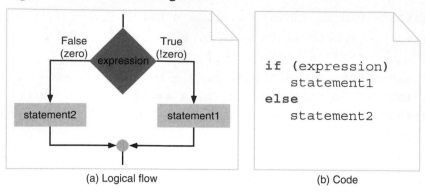

(a) Logical flow

(b) Code

Important syntactical points about `if ... else` statements are summarized in **Table 5-4**.

Table 5-4 Syntactical rules for `if ... else` **statements**

1.	The expression must be enclosed in parentheses.
2.	No semicolon (`;`) is needed for an `if ... else` statement; statement 1 and statement 2 may have a semicolon as required by their types.
3.	The expression can have a side effect.
4.	Both the true and the false statements can be any statement (even another `if ... else` statement) or they can be a `null` statement.
5.	Both `statement1` and `statement2` must be one and only one statement. Remember, however, that multiple statements can be combined into a compound statement through the use of braces.
6.	We can swap the position of `statement1` and `statement2` if we use the complement of the original expression.

The first rule in Table 5-4—that the expression must be enclosed in parentheses—is simple and needs no further discussion. The second rule is also simple, but it tends to cause more problems. We have, therefore, provided an example in **Figure 5-7**. In this example, each action is a single statement that either adds or subtracts 1 from the variable a. Note that the semicolons belong to the arithmetic statements, not the `if ... else` statement.

Figure 5-7 A simple `if ... else` statement

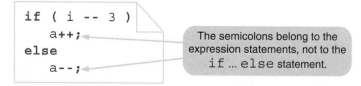

```
if ( i -- 3 )
    a++;
else
    a--;
```

The semicolons belong to the expression statements, not to the `if ... else` statement.

The third rule in Table 5-4 requires more discussion. It is quite common in C to code expressions that have side effects. For example, we often use expressions that read data as a side effect. As an example, consider what happens when we are writing a series of numbers, and when we have written ten numbers we want to go to a new line. A simple solution increments a line count and tests the limit in the same statement. The code for this logic could be written as shown in the following example.

```
if (++lineCnt > 10)
    {
    printf("\n");
```

```
        lineCnt = 0;
    } end true
printf( ... );
```

Rules 4 and 5 in Table 5-4 are closely related. The fact that any statement can be used in an `if ... else` is straightforward, but often new C programmers will forget to use a compound statement for complex logic. The use of compound statements is seen in **Figure 5-8**. The first example shows a compound statement only for the true condition. The second example shows compound statements for both conditions. Note that the compound statements begin with an open brace and end with a close brace.

Figure 5-8 Compound statements in an `if ... else`

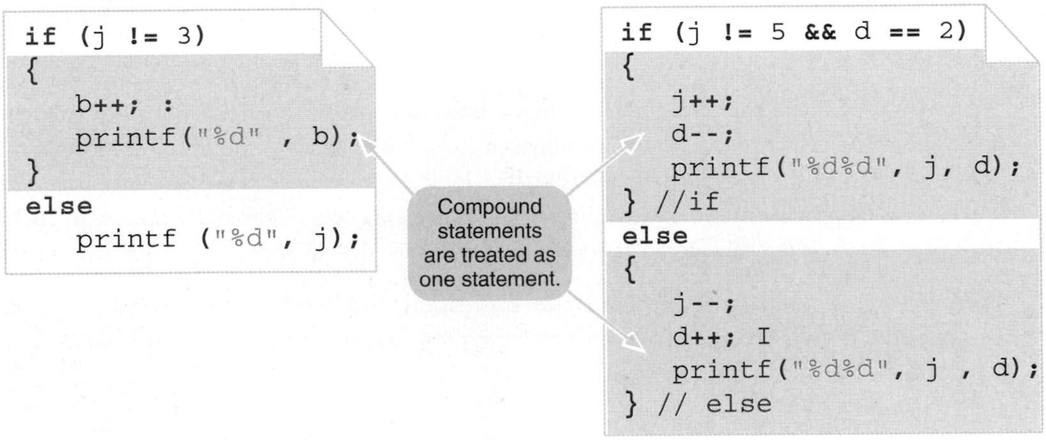

```
if (j != 3)
{
    b++; :
    printf("%d" , b);
}
else
    printf ("%d", j);
```

Compound statements are treated as one statement.

```
if (j != 5 && d == 2)
{
    j++;
    d--;
    printf("%d%d", j, d);
} //if
else
{
    j--;
    d++; I
    printf("%d%d", j , d);
} // else
```

The sixth rule states that the true and false statements can be exchanged by complementing the expression. Recall from our discussion of relational operators on "Comparative Operators" in Section 5.1 that any expression can be complemented. When we find that we need to complement an `if ... else` statement, all we have to do is to switch the true and false statements. An example of this operation is shown in **Figure 5-9**.

Figure 5-9 Complemented `if ... else` statements

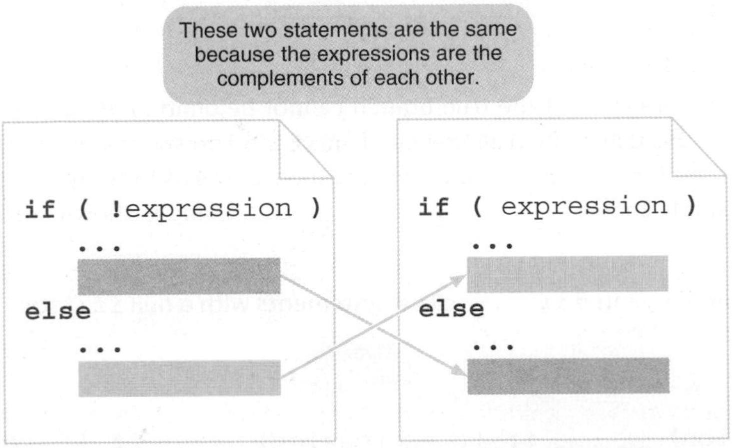

These two statements are the same because the expressions are the complements of each other.

```
if ( !expression )
    . . .

else
    . . .
```

```
if ( expression )
    . . .

else
    . . .
```

(a) Original   (b) Complemented

Null `else` Statement

Although there are always two possible actions after a decision, sometimes we do not care about both of them. In this case, the `else` action is usually left out. For example, assume we are processing numbers as they are being read. However, for some reason, the logic requires that we process only numbers greater than zero. As we read a number, we test it for greater than zero. If the test is true, we include it in the process. If it is false, we do nothing.

If the `else` condition is not required—that is, if it is null—it can be omitted. This omission can be shown as a null `else` statement (a null statement consists of only a semicolon); more commonly, the `else` statement is simply omitted entirely, as shown in **Figure 5-10**.

Figure 5-10 A null `else` statement

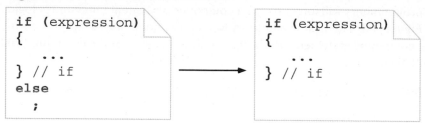

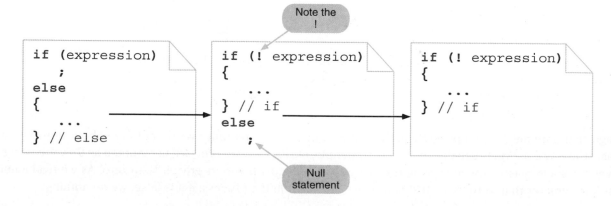

Note

When we design the logical flow of a program, we often have a situation in which the *not* operator is in front of a logical expression enclosed in the parentheses. Human engineering studies tell us, however, that positive logic is easier to read and understand than negative logic. In these cases, therefore, if we want to make the total expression positive by removing the parentheses, we apply the *not* operator directly to each operand. De Morgan's rule governs the complementing of operators in this situation. This rule is defined as follows:

When we remove the parentheses in a logical expression preceded by the *not* operator, we must apply the *not* operator to each expression while changing the logical operators—that is, changing *and* (&&) to *or* (||) and changing *or* (||) to *and* (&&).

Consider the following expression:

```
!(x && y) → !x || !y
!(x || y) → !x && !y
```

If the expression has been properly complemented according to De Morgan's rule, then the result of the first expression (true or false) will be the same as the result of the second expression for any given set of values for x and y. It is important to recognize, however, that in more complex situations, the C rules of precedence can affect De Morgan's rule.

It is possible to omit the false branch, but the true branch cannot be omitted. It can be coded as a null statement; normally, however, we do not use null in the true branch of an `if ... else` statement. To eliminate it, we can use Rule 6 in Table 5-4, "Syntactical Rules for `if ... else` Statements," which allows us to complement the expression and swap the two statements. The result is known as a complemented `if ... else` and is shown in **Figure 5-11**.

Figure 5-11 Complemented `if ... else` statements with a null `if` statement

Program 5-3 contains an example of a simple two-way selection. It displays the relationship between two numbers read from the keyboard.

Program 5-3 | Two-way selection

```
1   /* Two-way selection.
2      Written by:
3      Date:
4   */
5   # include <stdio.h>
6
7   int main (void)
8   {
9   // Local Declarations
10     int a;
11     int b;
12
13  // Statements
14     printf("Please enter two integers: ");
15     scanf("%d%d", &a, &b);
16
17     if (a <= b)
18        printf("%d <= %d\n", a, b);
19     else
20        printf("%d > %d\n", a, b);
21
22     return 0;
23  } // main
```

Output
```
Please enter two integers: 10 15

10 <= 15
```

Nested `if` Statements

As we stated previously, for the if ... else, the statements may be any statement, including another if ... else. When an if ... else is included within an if ... else, it is known as a nested if statement. **Figure 5-12** shows a nested if statement. There is no limit to how many levels can be nested, but if there are more than three, they can become difficult to read.

Figure 5-14 Dangling `else` solution

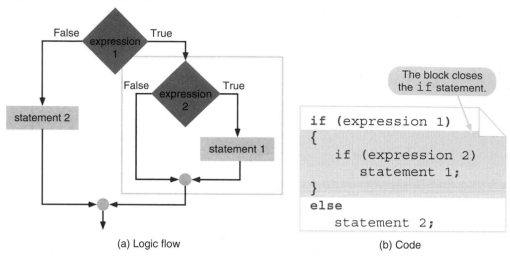

(a) Logic flow   (b) Code

Simplifying `if` Statements

By now you should recognize that `if ... else` statements can become quite complex. This discussion gives you some ideas on simplifying `if` statements. Usually, the purpose of simplification is to provide more readable code.

Sometimes the control expression itself can be simplified. For example, the two statements in **Table 5-5** are exactly the same. The simplified statements, however, are much preferred by experienced C programmers. When the simplified code becomes a natural way of thinking, you have begun to internalize the C concepts; that is, you are beginning to think in C!

Table 5-5 Simplifying the condition

ORIGINAL STATEMENT	SIMPLIFIED STATEMENT

`if (a != 0)`
    `statement`
	`if (a)`
	    `statement`

`if (a == 0)`
    `statement`
	`if (!a)`
	    `statement`

Because the simplified statements in Table 5-5 are new, let's look at them a little more carefully. The expression `a != 0` evaluates to either *true* or *false*. If a is anything other than zero, then the expression is true and `statement1` is executed. However, any integer can be used to represent true or false. In this case, if a contains any value other than zero, it is true; otherwise, it is false. (See Figure 5-1.) Therefore, because we want to execute `statement2` whenever a is not zero, and because anything other than zero is true, we code the expression as (a)—that is, as "a is true." Similarly, if we want to test for a equal to zero, we simply complement the expression, making it `!a`.

Conditional Expressions

C provides a convenient alternative to the traditional `if ... else` for two-way selection—the ternary conditional expression has a precedence of 3.

The **conditional expression** has three operands and a two-token operator. Each operand is an expression. The first token, a question mark (?), separates the first two expressions. The second token, a colon (:), separates the last two expressions. This gives it the following format:

```
expression ? expression1 : expression2
```

To evaluate this expression, C first evaluates the leftmost expression. If the expression is *true,* then the value of the conditional expression is the value of expression1. If the expression is *false,* then the value of the conditional expression is the value of expression2.

Let's look at an example.

```
a == b ? c++ : d++;
```

In this expression, only one of the two side effects take place. If a is equal to b, c++ is evaluated and one is added to c; expression2 is ignored. On the other hand, if a is not equal to b, then d++ is evaluated and 1 is added to d; expression1 is ignored. If this sounds much like a simplified if ... else, that's because it is! **Figure 5-15** shows the flowchart for the expression, which could easily be coded as an if ... else.

Figure 5-15 Conditional expression

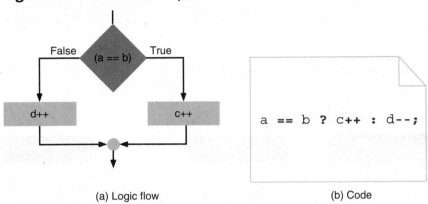

(a) Logic flow   (b) Code

The conditional expression, like any other expression, can be used in an assignment expression. Suppose that we have a program that can write either to a printer or to the system monitor. When we write to the monitor, we can write ten numbers to a line. When we write to the printer, we can write 15 numbers to a line. Given that fileFlag is a variable that indicates either the monitor (M) or printer (P), we could set the numbers per line as follows. (The parentheses are not necessary but make the statement more readable.)

```
numPerLine = (fileFlag == 'M' ? 10 : 15);
```

One final note: Although we can nest conditional expressions, it is not recommended. When the logic begins to get complex, remember the KISS (Keep It Simple and Short) principle and use nested if statements.

Two-Way Selection Example

To demonstrate two-way selection, let's look at a program that calculates income taxes. A brief explanation of progressive tax brackets may be helpful. In a progressive bracket system, the higher the income, the higher the tax rate. However, the higher rates are applied only to the income in the bracket level. Thus, if you examine two incomes, they will both pay the same amount of taxes at the lower rates. This concept of marginal tax rates is shown in **Table 5-6**.

Table 5-6 Examples of marginal tax rates

CASE 1: TOTAL INCOME 23,000			CASE 2: TOTAL INCOME 18,000		
INCOME IN BRACKET	TAX RATE	TAX	INCOME IN BRACKET	TAX RATE	TAX
(1) 10,000	2%	200	(1) 10,000	2%	200
(2) 10,000	5%	500	(2) 8,000	5%	400
(3) 3,000	7%	210	(3) none	7%	0
Total Tax		910	Total Tax		600

The design for the program to calculate taxes is shown in the structure chart in **Figure 5-16**. The design has only four functions besides `main`. The notation for `bracketTax` is somewhat unusual: In the final code, it is called five times in one expression. Therefore, we show it as a nested set of calls.

Figure 5-16 Design for calculate taxes

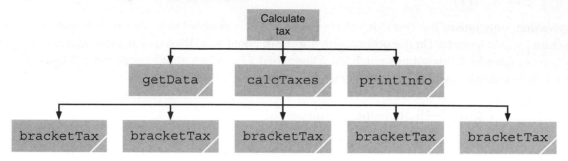

The design for each of the functions is shown in **Figure 5-17**.

Figure 5-17 Design for **Program 5-5**

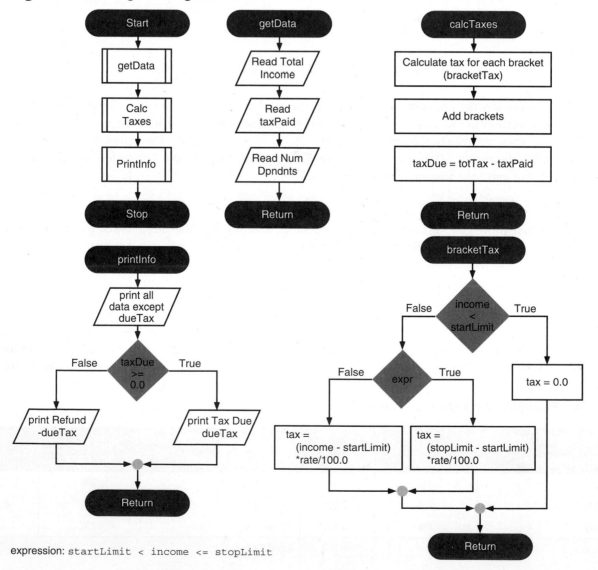

expression: `startLimit < income <= stopLimit`

The logic for calculating the tax information requires three major steps:

(1) Calculate the taxable income. Taxable income is total income adjusted for the number of dependents. In our example, we subtract $1,000 for each dependent.

(2) Calculate the taxes. The tax due calculation uses the progressive bracket system described at the beginning of the section. Our example uses five brackets.

(3) Calculate the taxes due or to be refunded. Note that if more taxes were withheld than are due, the taxes due is a negative number, indicating a refund.

The code is seen in **Program 5-5**.

Program 5-5 | Calculate taxes

```
1   /* Calculate the tax due or the refund for a family based
2      on the following imaginary formula.
3      1. For each dependent deduct $1,000 from income.
4      2. Determine tax rate from the following brackets:
5      bracket taxable income tax rate
6         1   <= 10000     2%
7         2  10001 - 20000   5%
8         3  20001 - 30000   7%
9         4  30001 - 50000  10%
10        5  50001 and up 15%
11     Then print the amount of tax or the refund.
12
13     Written by:
14     Date:
15 */
16 #include <stdio.h>
17
18 #define LOWEST 0000000.00
19 #define HIGHEST 1000000.00
20
21 #define LIMIT1 10000.00
22 #define LIMIT2 20000.00
23 #define LIMIT3 30000.00
24 #define LIMIT4 50000.00
25
26 #define RATE1 02
27 #define RATE2 05
28 #define RATE3 07
29 #define RATE4 10
30 #define RATE5 15
31
32 #define DEDN_PER_DPNDNT 1000
33
34 // Function Declarations
```

(continue)

Program 5-5 Calculate taxes *(continued)*

```c
35  void getData (double* totalIncome, double* taxPaid,
36                   int* numOfDpndnts);
37
38  void calcTaxes (double totalIncome,
39                   double taxPaid,
40  int  numOfDpndnts,
41  double* taxableIncome,
42  double* totalTax,
43  double* taxDue);
44
45  void printInformation (double totalIncome,
46                          double taxPaid,
47                          int numOfDpndnts,
48                          double totalTax,
49                          double paidTax,
50                          double taxDue);
51
52  double bracketTax (double income,
53                       double startLimit,
54                       double stopLimit,
55                       int rate);
56
57  int main (void)
58  {
59  // Local Declarations
60     int numOfDpndnts;
61     double taxDue;
62     double taxPaid;
63     double totalIncome;
64     double taxableIncome;
65     double totalTax;
66
67  // Statements
68     getData (&totalIncome, &taxPaid, &numOfDpndnts);
69     calcTaxes (totalIncome, taxPaid, numOfDpndnts,
70              &taxableIncome, &totalTax, &taxDue);
71     printInformation (totalIncome, taxableIncome,
72                       numOfDpndnts, totalTax,
73                       taxPaid, taxDue);
74     return 0;
75  } // main
76
77  /* ------------------- getData ------------------
78      This function reads tax data from the keyboard.
```

(continue)

Program 5-5 Calculate taxes *(continued)*

```
79       Pre Nothing
80       Post Reads totalIncome, taxPaid, & numOfDpndnts
81 */
82 void getData ( double* totalIncome, double* taxPaid,
83                int* numOfDpndnts)
84 {
85 // Statements
86    printf("Enter your total income for last year: ");
87    scanf ("%lf", totalIncome);
88
89    printf("Enter total of payroll deductions : ");
90    scanf ("%lf", taxPaid);
91
92    printf("Enter the number of dependents  : ");
93    scanf ("%d", numOfDpndnts);
94    return;
95 }  // getData
96
97  /*  ============ calcTaxes ============
98     This function calculates the taxes due.
99     Pre Given-income, numOfDpndnts, & taxPaid
100    Post Tax income, total tax, and tax due
101    calculated
102 */
103 void calcTaxes (double totInc,
104                double taxPaid,
105                int  numOfDpndnts,
106                double* taxableInc,
107                double* totTax,
108                double* taxDue)
109 {
110 // Statements
111    *taxableInc = totInc -
112       (numOfDpndnts * DEDN_PER_DPNDNT);
113    *totTax =
114       bracketTax(*taxableInc, LOWEST, LIMIT1, RATE1)
115     + bracketTax(*taxableInc, LIMIT1, LIMIT2, RATE2)
116     + bracketTax(*taxableInc, LIMIT2, LIMIT3, RATE3)
117     + bracketTax(*taxableInc, LIMIT3, LIMIT4, RATE4)
118     + bracketTax(*taxableInc, LIMIT4, HIGHEST, RATE5);
119
120    *taxDue = *totTax - taxPaid;
121    return;
```

(continue)

Program 5-5   Calculate taxes *(continued)*

```
122 } // calcTaxes
123
124 /*  ============ printInformation ============
125     This function prints a table showing all information.
126     Pre The parameter list
127     Post Prints the table
128 */
129 void printInformation (double totalIncome,
130                        double income,
131                        int numDpndnts,
132                        double totalTax,
133                        double paidTax,
134                        double dueTax)
135 {
136 // Statements
137    printf("\nTotal income        :%9.2f\n",
138          totalIncome);
139    printf("Number of dependents :%9d\n", numDpndnts);
140    printf("Taxable income       :%9.2f\n", income);
141    printf("Total tax            :%9.2f\n", totalTax);
142    printf("Tax already paid     :%9.2f\n", paidTax);
143
144    if (dueTax >= 0.0)
145       printf("Tax due              :%9.2f\n", dueTax);
146    else
147       printf("Refund               :%9.2f\n", -dueTax);
148    return;
149 } // printlnformation
150
151 /*  ----------------- bracketTax -----------------
152     Calculates the tax for a particular bracket.
153     Pre The taxableIncome
154     Post Returns the tax for a particular bracket
155 */
156 double bracketTax (double income, double startLimit,
157                    double stopLimit, int rate)
158 {
159 // Local Declarations
160    double tax;
161
162 // Statements
163    if (income <= startLimit)
164       tax = 0.0;
```

(continue)

Program 5-5   Calculate taxes *(continued)*

```
165    else
166        if (income > startLimit && income <= stopLimit)
167            tax = (income - startLimit) * rate / 100.00;
168        else
169            tax = (stopLimit - startLimit) * rate / 100.00;
170
171    return tax;
172 } // bracketTax
```

Output
```
Enter your total income for last year: 15000

Enter total of payroll deductions    : 250

Enter the number of dependents       : 2

Total income         : 15000.00

Number of dependents :        2

Taxable income       : 13000.00

Total tax            :   350.00

Tax already paid     :   250.00

Tax due              :   100.00
```

Note that Program 5-5 contains extensive internal documentation. This documentation includes a series of comments at the beginning of the program, the define statements used to set some of the key values in the program, and the prototype statements.

Next examine the structure of the program; main contains no detail code; it simply calls three functions to get the job done. Because two of the functions must pass data back to main, they use the address (&) and indirection (*) operators. The call to getData in statement 68 uses the address operator to pass the address of the three variables that need to be read from the keyboard. Then, statements 82–83 in the getData header statement use the asterisk to specify that the type is an address. Because the parameters are already addresses, the scanf statements do not need an address operator. You must always consider what type of parameter you are using, data or address, and use the correct operators for it. Do not automatically use the address operator with scanf.

Examine the code for calcTaxes. The function header (starting at statement 103) specifies that the first three formal parameters are passed as values and the last three are passed by address. The last three are address parameters because they are calculated values that need to be passed back to main for later printing. Note that all references to them in the function are prefaced with the indirection operator, which tells the compiler that it must use the variables in main.

Note the use of the type double throughout the program. If you examine the conversion specifications in the format strings, you will note that they are If for input and f for output.

Finally, and the main point of this example, note how we used the function bracketTax to calculate the tax. This function was designed so that it could calculate the tax for any bracket. This is a much simpler design than writing complex code for different brackets and demonstrates how keeping it simple and short (KISS) makes for better programs.

5.3 Multiway Selection

In addition to two-way selection, most programming languages provide another selection concept known as multiway selection. A multiway selection statement chooses among several alternatives. The decision logic for the multiway statement is seen in **Figure 5-18**.

Figure 5-18 Switch decision logic

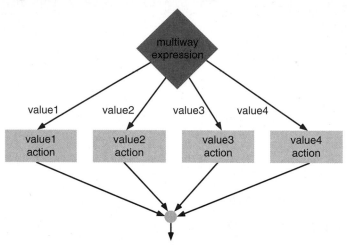

C has two different ways to implement multiway selection. The first is by using the switch statement. The other is a programming technique known as the else ... if that provides a convenient style to nest if statements. The switch statement can be used only when the selection condition reduces to an integral expression. Many times, however, such as when the selection is based on a range of values, the condition is not an integral. In these cases, we use the else ... if.

The switch Statement

The switch statement is a composite statement used to make a decision between many alternatives. **Figure 5-19** shows the switch statement syntax. Syntactically, the block in the switch statement is not needed if only one case is required. However, a simple if statement should be used if only one choice is available.

Figure 5-19 Switch statement syntax

```
switch (expression)
{
    case constant-1 : statement
                      ...
                      statement
    case constant-2 : statement
                      ...
                      statement
    case constant-n : statement
    default         : statement
                      ...
                      statement
} // end switch
```

Although the switch expression can use any expression that reduces to an integral value, the most common is a unary expression in the form of an integral identifier. The selection alternatives, known as case label, must be C integral constants. For every possible value in the switch expression, a separate case label is defined. Figure 5-19 also shows the format for the case label. Associated with each possible case is zero or more statements. Everything from a case label to the next case label is a sequence. The case label simply provides an entry point to start executing the code.

The default label is a special form of the case label. It is executed whenever none of the other case values matches the value in the switch expression. Note, however, that default is not required. If we do not provide a default, the compiler will simply continue with the statement after the closing brace in the switch.

The switch statement is a puzzle that must be solved carefully to avoid confusion. Think of the switch statement as a series of drawbridges, one for each case and one for the default. As a result of the switch evaluation, one and only one of the drawbridges will be closed, so that there will be a path for the program to follow. (If none of the drawbridges is closed, then the statement is skipped and the program continues with the next statement after the switch.) The switch flow is shown in **Figure 5-20**.

Figure 5-20 Switch flow

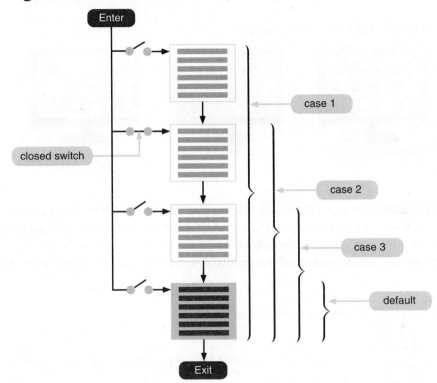

Pay careful attention to what happens once the program flow enters a case label. When the statements associated with one case have been executed, the program flows to the statements for the next case. In other words, after the program enters through a closed switch, it executes the code for all of the following cases until the end. While we occasionally need this flexibility, it is not always what we want. We show how to break the flow shortly, but let's look at an example first. **Program 5-6** demonstrates the switch statement. Can you figure out what it prints?

Program 5-6 | Demonstrate the switch statement

```
1  // Program fragment to demonstrate switch
2  switch (printFlag)
3  {
4     case 1: printf("This is case 1\n");
5
6     case 2: printf("This is case 2\n");
7
8     default: printf("This is default\n");
9  } // switch
```

Program 5-6 has three different `case` labels. The first `case` identifies the entry point to be used when `printFlag` is a 1. The second `case` identifies the entry point when `printFlag` is a 2. And finally, the `default` identifies the entry point when `printFlag` is neither a 1 nor a 2. While `default` is not a required condition in a `switch` statement, it should be included when all possible situations have not been covered by the `case` labels.

Have you figured out what is printed by Program 5-6? The answers are in **Figure 5-21**. Three results are possible, depending on the value in `printFlag`. If `printFlag` is a 1, then all three `print` statements are executed. If `printFlag` is a 2, then the first `print` statement is skipped and the last two are executed. Finally, if `printFlag` is neither a 1 nor a 2, then only the statements defined by the `default` are executed. This results in the first two `print` statements being skipped and only the last one being executed.

Figure 5-21 `Switch` results

(a) `printFlag` is 1   (b) `printFlag` is 2   (c) `printFlag` is not 1 and 2

But what if we want to execute only one of the case-label sequences? To do so, we must use `break` statements. The `break` statement causes the program to jump out of the `switch` statement—that is, to go to the closing brace and continue with the code that follows the `switch`. If we add a `break` as the last statement in each `case`, we have **Figure 5-22**. Now, only one `print` statement will be executed, regardless of the value of `printFlag`.

Figure 5-22 A `switch` with `break` statements

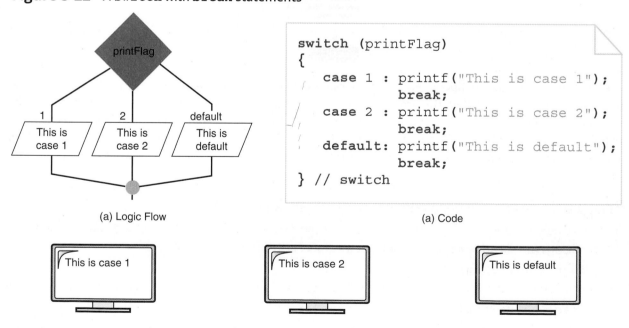

(a) Logic Flow

```
switch (printFlag)
{
    case 1 : printf ("This is case 1");
             break;
    case 2 : printf ("This is case 2");
             break;
    default: printf ("This is default");
             break;
} // switch
```

(a) Code

Two or more `case` labels can be associated with the same set of actions. In **Program 5-7**, for example, we print a message depending on whether `printFlag` is even or odd.

Program 5-7 | Multivalued `case` statements

```
 1   /* Program fragment that demonstrates multiple
 2      cases for one set of statements
 3   */
 4   switch (printFlag)
 5   {
 6       case 1:
 7       case 3:  printf("Good Day\n");
 8                printf("Odds have it!\n");
 9                break;
10       case 2:
11       case 4:  printf("Good Day\n");
12                printf("Evens have it!\n");
13                break;
14       default: printf("Good Day, I'm confused!\n");
15                printf("Bye!\n");
16                break;
17   } // switch
```

As a matter of style, the last statement in the `switch` does not require a `break`. We recommend, however, that you get in the habit of using it, especially when the last statement is not the `default`. This good habit will eventually save you hours of debugging time because you will not forget to add it when you add a new `case` to the `switch` statement.

The following list summarizes some points you must remember about the `switch` statement.

  1. The control expression that follows the keyword switch must be an integral type.

  2. Each case label is the keyword case followed by a constant expression.

  3. No two case labels can have the same constant expression value.

  4. But two case labels can be associated with the same set of actions.

  5. The `default` label is not required. If the value of the expression does not match with any labeled constant expression, the control transfers outside of the switch statement. However, we recommend that all switch statements have a `default` label.

  6. The switch statement can include at most one `default` label. The `default` label may be coded anywhere, but it is traditionally coded last.

Program 5-8 converts a numeric score to a letter grade. The grading scale is the rather typical "absolute scale," in which 90% or more is an A, 80%–89% is a B, 70%–79% is a C, and 60%–69% is a D. Anything below 60% is an F.

Program 5-8 | Student grading

```
1   /* This program reads a test score, calculates the letter
2      grade for the score, and prints the grade.
3      Written by:
4      Date:
5   */
6   #include <stdio.h>
7
8   // Function Declarations
9      char scoreToGrade (int score);
10
11  int main (void)
12  {
13  // Local Declarations
14     int score;
15     char grade;
16
17  // Statements
18     printf("Enter the test score (0-100): ");
19     scanf ("%d", &score);
20
21     grade = scoreToGrade (score);
22     printf("The grade is: %c\n", grade);
23
24     return 0;
25  } // main
26  /*  ==========score ToGrade==========
27     This function calculates the letter grade for a score.
28     Pre the parameter score
29     Post returns the grade
30  */
31  char scoreToGrade (int score)
32  {
33  // Local Declarations
34     char grade;
35     int temp;
36
37  // Statements
38     temp = score / 10;
39     switch (temp)
```

(continue)

Program 5-8   Student grading *(continued)*

```
40      {
41          case 10:
42          case 9 : grade = 'A';
43                   break;
44          case 8 : grade = 'B';
45                   break;
46          case 7 : grade = 'C';
47                   break;
48          case 6 : grade = 'D';
49                   break;
50          default: grade = 'F';
51      } // switch
52      return grade;
53 } // scoreToGrade
```

Output
```
Enter the test score (0-100): 89

The grade is: B
```

This example shows how we can use the integer division operator (/) to change a range of numbers to individual points to be used by the `switch` statement. The problem definition requires that if the score is between 80% and 89%, it must be changed to letter grade 'B.' This condition cannot be used in a `switch` statement. But if we divide the score by 10 (integer division), the entire range (such as 80–89) can be changed to one single number (8), which can be used as a constant in the `case` label.

Note how the `break` statement works. This is an important part of the logic for `switch` statements. Without the `break`, we would have determined and assigned the score, and then proceeded to assign all of the lower scores down to 'F,' with the result that everyone would have failed. The `break` allows us to leave the body of the `switch` as soon as we have completed the grade assignment.

One word of caution. If the user enters an invalid score, such as 110, this program gives invalid results.

The `else ... if`

The `switch` statement only works when the constant expression in the `case` labels are integral. What if we need to make a multiway decision on the basis of a value that is not integral? The answer is the `else ... if`. There is no such C construct as the `else ... if`. Rather, it is a style of coding that we use when we need a multiway selection based on a value that is not integral.

Suppose we need a selection based on a range of values. We code the first `if` condition and its associated statements, and then we follow it with all other possible values using `else ... if`. The last test in the series concludes with an `else`. This is the default condition; that is, it is the condition that is to be executed if all other statements are false. A sample of the `else ... if` logic design is shown in **Figure 5-23**.

Figure 5-23 The else … if logic design for Program 5-9

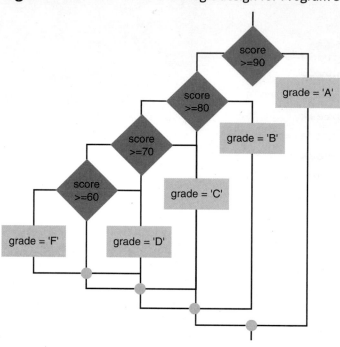

What is different about the else … if code? As we said, it is really nothing more than a style change. Rather than indenting each if statement, we code the else … if on a single line and align it with the previous if. In this way we simulate the same formatting that we see in the switch and its associated case label. This style format is as follows:

```
if (score >= 90)
    grade = 'A';
else if (score >= 80)
    grade = 'B';
```

One important point about the else … if: Use it only when the same basic expression is being evaluated. In Figure 5-23, the expressions are all based on the variable score. If different variables were being evaluated, we would use the normal nesting associated with the if … else statement. Do not use the else … if format with nested if statements.

Note	The else … if is an artificial C construct that is only used when: 1. The selection variable is not an integral, and 2. The same variable is being tested in the expressions.

Program 5-9 is the same as the switch example in Program 5-8, but this time, we use the else … if to solve the problem. It shows how we can use multiway selection and the else … if construct to change a numeric score to a letter grade.

Program 5-9 | Convert score to grade

```c
 1  /* This program reads a test score, calculates the letter
 2     grade based on the absolute scale, and prints it.
 3     Written by:
 4     Date:
 5  */
 6  #include <stdio.h>
 7
 8  // Function Declarations
 9  char scoreToGrade (int score);
10
11  int main (void)
12  {
13  // Local Declarations
14     int score;
15     char grade;
16
17  // Statements
18     printf("Enter the test score (0-100): ");
19     scanf ("%d", &score);
20
21     grade = scoreToGrade (score);
22     printf("The grade is: %c\n", grade);
23
24     return 0;
25  } // main
26
27  /* ================ scoreToGrade ================
28     This function calculates letter grade for a score.
29     Pre the parameter score
30     Post returns the grade
31  */
32  char scoreToGrade (int score)
33  {
34  // Local Declarations
35     char grade;
36
37  // Statements
38     if (score >= 90)
39        grade = 'A';
40     else if (score >= 80)
41        grade = 'B';
```

(continue)

Program 5-9   Convert score to grade *(continued)*

```
42      else if (score >= 70)
43          grade = 'C';
44      else if (score >= 60)
45          grade = 'D';
46      else
47          grade = 'F';
48      return grade;
49 } // scoreToGrade
```

Output
```
Enter the test score (0-100): 90

The grade is: A
```

We used the `else ... if` construct because our condition was not an integral; rather, it tested several ranges of the same variable, score. Study the code carefully. Note that, once the correct range is located, none of the following conditions will be tested. For instance, if a score of 85 is entered, the test against 90% is false, so we execute the `else ... if` test for a score greater than 80%. Because this condition is true, we set grade to `'B'` and skip all the remaining tests.

Also, note how the tests are ordered. In this case we first eliminate those scores equal to or greater than 90%; then we check 80%, 70%, and 60% in turn. Because we were checking for greater than, we could not have coded it in the reverse, 60% first.

This is an important design concept: When checking a range using greater than, start with the largest value; when checking a range using less than, start with the lowest value.

The **Table 5-7** presents a summary of all conditional statements, their use, and an example of each conditional statement. This table will help you select the most appropriate conditional statement to select for your specific scenario.

Table 5-7   Summary of conditional statements

DECISION-MAKING STRUCTURE	SITUATION	C CODE	SCENARIO
Simple `if`	Used to execute one or more statements when a specific condition is met (true). This is the simplest form of a decision-making structure.	`if ( bal > limit )` `    acct_status = -1;`	Deactivate account when credit limit is reached.

If ... else	Used to check a specific condition. If the condition is met (true) then one block of statements is executed. If the condition is not met (false), then another block of statements is executed instead.	`if ( score >= 65 )`
		`    printf("Passed");`
		`else`
		`    printf("Failed");`
			Grant a passing grade if `score` is greater than 65. Otherwise, assign a failing grade.

DECISION-MAKING STRUCTURE	SITUATION	C CODE	SCENARIO

Nested `if ... else`	Used when a series of conditions must be tested to execute a specific action.	```if (rate > 8)```
		``` printf("Excellent\n");```
		```else if (rate > 2= && rate <= 8)```
		``` printf("Average\n");```
		```else if (rate >= 0 && rate <= 2)```
		``` printf("Poor\n")```
		```else```
		``` printf("invalid rate\n");```
			Display movie review status based on the value of the rating it obtained.

`if ... else` ladder `else ... if`	Used to execute an action from a multiple of actions. This is known as multi-way. If the first condition is not met, then check the next one until one of the conditions is true. Otherwise, execute the `else` statement.	```if (rooms > 5)```
		``` property_tax = 0.40;```
		```else if (rooms > 4)```
		``` property_tax = 0.35;```
		```else if (rooms > 3)```
		``` property_tax = 0.25;```
		```else if (rooms > 2)```
		``` property_tax = 0.10;```
		```else```
		``` property_tax = 0.0;```
			Determine the property tax rate based on number of rooms.

Nested `if` statements	Used when a series of conditions must be tested to execute specific statements. Either *and* or *or* operators could be used to replace nested `if` statements.	```if (member == 'Y')```
		``` if (duration >= 10)```
		``` if (status == 'P')```
		``` printf("Discount is 50%\n");```
		``` else```
		``` if (duration >= 5)```
		``` if (status == 'P')```
		``` printf("Discount is 40%\n");```
		``` else if (status == 'G')```
		``` printf("Discount is 30%\n");```
		``` else if (status == 'S')```
		``` printf("Discount is 20%\n");```
		``` else if (status == 'B')```
		``` printf("Discount is 10%\n");```
		``` else```
		``` printf("Discount is 5%\n");```
		```else```
		``` printf("No Discount%\n");```
			Determine discount based on whether an individual is a member of airlines rewards club, length of membership, and membership status.

Conditional expression	Used to replace a simple `if ... else` statement and assign the result of the expression to a variable.	```Discount = age > 64 ? 35 : 15;```	`Discount` is 35% if age is greater than 64. Otherwise `Discount` is 15%.

(continue)

Table 5-7 Summary of conditional statements *(continued)*

DECISION-MAKING STRUCTURE	SITUATION	C CODE	SCENARIO

switch	Used to execute a specific action when a choice from the option list is matched in the case statements.	```switch (choice)
		{
		    case 1: DoMenuOptionOne; break;
		    case 2: DoMenuOptionTwo; break;
		    case 3: DoMenuOptionThree; break;
		    case 4: DoMenuOptionFour; break;
		    case 5: DoMenuOptionFive; break;
		    default: DoMenuOptionDefault;
		}```
			Select a choice from a menu of options. For example, the menu might list the following:
			• **Option 1:** calculate loan interest
			• **Option 2:** early loan settlement charges
			• **Option 3:** loan deferment charges
			• **Option 4:** loan extension
			• **Option 5:** loan top-up interest charges
			• **Default display:** wrong option

5.4 More Standard Functions

One of the assets of the C language is its rich set of standard functions that make programming much easier. You are already familiar with some of these standard functions. Now that we have studied selection, we can discuss two other libraries of standard functions that are closely related to selection statements.

C18 has two parallel but separate header files for manipulating characters. The first, ctype.h, supports the ASCII character set. The second, wctype.h, supports wide characters. While the wide-character library (wctype.h) contains some functions not found in the ASCII character library (ctype.h), they follow a common naming format. For example, the ASCII library contains a function, islower, to test for lowercase alphabetic characters. The equivalent function in the wide-character library is iswlower. Therefore, if we know the name for one library, we know it for the other.

Standard Characters Functions

The character libraries are divided into two major groups: classifying functions and converting functions. The prototypes of these functions are in the ctype.h or wctype.h header files. Before looking at these functions, make sure you understand the classification of characters that C uses. This breakdown of classes is shown in **Figure 5-24**, which uses a tree to show how characters are classified. You read the tree much like a structure chart, starting at the top and following the branches to the bottom.

Characters are first broken down into control characters, such as carriage return and end of file, or into printable characters. This tells us that control characters are not printable. The printable characters are either a space or the rest of the printable characters, which are classified as graphical. In turn, the graphical characters are broken down into alphanumeric and punctuation characters. Alphanumeric means either an alphabetic character or a digit. Finally, alphabetic characters are either upper- or lowercase.

Figure 5-24   Classifications of the character type

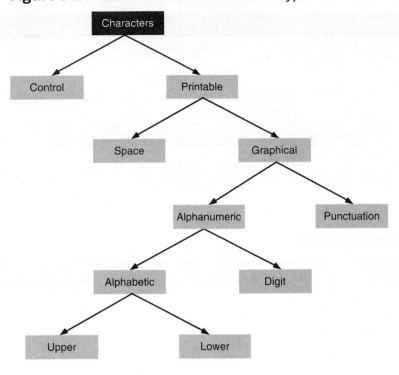

Classifying Functions

A classifying function examines a character and returns its given classification, if it has one. They all start with the prefix is and return true if the actual parameter is in the specified class. They return false if it is not. The prototypes of these functions are found in the ctype.h and cwtype.h files. The general form of the prototype function is

```
int is... (int testChar)
```

where the function name starts with is or isw. (The second option, isw , is used for wide-character functions.) One example is iscntrl, which stands for "is a control character."

All of the classifying functions return true or false. If the character matches the set being tested by the function, it returns true; if it doesn't, it returns false. For example, the isdigit function tests the character against the decimal digits (0 through 9). If the character is a decimal digit, it returns true; if the character is not a decimal digit, it returns false. **Table 5-8** summarizes each function with a brief explanation.

Table 5-8   Classifying functions

FUNCTION	DESCRIPTION
iscntrl	Control characters
isprint	Printable character, that is a character with an assigned graphic
isspace	Whitespace character: space character (32), horizontal tab (9), line feed (10), vertical tab (11), form feed (12), and carriage return (13)
isgraph	Character with printable graphic; all printable characters except space
isalnum	Alphanumeric: any alphabetic or numeric character

(continue)

Table 5-8 Classifying functions *(continued)*

FUNCTION	DESCRIPTION
`ispunct`	Any graphic character that is not alphanumeric
`isalpha`	Any alphabetic character, upper- or lowercase
`isupper`	Only uppercase alphabetic
`islower`	Only lowercase alphabetic
`isdigit`	Decimal digits (0 ... 9)
`isxdigit`	Hexadecimal digits (0 ... 9, a ... f, A ... F)
`Isodigit`	Octal digits (0 ... 7)

Character Conversion Functions

Two converting functions are used to convert a character from one case to another. These functions start with prefix `to` or `tow` (for wide characters) and return an integer that is the value of the converted character. Their basic format is

```
int to... (int oldChar)
```

Table 5-9 summarizes each function with a brief explanation.

Table 5-9 Conversion functions

FUNCTION	DESCRIPTION
`toupper`	Converts lower- to uppercase. If not lowercase, returns it unchanged.
`tolower`	Converts upper- to lowercase. If not uppercase, returns it unchanged.

A Classification Program

Let's write a program that uses classification functions to examine a character input from the keyboard. If you study Figure 5-24, carefully, you will note that most characters fall into more than one classification. For instance, a digit is printable, graphical, alphanumeric, and a digit.

Our program tests from the bottom up, so that only one classification will be printed for each character. For a digit, only the fact that it is a digit will be printed. Because it is a relatively simple demonstration of the classification functions, we wrote it using only `main`. The solution is shown in **Program 5-10**.

Program 5-10 | Demonstrate classification functions

```
1   /* This program demonstrates the use of the character
2      classification functions found in the c-type library.
3      Given a character, it displays the highest
4      classification for the character.
5      Written by:
6      Date:
```

(continue)

First Increment: ma

Program 5-11 begins th

Program 5-

```
1  /* This pro
2     multiply
3     Written
4     Date:
5  */
6  #include <s
7  #include <s
8
9  // Functior
10 int getOpti
11
12 int main (\
13 {
14 // Local De
15    int opti
16
17 // Statemer
18    option :
19
20    printf('
21
22    return (
23 } // main
24
25 /* =======:
26    This fur
27    Pre Notl
28    Post re
29 */
30 int getOpt
31 {
32 // Local D
33    int opt
34
35 // Stateme
36    printf
37    printf(
38    printf(
```

Program 5-10   Demonstrate classification functions (*continued*)

```
7   */
8
9   #include <stdio.h>
10  #include <ctype.h>
11
12  int main (void)
13  {
14  // Local Declarations
15     char charIn;
16
17  // Statements
18     printf("Enter a character to be examined: ");
19     scanf ("%c", &charIn);
20
21     if (islower(charIn))
22        printf("You entered a lowercase letter.\n");
23     else if (isupper(charIn))
24        printf("You entered an uppercase character.\n");
25     else if (isdigit(charIn))
26        printf("You entered a digit.\n");
27     else if (ispunct(charIn))
28        printf("You entered a punctuation character.\n");
29     else if (isspace(charIn))
30        printf("You entered a whitespace character.\n");
31     else
32        printf("You entered a control character.\n");
33  return 0;
34  } // main
```

Output
```
Enter a character to be examined: a

You entered a lowercase letter.
```

Note the use of the else ... if in this program. While it may not appear so at first analysis, this is actually a range analysis problem, which makes it suitable for multiway selection.

Handling Major Errors

One of the better known computer acronyms is GIGO—garbage in, garbage out. In writing programs, we must decide how to handle errors to prevent garbage from corrupting the data. Sometimes, as we will see later in this text, we can recover from the error by having the user re-enter it. Other times, there is no way to recover.

When we can't recover, C provides two functions that allow us to terminate the functions: exit and abort. Both functions are found in the standard library (stdlib.h).

exit

Whereas return terminate
cuted. While we use it to terr
this reason, the termination
The exit prototype statemen

```
void exit (int terr
```

There is one parameter to th
acceptable, it is usually a nc
exit function later in this cl

abort

The abort function is used
the output streams are not fl
go directly to jail, you do no
goes to the operating system

The abort function has no p

```
void abort (void);
```

Programming
Development

In previous chapters, we intr
continue the discussion by a

Calculator Design

Although it is an elementary e
municate with a user through
demonstrates incremental dev

Calculator Incremen

Good structured programming
things: (1) We must ask the us
the calculation, and finally (4)
calc calls one of four function

Program 5-11 Menu-driven calculator—first increment *(continued)*

```
39      printf("\n\t* 1. ADD                    *");
40      printf("\n\t* 2. SUBTRACT               *");
41      printf("\n\t* 3. MULTIPLY               *");
42      printf("\n\t* 4. DIVIDE                 *");
43      printf("\n\t*                           *");
44      printf("\n\t*****************************");
45
46      printf("\nPlease type your choice ");
47      printf("and key return: ");
48      scanf ("%d", &option);
49      printf("**You selected option %d\n", option);
50      return option;
51 } // getOption
```

```
Output
*********************************

*    MENU                        *

*                                *

*    1. ADD                      *

*    2. SUBTRACT                 *

*    3. MULTIPLY                 *

*    4. DIVIDE                   *

*                                *

*********************************

Please type your choice and key return: 3

**You selected option 3

**You selected option 3
```

We use the same approach that we used previously. In main we call the get option function. Just before returning, we print the option and then we re-print it in main so that we can easily verify the results.

We incorporate one new style. Because it can be difficult to find the debugging statements in a large function, we do not indent them in the function. Rather we leave them flush to the left margin so that they are easy to find and remove and we continue the incremental development.

Second Increment: getData

Following the structure chart, we next write and debug getData. Because we wrote and debugged the getData function previously, we do not need to include it here. We simply copy it into our new program.

Third Increment: Calculate

The third function is calculate (`calc`). This is the first example of a subfunction that calls other subfunctions: `add`, `subtract`, `multiply`, and `divide`. In this case, we write the complete function except for the subfunction calls.

The design for the calculate function requires a `switch` statement to select the correct subfunction. In place of the actual calls, we return dummy values: 1.0 for add, 2.0 for subtract, 3.0 for multiply, and 4.0 for divide. You should recognize these as the option numbers. When testing a program, use test data that is easy to remember and that can be easily verified. The code is shown in **Program 5-12**.

Program 5-12 | Menu-driven calculator—third increment

```
1   /* This program uses a menu to allow the user to add,
2       multiply, subtract, or divide two integers.
3       Written by:
4       Date:
5   */
6   #include <stdio.h>
7   #include <stdlib.h>
8
9   // Function Declarations
10  int getOption (void);
11  void getData (int* num1, int* num2);
12  float calc  (int option, int num1, int num2);
13
14  int main (void)
15  {
16  // Local Declarations
17      int option;
18      int num1;
19      int num2;
20      float result;
21
22  // Statements
23      option = getOption();
24      getData (&num1, &num2);
25      result = calc  ( option, num1, num2);
26      printf("**In main result is: %6.2f", result);
27
28      return 0;
29  } // main
30
31  /*  -------------------- getOption --------------------
```

(continue)

Program 5-12 Menu-driven calculator—third increment *(continued)*

```
32      This function shows a menu and reads the user option.
33      Pre     Nothing
34      Post    returns the option
35  */
36  int getOption (void)
37  {
38  // Local Declarations
39     int option;
40
41  // Statements
42     printf("\t*********************************");
43     printf("\n\t*      MENU                    *");
44     printf("\n\t*                              *");
45     printf("\n\t* 1. ADD                       *");
46     printf("\n\t* 2. SUBTRACT                  *");
47     printf("\n\t* 3. MULTIPLY                  *");
48     printf("\n\t* 4. DIVIDE                    *");
49     printf("\n\t*                              *");
50     printf("\n\t*********************************");
51
52     printf("\nPlease type your choice ");
53     printf("and key return: ");
54     scanf ("%d", &option);
55     return option;
56  } // getOption
57
58  /* ================ getData ================
59     This function reads two integers from the keyboard.
60     Pre Parameters a and b are addresses
61     Post Data read into parameter addresses
62  */
63  void getData (int* a, int* b)
64  {
65     printf("Please enter two integer numbers: ");
66     scanf("%d %d", a, b);
67     return;
68  } // getData
69
70  /* ================ calc ================
71     This function determines the type of operation
72     and calls a function to perform it.
```

(continue)

Program 5-12   Menu-driven calculator—third increment *(continued)*

```
73     Pre option contains the operation
74     num1 & num2 contains data
75     Post returns the results
76  */
77  float calc (int option, int num1, int num2)
78  {
79  // Local Declarations
80     float result;
81
82  // Statements
83     printf("**In calc input is: %d %d %d\n",
84             option, num1, num2);
85     switch(option)
86     {
87       case 1: result = 1.0;    // Add
88               break;
89       case 2: result =2.0;     // Subtract
90               break;
91       case 3: result =3.0;     // Multiply
92               break;
93       case 4: if (num2 ==0.0)  // Divide
94               {
95                   printf("\n\a\aError: ");
96                   printf("division by zero ***\n");
97                   exit (100);
98               } // if
99               else
100                  result = 4.0;
101              break;
102        /* Better structured programming would validate
103           option in getOption. However, we have not
104           yet learned the technique to code it there.
105        */
106       default: printf("\aOption not available\n");
107                exit (101);
108     } // switch
109     printf("**In calc result is: %6.2f\n", result);
110     return result;
111  } // calc
```

(continue)

Program 5-13   Menu-driven calculator—fifth increment *(continued)*

```
41   // Local Declarations
42      int option;
43
44   // Statements
45      printf("\n\t*********************************");
46      printf("\n\t*     MENU                    *");
47      printf("\n\t*                             *");
48      printf("\n\t* 1. ADD                      *");
49      printf("\n\t* 2. SUBTRACT                 *");
50      printf("\n\t* 3. MULTIPLY                 *");
51      printf("\n\t* 4. DIVIDE                   *");
52      printf("\n\t*                             *" );
53      printf("\n\t*********************************");
54
55      printf("\nPlease type your choice ");
56      printf("and key return: ");
57      scanf ("%d", &option);
58      return option;
59   } // getOption
60
61   /* ================ getData ================
62      This function reads two integers from the keyboard.
63      Pre Parameters a and b are addresses
64      Post Data read into parameter addresses
65   */
66   void getData (int* a, int* b)
67   {
68      printf("Please enter two integer numbers: ");
69      scanf("%d %d", a, b);
70      return;
71   } // getData
72
73   /* ================ calc ================
74      This function determines the type of operation
75      and calls a function to perform it.
76      Pre option contains the operation
77      num1 & num2 contains data
78      Post returns the results
79   */
80   float calc (int option, int num1, int num2)
81   {
```

(continue)

Program 5-13 Menu-driven calculator—fifth increment *(continued)*

```
82  // Local Declarations
83     float result;
84
85  // Statements
86     switch(option)
87     {
88        case 1: result = add  ( num1,  num2);
89
90              break;
91        case 2: result = sub  ( num1,  num2);
92              break;
93        case 3: result =3.0;     // Multiply
94              break;
95        case 4: if (num2 ==0.0)   // Divide
96              {
97                  printf("\n\a\aError: ");
98                  printf("division by zero ***\n");
99                  exit (100);
100             } // if
101             else
102                 result = 4.0;
103                 break;
104     /* Better structured programming would validate
105        option in getOption. However, we have not
106        yet learned the technique to code it there.
107     */
108     default: printf("\aOption not available\n");
109              exit (101);
110     } // switch
111     printf("**In calc result is: %6.2f\n", result);
112     return result;
113 } // calc
114
115 /* ================= add =================
116    This function adds two numbers and returns the sum.
117    Pre a and b contain values to be added
118    Post Returns a + b
119 */
120 float add (int a, int b)
121 {
122 // Local Definitions
123    float sum;
```

(continue)

Program 5-13 Menu-driven calculator—fifth increment *(continued)*

```
124
125 // Statements
126     sum = a + b;
127     return sum;
128 } // add
129
130 /* ================sub ================
131     This function subtracts two numbers
132     Pre a and b contain values to be subtracted
133     Post Returns a + b
134 */
135 float sub (int a, int b)
136 {
137
138 // Local Definitions
139     float dif;
140
141 // Statements
142     dif = a - b;
143     printf("**In sub result is: %6.2f\n", dif);
144     return dif;
145 } // sub
```

Output

```
************************************
*      MENU                        *
*                                  *
* 1. ADD                           *
* 2. SUBTRACT                      *
* 3. MULTIPLY                      *
* 4. DIVIDE                        *
*                                  *
************************************
Please type your choice and key return: 2
Please enter two integer numbers: 13 8
**In sub result is:    5.00
**In calc result is:    5.00
**In main result is:    5.00
```

Note how we display the results up the program to `main`. This verifies that the upward communication is correct. If there should be a problem, we will know exactly where it occurred.

Remaining Increments

At this point, we have demonstrated the incremental development concepts for programs using multiple levels of subprograms. To complete the program, we must write and debug the final three increments:

> **Increment 6:** multiply

> **Increment 7:** divide

> **Increment 8:** print results

We leave the completion of the program for you as a problem at the end of the chapter.

Software Engineering

Several statements in the C language control other statements that follow them. The `if...else` is the first of these statements that we have seen. Whenever one statement controls or influences statements that follow it, good structured programming style indents the dependent statement (or statements) to show that the indented code is dependent on the controlling statement. The compiler does not need the indentation—it follows its syntactical rules regardless of how a program is formatted—but good style makes for readable programs.

To illustrate the point, consider the two versions of the code for the function in **Program 5-14**. They both accomplish the same task. To make this exercise even more meaningful, cover up the right half of the program and predict the results that will be produced when the ill-formed code executes. Then look at the well-structured code.

Program 5-14 | Examples of poor and good nesting styles

```
              Poor Style                          Good Style
1     int someFun (int a, int b)        int someFun (int a, int b)
2     {                                 {
3     int x;                            int x;
4
5         if (a < b)                        if (a < b)
6             x = a;                         x = a;
7         else
8             x = b;                             x = b;
9         x *= .5f;                          x *= .5f;
10        return x;                          return x;
11    } // someFun                       } // someFun
```

Assume that in this example, a has a value of 10 and b has a value of 20. What value will be returned? First, look at statement 6. The assignment of x in this example is dependent on the if in statement 5. Because statement 6 is not indented, however, it is difficult to see the dependency. Because the value of a (10) is less than the value of b (20), x will be assigned the value 10.

Now examine statement 9. It is indented and therefore appears to be dependent on the else statement. But is it? The answer is no. It just looks that way and is therefore misleading. Statement 9 will therefore execute regardless of the expression in the if statement. This relationship is much more clearly seen in the well-styled code on the right. The code on the right is properly indented to show the relationships among the statements, and therefore the chance of misreading the code is minimal.

Pay attention to the following rules when deciding how to indent lines of code:

1. Indent statements that are dependent on previous statements. The indentations are at least three spaces from the left end of the controlling statement.

2. Align else statements with their corresponding if statements. (See Figure 5-12.)

3. Place the opening brace identifying a body of code on a separate line. Indent the statements in the body of the code one space to the right of the opening brace.

4. Align the closing brace identifying a body of code with the opening brace, and place the closing brace on a separate line. Use a comment to identify the block being terminated.

5. Align all code on the same level, which is dependent on the same control statement.

6. Further indent nested statements according to the above rules.

7. Surround operators with whitespace.

8. Code only one definition or statement on a single line.

9. Make your comments meaningful at the block level. Comments should not simply parrot the code.

Negative Logic

The term **negative logic** refers to any expression that begins with not or that contains multiple not expressions within. Like the proverbial double-negative in the English language, interpreting negative logic can be difficult. We therefore try to avoid it.

In the discussion of Figure 5-11 and in the section on simplifying the if statement, one technique that we proposed was complementing a conditional statement. This requires making a positive statement negative and a negative statement positive. This can be done by following Rule 6 in Table 5-4, "Syntactical rules for if … else statements," which states that the positions of the statements in an if … else can be swapped if the original control expression is complemented. The concept of complementing the if statement was shown in Figure 5-9, "Complemented if … else statements."

Remember, however, that simple code is the clearest code. This concept has been formulated into the KISS acronym (Keep It Simple and Short). Unfortunately, negative logic is not always simple. In fact, it can get extremely confusing. It is highly recommended to avoid compound negative statements. We have seen professional programmers work for hours trying to debug negative logic.

When you complement an expression, make sure that the resulting statement is readable. Complementing an expression can be more difficult than simply making the condition negative. Examine the third statement in **Table 5-10** carefully. Note that the complement of the *not* (!) is *not-not* (!!), which in effect cancels the *not*. In general, you should avoid compound negative statements. In this case, therefore, the complemented statement is greatly preferred.

Table 5-10 Complementing expressions

ORIGINAL STATEMENT	COMPLEMENTED STATEMENT
if (x <= 0)	if (x > 0)
if (x != 5)	if (x == 5)
if (!(x <= 0 || !flag))	if (x > 0 && flag)

Rules for Selection Statements

For selection statements, you need to consider three other rules. Because these rules are sometimes conflicting, they are listed here in order of importance.

1. Code positive statements whenever possible.
2. Code the normal/expected condition first.
3. Code the most probable conditions first.

Human engineering studies have shown that people make fewer errors when reading positive statements than when reading negative statements. This is especially true when complex, compound Boolean statements are involved. Therefore, the first rule is, whenever possible, code your selection statements using positive conditions.

The second rule concerns the human expectations about what will follow. People have a tendency to anticipate things. They will, therefore, be less confused if what follows is what they expect. In most cases, this means coding the anticipated condition first.

Finally, the third rule concerns the efficiency of the resulting program. Coding the most probable conditions first is especially important in a multiway selection, such as the else ... if. When you code the most probable test first, then the program can skip the rest of the statements. Obviously, the more statements skipped, the more efficient the resulting program.

As we mentioned previously, these rules often conflict with each other. We have listed them in their order of importance from a human engineering point of view. Unless there are overriding circumstances, you should select the higher option (Rule 1 before Rule 2 before Rule 3) in case of conflicts. But remember the overriding principle: KISS—Keep It Simple and Short.

Selection in Structure Charts

At this point you understand the basic concepts of structure charts. In this section we extend the discussion to selection in structure charts. **Figure 5-26** shows two symbols for a function that is called by a selection statement, the condition and the exclusive *or*.

Figure 5-26 Structure chart symbols for selection

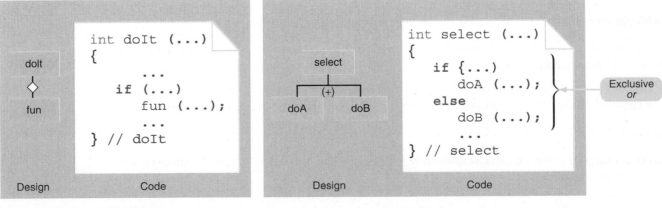

(a) Conditional

(b) Exclusive *or*

In Figure 5-26(a), the function doIt contains a conditional call to a subfunction, fun. If the condition in the if statement is true, we call doIt. If it is not true, we skip doIt. This situation is represented in a structure chart as a small diamond on the vertical line between the two function blocks.

Figure 5-26(b) represents the selection between two different functions. In this example, the function select chooses between doA and doB. One and only one of them will be called each time the conditional statement is executed. This is known as an exclusive *or*. One of the two alternatives is executed to the exclusion of the other. The exclusive or is represented by a plus sign between the processes.

Now consider the design found when a series of functions can be called exclusively. This occurs when a multiway selection contains calls to several different functions. **Figure 5-27** contains an example of a switch statement that calls different functions based on color.

Figure 5-27 Multiway selection in a structure chart

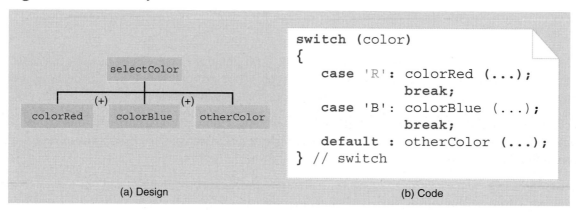

```
switch (color)
{
    case 'R': colorRed (...);
            break;
    case 'B': colorBlue (...);
            break;
    default : otherColor (...);
} // switch
```

(a) Design   (b) Code

The structure charts in this section adhere to the following rules:

1. Conditional calls are indicated by a diamond above the called function rectangle.

2. Exclusive or calls are indicated by a (+) between functions.

Tips and Common Programming Errors

1. The complement of < is >=, and the complement of > is <=.

2. Dangling else statements are easily created and difficult to debug. One technique for avoiding dangling *else* statements is to use braces, even when they are not needed.

3. The expression in the control expression in the if ... else statement may have a side effect, as follows:

   ```
   if (a++)
   ```

4. Encapsulate the statements inside braces if you have more than one statement after if or else in an if ... else statement.

5. Do not use the equal operator with a floating-point number. Floating-point numbers are seldom exactly equal to a required value. When you need to test for equality, such as a == b, use this expression:

   ```
   if (fabs (a - b) < .0000001)
   ```

6. Do not forget to use a break statement when the cases in a switch statement are exclusive.

7. While not necessarily an error, it is poor programming practice to write a `switch` statement without a `default` label. If the logic doesn't require one, code it with an error message to guard against unanticipated conditions. This is shown below.

```
default: printf("\aImpossible default\n");

exit (100);
```

8. The most common C error is using the assignment operator (=) in place of the equal operator (==). One way to minimize this error is to get in the habit of using the term "assignment operator" when reading the code. For example, say "a is assigned b," not "a equals b."

9. It may be an error to place a semicolon after the `if` expression.
   a. The semicolon terminates the `if` statement, and any statement that follows it is not part of the `if`.
   b. It is a compile error to code an `else` without a matching `if`. This error is most likely created by a misplaced semicolon.

```
if (a == b); // if terminated here
    printf (...);
else // No matching if
    printf (...);
```

10. It is a compile error to forget the parentheses in the `if` expression.

11. It is a compile error to put a space between the following relational operators: `==`, `! =`, `>=`, `<=`. It is also a compile error to reverse them.

12. It is a compile error to use a variable rather than an integral constant as the value in a `case` label.

13. It is a compile error to use the same constant in two `case` labels.

14. The logical operators require two ampersands (`&&`) or two bars (`| |`). It is a logic error to code them with only one. (Single operators are bitwise operators and are, therefore, valid code.)

15. It is generally a logic error to use side effects in the second operand in a logical binary expression, as shown in the following, because the second operand may not be evaluated.

```
(a++ && --b)
```

Summary

> Data are called logical if they convey the idea of true or false.

> C99 implements the logical type, `bool`. It also supports integer logical data: if a data item is nonzero, it is considered true; if it is zero, it is considered false.

> C has three operators for combining logical values to create new values: *not, and,* and *or.*

> Six comparative operators are used in C: `<`, `<=`, `>`, `>=`, `==`, and `!=`.

> Selection in C is done using two statements: `if ... else` and `switch`.

> The `if ... else` construct is used for selection between two alternatives.

> You can swap the statements in the true and false branches if you use the complement of an expression in an `if ... else` statement.

> If the false statement is not required in an `if ... else`, it is omitted and the keyword `else` dropped.

> If an `else` is dangling, it will be paired with the last unpaired `if`.

> Multiway selection can be coded using either the `switch` statement or an `else ... if` construct.

> The `switch` statement is used to make a decision between many alternatives when the different conditions can be expressed as integral values.

> The `else ... if` format is used to make multiple decisions when the item being tested is not an integral and therefore a `switch` statement cannot be used.

> A labeled statement is used for selection in a `switch` statement.

> A `default` label is used as the last label in a `switch` statement, to be executed when none of the `case` alternatives match the tested value.

> Indenting the controlled statements in C is good style that enhances the readability of a program.

> Selection is used in a structure chart only when it involves a call to another function.

> The structure chart for selection shows the paths taken by the logic flow. You cannot always tell by looking at the structure chart which selection will be used (two-way or multiway).

    a. A simple `if` is indicated by a diamond below the calling function.

    b. An `if ... else` and `switch` are indicated by the exclusive *or* (+).

Key Terms

`break` statement	dangling `else`	multiway selection statement
case label	`default` label	negative logic
classifying function	De Morgan's rule	nested `if` statement
complemented `if ... else`	dependent statement	selection statement
conditional expression	exclusive *or*	`switch` statement
converting functions	logical operators	two-way selection statement

Review Questions

1. Logical data are data that can be interpreted as true or false.
     a. True   **b.** False

2. The expression in a selection statement can have no side effects.
     a. True   **b.** False

3. Each labeled statement may identify one or more statements.
     a. True   **b.** False

4. The character classification functions are found in the standard library (`stdlib.h`).
     a. True
     b. False

5. To ensure that a character is uppercase, the `toupper` conversion function is used.
     a. True   **b.** False

6. The _____ logical operator is true only when both operands are true.
     a. and (`&&`)
     b. greater than (`>`)
     c. less than (`<`)
     d. or (`||`)
     e. not (`!`)

7. Which of the following is not a comparative operator in C?
     a. `<`   **c.** `=`   **e.** `>=`
     b. `<=`   **d.** `>`

8. Two-way selection is implemented with the
   _____ statement.
   a. `case`
   b. `else if`
   c. `switch`
   d. the `if ... else` and the `switch`
   e. `if ... else`

9. Which of the following is not a syntactical rule for
   the `if ... else` statement?
   a. Any expression can be used for the `if`
      expression.
   b. Only one statement is allowed for the true and
      the false actions.
   c. The true and the false statements can be
      another `if ... else` statement.
   d. The expression must be enclosed in parentheses.
   e. The selection expression cannot have a side effect.

10. Which of the following statements creates the
    "dangling `else` problem"?
    a. A nested `if` statement without a false
       statement
    b. A nested `if` statement without a true
       statement
    c. A `switch` statement without a default
    d. An `if` statement without a true or a false
       statement
    e. Any nested `if` statement

11. There are two different ways to implement a
    multiway selection in C. They are
    a. `if ... else` and `switch`.
    b. `else ... if` and `switch`.
    c. `if ... else` and `else ... if`.

d. `else ... if` and `case`.
e. `switch` and `case`.

12. Which of the following statements about `switch`
    statements is false?
    a. No two `case` labels can have the same value.
    b. The `switch` control expression must be an
       integral type.
    c. The `case`-labeled constant can be a constant or
       a variable.
    d. Two `case` labels can be associated with the
       same statement series.
    e. A `switch` statement can have at most one
       default statement.

13. Which of the following statements about the
    `else ... if` is false?
    a. Each expression in the `else ... if` must test
       the same variable.
    b. The `else ... if` is a coding style rather than a
       C construct.
    c. The `else ... if` requires integral values in its
       expression.
    d. The `else ... if` is used for multiway selections.
    e. The last test in the `else ... if` series concludes
       with a single `else`, which is the default
       condition.

14. Which of the following is not a character
    classification in the C language?
    a. Ascii
    b. Control
    c. Digit
    d. Graphical
    e. Space

Exercises

15. Evaluate the following expressions to true or false. Show how you arrived at your answer by first adding the default
    parentheses and then showing the value of each expression as it would be evaluated by C, one expression to a line.
    a. `! (3 + 3 >= 6)`
    b. `1 + 6 == 7 || 3 + 2 == 1`
    c. `1 > 5 || 6 < 50 && 2 < 5`
    d. `14 != 55 && 1(13 < 29) | | 31 > 52`
    e. `6 < 7 > 5`

16. If x = 0, y = 5, z = 5, what is the value of x, y, and z for each of the following code fragments? (Assume that x,
    y, and z are their original values for each fragment.)
    a. ```
       if (z != 0)
           y = 295;
       else
           x = 10;
       ```
       ```

b.
```
if (y + z > 10)
    y = 99;
z = 8;
x = ++z;
```
c.
```
if (x == 0)
{
    x = x - 3;
    z = z + 3;
}
else
    y = 99;
```

17. If x = 3, y = 0, and z = −4, what is the value of the following expressions?

    a. `x && y || zx || y && z`

    b. `(x && y) || z`

    c. `(x || y) && z`

    d. `(x && z) || y`

18. Simplify the following expressions by removing the ! operator and the parentheses:

    a. `! (x < y)`

    b. `! (x >= y)`

    c. `!(x == y)`

    d. `!(x != y)`

    e. `!(<(x > y))`

19. If x = −2, y = 5, z = 0, and t = −4, what is the value of each of the following expressions?

    a. `x + y < z + t`

    b. `x-2*y + y < z*2/3`

    c. `3 * y / 4 % 5 && y`

    d. `t || z < (y + 5) && y`

    e. `!(4 + 5 *y>=z - 4) && (z-2)`

20. If originally x = 4, y = 0, and z = 2, what is the value of x, y, and z after executing the following code?

```
if (x != 0)
    y = 3;
else
    z = 2;
```

21. If originally x = 4, y = 0, and z = 2, what is the value of x, y, and z after executing the following code?

```
if (z == 2)
    y = 1;
else
    x = 3;
```

22. If originally x = 4, y = 0, and z = 2, what is the value of x, y, and z after executing the following code?

```
if (x && y)
    x = 3;
else
    y = 2;
```

23. If originally x = 4, y = 0, and z = 2, what is the value of x, y, and z after executing the following code?

```
if (x || y || z)
    y = 1;
else
    z = 3;
```

24. If originally x = 0, y = 0, and z = 1, what is the value of x, y, and z after executing the following code?

```
if (x)
    if (y)
    z = 3;
else
    z = 2;
```

25. If originally x = 4, y = 0, and z = 2, what is the value of x, y, and z after executing the following code?

```
if (z == 0 || x && !y)
    if (!z)
    y = 1;
else
    x = 2;
```

26. If originally x = 0, y = 0, and z = 1, what is the value of x, y, and z after executing the following code?

```
if (x)
    if (y)
        if (z)
            z = 3;
        else
            z = 2;
```

27. If originally x = 0, y = 0, and z = 1, what is the value of x, y, and z after executing the following code?

```
if (z < x || y >= z && z == 1)
    if (z && y)
        y = 1;
else
    x = 1;
```

28. If originally x = 0, y = 0, and z = 1, what is the value of x, y, and z after executing the following code?

```
if (z = y )
    {
        y++;
        z--;
    }
else
    --x;
```

29. If originally x = 0, y = 0, and z = 1, what is the value of x, y, and z after executing the following code?

```
if (z = x < y)
    {
        x += 3;
        y -= 1;
    }
else
    x = y++;
```

30. If originally x = 0, y = 0, and z = 1, what is the value of x, y, and z after executing the following code?

```
switch (x)
    {
case 0 : x = 2;
    y = 3;
case 1 : x = 4;
default : y = 3;
    x = 1;
}
```

31. If originally x = 2, y = 1, and z = 1, what is the value of x, y, and z after executing the following code?

```
switch ( x )
{
    case 0 : x = 2;
        y = 3;
    case 1 : x = 4;
            break;
    default: y = 3;
            x = 1;
}
```

32. If originally x = 1, y = 3, and z = 0, what is the value of x, y, and z after executing the following code?

```
switch ( x )
{
    case 0 : x = 2;
        y = 3;
            break;
    case 1 : x = 4;
            break;
    default: y = 3;
            x = 1;
}
```

33. Evaluate the value of the following expressions:

    a. `tolower ('c')`

    b. `tolower ('?')`

    c. `tolower ('c')`

    d. `tolower ('5')`

34. Evaluate the value of the following expressions:

    a. `toupper ('c')`

    b. `toupper ('c')`

    c. `toupper ('?')`

    d. `toupper ('7')`

Programs

35. Write an `if` statement that will assign the value 1 to the variable best if the integer variable score is 90 or greater.

36. Repeat Problem 35 using a conditional expression.

37. Write the code to add 4 to an integer variable, num, if a float variable, amount, is greater than 5.4.

38. Print the value of the integer num if the variable `flag` is true.

39. Write the code to print either zero or not zero based on the integer variable num.

40. If the variable `divisor` is not zero, divide the variable `dividend` by `divisor`, and store the result in `quotient`. If `divisor` is zero, assign it to `quotient`. Then print all three variables. Assume that `dividend` and `divisor` are integers and `quotient` is a double.

41. If the variable `flag` is true, read the integer variables a and b. Then calculate and print the sum and average of both inputs.

42. Rewrite the following code using one `if` statement:

```
if (aChar == 'E')
    c++;
if (aChar == 'E')
    printf ("Value is E\n");
```

43. Rewrite the following code fragment using one `switch` statement:

```
if (ch == 'E' | ch == 'e')
    countE++;
else if (ch == 'A' || ch == 'a')
    countA++
else if (ch == 'I' || ch == 'I')
    countI++;
else
    print ("Error—Not A, E, or I\a\n");
```

44. Write a code fragment that tests the value of an integer num1. If the value is 10, square num1. If it is 9, read a new value into num1. If it is 2 or 3, multiply num1 by 99 and print out the result. Implement your code using nested if statements, not a switch.

45. Rewrite Problem 44 using a switch statement.

46. Write a code fragment for the flowchart shown in **Figure 5-28**. Assume that the variables x and y are integers and z is a float-point number.

Figure 5-28 Flowchart for Problem 46

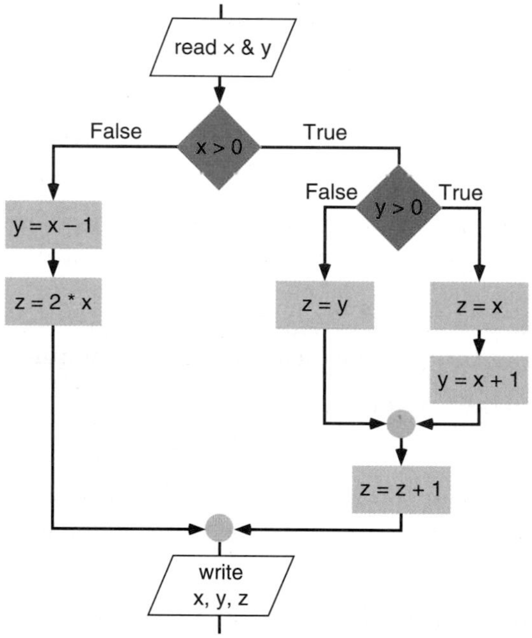

47. Write a function called smallest that, given three integers, returns the smallest value.

48. Write a function called day_of_week that, given an integer between 0 and 6, prints the corresponding day of the week. Assume that the first day of the week (0) is Sunday.

49. Write a function called month_of_year that, given an integer between 1 and 12, prints the corresponding month of the year.

50. Write a function called parkingCharge that, given the type of vehicle (c for car, b for bus, t for truck) and the hours a vehicle spent in the parking lot, returns the parking charge based on the following rates:

   car: $2 per hour

   bus: $3 per hour

   truck: $4 per hour

51. Write a function to find the smallest of four integers.

Projects

52. Complete the incremental implementation of Program 5-13. First write the code to implement the multiply function, then the divide function, and finally the print results function. The print results function should use a switch to determine which option was requested and then print the results in the following format:

   number **operator** number = result

53. Write a program that determines a student's grade. It reads three test scores (between 0 and 100) and calls a function that calculates and returns a student's grade based on the following rules:

   a. If the average score is 90% or more, the grade is A.

   b. If the average score is 70% or more and less than 90%, it checks the third score. If the third score is more than 90%, the grade is A; otherwise, the grade is B.

   c. If the average score is 50% or more and less than 70%, it checks the average of the second and third scores. If the average of the two is greater than 70%, the grade is C; otherwise, it is D.

   d. If the average score is less than 50%, then the grade is F.

   The program's `main` is to contain only `call` statements. At least three subfunctions are required: one to read scores, one to determine the grade, and one to print the results.

54. In Program 4-7, "Acme college fees," we wrote a program to calculate college fees. Modify this program for Typical College. At Typical College, the students pay a fee of $10 per unit for up to 12 units; after they have paid for 12 units, they have no additional per-unit fee. The registration fee remains $10 but is assessed only if courses are taken in the term.

55. Given a point, a line from the point forms an angle with the horizontal axis to the right of the line. The line is said to terminate in one of four quadrants based on its angle (α) from the horizontal, as shown in **Figure 5-29**.

Figure 5-29 Quadrants for Project 55

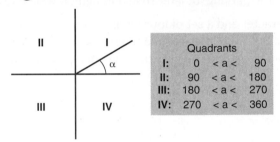

Write a program that determines the quadrant, given a user-input angle. Use a function to read and validate the angle. Note: If the angle is exactly 0°, it is not in a quadrant but lies on the positive X-axis; if it is exactly 90°, it lies on the positive Y-axis; if it is exactly 180°, it lies on the negative X-axis; and if it is exactly 270°, it lies on the negative Y-axis. Test your program with the following data:

0°, 48.3°, 90°, 179.8°, 180°, 186°, 270°, 300°, and 360°

56. How many values of the variable `num` must be used to completely test all branches of the following code fragment?

```
if (num > 0)
    if (value < 25)
    {
        value = 10 * num;
        if (num < 12)
            value = value / 10;
    }   // if value
    else
        value = 20 * num;
else
    value = 30 * num;
```

57. Write a program that asks the user to enter the current date and a person's birth date in the form month, day, year. The program then calculates the person's age in integral years. Use separate functions to enter the dates (pass by address), calculate the person's age, and print the results. Test your program with the following dates: 11/14/1990, 5/10/1995, and 1/5/2020.

58. Write a C program to calculate the parking fare for customers who park their cars in a parking lot when the following information is given:

   a. A character showing the type of vehicle: C for car, B for bus, T for truck.

   b. An integer between 0 and 24 showing the hour the vehicle entered the lot.

   c. An integer between 0 and 60 showing the minute the vehicle entered the lot.

   d. An integer between 0 and 24 showing the hour the vehicle left the lot.

   e. An integer between 0 and 60 showing the minute the vehicle left the lot.

This is a public lot. To encourage people to park for a short period of time, the management uses two different rates for each type of vehicle, as shown in **Table 5-11**.

Table 5-11   Rates for Project 58

VEHICLE	FIRST RATE	SECOND RATE
CAR	$0.00/hr first 3 hr	$1.50/hr after 3 hr
TRUCK	$1.00/hr first 2 hr	$2.30/hr after 2 hr
BUS	$2.00/hr for first hr	$3.70/hr after first hr

No vehicle is allowed to stay in the parking lot later than midnight; it will be towed away.

The input data consist of a character and a set of four integers representing the type of vehicle and the entering and leaving hours and minutes. But these pieces of data must be input into the computer in a user-friendly way. In other words, the computer must prompt the user to enter each piece of data as shown below. (Color indicates typical data.)

```
Type of vehicle? C
Hour vehicle entered lot        (0 - 24)? 14
Minute vehicle entered lot      (0 - 60)? 23
Hour vehicle left lot           (0 - 24)? 18
Minute vehicle left lot         (0 - 60)? 8
```

The output format is shown below.

```
                                PARKING LOT CHARGE
Type of vehicle: Car            or Bus or Truck
TIME-IN                         XX : XX
TIME-OUT                        XX : XX
PARKING TIME                    XX : XX
ROUNDED TOTAL                   XX
TOTAL CHARGE                    $XX.XX
```

This program must first calculate the actual time spent in the parking lot for each vehicle. This means using modulo arithmetic to handle time calculation. We can calculate this in many ways, one of which is shown below. To calculate the time spent in the parking lot, use the following algorithm:

   a. Compare the minute portion of the leaving and the entering time.

      If the first one is smaller than the second,

      • Add 60 to the minute portion of the leaving time.

      • Subtract 1 from the hour portion of the leaving time.

   b. Subtract the hour portions.

   c. Subtract the minute portions.

   d. Because there are no fractional hour charges, the program must also round the parking time up to the next hour before calculating the charge. The program should use the switch statement to distinguish between the different types of vehicles.

A well-structured program design is required. A typical solution will use several functions besides `main`. Before you start programming, prepare a structure chart. Run your program six times with the data shown in **Table 5-12**.

Table 5-12   Test data for Project 58

TEST	TYPE	HOUR IN	MINUTE IN	HOUR OUT	MINUTE OUT
1	C	12	40	14	22
2	B	8	20	8	40
3	T	2	0	3	59
4	C	12	40	16	22
5	B	8	20	14	20
6	T	2	0	12	0

59. This program is a simple guessing game. The computer is to generate a random number between 1 and 20. The user is given up to five tries to guess the exact number. After each guess, you are to tell the user if the guessed number is greater than, less than, or equal to the random number. If it is equal, no more guesses should be made. If the user hasn't guessed the number after five tries, display the number with a message that the user should know it by now and terminate the game.

A possible successful dialog:

```
I am thinking of a number between 1 and 20.
Can you guess what it is?            10
Your guess is low. Try again:        15
Your guess is low. Try again:        17
Your guess is high. Try again:       16
Congratulations! You did it.
```

A possible unsuccessful dialog:

```
I am thinking of a number between 1 and 20.
Can you guess what it is? 10
Your guess is low. Try again:               20
Your guess is high. Try again:              10
Your guess is low. Try again:               18
Your guess is high. Try again:              12
Sorry. The number was 15.
You should have gotten it by now.
Better luck next time.
```

Your design for this program should include a separate function to get the user's guess, a function to print the unsuccessful message, one to print the successful message, and one to print the sorry message.

60. Write a program that, given a person's birth date (or any other date in the Gregorian calendar), will display the day of the week the person was born.

To determine the day of the week, you will first need to calculate the day of the week for December 31 of the previous year. To calculate the day for December 31, use the following formula.

$$\left((year-1) \times 365 + \frac{[year-1]}{4} - \frac{[year-1]}{100} + \frac{[year-1]}{400} \right) \%7$$

The formula determines the day based on the values as shown below.

Day 0: Sunday

Day 1: Monday

Day 2: Tuesday

Day 3: Wednesday

Day 4: Thursday

Day 5: Friday

Day 6: Saturday

After you know the day for December 31, you simply calculate the days in the year before the month in question. Use a `switch` statement to make this calculation. (Hint: Use `case 12` first, and then fall into `case 11, 10 ... 2`.) If the desired month is 12, add the number of days for November (30). If it is 11, add the number of days for October (31). If it is 3, add the number of days for February (28). If it is 2, add the number of days for January (31). If you do not use a `break` between the months, the `switch` will add the days in each month before the current month.

To this figure, add the day in the current month and then add the result to the day code for December 31. This number modulo seven is the day of the week.

There is one more refinement. If the current year is a leap year, and if the desired date is after February, you need to add 1 to the day code. The following formula can be used to determine if the year is a leap year.

```
(!(year % 4) && (year % 100)) || !(year % 400)
```

Your program should have a function to get data from the user, another to calculate the day of the week, and a third to print the result.

To test your program, run it with the following dates:

a. February 28, 1900, and March 1, 1900

b. February 28, 1955, and March 1, 1955

c. February 28, 1996, and March 1, 1996

d. February 28, 2000, and March 1, 2000

e. December 31, 1996

f. The first and last dates of the current week.

61. Write a program that calculates the change due a customer by denomination; that is, how many pennies, nickels, dimes, etc. are needed in change. The input is to be the purchase price and the size of the bill tendered by the customer ($100, $50, $20, $10, $5, $1).

62. Write a menu-driven program that allows a user to enter five numbers and then choose between finding the smallest, largest, sum, or average. The menu and all the choices are to be functions. Use a `switch` statement to determine what action to take. Provide an error message if an invalid choice is entered.

Run the program five times, once with each option and once with an invalid option. Use the following set of data for each run:

16, 21, 7, 54, 9

63. Write a program that tests a user-entered character and displays its classification according to the ASCII classifications shown in Figure 5-24, "Classifications of the character type." Write the program starting at the top of the classification tree and display all classifications that the character belongs to. For instance, if the user enters a digit, you should display that it is printable, graphical, alphanumeric, and a digit.

64. Write a program to compute the real roots of a quadratic equation ($ax^2 + bx + c = 0$). The roots can be calculated using the following formulas:

$$x1 = \frac{-b + \sqrt{b^2 - 4ac}}{2a} \quad \text{and} \quad x2 = \frac{-b - \sqrt{b^2 - 4ac}}{2a}$$

Your program should prompt the user to enter the constants (a, b, c). It should then display the roots based on the following rules:

   a. If both a and b are zero, there is no solution.
   b. If a is zero, there is only one root (−c / b).
   c. If the discriminate ($b^2 − 4ac$) is negative, there are no real roots.
   d. For all other combinations, there are two roots.

   Test your program with the data in **Table 5-13**.

Table 5-13   Test data for Project 64

a	b	c
3	8	5
−6	7	8
0	9	−10
0	0	11

Repetition

Learning Objectives

When you complete this chapter, you will be able to:

6.1 Explain basic loop concepts

6.2 Describe pretest loops and posttest loops

6.3 Implement loop initialization and updating

6.4 Explain event- and counter-controlled loops

6.5 Write programs that use the `while`, `for`, or `do ... while` statements

6.6 Select the best loop construct for a given problem

6.7 Use `break`, `continue`, and `goto` statements in loops

6.8 Identify the four common applications for loops: summation, product, smallest or largest, and inquiries

6.1 Concept of a Loop

The real power of computers is in their ability to repeat an operation or a series of operations many times. This repetition, called looping, is one of the basic structured programming concepts. The concept of a loop is shown in the flowchart segment in **Figure 6-1**. In this flowchart, the action is repeated over and over again. It never stops.

Figure 6-1 Concept of a loop

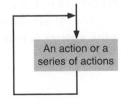

An action or a series of actions

Since the loop in Figure 6-1 never stops, it is the computer version of the perpetual motion machine. The action (or actions) will be repeated forever. We definitely do not want this to happen. We want our loop to end when the work is done. To make sure that it ends, we must have a condition that controls the loop. In other words, we must design the loop so that before or after each iteration, it checks to see if the task is done. If it is not done, the loop repeats one more time; if the task is done, the loop terminates. This test is known as a loop control expression.

6.2 Pretest and Posttest Loops

We have established that we need to test for the end of a loop, but where should we check it—before or after each iteration? Programming languages allow us to check the loop control expression either before *or* after each iteration of the loop. In other words, we can have either a pre- or a posttest terminating condition. In a pretest loop, the condition is checked before we start and at the beginning of each iteration. If the test condition is true, we execute the code; if the test condition is false, we terminate the loop.

The posttest loop always executes the action at least once. The loop control expression is then tested. If the expression is true, the loop repeats; if the expression is false, the loop terminates. The flowcharts in **Figure 6-2** show these two loop types.

Figure 6-2 Pretest and posttest loops

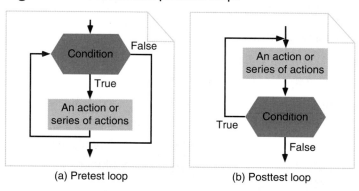

(a) Pretest loop   (b) Posttest loop

> **Note**
>
> **Pretest Loop:** In each iteration, the control expression is tested first. If it is true, the loop continues; otherwise, the loop is terminated.
>
> **Posttest Loop:** In each iteration, the loop action(s) are executed. Then the control expression is tested. If it is true, a new iteration is started; otherwise, the loop terminates.

To help you envision how looping works, imagine you are ready to start your daily exercises. Your exercise program requires you to do as many push-ups as possible. You can check your limit using either a pretest or a posttest condition. In the pretest strategy, you first check to see if you have enough energy to start. In the posttest strategy, you do one push-up and then you test to see if you have enough energy to do another one. Note that in both cases the question is phrased so that if the answer is true you continue the loop. The two strategies are shown in **Figure 6-3**.

Figure 6-3 Two strategies for doing exercises

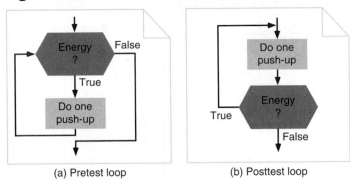

(a) Pretest loop   (b) Posttest loop

As you can see, in the first strategy, you may not do any push-ups. If you are tired when you start and don't have the energy for at least one push-up, you are done. In the second strategy, you must do at least one push-up. In other words, in a pretest loop, the action may be done zero, one, or more times; in a posttest loop, the action is done one or more times. This major difference between a pretest and a posttest loop, which you must clearly understand, is shown in **Figure 6-4**.

Figure 6-4 Minimum number of iterations in two loops

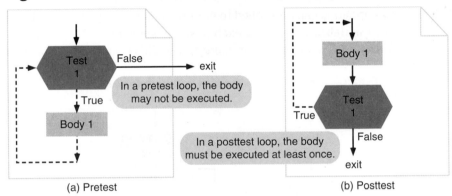

(a) Pretest   (b) Posttest

6.3 Initialization and Updating

In addition to the loop control expression, two other processes, initialization and updating, are associated with almost all loops.

Loop Initialization

Before a loop can start, some preparation is usually required. We call this preparation loop initialization. Initialization must be done before the first execution of the loop body. It sets the stage for the loop actions. **Figure 6-5** shows the initialization as a process box before the loop.

Initialization may be explicit or implicit. Explicit initialization is much more common. When the initialization is explicit, we include code to set the beginning values of key loop variables. Implicit initialization provides no direct initialization code; rather, it relies on a preexisting situation to control the loop.

Loop Update

How can the condition that controls the loop be true for a while and then change to false? The answer is that something must happen inside the body of the loop to change the condition. Otherwise, we would have an infinite loop, which is a loop that does not terminate. For example, in the loops shown in Figure 6-3, you gradually lose your energy until a point comes when you cannot continue the push-ups. This changes the resulting condition from true to false. The action that causes this change is known as a loop update. Updating is done in each iteration, usually as the last action. If the body of the loop is repeated *m* times, then the updating is also done *m* times.

Figure 6-5 Loop initialization and updating

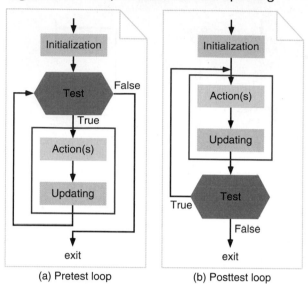

(a) Pretest loop (b) Posttest loop

The concepts of initialization and updating can be applied to our previous push-up example. In this case, initialization is created by nutrition, an implicit initialization. During each push-up, some of the initial energy is consumed in the process and your energy is reduced, which updates your energy level. This is shown in **Figure 6-6**.

Figure 6-6 Initialization and updating for exercise

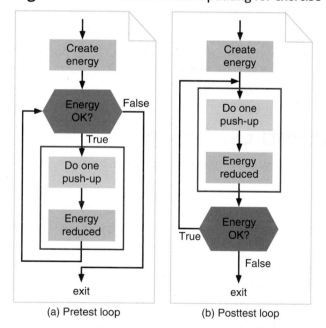

(a) Pretest loop (b) Posttest loop

6.4 Event- and Counter-Controlled Loops

All the possible expressions that can be used in a loop limit test can be summarized into two general categories: event-controlled loops and counter-controlled loops.

Event-Controlled Loops

In an event-controlled loop, an event changes the control expression from true to false. For example, when reading data, reaching the end of the data changes the expression from true to false. In event-controlled loops, the updating process can be explicit or implicit. If it is explicit, such as finding a specific piece of information, it is controlled by the loop. If it is implicit, such as the temperature of a batch of chemicals reaching a certain point, it is controlled by some external condition. The event-controlled loop is shown in **Figure 6-7**.

Figure 6-7   Event-controlled loop concept

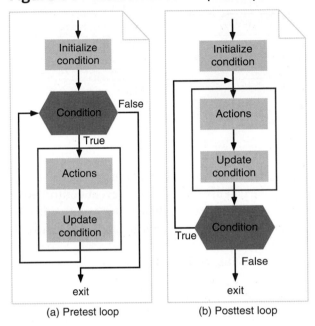

(a) Pretest loop   (b) Posttest loop

Counter-Controlled Loops

When we know the number of times an action is to be repeated, we use a counter-controlled loop. We must initialize, update, and test the counter. It can also be a variable or a calculated value. The update can be an increment, in which case we are counting up, or a decrement, in which case we are counting down. The counter-controlled loop is shown in **Figure 6-8**.

Figure 6-8   Counter-controlled loop concept

(a) Pretest loop   (b) Posttest loop

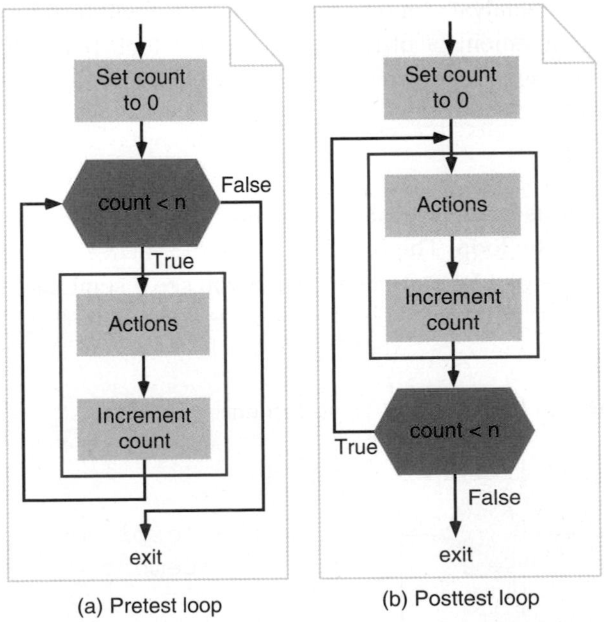

Loop Comparison

The number of iterations of a loop is given as n. In a pretest loop, when we come out of the loop, the limit test has been executed $n + 1$ times. In a posttest loop, when we come out of the loop, the limit test has been executed only n times. A summary of the two different loop concepts is shown in **Table 6-1**.

Table 6-1 Loop comparisons

PRETEST LOOP		POSTTEST LOOP	
Initialization:	1	Initialization:	1
Number of tests:	$n + 1$	Number of tests:	n
Action executed:	n	Action executed:	n
Updating executed:	n	Updating executed:	n
Minimum iterations:	0	Minimum iterations:	1

6.5 Loops in C

C has three loop statements: the `while` loop, the `for` loop, and the `do ... while` loop. The first two are pretest loops, and the `do ... while` is a posttest loop. We can use all of them for event-controlled and counter-controlled loops. The `while` loop and the `do ... while` loops are most commonly used for event-controlled loops, and the `for` loop is usually used for counter-controlled loops. These loop constructs are shown in **Figure 6-9**.

Figure 6-9 C loop constructs

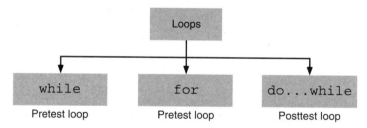

Note that all three of these loop constructs continue when the limit control test is true and terminate when it is false. This consistency of design makes it easy to write the limit test in C. On the other hand, general algorithms are usually written just the opposite because analysts tend to think about what will terminate the loop rather than what will continue it. Therefore, we must complement or otherwise modify the limit test when we write our program. This is one place where "De Morgan's Rule," discussed previously, is very handy.

The `while` Loop

The `while` loop is a pretest loop. It uses an expression to control the loop. Because it is a pretest loop, it tests the expression before every iteration of the loop. The basic syntax of the `while` statement is shown in **Figure 6-10**. No semicolon is needed at the end of the `while` statement. When you see a semicolon, it actually belongs to the statement within the `while` statement.

Figure 6-10 The `while` statement

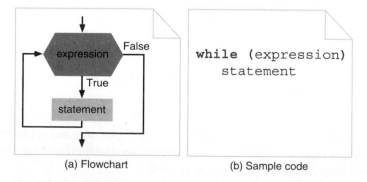

(a) Flowchart   (b) Sample code

Note that the sample code in Figure 6-10 shows that the loop body is a single statement; that is, the body of the loop must be one, and only one, statement. If we want to include multiple statements in the body, we must put them in a compound statement (block). This concept is shown in **Figure 6-11**.

Figure 6-11   Compound `while` statement

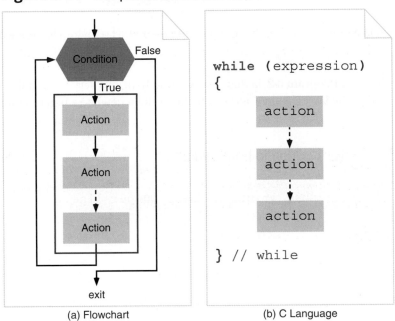

(a) Flowchart   (b) C Language

Process-Control Loops

Perhaps the simplest loop is the loop that never ends. While it is virtually never used in data processing, it is common in process-control loops such as network servers, environmental systems, and manufacturing systems. A simple process-control system that might be used to control the temperature in a building is shown in **Program 6-1**.

Program 6-1 | Process-control system example

```
1   while (true)
2   {
3       temp = getTemperature();
4       if (temp < 68)
5           turnOnHeater();
6       else if (temp > 78)
7           turnOnAirCond();
8       else
9       {
10          turnOffHeater();
11          turnOffAirCond();
12      } // else
13  } // while true
```

The limit test in this simple program is a literal constant. It cannot be changed. Therefore, no update is required. Because the limit test in the `while` statement is always true, it will never stop. We must emphasize, however, that this is not a good construct for anything other than a loop that truly never ends.

As an aside, what would be the effect in Program 6-1 if the following `while` statement were used?

```
while (0)
```

Because the limit condition is a constant false, the loop would never start. Obviously, this would be a logic error.

Print Loops

A common `while` loop is shown in **Program 6-2**. In this case we want to print a series of numbers in descending order. To keep from running off the end of the line, we have added a test to write a newline when ten numbers have been written.

Program 6-2 | A `while` loop to print numbers

```c
1   /* Simple while loop that prints numbers 10 per line.
2      Written by:
3      Date:
4   */
5   #include <stdio.h>
6
7   int main (void)
8   {
9   // Local Declarations
10     int num;
11     int lineCount;
12
13  // Statements
14     printf ("Enter an integer between 1 and 100: ");
15     scanf ("%d", &num);  // Initialization
16
17     // Test number
18     if (num > 100)
19        num = 100;
20
21     lineCount = 0;
22     while (num > 0)
23     {
24        if (lineCount < 10)
25           lineCount++;
26        else
27        {
28           printf("\n");
29           lineCount = 1;
30        } // else
31        printf("%4d", num--);  // num-- updates loop
```

(continue)

Program 6-2   A while loop to print numbers *(continued)*

```
32      } // while
33      return 0;
34 } // main
```

Output
```
Enter an integer between 1 and 100: 15

15   14   13   12   11   10   9    8    7    6

5    4    3    2    1
```

Find the basic elements of a loop in this program. First, look for loop initialization, then the limit test, and finally the update.

The initialization is done by asking the user to enter an integer in Statement 14, which is stored as num. Note how we make sure that the user enters a number that is not too large. If the number is over 100, we simply set it to 100, which is the maximum we told the user to enter. The limit test is in Statement 22. As long as num is greater than 0, we continue printing out the number series. The update is hidden in Statement 31; after printing num, we subtract 1 from it. Although this is a common C programmer trick, the program would have been easier to read if we had put the update (num--) on the line after the print. That way it would have been obvious.

File Loops

One of the most common loop applications in any language is reading data until all the data have been processed— that is, until the end of file is reached. In C, the scanf function returns the system constant EOF when it detects an end-of-file.

Consider this application of the scanf feature: suppose we want to read and process a list of numbers from the keyboard. We type all the numbers, each one on a separate line. At the end, we can type end-of-file (<ctrl+d> in UNIX or <ctrl+z> in DOS). This loop logic is shown in the next example.

```
ioResult = scanf ("%d", &a);
while (ioResult != EOF)
    {
    // Action: Process data

    ioResult = scanf ("%d", &a);
    } // while
```

But no one codes a while loop like this. Let's simplify it. In the revised version of the loop, we have moved the scanf to the conditional expression in the while statement itself. We can do this because the initialization and the update are identical. The initialization and updating are now both self-contained parts of the while statement. This change is as follows:

```
while ((ioResult = scanf ("%d", &a)) != EOF)
{
    // Process data
} // while
```

But we can simplify this loop even further. Because the scanf function returns a value, we can test for end-of-file in the while expression. We don't need the variable, ioResult, so we can simply use the function value and discard it after it has been checked. The result is the standard C loop for reading and processing data from a file shown in **Program 6-3**, which adds a list of integers read from the keyboard and displays their sum.

Program 6-3 | Adding a list of numbers

```
1   /* Add a list of integers from the standard input unit
2        Written by:
3        Date:
4   */
5   #include <stdio.h>
6   int main (void)
7   {
8   // Local Declarations
9        int x;
10       int sum = 0;
11
12  // Statements
13       printf("Enter your numbers: <EOF> to stop.\n");
14       while (scanf ("%d", &x) != EOF)
15          sum += x;
16       printf ("\nThe total is: %d\n", sum);
17       return 0;
18  } // main
```

Output
```
Enter your numbers: <EOF> to stop.

15

22

3^d

The total is: 40
```

Note that a compound statement (block) is not needed in the `while` loop, because the addition can be done in one statement. Another important point is that the statement to print the sum is outside the loop. Because the user can see the input values on the screen, all we need to show is the sum.

The `for` Loop

The `for` statement is a pretest loop that uses three expressions. The first expression contains any initialization statements, the second contains the limit-test expression, and the third contains the updating expression. **Figure 6-12** shows a flowchart, and an expanded interpretation, for a sample `for` statement.

Expression 1 is executed when the `for` loop starts. Expression 2 is the limit-test expression. As shown in the expanded flowchart, it is tested *before* every iteration. Remember that since the `for` is a pretest loop, the body is not executed if the limit condition is false at the start of the loop.

Finally, Expression 3 is the update expression. It is executed at the end of each loop. Note that the code in the `for` statement must be expressions. This means that you cannot use statements, such as `return`, in the `for` statement itself. Like the `while` statement, the `for` statement does not need a semicolon.

Figure 6-12   The `for` statement

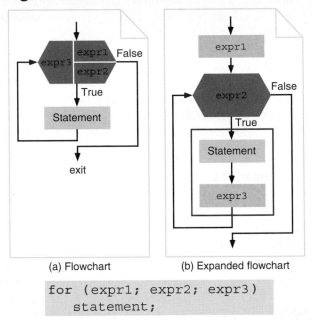

| (a) Flowchart | (b) Expanded flowchart |

```
for (expr1; expr2; expr3)
    statement;
```

C allows the limit test in Expression 2 to be a variable. It also allows us to change the value of the variable during the execution of the loop. We do not recommend changing it in the loop, however. It is not a good structured programming style and can lead to errors and perpetual loops.

The body of the `for` loop must be one, and only one, statement. If we want to include more than one statement in the body, we must code them in a compound statement. A `for` statement with a compound statement is shown in **Figure 6-13**.

Figure 6-13   Compound `for` statement

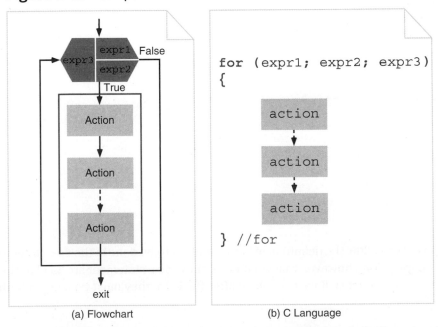

| (a) Flowchart | (b) C Language |

Unlike some languages, C allows the loop control expression to be controlled inside the `for` statement itself. This means that the updating of the limit condition can be done in the body of the `for` statement. In fact, Expression 3 can be null and the updating controlled entirely within the body of the loop. This is not a recommended structured programming coding technique, although it is required in some situations.

Although the `for` loop can be used anywhere a pretest loop is required, it is most naturally used for counter-controlled loops (see "Counter-Controlled Loops" in Section 6.4). Its self-contained design makes it ideal for count logic.

> | **Note** | A for loop is used when a loop is to be executed a known number of times. We can do the same thing with a while loop, but the for loop is easier to read and more natural for counting loops.

Let's compare the while and the for loops. **Figure 6-14** shows a graphical representation of each side by side. Note that the for loop contains the initialization, update code, and limit test in one statement. This makes for very readable code. All the control steps, initialization, end-of-loop test, and updating are done in one place. This is a variation of the structured programming concepts of encapsulation, in which all code for a process is placed in one module. Another way of looking at it is that a for loop communicates better and is more compact.

Figure 6-14 Comparing for and while loops

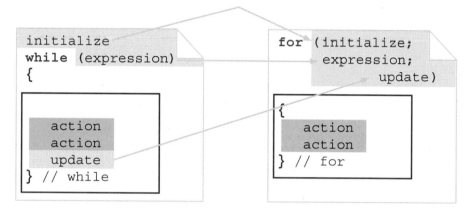

Now let's solve the same problem using both a while and a for loop. The following code contains a loop that reads 20 numbers from the keyboard and finds their sum. This can be done both in a while loop and a for loop. But as you can see, the for loop is more self-documenting.

```
i = 1;
sum = 0;       sum = 0;
while (i <= 20)
{
   for (i = 1; i <= 20; i++)
   {
      scanf("%d", &a);         scanf ("%d", &a);
      sum += a;          sum += a;
      i ++;
   } // for
} // while
```

C99 modified the for syntax to allow the definition of loop variables to be done in the for statement itself. This syntax is shown in the next example. Note, however, that definitions of the for statement are local to the loop body; they are not in scope when the loop terminates. If we need them after the loop, they must be defined in the local declarations section.

To demonstrate the for loop, let's write a program that asks the user for a number and then prints the series of numbers starting at one and continuing up to and including the user-entered number. The code is in **Program 6-4**.

Program 6-4 | Example of a `for` loop

```c
 1  /* Print number series from 1 to user-specified limit.
 2     Written by:
 3     Date:
 4  */
 5  #include <stdio.h>
 6  int main (void)
 7  {
 8  // Local Declarations
 9     int limit;
10
11  // Statements
12     printf ("Please enter the limit: ");
13     scanf ("%d", &limit);
14     for (int i = 1; i <= limit; i++)
15         printf("\t%d\n", i);
16     return 0;
17  } // main
```

Output
```
Please enter the limit: 3

    1

    2

    3
```

This simple program is the model for many looping functions. Let's look at three simple modifications to it. First, how would you print only odd numbers? This requires a change only to the update in the `for` statement.

```c
for (i = 1; i <= limit; i += 2)
```

Now let's change it to print the numbers backward. In this case, all the statements in the `for` statement must be changed, but the rest of the program is still unchanged.

```c
for (i = limit; i >= 1; i--)
```

For the final example, let's print the numbers in two columns, the odd numbers in the first column and the even numbers in the second column. We must modify the update statement in the `for` statement and also the print statement as follows.

```c
for (i = 1; i <= limit; i += 2)
    printf("\t%2d\t%2d\n", i, i + 1);
```

We have used tabs and width specifications to align the output in columns. Note that the second print value ($i + 1$) is an expression. It does *not* change the value of i. There is no side effect, it is just a value.

Nested `for` Loops

Any statement, even another `for` loop, can be included in the body of a `for` statement. Using nested loops can create some interesting applications. Let's look at a very simple one here. We will give other examples in Section 6.8 "Looping Applications," later in the chapter.

Program 6-5 uses a nested loop to print a series of numbers on multiple lines.

Program 6-5 | A simple nested `for` loop

```
1   /* Print numbers on a line.
2      Written by:
3      Date:
4   */
5   #include <stdio.h>
6
7   int main (void)
8   {
9   // Statements
10     for (int i = 1; i <= 3; i++)
11     {
12        printf("Row %d: ", i);
13        for (int j = 1; j<= 5; j++)
14           printf("%3d", j);
15        printf("\n");
16     } // for i
17     return 0;
18  } // main
```

Output
```
Row 1:    1  2  3  4  5

Row 2:    1  2  3  4  5

Row 3:    1  2  3  4  5
```

The `do ... while` Loop

The `do ... while` statement is a posttest loop. Like the `while` and `for` loops, it also uses an expression to control the loop, but it tests this expression *after* the execution of the body. The format of the `do ... while` statement is shown in **Figure 6-15**.

The body of the `do ... while` loop must be one, and only one, statement. If we need to include multiple statements in the body, we must put them in a compound statement. The second example in Figure 6-15 shows the logic flow and code for a `do ... while` statement that uses a compound statement. Look carefully at the code block in the second example. Note that the `do` and the `while` braces are aligned. Note also that the `while` expression follows the brace on the same line. This is a good style because it makes it easy for the reader to see the statement. Finally, note that the `do ... while` is concluded with a semicolon. This differs from the other looping constructs that we have seen.

Figure 6-15 `do ... while` statement

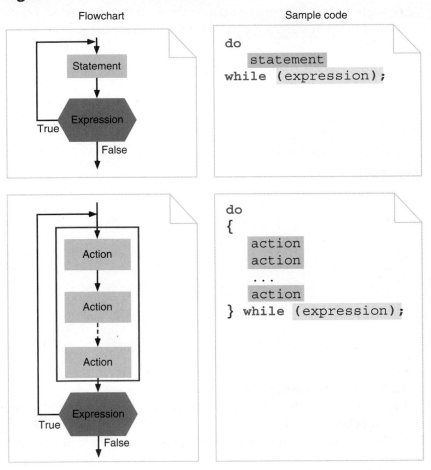

Let's look at a simple program that uses a loop to print five numbers. We code two loops, first a `while` loop and then a `do ... while`. Although one loop is a pretest and the other is a posttest, both print the same series. The code is seen in **Program 6-6**.

Program 6-6 | Two simple loops

```
1   /* Demonstrate while and do...while loops.
2      Written by:
3      Date:
4   */
5   #include <stdio.h>
6
7   int main (void)
8   {
9   // Local Declarations
10     int loopCount;
11
12  // Statements
13     loopCount = 5;
14     printf("while loop:     ");
```

(continue)

Program 6-6   Two simple loops *(continued)*

```
15      while (loopCount > 0)
16          printf ("%3d", loopCount--);
17      printf("\n\n");
18
19      loopCount = 5;
20      printf("do...while loop: ");
21      do
22          printf ("%3d", loopCount--);
23      while (loopCount > 0);
24      printf("\n");
25      return 0;
26 } // main
```

Output
```
while loop :        5  4  3  2  1

do...while loop:    5  4  3  2  1
```

Because the do ... while limit test isn't done until the end of the loop, we use it when we know that the body of the loop must be done at least once. To demonstrate the impact of the two loops, study the code in **Figure 6-16**. In the while loop, the message is not printed, because the limit condition is tested first. In the do ... while loop, even though the limit test is false, the message is printed because the message is printed before the limit test.

Figure 6-16   Pre- and posttest loops

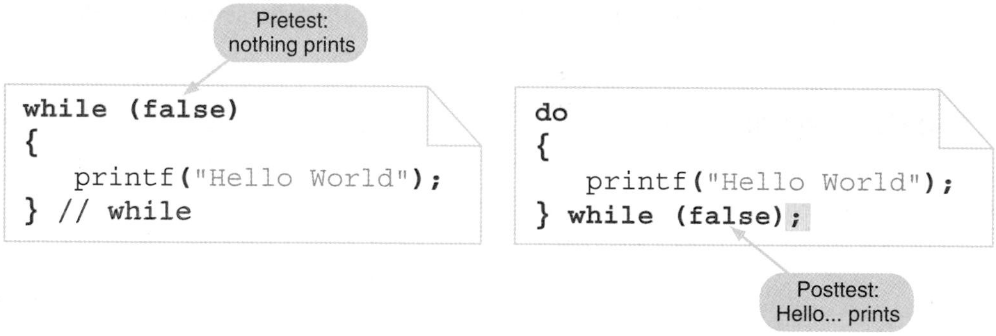

```
while (false)
{
    printf("Hello World");
} // while
```
Pretest: nothing prints

```
do
{
    printf("Hello World");
} while (false);
```
Posttest: Hello... prints

Programmers commonly use the do ... while loop in data validation to make a program robust. For example, consider an application that requires that we read an integer between 10 and 20. We can use the do ... while loop as shown in the next example.

```
do
{
    printf ("Enter a number between 10 & 20: ");
    scanf ("%d", &a);
} while (a < 10 || a > 20);
```

To demonstrate the do ... while, let's rewrite Program 6-3, "Adding a List of Numbers." The modified code is shown in **Program 6-7**.

Program 6-7   Adding a list with the do ... while

```c
 1   /* Add a list of integers from the standard input unit
 2         Written by:
 3         Date:
 4   */
 5   #include <stdio.h>
 6
 7   int main (void)
 8   {
 9   // Local Declarations
10       int x;
11       int sum =0;
12       int testEOF;
13
14   // Statements
15       printf("Enter your numbers: <EOF> to stop.\");
16       do
17       {
18          testEOF = scanf("%d", &x);
19          if (testEOF != EOF)
20             sum += x;
21       } while (testEOF != EOF);
22       printf ("\nTotal: %d\n", sum);
23       return 0;
24   } // main
```

Output

Run 1:

    Enter your numbers: <EOF> to stop.

    10 15 20 25 ^d

    Total: 70

Run 2:

    Enter your numbers: <EOF> to stop.

    ^d

    Total: 0

Because the do ... while always executes the body of the loop at least once, we had to make some changes. Compare Program 6-3 and Program 6-7 carefully. Note that the scanf is no longer in the loop limit test. Because the limit test is after the loop body, the scanf must be moved to the beginning of the loop. The result of the input is saved in a new variable, testEOF. Finally, before we can add the value we read to the accumulator, we must ensure we are not at the end of the file. The add statement is therefore guarded by an `if` statement. Although Program 6-7 is a little less efficient than Program 6-3, it does the same job.

The Comma Expression

A comma expression is a complex expression made up of two expressions separated by a comma. Although it can legally be used in many places, it is most often used in `for` statements. The expressions are evaluated left to right. The value and type of the expressions are the value and type of the right expression; the left expression is included only for its side effect. The comma operator has the lowest priority of all operators, priority 1.

The following statement is a modification of the `for` statement code shown in Program 6-7. It uses a comma expression to initialize the accumulator, sum, and the index, i, in the loop. In this example, the value of the comma expression is discarded. This is a common use of the comma operator.

```
for (sum = 0, i = 1; i <= 20;)
{
    scanf("%d", &a);
    sum += a;
} // for
```

Comma expressions can be nested. When they are nested, all expression values other than the last are discarded. **Figure 6-17** shows the format of a nested comma expression.

Figure 6-17   Nested comma expression

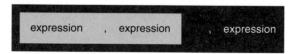

A final word of caution. Remember that the value of the expression is the value of the rightmost expression. Although it is not recommended, if you use a comma expression for the second expression in a `for` loop, make sure that the loop control is the last expression.

Let's use the comma expression to demonstrate the difference between the `while` and the `do … while`. As shown in Table 6-1, "Loop comparisons," the only difference is the number of limit tests that are made. Program 6-6 shows that the same job can be done by either loop. **Program 6-8** uses both loops to count from 1 to 10. It uses the comma expression to count the number of limit tests in each loop.

> ## Program 6-8 | Comparison of `while` and `do … while`

```
1   /* Demonstrate while and do...while loops.
2      Written by:
3      Date:
4   */
5   #include <stdio.h>
6
7   int main (void)
```

(continue)

Program 6-8   Comparison of while and do ... while *(continued)*

```
 8  {
 9  // Local Declarations
10     int loopCount;
11     int testCount;
12
13  // Statements
14     loopCount = 1;
15     testCount = 0;
16     printf("while loop:   ");
17     while (testCount++, loopCount <= 10)
18        printf("%3d", loopCount++);
19     printf("\nLoop Count:  %3d\n", loopCount);
20     printf("Number of tests: %3d\n", testCount);
21
22     loopCount = 1;
23     testCount = 0;
24     printf("\ndo...while loop: ");
25     do
26        printf("%3d", loopCount++);
27     while (testCount++, loopCount <= 10);
28
29     printf("\nLoop Count:  %3d\n", loopCount);
30     printf("Number of tests: %3d\n", testCount);
31     return 0;
32  } // main
```

```
Output
while loop:     1  2  3  4  5   6  7  8  9 10

Loop Count:    11

Number of tests:   11


do...while loop:    1  2  3  4  5  6  7  8  9 10

Loop Count:    11

Number of tests:   10
```

Look at statements 17 and 27 carefully. They both contain comma expressions. This technique of combining the counter and the limit test in one expression ensures that the count will be accurate. Because the value of the whole comma expression is the value of its last expression, however, the limit test must be coded last.

The results demonstrate that both loops count from one to ten. Because they are doing exactly the same job, we expect that the loop bodies would also execute the same number of times. As predicted in Table 6-1 the only difference is in the number of tests: the while loop control expression was evaluated 11 times; the do ... while control expression was evaluated only 10 times.

6.6 Loop Examples

This section contains several short examples of loop applications. Each program demonstrates one or more programming concepts that you will find helpful in solving other problems.

for Loop: Calculate Compound Interest

One classic loop problem is calculating the value of an investment. We want to know the value of an investment over time, given its initial value and annual interest rate. **Program 6-9** displays a compound interest table.

Program 6-9 | Compound interest

```
1   /* Print report showing value of investment.
2      Written by:
3      Date:
4   */
5   #include <stdio.h>
6
7   int main (void)
8   {
9   // Local Declarations
10     double presVal;
11     double futureVal;
12     double rate;
13     int years;
14     int looper;
15
16  // Statements
17     printf("Enter value of investment: ");
18     scanf ("%1f", &presVal);
19     printf("Enter rate of return (nn.n): ");
20     scanf ("%1f", &rate);
21     printf("Enter number of years:  ");
22     scanf ("%d", &years);
23
24     printf("\nYear    Value\n");
25     printf("====    ========\n");
26     for (futureVal = presVal, looper = 1;
27          looper <= years;
28          looper++)
29     {
30        futureVal = futureVal * (1 + rate/100.0);
31        printf("%3d%11.21f\n", looper, futureVal);
```

(continue)

Program 6-9 Compound interest *(continued)*

```
32     } // for
33     return 0;
34 } // main
```

Output
```
Enter value of investment: 10000

Enter rate of return (nn.n): 7.2

Enter number of years:  5


Year    Value

====    ========

  1     10720.00

  2     11491.84

  3     12319.25

  4     13206.24

  5     14157.09
```

This program uses a `for` loop to calculate the value of the investment at the end of each year. Each iteration adds the current year's interest to the investment and then prints its current value.

Note how we prompted the user for input, especially the decimal return rate. Things like percentage rates can be confusing to enter. Is 7.2% entered as 7.2 or .072? Make sure you give the user a sample of how the data should be entered.

Now study the way we created a caption for the reports, using equal signs to underscore the captions and spaces with width specifications to align the values in columns. This rather simple technique makes the results quite readable.

One final point. When defining multiple variables in one statement, they must all have the same type. Notice that we defined the `for` loop variables in the definition sections. To define multiple variables in a `for` statement, they must all be the same type because they are treated as a type list.

Nested `for` Loops: Print a Right Triangle

Let's write a program that will print a series of numbers in the form of a right triangle. We ask the user to enter a one-digit number. Each line, from the first to the limit entered by the user, then prints a number series from one to the current line number. For example, if a user enters 6, the program prints

```
1
12
123
1234
12345
123456
```

The flowchart and pseudocode for the loop are shown in **Figure 6-18**.

Figure 6-18 Print right triangle flowchart and pseudocode

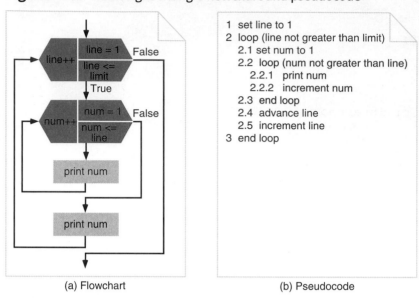

(a) Flowchart   (b) Pseudocode

The completed program is shown in **Program 6-10**.

Program 6-10 | Print right triangle using nested `for` loops

```
1   /* Print a number series from 1 to a user-specified limit
2      in the form of a right triangle.
3      Written by:
4      Date:
5   */
6   #include <stdio.h>
7
8   int main (void)
9   {
10  // Local Declarations
11  int limit;
12
13  // Statements
14  // Read limit
15     printf("\nPlease enter a number between 1 and 9: ");
16     scanf("%d", &limit);
17
18     for (int lineCtrl = 1; lineCtrl <= limit; lineCtrl++)
19     {
20        for (int numCtrl = 1;
21           numCtrl <= lineCtrl;
22           numCtrl++)
23           printf("%ld", numCtrl);
```

(continue)

Program 6-10   Print right triangle using nested `for` loops *(continued)*

```
24
25        printf("\n");
26    } // for lineCtrl
27    return 0;
28 } // main
```

Output
```
Please enter a number between 1 and 9: 6

1

12

123

1234

12345

123456
```

Program 6-10 demonstrates the concept of a loop within a loop. Note how we use two `for` loops to print the triangle. The first or outer `for` controls how many lines we will print. The second or inner `for` writes the number series on one line. This use of nested loops is a very important programming concept.

Also note the name we used in the loops. Often programmers will use `i` and `j` to control `for` loops. But notice how much more readable the code is when meaningful names are used. When we use `lineCtrl` rather than `i` in the outer loop, we know that the `for` is controlling the number of lines we are printing. Likewise, the name `numCtrl` clearly tells the reader that the `for` loop is controlling the numbers.

Nested `for` Loops: Print a Rectangle

Now let's write a program that prints the triangle pattern in the previous example, but now filled out with asterisks to form a rectangle. For example, if a user enters 6, **Program 6-11** prints the rectangle shown in the results.

Program 6-11 | Print number series using user-specified limit

```
1  /* Print number series from 1 to a user-specified limit
2     in the form of a rectangle.
3     Written by:
4     Date:
5  */
6  #include <stdio.h>
7
8  int main (void)
9  {
```

(continue)

Program 6-11   Print number series using user-specified limit *(continued)*

```
10 // Local Declarations
11 int limit;
12
13 //Statements
14 // Read limit
15    printf("Please enter a number between 1 and 9: ");
16    scanf("%d", &limit);
17
18    for (int row = 1; row <= limit; row++)
19    {
20       for (int col = 1; col <= limit; col++)
21          if (row >= col)
22             printf("%d", col);
23          else
24             printf("*");
25       printf("\n");
26    } // for row ...
27    return 0;
28 } // main
```

Output
```
Please enter a number between 1 and 9: 6

1*****

12****

123***

1234**

12345*

123456
```

This program is an interesting variation of the previous program. Compare its inner loop to the inner loop in Program 6-10. This is the only part of the program that is different. The first thing you should note is that the limit test expression is different; it always goes to the maximum number of print positions. Within the inner loop, we test the column number (col) to determine how many digits we print on the line. If the expression is true, we print a digit. If it is false, we print an asterisk.

`for` Loop: Print a Calender Month

As a final example of a `for` loop, let's print a calendar month. In **Program 6-12**, the function `printMonth` receives only the start day of the month—Sunday is 0, Monday is 1 ... Saturday is 6—and the number of days in the month. This is all that the program needs to print any month of the year.

Program 6-12 | Print calendar month

```
1  /* Test driver for function to print a calendar month.
2     Written by:
3     Date:
4  */
5  #include <stdio.h>
6
7  // Prototype Declarations
8  void printMonth (int startDay, int days);
9
10 int main (void)
11 {
12 // Statements
13    printMonth (2, 29);   // Day 2 is Tuesday
14    return 0;
15 } // main
16
17 /* ============== printMonth ==============
18    Print one calendar month.
19    Pre startDay is day of week relative
20        to Sunday (0)
21    days is number of days in month
22    Post Calendar printed
23 */
24 void printMonth (int startDay, int days)
25 {
26 // Local Declarations
27    int weekDay;
28
29 // Statements
30 // print day header
31    printf("Sun Mon Tue Wed Thu Fri Sat\n");
32    printf ("-----------------------------------\n" );
33
34 // position first day
35    for (weekDay = 0; weekDay < startDay; weekDay++)
36      printf("    ");
37
38    for (int dayCount = 1; dayCount <= days; dayCount++)
39    {
40        if (weekDay > 6)
```

(continue)

Program 6-12   Print calendar month *(continued)*

```
41          {
42              printf("\n");
43              weekDay = 1;
44          } // if
45          else
46              weekDay++;
47          printf("%3d ", dayCount);
48      } // for
49      printf ("\n----------------------------------\n" );
50      return;
51 } // printMonth
```

Output
```
Sun Mon Tue Wed Thu Fri Sat

    ------------------------------------

            1   2   3   4   5

     6   7   8   9  10  11  12

    13  14  15  16  17  18  19

    20  21  22  23  24  25  26

    27  28  29

    ------------------------------------
```

This program is interesting for two reasons: first, it requires two `for` loops, one to position the printing for the first day of the month and one to print the dates. Second, the logic to control the days of the week is simple yet efficient. In an effort to eliminate one variable (`weekDay`), many programmers would use the modulo statement as follows to determine the day of the week.

```
(dayCount + startDay) % 7
```

Although this logic works, it is very inefficient. Using a separate variable to control the days of the week requires simple addition, which is much more efficient. It also avoids another poor programming style: using one variable to control two processes. Although using one variable to control two processes may work initially, it often leads to subtle bugs when the program is changed.

One final point. Examine the initialization in the two `for` loops. Do you see a difference? Because `weekday` is used in both loops, it cannot be declared local to the first loop. We must declare it in the definition section.

> **Note** | Never use *one* variable to control *two* processes.

`while` Loop: Print the Sum of Digits

This section and the next each contain an example of a `while` loop. The first prints the sum of the digits in an integer entered from the keyboard. The second prints a number backwards. **Program 6-13** accepts an integer from the keyboard and then prints the number of digits in the integer and the sum of the digits.

Program 6-13 | Print sum of digits

```
 1  /* Print the number and sum of digits in an integer.
 2     Written by:
 3     Date:
 4  */
 5  #include <stdio.h>
 6
 7  int main (void)
 8  {
 9  // Local Declarations
10     int number;
11     int count = 0;
12     int sum = 0;
13
14  // Statements
15     printf("Enter an integer: ");
16     scanf ("%d", &number);
17     printf("Your number is: %d\n\n", number);
18
19     while (number != 0)
20     {
21        count++;
22        sum += number % 10;
23        number /= 10;
24     } // while
25     printf("The number of digits is: %3d\n", count);
26     printf("The sum of the digits is: %3d\n", sum);
27     return 0;
28  } // main
```

Output
```
Enter an integer: 12345

Your number is: 12345

The number of digits is:    5

The sum of the digits is: 15
```

This problem requires that we "peel" off one digit at a time and add it to the total of the previous digits. We can solve this problem in a couple of ways, but by far the most straightforward is to use the modulus operator (%) to extract the rightmost digit and then to divide the number by ten to remove the right digit. For example, given the number 123, we first extract the 3 by

```
123 % 10
```

and then eliminate it by dividing by 10 to give 12. Note that because both the dividend and the divisor are integers, the result is an integer. We loop until there is only one digit left, at which time any digit divided by ten will result in zero and the loop terminates.

`while` Loop: Print a Number Backwards

Now let's look at an example of a loop that prints a number backward. We can solve this problem in several ways. Perhaps the easiest is to simply use modulo division, as shown in **Program 6-14**.

Program 6-14 | Print number backward

```
 1   /* Use a loop to print a number backward.
 2      Written by:
 3      Date:
 4   */
 5   #include <stdio.h>
 6
 7   int main (void)
 8   {
 9   // Local Declarations
10      long num;
11      int digit;
12
13   // Statements
14      printf("Enter a number and I'll print it backward: ");
15      scanf ("%d", &num);
16
17      while (num > 0)
18      {
19         digit = num % 10;
20         printf("%d", digit);
21         num = num / 10;
22      } // while
23      printf("\nHave a good day.\n");
24      return 0;
25   } // main
```

Output
```
Enter a number and I'll print it backward: 12345678

87654321

Have a good day.
```

do ... while Loop: Validate Data

This section contains an example of a program that uses a do ... while loop. While it is a simple problem, it demonstrates a classic data-validation technique. We'll write a program that reads an integer consisting of only zeros and ones (a binary number) and converts it to its decimal equivalent. Provide a function that ensures that the number entered is a binary number. The design for this program is shown in **Figure 6-19.**

Figure 6-19   Design for binary to decimal

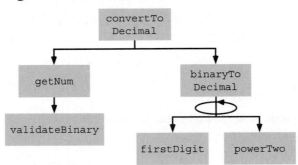

This design follows a classic program design: input–process–output. The input function is getNum; the process function is binaryToDecimal; and the output function is printResults. Study the design of binaryToDecimal. Note that it uses a loop and calls firstDigit and powerTwo in turn within the loop. How would you implement this loop? Think about it for a minute, and then look at Statement 65 in **Program 6-15** to see how we did it. If you are not sure of your binary arithmetic and binary conversions, study Appendix A, "Numbering Systems."

Program 6-15 | Convert binary to decimal

```
1   /* Convert a binary number to a decimal number.
2      Written by:
3      Date:
4   */
5   #include <stdio.h>
6   #include <stdbool.h>
7
8   // Function Declarations
9   long long getNum    (void);
10  long long binaryToDecimal (long long binary);
11  long long powerTwo  (long long num);
12  long long firstDigit  (long long num);
13  bool  validateBinary (long long binary);
14
15  int main (void)
16  {
17  // Local Declarations
18     long long binary;
```

(continue)

Program 6-15   Convert binary to decimal *(continued)*

```
19      long long decimal;
20
21 // Statements
22      binary = getNum ();
23      decimal = binaryToDecimal (binary);
24      printf("The binary number was: %lld", binary);
25      printf("\nThe decimal number is: %lld", decimal);
26      return 0;
27 } // main
28
29 /* ============ getNum ============
30     This function reads and validates a binary number
31     from the keyboard.
32     Pre nothing
33     Post a valid binary number is returned
34 */
35 long long getNum (void)
36 {
37 // Local Declarations
38     bool  isValid;
39     long long binary;
40
41 // Statements
42     do
43     {
44         printf("Enter a binary number (zeros and ones): ");
45         scanf ("%lld", &binary);
46         isValid = validateBinary (binary);
47         if (!isValid)
48             printf("\a\aNot binary. Zeros/ones only.\n\n");
49     } while (!isValid);
50     return binary;
51 } // getNum
52
53 /* ============ binaryToDecimal ============
54     Change a binary number to a decimal number.
55     Pre binary is a number containing only 0 or 1
56     Post returns decimal number
57  */
58 long long binaryToDecimal (long long binary)
59 {
60 // Local Declarations
61     long long decimal;
62
```

(continue)

Program 6-15 Convert binary to decimal *(continued)*

```
63  // Statements
64     decimal = 0;
65     for (int i = 0; binary != 0; i++)
66     {
67        decimal += firstDigit (binary) * powerTwo (i);
68        binary /= 10;
69     } // for i
70     return decimal;
71  } // binaryToDecimal
72
73  /* ============ validateBinary ============
74     Check the digits in a binary number for only 0 and 1.
75     Pre binary is a number to be validated
76     Post returns true if valid; false if not
77  */
78  bool validateBinary (long long binary)
79  {
80  // Statements
81     while (binary != 0)
82     {
83        if (! (binary % 10 == 0 || binary % 10 == 1))
84           return false;
85        binary /= 10;
86     } // while
87     return true;
88  } // validateBinary
89
90  /* ============ powerTwo ============
91     This function raises 2 to the power num
92     Pre num is exponent
93     Post Returns 2 to the power of num
94  */
95  long long powerTwo (long long num)
96  {
97  // Local Declarations
98     long long power = 1;
99
100 // Statements
101    for (int i = 1; i <= num; i++)
102       power *= 2;
103    return power;
104 } // powerTwo
105
106 /* ========= firstDigit =========
```

(continue)

Program 6-15   Convert binary to decimal *(continued)*

```
107       This function returns the rightmost digit of num
108       Pre the integer num
109       Post the right digit of num returned
110  */
111  long long firstDigit (long long num)
112  {
113  // Statements
114       return (num % 10);
115  } // firstDigit
```

Output
```
Enter a binary number (zeros and ones): 10001

The binary number was: 10001

The decimal number is: 17
```

This program has several interesting aspects. First, note the data validation that we use to ensure that the binary number that we read consists of nothing but zeros and ones. We used this series of modulus and divide statements previously in Program 6-13 and Program 6-14.

Then, note how we enclosed the call to the validation function in a do ... while that allows us to keep reading input until the user gives us a binary number. Again, note how we display an error message when the number is not valid. This is a standard data validation technique.

Next, study the `binaryToDecimal` function that converts the binary number to its decimal value. Note that when we extract a digit, it is either a zero or a one. We then multiply the extracted digit by 2 raised to the digit position we are currently evaluating, which gives us the binary value of that digit's position in the binary number. The value is then added to the decimal number. Of course, if the digit is a zero, then the product is zero and the value is unchanged. It is only when the digit is a one that we add to the decimal number.

Finally, note that throughout this program we used `long long` for the binary and decimal number. We did this because the decimal representation of a binary number can get very big very fast. On a personal computer, `long` might not be able to hold a large binary number.

6.7 Other Statements Related to Looping

Three other C statements are related to loops: `break, continue,` and `goto`. The last statement, `goto`, is not valid for structured programs and therefore is not discussed in this text.

break

We saw the `break` statement when we discussed `switch` previously. In a loop, the `break` statement causes a loop to terminate. It is the same as setting the loop's limit test to `false`. If we are in a series of nested loops, `break` terminates only the inner loop—the one we are currently in. **Figure 6-20** shows how `break` transfers control out of an inner `for` loop and continues with the next statement in the `while`. Note that the `break` statement needs a semicolon.

Figure 6-20 break and inner loops

```
while (condition)
{
   ...
   for ( ...; ...;  ... )
   {
      ...
      if (otherCondition)
         break;
      ...
   } // for
   // more while processing
   ...
} // while
```

> The break statement takes us out of the inner loop (the for loop). The while loop is still active.

The break statement can be used in any of the loop statements—while, for, and do ... while—and in the selection switch statement. However, good structured programming limits its use to the switch statement. It should not be used in any of the looping statements. If you feel you must use break, reexamine your design. You will usually find that you have not properly structured your logic. (Although this statement is generally true, as you study advanced programming concepts, such as parsing, you will find that break and continue are used to simplify the code.)

Program 6-16 shows two examples of poor loop situations and how to restructure them so that the break is not needed. The for statement shows a never-ending loop. As coded, there is no way to terminate the loop without the break. Although the break works, better documentation and style puts the limiting condition as the second expression in the for statement. After all, that is the use of the limit expression in the first place.

Program 6-16 | The for and while as perpetual loops

```
1  //A bad loop style
2  for ( ; ; )
3  {
4     ...
5     if (condition)
6        break;
7  } //for
```

```
//A better loop style
for ( ; ! condition ; )
{
   ...
} // for
```

```
1  while (x)
2  {
3     ...
4     if (condition)
5        break;
6     else
7        ...
8  } // while
```

```
while (x && !condition)
{
   ...
   if (!condition)
      ...;
} // while
```

Even if the break condition is in the middle of a block, it can be removed to the limit condition, as shown in the while example in Program 6-16. Note that in this case, we complement the condition, which then executes the else logic when the limit condition has not been reached.

Sometimes the limit condition is so complex that it cannot easily be put in the limit condition. In these cases, a flag is used. A flag is a logical variable that tracks the presence or absence of an event. In this case, the flag is set to 1 to indicate that the end of the loop has been reached. This is shown in the while example in **Program 6-17**.

> # Program 6-17 | Using a break flag

```
1   breakFlag = 0;
2   while (!breakFlag)
3   {
4       ...
5       if (x && !y || z)    // Complex limit test
6           breakFlag = 1;
7       else
8           ...;
9   } // while
```

On the other hand, too many flags can make a function overly complex. The use of break and flags needs to be tempered with simplicity and clarity of logic. Finally, note that the flag is called breakFlag, which is a generic name. You should choose a more descriptive name, such as accountFlag or timeLimitFlag.

continue

The continue statement does not terminate the loop but simply transfers to the testing expression in while and do ... while statements and transfers to the updating expression in a for statement. These jumps are shown in **Figure 6-21**. Although the transfer is to different positions in pretest and posttest loops, both can be logically thought of as a jump to the end of the loop's body.

Figure 6-21 The continue statement

```
while (expression)      do                      for (expr1; expr2; expr3)
{                       {                       {
    ...                     ...                     ...
    continue;               continue;               continue;
    ...                     ...                     ...
} // while              } while (expr);         } //for
```

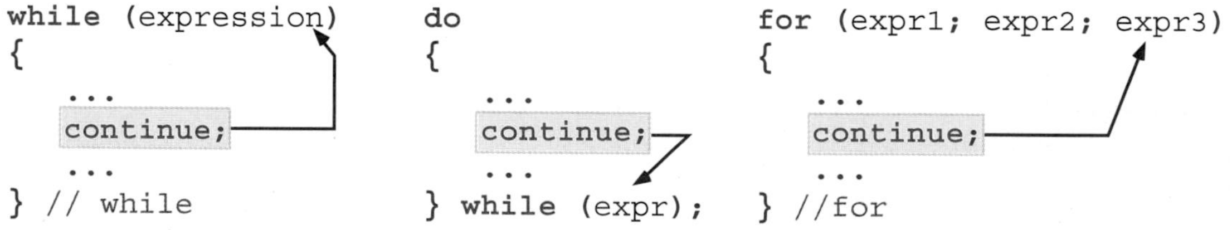

The use of the continue statement is also considered unstructured programming. If you think that you need a continue, your algorithm may not be well structured. A little study will show how to eliminate it. **Program 6-18** contains a common continue example found in many textbooks. In this function, the assignment is to read data and return the average of nonzero numbers read. In other words, it skips zeros. Note how simply reversing the conditional test eliminates the need for the continue.

Program 6-18 | Eliminating the need for the `continue` statement

```
1    float readAverage (void)
2    {
3    // Local Declarations
4       int count = 0;
5
6       int n;
7       float sum = 0;
8
9    // Statements
10       while(scanf("%d",&n) != EOF)
11       {
12          if (n == 0)
13             continue;
14          sum += n;
15          count++;
16       } // while
17
18       return (sum / count);
19    } // readAverage
```

```
float readAverage (void)
{
// Local Declarations
   int count = 0;

   int n;
   float sum = 0;

// Statements
   while(scanf("%d",&n) != EOF)
   {
      if (n != 0)
      {
         sum += n;
         count++;
      } // if
   } // while
   return (sum / count);
} // readAverage
```

6.8 Looping Applications

In this section, we examine four common applications for loops: summation, product, smallest or largest, and inquiries. Although the uses for loops are virtually endless, these problems illustrate many common applications. Note that a common design runs through all looping applications. With few exceptions, each loop contains initialization code, looping code, and disposition code. Disposition code handles the result of the loop, often by printing it, other times by simply returning it to the calling function.

Summation

As you have seen, we can add two or three numbers very easily. But how can we add many numbers or a variable series of numbers? The solution is simple: use the add operator in a loop. The concept of summation is graphically shown in **Figure 6-22**.

A sum function has three logical parts: (1) initialization of any necessary working variables, such as the sum accumulator; (2) the loop, which includes the summation code and any data validation code (for example, "only nonzero numbers are to be considered"); and (3) the disposition code to print or return the result. **Program 6-19** is a loop function that reads a series of numbers from the keyboard and returns their sum. In each loop, we read the next number and add it to the accumulator, sum. A similar application, counting, is a special case of summation in which we add 1 to a counter instead of adding the number we read to an accumulator.

Figure 6-22   Summation and product loops

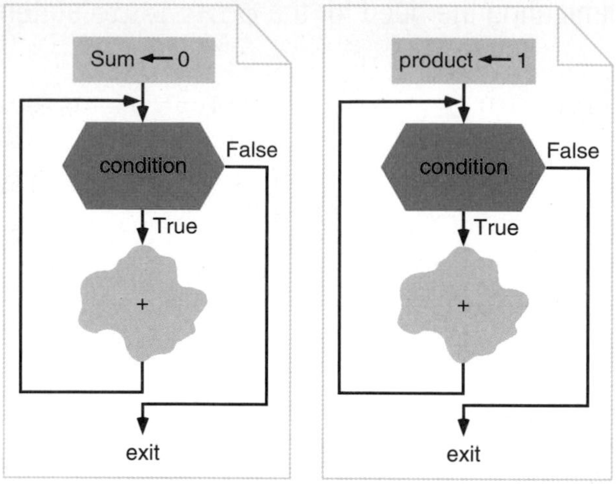

Summation	Product

Program 6-19 | Sum to EOF function

```
1   /* Read a series of numbers, terminated by EOF, and
2          return their sum to the calling program.
3          Pre nothing
4          Post data read and sum returned
5   */
6   int sumEOF (void)
7   {
8   // Local Declarations
9       int nmbr;
10      int sum;
11
12  // Statements
13      sum = 0;
14      printf ("Please enter an integer: ");
15
16      while (scanf("%d", &nmbr) != EOF)
17      {
18         sum += nmbr;
19         printf("Next integer <EOF> to stop: ");
20      } // while
21      return sum;
22  } // sumEOF
```

Powers

Just as we can add a series of numbers in a loop, we can perform any mathematical operation. A product loop is useful for two common applications: raising a number to a power and calculating the factorial of a number. For example, **Program 6-20** shows a function to return x^n. Notice that this function also includes initialization logic to validate the parameter list. If either of the parameters is invalid, we return zero as an error indicator.

Program 6-20 | Powers Function

```
1   /* Raise base to an integral power, exp. If the
2      exponent is zero, return 1.
3      Pre base & exp are both positive integer values
4      Post return either (a) the result of raising the
5      base to the exp power
6      or (b) zero if the parameters are invalid
7   */
8   int powers (int base, int exp)
9   {
10  // Local Declarations
11     int result = 1;
12
13  // Statements
14     if (base < 1 || exp < 0)
15        // Error Condition
16        result = 0;
17     else
18        for (int i = 1; i <= exp; i++)
19           result *= base;
20     return result;
21  } // powers
```

The summation and powers examples demonstrate a subtle point: initialization must be based on the application; it is not the same for every problem. For summation, the initialization sets the accumulator to 0. For product-based applications, such as powers, we must initialize it to 1. If we use 0, then the result is 0 because 0 multiplied by anything is 0.

Note | To find the *sum* of a series, the result is initialized to 0; to find the *product* of a series, the result is initialized to 1.

Smallest and Largest

We often encounter situations in which we must determine the smallest or largest among a series of data. This is also a natural looping structure.

We can write a statement to find the smaller of two numbers. For example,

```
result = a < b ? a : b;
```

But how can we find the smallest of several numbers? We simply put the same statement inside a loop. Each iteration then tests the current smallest to the next number. If this new number is smaller than the current smallest, we replace the smallest. In other words, we determine the smallest number by looping through a series while remembering the smallest number the loop has found. This concept is shown in **Figure 6-23**.

Figure 6-23 Smallest and largest loops

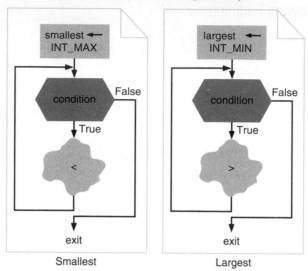

To find the smallest of a series, the initialization sets the initial value of smallest to the largest possible value for its type. In a C program, the largest value for an integer is given as INT_MAX, which is found in the limits library (limits.h). The loop then proceeds to read a series of numbers and tests each one against the previously stored smallest number. Because smallest starts with the maximum integer value, the first read number automatically becomes smallest. Thereafter, the result depends entirely on the data being read. The disposition simply returns the smallest value found.

Program 6-21 is the C implementation of smallest.

Program 6-21 | Smallest to EOF function

```
1   /* Read a series of numbers, terminated by EOF, and
2       pass the smallest to the calling program.
3       Pre nothing
4       Post data read and smallest returned
5   */
6   int smallestEOF (void)
7   {
8   // Local Declarations
9       int numIn;
10      int smallest;
11
12  // Statements
13      smallest = INT_MAX;  // requires <limits.h>
14
15      printf("Please enter an integer: ");
16
17      while (scanf("%d", &numIn) != EOF)
18      {
19          if (numIn < smallest)
```

(continue)

Program 6-21 Smallest to EOF function *(continued)*

```
20            smallest = numIn;
21            printf("Enter next integer <EOF> to stop: ");
22      } // while
23      return smallest;
24 }// smallestEOF
```

We can find the largest number by simply reversing the less than operator in the expression, making it greater than. We would also need to set the variable, renamed `largest`, to INT_MIN.

> **Note**
>
> To find the largest, we need to initialize the result (a variable named `largest`) variable to a very small number, such as INT_MIN.
>
> To find the smallest, we need to initialize the result (a variable named `smallest`) to a very large number, such as INT_MAX.

Inquiries

An inquiry is a request for information from a program. In programming, we often encounter one of two basic inquiry types: *any* and *all*. We use the inquiry type *any* when we have a list of data and we want to know if *at least one* of them meet a given criteria. The answer to the inquiry is yes if one or more data meet the criteria. The answer is no if none of the data meet the criteria.

We use *all* when we have a list of data and we want to make sure that *each and every one* of them meet some specified criteria. The concept of *any* and *all* in an inquiry is shown in **Figure 6-24**.

Figure 6-24 *any* and *all* inquiries

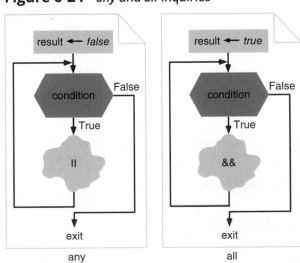

The *any* Inquiry

The *any* inquiry is an algorithm that determines if one item in a series satisfies a requirement, we can test them using *or* as shown in the next example.

```
result = (a == condition) || (b == condition);
```

If either or both of the equal expressions are true, `result` is set to `true`. This works fine for testing the first two items. To test the third item in the series, however, we need to include the result of the first two. This is easily done with the next example.

```
result = result || (c == condition);
```

Study this test carefully. If the previous tests were all false, then `result` contains `false` when the statement is executed. If the equal expression is false, then `result` is assigned `false`; however, if the equal expression is true, then `result` is assigned `true`. By placing this expression in a loop, we can test all of the values in the series. For example, to test a series to determine if any of the values are positive, we can use the following code.

```
result = false;
while (scanf("%d", &number)
{
    result = result || number > 0;
} // while
```

This code produces an accurate answer to the inquiry. However, it can be very inefficient, especially if the series is long. For example, suppose that the first item tested is greater than 0. In this case, it is not necessary to test the rest of the list; we already know the answer.

Program 6-22 is an example of an *any* inquiry. It reads a series of numbers and checks to see if any of the numbers in the list are greater than zero. The function terminates and returns `true` as soon as a positive number is read.

Program 6-22 | `anyPositive` to EOF function

```
1   /* Read number series to determine if any positive.
2      Pre nothing
3      Post return true if any number > zero
4          return false if all numbers <= zero
5   */
6   bool anyPositiveEOF (void)
7   {
8   // Local Declarations
9      bool anyPositive = false;
10     int num1n;
11
12  // Statements
13     printf("Determine if any number is positive\n")
14     printf("Enter first number: ");
15     while (scanf("%d", &num1n) != EOF)
16     {
17        anyPositive = num1n > 0;
18        if (anyPositive)
19           return true;
20        printf("Enter next number: ");
21     } // while
22     return false;
23  } // anyPositiveEOF
```

Note that anyPositive is a logical variable bool and is initialized to false. Because we do not need to read the entire number series, we can use a simple test to set anyPositive. If a positive number was entered, we return true; if not, we prompt for the next number and loop back to the while expression.

To use the bool type, we must include the stdbool.h library in the program. This library uses a define macro to declare the bool type and equate it to the C Boolean type, _bool. It also defines true and false.

The *all* Inquiry

The *all* inquiry is an algorithm that determines if two items in a series satisfy a requirement; we can test them using the *and* operator as shown in the next example.

```
result = (a == condition) && (b == condition);
```

If both of the equal expressions are true, result is set to true; if either of them is false, the result is false. This works fine for testing the first two items. To test the third item in the series, however, we need to include the result of the first two. This is easily done with the next example.

```
result = result && (c == condition);
```

Study this test carefully. If the previous tests were all true, then result contains true when the statement is executed. If the equal expression is also true, then result is assigned true; however, if the equal expression is false, then result is assigned false. By placing this expression in a loop, we can test all of the values in the series. For example, to test a series to determine if all of the values are positive, we can use the following code.

```
result = true;
while (scanf("%d", &number)
{
    result = result && number > 0;
} // while
```

Once again, for efficient processing we may not need to examine all of the numbers in the series. As soon as a nonpositive number is found, we know the result and can return false.

This function is seen in **Program 6-23**.

> **Program 6-23** | All positive function

```
1   /* Read number series, and determine if all are positive.
2       Pre nothing
3       Post return true if all numbers > zero
4       return false if any numbers <= zero
5   */
6
7   bool allPositiveEOF (void)
8   {
9   // Local Declarations
10      bool allPositive = true;
11      int numIn;
12
13  // Statements
```

(continue)

Program 6-23 All positive function *(continued)*

```
14     printf("Determine if all numbers are positive\n");
15     printf("Enter first number: ");
16     while (allPositive && (scanf("%d", &numIn) != EOF))
17     {
18        allPositive = numIn > 0;
19        if (!allPositive)
20           return false;
21        printf("Enter next number: ");
22     } // while
23     return true;
24  } // allPositiveEOF
```

Once again you should study how we initialize the Boolean flags in these two programs. To test for any item, we start with the flag `false`. If and when it becomes `true`, the result has been determined. Similarly, to test for all items, we initialize the Boolean flag to `true`. If and when it becomes `false`, the result has been determined.

> **Note** | To answer an *any* inquiry, the result is initialized to `false`; to answer an *all* inquiry, the result is initialized to `true`.

Programming Example: The Calculator Program

Let's return to the calculator program you worked on earlier in this text. We gave users the capability of selecting one of four options: add, subtract, multiply, or divide. However, if users needed to make two calculations, they had to run the program twice. We now add a loop that allows users to make as many calculations as needed (**Program 6-24**). We include only two functions, `main` and `getOption`, because, at this point, all of the others are the same.

Program 6-24 | The complete calculator

```
1   /* This program adds, subtracts, multiplies, and divides
2      two integers.
3      Written by:
4      Date:
5   */
6   #include <stdio.h>
7   #include <stdlib.h>
8
9   // Function Declaration
10  int getOption (void);
11  void getData (int* a,  int* b);
12  float calc  (int option, int num1, int num2);
13
```

(continue)

Program 6-24   The complete calculator *(continued)*

```c
14 float add (float num1, float num2);
15 float sub (float num1, float num2);
16 float mul (float num1, float num2);
17 float divn (float num1, float num2);
18
19 void printResult (float num1, float num2,
20                   float result, int option);
21
22 int main (void)
23 {
24 // Local Declarations
25    int done = 0;
26    int option;
27    float num1;
28    float num2;
29    float result;
30
31 // Statements
32    while (!done)
33    {
34       option = getOption();
35       if (option = = 5)
36          done = 1;
37       else
38       {
39          do
40          {
41             printf("\n\nEnter two numbers: ");
42             scanf("%f %f", snum1, &num2);
43             if (option == 4 && num2 == 0)
44             {
45                printf("\a\n *** Error *** ");
46                printf("Second number cannot be 0\n");
47             } // if
48          } while (option == 4 && num2 == 0);
49
50          switch (option)
51          {
52             case 1: result = add (num1, num2);
53                     break;
54             case 2: result = sub (num1, num2);
55                     break;
56             case 3: result = mul (num1, num2);
57                     break;
58             case 4: result = divn (num1, num2);
```

(continue)

Program 6-24   The complete calculator *(continued)*

```
59                } // switch
60
61              printResult (num1, num2, result, option);
62           } // else option != 5
63        } // while
64     printf("\nThank you for using Calculator.\n");
65        return 0;
66  } // main
67
68  /* =========== getOption ============
69     This function shows a menu and reads the user option.
70     Pre nothing
71     Post returns a valid option
72  */
73  int getOption (void)
74  {
75  // Local Declarations
76     int option;
77
78  // Statements
79     do
80     {
81        printf("\n******************");
82        printf("\n*   MENU          *");
83        printf("\n*                 *");
84        printf("\n* 1. ADD          *");
85        printf("\n* 2. SUBTRACT     *");
86        printf("\n* 3. MULTIPLY     *");
87        printf("\n* 4. DIVIDE       *");
88        printf("\n* 5. QUIT         *");
89        printf("\n*                 *");
90        printf("\n******************");
91
92        printf("\n\n\nPlease type your choice ");
93        printf("and press the return key : ");
94        scanf("%d", &option);
95
96        if (option < 1 || option > 5)
97            printf("Invalid option. Please re-enter.\n");
98
99     } while (option < 1 || option > 5);
100    return option;
101 } //getOption
```

As you look at the changes in this version of our program, first note the two loops in `main`. The first loop (statement 32) continues the calculator until the user says it's time to quit. The second loop (statement 39) gets and validates the numbers, making sure that the user isn't trying to divide by zero. (Your computer will get very upset if you divide by zero and will stop!)

We also modified our `getOption` function to add the `quit` option and to validate the options. If the user makes a mistake, we correct it in `getOption`. Extending the concept to a general principle, whenever we write a function to get data from a user, the function should handle all data validation. This makes for much simpler code in the rest of the program.

This simplification is also seen in the `switch` statement. Because we have validated the numbers before the `switch`, we no longer need to test for a valid divisor in the fourth `case` option. We also no longer need a `default`, because we know the options are valid. The result is a simpler statement, much more in line with the KISS principle.

Software Engineering

Loops in Structure Charts

Now that you understand how to write loops, let's look at how they are shown in a structure chart. The symbols are very simple. Loops go in circles, so the symbol we use is a circle. Programmers use two basic looping symbols. The first is a simple loop. It is represented by **Figure 6-25** (a). The other is the conditional loop, shown in Figure 6-25 (b).

Figure 6-25 Structure chart symbols for loops

```
dolt

fun

int doIt ( ... )
{
    while (expression)
        fun ( ... );
} // doIt
```
(a) Loop

```
select

doA

int select ( ... )
{
    ...
    while (expression)
    {
        if (condition)
            doA ( ... );
        ...
    } // while
    ...
} // select
```
(b) Conditional loop

When the function is called unconditionally, as in a `while` loop, the circle flows around the line above the called function. On the other hand, if the call is conditional, as in a function called in an `if ... else` statement inside a loop, then the circle includes a decision diamond on the line.

Figure 6-26 shows the basic structure for a function called `process`. The circle is below the function that controls the loop. In this example, the looping statement is contained in `process`, and it calls three functions, `A`, `B`, and `C`. The exact nature of the loop cannot be determined from the structure chart. It could be any of the three basic looping constructs. To help you better visualize the process, however, let's further assume that the loop is a `while` loop that contains a `scanf` that reads until the end of file. Within the `while` loop are three calls: the first to `A`, the second to `B`, and the third, conditionally, to `C`.

Figure 6-26 Structure chart for `process`

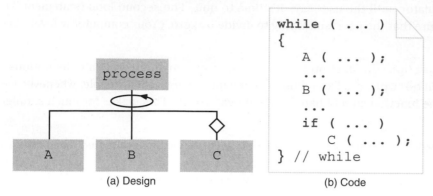

(a) Design

```
while ( ... )
{
    A ( ... );
    ...
    B ( ... );
    ...
    if ( ... )
        C ( ... );
} // while
```

(b) Code

Determining Algorithm Efficiency

There is seldom a single algorithm for any problem. When comparing two different algorithms that solve the same problem, we often find that one algorithm will be an order of magnitude more efficient than the other. In this case, it only makes sense that programmers have some way to recognize and choose the more efficient algorithm.

Although computer scientists have studied algorithms and algorithm efficiency extensively, the field has not been given an official name. In their book *Algorithmic Theory and Practice*, Brassard and Bratley coined the term *algorithmics,* which they define as "the systematic study of the fundamental techniques used to design and analyze efficient algorithms." We will use this term.

If a function is linear—that is, if it contains no loops—then its efficiency is a function of the number of instructions it contains. In this case, the function's efficiency depends on the speed of the computer and is generally not a factor in its overall efficiency in a program. On the other hand, functions that loop will vary widely in their efficiency. The study of algorithm efficiency is therefore largely devoted to the study of loops.

As we study specific examples, we will develop a formula that describes the algorithm's efficiency. We will then generalize the algorithm so that the efficiency can be stated as a function of the number of elements to be processed. The general format is

```
f(n) = efficiency
```

Linear Loops

Let's start with a simple loop. We want to know how many times the body of the loop is repeated in the following code:

```
for (int i = 1; i <= 1000; i++)
{
    BODY;
} // for
```

The answer is 1000 times. But the answer is not always straightforward as it is in the previous example. Consider the following loop. How many times is the body repeated in this loop? Here the answer is 500 times. Why?

```
for (int i = 1; i <= 1000; i += 2;)
{
    BODY;
} // for
```

In both cases, the number of iterations is directly proportionate to the limit test in the `for` loop. If we were to plot either of these loops, we would get a straight line. Thus, they are known as linear loops.

Because the efficiency is proportionate to the number of iterations, it is

$$f(n) = n$$

Logarithmic Loops

Now consider a loop in which the controlling variable is multiplied or divided in each loop. How many times will the body of the loops be repeated in the following program segments?

MULTIPLY LOOPS	DIVIDE LOOPS
| ```
i = 1;
while (i < 1000)
{
    BODY;
    i *= 2;
} // while
``` | ```
i = 1000;
while (i >= 1)
{
    BODY;
    i /= 2;
} //while
``` |

To help us understand this problem, **Table 6-2** below analyzes the values of *i* for each iteration.

Table 6-2   Analysis of multiply/divide loops

MULTIPLY		DIVIDE	
ITERATION	I	ITERATION	I
1	1	1	1000
2	2	2	500
3	4	3	250
4	8	4	125
5	16	5	62
6	32	6	31
7	64	7	15
8	128	8	7
9	256	9	3
10	512	10	1
(exit)	1024	(exit)	0

As can be seen, the number of iterations is 10 in both cases. The reason is that in each iteration the value of i doubles for the multiplication and is cut in half for the division. Thus, the number of iterations is a function of the multiplier or divisor; in this case, two. That is, the loop continues while the following condition is true.

multiply $\qquad\qquad\qquad 2^{\text{Iterations}} < 1000$

divide $\qquad\qquad\qquad 1000 / 2^{\text{Iterations}} >= 1$

Generalizing the analysis, we can say that the iterations in loops that multiply or divide are determined by the following formula:

$$f(n) = ceil\ (\log_2 n)$$

Nested Loops

When we analyze loops that contain loops, we must determine how many iterations each loop completes. The total is then the product of the number of iterations for the inner loop and the number of iterations in the outer loop.

```
Iterations = outer loop iterations * inner loop iterations
```

We now look at three nested loops: linear logarithmic, dependent quadratic, and quadratic.

Linear Logarithmic

The inner loop in the following code is a loop that multiplies. (To see the multiplication, look at the update expression in the inner `for` statement.)

```
for (int i= 1; i<= 10; i++)
    for (int j = 1; j <= 10; j *= 2)
    {
        BODY;
    } // for j
```

The number of iterations in the inner loop is therefore

ceil $(\log_2 10)$

However, since the inner loop is controlled by an outer loop, the above formula must be multiplied by the number of times the outer loop executes, which is 10. This gives us

10 (*ceil* $(\log_2 10)$)

which is generalized as

$f(n) = n(\text{ceil} (\log_2 n))$

Dependent Quadratic

Now consider the nested loop shown in the following example:

```
for (int i= 1; i<= 10; i++)
    for (int j = 1; j <= i; j ++)
    {
        BODY;
    } // for j
```

The outer loop is the same as the previous loop. However, the inner loop is executed only once in the first iteration, twice in the second iteration, three times in the third iteration, and so forth. The number of iterations in the body of the inner loop is mathematically stated as

```
1 + 2 + 3 + ... + 9 + 10 = 55
```

which is generalized to

$$f(n) = n\frac{(n + 1)}{2}$$

Quadratic

In the final nested loop, each loop executes the same number of times, as seen in the following example:

```
for (int i = 1; i <= 10; i ++)
    for (int j = 1; j <= 10; j ++)
```

```
{
    BODY;
} // for j
```

The outer loop—that is, the loop at the first `for` statement—is executed ten times. For each iteration, the inner loop is also executed ten times. The answer, therefore, is 100, which is 10 * 10, the square of the loops. This formula generalizes to

$$f(n) = n^2$$

Big-O Notation

With the speed of computers today, we are not concerned with an exact measurement of an algorithm's efficiency as much as we are with its general magnitude. If the analysis of two algorithms shows that one executes 15 iterations while the other executes 25 iterations, they are both so fast that we can't see the difference. On the other hand, if one iterates 15 times and the other 1500 times, we should be concerned.

We have shown that the number of statements executed in the function for n elements of data is a function of the number of elements, expressed as $f(n)$. Although the equation derived for a function may be complex, usually, a dominant factor in the equation determines the order of magnitude of the result. Therefore, we don't need to determine the complete measure of efficiency, only the factor that determines the magnitude. This factor is the big-O, as in On-the-Order-Of, and expressed as O(n), that is, on-the-order-of n.

This simplification of efficiency is known as big-O analysis. For example, if an algorithm is quadratic, we would say its efficiency is

$$O(n^2)$$

or on-the-order of n-squared.

The big-O notation can be derived from $f(n)$ using the following steps:

1. In each term, set the coefficient of the term to 1.
2. Keep the largest term in the function, and discard the others. Terms are ranked from lowest to highest, as follows:
   `Log n   n   n log n   n² n³ nᵏ 2ⁿ n!`

   For example, to calculate the big-O notation for

   $$f(n) = n\frac{n+1}{2} = \frac{1}{2}n^2 + \frac{1}{2}n$$

   we first remove all coefficients. This gives us

   $n^2 + n$

   which, after removing the smaller factors, gives us

   n^2

   which, in big-O notation, is stated as

   `O(f(n)) = O(n²)`

   To consider another example, let's look at the polynomial expression

   $$f(n) = a_j n^k + a_{j-1} n^{k-1} + \cdots + a_2 n^2 + a_1 n^1 + a_0$$

   We first eliminate all of the coefficients, as follows:

   $$f(n) = n^k + n^{k-1} + \cdots + n^2 + n + 1$$

The largest term in this expression is the first one, so we can say that the order of a polynomial expression is

$$O(f(n)) = O(n^k)$$

Standard Measures of Efficiency

Computer scientists have defined seven categories of algorithm efficiency. We list them in **Table 6-3** in order of decreasing efficiency. Any measure of efficiency presumes that a sufficiently large sample is being considered. If we are only dealing with ten elements and the time required is a fraction of a second, there will be no meaningful difference between two algorithms. On the other hand, as the number of elements processed grows, the difference between algorithms can be staggering. In Table 6-3, n is 10,000.

Returning to the question of why we should be concerned about efficiency, consider the situation in which we can solve a problem in three ways: one is linear, another is linear-logarithmic, and the third is quadratic. The order of their efficiency for a problem containing 10,000 elements is shown in Table 6-3, along with the other algorithmics. Obviously, we wouldn't want to use the quadratic solution.

Table 6-3   Measures of efficiency

EFFICIENCY	BIG-O	ITERATIONS
logarithmic	$O(\log n)$	14
linear	$O(n)$	10,000
linear logarithmic	$O(n(\log n))$	140,000
quadratic	$O(n^2)$	$10,000^2$
polynomial	$O(n^k)$	$10,000^k$
exponential	$O(c^n)$	$2^{10,000}$
factorial	$O(n!)$	10,000!

Looking at the problem from the other end, if we use a computer that executes a million instructions per second and the loop contains ten instructions, then we spend .00001 second for each iteration of the loop. Table 6-3 also contains an estimate of the time to solve the problem given different efficiencies.

Tips and Common Programming Errors

1. Be aware that the `while` and `for` loops are pretest loops. Their body may never be executed. If you want your loop to be executed at least once, use a `do ... while`.

2. Do not use equality and inequality for the control expression in loops; use limits that include less than or greater than. You may accidentally create an infinite loop, as follows:

```
...
i = 0;
while (i != 13)
{
   ...
   i++;     // sets i to 1, 3, 5, 13
   ...
```

```
    i++;     // sets i to 2, 4, 6, 14
    ...
} // while
```

3. It is a compile error to omit the semicolon after the expression in the `do ... while` statement.

4. It is most likely a logic error to place a semicolon after the expression in a `while` or `for` statement. (Some compilers warn you when you do.)

5. It is a compile error to code a `for` statement with commas rather than semicolons, as follows:

```
for (int i = 0, i < 10, i++)
```

6. It is a logic error to omit the update in the body of a `while` or `do ... while` loop. Without an update, either explicit or implicit, the loop never terminates.

7. It is a common logic error to miscode the limit test in `for` statements. The result is usually a loop that executes one extra time or terminates one iteration short. For example, the following statement executes nine times, not ten:

```
for (int i = 1; i < 10; i++)
```

8. It is generally a logic error to update the terminating variable in both the `for` statement and in the body of the loop, as follows.

```
for (int i = 0; i < 10; i++)
{
    ...
    i += 1;
} // for
```

Summary

> The real power of computers is in their ability to repeat an operation or a series of operations many times.

> To control the loop, we need a condition to determine if more processing is needed.

> In a pretest loop, in each iteration, we check the condition first. If it is true, we iterate once more; otherwise, we exit the loop.

> In a posttest loop, in each iteration, we do the processing. Then we check the condition. If it is true, we start a new iteration; otherwise, we exit the loop.

> In a pretest loop, the processing is done zero or more times.

> In a posttest loop, the processing is done one or more times.

> In a pretest loop, if the body is executed n times, the limit test is executed $n + 1$ times.

> In a posttest loop, if the body is executed n times, the limit test is executed n times.

> The control expression in a loop must be explicitly or implicitly initialized.

> If you know exactly the number of times the body must be repeated, use a counter-controlled loop; if an event must occur to terminate a loop, use an event-controlled loop.

› C has three loop statements: while, for, and do...while.

› The while loop is a pretest loop. It can be used for a counter-controlled or event-controlled loop, but it is usually used only for event control.

› The for loop is a pretest loop. It can be used for both counter-controlled and event-controlled loops, but it is used mostly in the first case.

› The loop variable in a for loop may be locally defined in the for statement.

› The do ... while loop is a posttest loop. It is usually used when the body must be executed at least once.

› We discussed two C statements that are related to looping: break and continue.

› The break statement is used to terminate a loop prematurely. We strongly recommend that you use the break statement only within switch statements.

› The continue statement is used to skip the rest of the statements in a loop and start a new iteration without terminating the loop. We strongly recommend that you never use the continue statement.

› The best loop for data validation is the do ... while loop.

› A loop in a structure chart is indicated by a circle on the line connecting it to the called functions. Only loops that call other functions are shown.

Key Terms

all inquiry	event-controlled loop	loop update
any inquiry	infinite loop	posttest loop
big-O analysis	initialization	pretest loop
comma expression	inquiry	process-control loops
comma operator	limit-test expression	summation
continue	loop body	while loop
counter-controlled loop	loop control expression	

Review Questions

1. In a pretest loop, the limit test condition is tested first.
   a. True   b. False

2. The action that causes the loop limit test to change from true to false is the loop update.
   a. True   b. False

3. The value of a comma expression is the value of the first expression.
   a. True   b. False

4. An inquiry is a request for information from a user.
   a. True   b. False

5. Which of the following statements about pretest loops is true?
   a. If a pretest loop limit test is false, the loop executes one more time.
   b. Pretest loop initialization is done first in the loop body.
   c. Pretest loops execute a minimum of one time.
   d. Pretest loops test the limit condition after each execution of the loop body.
   e. The update for a pretest loop must be a part of the loop body.

6. Which of the following statements about loop initialization is false?
   a. Explicit initialization includes code to set the initial values of loop variables.
   b. Implicit initialization relies on preexisting values for loop variables.
   c. Initialization code is explicitly required in all loops.
   d. Initialization is preparation required for proper execution of a loop.
   e. Initialization must be done before the first execution of the loop.

7. Which of the following statements about loop updates is false?
   a. A loop update changes key variable(s) in a loop, thus allowing the loop to terminate.
   b. Loop updates may be made before or after a loop iteration.
   c. Loops may use explicit or implicit updates.
   d. In a `for` loop, updates are generally found in the `for` statement itself.
   e. The number of updates always equals the number of loop iterations.

8. Which of the following statements about counter-controlled loops is false?
   a. Counter-controlled loops are generally pretest loops.
   b. Counter-controlled loops generally increment or decrement a counter.
   c. Counter-controlled loops require a limit test.
   d. The number of times a loop iterates must be a constant.
   e. The update in a counter-controlled loop is generally explicit.

9. Which of the C loops is a pretest loop?
   a. `do ... while`
   b. `for`
   c. `while`
   d. Both the `do ... while` and the `for`
   e. Both the `for` and the `while`

10. Which of the following statements about the `while` statement is true?
    a. Multiple statements are allowed in a `while` loop.

11. Which of the following statements about `for` and `while` statements is false?
    a. Both statements allow only one statement in the loop.
    b. Both statements are pretest loops.
    c. Both statements can be used for counter-controlled loops.
    d. Both statements include initialization within the statement.
    e. Both statements require an update statement.

b. The limit test in a `while` loop is made before each iteration.
   c. The update in a `while` statement is contained in the `while` statement expression itself.
   d. The `while` statement is a posttest loop.
   e. The `while` statement must be terminated with a semicolon.

12. Which of the following statements about the `do ... while` loop is false?
    a. A `do ... while` loop executes one or more iterations.
    b. Any statement may be used as the action in a `do ... while`.
    c. The `do ... while` is best suited for use as an event-controlled loop.
    d. The `do ... while` is the only loop that requires a semicolon.
    e. The limit test in a `do ... while` loop is executed at the beginning of each iteration.

13. Nested loops have a(an) _____ standard measure of efficiency.
    a. exponential
    b. linear
    c. linear logarithmic
    d. quadratic
    e. linear logarithmic or quadratic

14. The _____ standard measure of efficiency is considered the most efficient.
    a. exponential
    b. linear
    c. logarithmic
    d. quadratic
    e. polynomial

Exercises

15. What would be printed from each of the following program segments? Compare and contrast your answers to parts a, b, and c.

    a.

    ```
    x = 12;
    while (x > 7)
        printf("%d\n", x);
    ```

    b.

    ```
    for (int x = 12; x > 7;)
        printf("%d\n", x);
    ```

    c.

    ```
    x = 12;
    do
        printf("%d\n", x);
    while (x > 7);
    ```

16. What would be printed from each of the following program segments? Compare and contrast your answers to parts a, b, and c.

    a.

    ```
    x = 12;
    while (x > 7)
    {
        printf("%d\n", x);
        x—;
    }
    ```

    b.

    ```
    for (int x = 12; x > 7; x—)
        printf(" %d\n", x);
    ```

    c.

    ```
    x = 12;
    do
    {
        printf("%d\n", x);
        x—;
    } while (x > 7);
    ```

17. What would be printed from each of the following program segments? Compare and contrast your answers to parts a and b.

    a.

    ```
    x = 12;
    while (x > 7)
    {
        printf("%d\n", x);
    ```

```
      x -= 2;
   }
```

b.

```
for (int x = 12; x > 7; x -= 2)
   printf("%d\n", x);
```

18. What would be printed from each of the following program segments? Compare and contrast your answers to parts a, b, and c.

   a.

```
x = 12;
while (x < 7)
{
   printf("%d\n", x);
   x--;
} // while
```

   b.

```
for (int x = 12; x < 7; x--)
   printf ("%d\n", x);
```

   c.

```
x = 12;
do
{
   printf("%d\n", x);
   x--;
} while (x < 7);
```

19. Change the following while loops to for loops.

   a.

```
x = 0;
while (x < 10)
{
   printf("%d\n", x);
   x++;
}
```

   b.

```
scanf("%d", &x);
while (x != 9999)
{
   printf("%d\n", x);
   scanf("%d", &x);
}
```

20. Change the while loops in Exercise 19 to do ... while loops.

21. Change the following `for` loops to `while` loops:

    a.

    ```
    for (int x = 1; x < 100; x++)
        printf("%d\n", x);
    ```

    b.

    ```
    for (; scanf("%d", &x) != EOF;)
        printf("%d\n", x);
    ```

22. Change the `for` loops in Exercise 21 to do ... while loops.

23. Change the following do ... while loops to `while` loops.

    a.

    ```
    x = 0;
    do
    {
        printf("%d\n", x);
        x++;
    } while (x < 100);
    ```

    b.

    ```
    x = 0;
    do
    {
        res = scanf("%d", &x);
    } while (res != EOF);
    ```

24. Change the do ... while loops in Exercise 23 to `for` loops.

25. A programmer writes the following `for` loop to print the numbers 1 to 10. What is the output? If the output is incorrect, how would you correct it?

    ```
    for (num = 0; num < 10; num++)
        printf("%d", num);
    ```

26. Another programmer writes the following `for` loop to print the numbers 1 to 10. What is the output? If the output is incorrect, how would you correct it?

    ```
    for (int num = 0; num < 10; num++)
    {
        numOut = num + 1;
        printf("%d", numOut);
    } // for
    ```

27. What will be printed from the following program segments?

    a.

    ```
    for (int x = 1; x <= 20; x++)
        printf("%d\n", x);
    ```

b.

```
for (int x = 1; x <= 20; x++)
{
    printf("%d\n", x);
    x++;
} // for
```

28. What will be printed from the following program segments?

a.

```
for (int x = 20; x >= 10; x--)
    printf("%d\n", x);
```

b.

```
for (int x = 20; x >= 1; x--)
{
    printf("%d\n", x);
    x--;
} // for
```

29. What will be printed from the following program segments?

a.

```
for (int x = 1; x < 20; x++)
{
    for (int y = 1; y <= 5; y++)
        printf("%d", x);
    printf("\n");
} // for
```

b.

```
for (int x = 20; x >= 1; x--)
{
    for (int y = x; y >= 1; y--)
        printf("%3d", x);
    printf("\n");
} // for
```

30. What will be printed from the following program segments?

a.

```
for (int x = 1; x <= 20; x++)
{
    for (int y = 1; y < x; y++)
        printf (" ");
    printf ("%d\n", x);
} // for
```

b.

```
for (int x = 20; x >= 1; x--)
{
    for (int y = x; y >=1; y--)
        printf (" ");
    printf ("%d\n", x);
} // for
```

31. You find the following statement in a program you are maintaining.

```
for ( ; ; )
{
    ...
} // for
```

    a. Describe the implications behind the null expressions in the `for` statement.
    b. Because there is no limit condition, how can this statement be exited?
    c. Is this good structured programming style? Explain your answer.

Problems

32. Write a program that uses a `for` loop to print a line of 60 asterisks.

33. Write a `for` loop that will produce each of following sequences:
    a. 6, 8, 10, 12, 66
    b. 7, 9, 11, 13, 67
    c. The sum of the numbers 1 through 15 inclusive
    d. The sum of the odd numbers 15 through 45 inclusive
    e. The sum of the first 50 numbers in the series $(1 + 4 + 7 + 10 + \ldots)$

34. Write a program that prompts the user to enter an integer, n, and then n floating-point numbers. As the numbers are read, the program will calculate the average of the positive numbers.

35. Rewrite Problem 34 to average the negative numbers.

36. Write a program that asks the user to enter a list of integers. The program is to determine the largest value entered and the number of times it was entered. For example, if the following series is entered

```
5 2 15 3 7 15 8 9 5 2 15 3 7
```

it would output the largest value is 15 and it was entered 3 times.

37. Write a program that creates the following pattern:

```
1 2 3 4 5 6 7 8 9
1 2 3 4 5 6 7 8
1 2 3 4 5 6 7
1 2 3 4 5 6
1 2 3 4 5
1 2 3 4
1 2 3
1 2
1
```

38. Write a function that creates the following pattern, given the height (number of rows) and the width (asterisks per row):

```
* * * * * * * * * * * *
* * * * * * * * * * * *
* * * * * * * * * * * *
* * * * * * * * * * * *
```

39. Write a function that creates the following pattern, given the height (number of rows) and the width (print characters per line):

```
=====
*   *
*   *
*   *
*   *
*   *
=====
```

40. Write a function that creates the following pattern, given the height (number of rows):

```
*
* * *
* * * * *
* * * * * *
* * * * * * * *
* * * * * * * * * *
```

41. Write a function that creates the following pattern, given the height (number of rows):

```
* * * * * * * * * *
* * * * * * * *
* * * * * *
* * * *
* *
*
```

42. Write a function that creates the following pattern, given the height (number of rows):

```
*
* * *
* * * * *
* * * * * *
* * * * * * * *
* * * * * * * *
* * * * * *
* * * * *
* * *
*
```

43. Modify Program 6-3 to display the total as each number is entered. The format should be

```
Enter your numbers: <EOF> to stop.
5
Total: 5
17
Total: 22
8
Total: 30
```

44. Write a program that reads integer data from the standard input unit and prints the minimum integer read, maximum integer read, and the average of the list. Test your program with the following data.

{24 7 31 –5 64 0 57 –23 7 63 31 15 7 –3 2 4 6}

45. In "The do ... while Loop" in Section 6.5, we demonstrated the use of a do ... while to validate input. The code fragment contains no message to tell the user that an invalid number has been entered. Write a function that reads only positive even numbers from the keyboard. If a negative or odd number is entered, it should print an error message and ask the user to enter another number. Each call to the function is to read only one number. The valid number read is to be returned to the calling program. If the user enters EOF, the function should return it. Then write a short program to test the function using the following data. The valid numbers should be printed, either in a separate function or in main.

{2 18 –18 5 7 100 1 –1}

46. Write a function that reads integers from the keyboard. If any of the numbers are negative, it returns a negative number. If all the numbers are positive, it returns their average. (Hint: See Program 6-22.)

47. Program 6-19 uses a while loop to read a series of numbers from the keyboard. Because you will always have at least one number in this program, rewrite it to use the do ... while.

48. Program 6-21 uses INT_MAX from the limits.h library to initialize the smallest variable. Another solution is to read the first number and put its value in smallest, then go into the loop to read the rest of the numbers. Modify Program 6-21 to make this change.

49. Write a program that prompts the user to enter a number less than 100 then asks if the series of numbers to be produced is even or odd. The program will produce the series of number less than the entered one. For example:

```
Welcome to Even or Odd series generator
Please enter an integer number less than 100: 8
Would you like even (0) or odd (1)?: 1
```

Output

```
The following is the odd series below 8:

1 3 5 7
```

50. The value of pi (π) can be calculated by the following formula:

$$\theta = \sqrt{6\left(\frac{1}{1^2} + \frac{1}{2^2} + \frac{1}{3^2} + \cdots + \frac{1}{limit^2}\right)}$$

Write a function that uses this formula to calculate pi. Then write a test driver and run it once to test your function with a limit of 5 terms and a limit of 10 terms. Display the result of each test.

51. Write a program that reads an integer from the keyboard and then calls a function to print it out in reverse. For example, if the user enters 4762, it prints 2674.

52. Rewrite Exercise 26 using an iterative solution.

Projects

53. Statisticians use many different algorithms in addition to the arithmetic average. One other average is the harmonic mean, which is defined by the following formula:

$$\frac{n}{\dfrac{1}{x_1} + \dfrac{1}{x_2} + \cdots + \dfrac{1}{x_n}}$$

Write a program that reads a series of numbers and calculates the average and harmonic mean.

54. Write a C program that can create four different patterns of different sizes. The size of each pattern is determined by the number of columns or rows. For example, a pattern of size 5 has 5 columns and 5 rows. Each pattern is made of character $ and a digit, which shows the size. The size must be between 2 and 9. **Table 6-4** shows the four patterns in size 5.

Table 6-4   Patterns for Problem 54

PATTERN 1	PATTERN 2	PATTERN 3	PATTERN 4
5$$$$	$$$$5	$$$$$	$$$$$
$5$$$	$$$5$	$$$$5	5$$$$
$$5$$	$$5$$	$$$55	55$$$
$$$5$	$5$$$	$$555	555$$
$$$$5	5$$$$	$5555	5555$

Your program displays a menu and asks the user to choose a pattern and size. But note that it must be robust; it must prompt the user to choose an option only between 1 and 5, and a pattern size only between 2 and 9. You are to print the menu and the user's response. The following example shows all user menu responses, including potential errors:

```
    M E N U
1.  Pattern One
2.  Pattern Two
3.  Pattern Three
4.  Pattern Four
5.  Quit
Choose an option (between 1 and 5): 11
Your option is incorrect. Please try again.
Choose an option (between 1 and 5): 3
Choose a pattern size (between 2 and 9): 12
Your pattern size is incorrect. Try again.
Choose a pattern size (between 2 and 9): 4
```

The program must consist of a `main` function and six other functions called `getOption`, `getSize`, `patternOne`, `patternTwo`, `patternThree`, and `patternFour`.

Run your program *once* with the options and sizes shown in **Table 6-5**. Note that some options and sizes are missing because either the previous option or the size is invalid.

Table 6-5   Test data for Problem 54

	OPTION	SIZE
SET 1	1	2
SET 2	2	3
SET 3	3	4
SET 4	4	5
SET 5	6	
SET 5	3	6
SET 6	2	10
SET 6		7
SET 7	5	

55. Write a C program to create a calendar for a year. The program reads the year from the keyboard. It then calculates which day of the week (SUN, MON, TUE, WED, THU, FRI, SAT) is the first day of the year and prints the calendar for that year. After printing the year, it should ask if the user wants to continue. If the answer is yes, it will print the calendar for another year until the user is done.

The program prompts the user for the input, as shown in the next example.

```
Enter the year for your calendar : 2022
```

The output is a calendar for the whole year (12 months). One month is shown in the next example.

```
JANUARY                                                        2022
SUN         MON         TUE         WED         THU         FRI         SAT
                                                                        1
2           3           4           5           6           7           8
9           10          11          12          13          14          15
16          17          18          19          20          21          22
23          24          25          26          27          28          29
30          31
```

To print the correct calendar for the requested year, you must first find which day of the week is the first day of that year. This can be done with the following formula.

$$\left((year - 1) \times 365 + \frac{[year - 1]}{4} - \frac{[year - 1]}{100} + \frac{[year - 1]}{400} \right) \% 7$$

(For a complete explanation, see Chapter 5, Project 60.) Note that the Julian calendar was changed to our current (Gregorian) calendar in 1752. Although calendars before this date are valid Gregorian calendars, they do not represent the Julian calendar in use at that time.

```
(!(year % 4) && (year % 100)) || !(year % 400)
```

You also must calculate leap years.

Run your program once with the following sets of data:

SET 1: 2005

SET 2: 0

SET 3: 2000

SET 4: 123

56. Write a C program to help a prospective borrower calculate the monthly payment for a loan. The program also prints the amortization (payoff) table to show the balance of the loan after each monthly payment.

The program prompts the user for input, as shown in the following example:

```
Amount of the loan (Principal)? 10000.00
Interest rate per year (per cent)? 12
Number of years? 10
```

The program then creates an information summary and amortization table.

Banks and financial institutions use different formulas to calculate the monthly payment of a loan. For the purpose of this assignment, we use a simple formula

$$NM \quad = (NY * 12)$$
$$IM \quad = (IY / 12) / 100$$
$$P \quad = (1 + IM)^{NM}$$
$$Q \quad = (P / (P - 1))$$
$$MP \quad = (PR * IM * Q)$$

NY:	Scheduled number of years to amortize the loan
NM:	Scheduled number of months for the loan
IY:	Interest rate per year (as a percentage)
IM:	Interest rate/month (decimal)
PR:	Principal (the amount of the loan)
P:	The value of $(1 + IM)^{NM}$
Q:	The value of $P / (P - 1)$
MP:	Monthly payment

The `main` function must call three other functions: `calculateMonthlyPayment`, `printInformation`, and `printAmortizationTable`. Of course, the first function may also call other functions if necessary.

Because of the approximation used in calculation, the value of the new balance at the end of the last month may become nonzero. To prevent this, the last payment must be adjusted. It may be less or greater than the other months. It must be calculated by adding the principal paid to the interest paid for that month. The new balance at the end of the last month must be zero.

The following example shows the concept. The program has been run for a loan of $5000.00 at 11% interest rate for a period of 1 year. The input was

```
Amount of the loan (Principal)? 5000.00
Interest rate / year (per cent)? 11
Number of years? 1
```

Run your program once with the test data shown in **Table 6-6**.

Table 6-6   Test data for Problem 56

	AMOUNT	INTEREST	YEARS
Set 1	10,000.00	12	I
Set 2	5,000.00	10	2
Set 3	1,000.00	8	3

The output is shown in **Table 6-7**. Note: Your answer might differ by a few pennies because of different precision.

Table 6-7   Sample output from Project 57

The amount of the loan (principal):				5000.00	
Interest rate/year (percent):				11.0	
Interest rate/month (decimal):				0.009167	
Number of years:			1		
Number of months:			12		
Monthly payment:				441.91	
Month	Old Balance	Monthly Payment	Interest Paid	Principal Paid	New Balance
1	5000.00	441.91	45.83	396.08	4603.92
2	4603.92	441.91	42.20	399.71	4204.21
3	4204.21	441.91	38.54	403.37	3800.84
4	3800.84	441.91	34.84	407.07	3393.77
5	3393.77	441.91	31.11	410.80	2982.97
6	2982.97	441.91	27.34	414.57	2568.40
7	2568.40	441.91	23.54	418.37	2150.03
8	2150.03	441.91	19.71	422.20	1727.83
9	1727.83	441.91	15.84	426.07	1301.76
10	1301.76	441.91	11.93	429.98	871.78
11	871.78	441.91	7.99	433.92	437.86
12	437.86	441.87	4.01	437.86	0.00
Total amount paid: 5302.88					

57. Write a program that reads a list of integers from the keyboard and creates the following information:
    a. Finds and prints the sum and the average of the integers
    b. Finds and prints the largest and the smallest integer
    c. Prints a Boolean (true or false) if some of them are less than 20
    d. Prints a Boolean (true or false) if all of them are between 10 and 90

    The input data consist of a list of integers with a sentinel. The program must prompt the user to enter the integers, one by one, and enter the sentinel when the end of the list has been reached. The prompt should look like the following:

    Enter numbers with <return> (99999 to stop):

The output should be formatted as follows:

```
The number of integers is:            XXX
The sum of the integers is:           XXXX
The average of the integers is:       XXX.XX
The smallest integer is:              XXX
The largest integer is:               XXX
At least one number was < 20:         <true or false>
All numbers were (10 <= n >= 90):     <true or false>
```

58. The formula for converting centigrade temperatures to Fahrenheit is

$$F = 32 + \left(C \times \frac{180.0}{100.0} \right)$$

Write a program that prints out conversion tables for Celsius to Fahrenheit ($0°$ to $100°$). The output format is to fit on a standard monitor display, 80 columns by 20 rows.

CHAPTER 7

Text Input/Output

Learning Objectives

When you complete this chapter, you will be able to:

7.1 Describe the basic properties and characteristics of external files

7.2 Explain the C implementation of file I/O using streams

7.3 Use C input/output functions to open and close streams

7.4 Use formatting input/output functions to convert data values into text streams

7.5 Write programs that read and write text files using the C character I/O functions

7.1 Files

A program is a data processor: It accepts input data, processes data, and creates output data. Handling input/output is a complex task, largely because of the variety of devices and data formats. Data may come from many different sources and may go to different destinations. For example, data may come from such diverse sources as a keyboard, a file on the disk, a heating or air-conditioning system, or a communication channel (network or Internet). Data may also go to many destinations, such as a monitor or a file on the disk, or to a communication channel.

A file is an external collection of related data treated as a unit. The primary purpose of a file is to keep a record of data. Because the contents of primary memory are lost when the computer is shut down, we need files to store our data in a more permanent form. Additionally, the collection of data is often too large to reside entirely in main memory at one time. Therefore, we must have the ability to read and write portions of the data while the rest remain in the file.

> **Note** | A file is an external collection of related data treated as a unit.

Files are stored in auxiliary storage devices (also known as secondary storage devices). The two most common forms of secondary storage are disk (hard disk, CD, and DVD) and tape.

When the computer reads, the data move from the external device to memory; when it writes, the data move from memory to the external device. This data movement often uses a special work area known as a buffer. A buffer is a temporary storage area that holds data while they are being transferred to or from memory. The primary purpose of a buffer is to synchronize the physical devices with a program's needs, especially on large storage devices such as disk and tape. Because of the physical requirements of these devices, more data can be input at one time than a program can use. The buffer holds the extra data until the program or the user is ready for it. Conversely, the buffer collects data until there are enough to write efficiently. These buffering activities are taken care of by software known as device drivers or access methods provided by the supplier of the computer's operating system.

As a file is being read, there eventually comes a point when all the data have been input. At this point, the file is said to be at end of file. The end of file in an auxiliary device is detected automatically by the device and passed to the program. It is the programmer's job to test for end of file. This test is often done in a loop control statement.

File Name

Every operating system uses a set of rules for naming its files. When we want to read or write auxiliary storage files, therefore, we must use the operating system's rules when we name the files. We refer to the operating system's name as *the file name* in this text.

File Information Table

A program that reads or writes files needs to know several pieces of information, such as the operating system's name for the file, the position of the current character in the file, and so on. C has predefined a file structure to hold this information. The `stdio.h` header file defines the file structure; its identifier is `FILE`. When we need a file in our program, we declare it using the `FILE` type.

7.2 Streams

Although the source and destination of data is a file or a physical device in C, data are input to and output from a stream. A stream can be associated with a physical device, such as a terminal, or with a file stored in auxiliary memory. **Figure 7-1** illustrates this idea.

Figure 7-1 Streams

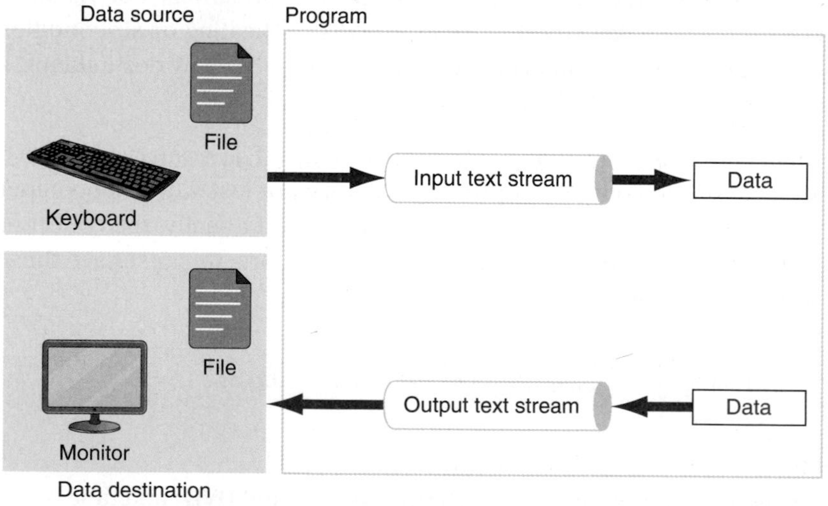

Text and Binary Streams

C uses two types of streams: text and binary. A text stream consists of a sequence of characters divided into lines, with each line terminated by a newline (\n). A binary stream consists of a sequence of data values such as integer, real, or complex using their memory representation. In this chapter, we discuss only text streams. You will learn about binary streams later.

Stream-File Processing

A file exists as an independent entity with a name known to the operating system. A stream is an entity created by the program. To use a file in our program, we must associate the program's stream name with the operating system's file name.

In general, there are four steps to processing a file:

1. We first create the stream.
2. We then open the file, which associates the stream name with the file name.
3. After the file is opened, we read or write data; that is, we process the file.
4. When the processing is complete, we close the file.

We describe the steps to make this association in the following sections.

Step 1: Create a Stream

We create a stream when we declare it. The declaration uses the FILE type as shown in the following example. The FILE type is a structure that contains the information needed for reading and writing a file.

```
FILE* spData;
```

In this example, spData is a pointer to the stream. Because of the importance of streams in a program, we provide a special notation to help us recognize them. The sp in the name stands for stream-pointer. We then follow it with a descriptive name for the data that flows through the stream. In this case we used the generic name, data. In our examples, we use more descriptive names.

Note that there is an asterisk after the file type (FILE). It indicates that spData is a pointer variable that contains the address of the stream we are creating. It is an error to omit the asterisk.

Step 2: Open a File

After the stream has been created, we are ready to associate the stream to a file. This is done, as we discuss in detail in the next section, through the standard open function. When the file is opened, the stream and the file are associated with each other, and the FILE type is filled with the pertinent file information. The **open function** returns the address of the file type, which is stored in the stream pointer variable, spData. The file open function creates the stream, which we then refer to by its name.

Step 3: Use the Stream Name

After we create the stream, we can use the stream pointer in all functions that need to access the corresponding file for input or output. For example, a function can use the stream pointer to read from the file through the corresponding stream.

Step 4: Close the Stream

When the file processing is complete, we close the file. Closing the file breaks the association between the stream name and the file name. After the close, the stream is no longer available and any attempt to use it results in an error. To close the association, we need to use a **close function** to release the file.

System-Created Streams

We discussed that a terminal—that is, the keyboard or monitor—can be the source or destination of a text stream. C provides standard streams to communicate with a terminal. These streams must be created and associated with their terminal devices just like files. The difference is that C does it automatically for us.

C declares and defines three stream pointers in the stdio.h header file. The first, stdin, points to the standard input stream; the second stdout, points to the standard output stream; and the third, stderr, points to the standard error stream. Note that these streams are created when the program starts and we cannot declare them.

> **Note** | Standard stream names have already been declared in the `stdio.h` header file and cannot be declared again in our program.

The association between the three standard streams and the keyboard and the monitor is also done automatically when the program starts. Therefore, we cannot open any of the standard streams in our code. Like file streams, the standard streams must be closed at the end of the program. However, they are closed automatically when the program terminates.

> **Note** | There is no need to open and close the standard streams. It is done automatically by the operating system.

C includes many standard functions to input data from the keyboard and output data to the monitor automatically without the need for explicitly using these standard streams. For these functions, the stream that connects our programs to the terminal is automatically created by the system and we do not have to do anything more. Examples of such functions are `scanf` and `printf`.

7.3 Standard Input/Output Functions: File Open and Close

The `stdio.h` header file contains several different input/output function declarations. (These are sometimes referred to as I/O functions.) They are grouped into eight different categories, as shown in **Figure 7-2**. The first three will be discussed in the following sections. You will learn about those shown in shaded boxes as you become a more experienced programmer.

Figure 7-2 Categories of standard input/output functions

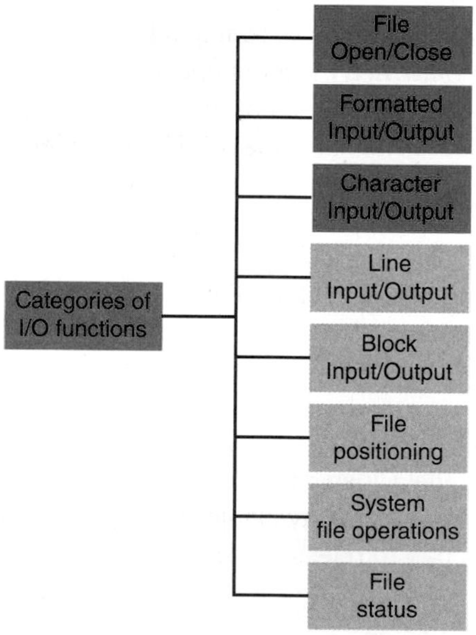

In this section we discuss the C functions to open and close streams.

File Open (`fopen`)

The function that prepares a file for processing is *fopen*. It does two things: First, it makes the connection between the physical file and the file stream in the program. Second, it creates a program file structure to store the information needed to process the file.

To open a file, we need to specify the physical filename and its mode, as shown in the following statement.

```
fopen("filename", "mode");
```

Let's examine this statement by starting on the right. The file mode is a string that tells C how we intend to use the file: Are we going to read an existing file, write a new file, or append to a file? We discuss file modes later in this section.

A filename is a string that supplies the name of the physical file as it is known to the external world. For example, when we work in a Microsoft Windows system, the file name consists of a name, a dot (period), and a three-character file extension.

The address of the file structure that contains the file information is returned by fopen. The actual contents of FILE are hidden from our view because we do not need to see them. All we need to know is that we can store the address of the file structure and use it to read or write the file. A complete open statement is shown in the following code. We could open it for output (writing) with the following open statements. The first is the basic format as it might be used for the current directory in UNIX or Windows; the second is the Windows version to open a file for drive A.

```
spData = fopen("MYDATA.DAT", "w");
spData = fopen("A:MYDATA.DAT", "w");
```

We see this open statement in the program in **Figure 7-3**. Some explanation of the program segment in the figure is in order. You should first note that the standard input/output library is called out at the beginning of the program.

Figure 7-3 File open results

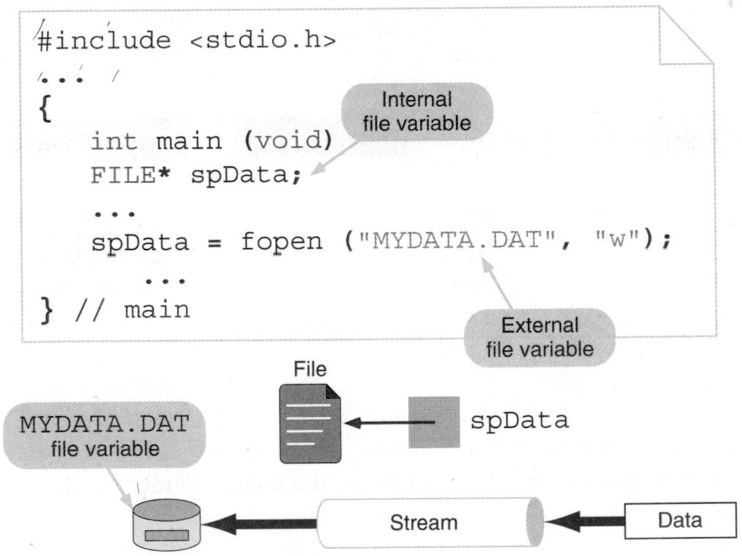

Next, note the name we have used for the file address. The sp stands for "stream pointer"; we use it in all of our stream identifiers. To the stream pointer abbreviation, we add the name of the file. Because this is a generic example, we use "Data." This combination gives a readable name that is easy to remember.

Our stream pointer variable, spData, is assigned the address of the file structure when we open the file; the return value from the fopen function contains the file structure address. Later in the program, when we need to read or write the file, we use this pointer.

File Modes

When we open a file, we explicitly define its mode. The mode shows how we will use the file: for reading, for writing, or for appending, which means adding new data at the end of the current file. C has six different file modes. The first three, which we discuss here, are used to read, write, or append a text file. As you become a more experienced programmer, you will learn about other modes, which allow both reading and writing in the same file. The mode codes discussed in this chapter are shown in **Table 7-1**.

Table 7-1 Text file modes

MODE	MEANING
R	Open text file in read mode • If file exists, the marker is positioned at beginning. • If file doesn't exist, error returned.
W	Open text file in write mode • If file exists, it is erased. • If file doesn't exist, it is created.
A	Open text file in append mode • If file exists, the marker is positioned at end. • If file doesn't exist, it is created.

Figure 7-4 describes the simple open modes.

Figure 7-4 File-opening modes

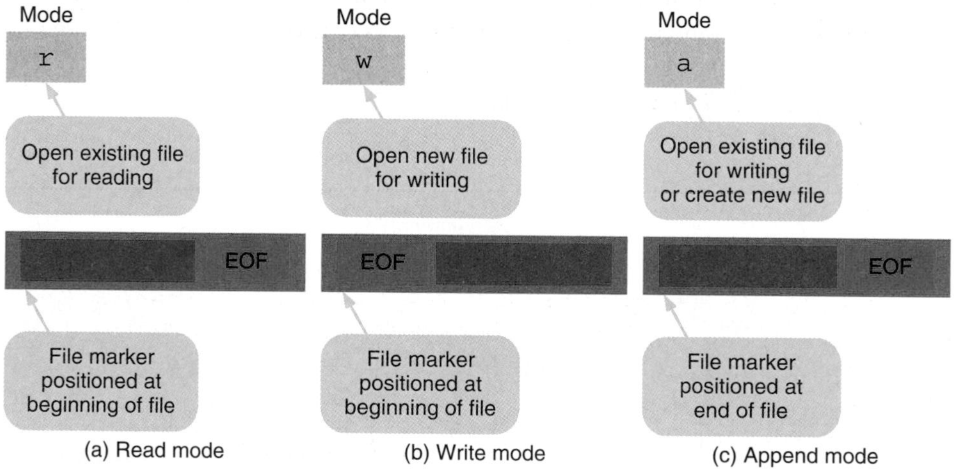

Mode	Mode	Mode
r	w	a
Open existing file for reading	Open new file for writing	Open existing file for writing or create new file

| EOF | EOF | EOF |

| File marker positioned at beginning of file | File marker positioned at beginning of file | File marker positioned at end of file |
| (a) Read mode | (b) Write mode | (c) Append mode |

Read Mode

The read mode (r) opens an existing file for reading. When a file is opened in this mode, the file marker is positioned at the beginning of the file (the first character). The file marker is a logical element in the file structure that keeps track of our current position in the file.

The file must already exist: If it does not, NULL is returned as an error. Files opened for reading are shown in Figure 7-4a. If we try to write to a file opened in the read mode, we get an error message.

Write Mode

The write mode (w) opens a file for writing. If the file doesn't exist, it is created. If it already exists, it is opened and all its data are deleted; that is, it assumes the status of an empty file. It is an error to try to read from a file opened in write mode. A file opened for writing is shown in Figure 7-4b.

Append Mode

The append mode (a) also opens an existing file for writing. Instead of creating a new file, however, the writing starts after the last character; that is, new data are added, or appended, at the end of the file.

If the file doesn't exist, it is created and opened. In this case, the writing will start at the beginning of the file; the result will be logically the same as opening a new file for writing. Files opened in append mode are shown in Figure 7-4c. If we try to read a file opened for write append, we get an error message.

File Close (`fclose`)

When we no longer need a file, we should close it to free system resources, such as buffer space. A file is closed using the close function, `fclose`, as shown in the following section. Note that some operating systems allow a file to be opened by only one application program at a time. In that case, closing the file allows other application programs to have access to the file.

```
#include <stdio.h>
...
int main (void)
{
// Local Declarations
    FILE* spTemp;
// Statements
    ...
    spTemp = fopen ("MYDATA.DAT", "w");
    ...
    fclose(spTemps);
    ...
```

Open and Close Errors

What if the open or close fails? Open and close errors occur for a number of reasons. One of the most common errors occurs when the external filename in the open function call does not match a name on the disk. When we create a new file, the open fails if there isn't enough room on the disk.

Always check to make sure that a stream has opened successfully. If it has, then we have a valid address in the file variable. But if it failed for any reason, the stream pointer variable contains NULL, which is a C-defined constant for no address in `stdio.h`.

Similarly, we can test the return value from the close to make sure it succeeded. The `fclose` function returns an integer that is zero if the close succeeds and EOF if there is an error. EOF is defined in the standard input/output header file. Traditionally, it is –1, but the standard defines it as any noncharacter value. To ensure that the file opened or closed successfully, we use the function as an expression in an `if` statement, as shown in **Program 7-1**.

Program 7-1 | Testing for open and close errors

```
1   #include <stdio.h>
2   #include <stdlib.h>
3   ...
4
5   int main (void)
6   {
7   //  Local Declarations
8       FILE* spTemps;
9
10  // Statements
11      ...
```

(continue)

Program 7-1   Testing for open and close errors *(continued)*

```
12
13    if ((spTemps = fopen("TEMPS.DAT", "r")) == NULL)
14    {
15        printf("\aERROR opening TEMPS.DAT\n");
16        exit (100);
17    } // if open
18    ...
19
20    if (fclose(spTemps) == EOF)
21    {
22        printf("\aERROR closing TEMPS.DAT\n");
23        exit (102);
24    } // if close
25    ...
26
27 } // main
```

The most common mistake in testing for a successful open is getting the parentheses wrong, as shown here:

```
if (spTemps = fopen("TEMPS.DAT", "w") == NULL)
```

The above statement is syntactically correct (we do not get a compile error) but invalid. You must test the address returned by `fopen` after it has been assigned to `spTemps`. In the above statement, `spTemps` is assigned the logical value of the expression

```
fopen("TEMPS.DAT", "W") == NULL
```

because the equal operator has a higher precedence than the assignment operator. Study the open file function in Program 7-1 carefully, and make sure you understand the difference between it and the incorrect version shown in the previous example.

The error testing for the close is much simpler; we can use a simple test for the error code, `EOF`. Note that we have assigned a different return code to distinguish the open failure from the close failure.

7.4 Standard Input/Output Functions: Formatting Input/Output Functions

Previously, we introduced two formatting input/output functions, `scanf` and `printf`. The `scanf` function receives a text stream from the keyboard and converts it to data values to be stored in variables. The `printf` function receives data values from the program and converts them into text stream to be displayed on the monitor.

These two functions can be used only with the keyboard and monitor. The C library defines two more general functions, `fscanf` and `fprintf`, that can be used with any text stream. **Table 7-2** compares these four input/output functions.

Stream Pointer

The first argument in the text input/output function, stream pointer, is the pointer to the streams that has been declared and associated with a text file. The example that follows Table 7-2 demonstrates the use of an input stream.

Table 7-2 Formatting functions

TERMINAL INPUT/OUTPUT
scanf ("control string", …);
printf ("control string", …);
GENERAL INPUT/OUTPUT
fscanf (stream_pointer, "control string", …) ;
fprintf (stream_pointer, "control string", …);

Although we normally read data from the terminal keyboard using scanf, we can also use fscanf. When we use fscanf we must specify that the stream pointer is stdin, as shown in the following example.

```
fscanf(stdin, "format string", address list);
```

The following example demonstrates the use of an output stream.

```
FILE* spIn;
…
spIn = fopen("file name", "r");
…
fscanf(spln, "format string", address list);
```

Similarly, we can use fprintf to print to the terminal monitor by specifying that the stream is stdout, as shown in the following example.

```
fprintf(stdout, "format string", value list);
```

Format Control Strings

Input and output functions for text files use a format string to describe how data are to be formatted when read or written. The format control string consists of three types of data, which may be repeated: whitespace, text characters, and the most important of the three, the conversion specification that describes how the data are to be formatted as they are read or written.

Whitespace

Format control string whitespace is handled differently for input and output. In an input function, one or more whitespaces in the format string cause zero, one, or more whitespaces in the input stream to be read and discarded. Thus, any sequence of consecutive whitespace characters in the format string will match any sequence of consecutive whitespace characters, possibly of different length, in the input stream.

Note | A whitespace character in an input format string causes leading whitespace characters in the input to be discarded. A whitespace character in an output format string is copied to the output stream.

Whitespace in an output function is simply copied to the output stream. Thus, a space character is placed in the output stream for every space character in the format string. Likewise, tabs in the format string are copied to the output stream. This is not a good idea, however, because we can't see tabs in the format string. It is better to use the tab escape character (\t) so that we can see the tabs.

Text

Any text character other than a whitespace in an input format string must match exactly the next character of the input stream. If it does not match, a conflict occurs that causes the operation to be terminated. The conflicting input character remains in the input stream to be read by the next input operation on that stream. We therefore recommend that you do not use text characters in an input format string.

Text characters in an output format string are copied to the output stream. They are usually used to display messages to the user or to label data being output.

Conversion Specification

The conversion specification consists of a percent character (%), optional formatting instructions, and a conversion code. With one exception, each conversion specification must have a matching parameter in the parameter list that follows the format string. The type in the conversion specification and the type of the parameter must match.

> **Note** | The number, order, and type of the conversion specifications must match the number, order, and type of the parameters in the list. Otherwise, the result will be unpredictable and may terminate the input/output function.

Conversion specifications can have up to six elements, as shown in **Figure 7-5**. (Note that for input there are only five; precision is not allowed.) The first element is a conversion specification token (%). The last element is the conversion code. Both of these elements are required; the other elements are optional. Generally, the meaning and usage of each element is the same for both input and output. The exceptions are noted in the following discussion.

Figure 7-5 Conversion specifications

```
scanf/fscanf
```

```
printf/fprintf
```

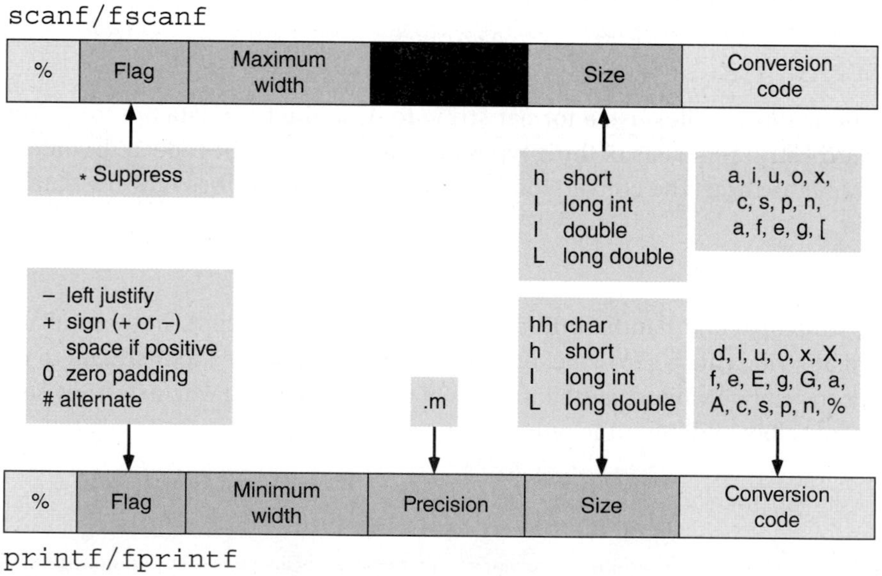

The conversion code specifies the type of data that are being formatted. For input, it specifies the type of variable into which the formatted data are stored. For output, it specifies the type of data in the parameter associated with the specification. It is the programmer's responsibility to ensure that the data are of the right type. If they are not, strange formatting may result. Conversion codes are discussed in detail in the "Input Formatting (scanf and fscanf)" and "Output Formatting (printf and fprintf)" sections that follow.

Input Formatting (`scanf` and `fscanf`)

The `scanf` and `fscanf` functions read text data and convert the data to the types specified by a format string. The only difference between them is that `scanf` reads data from the standard input unit (the keyboard by default) and `fscanf` reads the input from a file specified by the first parameter. This file can be standard input (`stdin`).

> **Note** | `scanf` reads from stdin; `fscanf` reads from a user-specified stream.

The name `scanf` stands for "scan formatted"; the name `fscanf` stands for "file scan formatted." These functions have the following formats:

```
scanf ("format string", address list);
fscanf(sp, "format string", address list);
```

where sp is the address of a stream defined as type `FILE*`, "`format string`" is a string containing formatting instructions, and the address list specifies the addresses where the data are to be stored after they have been formatted. A comma must separate the format string from the variable list. If more than one variable is present, then separate the variables from each other by commas.

We must include a variable address in the address list for every conversion specification in the format string that requires data. If we do not, the result is "unpredictable and undefined." This is a standard disclaimer that means anything can happen. The usual result is that the program doesn't do what we expect and often crashes.

Input Data Formatting

The conversion operation processes input characters until any of the following occur:

1. End of file is reached.
2. An inappropriate character is encountered.
3. The number of characters read is equal to an explicitly specified maximum field width.

Input Conversion Specification

Previously, we introduced some of the conversion specifications. We discuss the rest here. **Table 7-3** shows the type of the pointer argument, size, and conversion codes for `scanf` family. Note that we have not shown a flag specification in the table, because there is only one flag, suppress (*), which can be used with all input format codes.

Table 7-3 Sizes and conversion code for `scanf` family

ARGUMENT TYPE	SIZE SPECIFIER	CODE
Integral	hh (char), h (short), none (int), l (long), ll (long long)	I
Integer	h (short), none (int), l (long), ll (long long)	D
Unsigned int	hh (char), h (short), none (int), l (long), ll (long long)	U
Character octal	hh (unsigned char)	O
Integer hexadecimal	h (short), none (int), l (long), ll (long long)	X

(continue)

Table 7-3   Sizes and conversion code for `scanf` family (*continued*)

ARGUMENT TYPE	SIZE SPECIFIER	CODE
Real	none (float), l (double), L (long double)	F
Real (scientific)	none (float), l (double), L (long double)	E
Real (scientific)	none (float), l (double), L (long double)	G
Real (hexadecimal)	none (float), l (double), L (long double)	A
Character	none (char), l (wchar_t)	c
String	none (char string), l (wchar_t string)	s
Pointer		P
Integer (for count)	none (int), hh (char), h (short), l (long), ll (long long)	n
Set	none (char), l (wchar_t)	[

Flag

There is only one flag for input formatting, the assignment suppression flag (*). More commonly associated with text files, the assignment suppression flag tells `scanf` that the next input field is to be read but not stored. It is discarded. The following `scanf` statement reads an integer, a character, and a floating point number from the input stream. The character is read and discarded. The other fields are read, formatted, and stored. Note that there is no matching address parameter for the data to be discarded.

```
scanf ("%d %*c %f", &x, &y);
```

Width

The width specifies the maximum width of the input (in characters). This allows us to break out a code that may be stored in the input without spaces. Consider what happens when we read a Social Security number from a file and the number has no formatting; it is just nine digits in a row, followed by a space. We could read it into three variables, thus allowing us to format it with dashes in our output, with the following format specifications:

```
scanf ("%3d%2d%4d...", &ssn1, &ssn2, &ssn3, ...);
```

Note that the width is a maximum. If the amount of data is less than required, the scan terminates. What determines the end of the data depends on the type of data, but generally whitespace will terminate most scans.

Size

The size specification is a modifier for the conversion code. Used in combination with the conversion code, it specifies the type of the associated variable, for example, a `long double` (`Lf`). The size codes, along with their associated conversion codes, are explained in Table 7-3.

Conversion Codes

With the exception of string and pointer, this section discusses the input conversion codes.

> **Integer (d)** The decimal (d) format code accepts a value from the input stream and formats it into the specified variables. It reads only decimal digits and an optional plus or minus sign as the first character of the value.

> **Integer (i)** The integer format code (i) allows the user to key a decimal, octal, or hexadecimal number. Numbers starting with any digit other than zero are read and stored as decimal values. Numbers starting with zero are interpreted as octal values and are converted to decimal and stored. Hexadecimal numbers must be prefixed with 0x or 0X; the hexadecimal value is converted to decimal and stored. We strongly recommend that the integer format code be used only when nondecimal data is being entered—such as when programmers are entering technical data; in all other cases, the decimal format code (d) should be used.

> **Octal and Hexadecimal (o, x)** The octal (o) and hexadecimal (x) conversion codes perform unsigned conversion. For octal, the only valid input digits are 0...7. For hexadecimal input, the valid digits are 0...9, a...f, and A...F. If you are not familiar with octal or hexadecimal numbers, see Appendix A, "Numbering Systems."

> **Scientific Notation (e, g, a)** The C language uses three real format codes for scientific notation. In scientific notation, the significant and exponent are specified separately. The significant part is a floating-point number that contains as many significant digits as possible. For example, if it contains six digits, then the number is significant only to six digits; if it has twelve digits, then it is significant to twelve digits. The larger the significance, the greater the precision. Therefore, `long double` may be more precise than `double`, which may be more precise than `float`.

The exponent specifies the magnitude of the number. It may be either positive or negative. If it is positive, then the number is the significant times ten to the power of the exponent, which may be a very large number. If it is negative, then the number is the significant times the reciprocal of the base ten exponent, which may be a very small number. These forms are as follows:

$$123e03 \rightarrow 123*10^3 \qquad\qquad 123e-03 \rightarrow 123*10^{-3}$$

All of the following numbers are in scientific notation:

```
3e -1.0e-3 0.1+e1 2e2
```

For input, all conversion codes (`f`, `e`, `g`, `a`) accept all three scientific notations as well as algebraic notation.

> **Count (n)** To verify the number of input characters, we use the n conversion code. This code requires a matching variable address into which `scanf` places the count of the characters input. In the following example, count is a short integer that is to receive the number of characters read:

```
scanf("%d %8.2f %d %hn", &i, &x, &j, &count);
```

Input Side Effect and Value

When the `scanf` function is called, it can create a side effect and return a value. The side effect is to read characters from a file and format them into variables supplied in the parameter list. It continues until the end of the line is reached or until there is a conflict between the format string and a character read from the input stream. In either case, the scan returns the number of successfully formatted values before termination. If the scan detects the end-of-file before any conflict or assignment is performed, then the function returns EOF. The difference between the side effect and the value is seen in **Figure 7-6**.

Figure 7-6   Side effect and value of `scanf` and `fscanf`

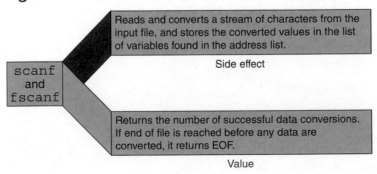

This leads us to a common example of a **value error**. Suppose we want to read two numbers with one scan statement. If we succeed, the scan function returns a 2, indicating that both were read correctly. If the user makes a mistake with the first number, the scan function returns a 0. If there is a mistake with the second entry, `scanf` returns a 1. This allows us to validate that at least the correct amount and type of data were read. An error reading the second piece of data is shown in **Figure 7-7**.

Figure 7-7 Another common error

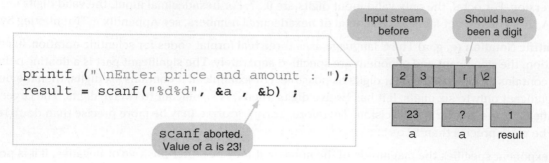

When we read data, we should verify that the data were read correctly. This is easily done by checking the return value from the scan function. **Program 7-2** is a program fragment that shows how the two numbers in Figure 7-7 could be checked.

Program 7-2 | Checking `scanf` results

```
1   #define FLUSH while (getchar()!= 'n')
2   #define ERR1 "\aPrice incorrect. Re-enter both fields\n"
3   #define ERR2 "\aAmount incorrect. Re-enter both fields\n"
4
5   // Read price and amount
6      do
7      {
8         printf("\nEnter amount and price: ");
9         ioResult = scanf("%d%f", &amount, &price);
10
11        if (ioResult != 2)
12        {
13           FLUSH;
14           if (ioResult == 1)
15              printf(ERR1);
16           else
17              printf(ERR2);
18        } // if
19     } while (ioResult != 2);
```

```
Output
Enter amount and price: ? 15.25

Amount incorrect. Re-enter both fields

Enter amount and price: 100?

Price incorrect. Re-enter both fields

Enter amount and price: 100 15.25
```

We have introduced a new define statement, FLUSH, in this program segment.

```
#define FLUSH while (getchar( ) != '\n')
```

Why is this statement necessary? Recall that when scanf encounters an error, it leaves the invalid data in the input stream. If we simply print the user messages and then return to the scanf statement, the invalid data are still there. We need to get rid of them somehow! This is the purpose of the FLUSH statement. It reads all data from the invalid input to the end of the line. For a complete discussion of the flush statement, see "Testing for Valid User Input" in the software engineering section.

Also note how the error messages tell the user exactly what went wrong, rather than giving a general "The numbers entered are incorrect" type of message. Whenever possible, you should tell the user exactly what went wrong.

Two Common Input Format Mistakes

There are as many mistakes to be made as there are programmers programming. Two are so common that they need to be emphasized.

Invalid Address

The first common mistake is to use a data value rather than an address for the input parameter. The scan function places the formatted input at the address specified in the parameter list. When we pass data rather than an address, C interprets the data as an address. This causes a part of memory to be destroyed. If we are lucky, our program fails immediately. If we are unlucky, it runs until the destroyed part of the program is needed and then fails. This problem is shown in **Figure 7-8**.

Figure 7-8   Missing address operator in `scanf`

```
...
printf ("\nPlease enter number of dependents : ");
scanf ("%4d", a);
...
```

A missing address operator will cause your program to fail.

Data Type Conflict

The second common mistake is a conflict between the format string and the input stream. This occurs, for example, when the format string calls for a numeric value and the input stream contains an alphabetic character. If any conflict occurs between the format string and the input stream, the scanf operation aborts. The character that caused the conflict stays in the input stream, and the rest of the input stream (including the troublemaker) remains waiting to be processed. The problem is that the input stream cannot be filled again until it has been completely processed or flushed by the program. The next input operation will read from the unused stream instead of reading from a new input stream. The result: Everything is a mess!

In **Figure 7-9**, the user meant to enter the number 235 but instead entered 23r. (This is a common error. Note that the r key is just below and to the left of the 5 on the keyboard.) When scanf reads the input stream, it interprets the number 23 but stops with the r and returns 1, indicating that one decimal number was successfully formatted. The r remains in the input stream, waiting for the next scanf. The typical result of this error is a perpetual loop looking for an integer value. Even if we detect and flush the error when the r is read, we still have processed the wrong data (23, not 235) in the first read!

Figure 7-10 contains three more examples that show the operation of a fscanf function. In the first example, the format string requests that two integers be read, and two are successfully read. The value returned by the scanf function is 2. In the second example, two more numbers are requested, but only one is available in the input stream. In this case, the value of the scanf expression is 1. The third example shows the result if all the data have been read and the input file is at end of file.

Figure 7-9 Data type conflict

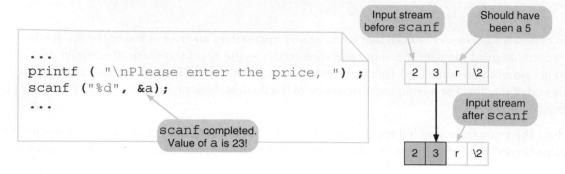

Figure 7-10 `fscanf` examples

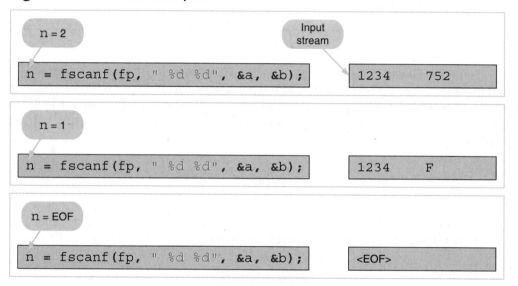

Input Examples

In this section, we present several examples of scanf formatting. Some of them are rarely used, but they illustrate some of the finer points of formatting. We suggest that you cover up the answer until you have tried to write the statement yourself.

Example: scanf Statement 1

Write the scanf statement that will read three values—a real number, an integer, and a character— from the standard input file. The input is

```
3.1416 31416 x
scanf("%f %d %c", &fNum, &iNum, &aChr);
```

Example: scanf Statement 2

Write the scanf statement that will read three values—a real number, an integer, and a character—from the standard input file. All data are on different lines. The input is

```
3.1416
31416
X
scanf("%f %d %c", &fNum, &iNum, &aChr);
```

Note that this statement is the same as the first example. Because the newline is whitespace, it makes no difference if the data are separated by newlines, spaces, or tabs. However, the following code fails when it tries to read the character!

```
scanf("%f%d%c", &fNum, &iNum, &aChr);
```

Do you see the mistake? Recall that the character conversion code (c) does not skip whitespace. Therefore, it reads the return character from the integer input. To prevent this problem, code a space before the character format specification. The space discards all whitespace characters before it reads the character.

Example: scanf Statement 3

Write the scanf statement that will read two fractions, such as 14/26 and 25/ 66, from the standard input unit and place the numerators and denominators in integer variables.

```
scanf("%d/%d %d/%d", &n1, &d1, &n2, &d2);
```

Example: fscanf Statement 1

Write the fscanf statement that will read a date, such as 5-10-1936, formatted with dashes (-) into three different integer fields. The input is to be read from a file opened as spData.

```
fscanf(spData, "%d-%d-%d", &month, &day, &year);
```

Note that with this statement, an error results if the user enters 5/10/2022.

Example: fscanf Statement 2

Write the fscanf statement that will read three integers from a file opened as spData and assign the number of successfully formatted variables to the identifier result.

```
result = fscanf(spData, "%d %d %d", &i, &j, &k);
```

Example: fscanf Statement 3

Given a file with four integers in each line, write a fscanf statement to read only the first, second, and fourth integer from a line; that is, discard the third element. Read the data from the file spData.

```
result = fscanf(spData, "%d%d%*d%d", &a, &b, &d);
```

Example: fscanf Statement 4

Write the fscanf statement that will read three integers from a file opened as spData and assign the number of successfully formatted variables to the identifier result. Use a defined constant for the format string.

```
#define FORMAT_3D "%d %d %d"
result = fscanf(spData, FORMAT_3D, &i, &j, &k);
```

Input Stream Concerns

There are three more points we need to discuss about scanf and how it handles the input stream.

1. The input stream is buffered. The operating system does not pass the data in the input stream until we press the return key. This means that there is always a return character at the end of the stream.

2. The scanf function leaves the return character in the buffer by default. If we want the buffer to be empty, we must read the return character and discard it. We read it using a character conversion specification with a suppress flag. When the return character remains in the buffer, the next scanf discards it for all conversion codes

except character and scan set. Alternatively, we can force it to be discarded by placing a space at the beginning of the format string or before a conversion specification.

3. The scanf function does not terminate until the format string is exhausted—that is, until all specified operations are complete. Whitespace characters in the format string cause whitespace characters in the buffer to be read and discarded. When a whitespace character occurs at the end of the format string, scanf reads and discards the return character in the buffer and then waits for more input. It cannot terminate until it finds a nonwhitespace character.

Let's look at some examples.

Example: fscanf Statement 5

In this example, we have just one scanf call in our program that reads two integers. In this case, the return character remains in the buffer, but it is not a problem. When the program terminates, the operating system flushes all buffers.

```
scanf ("%d %d", &a, &b);
```

Example: fscanf Statement 6

In this example, we explicitly consume the return character by reading and suppressing it.

```
scanf ("%d %d %*c", &a, &b);
```

Example: fscanf Statement 7

In this example, we let the return key stay in the buffer and let the second call discard it. Note that in this case, it does not matter if the next scanf follows immediately or after several lines of code. The first conversion specification (%d) at the beginning of the second scanf discards the return character left by the first scanf. The return character for the second input stream, however, remains in the buffer.

```
scanf ("%d %d", &a, &b);
scanf ("%d %d", &c, &d);
```

Example: fscanf Statement 8

When the first format specification in a scanf format string uses a character or edit set conversion code, any return character left in the buffer by a previous scanf operation must be manually consumed. This can be problematic because the leftover return character is read first, as follows:

```
// Does not work because %c reads the left-over return
scanf ("%d %d", &num1, &num2);
scanf ("%c %d" &aChr, &num1);
```

One solution is to put a whitespace character at the beginning of the second scanf to discard the previous return character. The whitespace before %c in the second scanf discards the return character.

```
// Preferred Solution
scanf ("%d %d", &num1, &num2);
scanf (" %c %d", &aChr, &num1);
```

Another solution is to discard the return character at the end of the previous format string. Note that as the number of scanf statements in a program grow, the safer and preferred method is to discard the return character at the beginning of the format string. In the following code, the character conversion specification (%*c) consumes the newline character at the end of the stream.

```
// Alternate Solution:
scanf ("%d %d%*c", &num1, &num2);
scanf ("%c %d", &aChr, &num1);
```

Example: `fscanf` Statement 9

The `scanf` function can hang our program. For example, in the following fragment of code, we expected that the `printf` function would be called after we entered two integers. The program, however, hangs. The reason is that the whitespace at the end of the control string tells `scanf` to discard any whitespace it sees in the buffer. Therefore, `scanf` deletes our return character. But, to complete its operation, `scanf` must find a return character. It does not matter how many return keys we enter on the keyboard, `scanf` discards all of them looking for a nonwhitespace character.

```
// Note space at end of first format string.
scanf ("%d %d ", &a, &b);
printf("Data entered: %d %d\n" , a, b);
scanf ("%d %d", &c, &d);
Sample run:
10 20<return>
<return>
```

We can force `scanf` to complete by entering any nonwhitespace character. Because `scanf` wants to format only two numbers, any character causes it to complete successfully. The following example demonstrates how we can force `scanf` to complete.

```
// Note space at end of first format string.
scanf ("%d %d ", &a, &b);
printf("Data entered: %d %d\n", a, b);
scanf ("%d %d", &c, &d);
Sample run:
10 20<return>    // scanf hangs here
x<return>        // extra character to force end
Data entered: 10 20
```

Note, however, that the extra character we enter (x) remains in the buffer and will be read next time `scanf` is executed. This extra character is undoubtedly not valid for the next read, which means that our program will produce invalid results.

Note | Discarding the return character is different from consuming it. Discarding can be done by whitespaces in the control string; consuming can only be done by reading the return character with a `%c`.

Output Formatting (`printf` and `fprintf`)

Two print formatted functions display output in human readable form under the control of a format string that is very similar to the format string in `scanf`. When necessary, internal formats are converted to character formats. In other words, it is the opposite of the scan formatted functions.

These functions have the following format:

```
printf("format string", value list)
fprintf(sp, "format string", value list)
```

One of the first differences to note is that the value list is optional. Whereas you always need a variable when you are reading, in many situations, such as user prompts, you display strings without a value list.

Three examples of `printf` output that might be found in a program are shown in the following code. The first is a greeting message at the start of the program, the second displays the result of a calculation, and the last is a closing message.

```
printf ("\nWelcome to Calculator.\n");
printf ("\nThe answer is %6.2f\n", x);
printf ("Thank you for using Calculator");
```

The `fprintf` function works just like `printf` except that it specifies the file in which the data will be displayed. The file can be the standard output (`stdout`) or standard error (`stderr`) files. For example, to write the three previous lines to a report file, we use the following code:

```
fprintf (spReport, "\nWelcome to Calculator.\n");
fprintf (spReport, "\nThe answer is %6.2f\n", x);
fprintf (spReport, "Thank you for using Calculator");
```

Print Conversion Specifications

Previously, we introduced some of the conversion codes. **Table 7-4** shows the flags, sizes, and conversion code for the `printf` family.

Table 7-4   Flags, sizes, and conversion codes for `printf` family flag

ARGUMENT TYPE	FLAG	SIZE SPECIFIER	CODE
Integer	-, +, 0, space	hh (char), h (short), none (int), l (long), ll (long long)	d, i
Unsigned integer	-, +, 0, space	hh (char), h (short), none (int), l (long), ll (long long)	u
Integer (octal)	-, +, 0, #, space	hh (char), h (short), none (int), l (long), ll (long long)	o
Integer (hex)	-, +, 0, #, space	hh (char), h (short), none (int), l (long), ll (long long)	x, X
Real	-, +, 0, #, space	none (float), l (double), L (long double)	f
Real (scientific)	-, +, 0, #, space	none (float), l (double), L (long double)	e, E, g, G
Real (hexadecimal)	-, +, 0, #, space	none (float), l (double), L (long double)	a, A
Character	-	none (char), l (w-char)	c
String	-	none (char string), l (w-char string)	s
Pointer			p
Integer (for count)		none (int), h (short), l (long)	n
To print %			%

Flag

There are four output flags: justification, padding, sign, and alternate form. **Table 7-5** shows the output flag options.

Table 7-5   Flag formatting options

FLAG TYPE	FLAG CODE	FORMATTING
Justification	none	right justified
	-	left justified
Padding	none	space padding
	0	zero padding
Sign	none	positive value: no sign negative value: –
	+	positive value: +
		negative value: –
	space	positive value: space negative value: –
Alternate	#	print alternative format for real, hexadecimal, and octal

Justification

The justification flag controls the placement of a value when it is shorter than the specified width. Justification can be left or right. If there is no flag and the defined width is larger than required, the value is right justified. The default is right justification. To left justify a value, the flag is set to minus (–).

Padding

The padding flag defines the character that fills the unused space when the value is smaller than the print width. It can be a space, the default, or zero. If there is no flag defined for padding, the unused width is filled with spaces; if the flag is 0, the unused width is filled with zeros. Note that the zero flag is ignored if it is used with left justification because adding zeros after a number changes its value.

Sign Flag

The sign flag defines the use or absence of a sign in a numeric value. We can specify one of three formats: default formatting, print signed values, or prefix positive values with a leading space. Default formatting inserts a sign only when the value is negative. Positive values are formatted without a sign. When the flag is set to a plus (+), signs are printed for both positive and negative values. If the flag is a space, then positive numbers are printed with a leading space and negative numbers with a minus sign.

Alternate Flag

The alternate flag (#) is used with the real, engineering, hexadecimal, and octal conversion codes. The alternate flag is discussed with the conversion codes to which it applies.

Width

The meaning of the width field for input is the conceptual opposite of the width field for output. For input, the width specifies the maximum width. For output specifications, the width provides the minimum output width. However, if the data are wider than the specified width, C prints all the data.

Precision

Precision is specified as a period followed by an integer. Precision has meaning only for output fields, and it is an error to use it for input. Precision can control the following:

1. The minimum number of digits for integers. If the number has fewer significant digits than the precision specified, leading zeros will be printed.

2. The number of digits after the decimal point in float.

3. The number of significant digits in g and G output.

Size

The size specification is a modifier for the conversion code. Used in combination with the conversion code, it specifies the type of the associated variable, for example, a `long double` (`Lf`). The size codes with their associated conversion codes are explained in Table 7-4.

Conversion Codes

This section discusses all the input conversion codes except string and pointer, which you will learn about as you become a more experienced programmer.

> **Integer** (`d` and `i`) The value is formatted as a signed decimal number. The integer format code (`i`) is identical to the decimal code (`d`) for output.

> **Unsigned** (`u`) The value is formatted as an unsigned decimal number.

> **Octal and Hexadecimal** (`o`, `x`, `X`) The value is formatted in either octal or hexadecimal, as indicated by the conversion code. The alpha hexadecimal codes are printed in lowercase if the x code is used and in uppercase for the X code. If you are not familiar with octal or hexadecimal numbers, see Appendix A, "Numbering Systems." When the alternative format flag is used, the hexadecimal values are prefixed with `ox` or `OX` and octal numbers are printed with a zero prefix.

> **Real** (`f`) The real format code (`f`) was discussed earlier. If the precision is 0, the decimal point is printed only if the alternate flag (`#`) is also present.

> **Scientific notation** (`e`, `E`, `g`, `G`, `a`) These codes are the same as described for the `scanf`. The e and E codes format the number using (`f`), precision may be used to control the number of digits after the decimal point. If no precision is specified, six digits are used. If the precision is 0, no digits are used after the decimal point and the decimal point itself is shown only when the alternate form flag (`#`) is used. The g and G codes are also scientific notation. However, the scientific notation is used only when the exponent is less than −4 or greater than the specified precision. Otherwise, the real formatting rules are used. When the value is formatted in scientific notation, the uppercase G formats the number with an uppercase E. The (a and A) codes generate signed hexadecimal fractional representations with a decimal power-of-two exponent. The formatted result with A is formatted as `±0Xh.hhhP±dd`, where h represents hexadecimal digits and d represents decimal digits.

> **Count** (`n`) To verify the number of output characters, we use the n conversion code. This code requires a matching variable into which `printf` places the count of the characters output. Because the operation places the results in the variable, its address must be used in the parameter list. In the following example, count is a short integer that is to receive the number of characters written (note the address operator):

```
printf("%d %8.2f %d %hn", i, x, j, &count);
```

> **Percent** (`%`) The percent sign as a conversion code is used to output a percent sign. For example, assume that grade contains a student's score expressed as a percentage. The following statement could then be used to print the grade in the format 93.5%. Note that there is no output value for the percent conversion code.

```
printf("%4.1f%%", grade);
```

Example: Scientific Formatting

The following code fragment demonstrates the use of scientific formatting. We print the same real number first in real number format (`%f`), then in three scientific notations (`%e`, `%G`, and `%a`).

```
double x = 1234.5678;
printf("|%#.4f| |%#.4e| |%#.4G| |%#.4a|", x, x, x, x);
```

Output

```
|1234.5678| |1.2346e+03| | 1235 . | |0X1.34A4P+10|
```

The fourth output needs a little discussion. To verify that it is correct, we must convert the hexadecimal number to decimal. Using the following calculation, we see that 1.34A4 is approximately equal to 1234.56.

$$(1 \times 16^0 + 3 \times 16^{-1} + 4 \times 16^{-2} + A \times 16^{-3} + 4 \times 16^{-4}) \times 2^{10}$$

Output Side Effect and Value

The side effect of the print functions is to write text data to the output file. The value it returns is the number of characters written. If an error occurs, EOF, which is defined in the `stdio.h` header file, is returned. These concepts, which are summarized in **Figure 7-11**, are similar to the side effects and value discussed with scan functions.

Figure 7-11   Side effect and value of `printf`

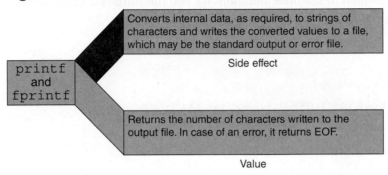

In this section we present several examples of `print` formatting. Although some of them are rarely used, they do illustrate some of the finer points of formatting. The sample output is shown in bold characters. You may want to cover up the answer until you have answered the question yourself.

Example: Output 1

Write the `print` statement that prints three columns of numbers. The first column contains a two-digit integer, the second column contains up to seven digits, and the third column contains a float with four integral numbers and three decimal places.

```
15   10   15.010
78   1234567 1234.123
printf("%2d %7ld %8.3f", i, j, x);
```

Example: Output 2

Write the `print` statement that prints the tax due as stored in a float named x. The output is

```
The tax is: 233.12
printf("The tax is: %8.2f\n", x);
```

Example: Output 3

Modify the previous example to add the words "dollars this year" after the numeric value. The output will then be

```
The tax is 233.12 dollars this year.
printf("The tax is %8.2f dollars this year\n", x);
```

Example: Output 4

Write the `print` statement that prints three integer variables to a file opened as `spOut`. Each write is to append a newline character (¬) to the output.

```
100 200 300
fprintf(spOut, "%d %d %d\n", i, j, k);
```

Example: Output 5

Write the `print` statement that prints three floating-point values. The first is a `float` with two places of precision; the second is a `double`, printed in scientific notation (G); and the third is a `long double`, printed using scientific notation (E). Each value prints on a separate line.

```
3.14
200
4.408946e+00
fprintf(spOut, "%.2f\n%G\n%E\n", i, j, k);
```

Example: Output 6

Write the `print` statement that prints three integral values. The first is a `short`, printed in octal: the second is an `int`, printed using lowercase hexadecimal digits; and the third is a `long`, printed using uppercase hexadecimal digits. End the line with a newline character.

```
25547 7e44 7864CB
fprintf(spOut, "%ho %x %lX\n", i, j, k);
```

Example: Output 7

Write the `print` statement that prints three real numbers in scientific notation (e or g) as shown in the following code. Use the alternate format flag so that the value prints with a decimal point even if it is zero.

```
3.1 7.893E-05 0.
printf("%#5.2g %#9.4G %#5.0g\n", i, j, k);
```

Example: Output 8

Write the `print` statement that prints a decimal number in decimal, hexadecimal, and octal format.

```
256 0X100 0400
printf("%5d %#5X %#5o\n", x, x, x);
```

In the following sections we develop four small programs that demonstrate various aspects of reading and writing files.

Read and Print File

Program 7-3 is a simple program that reads a file of integers and prints them out.

Note how we open the file in this small program. To make it easier to read the code, we split the file open and the test for successful open into two statements. This does not affect the program's efficiency and makes it much easier to code and read the statements.

Program 7-3 | Read and print text file of integers

```c
 1   /* Read a text file of integers, and print the contents.
 2      Written by:
 3      Date:
 4   */
 5   #include <stdio.h>
 6
 7   #include <stdlib.h>
 8   int main (void)
 9   {
10   // Local Declarations
11      FILE* spIn;
12      int numIn;
13
14   // Statements
15      spIn = fopen ("P07-03.DAT", "r");
16      if (spIn != NULL)
17      {
18         printf("Could not open file\a\n");
19         exit (101);
20      } // if open fail
21
22      while ((fscanf(spIn, "%d", &numIn)) == 1)
23         printf("%d ", numIn);
24
25      return 0;
26   } // main
```

Output

```
1 2 3 4 5 6 7 8 9 10
```

Now look at the read in the `while` loop. We loop as long as the `fscanf` succeeds, as indicated by a return value of 1. When the end of file is reached, the `while` statement will be false and the program terminates. There is one slight risk to this program: If a read error is caused by a bad disk, we get the same results. As you become a more experienced programmer, you will learn how to detect this type of error.

Copy File

In **Program 7-4**, we copy a text file of integers to a new file.

Because this program has no display output, we start with a message that says we will copy a file, and we end with a message that says the copy succeeded. Users need to know that the program ran; if we don't print these messages, users will not know. In fact, it is a good idea to print start and end messages with every program. This is a common standard in large production systems.

Program 7-5 Append data to file *(continued)*

```
14
15  // Statements
16      printf("This program appends data to a file\n");
17      spAppnd = fopen("P07-05.DAT", "a");
18      if (!spAppnd)
19      {
20          printf("Could not open input file\a\n");
21          exit (101);
22      } // if open fail
23
24      printf("Please enter first number: ");
25      while ((scanf("%d", &numIn)) != EOF)
26      {
27          fprintf(spAppnd, "%d\n", numIn);
28          printf("Enter next number or <EOF>: ");
29      } // while
30
31      closeResult = fclose(spAppnd);
32      if (closeResult == EOF)
33      {
34          printf("Could not close output file\a\n");
35          exit (201);
36      } // if close fail
37
38      printf("\nFile append complete\n");
39      return 0;
40  } // main
```

```
Output
This program appends data to a file

Please enter first number: 1

Enter next number or <EOF>: 2

Enter next number or <EOF>: 3

Enter next number or <EOF>:^d

File append complete
```

This program differs from Program 7-4 in two ways. First, this program has only one disk file. While we could have read the data to be appended from a file, it is more interesting and more flexible to get the data from the keyboard. The second change is the read loop to get the data. Because we are reading from the keyboard, we need to provide prompts for the user.

Student Grades

Programs 7-3 to 7-5 were all written in `main`. As our last example, let's write a program that reads and writes a student grades file to be turned in at the end of the term. The code is shown in **Program 7-6**.

Program 7-6 | Student grades

```c
1   /* Create a grades file for transmission to Registrar.
2      Written by:
3      Date:
4   */
5
6   #include <stdio.h>
7   // Function Declarations
8   int getStu (FILE* spStu,
9               int* stuID, int* exam1,
10              int* exam2, int* final);
11  int writeStu (FILE* spGrades,
12                int stuID, int avrg, char grade);
13  void calcGrade (int exam1, int exam2, int final,
14                  int* avrg, char* grade);
15
16  int main (void)
17  {
18  // Local Declarations
19     FILE* spStu;
20     FILE* spGrades;
21
22     int stuID;
23     int exam1;
24     int exam2;
25     int final;
26     int avrg;
27
28     char grade;
29
30  // Statements
31     printf("Begin student grading\n");
32     if (!(spStu = fopen ("P07-06.DAT", "r")))
33     {
34        printf("\aError opening student file\n");
35        return 100;
36     } // if open input
37
```

(continue)

Program 7-6   Student grades *(continued)*

```
38      if (!(spGrades = fopen ("P07-06Gr.DAT", "w")))
39      {
40          printf("\aError opening grades file\n");
41          return 102;
42      } // if open output
43
44      while (getStu(
45                      spStu, &stuID, &exam1, &exam2, &final))
46      {
47          calcGrade (exam1, exam2, final, &avrg, &grade);
48          writeStu (spGrades, stuID, avrg, grade);
49      } // while
50
51      fclose (spStu);
52      fclose (spGrades);
53
54      printf("End student grading\n");
55      return 0;
56  } // main
57
58  /*=================getStu==================
59     Reads data from student file.
60     Pre spStu is an open file.
61     stuID, exam1, exam2, final pass by address
62     Post reads student ID and exam scores
63     if data read —returns 1
64     if EOF or error—returns 0
65  */
66  int getStu (FILE* spStu, int* stuID, int* exam1,
67  int* exam2, int* final)
68  {
69  // Local Declarations
70     int ioResult;
71
72  // Statements
73     ioResult = fscanf(spStu, "%d%d%d%d", stuID,
74                        exam1, exam2, final);
75     if (ioResult == EOF)
76        return 0;
77     else if (ioResult != 4)
78     {
79        printf("\aError reading data\n");
80        return 0;
```

(continue)

Program 7-6   Student grades *(continued)*

```
 81      } // if
 82      else
 83         return 1;
 84 } // getStu
 85
 86 /*================ calcGrade================
 87    Determine student grade based on absolute scale.
 88    Pre exam1, exam2, and final contain scores
 89    avrg and grade are addresses of variables
 90    Post Average and grade copied to addresses
 91 */
 92 void calcGrade (int exam1, int exam2, int final,
 93 int* avrg, char* grade)
 94 {
 95 // Statements
 96    *avrg = (exam1 + exam2 + final) / 3;
 97    if (*avrg >= 90)
 98       *grade = 'A';
 99    else if (*avrg >= 80)
100       *grade = 'B';
101    else if (*avrg >= 70)
102       *grade = 'C';
103    else if (*avrg >= 60)
104       *grade = 'D';
105    else
106       *grade = 'F';
107    return;
108 } // calcGrade
109
110 /*================writeStu================
111    Writes student grade data to output file.
112    Pre spGrades is an open file
113    stuID, avrg, and grade have values to write
114    Post Data written to file
115 */
116 int writeStu (FILE* spGrades, int stuID,
117                int avrg,  char grade)
118 {
119 // Statements
120    fprintf(spGrades, "%04d %d %c\n",
121            stuID, avrg, grade);
122    return 0;
123 } // writeStu
```

(continue)

Program 7-6   Student grades *(continued)*

Output
```
Begin student grading
End student grading
Input----------------------
0090    90  90  90
0089    88  90  89
0081    80  82  81
0079    79  79  79
0070    70  70  70
0069    69  69  69
0060    60  60  60
0059    59  59  59
Output---------------
0090    90  A
0089    89  B
0081    81  B
0079    79  C
0070    70  C
0069    69  D
0060    60  D
0059    59  F
```

This program illustrates several important points. Let's start at the top. We open and close the files in main. Often, programmers write subfunctions for program initialization and conclusion, but in this case we decided to write them in main. The processing loop uses the return value from getStu to control the loop (see statement 44). If data are read, then the return value is true (1); if there is an error or all data have been read, the return value is false (0). This design results in a very simple while loop.

Within the loop are three calls: one to read the student data (in the while limit test), one to calculate the grade, and one to write the grades file. Study the parameters carefully. We have used a combination of data values and addresses. Note especially the file parameters. In the function headers, the file parameters are coded as FILE*, which you should recognize as a file address. We do not use an address operator when we pass the files, however, because they are already addresses. (See statements 44 and 48.)

Now study the results. The student ID is written as four digits with leading zeros because it is really a code, not a number. Note how we created the test data to verify that all of the boundaries in our multiway selection work correctly. To make it easy to verify, we made the student ID the same as the average. With these clues to the expected output, it only takes a quick review of the results to confirm that the program ran successfully.

7.5 Standard Input/Output Functions: Character

Character input functions read one character at a time from a text stream. Character output functions write one character at the time to a text stream. These functions can be divided into two general groups: input/output functions used exclusively with a terminal device and input/output functions that can be used with both terminal devices and text files. They are summarized in **Figure 7-12**.

Figure 7-12   Character input/output functions

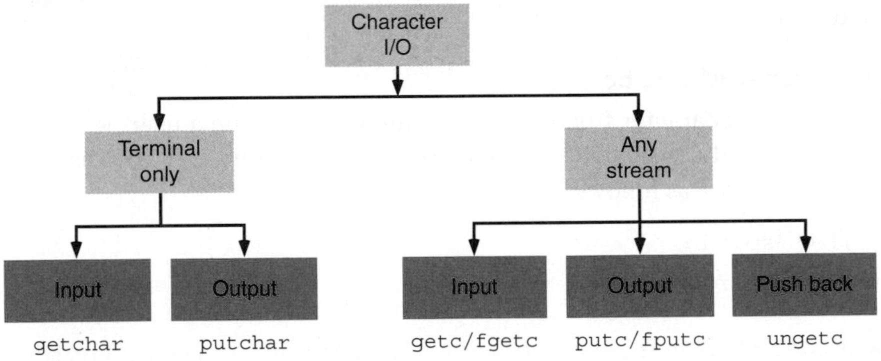

C provides two parallel sets of functions, one for characters and one for wide-characters. They are virtually identical except for the type. Because wide-characters are not commonly used and because their functions operate identically, we limit our discussion to the character type.

Terminal Character I/O

C declares a set of character input/output functions that can only be used with the standard streams: standard input (stdin), standard output (stdout).

Read a Character: getchar

The get character function (getchar) reads the next character from the standard input stream and returns its value. Only two input conditions stop it: end of file or a read error. If the end of file condition results, or if an error is detected, the functions return EOF. It is our responsibility to determine if some condition other than end of file stopped the reading. The function declaration is shown in the following code:

```
int getchar (void);
```

Note that the return type is an integer and not a character as you might expect. The return type is an integer because EOF is defined as an integer (int) in the standard definition stddef.h and other header files. There is another reason for this: C guarantees that the EOF flag is not a character. This is true regardless of what character set it is using: ASCII, EBCDIC, or whatever. If you examine the control characters in ASCII, you will find none for end of file. Traditionally, EOF is defined as –1, but this is not prescribed by ANSI/ISO. An individual implementation could therefore choose a different value.

Write a Character: putchar

The put character function (putchar) writes one character to the monitor. If any error occurs during the write operation, it returns EOF. This may sound somewhat unusual, as EOF is normally thought of as an input file consideration, but in this case it simply means that the character couldn't be written. The function declaration is as follows:

```
int putchar (int out_char);
```

Again the type is integer. An interesting result occurs with this function: When it succeeds, it returns the character it wrote as an integer!

Terminal and File Character I/O

The terminal character input/output functions are designed for convenience; we don't need to specify the stream. In this section, we describe a more general set of functions that can be used with both the standard streams and a file.

These functions require an argument that specifies the stream associated with a terminal device or a file.

1. When used with a terminal device, the streams are declared and opened by the system—the standard input stream (stdin) for the keyboard and the standard output stream (stdout) for the monitor.

2. When used with a file, we need to explicitly declare the stream. It is our responsibility to open the stream and associate it with the file.

Read a Character: getc and fgetc

The get functions read the next character from the file stream, which can be a user-defined stream or stdin, and convert it to an integer. If the read detects an end of file, the functions return EOF. EOF is also returned if any error occurs. The prototype functions are as follows:

```
int getc    (FILE* spIn);
int fgetc   (FILE* spIn);
```

Although the getc and fgetc functions operate basically the same way, for technical reasons we recommend that only fgetc be used. An example of fgetc is shown in the following section.

```
nextChar = fgetc (spMyFile);
```

Write q Character: *pi/fr* and *fputc*

The put functions write a character to the file stream specified, which can be a user-defined stream, stdout, or stderr. For fputc, the first parameter is the character to be written and the second parameter is the file. If the character is successfully written, the functions return it. If any error occurs, they return EOF. The prototype functions are as follows:

```
int putc (int oneChar, FILE* spOut);
int fputc (int oneChar, FILE* spOut);
```

Once again, we recommend that only fputc be used as in this example:

```
fputc (oneChar, spMyFile);
```

Note that we have discarded the return value. Although we may occasionally find a use for it, it is almost universally discarded.

Push a Character Back: *ungetc*

The push back functions insert one or more characters into a stream that has been opened for input; that is, they write to an input stream. When multiple characters are pushed back, they are then read in reverse order; that is the last character pushed is the first character read. Although multiple characters can be pushed back, we cannot push back more characters than we read. After a successful push back, when the stream is next read, the character pushed back will be read.

If the operation succeeds, the functions return the character; if they do not succeed, as with too many characters being pushed into the stream, they return EOF.

The unget character functions require that the first parameter be a character and that the second parameter be an input stream. The function declarations are as follows:

```
int ungetc (int oneChar, FILE* spData);
```

The intent of these functions is to return one or more characters to the input stream for a subsequent read. This situation might occur when we are reading characters that prompt action, such as in a menu system, and the wrong character is read as in the following code. In these situations, it is cleaner to reinsert the character into the input stream than to set a flag or otherwise pass the character through several functions.

In the following example, we want to process any option that is a character. Numeric options are processed in another function. Therefore, if we detect that an option is numeric, we put it back on the input stream and exit the function.

```c
option = fgetc (stdin);
if (isdigit(option))
   ungetc (option, stdin);
else
{

   ...

}
```

Programming Example: Character Input/Output

This section contains examples of common text file applications.

Create Text File

Program 7-7 reads text from the keyboard and creates a text file. All data are stored in text format with newlines only where input by the user.

Program 7-7 | Create text file

```c
1   /* This program creates a text file.
2      Written by:
3      Date:
4   */
5   #include <stdio.h>
6   int main (void)
7   {
8   // Local Declarations
9      FILE* spText;
10     int c;
11     int closeStatus;
12
13  // Statements
14     printf("This program copies input to a file.\n");
15     printf("When you are through, enter <EOF>.\n\n");
16
17     if (!(spText = fopen("P07-07.DAT","w")))
18     {
19        printf("Error opening P07-07.DAT for writing");
20        return (1);
21     } // if open
```

(continue)

Program 7-7   Create text file *(continued)*

```
22
23     while ((c = getchar()) != EOF)
24        fputc(c, spText);
25
26     closeStatus = fclose(spText);
27     if (closeStatus == EOF)
28     {
29        printf("Error closing file\a\n");
30        return 100;
31     } // if
32
33     printf("\n\nYour file is complete\n");
34     return 0;
35 } // main
```

Output

```
This program copies input to a file.

When you are through, enter <EOF>.



Now is the time for all good students

To come to the aid of their college. ^d



Your file is complete
```

This simple program is the beginning of a text editor. The biggest element missing is word wrap. Word wrap prevents a word from being split between two lines on a page.

Study the program carefully and note that we used integer for the character type (c) in statement 10. This is an important point whenever you are checking for end of file, as we did in statement 23. Because EOF will not be correctly represented in a character, we must use integer. But, what about when we have a character? C automatically casts the integer to a character wherever it is necessary.

Copy Text File

Program 7-8 will copy one text file to another text file. It is more generalized than Program 7-4, "Copy text file of integers," because it will copy any file data, not just integers.

Program 7-8 | Copy text file

```
1  /* This program copies one text file into another.
2        Written by:
3        Date:
4  */
```

(continue)

Program 7-8   Copy text file *(continued)*

```
 5  #include <stdio.h>
 6  int main (void)
 7  {
 8  // Local Declarations
 9     int c;
10     int closeStatus;
11     FILE* sp1;
12     FILE* sp2;
13
14  // Statements
15     printf("Begin file copy\n");
16
17     if (!(sp1 = fopen ("P07-07.DAT", "r")))
18     {
19        printf("Error opening P07-07.DAT for reading");
20        return (1);
21     } // if open input
22     if (!(sp2 = fopen ("P07-08.DAT", "w")))
23     {
24        printf("Error opening P07-08.DAT for writing");
25        return (2);
26     } // if open output
27
28     while ((c = fgetc(sp1)) != EOF)
29        fputc(c, sp2);
30
31     fclose(sp1);
32     closeStatus = fclose(sp2);
33     if (closeStatus == EOF)
34     {
35        printf("File close error.\a\n");
36        return 201;
37     } // if close error
38     printf("File successfully created\n");
39     return 0;
40  } // main
```

This program contains two notable style points. First, we have used generic names for the files, sp1 and sp2. Because this program simply copies and creates text files, we cannot give the files names that reflect their data. Better names might be spIn and spOut, but they are also generic.

Second, the program has two potential file open errors. We use different error codes for those operating systems whose job control can distinguish between different completion codes. We have also included the file names in the error messages so that the user knows exactly which file had the problem.

Finally, a subtle point: Note that we have arranged the local declarations in order of increasing complexity. First, we define the character and integer types: then we define the files. It is good practice to group the definitions by type and in order of increasing complexity.

Count Characters and Lines

Program 7-9 counts the number of characters and lines in a program. Lines are designated by a newline. Also note that the program guards against a file that ends without a newline for the last line.

Program 7-9 | Count characters and lines

```
1   /* This program counts characters and lines in a program.
2      Written by:
3      Date:
4   */
5   #include <stdio.h>
6   int main (void)
7   {
8   // Local Declarations
9      int curCh;
10     int preCh;
11     int countLn = 0;
12     int countCh = 0;
13     FILE* sp1;
14
15  // Statements
16     if (!(sp1 = fopen ("P07-07.DAT", "r")))
17     {
18        printf ("Error opening P07-07.DAT for reading");
19        return (1);
20     } // if open error
21
22     while ((curCh = fgetc(sp1)) != EOF)
23     {
24        if (curCh != '\n')
25           countCh++;
26        else
27           countLn++;
28        preCh = curCh;
29     } // while
30
31     if (preCh != '\n')
32        countLn++;
33
34     printf ("Number of characters: %d\n", countCh);
```

(continue)

Program 7-9   Count characters and lines *(continued)*

```
35      printf("Number of lines  : %d\n", countLn);
36      fclose(sp1);
37      return 0;
38 } // main
```

Output

```
Number of characters: 74

Number of lines:     2
```

Program 7-9 is rather straightforward. The only real problem is in making sure that the last line is counted even if there is no newline. We can check this at the end of the file by making sure that the last character we read, stored in preCh, was a newline. If it isn't, we add 1 to the line count.

Once again, we have used the integer type for our input character. Everything works correctly, even statement 31, which compares the integer type (preCh) to a character literal.

Count Words in File

Program 7-10 counts the number of words in a file. A word is defined as one or more characters separated by one or more whitespace characters—that is, by a space, a tab, or a newline.

Program 7-10 | Count words

```
1  /* Count number of words in file. Words are separated by
2     whitespace characters: space, tab, and newline.
3     Written by:
4     Date:
5  */
6
7  #include <stdio.h>
8  #define WHT_SPC\
9      (cur == ' ' || cur == '\n' || cur == '\f' )
10 int main (void)
11 {
12 // Local Declarations
13    int cur;
14    int countWd = 0;
15    char word = '0';    // O out of word: I in word
16    FILE* sp1;
17
18 // Statements
19    if (!(sp1 = fopen("P07-07.DAT", "r")))
20    {
```

(continue)

Program 7-10   Count words *(continued)*

```
21          printf("Error opening P07-07.DAT for reading");
22          return (1);
23    } // if file open error
24    while ((cur = fgetc(sp1)) != EOF)
25    {
26       if (WHT_SPC)
27          word = '0';
28       else
29          if (word == '0' )
30          {
31             countWd++;
32             word = 'I';
33          } // else
34    } // while
35    printf("The number of words is: %d\n", countwd);
36
37    fclose(sp1);
38    return 0;
39 } //main
```

Output

```
The number of words is: 15
```

The selection logic for this problem is similar to the previous program. We must determine when we are in a word and when we are between words. We are between words when we start the program and whenever we are at whitespace. To keep track of where we are, we use a flag, word. When word contains the letter I, we are in a word; when it contains the letter O, we are out of a word. We increment the counter only at the beginning of a word, when we set the word flag to I.

Note that the problem handles multiple whitespace characters by simply setting the word flag to O. Note also how we use a preprocessor define statement to define whitespace. This has no effect on the efficiency of the program, but it makes it easier to read.

Software Engineering

Testing Files

Testing files can be a very difficult task for two reasons. First, normal testing cannot reveal all errors. For example, testing can't reveal errors created by physical media that has become unreadable. Good programs test for these types of errors, but they are difficult to find.

Second, there are so many ways things can go wrong. The test plan therefore needs to ensure that all possibilities have been tested. Chief among them is the situation in which a user enters a nonnumeric character while trying to enter a number. If we don't provide for this situation, our program will not work properly. In fact, in some situations, it will not work at all.

Testing for Valid User Input

Consider the following code to read an integer value. If the user miskeys the data, the program will go into an infinite loop.

```
printf("\nPlease enter Number of Units Sold: ");
while (scanf("%d", SunitsSold) != 1) \
    // scanf returns 1 if number read correctly
    printf("\nInvalid number. Please re-enter.\n");
```

In this case, it looks as if the programmer has done everything correctly. The program checks for valid data being returned. A user prompt shows what data should be entered; the program checks for valid data being read; and if there were errors, provides the user with a good error message and repeats the scanf. What is wrong?

The problem lies in what scanf does when it finds an invalid first digit. If the number is entirely wrong, it leaves the data pending in the input stream. This means that while the user sees the error message, the invalid data are still in the input stream waiting for a scanf that will properly read and process them. Remember that scanf thinks that these "invalid data" are the beginning of the next field. It is our job as a programmer to get rid of the "bad data." We can do this with a small piece of code that is commonly named FLUSH. Its purpose is to read through the input stream looking for the end of a line. When it finds the end of the line, it terminates. Let's first look at the code, then we will look at an easy way to implement it.

```
while (getchar( ) != '\n')
    ;
```

Examine this statement carefully. All it does is get a character and then throw it away. That is, the character it reads is not saved. Now examine the expression that is controlling the while. If getchar reads any character other than a newline, the statement is true. If it reads a newline, then the statement is false. The while statement will, therefore, read the input stream and throw away all characters until it sees a newline. When it finds the newline, it will throw it away too, but at that point, the loop stops. In other words, it flushes the input stream to a newline character. This is exactly what we want to do when the user accidentally keys the wrong character when the program expects a digit.

One more point. Note that we coded the null statement on its own line. This is to make it clear that we intended to code a null statement. It also eliminates a warning message from the compiler—good compilers look for common errors like unintended semicolons.

Now, what's the easiest way to implement this handy statement? Well, we could simply code it everywhere you need it, but chances are that we would make some mistakes that would have to be found and debugged. A better solution is to use the preprocessor define declarative and code the statement only once, as shown below.

```
#define FLUSH while (getchar( ) != '\n')
```

Note that there is no semicolon at the end of the define declarative. We could have put one there, but it's better to put the semicolon after the FLUSH in the program. Our error code can now be changed to handle this type of error, as shown in **Program 7-11**.

> ## Program 7-11 | Handling errors the right way

```
1   #define FLUSH while (getchar() != '\n')
2   ...
3   printf("\nPlease enter Number of Units Sold: ");
4   while (scanf("%d", &unitsSold) != 1)
5   {
```

(continue)

Program 7-11   Handling errors the right way *(continued)*

```
 6      // scanf returns 1 if number read correctly
 7      FLUSH;
 8      printf("\nInvalid number. Please re-enter: ");
 9  } // while
```

Value Errors

Previously, we discussed some of the techniques for data validation. But the subtleties of data validation can be quite complex. Consider another type of human error, the partially correct input. In our program above, we assumed that the user entered invalid data for the first digit of the number. What if the error occurs on the second or third digit? Then the scanf function is happy, for the time being anyway, and returns a 1, indicating that it read one number successfully. How do we guard against this?

The best way is to echo the input to the user and ask for verification that it is correct. Although this greatly slows down the input process, for critical data it is necessary. The code for this situation is shown in **Program 7-12**. Here we present it as a complete function.

Program 7-12 | Handling errors with explanations

```
 1  /* This function reads the units sold from the keyboard
 2      and verifies the data with the user.
 3      Pre nothing
 4      Post units Sold read, verified, and returned
 5  */
 6  int getUnitsSold (void)
 7  {
 8  // Local Declarations
 9      int unitsSold;
10      bool valid;
11
12  // Statements
13      do
14      {
15          printf("\nPlease enter Number of Units Sold: ");
16          while (scanf("%d", &unitsSold) != 1)
17          {
18              FLUSH;
19              printf("\aInvalid number. Please re-enter: ");
20          } // while
21          printf("\nVerify Units Sold: %d: ", unitsSold);
22          printf("<Y> correct: <N> not correct: \n");
```

(continue)

Program 7-12   Handling errors with explanations *(continued)*

```
23          FLUSH;
24          if (toupper(getchar ()) == 'Y' )
25              valid = true;
26          else
27          {
28              FLUSH;
29              printf("\nYou responded 'no. ' ");
30              printf("Please re-enter Units Sold\n");
31              valid = false;
32          } // if
33      } while (!valid);
34      return unitsSold;
35 } // getUnitsSold
```

This function merits some discussion. First, note the good user communication throughout the function. It begins with a complete prompt and provides clear error messages whenever problems are detected.

We have implemented this logic with a do … while statement, which always loops at least once, because we know that there will always be input. This is the standard loop for validating user input. Within the loop are two different validation steps. The first tests for totally invalid input, the second asks the user to verify the input. If either test indicates a problem, the input is flushed. Note that the user messages are different depending on the circumstances.

The function cannot end unless the valid flag is true. The if statement in the loop will set it true if the user replies positively. Otherwise, it is set false and the input is flushed. This code again demonstrates two principles of good human engineering. The if statement is coded in a positive manner, and the expected event, good input, is checked first.

Many other things can go wrong when we are reading a file, but these two examples cover most of them.

Data Terminology

Computer specialists who deal with data use a set of specific terms to describe their data. These terms deal with data that are stored in files. What we call a variable in our program, they call a field or a data item. A field is the smallest named unit of data in a file. If we were working with data about the ten western states in the continental United States, we would have data like Name, Capital, Number, Square Miles, Population, and Number of Counties. The first two fields are strings and the last four are integers.

These six fields grouped together make up a state record. A record is a collection of related data, in this case state data, treated as a unit. Each record has a key, one or more fields that uniquely identify the record. In our state's record, the key could be the name. Names normally do not make good keys, because they are not guaranteed to be unique. A better choice is the state number, which represents the order in which the states entered the union. This field is guaranteed to be unique.

With text files we cannot create a record. We must wait for binary files and structures to do that. But we can simulate a record by grouping these data on the same line, with each field separated from the next by whitespace. The whitespace acts as a delimiter to determine the field width. The data for the ten western states are shown in **Table 7-6.**

Data can be logically organized to provide more meaning. Although computer scientists normally store this type of data using binary files, there is no reason it can't be stored in a text file as well. We will return to the discussion again when we study strings.

Table 7-6 Ten western states (2010 Census)

State	Capital	No.	Sq. Miles	Population	No. Counties
Arizona	Phoenix	48	113,508	6,392,017	15
California	Sacramento	31	156,299	37,253,956	58
Colorado	Denver	38	103,595	5,029,196	63
Idaho	Boise	43	82,412	1,567,582	44
Montana	Helena	41	145,388	989,415	56
Nevada	Carson City	36	109,894	2,700,551	16
New Mexico	Santa Fe	47	121,335	2,059,179	33
Oregon	Salem	33	96,184	3,831,074	36
Washington	Olympia	42	66,511	6,724,540	39
Wyoming	Cheyenne	44	96,989	563,626	23

Tips and Common Programming Errors

1. To print a percent sign, you need to use two tokens (`%%`).

2. After you have finished working with a file, you should close it.

3. If you open a file for writing, a new file will be created. This means that if you already have an existing file with the same name, it could be deleted.

4. If you want to write at the end of an existing text file, open the file for appending, not for writing.

5. C output is right justified when using `printf` and `fprintf` functions. If you want your data to be left justified, use the left-justify flag (–) explicitly.

6. It is a compile error to misplace the file pointer in the parameter list. The file pointer is coded last in all file functions except `fscanf` and `fprintf`, in which it is coded first.

7. An error that may cause your program run to terminate is to use a format code that does not match the variable type being read.

8. An error that will give invalid output is to use a format code that does not match the variable being printed.

9. Several common errors are created when a file operation is included in a selection statement. Three are shown below.

   a. The following code does not properly test to make sure that the file was opened correctly:

   ```
   if (sp = fopen() != NULL)      // logic error
   if ((sp = fopen()) != NULL)       // good code
   ```

   b. The following code does not store the character read in `ch`. It stores the logical result of the compare in `ch`.

   ```
   if (ch = getchar() != '\n')      // logic error
   if ((ch = getchar()) != '\n')    // good code
   ```

   c. In a similar way, the following code is invalid:

   ```
   // logic error
   while (ioResult = scanf (...)!= EOF)
   // good code
   while ((ioResult = scanf(...))!= EOF)
   ```

d. It is a logic error to define ioResult in the above statement as a character because EOF (−1) cannot be stored in a character.

10. It is a logic error to code a whitespace character at the end of a scanf statement.

11. It is a run-time error to attempt to open a file that is already opened.

12. It is a run-time error to attempt to read a file opened in the write mode or to write a file opened in the read mode.

Summary

> A file is a collection of related data treated as a unit.

> Data in a text file are stored as human-readable characters. The data in a text file are usually divided into lines separated by a newline character.

> A stream is a sequence of elements in time.

> A stream is associated with a file in C.

> There are three standard file streams in C: standard input, standard output, and standard error.

> The standard input is associated with the keyboard. The standard output and the standard error are associated with the monitor.

> The standard file streams can be accessed respectively using stdin, stdout, and stderr. These are pointers (addresses) to tables (structures) containing the information about the standard streams.

> To manipulate and access files, there are different types of input/output functions.

> The open/close functions, fopen and fclose, are used to open and close the association between external files and internal streams.

> A file in C can be any of the three basic modes: reading, writing, and appending.

> When a file is opened in reading mode, the file marker is positioned at the beginning of the existing file. The file is ready to be read.

> When a file is opened for writing, the file marker is positioned at the beginning of a newly created empty file, before the end-of-file character. The file is ready to be written.

> When a file is opened for appending, the marker is positioned at the end of the existing file (or at the beginning of a newly created file), before the end-of-file marker. The file is then ready to be written.

> Formatted input/output functions allow us to read data from and write data to files character by character while formatting them to the desired data types such as char, int, and float. The functions scanf and fscanf are used for reading. The functions printf and fprintf are used for writing.

> Character input/output functions allow us to read or write files character by character. The functions fgetc, getc, and getchar can be used for reading. The functions fputc, putc, and putchar can be used for writing.

> C99 added a set of wide character functions. They are fgetwc, getwc, getwchar, fputwc, putwc, and putwchar.

> When we are reading data from files, we should validate the data.

Key Terms

alternate flag	file mode	sign flag
append mode	filename	signed
auxiliary storage devices	justification flag	size specification
binary files	key	standard error
buffer	open function	text file
close function	padding flag	value error
end of file	precision	width
field	read mode	write mode
field width	record	
file	secondary storage devices	

Review Questions

1. User files are created using the `FILE` type.
   a. True   **b.** False

2. If a file does not exist, the append mode returns an error.
   a. True   **b.** False

3. The conversion specification starts with an asterisk (*) and ends with the conversion code.
   a. True   **b.** False

4. The space flag is used to left-justify output in the `printf` function.
   a. True   **b.** False

5. One of the problems with testing files is that some errors, such as physically bad media, cannot be created so that they can be tested.
   a. True   **b.** False

6. Which of the following is considered auxiliary storage?
   a. Disk
   b. Random access memory (RAM)
   c. Read only memory (ROM)
   d. Tape
   e. Both disk and tape

7. Which of the following is not a standard file stream?
   a. `stdin`
   b. `stderr`
   c. `stdfile`
   d. `stdout`

8. The C library that contains the prototype statements for file operations is _____.
   a. `file.h`
   b. `proto.h`
   c. `stdfile.h`
   d. `stdio.h`
   e. `stdlib.h`

9. If a file is opened in the `r` mode, C _____.
   a. opens the file for reading and sets the file marker at the beginning
   b. opens the file for reading and sets the file marker at the end
   c. opens the file for writing and sets the file marker at the beginning
   d. opens the file for writing and sets the file marker at the end
   e. returns a null file address indicating an error if the file exists

10. If a file is not opened successfully, C _____.
   a. aborts the program
   b. continues processing with the next statement after the open
   c. changes the file mode to write and opens a new file
   d. displays a message and waits for an answer
   e. returns a file address

11. The _____ specifies the type of data that are being formatted in formatted input/output.
    a. conversion code
    b. data code
    c. field code
    d. format code
    e. pcode

12. The input functions that read text data and convert the data to the types specified by a format string are _____.
    a. `fread` and `readd`. `read` and `readf`
    b. `fscanf` and `fprintf`. `scanf` and `printf`
    c. `fscanf` and `scanf`

13. Which of the following statements about the formatted input function (`scanf`) is false?
    a. `scanf` implicitly casts data to match the conversion code and its corresponding address parameter.
    b. `scanf` reads data from the keyboard and formats it according to conversion specifications.
    c. `scanf` returns an integer containing the number of variables successfully formatted for EOF.

    d. `scanf` stops formatting data when an inappropriate character for the type being formatted is encountered.
    e. To function properly, `scanf` requires at least one address.

14. The _____ function reads the next character from the standard input stream and returns its value.
    a. `fgetc`
    b. `getc`
    c. `getchar`
    d. `readchar`
    e. `ungetc`

15. When `scanf` finds invalid data in the input stream, it _____.
    a. flushes the input to a newline
    b. prints an error message and terminates the program
    c. prints an error message and terminates the `scanf` function
    d. skips the data and formats the next conversion specification, if any
    e. terminates the `scanf` function and leaves the invalid character in the input stream

Exercises

16. Given the following declaration:

```
int   i1;
int   i2;
float  f1;
char  c1;
char  c2;
char  c3;
```

and the following line of data

```
14 23 76 CD
```

what would be the value of i1, i2, f1, c1, c2, and c3 after the following statement?

```
scanf("%d %d %f %c %c %c",
    &i1, &i2, &f1, &c1, &c2, &c3);
```

17. Given the following declaration:

```
int i1;
int i2;
float f1;
char c1;
char c2;
```

and the following line of data

```
14.2 67 67.9
```

what would be the value of i1, i2, f1, c1, and c2 after the following statement?

```
scanf("%d %c %c %i %f ",
    &i1, &c1, &c2, &i2, &f1);
```

18. Given the following declaration:

```
int i1;
int i2;
int i3;
char c1;
char c2;
char c3;
```

and the following line of data:

```
C145d123 34.7
```

what would be the value of i1, i2, i3, c1, c2, and c3 after the following statement?

```
scanf("%c%c%d%c%d%d",
    &c1, &c2, &i1, &c3, &i2, &i3);
```

19. What would be printed from the following program segment?

```
int i1 = 123;
int i2 = -234;
int i3 = -7;
float f1 = 23.5;
float f2 = 12.09;
float f3 = 98.34;
char c1 = 65;
char c2 = ' \n' ;
char c3 = 'E';
printf("%06d, %06d, %06d %c",
    i1, i2, i3, c2);
printf("%-6d, %%, \", \\t, %-06d", i2, i1);
printf("%c %d ", c1, c2);
printf("%c %c %#x", c1 + 32, c3 + 3, c2 + 5);
```

20. What output is produced from the following program? Include in your answer the contents of any files created.

```c
#include <stdio.h>
int main (void)
{
    FILE* sp; int i;
    char ch;
    sp = fopen("TEST.DAT", "w");
    for (i=2; i<20; i+=2)
        fprintf(sp, "%3d", i);
        fclose(sp);
    sp = fopen("TEST.DAT", "r");
    while ((ch = fgetc(sp)) != EOF)
        if (ch == ' ')
            fputc('*', stdout);
        else
            fputc(ch, stdout);
    return 0;
} // main
```

Problems

For the problems and projects in this chapter, you need to create a test file using your text editor. End each line with a newline character; do not write in paragraph format. We suggest the Gettysburg Address as a suitable subject for these files:

Four score and seven years ago our fathers brought forth on this continent a new nation, conceived in liberty, and dedicated to the proposition that all men are created equal. Now we are engaged in a great civil war, testing whether that nation, or any nation so conceived and so dedicated, can long endure. We are met on a great battlefield of that war. We have come to dedicate a portion of that field as a final resting-place for those who here gave their lives that that nation might live. It is altogether fitting and proper that we should do this. But in a larger sense, we cannot dedicate, we cannot consecrate, we cannot hallow, this ground. The brave men, living and dead, who struggled here have consecrated it far above our poor power to add or detract. The world will little note, nor long remember what we say here, but it can never forget what they did here. It is for us the living, rather to be dedicated here to the unfinished work which they who fought here have thus far so nobly advanced. It is rather for us, to be here dedicated to the great task remaining before us, that from these honored dead we take increased devotion to that cause for which they gave the last full measure of devotion; that we here highly resolve that these dead shall not have died in vain; that this nation, under God, shall have a new birth of freedom, and that government of the people, by the people, for the people, shall not perish from the earth.

21. Write a function that appends one file at the end of the other.

22. Write a function that appends a file to itself.

23. Write a function that accepts a file of varying-length lines and changes it to a formatted file with 60 characters in each line.

24. Write a function that calculates the average number of characters per line in a file.

25. Write a function that deletes the last line of any file.

26. Write a function that deletes the blank lines in a file. A blank line is a line with only one single character in it: newline.

27. Write a program that prints itself.

28. Write a program that copies one text file to another and inserts blank lines between paragraphs in the new file. Paragraphs are identified by a newline character.

29. Write a program to copy only lines beginning with a user-specified character.

30. Write a program to parse words onto separate lines; that is, locate and write each word to its own line. Words are defined as one or more characters separated by whitespace.

31. When `scanf` encounters an error, the invalid data are left in the input stream, sometimes making it impossible to continue. Write a function that reads three pieces of numeric data. If an error is detected (return value not EOF but less than 3), flush the erroneous data. (See "Software Engineering" for details on how to write a flush statement.) Then test the function by entering numeric data and alphabetic data in different sequences.

32. Write a program to insert a blank line after the seventh line in a file.

33. Write a program to delete the sixth line in a file. Do not change the sixth line to a blank line; delete it completely.

34. Write a program to insert a blank line after each line in a file. In other words, double-space the text.

35. Write a program to duplicate the fourth line in a file.

36. Write a program to copy a file, deleting the first two characters of each line. (Do not replace the characters with blanks.)

37. Write a program to copy a file, inserting two space characters at the beginning of each line. In other words, each line will be shifted two characters to the right.

38. Write a program that copies the 21st character of each line in a file to a new file. All extracted characters are to be on the same line. If a line in the input file has fewer than 21 characters, write the last character. If a line is blank—that is, if it consists of only whitespace—then copy nothing. At the end of file, write a newline to the new file and close it.

39. Write a program that writes the odd-numbers between 300 and 500 to a text file.

40. Write a function that writes the multiples of num between `lowLimit` and `highLimit` to a text file. Assume that `lowLimit` < `highLimit` and that num is not equal to zero. Then write a test driver to validate your function.

41. Write a program to read a set of scores from a text file, count the scores over 90, copy the scores over 90 to a new file, and print the number of scores over 90 to the monitor.

42. Modify Problem 41 to count and create a file for the ranges 0 to 30, 31 to 60, 61 to 90, and over 90. Print the statistics for each range at the end of the program.

Projects

43. Write a program that will read a text file and count the number of alphabetic characters (`isalpha`), digits (`isdigit`), punctuation characters (`ispunct`), and whitespace characters (`isspace`) in the file. At the end of the file, the program is to display an appropriate report.

44. Write a text analyzer program that reads any text file. The program prints a menu that gives the user the options of counting lines, words, characters, or sentences (one or more words ending in a period), or all of the above. Provide a separate function for each option. At the end of the analysis, write an appropriate report.

45. Write a menu-driven text utility program. The program should be able to:

   a. Copy a user-named file to a new file.

   b. Append a user-named file to another user-named file.

   c. Change the file format to be double-spaced.

   d. Display the contents of the file as a series of 60 character lines with no words split between lines.

46. Using an editor, create an inventory file using the data shown in **Table 7-7** (do not include the column captions, just the data).

Table 7-7   Inventory file data for Project 46

PART NO.	PRICE	QUANTITY ON HAND	REORDER POINT	MINIMUM ORDER
0123	1.23	23	20	20
0234	2.34	34	50	25
3456	34.56	56	50	10
4567	45.67	7	10	5
5678	6.78	75	75	25

Write a program to read the inventory file and create an inventory report. The report will contain the part number, price, quantity on hand, reorder point, minimum order, and order amount. The order amount is calculated when the quantity on hand falls below the reorder point. It is calculated as the sum of the reorder point and the minimum order less the quantity on hand. Provide a report heading, such as "Inventory Report," captions for each column, and an "End of Report" message at the end of the report. Print the part number with leading zeros.

47. Using an editor, create the employee file shown in **Table 7-8**.

Table 7-8   Employee file data for Project 47

EMPLOYEE NO.	DEPARTMENT	PAY RATE	EXEMPT	HOURS WORKED
0101	41	8.11	Y	49
0722	32	7.22	N	40
1273	23	5.43	Y	39
2584	14	6.74	N	45

Write a program to read the employee file and create a payroll register. The register should contain the following data:

   a. Employee number (print left-justified)

   b. Department

   c. Pay rate

   d. Exempt

   e. Hours worked

   f. Base pay (pay rate * hours worked)

Arrays

Learning Objectives

When you complete this chapter, you will be able to:

8.1 Describe basic concepts and uses of arrays

8.2 Declare and define an array in C

8.3 Explain how to pass arrays and array elements to functions

8.4 Apply arrays in C using frequency arrays and random number permutations

8.5 Write programs that sort data using the three classical sorting algorithms: selection, bubble, and insertion sorting

8.6 Design programs that use the two classical search algorithms: sequential and binary

8.7 Store data using two-dimensional arrays

8.8 Use a multidimensional array to store data in three or more dimensions

---

8.1 Concepts

Figure 8-1 recaps the six derived types you've learned about so far. In this chapter we will cover the concept of arrays.

Figure 8-1 Derived types

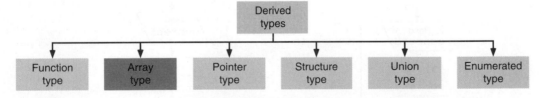

Imagine we have a problem that requires us to read, process, and print 10 integers. We must also keep the integers in memory for the duration of the program. To begin, we can declare and define 10 variables, each with a different name, as shown in **Figure 8-2**.

Having 10 different names, however, creates a problem: How can we read 10 integers from the keyboard and store them? To read 10 integers from the keyboard, we need 10 read statements, each to a different variable.

Figure 8-2 Ten variables

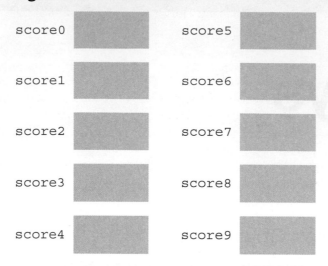

Furthermore, after we have them in memory, how can we print them? To print them, we need 10 write statements. The flowchart in **Figure 8-3** shows a design for reading, processing, and printing these 10 integers.

Although this approach may be acceptable for 10 variables, it is definitely not acceptable for 100 or 1,000 or 10,000. To process large amounts of data we need a powerful data structure, the array. An array is a collection of elements of the same data type.

Figure 8-3 Process 10 variables

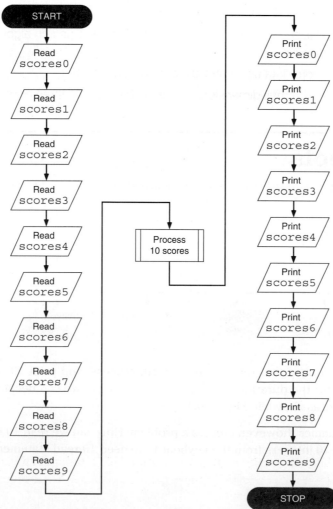

Because an array is a sequenced collection, we can refer to the elements in the array as the first element, the second element, and so forth until we get to the last element. Thus, when we put the 10 integers of our problem into an array, the address of the first element is 0 as follows:

scores$_0$

In a similar fashion, we refer to the second score as scores$_1$ and the third score as scores$_2$. Continuing the series, the last score would be scores$_9$. We can generalize this concept in the following fashion where a subscript indicates the ordinal number of the element counting from the beginning of the array:

scores$_0$, scores$_1$, …, scores$_{n-1}$

What we have seen is that the elements of the array are individually addressed through their subscripts, a concept shown graphically in **Figure 8-4**. The array as a whole has a name, scores, but each member can be accessed individually using its subscript.

Figure 8-4   An array of scores

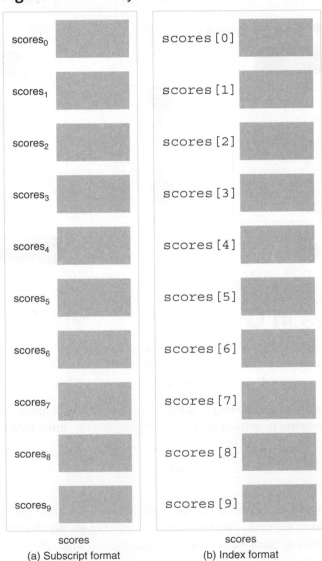

(a) Subscript format   (b) Index format

The advantages of the array would be limited if we didn't also have programming constructs that would allow us to process the data more conveniently. Fortunately, there is a powerful set of programming constructs—loops—that makes array processing easy.

We can use loops to read and write the elements in an array; to add, subtract, multiply, and divide the elements; and even for more complex processing such as calculating averages, searching, or sorting. Now it does not matter if there are 1, 10, 100, 1,000, or 10,000 elements to be processed, because loops make it easy to handle them all.

One question remains: How can we write an instruction so that one time it refers to the first element of an array and the next time it refers to another element? The answer is really quite simple: We simply borrow from the subscript concept we have been using. Rather than using subscripts, however, we will place the subscript value in brackets. This format is known as indexing. Using the index notation, we would refer to $scores_0$ as

```
scores[0]
```

Following the convention, $scores_0$ becomes `scores[0]` and $scores_9$ becomes `scores[9]`. Using a typical reference, we now refer to our array using the variable `i`.

```
scores[i]
```

The flowchart showing the loop used to process our 10 scores using an array is seen in **Figure 8-5**.

Figure 8-5 Loop for 10 scores

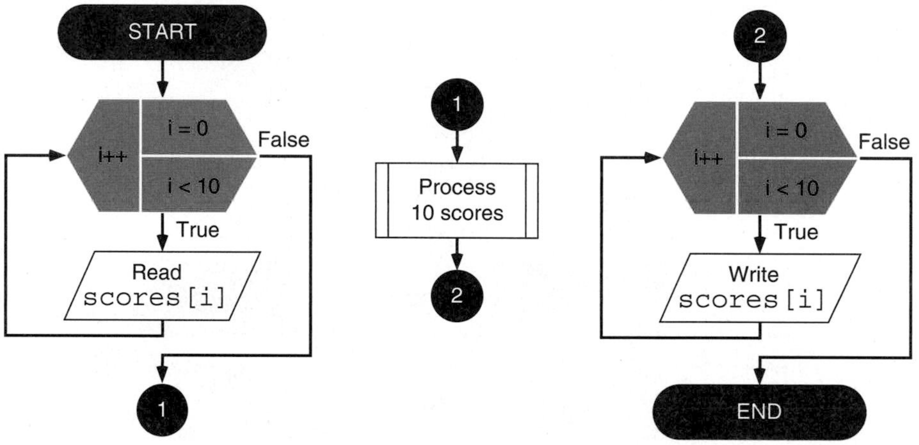

8.2 Using Arrays in C

In this section, we first show how to declare and define arrays. Then we present several typical applications using arrays including reading values into arrays, accessing and exchanging elements in arrays, and printing arrays. **Figure 8-6** shows a typical array, named `scores`, and its values.

C provides for two different array types, fixed-length array and variable-length array. In a fixed-length array, the size of the array is known when the program is written. In a variable-length array, introduced in C99, the size of the array is not known until the program is run.

Declaration and Definition

An array must be declared and defined before it can be used. Array declaration and definition tell the compiler the name of the array, the type of each element, and the size or number of elements in the array. In a fixed-length array, the size of the array is a constant and must have a value at compilation time. The declaration format is shown in the following example:

```
type arrayName [arraySize]
```

Figure 8-7 shows three different fixed-length array declarations: one for integers, one for characters, and one for floating-point numbers.

Figure 8-6 The scores array

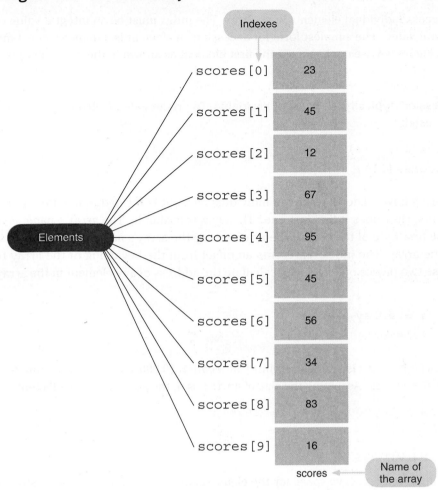

Figure 8-7 Declaring and defining arrays

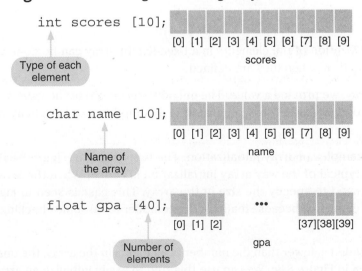

The declaration format for a variable-length array is the same as for a fixed-length array except that the array size is a variable. When the program is executed, the array size is determined and the array is defined. Once defined, its size cannot be changed. Following standard C syntax rules, the array size must be declared and initialized before it is used in the variable-length array definition.

```
float salesAry [arySize];
```

Accessing Elements in Arrays

C uses an index to access individual elements in an array. The index must be an integral value or an expression that evaluates to an integral value. The simplest form for accessing an element is a numeric constant. For example, given the scores array in Figure 8-6, we could access the first element as shown in the next example:

```
scores[0]
```

The index is an expression, typically the value of a variable. To process all the elements in scores, a loop similar to the following code is used:

```
for (i = 0; i < 10; i++)
    process (scores[i]);
```

You might be wondering how C knows where an individual element is located in memory. In scores, for example, there are nine elements. How does it find just one? The answer is simple. The array's name is a symbolic reference for the address to the first byte of the array. Whenever we use the array's name, therefore, we are actually referring to the first byte of the array. The index represents an offset from the beginning of the array to the element being referenced. With these two pieces of data, C can calculate the address of any element in the array using the following simple formula:

```
element address = array address
       + (sizeof (element) * index)
```

For example, assume that scores is stored in memory at location 10,000. If scores is an integer of type int, the size of one element is the size of int. Assuming the size of an int is 4, the address of the element at index 3 is

```
element address = 10,000 + 4 * 3 = 10,012
```

Storing Values in Arrays

Declaration and definition only reserve space for the elements in the array. No values are stored. If we want to store values in the array, we must either initialize the elements, read values from the keyboard, or assign values to each individual element.

Initialization

Just as with variables, initialization of the elements in a fixed-length array can be done when it is defined. Variable-length arrays cannot be initialized when they are defined.

For each element in the array, we provide a value. The only difference is that the values must be enclosed in braces and, if there is more than one, separated by commas. It is a compile error to specify more values than there are elements in the array.

Figure 8-8 contains four examples of array initialization. The first example (Figure 8-8a) is a simple array declaration of five integers and is typical of the way array initialization is coded. When the array is completely initialized, the programmer does not need to specify the size of the array. This case is seen in Figure 8-8b. It is a good idea, however, to define the size explicitly, because it allows the compiler to do some checking for errors and is also good documentation.

If the number of values provided is fewer than the number of elements in the array, the unassigned elements are filled with zeros. This case is seen in Figure 8-8c. We can use this rule to easily initialize an array to all zeros by supplying just the first zero value, as shown in the last example in Figure 8-8d.

> **Note** | Only fixed-length arrays can be initialized when they are defined. Variable-length arrays must be initialized by inputting or assigning the values.

Figure 8-8 Initializing arrays

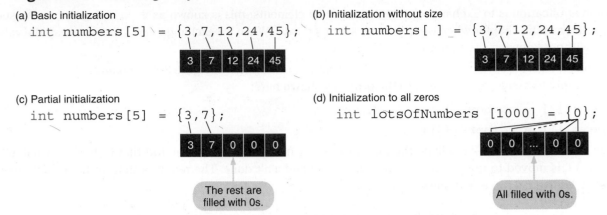

(a) Basic initialization
```
int numbers[5] = {3,7,12,24,45};
```
| 3 | 7 | 12 | 24 | 45 |

(b) Initialization without size
```
int numbers[ ] = {3,7,12,24,45};
```
| 3 | 7 | 12 | 24 | 45 |

(c) Partial initialization
```
int numbers[5] = {3,7};
```
| 3 | 7 | 0 | 0 | 0 |

The rest are filled with 0s.

(d) Initialization to all zeros
```
int lotsOfNumbers [1000] = {0};
```
| 0 | 0 | ... | 0 | 0 |

All filled with 0s.

Inputting Values

Another way to fill the array is to read the values from the keyboard or a file. This method of inputting values can be done using a loop. When the array is to be completely filled, the most appropriate loop is the for loop because the number of elements is fixed and known.

```
for (i = 0; i < 10; i++)
    scanf ("%id", &scores [i]);
```

Several concepts need to be studied in this simple statement. First, we start the index, i, at 0. Because the array has 9 elements, we must load the values from index locations 0 through 8. The limit test, therefore, is set at i < 9, which conveniently is the number of elements in the array. Then, even though we are dealing with array elements, the address operator (&) is still necessary in the scanf call.

Finally, if all the elements might not be filled, then we use one of the event-controlled loops (while or do...while). Which loop we use depends on the application.

Assigning Values

We can assign values to individual elements using the assignment operator. Any value that reduces to the proper type can be assigned to an individual array element. The following is a simple assignment statement for scores.

```
scores [4] = 23;
```

On the other hand, we cannot assign one array to another array, even if they match fully in type and size. We have to copy arrays at the individual element level. For example, to copy an array of 25 integers to a second array of 25 integers, we could use a loop, as follows:

```
for (i = 0; i < 25; i++)
    second[i] = first[i];
```

If the values of an array follow a pattern, we can use a loop to assign values. For example, the following loop assigns a value that is twice the index number to array scores:

```
for (i = 0; i < 25; i++)
    scores [i] = i * 2;
```

It should be noted that one array cannot be copied to another using assignment. For another example, the following code assigns the odd numbers 1 through 17 to the elements of an array named value:

```
for (i = 0; i < 9; i++)
    value [i] = (i * 2) + 1;
```

Exchanging Values

A common application is to exchange the contents of two elements; this is known as **exchanging values**. We see this operation later in the chapter when we talk about sorting arrays. When we exchange variables, we swap the values of elements without knowing what's in them.

For example, imagine we want to swap numbers[3] and numbers[1] in Figure 8-8. A common beginner's mistake would be simply to assign each element to the other, as shown here:

```
numbers [3] = numbers [1]; // Error
numbers [1] = numbers [3];
```

Although this code looks as if it will do the job, if we trace the code carefully, we find that it does only half the job. numbers[1] is moved to numbers[3], but the second half isn't done. The result is that both elements have the same value. **Figure 8-9** traces the steps.

Figure 8-9 Exchanging scores—the wrong way

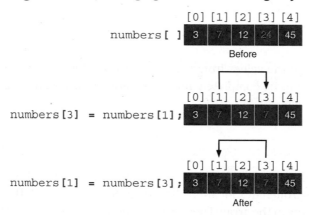

Figure 8-9 shows that the original value of numbers[3] is destroyed before we can move it. The solution is to use a temporary variable to store the value in numbers[3] before moving the data from numbers[1].

```
temp = numbers[3];
numbers [3] = numbers [1];
numbers [1] = temp;
```

This technique is shown in **Figure 8-10**.

Figure 8-10 Exchanging scores with temporary variable

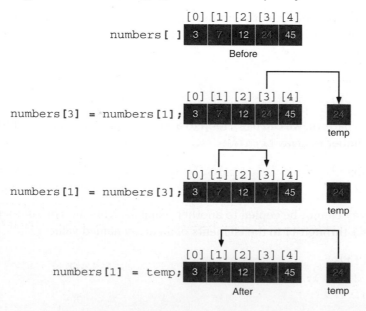

Printing Values

Another common application is printing the contents of an array. This is easily done with the following `for` loop:

```
for (i = 0; i < 9; i++)
    printf ("%d ", scores [i]);
printf ("\n");
```

In the example in **Program 8-1**, all the data are printed on one line. After the `for` loop completes, a final `printf` statement advances to the next line. But what if we had 100 values to be printed? In that case, we couldn't put them all on one line. Given a relatively small number width, however, we could put 10 on a line. We would then need 10 lines to print all the data. This rather common situation is easily handled by adding a counter to track the number of elements we have printed on one line. This logic is shown in Program 8-1.

Program 8-1 | Print ten numbers per line

```
 1   // a program fragment
 2   #define MAX_SIZE 25
 3
 4   // Local Declarations
 5       int list [MAX_SIZE];
 6
 7   // Statements
 8
 9       numPrinted = 0;
10       for (int i = 0; i < MAX_SIZE; i++)
11       {
12          printf("%3d", list[i]);
13          if (numPrinted < 9)
14              numPrinted++;
15          else
16          {
17              printf("\n");
18              numPrinted = 0;
19          } // else
20       } // for
```

Precedence of Array References

References to elements in arrays are postfix expressions. By looking at the precedence table in Chapter 3, we see that array references have a priority of 16, which is very high. What is not apparent from the table, however, is that the opening and closing brackets are actually operators. They create a postfix expression from a primary expression. With a little thought, you should recognize that this is exactly as it must be: When we index an array element in an expression, the value must be determined immediately.

Referring to the original array in Figure 8-10, what will be the result of the following code?

```
numbers [3] = numbers [4] + 15;
```

In this case, `numbers[4]` has a higher precedence (16) than the addition operator (12), so it is evaluated first. The result is then

```
numbers[3] = 45 + 15;
```

After this statement has been executed, `numbers[3]` has been changed from 24 to 60.

Index Range Checking

The C language does not check the boundary of an array. It is our job as programmers to ensure that all references to indexed elements are valid and within the range of the array. If we use an invalid index in an expression, we get unpredictable results. (The results are unpredictable because we have no way of knowing the value of the indexed reference.)

When we use an invalid index in an assignment, we destroy some undetermined portion of the program. Usually, but not always, the program continues to run and either produces unpredictable results or eventually aborts.

An example of a common out-of-range index is seen in the code to fill an array from the keyboard. For this example, we have reproduced the code we used to fill the `scores` array earlier; only this time we have made a common mistake! Can you spot it?

```
for (i = 1; i <= 9; i++)     // Error
    scanf ("%d", scores[i]);
```

When dealing with array processing, be very careful at the beginning and end of the array. A careful examination of the previous code discloses that we erroneously started at 1 instead of 0. So we fix it as follows, only to find that it still doesn't work!

```
for (i = 0; i <= 9; i++)
    scanf ("%d", &scores [i]);
```

The moral of this example is to examine our logic. If we made one mistake, we may well have made two. Although we corrected the error for initialization (the beginning of the array), there is still an error at the other end. If you can't see it, check the original code in "Inputting Values."

The result of both versions of this error is that the data stored in memory after the `scores` array are erroneously destroyed. In the first version of the error, the first element of the array was not initialized.

The problems created by unmanaged indexes are among the most difficult to solve, even with today's powerful programming workbenches. So we want to plan our array logic carefully and fully test it.

Let's write a program that uses arrays. **Program 8-2** uses a `for` loop to initialize each element in an array to the square of the index value and then prints the array.

Program 8-2 | Squares array

```
1   /* Initialize array with square of index and print it.
2      Written by:
3      Date:
4   */
5   #include <stdio.h>
6
7   #define ARY_SIZE 5
```

(continue)

Program 8-2 Squares array *(continued)*

```c
 8  int main (void)
 9  {
10  // Local Declarations
11     int sqrAry[ARY_SIZE];
12
13  // Statements
14     for (int i = 0; i < ARY_SIZE; i++)
15        sqrAry[i] = i * i;
16
17     printf ("Element\tSquare\n");
18     printf ("=======\t======\n");
19     for (int i = 0; i < ARY_SIZE; i++)
20        printf ("%5d\t%4d\n", i, sqrAry[i]);
21     return 0;
22  } // main
```

Output
```
Element      Square
    0           0
    1           1
    2           4
    3           9
    4          16
```

As another example of an array program, let's read a series of numbers from the keyboard and print them in reverse order; that is, if we read 1 2 3 4, we want to print them 4 3 2 1. With a little thought, it should be obvious that we must read all of the numbers before we can begin printing them. This definitely sounds like a problem for an array.

In **Program 8-3**, we read up to 50 integers and then print them reversed, 10 to a line.

Program 8-3 | Print input reversed

```c
1  /* ========== selectionSort ==========
2     Sorts by selecting smallest element in unsorted
3     portion of array and exchanging it with element at
4     the beginning of the unsorted list.
5     Pre  list must contain at least one item
6          last contains index to last element in list
7     Post list rearranged smallest to largest
8  */
```

(continue)

Program 8-3   Print input reversed *(continued)*

```
 9  void selectionSort (int list[], int last)
10  {
11  // Local Declarations
12      int smallest;
13      int tempData;
14
15  // Statements
16      // Outer Loop
17      for (int current = 0; current < last; current++)
18      {
19          smallest = current;
20          // inner Loop: One sort pass each loop
21          for (int walk = current + 1;
22               walk <= last;
23               walk++)
24             if (list[walk] < list[smallest])
25                 smallest = walk;
26          // Smallest selected: exchange with current
27          tempData       = list[current];
28          list[current]  = list[smallest];
29          list[smallest] = tempData;
30      } // for current
31      return;
32  } // selectionSort
```

Output
```
You may enter up to 50 integers:
How many would you like to enter? 12
Enter your numbers:
1 2 3 4 5 6 7 8 9 10 11 12
Your numbers reversed are:
12 11 10 9 8 7 6 5 4 3
2 1
```

First, note how we validate the number of integers to be read. If the user requests more than 50, we simply set readNum to 50. This ensures that we will not run off the end of the array.

This is an interesting loop because we start at the end and work to the front. Although many arrays are processed from the beginning, it is often necessary to process from the end. You will see more in the sorting functions later in the chapter.

Finally, note that we incorporate the logic from Program 8-1 to print ten numbers per line. Had we made Program 8-1 a function, we could have reused the code rather than repeating it.

8.3 Inter-function Communication

To process arrays in a large program, we have to be able to pass them to functions. We can pass arrays in two ways: pass individual elements or pass the whole array. In this section we discuss first how to pass individual elements and then how to pass the whole array.

Passing Individual Elements

As you have learned, we can pass individual elements by either passing their data values or by passing their addresses.

Passing Data Values

We pass data values, that is individual array elements, just like we pass any data value.

As long as the array element type matches the function parameter type, it can be passed. The called function cannot tell whether the value it receives comes from an array, a variable, or an expression. **Figure 8-11** demonstrates how an array value and a variable value can be passed to the same function.

Figure 8-11   Passing array elements

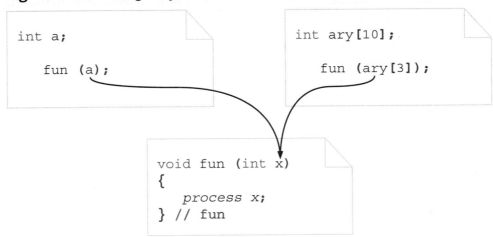

Note how only one element is passed by using the indexed expression, `ary[3]`. Because the value of this expression is a single integer, it matches the formal parameter type in fun. As far as fun is concerned, it doesn't know or care that the value it is working with came from an array.

Passing Addresses

As you know, we can use two-way communication by passing an address. We can pass the address of an individual element in an array just like we can pass the address of any variable.

To pass an array element's address, we prefix the address operator to the element's indexed reference. Thus, to pass the address of `ary[3]`, we use the code shown in the following example.

```
&ary[3]
```

Passing an address of an array element requires two changes in the called function. First, it must declare that it is receiving an address. Second, it must use the indirection operator (*) to refer to the elements value. These concepts are shown in **Figure 8-12**. Note that when we pass an address, it is two-way communication.

Passing the Whole Array

Here we see the first situation in which C does not pass values to a function. The reason for this change is that a lot of memory and time would be used in passing large arrays every time we wanted to use one in a function. For example, if an array containing 20,000 elements were passed by value to a function, another 20,000 elements would have to be

Program 8-4 | Calculate array average

```
 1  /* Calculate the average of the number in an array.
 2     Written by:
 3     Date:
 4  */
 5
 6  #include <stdio.h>
 7  // Function Declaration
 8  double average (int ary[ ]);
 9
10  int main (void)
11  {
12  // Local Declarations
13     double ave;
14     int base[5] = {3, 7, 2, 4, 5};
15
16  // Statement
17     ave = average(base);
18     printf("Average is: %1f\n", ave);
19     return 0;
20  } // main
21
22  /* ============ average ============
23     Calculate and return average of values in array.
24     Pre Array contains values
25     Post Average calculated and returned
26  */
27  double average (int ary [ ] )
28  {
29  // Local Declarations
30     int sum = 0;
31
32  // Statement
33     for (int i = 0; i < 5; i++)
34        sum += ary[i];
35
36     return (sum / 5.0);
37  } // average
```

In the example in **Program 8-5**, we average the elements in a variable-length array. However, because a variable-length array cannot be initialized, we read the data from the keyboard. Also, note that to keep the program as simple as possible, we create the array in a block. This is necessary because the size of the array must be known before it is declared. This concept is shown in Program 8-5.

Program 8-5 | Average elements in variable-length array

```
1   /* Calculate average of numbers in variable-length array.
2
3      Written by:
4      Date:
5   */
6
7   #include <stdio.h>
8   // Function Declaration
9   double average (int size, int ary[*]);
10
11  int main (void)
12  {
13  // Local Declarations
14     int size;
15     double ave;
16
17  // Statements
18     printf("How many numbers do you want to average? ");
19     scanf ("%d", &size);
20
21     // Create and fill variable-length array
22     {
23     // Local Declaration
24        int ary[size];
25
26        // Fill array
27        for (int i = 0; i < size; i++)
28        {
29           printf("Enter number %2d: ", i + 1);
30           scanf ("%d", &ary[i]);
31        } // for
32        ave = average(size, ary);
33     } // Fill array block
34
35     printf("Average is: %1f", ave);
36     return 0;
37  } // main
38
39  /*================average================
40     Calculate and return average of values in array.
41     Pre  Array contains values
```

(continue)

Program 8-5   Average elements in variable-length array *(continued)*

```
42    Post Average calculated and returned
43 */
44 double average (int size, int ary[size])
45 {
46 // Local Declarations
47    int sum = 0;
48    double ave;
49
50 // Statement
51    for (int i = 0; i < size; i++)
52       sum += ary[i];
53
54    ave = (double)sum / size;
55    return ave;
56 } // average
```

Output
```
How many numbers do you want to average? 5
Enter number 1: 3
Enter number 2: 6
Enter number 3: 9
Enter number 4: 2
Enter number 5: 8
Average is: 5.600000
```

There are two points to study in this program. First, in `main`, we use a variable-length array. This requires that the array size be known before the array is declared. We accomplish this by using a block within `main`. The array size is declared in `main`'s local declarations; the array itself is declared in the block local declarations.

Second, note how the variable array is declared in the function definition. We can do it by just declaring it as a variable array with an asterisk in the array brackets, or we can put the variable size in the brackets. Using size is better documentation because it declares our intent. When we use size, however, it must be declared before the array, in this case as the first parameter.

The previous examples involved one-way communication. In **Program 8-6** we demonstrate two-way communication by changing the values in the array. As you study it, note that no special code is required when we want to change the values in an array. Because the array's address is passed, we can simply use index notation to change it.

Program 8-6 | Change values in an array

```
1 /* Multiply each element in an array by 2.
2    Written by:
3    Date:
4 */
```

(continue)

Program 8-6   Change values in an array *(continued)*

```c
 5 #include <stdio.h>
 6 // Function Declaration
 7 void multiply2 (int x[]);
 8
 9 int main (void)
10 {
11 // Local Declarations
12    int base[5] = {3, 7, 2, 4, 5};
13
14 // Statements
15    multiply2 (base);
16
17    printf("Array now contains: ");
18    for (int i = 0; i < 5; i++)
19    printf("%3d", base[i]);
20    printf("\n");
21    return 0;
22 } // main
23
24 /* =============== multiply2 ================
25    Multiply each element in array by 2.
26    Pre array contains data
27    Post each element doubled
28 */
29 void multiply2 (int ary[ ])
30 {
31 // Statements
32    for (int i = 0; i < 5; i++)
33       ary[i] *= 2;
34    return;
35 } // multiply2
```

8.4 Array Applications

In this section, we study two array applications: frequency arrays with their graphical representations and random number permutations.

Frequency Arrays

Two common statistical applications that use arrays are frequency distributions and histograms. A frequency array shows the number of elements with an identical value found in a series of numbers. For example, suppose we have taken a sample of 100 values between 0 and 19. We want to know how many of the values are 0, how many are 1, how many are 2, and so forth up through 19.

We can read these numbers into an array called numbers. Then we create an array of 20 elements that will show the frequency of each number in the series. This design is shown in **Figure 8-14**.

Figure 8-14 Frequency array

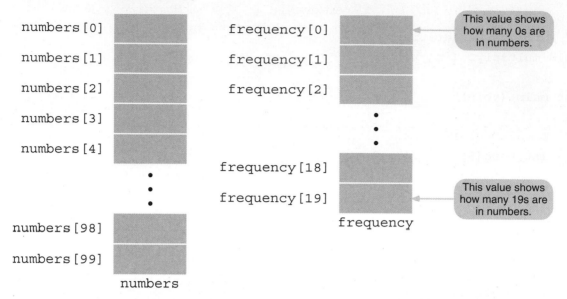

With the data structure shown in Figure 8-14 in mind, how do we write the application? Because we know that there are exactly 100 elements, we can use a `for` loop to examine each value in the array. But how can we relate the value in numbers to a location in the frequency?

One way to do it is to assign the value from the data array to an index and then use the index to access the `frequency` array. This technique is as follows:

```
f = numbers[i];
frequency [f]++;
```

Because an index is an expression, however, we can simply use the value from our data array to index us into the `frequency` array as shown in the next example. The value of `numbers[i]` is determined first, and then that value is used to index into frequency.

```
frequency [numbers [i]]++;
```

The function first initializes the `frequency` array and then scans the data array to count the number of occurrences of each value.

Histograms

A histogram is a pictorial representation of a `frequency` array. Instead of printing the values of the elements to show the frequency of each number, we print a histogram in the form of a bar chart. For example, **Figure 8-15** is a histogram for a set of numbers in the range 0 . . . 19. In this example, asterisks (*) are used to build the bar. Each asterisk represents one occurrence of the data value.

Figure 8-15 Frequency histogram

```
0    0
1    4    * * * *  ←———  Four 1s
2    7    * * * * * * *
3    7    * * * * * * *  ←———  Seven 3s
     .
     .
     .
18   2
19   0    * *  ←———  Zero 19s
```

Let's write a program that builds a frequency array for data values in the range 0 ... 19 and then prints their histogram. The data are read from a file. To provide flexibility, the getData function may only partially fill the array. The function that loads it also guards against too much data. The design for the program is shown in **Figure 8-16**.

Figure 8-16   Histogram program design

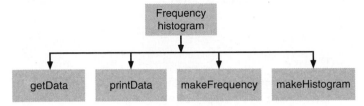

The code is shown in **Program 8-7**.

Program 8-7 | Frequency and histogram

```
 1  /* Build frequency array & print data in histogram.
 2     Written by:
 3     Data:
 4  */
 5  #include <stdio.h>
 6
 7  #include <stdlib.h>
 8  #define MAX_ELMNTS 100
 9  #define ANLYS_RNG 20
10
11  // Function Declarations
12  int getData (int numbers[ ], int size, int range);
13
14  void printData (int numbers[],
15                     int size, int lineSize);
16  void makeFrequency (int numbersf[], int size,
17                         int frequency[], int range);
18  void makeHistogram (int frequency[], int range);
19
20  int main (void)
21  {
22  // Local Declarations
23     int size;
24     int nums   [MAX_ELMNTS];
25     int frequency [ANLYS_RNG];
26
27  // Statements
28     size = getData (nums, MAX_ELMNTS, ANLYS_RNG);
```

(continue)

Program 8-7 Frequency and histogram *(continued)*

```
29      printData (nums, size, 10);
30
31      makeFrequency(nums, size, frequency, ANLYS_RNG);
32      makeHistogram(frequency, ANLYS_RNG);
33      return 0;
34 }   // main
35
36 /* ================== getData ===============
37      data from file into array. The array
38      does not have to be completely filled.
39      Pre data is an empty array
40      size is maximum elements in array
41      range is highest value allowed
42      Post array is filled. Return number of elements
43 */
44 int getData (int data [], int size, int range)
45 {
46 // Local Declarations
47      int dataIn;
48      int loader = 0;
49      FILE* fpData;
50
51 // Statements
52      if (!(fpData = fopen ("P08-07.dat", "r")))
53         printf("Error opening file\a\a\n"), exit (100);
54
55      while (loader < size
56            && fscanf(fpData, "%d", &dataIn) != EOF)
57         if (dataIn >= 0 && dataIn < range)
58            data[loader++] = dataIn;
59         else
60            printf("\nData point %d invalid. Ignored. \n",
61                    dataIn);
62
63      // Test to see what stopped while
64      if (loader == size)
65         printf("\nToo much data. Process what read.\n");
66      return loader;
67 }   // getData
68
69 /* =============== printData ===============
70      Prints the data as a two-dimensional array.
71      Pre data: a filled array
```

(continue)

Program 8-7   Frequency and histogram *(continued)*

```
72     size: number of elements in array
73     lineSize: number of elements printed/line
74     Post the data have been printed
75  */
76  void printData (int data[], int size, int lineSize)
77  {
78  // Local Declarations
79     int numPrinted = 0;
80     int i;
81  // Statements
82     printf("\n\n");
83     for (i = 0; i < size; i++)
84     {
85        numPrinted++;
86        printf("%2d ", data[i]);
87        if (numPrinted >= lineSize)
88        {
89           printf("\n");
90           numPrinted = 0;
91        } // if
92     } // for
93     printf("\n\n");
94     return;
95  } // printData
96
97  /* ===========makeFrequency===========
98     analyze the data in nums and build their frequency
99     distribution
100    Pre nums: array of validated data to be analyzed
101    last: number of elements in array
102    frequency: array for accumulation.
103    range: maximum index/value for frequency
104    Post Frequency array has been built.
105 */
106 void makeFrequency (int nums[], int last,
107                     int frequency[], int range)
108 {
109    int i, f;
110 // Statements
111    // First initialize the frequency array
112    for (f = 0; f < range; f++)
113       frequency [f] = 0;
114
```

(continue)

Program 8-7   Frequency and histogram *(continued)*

```
115     // Scan numbers and build frequency array
116     for (i = 0; i < last; i++)
117         frequency [nums [i]]++;
118     return;
119 } // makeFrequency
120
121/ * ============= makeHistogram =============
122     Print a histogram representing analyzed data.
123     Pre freq contains times each value occurred
124     size represents elements in frequency array
125     Post histogram has been printed
126 */
127 void makeHistogram (int freq[], int range)
128 {
129     int i, j;
130 //   Statements
131     for (i = 0; i < range; i++)
132     {
133         printf ("%2d %2d ", i, freq[i]);
134         for (j = 1; j <= freq[i]; j++)
135             printf ("*");
136         printf ("\n");
137     } // for i...
138     return;
139 } // makeHistogram
140 // ======== End of Program ==============
```

Output
```
Data point 20 invalid. Ignored.
Data point 25 invalid. Ignored.
1    2 3 4 5 6 7 8 7 10
2    12 13 13 15 16 17 18 17 7
3    4 6 8 10 2 4 6 8 10
4    3 5 7 1 3 7 7 11 13
5    10 11 12 13 16 18 11 12 7
6    1 2 2 3 3 3 4 4 4
7    7 8 7 6 5 4 1 2 2
8    11 11 13 13 13 17 17 7 7
13   17   17 15 15
0    0
1    4    ****
2    7    *******
```

(continue)

Program 8-7   Frequency and histogram *(continued)*

```
3    7    * * * * * *
4    8    * * * * * * *
5    4    * * * *
6    5    * * * * *
7    12   * * * * * * * * * * * *
8    5    * * * * *
9    0
10   4    * * * *
11   5    * * * * *
12   3    * * *
13   8    * * * * * * *
14   0
15   3    * * *
16   2    * *
17   6    * * * * * *
18   2    * *
19   0
```

Remember our discussion of what happens when an index gets out of range? What if one of the numbers in our data is greater than 19? We would destroy some other part of our program! To protect against this possibility, we test each data value to make sure that it is within the indexing range of frequency. If it is not, we display an error message and read the next number.

Similarly, we guard against too much data. If the file contains more than 100 valid numbers, then we stop reading. After the read loop, we test to make sure we are processing all of the data. If there were too many numbers, we print an error message. Finally, note that we print the data to make it easy to verify the results.

Random Number Permutations

A random number permutation is a set of random numbers in which no numbers are repeated. For example, given a random number permutation of 10 numbers, the values from 0 to 9 would all be included with no duplicates.

At this point, you know how to generate a set of random numbers. To generate a permutation, we need to eliminate the duplicates. Borrowing from the histogram concept in the previous section, we can solve the problem most efficiently by using two arrays. The first array contains the random numbers. The second array contains a logical value that indicates whether or not the number represented by its index has been placed in the random number array. This design is shown in **Figure 8-17**.

As you study Figure 8-17, note that only the first five random numbers have been placed in the permutation. For each random number in the random number array, its corresponding location in the have-random array is set to 1. Those locations representing numbers that have not yet been generated are still set to 0. The implementation of the design is shown in **Program 8-8**. The numbers generated by this program are a repeating series. To make them different with each run, we would use the srand function and set it to the time of day.

Figure 8-17 Design for random number permutations

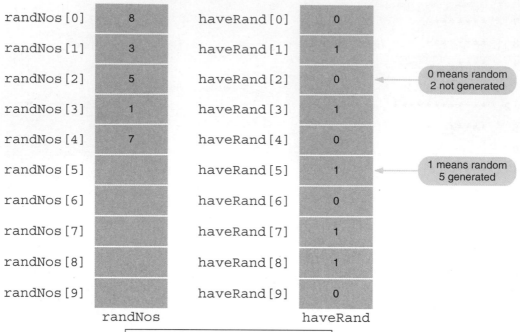

After first five random numbers generated

Program 8-8 | Generate a permutation

```
1  /* Generate a random number permutation.
2     Written by:
3     Date:
4  */
5  #include <stdio.h>
6
7  #include <stdio.h>
8
9  #define ARY_SIZE 20
10 // Function Declarations
11 void bldPerm (int randNos[]);
12 void printData (int data[], int size, int lineSize);
13
14 int main (void)
15 {
16 // Local Declarations
17    int randNos [ARY_SIZE];
18
19 // Statements
20    printf("Begin Random Permutation Generation\n");
21
22    bldPerm (randNos);
```

(continue)

Program 8-8   Generate a permutation *(continued)*

```
23      printData (randNos, ARY_SIZE, 10);
24
25      return 0;
26 }   // main
27
28 /* ==========bldPerm==========
29    Generate a random number permutation in array.
30    Pre randNos is array to receive permutations
31    Post randNos filled
32 */
33 void bldPerm (int randNos[])
34 {
35 // Local Declarations
36    int oneRandNo;
37    int haveRand[ARY_SIZE] = {0};
38
39 // Statements
40    for (int i = 0; i < ARY_SIZE; i++)
41    {
42       do
43       {
44          oneRandNo = rand() % ARY_SIZE;
45       } while (haveRand[oneRandNo] == 1);
46       haveRand[oneRandNo] = 1;
47       randNos[i] = oneRandNo;
48    } // for
49    return;
50 } // bldPerm
51
52 /* ============== printData ==============
53    Prints the data as a two-dimensional array.
54    Pre data: a filled array
55    last: index to last element to be printed
56    lineSize: number of elements on a line
57    Post data printed
58 */
59 void printData (int data[], int size, int lineSize)
60 {
61 // Local Declarations
62    int numPrinted = 0;
63
64 // Statements
65    printf("\n");
66    for (int i = 0; i < size; i++)
67    {
```

(continue)

Program 8-8   Generate a permutation *(continued)*

```
68          numPrinted++;
69          printf("%2d ", data[i]);
70          if (numPrinted >= lineSize)
71          {
72             printf("\n");
73             numPrinted = 0;
74          } // if
75       } // for
76       printf("\n");
77       return;
78 } // printData
```

Output
```
Begin Random Permutation Generation
18 13 15 11 7 10 19 12 6 9
 4 0 5 3 17 14 2 16 1 8
```

8.5 Sorting

One of the most common applications in computer science is sorting—the process through which data are arranged according to their values. We are surrounded by data. If the data are not ordered, we would spend hours trying to find a single piece of information. Imagine the difficulty of finding someone's telephone number in a telephone book that is not ordered in name sequence!

In this chapter we introduce three sorting algorithms: the selection sort, bubble sort, and insertion sort. In each section we will first introduce the basic concept, then use the idea in an example, and finally develop the code for the algorithm.

One programming concept common to the sorting algorithms we discuss in this section is the swapping of data between two elements in a list. You might want to review our discussion in "Exchanging Values" in Section 8.2.

Selection Sort

In the selection sort, the list is divided into two sublists, sorted and unsorted, which are divided by an imaginary wall. We find the smallest element from the unsorted sublist and swap it with the element at the beginning of the unsorted sublist. After each selection and swapping, the wall between the two sublists moves one element ahead, increasing the number of sorted elements and decreasing the number of unsorted ones. Each time we move one element from the unsorted sublist to the sorted sublist, we say that we have completed a sort pass If we have a list of n elements, we need n – 1 passes to completely rearrange the data. The selection sort is graphically presented in **Figure 8-18**.

Figure 8-18   Selection sort concept

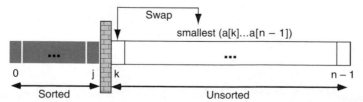

Figure 8-19 traces a set of six integers as we sort them. It shows how the wall between the sorted and unsorted sublists moves in each pass. As you study the figure, you will see that the array is sorted after five passes, which is one fewer than the number of elements in the array. This means that our sort loop has one less iteration than the number of elements in the array.

Figure 8-19 Selection sort example

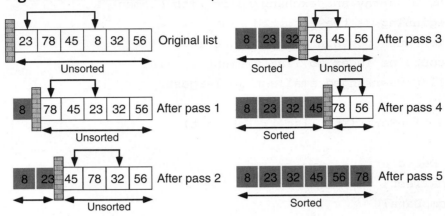

The program design is a rather straightforward algorithm. Starting with the first item in the list, it uses an inner loop to examine the unsorted items in the list for the smallest element. In each pass, the smallest element is "selected" and exchanged with the first unsorted element. The outer loop is repeated until the list is completely sorted. The design is shown in **Figure 8-20**.

Figure 8-20 Design for selection sort

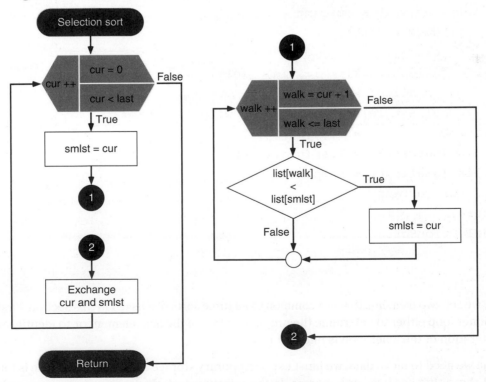

The code is shown in **Program 8-9**. We have highlighted the inner loop to make it easy to follow the logic.

Program 8-9 | Selection sort

```
 1  /* =========== selectionSort ===========
 2     Sorts by selecting smallest element in unsorted
 3     portion of array and exchanging it with element at
 4     the beginning of the unsorted list.
 5     Pre  list must contain at least one item
 6          last contains index to last element in list
 7     Post list rearranged smallest to largest
 8  */
 9  void selectionSort (int list[], int last)
10  {
11  // Local Declarations
12     int smallest;
13     int tempData;
14
15  // Statements
16     // Outer Loop
17     for (int current = 0; current < last; current++)
18     {
19        smallest = current;
20        // inner Loop: One sort pass each loop
21        for (int walk = current + 1;
22             walk <= last;
23             walk++)
24          if (list[walk] < list[smallest])
25             smallest = walk;
26        // Smallest selected: exchange with current
27        tempData       = list[current];
28        list[current]  = list[smallest];
29        list[smallest] = tempData;
30     } // for current
31     return;
32  } // selectionSort
```

In this algorithm, we see two elements that are common to all three sorts discussed in this section. First, each algorithm makes use of an inner loop either to determine the proper location of the next element or to identify and exchange two elements. Each iteration of the inner loop is one sort pass.

Second, each time we need to move data, we must use a temporary storage area. This technique is found in every sort algorithm except those that use two sorting areas. In the selection sort, the temporary area is used to exchange the two elements.

Bubble Sort

In the bubble sort, the list is divided into two sublists, sorted and unsorted. The smallest element is bubbled from the unsorted sublist and moved to the sorted sublist. After moving the smallest element to the sorted list, the wall moves one element ahead, increasing the number of sorted elements and decreasing the number of unsorted ones. Each time an element moves from the unsorted sublist to the sorted sublist, one sort pass is completed. Given a list of n elements, the bubble sort requires up to `n - 1` passes to sort the data. The bubble concept is seen in **Figure 8-21**.

Figure 8-21   Bubble sort concept

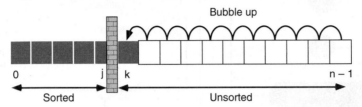

Figure 8-22 shows how the wall moves one element in each pass. Looking at the first pass, we start with 56 and compare it to 32. Because 56 is not less than 32, it is not moved and we step down one element. No exchanges take place until we compare 45 to 8. Because 8 is less than 45, the two elements are exchanged and we step down 1 element. Because 8 was moved down, it is now compared to 78 and these two elements are exchanged. Finally, 8 is compared to 23 and exchanged. This series of exchanges places 8 in the first location and the wall is moved up one position.

Figure 8-22   Bubble sort example

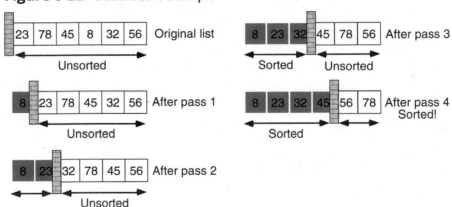

The bubble sort was originally written to "bubble up" the highest element in the list. From an efficiency point of view, it makes no difference whether the high element is bubbled or the low element is bubbled. From a consistency point of view, however, it makes comparisons between the sorts easier if all three of them work in the same manner. For that reason, we have chosen to bubble the lowest key in each pass.

Like the selection sort, the bubble sort is quite simple. In each pass through the data, controlled by the outer `for` loop, the lowest element is bubbled to the beginning of the unsorted segment of the array. The bubbling process is done in the inner loop.

Each time it is executed, the inner `for` loop makes one pass through the data. Whenever it finds two elements out of sequence, it exchanges them. It then continues with the next element. This process allows the smallest element to be bubbled to the beginning of the array, while at the same time adjacent elements along the way are rearranged. The design is shown in **Figure 8-23**.

Figure 8-23 Bubble sort design

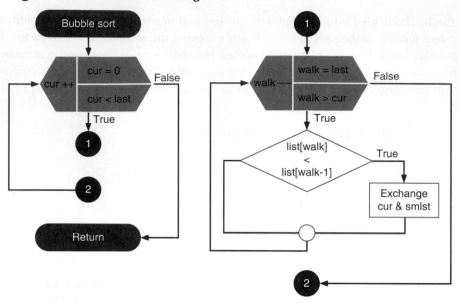

The bubble sort is shown in **Program 8-10**.

Program 8-10 | Bubble sort

```
1   /* =============== bubbleSort ==========
2      Sort list using bubble sort. Adjacent elements are
3      compared and exchanged until list is ordered.
4      Pre  list must contain at least one item
5      last contains index to last element in list
6      Post list rearranged in sequence low to high
7   */
8   void bubbleSort (int list [], int last);
9   {
10  // Local Declarations
11     int temp;
12
13  // Statements
14     // Outer loop
15     for(int current = 0; current < last; current++)
16     {
17        // Inner loop: Bubble up one element each pass
18        for (int walker = last; walker > current; walker--)
19           if (list[walker] < list[walker - 1])
20           {
21              temp       = list[walker];
22              list[walker]   = list[walker - 1];
```

(continue)

Program 8-10   Bubble sort *(continued)*

```
23                  list[walker -1] = temp;
24              } // if
25          } // for current
26      return;
27 } // bubbleSort
```

If the data being sorted are already in sequence, the inner loop still goes through the array element by element. One common modification is to stop the sort if there are no exchanges in the inner loop. This change requires the addition of a "sorted" flag. We leave this modification to the problem sets at the end of the chapter.

Insertion Sort

The insertion sort algorithm is one of the most common sorting techniques used by card players. As they pick up each card, they insert it into the proper sequence in their hand. (As an aside, card sorting is an example of a sort that uses two pieces of data to sort: suit and rank.)

In the insertion sort, the list is divided into two parts: sorted and unsorted. In each pass, the first element of the unsorted sublist is picked up and transferred into the sorted sublist by inserting it at the appropriate place. If we have a list of n elements, it will take at most n – 1 passes to sort the data (**Figure 8-24**).

Figure 8-24   Insertion sort concept

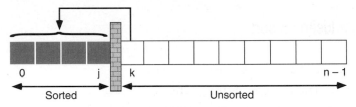

Figure 8-25 traces the insertion sort through our list of six numbers. Each pass moves the wall as an element is removed from the unsorted sublist and inserted into the sorted sublist.

Figure 8-25   Insertion sort example

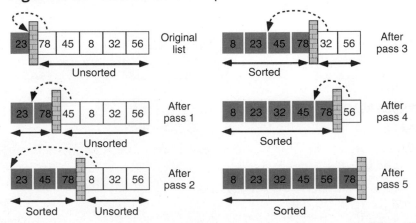

The design of the insertion sort follows the same pattern we saw in both the selection sort and the bubble sort; each iteration of the outer loop is a sort pass. The inner loop inserts the first element from the unsorted list into its proper position relative to the rest of the data in the sorted list. The design is shown in **Figure 8-26**.

Figure 8-26 Insertion sort design

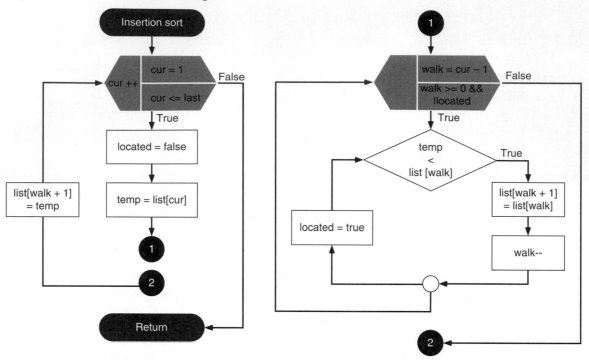

Program 8-11 shows the insertion sort.

Program 8-11 | Insertion sort

```
1 /* ============ insertionSort ============
2    Sort list using Insertion Sort. The list is divided
3    into sorted and unsorted lists. With each pass, first
4    element in unsorted list is inserted into sorted list.
5    Pre list must contain at least one element
6    last contains index to last element in list
7    Post list has been rearranged
8 */
9 void insertionSort (int list[], int last)
10 {
11 // Statements
12 // Local Declarations
13    int walk;
14    int temp;
15    bool located;
16
17 // Statements
18    // Outer loop
19    for (int current = 1; current <= last; current++)
20    {
```

Program 8-11   Insertion sort *(continued)*

```
21           // Inner loop: Select and move one element
22           located = false;
23           temp = list[current];
24           for (walk = current -1; walk >= 0 && !located;)
25              if (temp < list[walk])
26              {
27                 list[walk + 1] = list[walk];
28                 walk-;
29              } // if
30              else
31                 located = true;
32           list [walk + 1] = temp;
33        } // for
34        return;
35  } // insertionSort
```

Note how the exchange is worked in this sort. Before the inner loop starts, we put the data from the current element into the hold area (temp). This is the first step in the exchange. The loop then determines the correct position to place the element by starting with the largest element in the sorted list and working toward the beginning. As it searches, it spreads the sorted portion of the list by shifting each element one position higher in the list. When it locates the correct position, therefore, the data have already been moved right one position and the current location is "empty"; the sort, therefore, simply places the saved element in its proper location, completing the exchange.

Testing Sorts

Now that we have written three sorts, how do we test them? The answer is that we write a simple test driver. The same test driver can be used for all three sorts. The only changes necessary are in the include statement, the prototype statement, and the function call (see highlighted statements). **Program 8-12** is set up to test the insertion sort.

> ## Program 8-12 | Testing sorts

```
1   /* Test driver for insertion sort.
2      Written by:
3      Date:
4   */
5   #include <stdio.h>
6   #include <stdbool.h>
7
8   #include "P08-11.C"
9   #define MAX_ARY_SIZE 15
10
11  // Function Declarations
12  void insertionSort (int list[], int last);
```

(continue)

Program 8-12   Testing sorts *(continued)*

```
13
14 int main (void)
15 {
16 // Local Declarations
17    int ary[MAX_ARY_SIZE] = { 89, 72, 3, 15, 21,
18                                   57, 61, 44, 19, 98,
19                                    5, 77, 39, 59, 61 };
20 // Statements
21    printf("Unsorted: ");
22    for (int i = 0; i < MAX_ARY_SIZE; i++)
23       printf("%3d", ary[i]);
24
25    insertionSort (ary, MAX_ARY_SIZE - 1);
26
27    printf("\nSorted : ");
28    for (int i = 0; i < MAX_ARY_SIZE; i++)
29       printf("%3d", ary[i]);
30    printf("\n");
31    return 0;
32 } // main
```

```
Output
Unsorted: 89 72 3 15 21 57 61 44 19 98 5 77 39 59 61
Sorted: 3 5 15 19 21 39 44 57 59 61 61 72 77 89 98
```

Sorts Compared

It is interesting to compare the three sorting algorithms. All three use two nested loops. The outer loop is the same in all three; it moves the wall one element toward the beginning of the array. The processing in the inner loop, however, changes with each sort.

In the selection sort, the inner loop starts at the unsorted portion of the array and finds the smallest element in the unsorted area. Once located, it swaps the smallest element with the first unsorted element. It then moves the wall and continues the sort. Note that all exchanges take place in the unsorted portion of the array; the sorted elements are never touched.

While the selection sort starts at the beginning of the unsorted portion of the array, the bubble sort starts at the end. Another difference between the two is that the bubble sort may make multiple exchanges in each pass. While bubbling its way to the beginning of the array, it exchanges all elements that are out of sequence. Like the selection sort, once the wall is moved, the sorted data is never touched.

The insertion sort takes a completely different approach. In each pass, the first unsorted element is inserted into the sorted portion of the array. While it might appear that there are no exchanges in the insertion sort, there are. As explained previously, the first unsorted element is moved to a hold area. This is the first step in an exchange. Then, as it loops through the unsorted portion of the array, elements are shifted higher. Each shift is the equivalent of the second step in an exchange. Finally, when the correct location is found, the third step of the exchange moves the temporarily stored element to its correct position.

Table 8-1 summarizes the exchange and shift characteristics of these three sorts.

Table 8-1 Sort exchanges and passes

SORT	EXCHANGES	SHIFTS
Selection	Once for each pass	
Bubble	Several in each pass	
Insertion	Only partially in loop	Zero or more in each pass

Sort Conclusions

In this section, we have covered three classic sorts. With the exception of the insertion sort, you generally will not find them implemented in production systems. The insertion sort is used as a subfunction in both Quicksort and Singleton's variation, Quickersort, which are considered the best general-purpose sorts.

Historically, however, these three sorts are the foundation of improved and faster sorting methods that you will study in a data structures course. The selection sort is the foundation of a sorting method called the heap sort; the bubble sort is the foundation for Quicksort and Quickersort; and the insertion sort is the foundation of a sorting method called Shell Sort.

8.6 Searching

Another common operation in computer science is searching, which is the process used to find the location of a target among a list of objects. In the case of an array, searching means that given a value, we want to find the location (index) of the first element in the array that contains that value. The search concept is shown in **Figure 8-27**.

Figure 8-27 Search concept

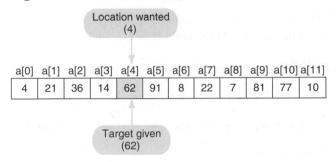

The algorithm used to search a list depends to a large extent on the structure of the list. Because our structure is currently limited to arrays, we will study searches that work with arrays. As we study other structures, we will study different search techniques.

There are two basic searches for arrays: the sequential search and the binary search. The sequential search can be used to locate an item in any array. The binary search, on the other hand, requires the list to be sorted.

Sequential Search

The **sequential search** is used whenever the list is not ordered. Generally, we use the technique only for small lists or lists that are not searched often. In other cases we would first sort the list and then search it using the binary search discussed later.

In the sequential search, we start searching for the target from the beginning of the list, and we continue until we find the target or until we are sure that it is not in the list. This gives us two possibilities; either we find it or we reach the end of the list. **Figure 8-28** traces the steps to find the value 62. We first check the data at index 0, then 1, 2, and 3 before finding the 62 in the fifth element (index 4).

Figure 8-28 Locating data in unordered list

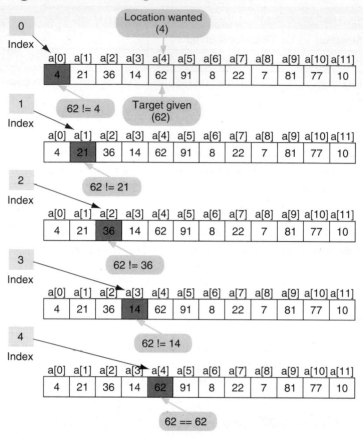

But what if the target is not in the list? Then we have to examine each element until we reach the end of the list. **Figure 8-29** traces the search for a target of 72. When we detect the end of the list, we know that the target does not exist.

Figure 8-29 Unsuccessful search in unordered list

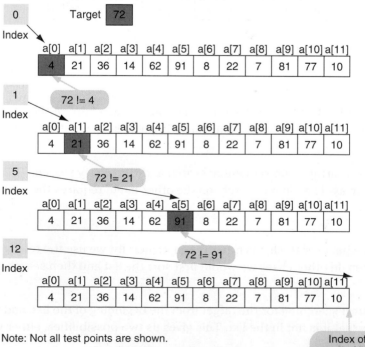

Note: Not all test points are shown.

Let's write the sequential search function. A search function needs to tell the calling function two things: Did it find the data it was looking for? If it did, what is the index at which the data were found?

But a function can return only one value. For search functions, we use the return value to designate whether we found the target or not. To "return" the index location where the data were found, we will use call-by-address.

The search function requires four parameters: the list we are searching, the index to the last element in the list, the target, and the address where the found element's index location will be stored. Although we could write it without passing the index to the last element, that would mean the search would have to know how many elements are in the list. To make the function as flexible as possible, therefore, we pass the index of the last data value in the array. This is also a good structured design technique. With this information, we are now ready to create the design. It is shown in **Figure 8-30**.

Figure 8-30   Sequential search design

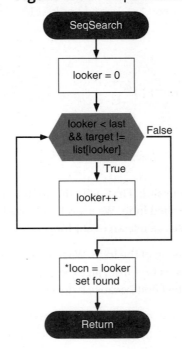

The code is shown in **Program 8-13**.

Program 8-13 | Sequential search

```
 1 /* ========== seqSearch ==========
 2    Locate target in an unordered list of size elements.
 3    Pre  list must contain at least one item
 4    last is index to last element in list
 5    target contains the data to be located
 6    locn is address for located target index
 7    Post Found: matching index stored in locn
 8    return true (found)
 9    Not Found: last stored in locn
10    return false (not found)
11 */
```

(continue)

Program 8-13   Sequential search *(continued)*

```
12 bool seqSearch (int list[], int last,
13                     int target, int* locn)
14 {
15 // Local Declarations
16    int looker;
17    bool found;
18
19 // Statements
20    looker = 0;
21    while (looker < last && target != list[looker])
22       looker++;
23
24    *locn = looker;
25    found = (target == list[looker]);
26    return found;
27 } // seqSearch
```

Program 8-13 is simple, but it does merit some discussion. First, why did we use a `while` statement? Even though we know the limits of the array, it is still an event-controlled loop. We search until we find what we are looking for or reach the end of the list. Finding something is an event, so we use an event loop.

Next, note that there are two tests in the limit expression of the loop. We have coded the test for the end of the array first. In this case, it doesn't make any difference which test is first from an execution point of view, but in other search loops it might. You should get in the habit of coding the limit test first because it doesn't use an indexed value and is therefore safer.

The call-by-address use for `locn` also merits discussion. Because we need to pass the found location back to the variable in the calling program, we need to pass its address to the function. A typical call to the search would look like the following statement:

```
found = seqSearch (stuAry, lastStu, stuID, &locn);
```

Notice how succinct this function is. In fact, there are more lines of documentation than there are lines of code. The entire search is contained in one `while` statement. With this short code, you might be tempted to ask, "Why write the function at all? Why not just put the one line of code wherever it is needed?" The answer lies in the structured programming concepts that each function should do only one thing and in the concept of reusability. By isolating the search process in its own function, we separate it from the process that needs the search. This is better structured programming. This also makes the code reusable in other parts of the program and portable to other programs that need searching; **reusable code** can be used by more than one process.

One final point: This function assumes that the list is not ordered. If the list were ordered, we could improve the search slightly when the data we were looking for were not in the list. We will leave this improvement for a problem at the end of the chapter.

Binary Search

The sequential search algorithm is very slow. If we have an array of 1 million elements, we must do 1 million comparisons in the worst case. If the array is not sorted, this is the only solution. But if the array is sorted, we can use a more efficient algorithm called the **binary search**. Generally speaking, we should use a binary search whenever the list starts to become large. The definition of large is vague. We suggest that you consider binary searches whenever the list contains more than 50 elements.

The binary search starts by testing the data in the element at the middle of the array. This determines if the target is in the first half or the second half of the list. If it is in the first half, we do not need to check the second half. If it is in the second half, we don't need to test the first half. In other words, either way we eliminate half the list from further consideration. We repeat this process until we find the target or satisfy ourselves that it is not in the list.

To find the middle of the list, we need three variables, one to identify the beginning of the list, one to identify the middle of the list, and one to identify the end of the list. We will analyze two cases: the target is in the list, and the target is not in the list.

Target Found

Figure 8-31 shows how we find 22 in a sorted array. We descriptively call our three indexes first, mid, and last. Given first as 0 and last as 11, we can calculate mid as follows:

```
mid = (first + last) / 2;
```

Figure 8-31   Binary search example

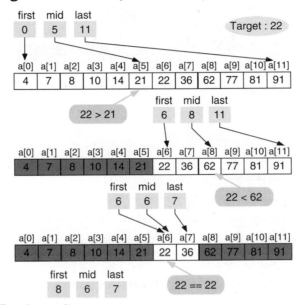

Function terminates

Note that this formula does not work if the number of elements in the array is greater than half MAX_INT. In that case, the correct formula is:

```
mid = first + (last - first) / 2
```

Because the index mid is an integer, the result will be the integral value of the quotient; that is, it truncates rather than rounds the calculation. Given the data in Figure 8-31, mid becomes 5 as a result of the first calculation.

```
mid = (0 + 11) / 2 = 11 / 2 = 5
```

At index location 5, we discover that the target is greater than the list value (22 > 21). We can, therefore, eliminate the array locations 0 through 5. (Note that mid is automatically eliminated.) To narrow our search, we assign mid + 1 to first and repeat the search.

The next loop calculates mid with the new value for first and determines that the midpoint is now 8.

```
mid = (6 + 11) / 2 = 17 / 2 = 8
```

Again we test the target to the value at mid, and this time we discover that the target is less than the list value (22 < 62). This time we adjust the ends of the list by setting last to mid −1 and recalculate mid. This eliminates elements 8 through 11 from consideration. We have now arrived at index location 6, whose value matches our target. This stops the search. (To terminate the search, we set first to last + 1. See **Program 8-14**.) Figure 8-31 traces the logic we have just described.

Target Not Found

A more interesting case occurs when the target is not in the list. We must construct our search algorithm so that it stops when we have checked all possible locations. This is done in the binary search by testing for `first` and `last` crossing; that is, we are done when `first` becomes greater than `last`. Thus, only two conditions terminate the binary search algorithm: Either the target is found or `first` becomes larger than `last`. For example, imagine we want to find 11 in our binary search array. This situation is shown in **Figure 8-32**.

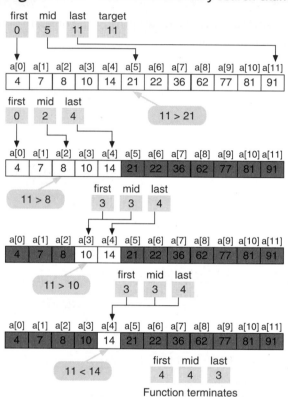

Figure 8-32 Unsuccessful binary search example

In this example, the loop continues to narrow the range as we saw in the successful search, until we are examining the data at index locations 3 and 4. These settings of `first` and `last` set the mid index to 3.

```
mid = (3 + 4) / 2 = 7 / 2 = 3
```

The test at index location 3 indicates that the target is greater than the list value, so we set first to `mid + 1` or 4. We now test the data at location 4 and discover that 11 < 14.

```
mid = (4 + 4) / 2 = 8 / 2 = 4
```

At this point, we have discovered that the target should be between two adjacent values; in other words, it is not in the list. We see this algorithmically because `last` is set to `mid - 1`, which makes first greater than last, the signal that the value we are looking for is not in the list.

Once we fully understand the logic, we can design the program. **Figure 8-33** contains the design in the form of a flowchart.

Program 8-14 contains the implementation of the binary search algorithm we have been describing. It is constructed along the same design we saw for the sequential search. The first three parameters describe the list and the target we are looking for, and the last parameter contains the address into which we place the located index. One point worth noting: When we terminate the loop with a not-found condition, the index returned is unpredictable—it may indicate the node greater than or less than the value in target.

Figure 8-33   Design for binary search

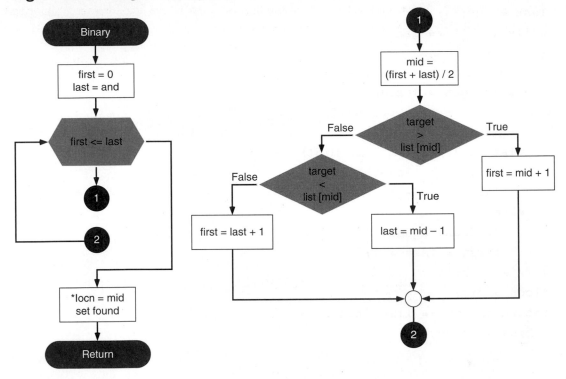

Program 8-14 | Binary search

```
 1 /* ============= binarySearch =============
 2    Search an ordered list using Binary Search
 3    Pre list must contain at least one element
 4        end is index to the largest element in list
 5        target is the value of element being sought
 6        locn is address for located target index
 7    Post Found: locn = index to target element
 8        return 1 (found)
 9    Not Found: locn = element below or above target
10        return 0 (not found)
11 */
12 bool binarySearch (int list[], int end,
13                    int target, int* locn)
14 {
15 // Local Declarations
16    int first;
17    int mid;
18    int last;
19
20 // Statements
21    first = 0;
```

(continue)

Program 8-14   Binary search *(continued)*

```
22      last = end;
23      while (first <= last)
24      {
25          mid = (first + last) / 2;
26          if (target > list[mid])
27              // look in upper half
28              first = mid + 1;
29          else if (target < list[mid])
30              // look in lower half
31              last = mid - 1;
32          else
33              // found equal: force exit
34              first = last + 1;
35      } // end while
36      *locn = mid;
37      return target == list [mid];
38 } // binarySearch
```

8.7 Two-Dimensional Arrays

The arrays we have discussed so far are known as one-dimensional arrays because the data are organized linearly in only one direction. Many applications require that data be stored in more than one dimension. One common example is a table, which is an array that consists of rows and columns. **Figure 8-34** shows a table, which is commonly called a two-dimensional array.

Figure 8-34   Two-dimensional array

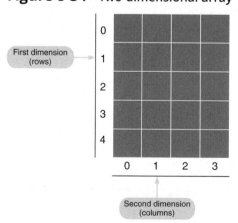

Although a two-dimensional array is exactly what is shown by Figure 8-34, C looks at it in a different way. It looks at the two-dimensional array as an array of arrays. In other words, a two-dimensional array in C is an array of one-dimensional arrays. This concept is shown in **Figure 8-35**.

Declaration

Two-dimensional arrays, like one-dimensional arrays, must be declared before being used. Declaration tells the compiler the name of the array, the type of each element, and the size of each dimension. Two-dimensional arrays can be either fixed length or variable length.

Figure 8-35 Array of arrays

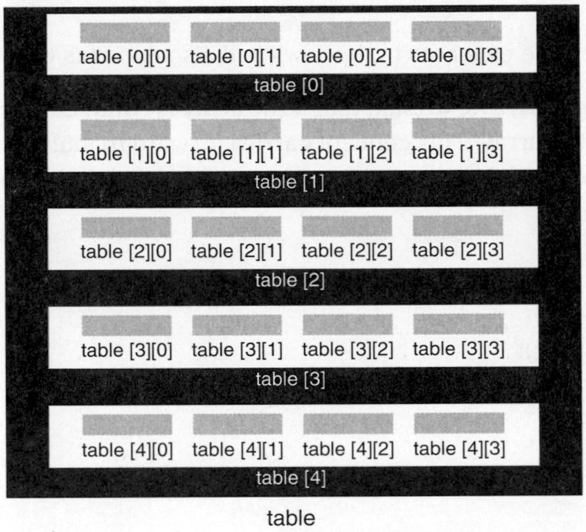

As we saw with the one-dimensional array, the size of a fixed-length array is a constant and must have a value at compilation time. For example, the array shown in Figure 8-35 can be declared and defined as follows:

```
int table[5][4];
```

By convention, the first dimension specifies the number of rows in the array. The second dimension specifies the number of columns in each row.

The rules for variable-length arrays follow the same concepts. To define a variable-length array, we would use the following statement.

```
int table5x4 [rows][cols];
```

Remember, however, that the dimensions must be set before the declaration or a compiler error occurs.

Initialization

As we noted before, the definition of a fixed-length array only reserves memory for the elements in the array. No values will be stored. If we don't initialize the array, the contents are unpredictable. Generally speaking, fixed-length arrays should be initialized.

Initialization of array elements can be done when the array is defined. As previously noted, variable-length arrays may not be initialized when they are defined. As with one-dimensional arrays, the values must be enclosed in braces. This time, however, there is a set of data for each dimension in the array. So for table, we will need 20 values. One way to initialize it is as follows:

```
int table[5][4] =   { 0,  1,  2,  3, 10, 11, 12, 13, 20, 21,
                     22, 23, 30, 31, 32, 33, 40, 41, 42, 43};
```

We highly recommend, however, that nested braces be used to show the exact nature of the array. For example, array table is better initialized as follows:

```
int table [5][4] =
    {
        { 0,  1,  2,  3},
        {10, 11, 12, 13},
        {20, 21, 22, 23},
        {30, 31, 32, 33},
        {40, 41, 42, 43}
    }
```

In this example, we define each row as a one-dimensional array of four elements enclosed in braces. The array of five rows also has its set of braces.

Note that we use commas between the elements in the rows and also commas between the rows.

When we discussed one-dimensional arrays, we said that if the array is completely initialized with supplied values, we do not need to specify the size of the array. This concept carries forward to multidimensional arrays, except that only the first dimension can be omitted. All others must be specified. The format is as follows:

```
int table[][4] =
    {
        { 0,  1,  2,  3},
        {10, 11, 12, 13},
        {20, 21, 22, 23},
        {30, 31, 32, 33},
        {40, 41, 42, 43}
    }; // table
```

To initialize the whole array to zeros, we need only specify the first value, as follows: **int** table [5][4] = {0};

Inputting Values

Another way to fill up the values is to read them from the keyboard. For a two-dimensional array, this usually requires nested for loops. If the array is an n by m array, the first loop varies the row from zero to n − 1. The second loop varies the column from zero to m − 1. The code to fill the array in Figure 8-35 is as follows:

```
for (row = 0; row < 5; row++)
    for (column =0; column < 4; column++)
        scanf ("%d", &table [row][column]);
```

When the program runs, we enter the 20 values for the elements and they are stored in the appropriate locations.

Outputting Values

We can also print the value of the elements one by one, using two nested loops. Again, the first loop controls the printing of the rows and the second loop controls the printing of the columns. To print the table in its table format, a newline is printed at the end of each row. The code to print Figure 8-35 is as follows:

```
for (row = 0; row < 5; row++)
{
    for (column = 0; column < 4; column++)
        printf("%8d", table [row][column]);
    printf("\n");
} // for
```

Accessing Values

Individual elements can be initialized using the assignment operator.

```
table[2][0] = 23;
table[0][1] = table[3][2] + 15;
```

Let's assume that we want to initialize our 5 × 4 array as follows:

```
00 01 02 03
10 11 12 13
20 21 22 23
```

```
30 31 32 33
40 41 42 43
```

One way to do this would be to code the values by hand. However, it is much more interesting to examine the pattern and then assign values to the elements in the array using an algorithm. What pattern do you see? One is that the value in each element increases by one from its predecessor in the row. Another is that the first element in each row is the row index times 10. With these two patterns, we should be able to write nested loops to fill the array. The code to initialize the patterns for the array is shown in **Program 8-15**.

Program 8-15 | Fill two-dimensional array

```
1  /* ========= fillArray =======
2     This function fills array such that each array element
3     contains a number that, when viewed as a two-digit
4     integer, the first digit is the row number and the
5     second digit is the column number.
6     Pre  table is array in memory
7          numRows is number of rows in array
8     Post array has been initialized
9  */
10 void fillArray (int table[] [MAX_COLS], int numRows)
11 {
12 // Statements
13    for (int row = 0; row < numRows; row++)
14    {
15       table [row] [0] = row * 10;
16       for (int col = 1; col < MAX_COLS; col++)
17          table [row] [col] = table [row] [col - 1] + 1;
18    } // for
19    return;
20 } // fillArray
```

Memory Layout

As discussed earlier, the indexes in the definition of a two-dimensional array represent rows and columns. This format maps to the way the data are laid out in memory. If we were to consider memory as a row of bytes with the lowest address on the left and the highest address on the right, then an array would be placed in memory with the first element to the left and the last element to the right. Similarly, if the array is a two-dimensional array, then the first dimension is a row of elements that are stored to the left. This is known as "row-major" storage and is seen in **Figure 8-36**. (At least one language, FORTRAN, reverses the data values placement in memory. It stores data by columns.)

To further examine how data are laid out in memory, look at **Program 8-16**, which converts a two-dimensional array to a one-dimensional array.

Figure 8-36   Memory layout

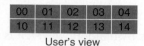

Memory view

Program 8-16 | Convert table to one-dimensional array

```
 1  /* This program changes a two-dimensional array to the
 2     corresponding one-dimensional array.
 3     Written by:
 4     Date:
 5  */
 6  #include <stdio.h>
 7  #define ROWS 2
 8
 9  #define COLS 5
10  int main (void)
11  {
12  // Local Declarations
13     int table [ROWS][COLS] =
14        {
15           {00, 01, 02, 03, 04},
16           {10, 11, 12, 13, 14}
17        }; // table
18     int line [ROWS * COLS];
19
20  // Statements
21     for (int row = 0; row < ROWS; row++)
22        for (int column = 0; column < COLS; column++)
23           line[row * COLS + column] = table[row][column];
24
25     for (int row = 0; row < ROWS * COLS; row++)
26        printf(" %02d ", line[row]);
27
28     return 0;
29  } // main
```

Output
```
00 01 02 03 04 10 11 12 13 14
```

In Program 8-16 we use nested `for` loops to make the conversion. The first loop controls the table rows, and the second loop controls the columns within each row. Because we know how many elements are in each row of the two-dimensional array, we can map it to the one-dimensional array by simply multiplying the row index by the number of elements in each row. When we are in row zero, we multiply the number of elements in one row (designed by the defined constant, COLS) by the row number (0) and add the result to the column. Doing so maps the elements in the two-dimensional array to the beginning of the receiving array. When we are in row 1, we add the number of elements in one row times the row (1) to the current column, which maps the elements to the next set (in this case, 5 … 9). To generalize, we add the product of the row and the number of elements in a row to the column to determine the receiving location.

Study the technique we used to define the number of elements in the rows and columns. Note how they are used not only to define the arrays but also to control the loop execution. Copy this program, and then run it with different row-column sizes to help understand the differences. (You will need to change the initialization also. You might want to consider initializing the values by assignments within for loops.)

Passing a Two-Dimensional Array

With two-dimensional arrays, we have three choices for passing parts of the array to a function. We can pass individual elements, as shown in "Passing Individual Elements" in Section 8.3. We can pass a row of the array. This is similar to passing an array, as we saw in "Passing the Whole Array" in Section 8.3. Finally, we can pass the whole array.

Passing a Row

Passing a row of the array is rather interesting. We pass a whole row by indexing the array name with only the row number. Referring to **Figure 8-37**, we see that a row is four integers. When we pass the row, therefore, the receiving function receives a one-dimensional array of four integers. The for loop in print_square prints the square of each of the four

Figure 8-37 Passing a row

```
#define MAX_ROWS 5
#define MAX_COLS 4
// Function Declarations
void print_square (int []);
int main (void)
{
int table [MAX_ROWS] [MAX_COLS]   =
          {
              { 0,   1,   2,   3},
              {10, 11,  12,  13},
              {20, 21,  22,  23},
              {30, 31,  32,  33},
              {40, 41,  42,  43}
          }; /* table */
  ...
  for (int row = 0; row < MAX_ROWS ; row++)
    print_square(table [row]);
  ...
  return 0;
} // main
```

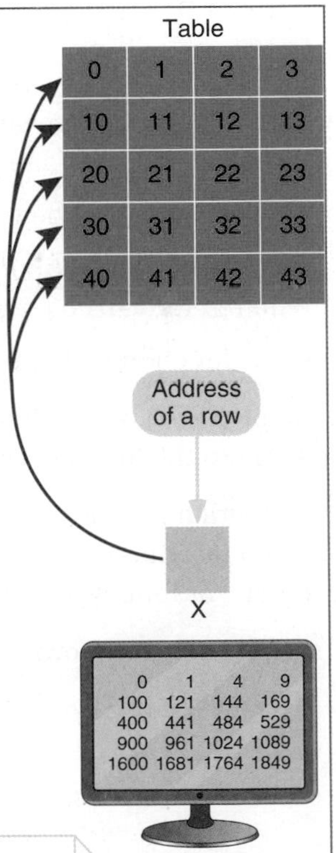

```
void print_square (int x[])
{
   for (int col = 0 ;col < MAX_COLS;
col++)
        printf ("%6d", x[col] * x[col]);
   printf ("\n ");

return;
} // print_ square
```

elements. After printing all the values, the function advances to the next line on the console and returns. The `for` loop in `main` calls `print_square` five times so that the final result is a table of the values squared shown on the monitor.

Note that we have declared the array dimensions as defined constants. This allows us to symbolically refer to the limits of the array in both the array definition and the `for` loops. Now, if we need to change the size of the array, all that is necessary is to change the `define` declarations, and any array initializers, and recompile the program.

We could code the `print` function array in Figure 8-37 as a variable-length array of one dimension. To do so, we would need to change the function definition and the calling statement to pass the array size as shown in the following example:

```
// Function call
print_square (MAX_COLS, table);
// Function definition
void print_square (int size, x[size])
{
  ...
} // print_square
```

Passing the Whole Array

When we pass a two-dimensional array to a function, we use the array name as the actual parameter just as we did with one-dimensional arrays. The formal parameter in the called function header, however, must indicate that the array has two dimensions. This is done by including two sets of brackets, one for each dimension, as follows:

```
double average (int table[][MAX_COLS]);
```

Note that again we do not need to specify the number of rows in a fixed-length array. It is necessary, however, to specify the size of the second dimension. Thus, we specified the number of columns in the second dimension (MAX_COLS). In summary, to pass two-dimensional arrays to functions:

1. The function must be called by passing only the array name.

2. In the function definition, the formal parameter is a two-dimensional array, with the size of the second dimension required for a fixed-length array.

3. In the function definition for a variable-length array, the size of all dimensions must be specified.

For example, we can use a function to calculate the average of the integers in an array. In this case, we pass the name of the array to the function as seen in **Figure 8-38**.

Write a program that fills the left-to-right diagonal of a square matrix (a two-dimensional array with an equal number of rows and columns) with zeros, the lower left triangle with − ls, and the upper right triangle with +ls. The output of the program, assuming a six-by-six matrix is shown in **Figure 8-39**.

The program code is shown in **Program 8-17**.

Figure 8-38   Calculate average of integers in array

```
#define MAX_ROWS 5
#define MAX_COLS 4
// Function Declarations
double average (int [][MAX_COLS]);

int main (void)
{
   double ave;
   int table[MAX_ROWS][MAX_COLS] =
      {
         {  0,  1,  2,  3},
         { 10, 11, 12, 13},
         { 20, 21, 22, 23},
         { 30, 31, 32, 33},
         { 40, 41, 42, 43}
      } ; // table
   ...
   ave = average(table);
   ...
   return 0;
} // main
```

```
double average (int x[][MAX_COLS])
{
   double sum = 0;
   for (int I = 0; i < MAX_ROWS; i++)
      for ( int j = 0; j < MAX_COLS; j++)
         sum += x [i] [j];
   return (sum / (MAX_ROWS * MAX_COLS));
} // average
```

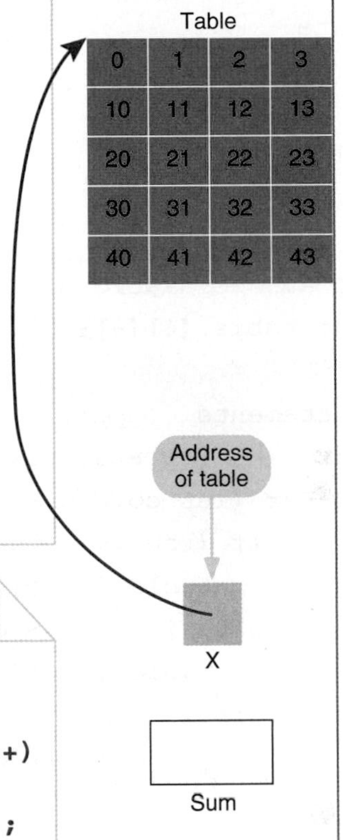

Table

0	1	2	3
10	11	12	13
20	21	22	23
30	31	32	33
40	41	42	43

Address of table

X

Sum

Figure 8-39   Example of filled matrix

0	1	1	1	1	1
−1	0	1	1	1	1
−1	−1	0	1	1	1
−1	−1	−1	0	1	1
−1	−1	−1	−1	0	1
−1	−1	−1	−1	−1	0

Program 8-17 | Fill matrix

```
 1   /* This program fills the diagonal of a matrix (square
 2       array) with 0, the lower left triangle with -1, and
 3       the upper right triangle with 1.
 4       Written by:
 5       Date:
 6   */
 7
 8   #include <stdio.h>
 9   int main (void)
10   {
11   // Local Declarations
12       int table [6][6];
13
14   // Statements
15       for (int row = 0; row < 6; row++)
16          for (int column = 0; column < 6; column++)
17              if (row == column)
18                  table [row][column] = 0;
19              else if (row > column)
20                  table [row][column] = -1;
21              else
22                  table [row][column] = 1;
23
24       for (int row = 0; row < 6; row++)
25       {
26          for (int column = 0; column < 6; column++)
27              printf ("%3d", table[row][column]);
28              printf ("\n");
29       } // for row
30       return 0;
31   }  // main
```

This is a rather simple pattern problem. The only difference is that now we are creating the pattern in array elements. Because there are two dimensions, we need two loops to control the pattern. If the row equals the column, we assign 0 to the element. If the row is greater than the column, then we are in the lower half of the matrix, so we assign −1. And if the row is less than the column, then we are in the upper half of the matrix and we assign +1.

8.8 Multidimensional Arrays

Multidimensional arrays can have three, four, or more dimensions. **Figure 8-40** shows an array of three dimensions. Note the terminology used to describe the array. The first dimension is called a plane, which consists of rows and columns. Arrays of four or more dimensions can be created and used, but they are difficult to draw.

Figure 8-40 Three-dimensional array (3×5×4)

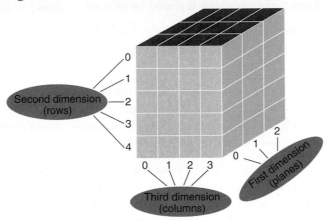

Although a three-dimensional array is exactly what is shown in Figure 8-40, the C language looks at it in a different way. It takes the three-dimensional array to be an array of two-dimensional arrays. It considers the two-dimensional array to be an array of one-dimensional arrays. In other words, a three-dimensional array in C is an array of arrays of arrays. This concept also holds true for arrays of more than three dimensions. The C view of a three-dimensional array is seen in **Figure 8-41**.

Figure 8-41 C view of three-dimensional array

| 200 | 201 | 202 | 203 |
| table[2][0][0] | table[2][0][1] | table[2][0][2] | table[2][0][3] |

| 100 | 101 | 102 | 103 | | 213 |
| table[1][0][0] | table[1][0][1] | table[1][0][2] | table[1][0][3] | | e[2][1][3] |

0	1	2	3		113		223
table[0][0][0]	table[0][0][1]	table[0][0][2]	table[0][0][3]		[1][1][3]		e[2][2][3]
table[0][0]							

10	11	12	13		123		233
table[0][1][0]	table[0][1][1]	table[0][1][2]	table[0][1][3]		[1][2][3]		e[2][3][3]
table[0][1]							

20	21	22	23		133		243
table[0][2][0]	table[0][2][1]	table[0][2][2]	table[0][2][3]		[1][3][3]		e[2][4][3]
table[0][2]						table[2]	

30	31	32	33		143
table[0][3][0]	table[0][3][1]	table[0][3][2]	table[0][3][3]		[1][4][3]
table[0][3]					table[1]

40	41	42	43
table[0][4][0]	table[0][4][1]	table[0][4][2]	table[0][4][3]
table[0][4]			table[0]

Declaring Multidimensional Arrays

Multidimensional arrays, like one-dimensional arrays, must be declared before being used. Declaration tells the compiler the name of the array, the type of each element, and the size of each dimension. The size of the fixed-length array is a constant and must have a value at compilation time. The three-dimensional array seen in Figure 8-41 can be declared as follows for a fixed-length array.

```
int table[3][5][4];
```

The definition for the same table as a variable-length array requires three variables, one for the rows, one for the columns, and one for the planes. Given these variables, it would be defined as shown in the following example:

```
int table[planes] [rows] [cols];
```

Initialization

As we said before, declaration and definition only reserve space for the elements in the array. No values will be stored in the array. If we want to store values, we must initialize the elements, read values from the keyboard, or assign values to each individual element. Following the rules we discussed for one- and two-dimensional arrays, only fixed-length multidimensional arrays can be initialized when they are defined.

Once more, initialization is simply an extension of the concept we saw for initializing a two-dimensional array (see "Initialization" in Section 8.7). For the three-dimensional array, we nest each plane in a set of brackets. For each plane, we bracket the rows as we did for the two-dimensional array. When we group the data by plane and row as we have done in the following code, the reader will be able to visualize the array with ease. We have added comments to make it even easier to read the values.

```
int table[3] [5] [4]  =
    {
      { // Plane 0
        { 0,   1,   2,   3}, // Row 0
        {10,  11,  12,  13}, // Row 1
        {20,  21,  22,  23}, // Row 2
        {30,  31,  32,  33}, // Row 3
        {40,  41,  42,  43}  // Row 4
      } ,
      { // Plane 1
        {100, 101, 102, 103}, // Row 0
        {110, 111, 112, 113}, // Row 1
        {120, 121, 122, 123}, // Row 2
        {130, 131, 132, 133}, // Row 3
        {140, 141, 142, 143}  // Row 4
      },
      { // Plane 2
        {200, 201, 202, 203}, // Row 0
        {210, 211, 212, 213}, // Row 1
        {220, 221, 222, 223}, // Row 2
        {230, 231, 232, 233}, // Row 3
        {240, 241, 242, 243}  // Row 4
      }
    }; // table
```

As we saw previously, the plane's size, and only the plane's size, does not need to be specified when we use explicit initialization. The size of all dimensions after the first must be explicitly stated.

Of course, if we want to initialize all the elements to zero, we can simply initialize only the first element to zero and let the compiler generate the code to initialize the rest of the array.

```
int table [3] [5] [4]  =  {0};
```

Programming Example: Calculating Averages

At this point, you are familiar with the software engineering concept of top-down development and the programming concept known as incremental development. In this chapter, we develop an example that contains many of the programming techniques found in array problems and implement it incrementally. It contains three arrays: a two-dimensional array of integers and two one-dimensional arrays of averages, one for rows and one for columns.

When we work with a large program with many different data structures (in this case, three arrays), it helps to draw a picture of the arrays. We can then see how the different arrays work together to solve the problem. A picture of the array structures and their relationships is shown in **Figure 8-42**.

Figure 8-42   Data structures for calculating row-column averages

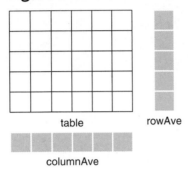

The program begins by requesting the user provide data for a two-dimensional array. After the array has been filled, the program calculates the average of each row and places it in a parallel array of row averages. It then calculates the average for each column and places it in an array of column averages. Although we have represented the column-average array horizontally and the row-average array vertically, they are both one-dimensional arrays.

When all the calculations are complete, the program calls a function to print the array with the row averages at the end of each row and the column averages at the bottom of each column. The structure chart for the program is seen in **Figure 8-43**.

Figure 8-43   Calculate row-column average design

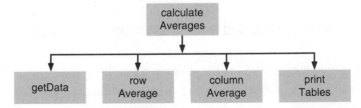

First Increment: `main`

In our previous examples, the first increment included `main` and its first sub-function. Because our data are more complex, we limit it to just `main` in this example. The first increment contains the global include statements we anticipate needing and the known data definitions. In `main` we define our local structures, including the three arrays. We then compile the program and correct any coding errors found by the compiler. Note that we don't run the program because it produces no output at this stage. **Program 8-18** contains the code.

Program 8-18 | Calculate row and column averages: `main`

```
1   /* Read values from keyboard into a two-dimensional
2      array. Create two one-dimensional arrays that
3      contain row and column averages.
4      Written by:
5      Date:
6   */
7
8   #include <stdio.h>
9   #define MAX_ROWS 5
10  #define MAX_COLS 6
11
12  int main (void)
13  {
14  // Local Declarations
15     int table [MAX_ROWS][MAX_COLS];
16
17     float rowAve [MAX_ROWS] = {0};
18     float columnAve [MAX_COLS] = {0};
19
20  // Statements
21     return 0;
22  } // main
```

Second Increment: `Get Data`

Having verified that `main` is error free, we are ready to write get data. At this point, we add the necessary function declaration and a print loop in `main` to display the table. The code is shown in **Program 8-19**.

Program 8-19 | Calculate row and column averages: `getData`

```
1   /* Read values from keyboard into a two-dimensional
2      array. Create two one-dimensional arrays that
3      contain row and column averages.
4      Written by:
5      Date:
6   */
7   #include <stdio.h>
8
9   #define MAX_ROWS 5
10  #define MAX_COLS 6
11
12  // Function Declaration
```

(continue)

Program 8-19   Calculate row and column averages: getData *(continued)*

```
13 void getData (int table[] [MAX_COLS]);
14
15 int main (void)
16 {
17 // Local Declarations
18    int table [MAX_ROWS] [MAX_COLS];
19
20    float rowAve [MAX_ROWS] = {0};
21    float columnAve [MAX_COLS] = {0};
22
23 // Statements
24    getData (table);
25
26    printf("\n**Tables built\n");
27    for (int i = 0; i < MAX_ROWS; i++)
28    {
29       for (int y = 0; y < MAX_COLS; y++)
30          printf("%4d", table[i] [y]);
31       printf("\n");
32    } // for i
33
34    return 0;
35 } // main
36
37 /*=============getData=============
38   Reads data and fills two-dimensional array.
39   Pre table is empty array to be filled
40   Post array filled
41 */
42 void getData (int table[] [MAX_COLS])
43 {
44 // Statements
45    for (int row = 0; row < MAX ROWS; row++)
46       for (int col = 0; col < MAX COLS; col++)
47       {
48          printf("\nEnter integer and <return>: ");
49          scanf("%d", &table[row] [col]);
50       } // for col
51    return;
52 } // getData
53 //=============End of Program=============
```

(continue)

Program 8-19   Calculate row and column averages: `getData` *(continued)*

Output
```
**Tables built
10  12  14  16  18  20
22  24  26  28  30  23
25  27  29  31  33  35
39  41  43  45  47  49
51  53  55  57  59  61
```

After running the program, we carefully examine the results to make sure that the new function worked correctly. Because we created our test data before we ran the program, we knew what the results should be. A simple comparison of the test data and the results verifies that the table was built correctly.

Third Increment: Calculate Row Averages

We are now ready to write the code for the averages. We begin with the calculation for the rows. This requires nested `for` loops, the outer loop steps through the rows and the inner loop steps through the columns within a row. The code is shown in **Program 8-20**.

Program 8-20 | Calculate row and column averages: `rowAverages`

```
1   /* Read values from keyboard into a two-dimensional
2      array. Create two one-dimensional arrays that
3      contain row and column averages.
4      Written by:
5      Date:
6   */
7
8   #include <stdio.h>
9   #define MAX_ROWS 5
10  #define MAX_COLS 6
11
12  // Function Declaration
13  void getData (int table[] [MAX_COLS]);
14  void rowAverage (int table[] [MAX_COLS],
15                   float rowAvrg [ ]);
16
17  int main (void)
18  {
19  // Local Declarations
20      int table [MAX_ROWS] [MAX_COLS];
21
```

(continue)

Program 8-20   Calculate row and column averages: rowAverages *(continued)*

```
22      float rowAve [MAX_ROWS] = {0};
23      float columnAve [MAX_COLS] = {0};
24
25  // Statements
26      getData (table);
27      rowAverage (table, rowAve);
28
29      printf ("\n**Tables built\n");
30      for (int i = 0; i < MAX_ROWS; i++)
31      {
32         for (int y = 0; y < MAX_COLS; y++)
33            printf ("%4d", table[i][y]);
34         printf ("\n");
35      } // for i
36      printf ("\n");
37
38      printf ("**Row averages\n");
39      for (int i = 0; i < MAX_ROWS; i++)
40          printf ("%6.If", rowAve[i]);
41      printf ("\n");
42
43      return 0;
44  } // main
45
46  /* ========== getData ==========
47     Reads data and fills two-dimensional array.
48     Pre table is empty array to be filled
49     Post array filled
50  */
51  void getData (int table[][MAX_COLS])
52  {
53  // Statements
54      for (int row = 0; row < MAX_ROWS; row++)
55         for (int col = 0; col < MAX_COLS; col++)
56         {
57             printf ("\nEnter integer and <return>: ");
58             scanf ("%d", &table[row][col]);
59         } // for col
60      return;
61  }    // getData
62
63  /* ============== rowAverage ==============
64     This function calculates the row averages for a table
65     Pre table has been filled with values
66     Post averages calculated and in average array
```

(continue)

Program 8-20   Calculate row and column averages: rowAverages *(continued)*

```
67 */
68 void rowAverage (int table[] [MAX_COLS],
69 float rowAvrg [])
70 {
71 // Statements
72    for (int row = 0; row < MAX_ROWS; row++)
73    {
74       for (int col = 0; col < MAX_COLS; col++)
75          rowAvrg[row] += table [row] [col];
76       rowAvrg [row] /= MAX_COLS;
77    } // for row
78    return;
79 } // rowAverage
80 //==================End of Program==================
```

Output
```
**Tables built
      10 12 14 16 18 20
      22 24 26 28 30 23
      25 27 29 31 33 35
      39 41 43 45 47 49
      51 53 55 57 59 61
**Row averages
      15.0 25.5 30.0 44.0 56.0
```

Fourth Increment: Calculate Column Averages

The calculation of the column averages is very similar to the calculation of the row averages. We leave its incremental development for a problem at the end of the chapter.

Fifth Increment: Print Tables

The final increment completes the program by printing the three tables. Note that we present the results with the row averages at the end of the rows and the column averages at the bottom of the columns. This is a natural and logical presentation from a user's perspective. The code for the fifth increment is shown in **Program 8-21**. Note that the column totals will be displayed as zero until the fourth increment is completed.

Program 8-21 | Calculate row and column averages: `printTables`

```
1  /* Read values from keyboard into a two-dimensional
2     array. Create two one-dimensional arrays that
3     contain row and column averages.
4     Written by:
5     Date:
6  */
7
8  #include <stdio.h>
9  #define MAX_ROWS 5
10 #define MAX_COLS 6
11
12 // Function Declaration
13 void getData (int table[][MAX_COLS]);
14 void rowAverage (int table[][MAX_COLS],
15                  float rowAvrg []);
16 void colAverage (int table[][MAX_COLS],
17                  float colAvrg []);
18 void printTables (int table[][MAX_COLS],
19                   float rowAvrg[],
20                   float colAvrg[]);
21
22 int main (void)
23 {
24 // Local Declarations
25    int table [MAX_ROWS][MAX_COLS];
26
27    float rowAve [MAX_ROWS] = {0};
28    float colAve [MAX_COLS] = {0};
29
30 // Statements
31    getData (table);
32    rowAverage (table, rowAve);
33 // colAverage (table, colAve);
34
35    printf("\n");
36    printTables (table, rowAve, colAve);
37    return 0;
38 }   // main
39
40 /* ============getData============
41    Reads data and fills two-dimensional array.
```

(continue)

Program 8-21   Calculate row and column averages: printTables *(continued)*

```
42      Pre table is empty array to be filled
43      Post array filled
44 */
45 void getData (int table[][MAX_COLS])
46 {
47 // Statements
48    for (int row = 0; row < MAX_ROWS; row++)
49       for (int col = 0; col < MAX_COLS; col++)
50       {
51          printf("\nEnter integer and <return>: ");
52          scanf("%d", &table[row][col]);
53       } // for col
54    return;
55 } // getData
56
57 /* ============= rowAverage==============
58    This function calculates the row averages for a table
59    Pre table has been filled with values
60    Post averages calculated and in average array
61 */
62 void rowAverage (int table[][MAX_COLS],
63       float rowAvrg [])
64 {
65 // Statements
66    for (int row = 0; row < MAX_ROWS; row++)
67    {
68       for (int col = 0; col < MAX_COLS; col++)
69          rowAvrg[row] += table [row][col];
70       rowAvrg [row] /= MAX_COLS;
71    } // for row
72    return;
73 } // rowAverage
74
75 /* ========== printTables==========
76    Print data table, with row average at end of each
77    row and average of columns below each column.
78    Pre each table filled with its data
79    Post tables printed
80 */
81 void printTables (int table[][MAX_COLS],
82                   float rowAvrg[],
83                   float colAvrg[])
84 {
```

(continue)

Program 8-21   Calculate row and column averages: printTables *(continued)*

```
85 // Statements
86    for (int row = 0; row < MAX_ROWS; row++)
87    {
88       for (int col = 0; col < MAX_COLS; col++)
89          printf("%6d", tablefrow][col]);
90       printf(" | %6.2f\n", rowAvrg [row]);
91    } // for row
92
93    printf ( "------------------------\n" );
94    printf(" ");
95    for (int col = 0; col < MAX_COLS; col++)
96       printf("%6.2f", colAvrg[col]);
97    return;
98 } // printTables
99 //==========End of Program==========
```

Output

```
10   12   14   16   18   20   |    15.00
22   24   26   28   30   23   |    25.50
25   27   29   31   33   35   |    30.00
39   41   43   45   47   49   |    44.00
51   53   55   57   59   61   |    56.00
0.00    0.00    0.00    0.00    0.00    0.00    |
```

Software Engineering

In this section, we discuss two basic concepts: testing and algorithm efficiency. To be effective, testing must be clearly thought out. We provide some concepts for testing array algorithms by studying sorting and searching. We then explore algorithm efficiency by studying sort and search algorithms as case studies.

Testing Sorts

As our programs become more complex, we need to spend more time creating test data that will completely validate them. In this section, we examine some techniques for testing sorts.

In general, we should conduct four tests: (1) sort a list of random values, (2) sort a list that is already in sequence, (3) sort a list that is in reverse order, (4) sort a nearly ordered list, such as one in which every tenth item is one position out of sequence. **Table 8-2** contains a summary of the tests that we should conduct and some sample test data to show the points.

Table 8-2 Recommended sort test cases

TEST CASE	SAMPLE DATA
Random data	5 23 7 78 22 6 19 33 51 11 93 31
Nearly ordered	5 6 7 21 19 22 23 31 29 33 51 93
Ordered – ascending	5 6 7 11 19 22 23 31 33 51 78 93
Ordered – descending	93 78 51 33 31 23 22 19 11 7 6 5

Testing Searches

When we test the sequential search, we need only four tests. Three deal with finding an element in the table—find the first, last, and any element in the middle. The last case deals with trying to find an element that is not in the list; look for any value that is not in the middle of the list. Whenever testing an array, always be sure that the test data access the first and last elements of the array. Many array processing errors occur at these locations.

> **Note** | When testing an array search, always access the first and last elements.

The binary search requires the four tests discussed above, plus three more. Because it uses an ordered list, we should try to find a target lower than the first element in the list and another target greater than the last element. Finally, we should find two elements that are in adjacent array locations, such as `list [0]` and `list [1]`. The reason for this test is that the binary search includes logic that divides by two. An error could result in being able to find only even- or only odd-numbered elements. Testing for adjacent locations ensures that such an error won't happen. These test cases are seen in **Table 8-3**.

Table 8-3 Test cases for searches

EXPECTED RESULTS	INDEX	TEST	SEARCH
found	0	target == list[0]	all
found	1	target == list[1]	binary only
found	n - 1	target == list[n-1]	all
found	0 < i < n	target == list[i]	all
not found	0	target < list[0]	binary only
not found	n - 1	target > list[n]	binary only
not found	0 < i < n	target != list[i]	all

Analyzing Sort Algorithms

We have developed three sort algorithms. We examine each of them in this section.

Bubble Sort Analysis

The bubble sort essentially contains the following block of code. Note that `exchange` in the code could be a function call or the three statements shown in Program 8-10.

```
for (current = 0; current < last; current++)
   for (walker = last; walker > current; walker--)
     if (list[walker] < list[walker - 1])
        exchange (walker, walker - 1);
```

To determine the relative efficiency, we need to analyze the two `for` statements. The first `for`, the outer loop, examines each entry in the sort array. It will, therefore, loop `n - 1` times.

The inner loop starts at the end of the array and works its way toward the current node as established by the outer loop. The first time it is called, it examines n – 1 elements; the second time, n – 2 elements, and so forth until it examines only one element. The average number of elements examined, therefore, is determined as follows:

$$(n - 1) + (n - 2) + \cdots + 2 + 1 = n\frac{(n - 1)}{2}$$

This is the nested dependent loop. Simplifying the previous formula we get

$$n\left(\frac{n - 1}{2}\right) = \frac{1}{2}(n^2 - n)$$

Discarding the coefficient and selecting the larger factor, we see that the dominant factor in the bubble sort is n^2, which in big-O notation would be stated as $O(n^2)$. The efficiency of the bubble sort is $O(n^2)$.

Selection Sort Analysis

Now let's examine the efficiency of the selection sort shown in Program 8-9. Again, its pivotal logic is essentially shown in the next example.

```
for (current = 0; current < last; current++)
    {
    for (walker = current + 1; walker <= last; walker++)
        if (list[walker] < list[smallest])
            smallest = walker;
    } // for current
```

This algorithm bears a strong resemblance to the bubble sort algorithm we discussed previously. Its first loop looks at every element in the array from the first element (current = 0) to the one just before the last. The inner loop moves from the current element, as determined by walker, to the end of the list. This is similar to the bubble sort, except that it works from the lower portion of the array toward the end. Using the same analysis, we see that it will test n(n - 1) / 2 elements, which means that the selection sort is also $O(n^2)$.

> **Note** | The efficiency of the selection sort is $O(n^2)$.

Insertion Sort Analysis

The last sort we covered was the insertion sort, Program 8-11. The nucleus of its logic is shown as follows:

```
for (current = 1; current <= last; current++)
    for (walker = current - 1; walker >= 0 && !located;)
        if (temp < list[walker])
            {
            list[walker + 1] = list[walker];
            walker--;
            } // if
```

Does the pattern look familiar? It should. Again we have the same basic nested for loop logic that we saw in the bubble sort and the selection sort. The outer loop is executed n times, and the inner loop is executed (n - 1) / 2 times, giving us $O(n^2)$.

As we have demonstrated, all three of these sorts are $O(n^2)$, which means that they should be used only for small lists or lists that are nearly ordered. You will eventually study sorts that are O(*nlogn*), which is much more efficient for large lists.

Analyzing Search Algorithms

All of the sort algorithms involved nested loops. We now turn our attention to two algorithms that have only one loop, the sequential search and the binary search. Recall that a search is used when we need to find something in an array or other list structure. The target is a value obtained from some external source.

Sequential Search Analysis

The basic loop for the sequential search is as follows:

```
while (looker < last && target != list[looker])
    looker++;
```

This is a classic example of a linear algorithm. In fact, in some of the literature, this search is known as a linear search. Because the algorithm is linear, its efficiency is O(n).

Binary Search Analysis

The binary search locates an item by repeatedly dividing the list in half. Its loop is

```
while (first <= last)
{
    mid = (first + last) / 2;
    if (target > list[mid])
        first = mid + 1;
    else if (target < list[mid])
        last = mid - 1;
    else
        first = last + 1;
} // while
```

This is obviously a loop that divides, and it is, therefore, a logarithmic loop. This makes the efficiency O($\log n$), which you should recognize as one of the more efficient of all the measures.

Comparing the sequential search and binary search, we see that, disregarding the time required to order the list, the binary search is obviously better for a list of any significant size (see **Table 8-4**). We therefore recommend the binary search for all but the smallest of lists—that is, lists with less than 50 elements.

Table 8-4   Comparison of binary and sequential searches

SIZE	BINARY	SEQUENTIAL (AVERAGE)	SEQUENTIAL (WORST CASE)
16	4	8	16
50	6	25	50
256	8	128	256
1,000	10	500	1,000
10,000	14	5,000	10,000
100,000	17	50,000	100,000
1,000,000	20	500,000	1,000,000

The big-O concept is generally interested only in the largest factor. This tends to significantly distort the efficiency of the sequential sort, in that it is always the worst case. If the search is always successful, it turns out that the efficiency of the sequential search is $1/2n$. We include the average in Program 8-3 for comparison. (The average for the binary search is only one less than the maximum, so it is less interesting.)

Tips and Common Programming Errors

1. In an array declared as array `[n]`, the index goes from 0 (not 1) to $n - 1$.

2. Three things are needed to declare and define an array: its name, type, and size.

3. The elements of arrays are not initialized automatically. You must initialize them if you want them to start with known values.

4. To initialize all elements in an array to zero, all you need to do is initialize the first element to zero.

5. To exchange the value of two elements in an array, you need a temporary variable.

6. You cannot copy all elements of one array into another with an assignment statement. You need to use a loop.

7. To pass the whole array to a function, you only use the name of the array as an actual parameter.

8. The most common logic error associated with arrays is an invalid index. An invalid index used with an assignment operator either causes the program to fail immediately or destroys data or code in another part of the program and causes it to fail later.

9. Invalid indexes are often created by invalid coding in a `for` statement. For example, given an array of ten elements, the following `for` statement logic error results in an index value of ten being used. Although it loops 10 times, the indexes are 1 through 10, not zero through 9.

   ```
   for (i = 1; i <= 10; i++)
   ```

10. Another cause of invalid indexes is an uninitialized index. Make sure your indexes are always properly initialized.

11. When initializing an array when it is defined, it is a compile error to provide more initializers than there are elements.

12. It is a compile error to leave out the index operators in an assignment statement, as follows:
    ```
    float costAry[20];

    ...

    costAry = quantity * price;
    ```

13. It is most likely a logic error to leave out the index operators in a `scanf` statement, as shown in the following example. In this case, `costAry` is the address of the array and the input will be placed in the first element of the array. Even when this is the desired result, you should code it with the index operators as shown.

    ```
    float costAry[20];

    ...

    scanf("%f", costAry);      // Poor Style
    scanf("%f", &costAry[0]);  // Clear code
    ```

14. It is a compile error to omit the array size in the parameter declaration for any array dimension other than the first.

15. To pass a variable-size array to a function, you need either to include the variable defining the array size or use an asterisk.

Summary

> A one-dimensional array is a fixed sequence of elements of the same type.

> We use indexes in C to show the position of the elements in an array.

> An array must be declared and defined before being used. Declaration and definition tell the compiler the name of the array, the type of each element, and the size of the array.

> Initialization of all elements of a fixed length array can be done at the time of the declaration and definition.

> If a one-dimensional array is completely initialized when it is declared, it is not necessary to specify the size, but it is recommended.

> When an array is partially initialized, the rest of the elements are set to zero.

> We can fill the elements of an array by using a loop to read the values from the keyboard or a file.

> We can access the individual elements of an array using the array name and the index.

> We can read or write the values of an array using a loop.

> An array reference is a postfix expression with the opening and closing brackets as operators.

> C does not do boundary checking on the elements of an array.

> We can pass an individual element of an array to a function either by value or by address.

> We can also pass the whole array to a function. In this case, only the address of the array will be passed. When this happens, the function has access to all elements in the array.

> A frequency array is an array whose elements show the number of occurrences of data values in another array.

> A histogram is a pictorial representation of a frequency array.

> A two-dimensional array is a representation of a table with rows and columns.

> We can pass a single element, a row, or the whole two-dimensional array to a function.

> A multidimensional array is an extension of a two-dimensional array to three, four, or more dimensions.

> An array can be sorted using a sorting algorithm.

> The selection sort divides the array into sorted and unsorted sublists. In each pass, the algorithm chooses the smallest element from the unsorted sublist and swaps it with the element at the beginning of the unsorted sublist.

> The bubble sort divides the array into sorted and unsorted sublists. In each pass, the algorithm bubbles the smallest element from the unsorted list into the sorted sublist.

> The insertion sort divides the array into sorted and unsorted sublists. In each pass, the algorithm inserts the first element from the unsorted list into the appropriate place in the sorted sublist.

> Searching is the process of finding the location of a target among a list of objects.

> The sequential search starts at the beginning of the array and searches until it finds the data or hits the end of the list. The data may be ordered or unordered.

> A binary search is a much faster searching algorithm. In the binary search, each test removes half of the list from further analysis. The data must be ordered.

> To pass a whole variable-length array to a function, you need to also pass its size.

Key Terms

array

binary search

bubble sort

exchanging values

fixed-length array

frequency array

histogram

index

insertion sort

linear search

multidimensional arrays

one-dimensional arrays

plane

reusable code

selection sort

sequential search

subscript

two-dimensional array

variable-length array

Review Questions

1. The type of all elements in an array must be the same.
   a. True   **b.** False

2. Any expression that evaluates to an integral value may be used as an index.
   a. True   **b.** False

3. When an array is defined, C automatically sets the value of its elements to zero.
   a. True   **b.** False

4. When an array is passed to a function, C passes the value for each element.
   a. True   **b.** False

5. Because of its efficiency, the binary search is the best search for any array, regardless of its size and order.
   a. True   **b.** False

6. The selection, insertion, and bubble sort are all $O(n^2)$ sorts.
   a. True   **b.** False

7. A(n) _____ is an integral value used to access an element in an array.
   a. constant
   b. element
   c. index
   d. number
   e. variable

8. Which of the following array initialization statements is valid?
   a. `int ary{ } = {1, 2, 3, 4};`
   b. `int ary[ ] = [1, 2, 3, 4];`
   c. `int ary[ ] = {1, 2, 3, 4};`
   d. `int ary{4} = [1, 2, 3, 4];`
   e. `int ary[4] = [1, 2, 3, 4];`

9. Which of the following statements assigns the value stored in x to the first element on an array, ary?

   a. `ary = x;`
   b. `ary = x[0];`
   c. `ary = x[1];`
   d. `ary[0] = x;`
   e. `ary[1] = x;`

10. Which of the following statements concerning passing array elements is true?
    a. Arrays cannot be passed to functions, because their structure is too complex.
    b. It is not possible to pass just a row of a two-dimensional array to a function.
    c. Only the size of the first dimension is needed when a two-dimensional array is declared in a parameter list.
    d. When an array is passed to a function, it is always passed by reference (only its address is passed).
    e. When a two-dimensional array is passed to a function, the size of the second dimension must be passed as a value parameter.

11. The process through which data are arranged according to their values is known as

    _____ .
    a. arranging
    b. listing
    c. parsing
    d. searching
    e. sorting

12. The _____ sort finds the smallest element from the unsorted sublist and swaps it with the element at the beginning of the unsorted data.
    a. bubble
    b. exchange
    c. insertion
    d. quick
    e. selection

13. The _____ search locates the target item by starting at the beginning and moving toward the end of the list.
    a. ascending
    b. binary
    c. bubble
    d. selection
    e. sequential

14. Which of the following statements about a sequential search is false?
    a. Any array can be searched using the sequential search.
    b. If the target is not found, every element in the list is tested.
    c. The efficiency of the sequential search is O(n).
    d. The list must be ordered.
    e. The sequential search is generally recommended only for small lists.

15. Which of the following statements about two-dimensional arrays is true?
    a. A two-dimensional array can be thought of as an array of one-dimensional arrays.
    b. Only the size of the second dimension needs to be declared when the array is used as a parameter.
    c. Two different types can be stored in a two-dimensional array.
    d. The first dimension is known as the column dimension.
    e. When passed to a function, the size of the second dimension must be passed as a value parameter.

Exercises

16. What would be printed by the following program?

```
#include <stdio.h>
int main (void)
{
// Local Declarations
   int list [10] = {0};
// Statements
   for (int i = 0; i < 5; i++)
      list [2*i + 1] = i + 2;
   for (int i = 0; i < 10; i++)
      printf ("%d\n", list [i]);
   return 0;
} // main
```

17. What would be printed by the following program?

```
#include <stdio.h>
int main (void)
{
// Local Declarations
   int list [10] = {2, 1, 2, 1, 1, 2, 3, 2, 1, 2};
// Statements
   printf ("%d\n", list [2]);
   printf ("%d\n", list [list [2]]);
   printf ("%d\n", list [list [2] + list [3]]);
   printf ("%d\n", list [list [list [2]]]);
   return 0;
} // main
```

18. What would be printed by the following program?

```
#include <stdio.h>
int main (void)
{
// Local Declarations
   int list [10] = {2, 1, 2, 4, 1, 2, 0, 2, 1, 2};
   int line [10];
// Statements
   for (int i = 0; i < 10; i ++)
      line [i] = list [9 - i];
   for (int i = 0; i < 10; i++)
      printf("%d %d\n", list [i], line [i]);
   return 0;
} // main
```

19. An array contains the following elements. The first two elements have been sorted using a selection sort. What would be the value of the elements in the array after three more passes of the selection sort algorithm?

```
7  8  26  44  13  23  98  57
```

20. An array contains the following elements. The first two elements have been sorted using a bubble sort. What would be the value of the elements in the array after three more passes of the bubble sort algorithm? Use the version of bubble sort that starts from the end and bubbles the smallest element.

```
7  8  26  44  13  23  57  98
```

21. An array contains the following elements. The first two elements have been sorted using an insertion sort. What would be the value of the elements in the array after three more passes of the insertion sort algorithm?

```
3  13  7  26  44  23  98  57
```

22. We have the following array:

```
47  3  21  32  56  92
```

After two passes of a sorting algorithm, the array has been rearranged as follows:

```
3  21  47  32  56  92
```

Which sorting algorithm is being used (selection, bubble, insertion)? Defend your answer.

23. We have the following array:

```
80  72  66  44  21  33
```

After two passes of a sorting algorithm, the array has been rearranged as follows:

```
21  33  80  72  66  44
```

Which sorting algorithm is being used (selection, bubble, insertion)? Defend your answer.

24. We have the following array:

```
47  3  66  32  56  92
```

After two passes of a sorting algorithm, the array has been rearranged as follows:

```
3  47  66  32  56  92
```

Which sorting algorithm is being used (selection, bubble, insertion)? Defend your answer.

25. An array contains the following elements. Using the binary search algorithm, trace the steps followed to find 88. At each loop iteration, including the last, show the contents of first, last, and mid.

```
8  13  17  26  44  56  88  97
```

26. An array contains the following elements. Using the binary search algorithm, trace the steps followed to find 20. At each loop iteration, including the last, show the contents of first, last, and mid.

```
8  13  17  26  44  56  88  97
```

27. Both the selection and bubble sorts exchange elements. The insertion sort does not. Explain how the insertion sort rearranges the data without exchanges.

Problems

28. We have two arrays A and B, each of 10 integers. Write a function that tests if every element of array A is equal to its corresponding element in array B. In other words, the function must check if A[0] is equal to B[0], A[1] is equal to B[1], and so forth. The function is to return true if all elements are equal and false if at least one element is not equal.

29. Write a function that reverses the elements of an array so that the last element becomes the first, the second from the last becomes the second, and so forth. The function is to reverse the elements in place—that is, without using another array. (It is permissible to use a variable to hold an element temporarily.) Then write a test driver to test your function. Test it twice, once with an even number of elements in the array and once with an odd number of elements in the array.

30. The Pascal triangle can be used to compute the coefficients of the terms in the expansion of $(a + b)^n$. Write a function that creates a two-dimensional matrix representing the Pascal triangle. In a Pascal triangle, each element is the sum of the element directly above it and the element to the left of the element directly above it (if any). The following is a Pascal triangle of size 7.

```
1
1    1
1    2    1
1    3    3    1
1    4    6    4    1
1    5    10   10   5    1
1    6    15   20   15   6    1
```

In the above example, the first element of row[0] and the first two elements of row[1] are set to 1. Then each of the following rows, up to the maximum size, are set with a loop as shown in the following pseudocode:

```
Algorithm PascalTriangle
1   pascal[0][0]    = 1
2   pascal[1][0]    = 1
3   pascal[1][1]    = 1
4   prevRow = 1
5   currRow = 2
6   loop (currRow <= size)
    6.1 pascal[row][0] = 1
    6.2 col = 1
    6.3 loop (col <= currRow)
        6.3.1 pascal[ row] [ col] =
```

```
          pascal[row - 1][col - 1]
            + pascal[row - 1][col]
      6.3.2 col = col + 1
    6.4 end loop
7   end loop
end PascalTriangle
```

Your program must be able to create the triangle of any size.

31. An international standard book number (ISBN) is used to uniquely identify a book. For books published after 2007, ISBNs consist of 13 digits. Prior to 2007, ISBNs consisted of 10 digits, as shown in **Figure 8-44**. Write a function that tests a 10-digit ISBN to see if it is valid. For an ISBN number to be valid, the weighted sum of the 10 digits must be evenly divisible by 11. The tenth digit may be x, which indicates 10.

Figure 8-44   ISBN for Problem 31

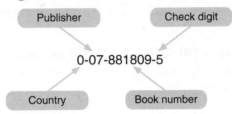

To determine the weighted sum, the value of each position is multiplied by its relative position, starting from the right, and the sum of the products is determined. The calculation of the weighted sum for the ISBN shown above is demonstrated in **Table 8-5**.

Table 8-5   Demonstration of ISBN calculation

CODE	WEIGHT	WEIGHTED VALUE
0	10	0
0	9	0
7	8	56
8	7	56
8	6	48
1	5	5
8	4	32
0	3	0
9	2	18
5	1	5
Weighted sum		220

Because the weighted sum modulus 11 is 0, the ISBN number is valid. Test your function with the above example and with the following number: 0-08-781809-5 (an invalid ISBN—the third and fourth digits are reversed).

32. Write a program to convert a 10-digit ISBN into a 13-digit ISBN. For example: 0-07-881809-5 would convert to 978-0-07-881809-7. Use the following ISBN conversion algorithm:

a. Remove the last digit from the ISBN.

b. Add 978 to the beginning of the new ISBN.

   c. Starting from the first digit, calculate the sum of each odd number and save it as SumOfOdd.

   d. Starting from the second digit, find the sum of each even number and save it as SumOfEven.

   e. Calculate TotalSum = SumOfOdd + (SumOfEven*3).

   f. Calculate NewCheckDigit = 10 − (TotalSum%10).

   g. New 13-digit ISBN = 978-(10 digits ISBN without old check digit)-NewCheckDigit.

Applying the above algorithm to the 10-digit ISBN 0-07-881809-5 yields the following:

   a. 007881809

   b. 978007881809

   c. SumOfOdd = 9+8+0+8+1+0 = 26

   d. SumOfEven = 7+0+7+8+8+9 = 39

   e. TotalSum = 26+(39*3) = 143

   f. NewCheckDigit = 10−(143%10) = 7

   g. New 13-digit ISBN = 978-0-07-881809-7

33. Write a function that copies a one-dimensional array of n elements into a two-dimensional array of k rows and j columns. The rows and columns must be a valid factor of the number of elements in the one-dimensional array; that is, k * j = n.

34. Write a program that creates an array of 100 random integers in the range 1 to 200 and then, using the sequential search, searches the array 100 times using randomly generated targets in the same range. At the end of the program, display the following statistics:

   a. The number of searches completed

   b. The number of successful searches

   c. The percentage of successful searches

   d. The average number of tests per search

To determine the average tests per search, you will need to count the number of tests for each search. Hint: Use the comma operator to count the compares.

35. Repeat Problem 34 using the binary search.

36. The sequential search assumes that a list is unordered. If it is used when the list is in fact ordered, the search can be terminated with the target not found whenever the target is less than the current element. Modify Program 8-13 to incorporate this logic.

37. Repeat Problem 34 with the modified search you created in Problem 36.

38. The binary search is a good algorithm to implement using recursion. Rewrite the binary search function using recursion. Then repeat Problem 35 using the recursive function.

39. Modify the bubble sort to stop as soon as the list is sorted. (See discussion in the analysis of Program 8-10.)

40. Modify the selection sort function to count the number of exchanges needed to order an array of 50 random numbers. Display the array before and after the sort. At the end of the program, display the total exchanges needed to sort the array.

41. Repeat Problem 40 using the bubble sort.

42. Program 8-7 builds a frequency array and its histogram. If there is an invalid data point in the input, it is displayed and ignored. Modify the program to make the frequency array one element larger than the data range, and use the last element of the array as a count of numbers not in the specified range.

43. Write a program that fills the right-to-left diagonal of a square matrix with zeros, the lower-right triangle with −1s, and the upper-left triangle with +1s. The output of the program, assuming a six-by-six matrix, is shown in **Figure 8-45**.

Figure 8-45 Matrix for Problem 43

44. Given an array of 100 random numbers in the range 1 ... 999, write a function for each of the following processes. In building the array, if the random number is evenly divided by 3 or 7, store it as a negative number.
    a. Print the array ten values to a line. Make sure that the values are aligned in rows.
    b. Print the odd values, ten to a line.
    c. Print the values at the odd numbered index locations, ten to a line.
    d. Return a count of the number of even values.
    e. Return the sum of all values in the array.
    f. Return the location of the smallest value in the array.
    g. Return the location of the largest value in the array.
    h. Copy all positive values to a new array. Then use process "a" above to print the new array.
    i. Copy all negative values to a new array. Then use process "a" above to print the new array.

45. Modify the sort of your choice to sort two parallel arrays. Parallel arrays are two or more arrays that contain related data. For example, one array might contain identification numbers, and a related array might contain corresponding scores in a tournament. The sort will sort only the array containing the identifiers; however, as each element in the sorted array is moved, its corresponding element in the data array must also be moved. After the arrays have been sorted, print out the following data:

    ```
    ID    Score
    1     72
    2     89
    3     98
    4     105
    ```

    Write a test driver to test your sort. Use the following data—the first value is an identifier and the second value is a score: {18, 90}, {237, 47}, {35, 105}, {5,25}, {76, 739}, {103, 26}, {189, 38}, {22, 110}, {156, 31}, {49, 245}.

46. Write the incremental implementation to calculate the column averages for the "Programming Example: Calculating Averages" section. Before testing the column average increment, determine the averages so that you will be able to verify that the correct values were calculated.

Projects

47. Write a C program that simulates a guessing game. Each turn, you choose among nine possible guesses. As many as five guesses may be made in a turn. For each turn, the program will generate a random number between 1 and 36. Each correct guess will be rewarded with points based on how many of your current points you risked.

    A game board divides the numbers into rows and columns, as shown in **Figure 8-46**. This board provides the basis for your guesses.

Figure 8-46 Guessing game board

	LEFT	CENTER	RIGHT
LOW	01	02	03
	04	05	06
	07	08	09
	10	11	12
MEDIUM	13	14	15
	16	17	18
	19	20	21
	22	23	24
HIGH	25	26	27
	28	29	30
	31	32	33
	34	35	36
	LEFT	CENTER	RIGHT

You can guess whether the random number is even or odd. In this case, you get 1 point for each point risked when you guess correctly. You can guess whether the number is low (1–12), medium (13–24), or high (25–36). In this case, you will get 2 points for each point risked. You can also guess left, center, or right, as shown in Figure 8-46. In this case, you get 2 points for each point risked when your guess is correct. Finally, you can guess a specific number between 0 and 36. In this case, you get 36 points for each point risked when your guess is correct.

To make the game more interesting, each round allows up to five guesses. None of the five may be correct, or any number up to all five may be correct. The program stops when the player quits or when the player is out of points.

The program first asks the number of points the user wants to start with, as follows:

```
How many points would you like? 2000
```

The program then prints the guess menu and allows up to five guesses, as shown in the following example:

```
Guesses Choices
O       Odd
E       Even
L       Low
M       Med
H       High
F       Left
C       Center
R       Right
N       Number
How many guesses would you like? 5
```

```
Guess 1 :
Enter your choice? L
Points at risk? 20
Guess 2 :
Enter your choice? H
Points at risk? 15
Guess 3 :
Enter your choice? N
Enter your number: 18
Points at risk? 20
Guess 4 :
Enter your choice? O
Points at risk? 120
Guess 5 :
Enter your choice? L
Points at risk? 0
```

After all guesses have been made, the program generates the random number and displays the following message:

```
My number is: 31
```

The program then prints the situation of the player:

```
Previous    Points: 2000
Guess       Type    Number   Amount   Won/Loss
    1       L                  20       -20
    2       H                  15       +30
    3       N        18        20       -20
    4       O                  120      +120
    5       N        20        10       -10
You won 100 points in this turn.
Your new balance is : 2100 points
Do you want to play again (Y or N)? Y
```

Some special rules: The minimum amount risked on a guess is 0. The maximum is the player's current balance. You need to verify that at no time are the points risked more than the player's current balance. Any combinations of guesses are allowed on a round as long as the total does not exceed the player's balance.

Some hints: You must use at least four arrays, each of five elements. The arrays hold the guess information for the kind of guess, chosen number (in case the player chooses a number), amount of the guess, and points won or lost.

Run your program twice, first with 2000 points and then with 500 points. Try different situations. Each run is to exercise each guess at least twice.

48. Write a program to keep records and perform statistical analysis for a class of students. The class may have up to 40 students. There are five quizzes during the term. Each student is identified by a four-digit student number.

The program will print the student scores and calculate and print the statistics for each quiz. The output is in the same order as the input; no sorting is needed. The input will be read from a text file. The output from the program should be similar to the following:

```
Student      Quiz 1 Quiz 2 Quiz 3 Quiz 4 Quiz 5
   1234        78     83     87     91     86
   2134        67     77     84     82     79
   3124        77     89     93     87     71
High Score     78     89     93     91     86
Low Score      67     77     84     82     71
  Average      73.4   83.0   88.2   86.6   78.6
```

Use one- and two-dimensional arrays only. Test your program with the quiz data in **Table 8-6**

Table 8-6   Test data for Project 48

STUDENT	QUIZ 1	QUIZ 2	QUIZ 3	QUIZ 4	QUIZ 5
1234	52	7	100	78	34
2134	90	36	90	77	30
3124	100	45	20	90	70
4532	11	17	81	32	77
5678	20	12	45	78	34
6134	34	80	55	78	45
7874	60	100	56	78	78
8026	70	10	66	78	56
9893	34	9	77	78	20
1947	45	40	88	78	55
2877	55	50	99	78	80
3189	22	70	100	78	77
4602	89	50	91	78	60
5405	11	11	0	78	10
6999	0	98	89	78	20

49. Rework Project 48, creating statistics for each student. Print the students' high, low, and average scores to the right of Quiz 5. Provide appropriate column headings.

50. Program 8-7 builds a frequency array. In the discussion of the algorithm, we noted that a potential problem occurs if any of the data are invalid.

Write a program that uses the random number generator, rand, to generate 100 numbers between 1 and 22. The array is then to be passed to a modified version of Program 8-7 that will count the number of values between 0 and 19. Add a 21st element in the array to count all numbers not in the valid range (0 to 19).

Print the input data in a 20 × 5 array—that is, 20 numbers in five rows—and then print the frequency diagram with a heading of the numbers as follows:

```
--0-  --1-  --2-  --3-  --4-  ...  -18-  -19-  Invalid
```

51. Modify the program you wrote in Project 50 to include a histogram printout of the data. Its format should be similar to Figure 8-15.

52. Using the data from Project 48, build a two-dimensional array of students. Then write a search function that uses the sequential search to find a student in the array and prints the students' scores, average score, and grade based on an absolute scale (90% is A, 80% is B, 70% is C, 60% is D, less than 60% is F). After each printout, give the user the opportunity to continue or stop.

53. Modify the program you wrote in Project 52 to sort the two-dimensional array of students. Then rewrite the search function to use a binary search.

54. Write a program that sorts a 50-element array using the selection sort, the bubble sort, and the insertion sort. Each sort is to be executed twice.

    a. For the first sort, fill the array with random numbers between 1 and 1000.

    b. For the second sort, fill the array with a nearly ordered list. Create the nearly ordered list by filling the array with sequential numbers and then subtracting 5 from every 10th number in the array.

    c. Each sort (selection, bubble, insertion) is to sort the same data. For each sort, count the number of comparisons and moves necessary to order this list.

    d. After each sort execution, print the unsorted data followed by the sort data in 5-by-10 matrixes (5 rows of 10 numbers each). After the sorted data, print the number of comparisons and the number of moves required to order the data. Provide appropriate headings for each printout.

    e. To make sure your statistics are as accurate as possible, you must analyze each loop limit condition test and each selection statement in your sort functions. The best way to count them is with a comma expression, as follows. Use similar code for the selection statements.

```
while ((count++, a) && (count++, b))
```

    f. Analyze the heuristics you generated, and write a few lines concerning what you discovered about these sorts. Put your comments in a box (asterisks) after your program documentation at the beginning of your program.

55. Write a program to compute the arithmetic mean (average), median, and mode for up to 50 test scores. The data are contained in a text file. The program will also print a histogram of the scores.

The program should start with a function to read the data file and fill the array. Note that there may be fewer than 50 scores. This will require that the read function return the index for the last element in the array.

To determine the average, write a function similar to Program 8-4. To determine the median, you must first sort the array. The median is the score in the middle of the range. This can be determined by selecting the score at last / 2 if last is an even index and by averaging the scores at the floor and ceiling of last / 2 if last is odd. The mode is the score that occurs the most often. It can be determined as a byproduct of building the histogram. After building the frequency array, use it to determine which score occurred most often. (Note that two scores can occur the same number of times.)

56. Write a menu-driven program that allows the user to fill an array of 50 integers with random numbers in the range 1 ... 999, sort it, and then search it to determine if a given random number was generated. The menu is as follows:

```
                    MENU
Select one of the following options:
1. Fill array with a random number series
2. Print the array
3. Sort the array
4. Query the array
5. Terminate the program
```

> Each time the fill option is executed it will fill the array with a new random number series.

> You may use any of the sorts discussed in the text.

> If the query locates the number, it will print a message that the number was located along with index location where it was found.

> If the query does not locate the number, it will print a message that the number was not in the list and then print the value and index location of the largest number less than the target and the smallest value greater than the requested number. Note that the first and last elements will not have both a smaller and larger value.

> If the array has been sorted, the query will use a binary search. If it is not sorted, it will use the sequential search.

To test the program:

a. Fill (F) the array.

b. Print (P) the unsorted array.

c. Search (Q) the first, last, and a middle element.

d. Refill (F) the array.

e. Sort (S) the array.

f. Print (P) the sorted array.

g. Search (Q) the first, last, and a middle element.

h. Search (Q) for a number less than the first, greater than the last, and not found in the middle of the list.

CHAPTER 9

Pointers

Learning Objectives

When you complete this chapter, you will be able to:

9.1 Describe how pointers are declared, defined, and initialized in C

9.2 Write programs that use pointers as parameters and return types

9.3 Define a pointer to point to other pointer variables

9.4 Describe the types and importance of pointer compatibility

9.5 Differentiate when to use an lvalue or an rvalue expression in C

9.6 Explain the relationship between arrays and pointers

9.7 Describe the design and concepts behind pointer arithmetic

9.8 Explain the design behind passing arrays to functions

9.9 Write C programs that use static and dynamic memory allocation

9.10 Implement ragged arrays using C

9.11 Learn how to code advanced programs using pointers

9.1 Understanding Pointers

Every computer has addressable memory locations. So far, all of our data manipulations, whether for inspection or alteration, used variable names to locate the data. In other words, we assigned identifiers to data and then manipulated their contents through the identifiers. In this chapter we explore the use of pointers to locate data instead. A pointer is a constant or variable that contains an address that can be used to access data.

Pointers have many uses in C. Besides being a very efficient method of accessing data, they provide efficient techniques for manipulating data in arrays, they are used in functions as pass-by-address parameters, and they are the basis for dynamic allocations of memory.

As shown in **Figure 9-1**, pointers are the third of the derived types.

We begin with the use of pointers in implementing arrays. This discussion includes the important topic of pointer arithmetic, which allows us to process data in an array by adding or subtracting from pointer addresses. Following a discussion of passing arrays to functions, we discuss one of the most powerful aspects of C, dynamic memory. We examine two different approaches to dynamic memory, static allocation and dynamic allocation, followed by sorting with pointers, ragged arrays, and pointer applications.

Figure 9-1 Derived types

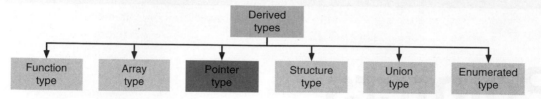

Pointers are built on the basic concept of pointer constants. To understand and use pointers, we must first understand this concept.

Pointer Constants

A pointer constant is a pointer whose contents cannot be changed. To get a better sense of what this means, let's compare character constants and pointer constants. We know that we can have a character constant, such as any letter of the alphabet, that is drawn from a universe of all characters. In most computers, this universe is ASCII. A character constant is a value and can be stored in a variable. Although the character constant is unnamed, the variable has a name that is declared in the program. This concept is shown in **Figure 9-2**.

Figure 9-2 Character constants and variables

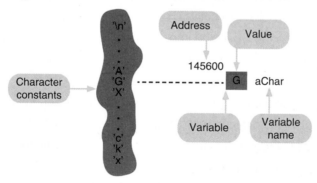

In Figure 9-2 we have a character variable, aChar. At this point, aChar contains the value 'G' that was drawn from the universe of character constants. The variable aChar has an address as well as a name. The name is created by the programmer; the address is the relative location of the variable with respect to the program's memory space. Assume, for example, that a computer has only 1 megabyte of memory (2^{20} bytes). Assume also that the computer has chosen the memory location 145600 as the byte to store this variable. This gives us the picture we see in Figure 9-2.

Like character constants, pointer constants cannot be changed. In **Figure 9-3** we see that the address for our character variable, aChar, was drawn from the set of pointer constants for our computer.

Figure 9-3 Pointer constants

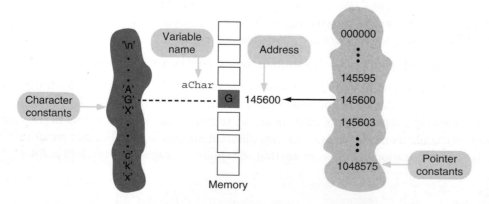

Although the addresses within a computer cannot change, be aware that the address of the variable, aChar, can and will change from one run of our program to another. This is because operating systems can put a program in memory wherever it is convenient when the program is started. Thus, while aChar is stored at memory location 145600 now, the next time the program is run, it could be located at 876050. It should be obvious, therefore, that even though addresses are constant, we cannot know what they will be. It is still necessary to refer to them symbolically.

Pointer Values

Having defined a pointer constant as an address in memory, we now turn our attention to saving this address. If we have a pointer constant, we should be able to save its value if we can somehow identify it. Not only is this possible, but we have been doing it since we wrote our first scanf statement with an address operator.

The address operator (&) extracts the address for a variable. The result is a unary expression, which is also known as an address expression. In **Table 9-1**, the address operator is listed in the unary category, with a precedence of 15.

Table 9-1   Precedence table

OPERATOR	DESCRIPTION	EXAMPLE	SIDE EFFECTS	ASSOC	PR
	Identifiers	amount	N	N/A	16
	Constants	3.14159			
	Parenthetical Expressions	(a + b)			
[ ]	Array Index	ary [i]	N	Left-Right	16
f (...)	Function Call	doIt(x, y)	Y		
.	Direct Member Selection	str.mem	N		
->	Indirect Member Selection	ptr->mem	N		
++ --	Postfix Increment • Decrement	a++	Y		
++ --	Prefix Increment • Decrement	++a	Y	Right-Left	15
sizeof	Size in Bytes	sizeof(int)	N		
~	Ones Complement	-a	N		
!	Not	!a	N		
+ -	Plus • Minus	+a	N		
&	Address	&a	N		
*	Dereference / Indirection	*ptr	N		
( )	Type Cast	(int)ptr	N	Right-Left	14
* / %	Multiply • Divide • Modulus	a * b	N	Left-Right	13
+ -	Addition • Subtraction	a + b	N	Left-Right	12
<< >>	Bit Shift Left • Bit Shift Right	a << 3	N	Left-Right	11
< <= > >=	Comparison	a < 5	N	Left-Right	10
== !=	Equal • Not Equal	a == b	N	Left-Right	9
&	Bitwise And	a & b	N	Left-Right	8
^	Bitwise Exclusive Or	a ^ b	N	Left-Right	7
|	Bitwise Or	a | b	N	Left-Right	6
&&	Logical And	a && b	N	Left-Right	5
||	Logical Or	a || b	N	Left-Right	4
? :	Conditional	a ? x : y	N	Right-Left	3

(continue)

Table 9-1 Precedence table—*(continued)*

OPERATOR	DESCRIPTION	EXAMPLE	SIDE EFFECTS	ASSOC	PR
`= += -=` `*= /= %=` `>>= <<=` `&= ^= |=`	Assignment	`a = 5` `a %= b` `a &= c` `a |= d`	Y	Right-Left	2
`,`	Comma	`a, b, c`	N	Left-Right	1

The address operator format is seen below.

`&variable_name`

Now let's write a program that defines two character variables and prints their addresses as pointers (conversion code `%p`). Depending on the operating system, this program may print different numbers each time we run it, as previously explained. The addresses would also be different in different computers. However, most of the time, the computer allocates two adjacent memory locations because we defined the two variables one after the other. If you are at your computer, take a moment to code and run the program in **Figure 9-4** to demonstrate the concept of address constants.

Figure 9-4 Print character addresses

```
// Print character addresses
#include <stdio.h>

int main (void)
{
// Local Declarations
    char a;
    char b;
// Statements
    printf("%p\n %p\n", &a, &b);
    return 0;
} // main
```

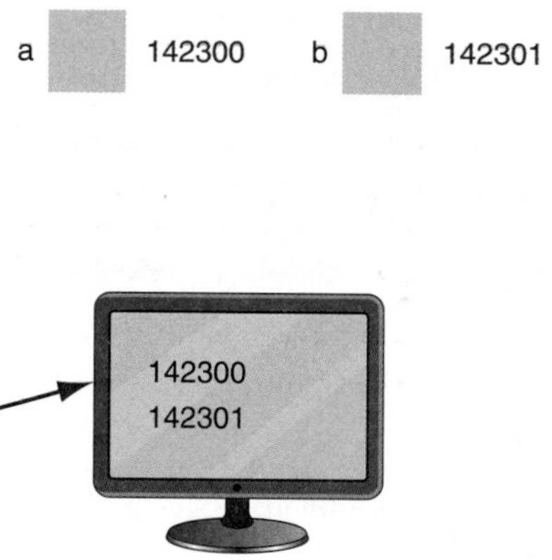

a   142300   b   142301

142300
142301

The situation changes slightly when we talk about integers. In most computers, the `int` type occupy 4 bytes. This means that each `int` variable occupies four memory locations. Which of these memory locations is used to find the address of the variable? In most computers, the location of the first byte is used as the memory address. For characters, there is only 1 byte, so its location is the address. For integers, the address is the first byte. This is shown in **Figure 9-5**.

Figure 9-5 Integer constants and variables

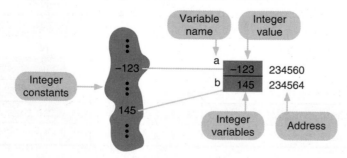

The same design applies to real and other data types. The address of a variable is the address of the first byte occupied by that variable.

Pointer Variables

If we have a pointer constant and a pointer value, then we can have a pointer variable. Thus, we can store the address of a variable into another variable, which is called a pointer variable. This concept is shown in **Figure 9-6**.

Figure 9-6   Pointer variable

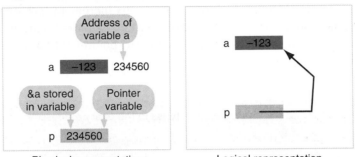

Physical representation   Logical representation

We must distinguish between a variable and its value. Figure 9-6 details the differences. In this figure we see a variable, a, with its value, –123. The variable a is found at location 234560 in memory. Although the variable's name and location are constant, the value may change as the program executes. This figure also has a pointer variable, p. The pointer has a name and a location, both of which are constant. Its value at this point is the memory location 234560. This means that p is pointing to a. In Figure 9-6, the physical representation shows how the data and pointer variables exist in memory. The logical representation shows the relationship between them without the physical details.

We can go even further and store a variable's address in two or more different pointer variables, as is shown in **Figure 9-7**. This figure has a variable, a, and two pointers, p and q. The pointers each have a name and a location, both of which are constant. Their value at this point is the memory location 234560. This means that both p and q are pointing to a. There is no limit to the number of pointer variables that can point to a variable.

Figure 9-7   Multiple pointers to a variable

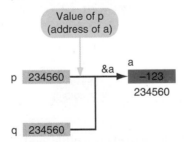

A final thought: If we have a pointer variable, but we don't want it to point anywhere, what is its value? C provides a special null pointer constant, NULL, in the standard input/output stdio.h header file for this purpose. It should be noted here that NULL is found technically in the stddef.h library. NULL is usually defined as a macro with a value of integer 0 or 0 cast to a void pointer (void*).

Accessing Variables through Pointers

Now that we have a variable and a pointer to the variable, how can we relate the two; that is, how can we use the pointer? Once again C has provided an operator for us. Right below the address operator in the unary expressions portion of Table 9-1, we find the indirection operator (*). When we dereference a pointer, we are using its value to reference (address) another variable. The indirection operator is a unary operator whose operand must be a pointer value. The result is an expression that can be used to access the pointed variable for the purpose of inspection or alteration. To access the variable a through the pointer p, we simply code *p. The indirection operator is shown below.

```
*p
```

Let's assume that we need to add 1 to the variable a. We can do this with any of the following statements, assuming that the pointer, p, is properly initialized (p = &a):

```
a++;   a = a + 1;   *p = *p + 1;   (*p)++;
```

In the last example, (*p)++, we need the parentheses. The postfix increment has a precedence of 16 in Table 9-1 while indirection, which is a unary operator, has a precedence of 15. The parentheses force the dereference to occur before the addition so that we add to the data variable and not to the pointer. Without the parentheses, we would add to the pointer first, which would change the address.

> **Note** | An indirect expression, one of the expression types in the unary expression category, is coded with an asterisk (*) and an Identifier.

Figure 9-8 expands the discussion. Let's assume that the variable x is pointed to by two pointers, p and q. The expressions x, *p, and *q all are expressions that allow the variable to be either inspected or changed. When they are used in the right-hand side of the assignment operator, they can only inspect (copy or compare). When they are used in the left-hand side of the assignment operator, they change the value of x.

Figure 9-8   Accessing variables through pointers

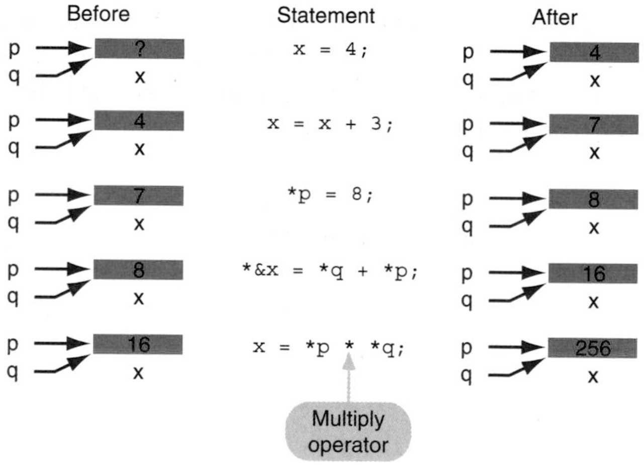

Before	Statement	After
p → ? / q → x	x = 4;	p → 4 / q → x
p → 4 / q → x	x = x + 3;	p → 7 / q → x
p → 7 / q → x	*p = 8;	p → 8 / q → x
p → 8 / q → x	*&x = *q + *p;	p → 16 / q → x
p → 16 / q → x	x = *p * *q; (Multiply operator)	p → 256 / q → x

The indirection and address operators are the inverse of each other, and when combined in an expression, such as *&x, they cancel each other. To see this, let's break down the expression. These two unary operators are evaluated from the right. The first expression is &x, the address of x, which, as we have seen, is a pointer value. The second expression, *(&x), dereferences the pointer constant, giving the variable (x) itself. Therefore, the operators effectively cancel each other (**Figure 9-9**). Of course, we would never code the expression *&a in a program; we use it in Figure 9-8 for illustration only.

Figure 9-9   Address and indirection operators

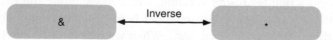

Pointer Declaration and Definition

As shown in **Figure 9-10**, we use the asterisk to declare pointer variables. When we use the asterisk in this way, it is really not an operator but rather a compiler syntactical notation.

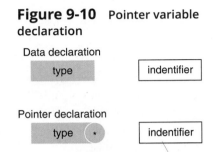

Figure 9-10 Pointer variable declaration

Figure 9-11 shows how we declare different pointer variables. Their corresponding data variables are shown for comparison. Note that in each case the pointer is declared to be of a given type. Thus, p is a pointer to characters, while q is a pointer to integers, and r is a pointer to floating-point variables.

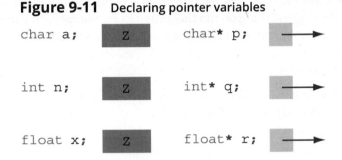

Figure 9-11 Declaring pointer variables

Program 9-1 stores the address of a variable in a pointer and then prints the data using the variable value and a pointer.

> ## Program 9-1 | Demonstrate use of pointers

```
 1   /* Demonstrate pointer use
 2      Written by:
 3      Date:
 4   */
 5   #include <stdio.h>
 6
 7   int main (void)
 8   {
 9   // Local Declarations
10       int a;
11       int* p;
12
13   // Statements
14       a = 14;
15       p = &a;
16
17       printf ("%d %p\n", a, &a);
18       printf ("%p %d %d\n", p, *p, a);
```

(continue)

Program 9-1 Demonstrate use of pointers *(continued)*

```
19
20    return 0;
21  } // main
```

Output

```
14 00135760
00135760 14 14
```

Program 9-1 requires a little explanation. First, we have defined an integer variable, a, and a pointer to integer, p, to which we assign a's address. We then print twice. The first print displays the contents of the variable a and its address (note the pointer conversion code). The second print uses the pointer, p. It prints the pointer value containing the address of a, followed by the contents of a, first referenced as a pointer and then as a variable. This demonstrates two ways to access the data. We suggest that you run this program for yourself. Of course, when you do, you will get a different address. Also, some compilers display addresses as integers, and some use hexadecimal numbers.

Declaration versus Redirection

We have used the asterisk operator in two different contexts: for declaration and for redirection. When an asterisk is used for declaration, it is associated with a type. For example, we define a pointer to an integer as

```
int* pa;
int* pb;
```

In this usage, the asterisk declares that the type of pa and pb is a pointer to an integer.

On the other hand, we also use the asterisk for redirection. When used for redirection, the asterisk is an operator that redirects the operation from the pointer variable to a data variable. For example, given two pointers to integers, pa and pb, sum is computed as

```
sum = *pa + *pb;
```

The first expression, *pa, uses the pointer value stored in the pointer variable, pa, to locate its value. The address in pa is not added; it is *redirected* through the asterisk operator to the desired value. Likewise, the address in the second expression, pb, is not added but used to locate the second expression's value. After both of the expressions have been evaluated, they can be added and the resulting expression value stored in sum.

Initialization of Pointer Variables

As we discussed in the previous section, the C language does not initialize variables. Thus, when we start our program, all of our uninitialized variables have unknown garbage in them.

The same is true for pointers. When the program starts, uninitialized pointers will have some unknown memory address in them. More precisely, they will have an unknown value that will be interpreted as a memory location. Most likely the value will not be valid for the computer you are using, or if it is, will not be valid for the memory you have been allocated. If the address does not exist, you will get an immediate run-time error. If it is a valid address, you often, but unfortunately not always, get a run-time error. (It is better to get the error when you use the invalid pointer than to have the program produce garbage.)

One of the most common causes of errors in programming, by novices and professionals alike, is uninitialized pointers. These errors can be very difficult to debug because the effect of the error is often delayed until later in the program execution. **Figure 9-12** shows both an uninitialized variable and an uninitialized pointer.

Figure 9-12 Uninitialized pointers

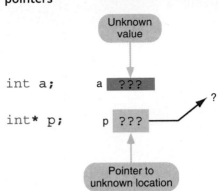

To correct the problem shown in Figure 9-12, we must always assign a valid memory address to the pointer, as shown in the next example.

```
int a; // int variable-value unknown
int* p = &a; // p has valid address
*p = 89; // a assigned value 89
```

As we saw with variables, it is also possible to initialize pointers when they are declared and defined. All that is needed is that the data variable be defined before the pointer variable. For example, if we have an integer variable, a, and a pointer to integer, p, then to set p to point to a at declaration time, we can code it as shown in **Figure 9-13**.

Figure 9-13 Initializing pointer variables

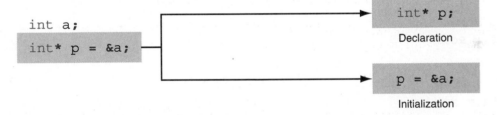

Note that in Figure 9-13, the initialization involves two different steps. First the variable is declared. Then the assignment statement to initialize the variable is generated. Some style experts suggest that you should not use an initializer in this way. Their argument is that it saves no code; that is, that the initializer statement is required either as a part of the declaration and initialization or as a separately coded statement in the statement section of the function. Putting the initialization in the declaration section tends to hide it and make program maintenance more difficult. We tend to agree with them.

We can also set a pointer to NULL, either during definition or during execution. The following statement demonstrates how we could define a pointer with an initial value of NULL.

```
int* p = NULL;
```

In most implementations, a null pointer contains address 0, which may be a valid or invalid address depending on the operating system. If we dereference the pointer p when it is NULL, we will most likely get a run-time error because NULL is not a valid address. The type of error we get depends on the system we are using.

Now let's write a program and have some fun with pointers. Our code is shown in **Program 9-2**. Do not try to figure out why this program is doing what it is doing; there is no reason. Rather, just try to trace the different variables and pointers as we change them.

Program 9-2 | Fun with pointers

```
1   /* Fun with pointers
2      Written by:
3      Date:
4   */
5   #include <stdio.h>
6
7   int main (void)
8   {
9   // Local Declarations
10     int a;
11     int b;
12     int c;
13     int* p;
14     int* q;
15     int* r;
16
17  // Statements
18     a = 6;
19     b = 2;
20     p = &b;
21
22     q = p;
23     r = &c;
24
25     p = &a;
26     *q = 8;
27
28     *r = *p;
29
30     *r = a + *q + *&c;
31
32     printf("%d %d %d \n",
33            a, b, c);
34     printf("%d %d %d",
35            *p, *q, *r);
36     return 0;
37  } // main
```

Output

```
6 8 20
6 8 20
```

When the program starts, all the variables and their pointers are uninitialized. The variables have garbage values, and the pointers have invalid memory locations.

The first thing the program does, therefore, is to assign values to a and b, and to initialize all three pointers. After statement 23, both p and g point to b, and r points to c.

Statement 25 assigns the address of a to p. All three pointers now point to different variables. Using the indirection operator, we dereference g (*q), and assign b the value 8.

Statement 28 demonstrates that both operands can be dereferenced when it assigns the contents of a (*p) to c (*r).

Finally, in statement 30, we use three different formats to sum the values in the variables, a variable name, a dereferenced pointer, and a dereferenced address operator. Using the figures in the program, trace these statements carefully to assure yourself that you understand how they work.

This example shows how we can use pointers to add two numbers. It explores the concept of using pointers to manipulate data. A graphic representation of the variables is shown in **Figure 9-14**. The code is shown in **Program 9-3**.

Figure 9-14 Add two numbers using pointers

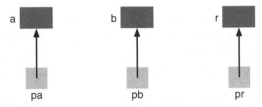

Program 9-3 | Add two numbers using pointers

```
1   /* This program adds two numbers using pointers to
2       demonstrate the concept of pointers.
3       Written by:
4       Date:
5   */
6   #include <stdio.h>
7
8   int main (void)
9   {
10  // Local Declarations
11      int a;
12      int b;
13      int r;
14      int* pa = &a;
15      int* pb = &b;
16      int* pr = &r;
17
18  // Statements
19      printf("Enter the first number : ");
```

(continue)

Program 9-3   Add two numbers using pointers *(continued)*

```
20      scanf ("%d", pa);
21      printf("Enter the second number: ");
22      scanf ("%d", pb);
23      *pr = *pa + *pb;
24      printf("\n%d + %d is %d", *pa, *pb, *pr);
25      return 0;
26 } // main
```

Output

```
Enter the first number : 15
Enter the second number: 51
15 + 51 is 66
```

This program is rather straightforward except for one thing. Look at statements 20 and 22 carefully. What is missing? When we discussed pass-by address in previous chapters in this text, we mentioned that when input areas are passed by address, we don't use the address operator in the scanf statement. This is because the pointer already contains an address. It would be an error to use the address operator on the pointers in this program.

We can use the same pointer to print the value of different variables. The variables and their pointer are shown in **Figure 9-15**.

Figure 9-15   Demonstrate pointer flexibility

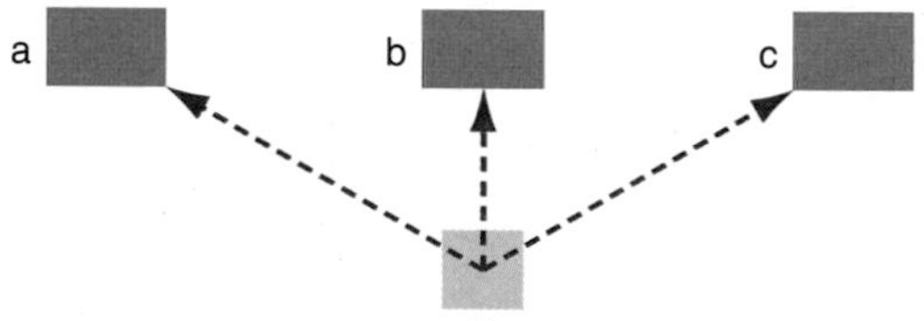

The code is in **Program 9-4**.

Program 9-4 | Using one pointer for many variables

```
1   /* This program shows how the same pointer can point to
2       different data variables in different statements.
3       Written by:
4       Date:
5   */
6   #include <stdio.h>
7
```

(continue)

Program 9-4   Using one pointer for many variables *(continued)*

```
8   int main (void)
9   {
10  // Local Declarations
11      int a;
12      int b;
13      int c;
14      int*p;
15
16  // Statements
17      printf("Enter three numbers and key return: ");
18      scanf ("%d %d %d", &a, &b, &c);
19      p = &a;
20      printf("%3d\n", *p);
21      p = &b;
22      printf("%3d\n", *p);
23      p = &c;
24      printf("%3d\n", *p);
25      return 0;
26  } // main
```

Output
```
Enter three numbers and key return: 10 20 30
 10
 20
 30
```

We can use different pointers to print the value of the same variable. The variable and its pointers are shown in **Figure 9-16**.

Figure 9-16   One variable with many pointers

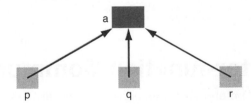

The code is shown in **Program 9-5**.

Program 9-5 | Using a variable with many pointers

```
 1   /* This program shows how we can use different pointers
 2         to point to the same data variable.
 3         Written by:
 4         Date:
 5   */
 6   #include <stdio.h>
 7
 8   int main (void)
 9   {
10   // Local Declarations
11       int a;
12       int* p = &a;
13       int* q = &a;
14       int* r = &a;
15
16   // Statements
17       printf("Enter a number: ");
18       scanf ("%d", &a);
19       printf("%d\n", *p);
20       printf("%d\n", *q);
21       printf("%d\n", *r);
22
23       return 0;
24   } // main
```

Output
```
Enter a number: 15
15
15
15
```

9.2 Pointers for Inter-function Communication

One of the most useful applications of pointers is in functions. When we discussed functions previously, we saw that C uses the pass-by-value for downward communication. For upward communication, the only direct way to send something back from a function is through the `return` value. We also saw that we can use upward and bidirectional communication by passing an address and using it to refer back to data in the calling program. When we pass an address, we are actually passing a pointer to a variable. In this section, we fully develop the bidirectional communication. We use two examples to demonstrate how pointers can be used in functions.

Passing Addresses

Figures 9-17 and 9-18 demonstrate the use of pointers. In **Figure 9-17**, we call the exchange function, passing it two variables whose values are to be exchanged. When we use downward communication, the data are exchanged in the called function, but nothing changes in the calling program.

Figure 9-17   An unworkable exchange

```
// Function Declarations
void exchange (int x, int y);

int main (void)
{
    int a = 5;
    int b = 7;
    exchange (a, b);
    printf("%d %d\n", a, b);
    return 0;
} // main
```

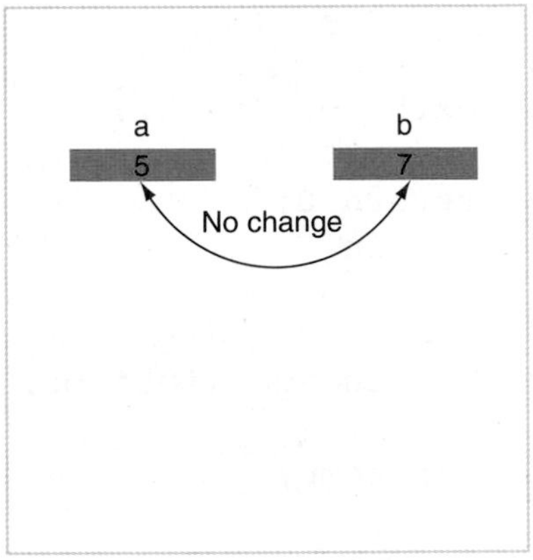

```
void exchange (int x, int y)
{
    int temp;

    temp = x;
    x    = y;
    y    = temp;
    return;
} // exchange
```

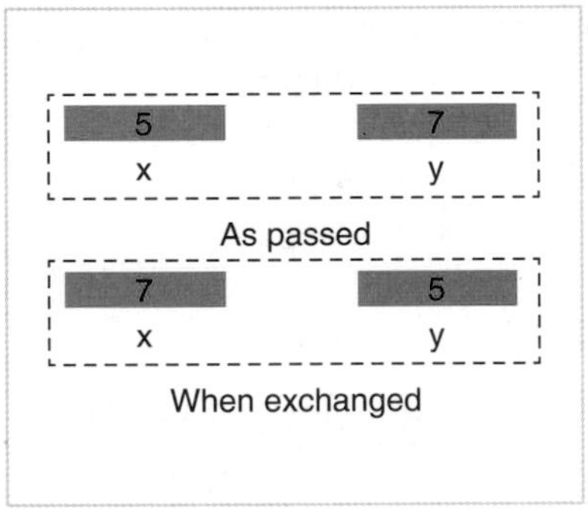

Rather than passing data to the called function, we need to pass addresses (pointers). Once we have a pointer to a variable, it doesn't make any difference if it is local to the active function, defined in `main`, or even if it is a global variable—we can change it! In other words, given a pointer to a variable anywhere in our memory space, we can change the contents of the variable.

Figure 9-18 shows the exchange using pointers. To create the pointers, we use the address operator (&) in the call, as shown below. We are now passing the address of a and b rather than their values.

```
exchange (&a, &b);
```

To pass addresses, the formal parameters in the called function are defined as a pointer to variables. This definition, which is shown below, completes the connection and allows us to indirectly reference the variables in the calling program through the pointers.

```
void exchange (int* px, int* py);
```

To assign a value to a, all that we need to use is the indirection operator in exchange. Using the indirection operator allows us to access data in the calling program.

We then call exchange using the address operator for the variables that we want to exchange. Note that exchange uses the two formal parameters, px and py, and one local variable, temp. By dereferencing the parameters, we make

Figure 9-18 Exchange using pointers

```
// Function Declarations
void exchange (int*, int*);

int main (void)
{
    int a = 5;
    int b = 7;

    exchange (a, b);
    printf("%d %d\n", a, b);
    return 0;
} // main
```

```
void exchange (int* px, int* py)
{
    int temp;

    temp = *px;
    *px = *py;
    *py = temp;

    return;
} // exchange
```

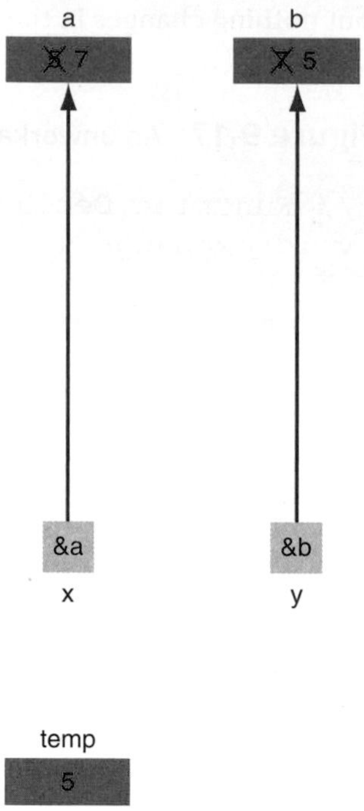

the exchange using the variables in main and the local variable, temp, in exchange. The correct logic is shown in Figure 9-18.

In summary, when we need to send more than one value back from a function, we use pointers. Using either upward or bi-directional communication, we can change any number of variables.

> **Note** Every time we want a called function to have access to a variable in the calling function, we pass the address of that variable to the called function and use the indirection operator to access it.

Functions Returning Pointers

We have shown you many examples of functions using pointers, but so far we have shown none that return a pointer. Nothing prevents a function from returning a pointer to the calling function. In fact, as you will see, it is quite common for functions to return pointers.

As an example, let's write a rather trivial function to determine the smaller of two numbers. In this case, we need a pointer to the smaller of two variables, a and b. Since we are looking for a pointer, we pass two pointers to the function, which uses a conditional expression to determine which value is smaller. Once we know the smaller value, we can return the address of its location as a pointer. The return value is then placed in the calling function's pointer, p, so that after the call it points to either a or b, based on their values. Both the code and a diagram of the variables and pointers are seen in **Figure 9-19**.

When we return a pointer, it must point to data in the calling function or a higher-level function. It is an error to return a pointer to a local variable in the called function, because when the function terminates, its memory may be used by

Figure 9-19 Functions returning pointers

```
// Prototype Declarations
int* smaller(int* p1, int* p2);

int main (void)
    int a;
    int b;
    int* p;
    ...
    scanf ( "&d &d ", &a, &b );
    p = smaller (&a, &b);
...
```

```
int* smaller(int* px, int* py)
{
    return (*px <*py ? px : py);
} // smaller
```

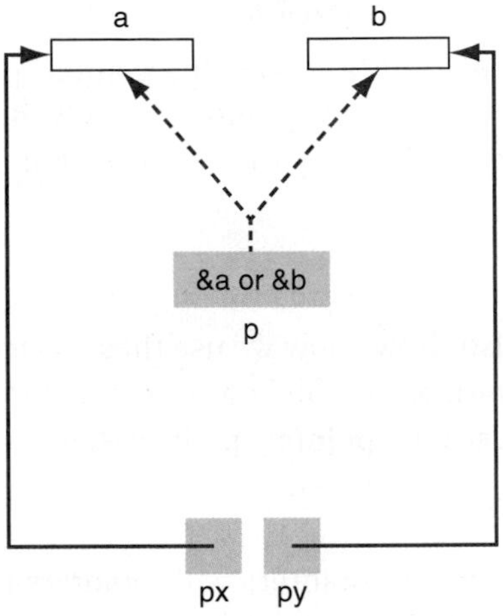

other parts of the program. Although a simple program might not notice the error because the space was not reused, a large program would either get the wrong answer or fail when the memory being referenced by the pointer was changed. It should be noted here that it is a serious error to return a pointer to a local variable.

9.3 Pointers to Pointers

So far, all our pointers have been pointing directly to data. It is possible—and with advanced data structures often necessary—to use pointers that point to other pointers. For example, we can have a pointer pointing to a pointer to an integer. This two-level indirection is seen in **Figure 9-20**. There is no limit as to how many levels of indirection we can use but, practically, we seldom use more than two.

Figure 9-20 Pointers to pointers

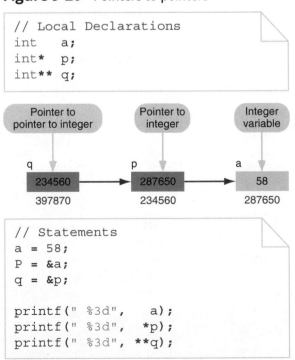

```
// Local Declarations
int    a;
int*   p;
int**  q;
```

```
// Statements
a = 58;
P = &a;
q = &p;

printf(" %3d",    a);
printf(" %3d",   *p);
printf(" %3d", **q);
```

Each level of pointer indirection requires a separate indirection operator when it is dereferenced. In Figure 9-20, to refer to a using the pointer p, we have to dereference it once, as shown below.

```
*p
```

To refer to the variable a using the pointer q, we have to dereference it twice to get to the integer a because there are two levels of indirection (pointers) involved. If we dereference it only once, we are referencing p, which is a pointer to an integer. Another way to say this is that q is a pointer to a pointer to an integer. The double dereference is shown below.

```
**q
```

Figure 9-20 also shows how we use these concepts in a C code fragment. All three references in the `printf` statements refer to the variable a. The first print statement prints the value of the variable a directly; the second uses the pointer p; the third uses the pointer q. The result is the value 58 printed three times, as shown below.

```
58 58 58
```

We can use different pointers with pointers to pointers and pointers to pointers to pointers to read the value of the same variable. A graphic representation of the variables is shown in **Figure 9-21**. The code is shown in **Program 9-6**.

Figure 9-21   Using pointers to pointers

r   q   p   a

> ## Program 9-6 | Using pointers to pointers

```
 1  /* Show how pointers to pointers can be used by different
 2     scanf functions to read data to the same variable.
 3     Written by:
 4     Date:
 5  */
 6  #include <stdio.h>
 7
 8  int main (void)
 9  {
10  // Local Declarations
11     int a;
12     int* p;
13     int** q;
14     int*** r;
15
16  // Statements
17     p = &a;
18     q = &p;
19     r = &q;
20
```

(continue)

Program 9-6 Using pointers to pointers *(continued)*

```
21     printf("Enter a number: ");
22     scanf ("%d", &a);          // Using a
23     printf("The number is : %d\n", a);
24
25     printf("\nEnter a number: ");
26     scanf ("%d", p);           // Using p
27     printf("The number is : %d\n", a);
28
29     printf("\nEnter a number: ");
30     scanf ("%d", *q);          // Using q
31     printf("The number is : %d\n", a);
32
33     printf("\nEnter a number: ");
34     scanf ("%d", **r);         // Using r
35     printf("The number is : %d\n", a);
36
37     return 0;
38 } // main
```

```
Output
Enter a number: 1
The number is : 1
Enter a number: 2
The number is : 2
Enter a number: 3
The number is : 3
Enter a number: 4
The number is : 4
```

In each successive read, we use a higher level of indirection. In the print statements, however, we always use the integer variable, a, to prove that the reads were successful.

9.4 Compatibility

It is important to recognize that pointers have a type associated with them. They are not just pointer types, but rather are pointers to a *specific* type, such as character. Each pointer takes on the attributes of the type to which it refers in addition to its own attributes.

Pointer Size Compatibility

The size of all pointers is the same. Every pointer variable holds the address of one memory location in the computer. On the other hand, the size of the variable that the pointer references can be different; it takes the attributes of the type being referenced. This is demonstrated by **Program 9-7**, which prints the size of each pointer and the size of the referenced object.

Program 9-7 | Demonstrate size of pointers

```
 1  /* Demonstrate size of pointers.
 2     Written by:
 3     Date:
 4  */
 5  #include <stdio.h>
 6
 7  int main (void)
 8  {
 9  // Local Declarations
10     char c;
11     char* pc;
12     int sizeofc  = sizeof(c);
13     int sizeofpc  = sizeof(pc);
14     int sizeofStarpc = sizeof(*pc);
15
16     int a;
17     int* pa;
18     int sizeofa  = sizeof(a);
19     int sizeofpa  = sizeof(pa);
20     int sizeofStarpa = sizeof(*pa);
21
22     double x;
23     double* px;
24     int sizeofx  = sizeof(x);
25     int sizeofpx = sizeof(px);
26     int sizeofStarpx = sizeof(*px);
27
28  // Statements
29     printf("sizeof(c): %3d | ", sizeofc);
30     printf("sizeof(pc): %3d | ", sizeofpc);
31     printf("sizeof(*pc): %3d\n", sizeofStarpc);
32
33     printf("sizeof(a): %3d | ", sizeofa);
34     printf("sizeof(pa): %3d | ", sizeofpa);
35     printf("sizeof(*pa): %3d\n", sizeofStarpa);
36
37     printf("sizeof(x): %3d | ", sizeofx);
38     printf("sizeof(px): %3d | ", sizeofpx);
39     printf("sizeof(*px): %3d\n", sizeofStarpx);
40
41     return 0;
42  } // main
```

(continue)

Program 9-7 Demonstrate size of pointers *(continued)*

Output
```
sizeof(c): 1 |   sizeof(pc): 4 |   sizeof(*pc): 1
sizeof(a): 4 |   sizeof(pa): 4 |   sizeof(*pa): 4
sizeof(x): 8 |   sizeof(px): 4 |   sizeof(*px): 8
```

What is this code telling us? First, note that the variables a, c, and x are never assigned values. This means that the sizes are independent of whatever value may be in a variable. In other words, the sizes are dependent on the type and not its values. It is worth noting that if you are running Program 9-7 on a 64-bit computer system, the output will differ—the size of the pointer is 8 bytes.

Now look at the size of the pointers. It is 4 in all cases, which is the size of an address in the computer on which this program was run. This makes sense: All computers today have more than *65,535* bytes, which is the maximum address that could be stored in 2 bytes.

But note what happens when we print the size of the type that the pointer is referring to: The size is the same as the data size! This means that in addition to the size of the pointer, the system also knows the size of whatever the pointer is pointing to. To confirm this, look at the size of the pointer, px, and what it is pointing to when dereferenced (*px).

Dereference Type Compatibility

The second issue in compatibility is the dereference type. The dereference type is the type of the variable that the pointer is referencing. With one exception (discussed later), it is invalid to assign a pointer of one type to a pointer of another type, even though the values in both cases are memory addresses and would, therefore, seem to be fully compatible. Although the addresses may be compatible because they are drawn from the same set, what is not compatible is the underlying data type of the referenced object.

In C, we can't use the assignment operator with pointers to different types; if we try to, we get a compile error. A pointer to a char is only compatible with a pointer to a char; and a pointer to an int is only compatible with a pointer to an int. We cannot assign a pointer to a char to a pointer to an int. Let's construct an example in which we have two variables: one int and one char. We also define one pointer to char and one pointer to int as shown in **Figure 9-22**.

Figure 9-22 Dereference type compatibility

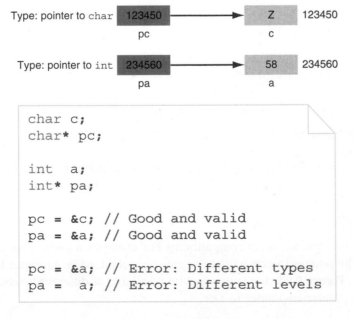

```
char c;
char* pc;

int  a;
int* pa;

pc = &c; // Good and valid
pa = &a; // Good and valid

pc = &a; // Error: Different types
pa =  a; // Error: Different levels
```

The first two assignments are valid. In the first assignment, we store the address of a character variable in a pointer to character variable. In the second assignment, we store the address of an integer (int) variable in a pointer to an integer (int) variable. We create an error in the third assignment because we try to store the address of a character variable into a pointer variable whose type is pointer to integer (int). We also get an error in the fourth assignment.

Pointer to Void

The exception to the reference type compatibility rule is the pointer to void. Recall that one of the types defined in C is void. Although the void type defines the lack of any other type when used with functions, its use with pointers is different. A pointer to void is a generic type that is not associated with a reference type; that is, it is not the address of a character, an integer, a real, or any other type. However, it is compatible, for assignment purposes only, with all other pointer types. Thus, a pointer of any reference type can be assigned to a pointer to void type and a pointer to void type can be assigned to a pointer of any reference type. There is, however, one restriction; since a void pointer has no object type, it cannot be dereferenced unless it is cast (see next section). The following shows how we can declare a variable of pointer to void type.

```
void* pVoid;
```

It is important to understand the difference between a null pointer and a variable of type pointer to void. A null pointer is a pointer of any type that is assigned the constant NULL. The reference type of the pointer will not change with the null assignment. A variable of pointer to void is a pointer with no reference type that can store only the address of any variable. We should remember that a void pointer cannot be dereferenced. The following examples show the difference:

```
void* pVoid; / Pointer to void type
int* pint = NULL; // Null pointer of type int
char* pChar = NULL; // Null pointer of type char
```

Casting Pointers

The problem of type incompatibility can be solved if we use casting. We can make an explicit assignment between incompatible pointer types by using a cast, just as we can cast an int to a char. For example, if we decided that we needed to use the *char* pointer, pc in the previous example, to point to an int (a), we could cast it as shown below.

```
pc = (char*) &a;
```

But in this case, *user beware!* Unless we cast all operations that use pc, we have a great chance of creating serious errors. In fact, with the exception of the void pointer, we should never cast a pointer. The following assignments are all valid, but they are extremely dangerous and must be used with a very carefully thought-out design.

```
// Local Declarations
   void* pVoid;
   char* pChar;
   int* pint;
// Statements
   pVoid = pChar;
   pint = pVoid;
   pint = (int*) pChar;
```

Another use of the cast is to provide a type for the void pointer. As noted in the previous section, a void pointer cannot be dereferenced because it has no object type. When we cast it, however, we provide the type.

Dereference Level Compatibility

Compatibility also includes dereference level compatibility. For example, a pointer to int is not compatible with a pointer-to-pointer to int. The pointer to int has a reference type of int, while a pointer-to-pointer to int has a reference type of pointer to int. **Figure 9-23** shows two pointers declared at different levels. The pointer pa is a pointer to int; the pointer ppa is a pointer-to-pointer to int.

Figure 9-23 Dereference level compatibility

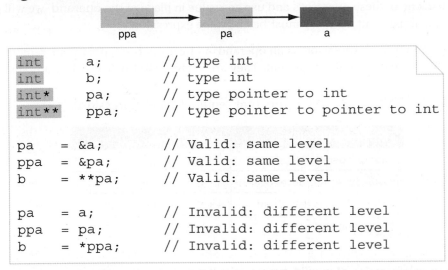

```
int      a;        // type int
int      b;        // type int
int*     pa;       // type pointer to int
int**    ppa;      // type pointer to pointer to int

pa   = &a;         // Valid: same level
ppa  = &pa;        // Valid: same level
b    = **pa;       // Valid: same level

pa   = a;          // Invalid: different level
ppa  = pa;         // Invalid: different level
b    = *ppa;       // Invalid: different level
```

9.5 Lvalue and Rvalue

In C, an expression is either an lvalue or an rvalue. As you know, every expression has a value. But the value in an expression (after evaluation) can be used in two different ways:

1. An lvalue expression must be used whenever the object is receiving a value; that is, it is being modified.

2. An rvalue expression can be used to supply a value for further use; that is, to examine or copy its value.

But how do you know when an expression is an lvalue and when it is an rvalue? Fortunately, only seven types of expressions are lvalue expressions. They are shown in **Table 9-2**.

Table 9-2 lvalue expressions

	EXPRESSION TYPE[a]	COMMENTS
1.	Identifier	Variable identifier
2.	expression [...]	Array indexing
3.	(expression)	Expression must already be lvalue
4.	*expression	Dereferenced expression
5.	expression.name	Structure selection
6.	Expression–>name	Structure indirect selection
7.	function call	If function uses *return* by address

[a]Expression types 5, 6, and 7 have not yet been covered.

For example, the following are lvalue expressions:

```
a = ...   a[5] = ...   (a) = ...     *p = ...
```

All expressions that are not lvalue expressions are rvalues. The following show some rvalue expressions:

```
5    a + 2    a * 6    a[2] + 3    a++
```

Note that even if an expression is an lvalue, if it is used as part of a larger expression in which the operators create only rvalue expressions, then the whole expression is an rvalue. For example, a[2] is an lvalue. But when it is used in the expression a[2] + 3, the whole expression is an rvalue, not an lvalue. Similarly, in the expression a++, the variable a is an lvalue while the whole expression (a++) is an rvalue.

You may ask, "Why worry so much about lvalues and rvalues?" The reason is that some operators need an lvalue as their operand. If we use one of these operators and use an rvalue in place of the operand, we will get a compile error. The right operand of an assignment operator must be an rvalue expression.

Only six operators need an lvalue expression as an operand: address operator, postfix increment, postfix decrement, prefix increment, prefix decrement, and assignment. They are shown in **Table 9-3** with examples of each.

Table 9-3   Operators that require lvalue expressions

TYPE OF EXPRESSION	EXAMPLES
Address operator	`&score`
Postfix increment/decrement	`x++` `y--`
Prefix increment/decrement	`++x` `--y`
Assignment (left operand)	`x = 1` `y += 3`

Table 9-4 contains several examples of invalid expressions that will create syntax errors because an rvalue is used when an lvalue is needed.

Table 9-4   Invalid rvalue expressions

EXPRESSION	PROBLEM
`a + 2 = 6;`	a + 2 is an rvalue and cannot be the left operand in an assignment; it is a temporary value that does not have an address; no place to store 6
`&(a + 2);`	a + 2 is an rvalue, and the address operator needs an lvalue; rvalues are temporary values and do not have addresses
`&4;`	Same as above (4 is an rvalue)
`(a + 2)++; ++(a + 2);`	Postfix and prefix operators require lvalues; (a + 2) is an rvalue

One final thought: A variable name can assume the role of either an lvalue or an rvalue depending on how it is used in an expression. In the following expression, a is an lvalue because it is on the left of the assignment and b is an rvalue because it is on the right of the assignment.

    a = b

We'll conclude this section with examples that demonstrate two ways we can use pointers when calling functions.

We begin with a simple function that converts time in seconds to hours, minutes, and seconds. While the function is simple, it does require three address parameters to return the values. The code is shown in **Program 9-8**.

Program 9-8 | Convert seconds to hours, minutes, and seconds

```
1   /*===========secToHours===========
2      Given time in seconds, convert it to hours, minutes,
3      and seconds.
4      Pre  time in seconds
5      addresses of hours, minutes, seconds
6      Post hours, minutes, seconds calculated
```

(continue)

Program 9-8   Convert seconds to hours, minutes, and seconds *(continued)*

```
 7      Return error indicator—1 success, 0 bad time
 8   */
 9   int secToHours (long time,
10                    int* hours, int* minutes, int* seconds)
11   {
12   // Local Declarations
13      long localTime;
14
15   // Statements
16      localTime = time;
17      *seconds = localTime % 60;
18      localTime = localTime / 60;
19
20      *minutes = localTime % 60;
21
22      *hours = localTime / 60;
23
24      if (*hours > 24)
25         return 0;
26      else
27         return 1;
28   } // secToHours
```

The first question you might ask when reading this simple function is "Why define a local variable for the time?" In this short function, it really wasn't necessary. However, a good programmer does not change a value parameter within the function, because its original value may be needed later. We have seen times when "later" turned out to be a maintenance change and hours were spent debugging the error when the wrong value was computed.

> **Note** | Create local variables when a value parameter will be changed within a function so that the original value will always be available for processing.

Another important design point: If you need to send back two values from a called function, *do not pass one back through a pointer and return the other.* Either use the `return` for some other reason, such as a status flag, or make the return `void`. Keeping your design consistent—in this case by using a consistent method of returning the values—makes your programs easier to understand and is an example of the KISS principle.

> **Note** | When several values need to be sent back to the calling function, use address parameters for all of them. Do not return one value and use address parameters for the others.

Let's look at a typical program design that reads, processes, and prints data. This is a processing cycle that is common to many, many programs. **Figure 9-24** shows its structure chart.

Figure 9-24 A common program design

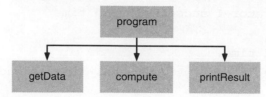

To demonstrate the universality of this design, let's compute the real roots for a quadratic equation. Recall that a quadratic equation has the form

$$ax^2 + bx + c = 0$$

Four possible situations can occur when you solve for the roots in a quadratic equation. First, it is an error if both a and b are 0: There is no solution. Second, if a is 0 and b is not 0, there is only one root:

$$x = \frac{-c}{b}$$

Third, if $b^2 - 4ac$ is 0 or positive, there are two, possibly equal, roots derived from the following equation:

$$x = -b \pm \frac{\sqrt{b^2 - 4ac}}{2a}$$

Finally, if $b^2 - 4ac$ is negative, the roots are imaginary.

Figure 9-25 diagrams the interaction of the variables and pointers for **Program 9-9**. In this short program, we use pointers to pass data from a read function, pass both values and pointers to a compute function, and finally pass the values to a print function.

Figure 9-25 Using pointers as parameters

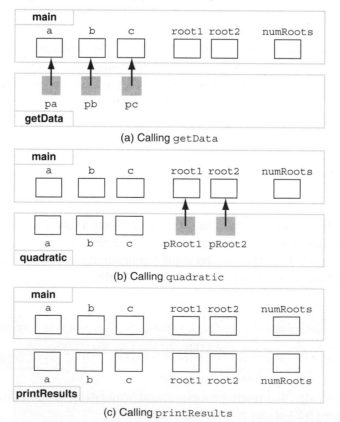

(a) Calling `getData`

(b) Calling `quadratic`

(c) Calling `printResults`

Program 9-9 | Quadratic roots

```c
1  /* Test driver for quadratic function.
2     Written by:
3     Date:
4  */
5  #include <stdio.h>
6  #include <math.h>
7
8  // Function Declarations
9  void getData   (int*, int*, int*);
10 int quadratic (int, int, int, double*, double*);
11 void printResults (int, int, int, int, double, double);
12
13 int main (void)
14 {
15 // Local Declarations
16    int a;
17    int b;
18    int c;
19    int numRoots;
20    double root1;
21    double root2;
22    char again = 'Y';
23
24 // Statements
25    printf("Solve quadratic equations.\n\n");
26    while (again == 'Y' || again == 'y')
27    {
28       getData (&a, &b, &c);
29       numRoots = quadratic (a, b, c, &root1, &root2);
30       printResults (numRoots, a, b, c, root1, root2);
31
32       printf("\nDo you have another equation (Y/N): ");
33       scanf (" %c", &again);
34    } // while
35    printf("\nThank you.\n");
36    return 0;
37 } // main
38
39 /*================getData==============
40    Read coefficients for quadratic equation.
```

(continue)

Program 9-9 Quadratic roots *(continued)*

```
41     Pre a, b, and c contains addresses
42     Post data read into addresses in main
43  */
44  void getData (int* pa, int* pb, int* pc)
45  {
46  // Statements
47     printf("Please enter coefficients a, b, & c: ");
48     scanf ("%d%d%d", pa, pb, pc);
49
50     return;
51  } // getData
52
53  /*================quadratic================
54     Compute the roots for a quadratic equation.
55     Pre a, b, & c are the coefficients
56     pRoot1 & pRoot2 are variable pointers
57     Post roots computed, stored in calling function
58     Return 2 two roots,
59            1 one root,
60            0 imaginary roots
61           -1 not quadratic coefficients.
62  */
63  int quadratic (int a, int b, int c,
64                    double* pRoot1, double* pRoot2)
65  {
66  // Local Declarations
67     int result;
68
69     double discriminant;
70     double root;
71
72  // Statements
73     if (a == 0 && b == 0)
74        result = -1;
75     else
76        if (a == 0)
77        {
78           *pRoot1 = -c / (double) b;
79           result = 1;
80        } // a == 0
81        else
```

(continue)

Program 9-9   Quadratic roots *(continued)*

```
82            {
83                discriminant = b * b -(4*a*c);
84                if (discriminant >= 0)
85                {
86                    root = sqrt(discriminant);
87                    *pRoot1 = ( -b + root) / (2 * a);
88                    *pRoot2 = ( -b - root) / (2 * a);
89                    result = 2;
90                } // if >= 0
91                else
92                    result = 0;
93            } // else
94        return result;
95  } // quadratic
96
97  /*================printResults================
98      Prints the factors for the quadratic equation.
99      Pre numRoots contains 0, 1, 2
100     a, b, c contains original coefficients
101     root1 and root2 contains roots
102     Post roots have been printed
103  */
104 void printResults (int numRoots,
105                    int a, int b, int c,
106                    double root1, double root2)
107 {
108 // Statements
109     printf("Your equation: %dx**2 + %dx + %d\n", a, b, c);
110     switch (numRoots)
111     {
112       case 2: printf("Roots are: %6.3f & %6.3f\n", root1, root2);
113             break;
114       case 1: printf("Only one root: %6.3f\n", root1);
115             break;
116       case 0: printf("Roots are imaginary.\n");
117             break;
118       default:printf("Invalid coefficients\n");
119             break;
120     } // switch
121     return;
122 } // printResults
123 //================End of Program================
```

(continue)

Program 9-9   Quadratic roots *(continued)*

Output
```
Solve quadratic equations.
Please enter the coefficients a, b, & c: 2 4 2
Your equation: 2x**2 + 4x + 2
Roots are: -1.000 & -1.000
Do you have another equation (Y/N): y
Please enter the coefficients a, b, & c: 0 4 2
Your equation: 0x**2 + 4x + 2
Only one root: -0.500
Do you have another equation (Y/N): y
Please enter the coefficients a, b, & c: 2 2 2
Your equation: 2x**2 + 2x + 2
Roots are imaginary.
Do you have another equation (Y/N): y
Please enter the coefficients a, b, & c: 0 0 2
Your equation: 0x**2 + 0x + 2
Invalid coefficients
Do you have another equation (Y/N): y
Please enter coefficients a, b, & c: 1 -5 6
Your equation: 1x**2 + -5x + 6
Roots are: 3.000 & 2.000
Do you have another equation (Y/N): n
Thank you.
```

This problem has many interesting points. The function `main` is a test driver—that is, code that will not be put into production. Therefore, we code much of the test logic in `main` rather than providing separate functions for it.

The `scanf` function used in `getData` does not have the usual address operator (&) in front of variables a, b, and c. Why? Because they are already pointer values pointing to variables in `main` and, therefore, are already addresses.

The variables in these examples are either integers or pointers to integers. Parameters that receive something from `main` are integers whose values will be filled when the call is made. Those that send data back to `main` are pointers to integers that will be filled with the addresses of the corresponding variables in `main`. As a general rule, if a value will be changed, it must be passed as a pointer. If it will not be changed, it should be passed as a value. This protects data from accidental destruction.

In `quadratic`, note the extensive testing to make sure that the coefficients are valid. To ensure valid code, they are all necessary. Look at how we calculated the square root of the discriminant separately (statement 89). Since square root is a complex function, it is more efficient to call it just once and save the value for later use. Note also that the function has only one `return` statement. This is proper structured code, though many professional programmers would simply return at statements 79, 89, 92, and 94.

Study our test data carefully. Note that this set of test data executes every line of code in the program. Designing test data that completely validates a function is not an easy task. Ensuring that all code has been executed is even more difficult and tedious. One way to make sure that all code has been tested is to use your debugger to set a break point at every statement and then clear them as the program executes. When all break points have been cleared, you know every instruction has been executed.

Executing every line of code does not ensure that the function has no bugs, however. With large programs, it is virtually impossible to test every possible combination of data. One of the advantages of structured programming is that by breaking the program down into separate functions we can test it better.

This program has a potential problem. Do you see it? Hint: What if the user enters invalid data? There is no error checking in `getData`. If this were a production program, it would contain code to check for errors. It would then return a status flag to indicate if `getData` was successful or not.

9.6 Arrays and Pointers

The name of an array is a pointer constant to the first element. Because the array's name is a pointer constant, its value cannot be changed. **Figure 9-26** shows an array with the array name as a pointer constant.

Figure 9-26 Pointers to arrays

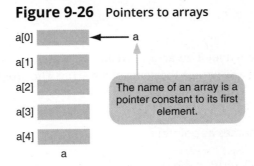

Since the array name is a pointer constant to the first element, the address of the first element and the name of the array both represent the same location in memory. Therefore, we can use the array name anywhere we can use a pointer, as long as it is being used as an rvalue. Specifically, this means that we can use it with the indirection operator. When we dereference an array name, we are dereferencing the first element of the array; that is, we are referring to `array[0]`. However, when the array name is dereferenced, it refers only to the first element, not the whole array.

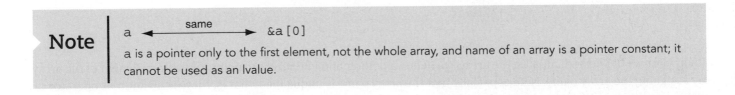

Note

a ←— same —→ &a[0]

a is a pointer only to the first element, not the whole array, and name of an array is a pointer constant; it cannot be used as an lvalue.

Prove this to yourself by writing a program with the code shown below. The code prints the address of the first element of the array (`&a[0]`) and the array name, which is a pointer constant. Note that we have used the format conversion code for a pointer (`%p`).

```
// Demonstrate that array name is pointer constant
   int a [5];
   printf("%p %p", &a[0], a);
```

We cannot tell you the values that this code will print, but they will be addresses in your computer. Furthermore, the first printed address (the first element in the array) and the second printed address (the array pointer) will be the same, proving our point.

A simple variation on this code is to print the value in the first element of the array using both a pointer and an index. This code is demonstrated in **Figure 9-27**. Note that the same value, 2, is printed in both cases, again proving our point that the array name is a pointer constant to the beginning of the array.

Figure 9-27   Dereference of array name

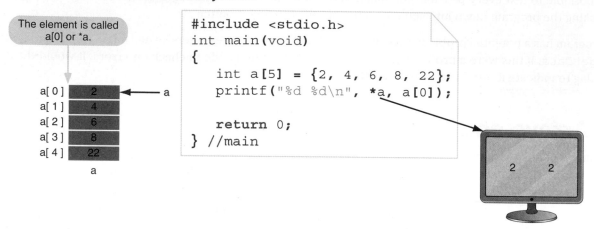

Let's investigate another point. If the name of an array is really a pointer, let's see if we can store this pointer in a pointer variable and use it in the same way we use the name of the array. The program that demonstrates this is shown in **Figure 9-28**.

Figure 9-28   Array names as pointers

```
#include <stdio.h>
int main(void)
{
    int a[5] = {2, 4, 6, 8, 22};
    int* p = a;
    ...
    printf("%d %d\n", a[0], *p);
    ...
    return 0;
} //main
```

Right after we define and initialize the array, we define a pointer and initialize it to point to the first element of the array by assigning the array name. Note especially that the array name is unqualified; that is, there is no address operator or index specification. We then print the first element in the array, first using an index notation and then a pointer notation.

Let's look at another example that explores the close relationship between an array and a pointer. We store the address of the second element of the array in a pointer variable. Now we can use two different names to access each element. This does not mean that we have two arrays; rather, it shows that a single array can be accessed through different pointers.

Figure 9-29 demonstrates the use of multiple names for an array to reference different locations at the same time. First, we have the array name. We then create a pointer to integer and set it to the second element of the array (a[1]). Now, even though it is a pointer, we can use it as an array name and index it to point to different elements in the array. We demonstrate this by printing the first two elements using first the array name and then the pointer. Note especially that, when a pointer is not referencing the first element of an array, the index can be negative [-1]. This is shown in the reference to p[-1]. Note that to access an array, any pointer to the first element can be used instead of the name of the array.

Figure 9-29   Multiple array pointers

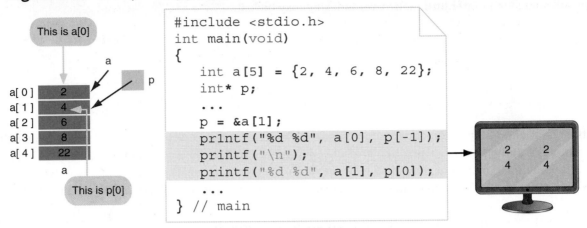

```
#include <stdio.h>
int main(void)
{
    int a[5] = {2, 4, 6, 8, 22};
    int* p;
    ...
    p = &a[1];
    printf("%d %d", a[0], p[-1]);
    printf("\n");
    printf("%d %d", a[1], p[0]);
    ...
} // main
```

9.7 Pointer Arithmetic and Arrays

Besides indexing, programmers use another powerful method of moving through an array: pointer arithmetic. Pointer arithmetic offers a restricted set of arithmetic operators for manipulating the addresses in pointers. It is especially powerful when we need to move through an array from element to element, such as when we are searching an array sequentially.

Pointers and One-Dimensional Arrays

If we have an array, a, then a is a constant pointing to the first element and a+1 is a constant pointing to the second element. Again, if we have a pointer, p, pointing to the second element of an array (see **Figure 9-30**), then p-1 is a pointer to the previous (first) element and p+1 is a pointer to the next (third) element. Furthermore, given a, a+2 is the address two elements from a, and a+3 is the address three elements from a. We can generalize the notation as follows: Given pointer, p, p±n is a pointer to the value n elements away. The following expressions are identical: *(a+n) and a[n]

Figure 9-30   Pointer arithmetic

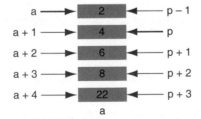

It does not matter how a and p are defined or initialized; as long as they are pointing to one of the elements of the array, we can add or subtract to get the address of the other elements of the array. This concept is portrayed in Figure 9-30.

But the meaning of adding or subtracting here is different from normal arithmetic. When we add an integer n to a pointer value, we get a value that corresponds to another index location, n elements away. In other words, n is an offset from the original pointer. To determine the new value, C must know the size of one element. The size of the element is determined by the type of the pointer. This is one of the prime reasons that pointers of different types cannot be assigned to each other.

If the offset is 1, then C can simply add or subtract one element size from the current pointer value. This may make the access more efficient than the corresponding index notation. If it is more than 1, then C must compute the offset by multiplying the offset by the size of one array element and adding it to the pointer value. This calculation is shown below.

```
address = pointer + (offset * size of element)
```

Depending on the hardware, the multiplication in this formula can make it less efficient than simply adding 1, and the efficiency advantage of pointer arithmetic over indexing may be lost.

We see the result of pointer arithmetic on different-sized elements in **Figure 9-31**. For char, which is usually implemented as 1 byte, adding 1 moves us to the next memory address (101). Assuming that integers are 4 bytes, adding 1 to the array pointer b moves us 4 bytes in memory (104). Finally, assuming the size of float is 6 bytes, adding 1 to array pointer c moves us 6 bytes in memory (106). In other words, a+1 means different things in different situations.

Figure 9-31 Pointer arithmetic and different types

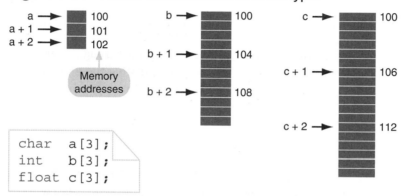

We've seen how to get the address of an array element using a pointer and an offset, now let's see how we can use that value. We have two choices: First, we can assign it to another pointer. This is a rather elementary operation that uses the assignment operator as shown below.

```
p = aryName + 5;
```

Second, we can use it with the indirection operator to access or change the value of the element we are pointing to. This possibility is seen in **Figure 9-32**.

Figure 9-32 Dereferencing array pointers

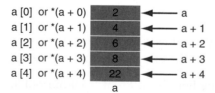

For practice, let's use pointers to find the smallest number among five integers stored in an array. **Figure 9-33** tracks the code as it works its way through the array.

We start with the smallest pointer (pSm) set to the first element of the array. The function's job is to see if any of the remaining elements are smaller. Since we know that the first element is not smaller than itself, we set the working pointer (pWalk) to the second element. The working pointer advances through the remaining elements, each time checking the element it is currently addressing against the smallest to that point (pSm). If the current element is smaller, its location is assigned to pSm.

Figure 9-33 Find smallest

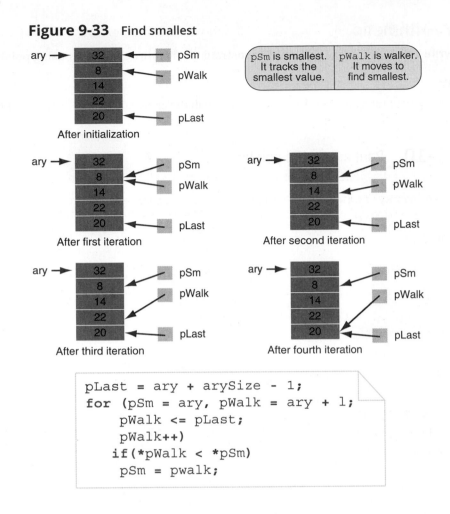

```
pLast = ary + arySize - 1;
for (pSm = ary, pWalk = ary + 1;
     pWalk <= pLast;
     pWalk++)
   if(*pWalk < *pSm)
     pSm = pwalk;
```

Arithmetic Operations on Pointers

Arithmetic operations involving pointers are very limited. Addition can be used when one operand is a pointer and the other is an integer. Subtraction can be used only when both operands are pointers or when the first operand is a pointer and the second operand is an index integer. We can also manipulate a pointer with the postfix and unary increment and decrement operators. All of the following pointer arithmetic operations are valid:

```
P + 5    5 + p    P - 5 pl - p2    p++ --p
```

When one pointer is subtracted from another, the result is an index representing the number of elements between the two pointers. Note, however, that the result is meaningful only if the two pointers are associated with the same array structure.

The relational operators (such as less than and equal) are allowed only if both operands are pointers of the same type. Two pointer relational expressions are shown below.

```
p1 >= p2    p1 != p2
```

The most common comparison is a pointer and the NULL constant, as shown in **Table 9-5**.

Table 9-5   Pointers and relational operators

LONG FORM	SHORT FORM
if (ptr == NULL)	if (!ptr)
if (ptr != NULL)	if (ptr)

Using Pointer Arithmetic

In this section, we write two small programs that demonstrate moving through arrays using pointers.

Printing an Array

Program 9-10 prints an array, first by adding 1 to advance through the array and then subtracting 1 to print it backward.

Program 9-10 | Print array with pointers

```
1   /* Print an array forward by adding 1 to a pointer. Then
2      print it backward by subtracting one.
3      Written by:
4      Date:
5   */
6   #include <stdio.h>
7
8   #define MAX_SIZE 10
9
10  int main (void)
11  {
12  // Local Declarations
13      int ary[] = {1, 2, 3, 4, 5, 6, 7, 8, 9, 10};
14      int* pWalk;
15      int* pEnd;
16
17  // Statements
18      // Print array forward
19      printf("Array forward : ");
20      for (pWalk = ary, pEnd = ary + MAX_SIZE;
21                  pWalk < pEnd;
22                  pWalk++)
23         printf ("%3d", *pWalk);
24      printf ("\n");
25
26      // Print array backward
27      printf ("Array backward: ");
28      for (pWalk = pEnd - 1; pWalk >= ary; pWalk--)
29          printf ("%3d", *pWalk);
30      printf ("\n");
31
32      return 0;
33  } // main
```

```
Output
Array forward :  1  2  3  4  5  6  7  8  9 10
Array backward: 10  9  8  7  6  5  4  3  2  1
```

While this program is quite simple, it does demonstrate one efficiency point. Note that before we printed the forward loop, we set pEnd. Many programmers would use the following test in the limit condition:

```
pWalk < ary + MAX_SIZE
```

While this logic works, some compilers will calculate the end address in each loop, an obvious inefficiency. Therefore, we recommend that whenever possible you calculate the end pointer in the loop initialization.

Searching with Pointers

The logic in Program 9-10 works well for the sequential search but not for the binary search. Recall that the binary search requires the calculation of the index or the address of the entry in the middle of a table. When we wrote the program using indexes, the calculation of the midpoint was done with the statement shown below.

```
mid = (first + last) / 2;
```

Since we cannot use addition with two pointers, this formula will not work. We need to come up with the pointer arithmetic equivalent. Another formula determines the midpoint in an array by calculating the number of elements from the beginning of the array. This method, known as the offset method, is shown below.

```
mid = first + (last - first) / 2;
```

The offset calculation works with pointers also. The subtraction of the first pointer from the last pointer will give us the number of elements in the array. The offset from the beginning of the array is determined by dividing the number of elements in the array by 2. We can then add the offset to the pointer for the beginning of the list to arrive at the midpoint. The pointer code is shown below.

```
midPtr = firstPtr + (lastPtr - firstPtr) / 2;
```

The pointer implementation of the binary search is shown in **Program 9-11**.

Program 9-11 | Pointers and the binary search

```
 1  /*==========binary Search==========
 2     Search an ordered list using Binary Search
 3     Pre list must contain at least one element
 4     endPtr is pointer to largest element in list
 5     target is value of element being sought
 6     Post FOUND: locnPtr pointer to target element
 7     return 1 (found)
 8     !FOUND: locnPtr = element below or above target
 9     return 0 (not found)
10  */
11  int binarySearch (int list[], int* endPtr,
12                    int target, int** locnPtr)
13  {
14  // Local Declarations
15     int* firstPtr;
16     int* midPtr;
17     int* lastPtr;
18
19  // Statements
```

(continue)

Program 9-11 Pointers and the binary search *(continued)*

```
20      firstPtr = list;
21      lastPtr = endPtr;
22      while (firstPtr <= lastPtr)
23      {
24          midPtr = firstPtr + (lastPtr - firstPtr) / 2;
25          if (target > *midPtr)
26              // look in upper half
27              firstPtr = midPtr + 1;
28          else if (target < *midPtr)
29              // look in lower half
30              lastPtr = midPtr - 1;
31          else
32              // found equal: force exit
33              firstPtr = lastPtr + 1;
34      } // end while
35      *locnPtr = midPtr;
36      return (target == *midPtr);
37 } // binarySearch
```

Although the code in this function is relatively simple, the coding for `locnPtr` merits some discussion. In the calling function, `locnPtr` is a pointer to the found location. Therefore, to store the pointer in `locnPtr`, we need to pass a pointer to a pointer to an integer (see statement 12). To create a pointer to pointer, the calling function must pass the address of its location pointer.

In addition to demonstrating the subtraction of two pointers, we also see the use of a relational operator with two pointers in statement 22.

Pointers and Two-Dimensional Arrays

The first thing to notice about two-dimensional arrays is that, just as in a one-dimensional array, the name of the array is a pointer constant to the first element of the array. In this case, however, the first element is *another array!* Assume that we have a two-dimensional array of integers. When we dereference the array name, we don't get one integer, we get an array of integers. In other words, the dereference of the array name of a two-dimensional array is a pointer to a one-dimensional array. **Figure 9-34** contains a two-dimensional array and a code fragment to print the array.

Each element in the figure is shown in both index and pointer notation. Note that `table [0]` refers to an array of four integer values. The equivalent pointer notation is the dereference of the array name plus 0, `*(table + 0)`, which also refers to an array of four integers.

```
table[0] is identical to *(table + 0)
```

To demonstrate pointer manipulation with a two-dimensional array, let's print the table in Figure 9-34. To print the array requires nested `for` loops. When dealing with multidimensional arrays, however, there is no simple pointer notation. To refer to a row, we dereference the array pointer, which gives us a pointer to a row. Given a pointer to a row, to refer to an individual element, we dereference the row pointer. This double dereference is shown below:

```
*(*(table))
```

Figure 9-34   Pointers to two-dimensional arrays

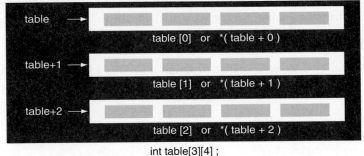

```
for (i=0; i<3; i++)
{
    for (j=0; j<4; j++)
        printf("%6d", *(*(table + i) + j));
    printf("\n");
} // for i
```

But the previous expression refers only to the first element of the first row. To step through all the elements, we need to add two offsets, one for the row and one for the element within the row. We use loop counters, i and j, as the offsets. This is the same logic we saw when we printed a two-dimensional array using indexes. To print an element, we use the array name, table, and adjust it with the loop indexes. This gives us the relatively complex expression shown below.

```
*(*(table + i) + j)
```

This pointer notation is equivalent to the index syntax, table[i][j]. With multidimensional arrays, the pointer arithmetic has no efficiency advantage over indexing. Because the pointer notation for multidimensional arrays is so complex and there is no efficiency advantage, most programmers find it easier to use the index notation.

9.8 Passing an Array to a Function

Now that we have discovered that the name of an array is actually a pointer to the first element, we can send the array name to a function for processing. When we pass the array, we do not use the address operator. Remember, the array name is a pointer constant, so the name is already the address of the first element in the array. A typical call would look like the following:

```
doIt (aryName);
```

The called program can declare the array in one of two ways. First, it can use the traditional array notation. This format has the advantage of telling the user very clearly that we are dealing with an array rather than a single pointer. This is an advantage from a structured programming and human engineering point of view.

```
int doIt (int ary[])
```

We can also declare the array in the function header as a simple pointer. The disadvantage to this format is that, while it is technically correct, it actually masks the data structure (array). For one-dimensional arrays, it is the code of choice among professional programmers.

```
int doIt (int* arySalary)
```

If you choose to code this way, use a good descriptive name for the parameter to minimize any reader confusion. The function documentation should also indicate clearly that an array is being passed.

Note, however, that when we pass a multidimensional array, we must use the array syntax in the header declaration and definition. The compiler needs to know the size of the dimensions after the first to calculate the offset for pointer arithmetic. Thus, to receive a three-dimensional array, we would use the following declaration in the function's header:

```
float doIt (int bigAry[][12][5])
```

To see how passing array pointers works, let's write a program that calls a function to multiply each element of a one-dimensional array by 2. The program's variables are shown in **Figure 9-35**, and the code is shown in **Program 9-12**.

Figure 9-35   Variables for multiply array elements by 2

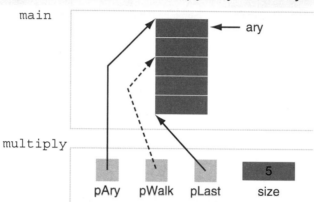

Program 9-12 | Multiply array elements by 2

```
1   /* Read from keyboard & print integers multiplied by 2.
2      Written by:
3      Date:
4   */
5   #include <stdio.h>
6   #define SIZE 5
7
8   // Function Declarations
9   void multiply (int* pAry, int size);
10
11  int main (void)
12  {
13  // Local Declarations
14      int ary [SIZE];
15      int* pLast;
16      int* pWalk;
17
18  // Statements
19      pLast = ary + SIZE - 1;
20      for (pWalk = ary; pWalk <= pLast; pWalk++)
21      {
```

(continue)

Program 9-12   Multiply array elements by 2 *(continued)*

```c
22          printf("Please enter an integer: ");
23          scanf ("%d", pWalk);
24    } // for
25
26    multiply (ary, SIZE);
27
28    printf ("Doubled value is: \n");
29    for (pWalk = ary; pWalk <= pLast; pWalk++)
30        printf (" %3d", *pWalk);
31
32    return 0;
33 } // main
34
35 /*=============multiply==============
36    Multiply elements in an array by 2
37    Pre array has been filled
38    size indicates number of elements in array
39    Post values in array doubled
40 */
41 void multiply (int* pAry, int size)
42 {
43 // Local Declarations
44    int* pWalk;
45    int* pLast;
46
47 // Statements
48    pLast = pAry + size - 1;
49    for (pWalk = pAry; pWalk <= pLast; pWalk++)
50        *pWalk = *pWalk * 2;
51    return;
52 } // multiply
53 //==============End of Program==============
```

Output
```
Please enter an integer: 1
Please enter an integer: 2
Please enter an integer: 3
Please enter an integer: 4
Please enter an integer: 5
Doubled value is:
  2    4    6    8   10
```

This program contains several points of interest. First, we have declared the array in the function declaration using the more common pointer notation, but we have given it a name that indicates it is a pointer to an array (pAry).

In the multiply function, we use a separate pointer (pWalk) to walk through the list. We could have used pAry, since it was not being used other than to identify the beginning of the array. All too often, however, this type of "shortcut" saves a line or two of code only to create hours of debugging when the program is changed later. As we have pointed out before, do not use formal parameters as variables unless their intent is to change a value in the calling program. This rule is especially important when the parameter is a pointer, as in this case.

Finally, note that we have passed the size of the array to the multiply function. We still need to know how much data we need to process, and we use the size to calculate the address of the last element in the list. As a variation on the limit test, however, we could have passed a pointer to the last element of the array, &ary[SIZE - 1]. This would save the calculation of pLast. From a style and efficiency point of view, neither method has an advantage over the other. The structure and needs of other parts of the program usually dictate which method is used.

Note

Understanding Complicated Declarations

Following the right–left rule will help you read and understand complicated declarations. Using this rule to interpret a declaration, you start with the identifier in the center of a declaration and "read" the declaration by alternatively going right and then left until all entities have been read. The basic concept is shown below.

			Identifier			
6	4	2	Start here	1	3	5

Consider the following simple declaration:

```
int x;
```

This is read as "x is ❑ an integer."*

```
int          x          ❑;
↑            ↑           ↑
2            0           1
```

Since there is nothing on the right, we simply go left.

Now consider the example of a pointer declaration. This example is read as "p is ❑ a pointer ❑ to integer."

```
int      *       p       ❑       ❑;
↑        ↑       ↑       ↑       ↑
4        2       0       1       3
```

Note that we keep going right even when there is nothing there until all the entities on the left have been exhausted. For a more complete discussion of complex declarations, see Appendix F.

*The box (❑) is just a place holder to show that there is no entry to be considered. Simply ignore it when you read each declaration.

9.9 Memory Allocation Functions

C gives us two choices when we want to reserve memory locations for an object: static allocation and dynamic allocation. **Figure 9-36** shows the characteristics of memory allocation.

Figure 9-36 Memory allocation

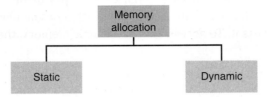

Memory Usage

To understand how dynamic memory allocation works, we must study how memory is used. Conceptually, memory is divided into program memory and data memory. Program memory consists of the memory used for `main` and all called functions. Data memory consists of permanent definitions, such as global data and constants, local declarations, and dynamic data memory. Exactly how C handles these different needs is a function of the operating system and the compiler writer's skills. We can, however, generalize the concepts.

Obviously, `main` must be in memory at all times. Beyond `main`, each called function must be in memory only while it or any of its called functions are active. As a practical matter, most systems keep all functions in memory while the program is running.

Although the program code for a function may be in memory at all times, the local variables for the function are available only when it is active. Furthermore, more than one version of the function can be active at a time. In this case, multiple copies of the local variables are allocated, although only one copy of the function is present. The memory facility for these capabilities is known as the stack memory.

In addition to the stack, a memory allocation known as the heap is available. Heap memory is unused memory allocated to the program and available to be assigned during its execution. It is the memory pool from which memory is allocated when requested by the memory allocation functions. This conceptual view of memory is shown in **Figure 9-37**.

Figure 9-37 A conceptual view of memory

![A conceptual view of memory showing Program memory containing main and function, and Data memory containing global, heap, and stack, all within Memory.]

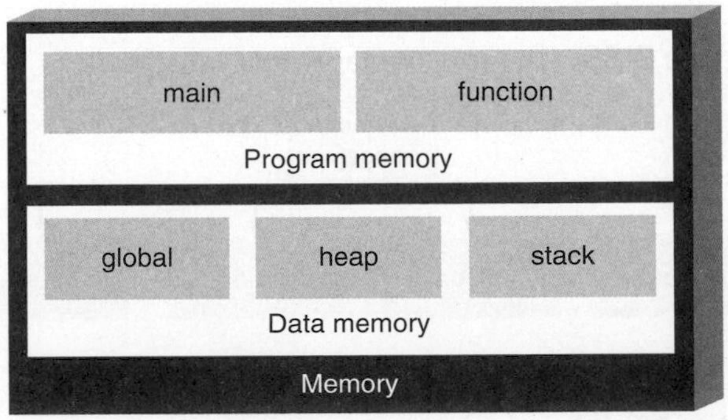

It is important to recognize that this is a conceptual view of memory. As we said before, implementation of memory is up to the software engineers who design the system. For example, nothing prevents the stack and the heap from sharing the same pool of memory. In fact, it would be a good design concept.

Static Memory Allocation

Static memory allocation requires that the declaration and definition of memory be fully specified in the source program. The number of bytes reserved cannot be changed during run time. This is the technique we have used to this point to define variables, arrays, pointers, and streams.

Dynamic Memory Allocation

Dynamic memory allocation uses predefined functions to allocate and release memory for data while the program is running. It effectively postpones the data definition, but not the data declaration, to run time. Note that we can refer to memory allocated in the heap only through a pointer.

To use dynamic memory allocation, we use either standard data types or derived types that we have previously declared. Unlike static memory allocation, dynamic memory allocation has no identifier associated with it; it has only an address that must be used to access it. To access data in dynamic memory, therefore, we must use a pointer. This concept is shown in **Figure 9-38**.

Figure 9-38   Accessing dynamic memory

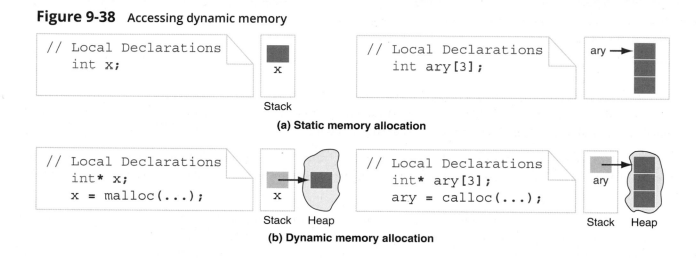

(a) Static memory allocation

(b) Dynamic memory allocation

Memory Allocation Functions

Four memory management functions are used with dynamic memory. Three of them, `malloc`, `calloc`, and `realloc`, are used for memory allocation. The fourth, `free`, is used to return memory when it is no longer needed. All the memory management functions are found in the standard library file (`stdlib.h`). The collection of memory functions is shown in **Figure 9-39**.

Figure 9-39   Memory management functions

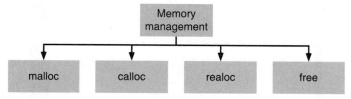

Block Memory Allocation (`malloc`)

The `malloc` function allocates a block of memory that contains the number of bytes specified in its parameter. It returns a `void` pointer to the first byte of the allocated memory. The allocated memory is not initialized. Therefore, we should assume that it will contain unknown values and initialize it as required by our program.

The `malloc` function declaration is shown below.

```
void *malloc (size_t size);
```

The type, size_t, is defined in several header files including stdio.h. The type is usually an unsigned integer, and by the standard it is guaranteed to be large enough to hold the maximum address of the computer.

To provide portability, the size specification in malloc's actual parameter is generally computed using the sizeof operator. For example, if we want to allocate an integer in the heap, we code the call as shown below.

```
pInt = malloc (sizeof (int));
```

As mentioned above, malloc returns the address of the first byte in the memory space allocated. However, if it is not successful, malloc returns a NULL pointer. An attempt to allocate memory from the heap when memory is insufficient is known as **overflow**. It is up to the program to check for memory overflow. If it doesn't, the program produces invalid results or aborts with an invalid address the first time the pointer is used.

Exactly what action should be taken when memory overflow is encountered is application dependent. If memory might be released by another portion of the program, the memory request can be held. Generally, however, the programmer must terminate the program and allocate more memory to the heap.

> **Note**
>
> Prior to C99, it was necessary to cast the pointer returned from a memory allocation function. While it is no longer necessary, it does no harm as long as the cast is correct. If you should be working with an earlier standard, the casting format is:
>
> pointer = (type*) malloc(size)

The malloc function has one more potential error. If we call malloc with a zero size, the results are unpredictable. It may return a NULL pointer, or it may return some other implementation-dependent value. *Never call malloc with a zero size.*

Figure 9-40 shows a typical malloc call. In this example, we are allocating one integer object. If the memory is allocated successfully, ptr contains a value. If it doesn't, there is no memory and we exit the program with error code 100.

Figure 9-40 malloc

```
if (!(pInt = malloc(sizeof(int))))
    // No memory available
    exit(100);
// Memory available
...
```

pInt

Stack   Heap

Contiguous Memory Allocation (calloc)

The second memory allocation function, calloc, is primarily used to allocate memory for arrays. It differs from malloc only in that it sets memory to null characters. The calloc function declaration is shown below.

```
void *calloc (size_t element-count,
              size_t element_size);
```

The result is the same for both malloc and calloc when overflow occurs and when a zero size is given.

A sample calloc call is shown in **Figure 9-41**. In this example, we allocate memory for an array of 200 integers.

Figure 9-41 `calloc`

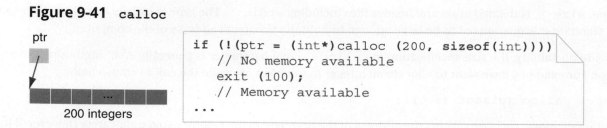

ptr

200 integers

```
if (!(ptr = (int*)calloc (200, sizeof(int))))
    // No memory available
    exit (100);
    // Memory available
...
```

Reallocation of Memory (`realloc`)

The `realloc` function can be highly inefficient and therefore should be used advisedly. When given a pointer to a previously allocated block of memory, `realloc` changes the size of the block by deleting or extending the memory at the end of the block. If the memory cannot be extended because of other allocations, `realloc` allocates a completely new block, copies the existing memory allocation to the new allocation, and deletes the old allocation. The programmer must ensure that any other pointers to the data are correctly changed. The operation of `realloc` is shown in **Figure 9-42**.

```
void* realloc (void* ptr, size_t newSize);
```

Figure 9-42 `realloc`

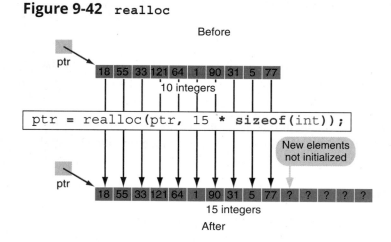

Before

ptr

| 18 | 55 | 33 | 121 | 64 | 1 | 90 | 31 | 5 | 77 |

10 integers

```
ptr = realloc(ptr, 15 * sizeof(int));
```

New elements not initialized

ptr

| 18 | 55 | 33 | 121 | 64 | 1 | 90 | 31 | 5 | 77 | ? | ? | ? | ? | ? |

15 integers

After

Releasing Memory (`free`)

When memory locations allocated by `malloc`, `calloc`, or `realloc` are no longer needed, they should be freed using the predefined function `free`. It is an error to `free` memory with a null pointer, a pointer to other than the first element of an allocated block, a pointer that is a different type than the pointer that allocated the memory; it is also a potential error to refer to memory after it has been released. The function declaration statement for `free` is shown below.

```
void free (void* ptr);
```

Figure 9-43 shows two examples. The first one releases a single element, allocated with a `malloc`, back to the heap. In the second example, the 200 elements were allocated with `calloc`. When we `free` the pointer in this case, all 200 elements are returned to the heap. You should note two things in this figure. First, it is not the pointers that are being released but rather what they point to. Second, to release an array of memory that was allocated by `calloc`, you need only release the pointer once. It is an error to attempt to release each element individually.

Figure 9-43 Freeing memory

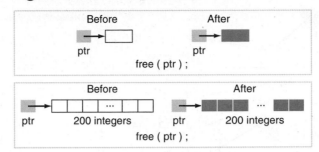

Releasing memory does not change the value in a pointer. It still contains the address in the heap. It is a *logic* error to use the pointer after memory has been released. The program may continue to run, but the data may be destroyed if the memory area is allocated for another use. This logic error is very difficult to trace. We suggest that immediately after you free memory you also clear the pointer by setting it to NULL. It is important to erase the content of the pointer address after its memory has been released—this is a common programming error. Guard against it by clearing the pointer.

One final thought: You should free memory whenever it is no longer needed. It is not necessary, however, to clear memory at the end of the program. The operating system will release all memory when your program terminates. Always remember that the pointer used to free memory must be of the same type as the pointer used to allocate the memory.

9.10 Array of Pointers

Another useful structure that uses arrays and pointers is an array of pointers. This structure is especially helpful when the number of elements in the array is variable.

To look at an example, **Table 9-6** is a two-dimensional array in which only one row (1) is full. The rest of the rows contain from one to four elements. This array is also known as a *ragged array* because the right elements in each row may be empty, giving it an uneven (ragged) right border.

Table 9-6 A ragged array

32	18	12	24			
13	11	16	12	42	19	14
22						
13	13	14				
11	18					

If we use a two-dimensional array for storing these numbers, we are wasting a lot of memory. The solution in this case is to create five one-dimensional arrays that are joined through an array of pointers. One implementation of this concept is seen in **Figure 9-44** along with the statements needed to allocate the arrays in the heap. Note that table is a pointer to a pointer to an integer and must be declared as shown below, not as an array.

```
int** table;
```

Program 9-13 in the next section, "Programming Example: Programming Applications," demonstrates the concept in a complete program. We will learn about other variations on this data structure as you become a more experienced programmer.

Figure 9-44 A ragged array

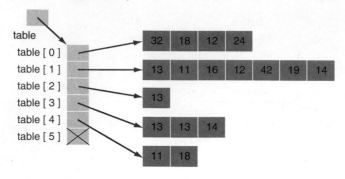

```
table = (int**)calloc (rowNum + 1, sizeof(int*));

table[0] = (int*)calloc (4, sizeof(int));
table[1] = (int*)calloc (7, sizeof(int));
table[2] = (int*)calloc (1, sizeof(int));
table[3] = (int*)calloc (3, sizeof(int));
table[4] = (int*)calloc (2, sizeof(int));
table[5] = NULL;;
```

Programming Example: Programming Applications

This section contains two applications. The first is a rewrite of the selection sort, this time using pointers. The second uses dynamic arrays.

Selection Sort Revisited

Let's revisit the selection sort we developed in the previous chapter. Now that we know how to use pointers, we can improve it in several ways. First, and perhaps most important, it is structured. The structure chart is shown in **Figure 9-45**. Note that main contains no detailed code. It simply calls the three functions that will get the job done. First, getData reads data from the keyboard and puts it into an array. Then selectSort calls two functions to sort the data. Finally, printData displays the result. The complete algorithm is shown in **Program 9-13**.

Figure 9-45 Selection sort with pointers—structure chart

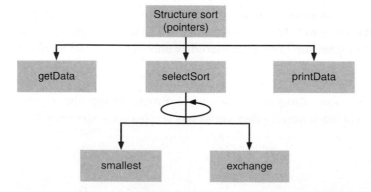

Program 9-13 | Selection sort revisited

```c
1  /* Demonstrate pointers with Selection Sort
2     Written by:
3     Date written:
4  */
5  #include <stdio.h>
6  #define SIZE 25
7
8  // Function Declarations
9  int* getData (int* pAry, int arySize);
10 void selectSort (int* pAry, int* last);
11 void printData (int* pAry, int* last);
12 int* smallest (int* pAry, int* pLast);
13 void exchange (int* current, int* smallest);
14
15 int main (void)
16 {
17 // Local Declarations
18    int ary[SIZE];
19    int* pLast;
20
21 // Statements
22    pLast = getData (ary, SIZE);
23    selectSort (ary, pLast);
24    printData (ary, pLast);
25    return 0;
26 } // main
27
28 /*==============getData==============
29   Reads data from keyboard into array for sorting.
30   Pre pAry is pointer to array to be filled
31   arySize is integer with maximum array size
32   Post array filled. Returns address of last element
33 */
34 int* getData (int* pAry, int arySize)
35 {
36 // Local Declarations
37    int ioResult;
38    int readCnt = 0;
39    int* pFill = pAry;
40
41 // Statements
42    do
```

(continue)

Program 9-13 Selection sort revisited *(continued)*

```
43    {
44        printf("Please enter number or <EOF>: ");
45        ioResult = scanf("%d", pFill);
46        if (ioResult == 1)
47        {
48           pFill++;
49           readCnt++;
50        } // if
51    } while (ioResult == 1 && readCnt < arySize);
52
53    printf("\n\n%d numbers read.", readCnt);
54    return (--pFill);
55 } // getData
56
57 /*==============selectSort==============
58    Sorts by selecting smallest element in unsorted
59    portion of the array and exchanging it with element
60    at the beginning of the unsorted list.
61    Pre array must contain at least one item
62    pLast is pointer to last element in array
63    Post array rearranged smallest to largest
64 */
65 void selectSort (int* pAry, int* pLast)
66 {
67 // Local Declarations
68    int* pWalker;
69    int* pSmallest;
70
71 // Statements
72    for (pWalker = pAry; pWalker < pLast; pWalker++)
73    {
74       pSmallest = smallest (pWalker, pLast);
75       exchange (pWalker, pSmallest);
76    } // for
77    return;
78 } // selectSort
79
80 /*==============smallest==============
81    Find smallest element starting at current pointer.
82    Pre pAry points to first unsorted element
83    Post smallest element identified and returned
84 */
85 int* smallest (int* pAry, int* pLast)
86 {
```

(continue)

Program 9-13 Selection sort revisited *(continued)*

```
87  // Local Declarations
88     int* pLooker;
89     int* pSmallest;
90
91  // Statements
92     for (pSmallest = pAry, pLooker = pAry + 1;
93          pLooker <= pLast;
94          pLooker++)
95       if (*pLooker < *pSmallest)
96           pSmallest = pLooker;
97     return pSmallest;
98  } // smallest
99
100 /*==============exchange==============
101   Given pointers to two array elements, exchange them
102   Pre p1 & p2 are pointers to exchange values
103   Post exchange is completed
104 */
105 void exchange (int* p1, int* p2)
106 {
107 // Local Declarations
108     int temp;
109
110 // Statements
111     temp = *p1;
112     *p1 = *p2;
113     *p2 = temp;
114     return;
115 } // exchange
116
117 /*==============printData==============
118   Given a pointer to an array, print the data.
119   Pre pAry points to array to be filled
120   pLast identifies last element in the array
121   Post data have been printed
122 */
123 void printData (int* pAry, int* pLast)
124 {
125 // Local Declarations
126     int nmbrPrt;
127     int* pPrint;
128
129 // Statements
130     printf("\n\nYour data sorted are: \n");
```

(continue)

Program 9-13   Selection sort revisited *(continued)*

```
131        for (pPrint = pAry, nmbrPrt = 0;
132             pPrint <= pLast;
133             nmbrPrt++, pPrint++)
134          printf ("\n#%02d %4d", nmbrPrt, *pPrint);
135        printf("\n\nEnd of List ");
136        return;
137 } // PrintData
138 //===============End of Program===============
```

Here are a few points you should note as you study this program. Note that we have used pointers and pointer arithmetic in all functions.

The getData function fills the array. Since the pointer, pFill, is always one ahead of the read, when we reach the end of file, it is pointing to an empty element. Therefore, when we return it we subtract 1.

The selectSort function advances through the array using a for statement. For each iteration, it selects the smallest element in the unsorted portion of the array and exchanges it with the first element in the unsorted portion of the array. Each loop, therefore, examines a smaller number of unordered elements. We stop at the element just before the last one because smallest always tests the first element and at least one element after the first one. When we are at the element just before the last, therefore, we are also testing the last element.

Finally, note the style used to code the for statement in both smallest and printData. Long for statements are more readable if you put each expression on a separate line.

Dynamic Array

This program creates a dynamic table that can store a ragged array. The column and the width of the dynamic array are tailored to the needs of the user. The program starts by asking the user for the number of rows that must be stored. After allocating the row pointers (using calloc), the program asks for the number of entries in each row. The table is then filled with data supplied by the user from the keyboard. To demonstrate the applications that could be used with this type of structure, we then determine the minimum, maximum, and average of each row of data. The design is shown in **Figure 9-46**.

Figure 9-46   Dynamic array structure chart

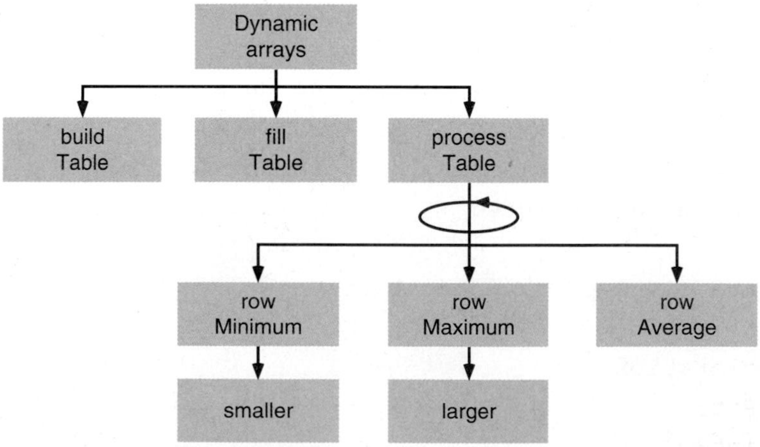

The data structure is shown in **Figure 9-47**. The table pointer points to the first pointer in an array of pointers. Each array pointer points to a second array of integers, the first element of which is the number of elements in the list. All arrays are allocated out of the heap, giving us a structure that is limited only by the computer's memory.

Figure 9-47   Ragged array structure

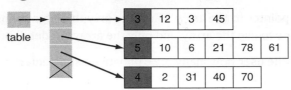

The complete set of programs to build and fill the table and some sample applications are shown in **Programs 9-14** through **9-22**. To compile these programs, they need to be put in one source file or combined using `include` statements.

Program 9-14 | Dynamic arrays: `main`

```
1  /* Demonstrate storing arrays in the heap. This program
2     builds and manipulates a variable number of ragged
3     arrays. It then calculates the minimum, maximum, and
4     average of the numbers in the arrays.
5     Written by:
6     Date:
7  */
8  #include <stdio.h>
9  #include <stdlib.h>
10 #include <limits.h>
11
12 // Function Declarations
13 int** buildTable (void);
14 void fillTable (int** table);
15 void processTable (int** table);
16 int smaller (int first, int second);
17 int larger (int first, int second);
18 int rowMinimum (int* rowPtr);
19 int rowMaximum (int* rowPtr);
20 float rowAverage (int* rowPtr);
21
22 int main (void)
23 {
24 // Local Declarations
25    int** table;
26
27 // Statements
28    table = buildTable();
29    fillTable (table);
30    processTable (table);
31    return 0;
32 } // main
```

The `main` function in Program 9-14 is a classic example of a well-designed program.

It contains only one variable: the pointer to the array. There are only three functions calls in `main`: The first returns the address of the array; the other two use the array, and only the array. All detail processing is done in subfunctions.

We begin **Program 9-15** by asking the user how many rows of data must be entered.

Program 9-15 | Dynamic arrays: `buildTable`

```
1   /* ==================buildTable==================
2       Create backbone of the table by creating an array of
3       pointers, each pointing to an array of integers.
4       Pre nothing
5       Post returns pointer to the table
6   */
7   int** buildTable (void)
8   {
9   // Local Declarations
10      int rowNum;
11      int colNum;
12      int** table;
13      int row;
14
15  // Statements
16      printf("\nEnter the number of rows in the table: ");
17      scanf ("%d", &rowNum);
18      table = (int**) calloc(rowNum + 1, sizeof(int*));
19      for (row =0; row < rowNum; row++)
20      {
21         printf("Enter number of integers in row %d: ",
22                 row + 1);
23         scanf ("%d", &colNum);
24         table[row] = (int*)calloc(colNum + 1,
25                                    sizeof(int));
26         table[row] [0] = colNum;
27      } // for
28      table[row] = NULL;
29      return table;
30  } // buildTable
```

Using the `calloc` function, we then allocate the memory for an array of pointers plus one extra pointer at the end. Each entry in the allocated table is used to point to an array of integers, also stored in the heap.

Filling the rows, **Program 9-16** requires a while statement to loop through the array pointers and a for statement to enter the data. We use the while statement because the pointer array is designed with a null pointer at the end, and we use it to tell we are at the end of the array. We use the for statement for filling the row because the user has already told us how many elements are in each row.

Program 9-16 | Dynamic arrays: `fillTable`

```
 1  /* ===================fillTable==================
 2      This function fills the array rows with data.
 3      Pre array of pointers
 4      Post array filled
 5  */
 6  void fillTable (int** table)
 7  {
 8  // Local Declarations
 9     int row = 0;
10
11  // Statements
12     printf("\n ==============================");
13     printf("\n Now we fill the table.\n");
14     printf("\n For each row enter the data");
15     printf("\n and press return: ");
16     printf("\n ============================\n");
17
18     while (table[row] != NULL)
19     {
20        printf("\n row %d (%d integers) -----> ",
21        row + 1, table[row][0]);
22        for (int column = 1;
23             column <= *table[row];
24             column++)
25          scanf("%d", table[row] + column);
26        row++;
27     } // while
28     return;
29  } // fillTable
```

Processing the table in **Program 9-17** calls three functions to show how you could use a dynamic structure such as this. Obviously, many more applications could be used. Remember the structure of this example. You will be able to use this structure in future applications. **Programs 9-18** through **9-22** continue the code for the functions.

Program 9-17 | Dynamic arrays: `processTable`

```c
 1   /*================processTable================
 2      Process the table to create the statistics.
 3      Pre table
 4      Post row statistics (min, max, and average)
 5   */
 6   void processTable (int** table)
 7   {
 8   // Local Declarations
 9   int row = 0;
10   int rowMin;
11   int rowMax;
12   float rowAve;
13
14   // Statements
15      while (table[row] != NULL)
16      {
17         rowMin = rowMinimum (table[row]);
18         rowMax = rowMaximum (table[row]);
19         rowAve = rowAverage (table[row]);
20         printf ("\nThe statistics for row %d ", row + 1);
21         printf("\nThe minimum: %5d", rowMin);
22         printf("\nThe maximum: %5d", rowMax);
23         printf("\nThe average: %8.2f ", rowAve);
24         row++;
25      } // while
26      return;
27   } // processTable
```

Program 9-18 | Dynamic arrays: find row minimum

```c
 1   /*================rowMinimum================
 2      Determines the minimum of the data in a row.
 3      Pre given pointer to the row
 4      Post returns the minimum for that row
 5   */
 6   int rowMinimum (int* rowPtr)
 7   {
 8   // Local Declarations
 9      int rowMin = INT MAX;
10
```

(continue)

Program 9-18   Dynamic arrays: find row minimum *(continued)*

```
11 // Statements
12    for (int column =1; column <= *rowPtr; column++)
13        rowMin = smaller (rowMin, *(rowPtr + column));
14    return rowMin;
15 } // rowMinimum
```

Program 9-19 | Dynamic arrays: find row maximum

```
1   /*=================rowMaximum=================
2     Calculates the maximum of the data in a row.
3     Pre given pointer to the row
4     Post returns the maximum for that row
5   */
6   int rowMaximum (int* rowPtr)
7   {
8   // Local Declarations
9      int rowMax = INT MIN;
10
11  // Statements
12     for (int column = 1; column <= *rowPtr; column++)
13        rowMax = larger (rowMax, *(rowPtr + column));
14     return rowMax;
15  } // rowMaximum
```

Program 9-20 | Dynamic arrays: find row average

```
1   /*=================rowAverage=================
2     This function calculates the average of data in a row.
3     Pre pointer to the row
4     Post returns the average for that row
5   */
6   float rowAverage (int* rowPtr)
7   {
8   // Local Declarations
9      float total = 0;
10     float rowAve;
11
12  // Statements
13     for (int column = 1; column <= *rowPtr; column++)
```

(continue)

Program 9-20   Dynamic arrays: find row average *(continued)*

```
14        total += (float)*(rowPtr + column);
15     rowAve = total / *rowPtr;
16     return rowAve;
17 } // rowAverage
```

Program 9-21 | Dynamic arrays: find smaller

```
1  /*================smaller=================
2    This function returns the smaller of two numbers.
3    Pre two numbers
4    Post returns the smaller
5  */
6  int smaller (int first, int second)
7  {
8  // Statements
9     return (first < second ? first : second);
10 } // smaller
```

Program 9-22 | Dynamic arrays: find larger

```
1  /*================larger=================
2    This function returns the larger of two numbers.
3    Pre two numbers
4    Post returns the larger
5  */
6  int larger (int first, int second)
7  {
8  // Statements
9     return (first > second ? first : second);
10 } // larger
```

9.11 Advanced Pointer Concepts

Now, just before we wrap up the chapter with software engineering fundamentals, let's touch on some important advanced pointer concepts that will aid you in developing advanced code using pointers for your future applications.

Pointers and Arrays

When you combine pointers and arrays, the complexity quickly becomes difficult. This is especially true when the array is multidimensional. Whenever possible, therefore, rather than passing a multidimensional array, pass just one row. This reduces the complexity significantly because the function is now dealing with a one-dimensional array. Not only are the references easier to work with, but passing a row also allows simple pointer arithmetic, which is usually more efficient.

When you must work with a two-dimensional array, use index rather than pointer notation. Index notation is much simpler to work with, and there is no difference in efficiency. If you are not sure of this recommendation, consider the following equivalent expressions. Which one would you rather find in a strange program?

```
*(*(ary + i) + j)  or  a[i][j]
```

Array Index Commutativity

Commutativity is a principle in mathematics that says the results of an expression do not depend on the order in which the factors are evaluated. For example, a + b is identical to b + a. Pointer addition is commutative; subtraction is not. Thus, the following two expressions are identical.

```
a + i      i + a
```

But we also know that a + i is identical to a[i]. Similarly, i + a would be equivalent to i[a]. Therefore, using the principle of commutativity, we see that

```
a[i] is identical to i[a]
```

A word of caution: Commutativity works in C because of the pointer concept and pointer arithmetic. Do not try this in another language.

Dynamic Memory: Theory versus Practice

Do not get carried away with dynamic memory. The programming complexity of dynamically managing memory is very high. What you will often find, therefore, is that memory is not fully reused. To test memory reusability in your system, run **Program 9-23**. (Note: This may not be a problem with today's compilers. When we reran this program for this edition, the memory was reused.)

> ## Program 9-23 | Testing memory reuse

```
1   /* This program tests the reusability of dynamic memory.
2      Written by:
3      Date:
4   */
5   #include <stdio.h>
6   #include <stdlib.h>
7
8   int main (void)
9   {
10  // Local Declarations
11      int looper;
12      int * ptr;
13
```

(continue)

Program 9-23   Testing memory reuse *(continued)*

```
14 // Statements
15    for (looper = 0; looper < 5; looper++)
16    {
17        ptr = malloc(16);
18        printf("Memory allocated at: %p\n", ptr);
19
20        free (ptr);
21    } // for
22    return 0;
23 } // main
```

Output in Personal Computer:
```
Memory allocated at: 0x00e80238
Memory allocated at: 0x00e8024a
Memory allocated at: 0x00e8025c
Memory allocated at: 0x00e8026e
Memory allocated at: 0x00380280
```

Output in UNIX system:
```
Memory allocated at: 0x00300f70
Memory allocated at: 0x00300f70
Memory allocated at: 0x00300f70
Memory allocated at: 0x00300f70
Memory allocated at: 0x00300f70
```

First look at the logic of this simple program. It loops five times, each time allocating 16 bytes and immediately freeing them. The program was run on two different systems, a personal computer and a UNIX network.

If the memory management is doing its job, the same 16 bytes would be allocated each time. What we see, however, is that for the personal computer, each address is different. It is also interesting to note that the difference between all the allocations except the first was 18 bytes, not 16.

The larger UNIX network system is more sophisticated, and it appears to reuse dynamic memory efficiently.

Software Engineering

Everyone claims to want the highest quality software available, and to listen to the creators of systems on the market, their systems are all perfect. Yet most software users acknowledge that even their favorite software is not as good as they would like. In this chapter, we discuss some of the attributes of a quality product and how you go about achieving quality.

Quality Defined

Quality software is defined as software that satisfies the user's explicit and implicit requirements, is well documented, meets the operating standards of the organization, and runs efficiently on the hardware for which it was developed.

Every one of these attributes of good software falls squarely on you, the system designer and programmer. Note that we place on you the burden of satisfying not only the users' explicit requirements, but also their implicit needs. Often, users don't fully know what they need. When this happens, it is your job to determine their implicit requirements, which are hidden in the background. This is a formidable task indeed.

Of course, it is also your job to document the software. If you are lucky, you will have a technical writer to help. However, even if you do, the final product is still your responsibility. And as an analyst and programmer, you are expected to know the standards of your organization and to implement them properly.

Finally, it is your program, so you are responsible for its efficiency. This means that you are expected to use appropriate and efficient algorithms, as you learned earlier when you learned how to analyze algorithms and how to use the big-O theory.

Quality software is not just a vague concept. If we want to attain it, we have to be able to measure it. Whenever possible, these measurements should be quantitative—that is, they should be numerically measurable. For example, if an organization is serious about quality, it should be able to tell you the number of errors (bugs) per thousand lines of code and the mean time between failures for every software system it maintains. These are measurable statistics.

On the other hand, some of the measurements may be qualitative, meaning that they cannot be numerically measured. Flexibility and testability are examples of qualitative software measurements. This does not mean that they can't be measured, but rather that they rely on someone's judgment in assessing the quality of a system.

Quality Factors

Software quality can be divided into three broad measures: operability, maintainability, and transferability. These measures can be broken down as shown in **Figure 9-48**.

Figure 9-48 Software quality

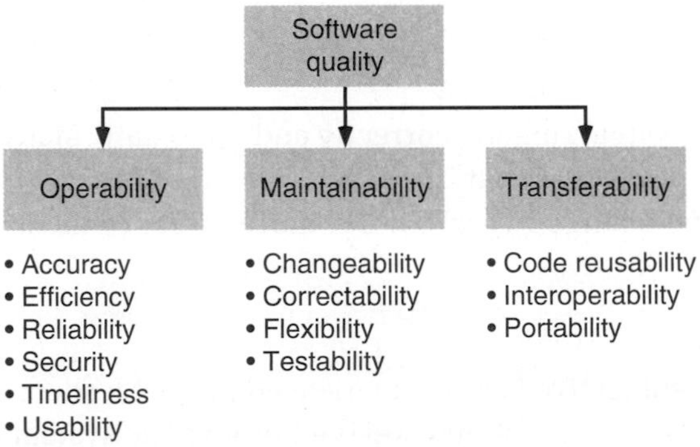

Software quality
- Operability
  - Accuracy
  - Efficiency
  - Reliability
  - Security
  - Timeliness
  - Usability
- Maintainability
  - Changeability
  - Correctability
  - Flexibility
  - Testability
- Transferability
  - Code reusability
  - Interoperability
  - Portability

Operability

Operability refers to the basic operation of a system. The first thing a user notices about a system is its "look and feel." This means, especially for an online, interactive system, how easy and intuitive it is to use. Does it fit well into the operating system it is running under? For example, if it is running in a Windows environment, its pull-down and pop-up menus should work the same way the operating system's menus do. In short, operability answers the question, "How does it drive?"

But these factors are subjective; they are not measurable. So let's look at the factors that make up operability. They are listed alphabetically.

Accuracy

A system that is not accurate is worse than no system at all. Most workers would rather rely on intuition and experience than a system that they know gives false and misleading information.

Any system that you develop must be thoroughly tested, both by you (whitebox) and by a systems test engineer and the user (blackbox). If you get the opportunity, take a course on software testing.

Accuracy can be measured by such metrics as mean time between failures, number of bugs per thousand lines of code, and number of user requests for change.

Efficiency

Efficiency is, by and large, a subjective term. In some cases the user will specify a performance standard, such as that a real-time response must be received within 1 second, 95% of the time. This is certainly measurable.

Reliability

Reliability is really the sum of the other factors. If users count on the system to get their job done and are confident in it, then it is most likely reliable. On the other hand, some measures speak directly to a system's reliability, most notably, mean time between failures.

Security

The security of a system refers to how easy it is for unauthorized persons to access the system's data. Although this is a subjective area, there are checklists that assist in assessing the system's security. For example, does the system have and require passwords?

Timeliness

Does the system deliver its output in a timely fashion? For online systems, does the response time satisfy the users' requirements? For batch systems, are the reports delivered in a timely fashion? It is also possible, if the system has good auditability, to determine if the data in the system are timely; that is, are data recorded within a reasonable time after the activity that creates them takes place?

Usability

Usability is also highly subjective. The best measure of usability is to watch the users and see if they are using the system. User interviews will often reveal problems with the usability of a system.

Maintainability

Maintainability refers to keeping a system running correctly and up to date. Many systems require regular changes, not because they were poorly implemented but because of changes in external factors. For example, the payroll system for a company must be changed yearly, if not more often, to meet changes in government laws and regulations.

Changeability

The ease of changing a system is a subjective factor. Experienced project leaders, however, can estimate how long a requested change will take. If it takes too long, it may well be because the system is difficult to change. This is especially true of older systems.

Current software measurement tools estimate a program's complexity and structure. These tools should be used regularly, and if a program's complexity is high, we should consider rewriting the program. Programs that have been changed many times may have often lost their structured focus and become difficult to change. They also should be rewritten.

Correctability

One measure of correctability is mean time to recovery—how long it takes to get a program back in operation when it fails. Although this is a reactive definition, there are currently no predictors of how long it will take to correct a program before it fails.

Flexibility

Users are constantly requesting changes in systems. This qualitative attribute attempts to measure how easy it is to make these changes. If a program needs to be completely rewritten to effect a change, it is not flexible. Fortunately, this factor became less of a problem with the advent of structured programming.

Testability

You might think that testability is a highly subjective area, but a test engineer has a checklist of factors that can be used to assess a program's testability.

Transferability

Transferability refers to the ability to move data and/or a system from one platform to another and to reuse code. In many situations, it is not an important factor. On the other hand, if you are writing generalized software, it can be critical.

Code Reusability

If functions are written so that they can be reused in different programs and on different projects, then they are highly reusable. Good programmers build libraries of reusable functions that they can use when they need to solve a similar problem.

Interoperability

Interoperability addresses the capability of sending data to other systems. In today's highly integrated systems, interoperability is a desirable attribute. In fact, it has become so important that operating systems now support the ability to move data between applications, such as between a word processor and a spreadsheet.

Portability

Portability addresses the ability to move software from one hardware platform to another; for example, from a Macintosh to a Windows environment or from an IBM mainframe to a VAX environment.

The Quality Circle

The first and most important point to recognize is that quality must be designed into a system. It can't be added as an afterthought. It begins at Step 1, determining the user requirements, and continues throughout the life of the system. Since quality is a continuous concept that, like a circle, never ends, we refer to it as the quality circle.

There are six steps to developing quality software: quality tools, technical reviews, formal testing, change control, standards, and measurement and reporting. These steps are shown in **Figure 9-49**.

Figure 9-49 The quality circle

Quality begins with the software engineers assigned to the team. But they can only achieve their goals if they have the quality tools required to develop a quality product. Fortunately, today's development tools are excellent. A whole suite of quality tools known as computer-assisted software engineering (CASE) guides software development through requirements, design, programming and testing, and into production. Programmers can use computer systems that not only assist in writing the program but also in testing and debugging. For example, some CASE tools track tests through a program and then determine which statements were executed and which were not. Tools such as these are invaluable for whitebox testing. Other development tools, known as Integrated Development Environments (IDE) are available for programmers for different computer languages, including C. These tools offer programming a slew of features such as advanced editor, built-on compilers, and ability to run the code with the click of a button. In this text, an open source Dev C++ IDE is used to compose, compile, and run all programs.

Another major step in quality software is the technical review. These reviews should be conducted at every step in the development process including requirements, design, programming, and testing. A typical program review begins after the programmer has designed the data structures and structure chart for a program. A design review board consisting of the systems analyst, test engineer, user representative, and one or two peers is then convened. Note that no one from management is allowed to attend a technical review. During the review, the programmer explains the approach and discusses interfaces to other programs while the reviewers ask questions and make suggestions.

Quality also requires formal testing. Formal testing ensures that the programs work together as a system and meet the defined requirements. After the programmer has completed unit testing, the program is turned over to another software engineer for integration and system testing. On a small project, this is most likely the systems analyst and/or the user. A large project will have a separate testing team.

Large systems take months and sometimes years to develop. It is only natural that, over extended periods of time, changes to the requirements and design become necessary. To ensure quality, each change should be reviewed and approved by a change control board. The impact of a change on each program needs to be assessed and properly planned. Uncontrolled change causes schedule and budget overruns and poor-quality products.

Finally, a good-quality environment measures all aspects of quality and regularly reports the results. Without measurement, you cannot tell if quality is good or bad, improving or deteriorating. At the same time, published standards provide the yardstick for many of the quality measurements.

Pointers and Function Calls

Pointer applications must be carefully designed to ensure they work correctly and efficiently. You must take great care in the program design, while also carefully considering the data structures inherent within the pointer applications. The design of data structures is beyond the scope of this text.

Before we discuss specific aspects of pointer applications, a word of caution: Remember the KISS principle. The complexity of pointers grows rapidly as you move from single references to double references to triple references. Keep it short and simple!

You should always pass by value when possible. If you have to use a pointer to pass back a value, however, whenever possible, pass a pointer to the ultimate object to be referenced. When the pointer refers to the data variable, it is a single dereference. Despite your best efforts, at times you will have to pass a pointer to a pointer. When a function opens a file whose file pointer is in the calling function, you must pass a pointer to the pointer to the file table. In Figure 9-41, we allocated a dynamic array of 200 integers. If the allocation is performed in a subfunction, then it must receive a pointer to the pointer to the array in memory so that it can store the address of the array.

Tips and Common Programming Errors

1. The address of a memory location is a pointer constant and cannot be changed.

2. Only an address (pointer constant) can be stored in a pointer variable.

3. Remember compatibility. Do not store the address of a data variable of one type into a pointer variable of another type. In other words, a variable of pointer to `int` can only store the address of an `int` variable, and a variable of pointer to `char` can only store the address of a `char` variable.

4. The value of a data variable cannot be assigned to a pointer variable. In other words, the following code creates an error:

```
int* p;
int a;
p = a; // ERROR
```

5. You must not use a pointer variable before it is assigned the address of a variable. In other words, the following lines create an error unless p is assigned an address:

```
int* p;
x = *p; // ERROR
*p = x; // ERROR
```

6. A pointer variable cannot be used to refer to a nonexistent pointer variable. For example, the following lines create a run-time error because p exists, but *p does not exist until it is assigned a value.

```
int* p;
*p = ...
```

7. You cannot dereference a pointer variable of type void*.

8. Remember that the definition for a pointer variable allocates memory only for the pointer variable, not for the variable to which it is pointing.

9. The address operator (&) must be used only with an lvalue.

10. A function that uses addresses as parameters needs a pointer to data as a formal parameter; the actual parameter in the function call must be a pointer value (address).

11. If you want a called function to change the value of a variable in the calling function, you must pass the address of that variable to the called function.

12. When using multiple definitions in one statement—a practice we do not recommend—the pointer token is recognized only with one variable. Therefore, in the following definition, only the first variable is a pointer to an integer; the rest are integers.

```
int* ptrA, ptrB, ptrC;
```

13. It is a compile error to initialize a pointer to a numeric constant.

```
int* ptr = 59;
```

14. Similarly, it is a compile error to assign an address to any variable other than a pointer.

```
int x = &y; // ERROR
```

15. It is a compile error to assign a pointer of one type to a pointer of another type without a cast. (Exception: If one pointer is a void pointer, it is permitted.)

16. It is a common compile error to pass values when addresses are required in actual parameters. Remember to use the address operator when passing identifiers to pointers in the called function.

17. It is a logic error to use a pointer before it has been initialized.

18. It is a logic error to dereference a pointer whose value is NULL.

19. If ary is the name of an array, then

```
ary is the same as &ary[0]
```

20. If ary is the name of an array, then

```
ary[i] is the same as *(ary + i)
```

21. Remember that we usually pass the name of an array as a pointer value to a function that needs to access the elements of the array.

22. Remember that `int* a[5];` is different from `int (*a)[5];`

23. Similar to array indexes, the most common pointer error is referencing a nonexistent element in an array. This is especially easy to do with pointer arithmetic.

24. It is a compile error to use pointer arithmetic with a pointer that does not reference an array.

25. It is a logic error to subtract two pointers that are referencing different arrays.

26. It is a compile error to subtract a pointer from an index.

27. It is a compile error to attempt to modify the name of an array using pointer arithmetic, such as

```
table++;      // Error: table is constant
table = …;    // Error: table is constant
```

28. The header file `stdlib.h` is required when using memory allocation functions.

29. It is a compile error to assign the return value from `malloc` or `calloc` to anything other than a pointer.

30. It is a logic error to set a pointer to the heap to `NULL` before the memory has been released.

31. It is a compile error to use pointer arithmetic with multiply, divide, or modulo operators.

Summary

> Every computer has addressable memory locations.

> A pointer is a derived data type consisting of addresses available in the computer.

> A pointer constant is an address that exists by itself. We cannot change it. We can only use it.

> The address operator (&) makes a pointer value from a pointer constant. To get the address of a variable, we simply use this operator in front of the variable name.

> The address operator can only be used in front of an lvalue. The result is an rvalue.

> A pointer variable is a variable that can store an address.

> The indirection operator (*) accesses a variable through a pointer containing its address.

> The indirection operator can only be used in front of a pointer value.

> Pointer variables can be initialized just like data variables. The initializer must be the address of a previously defined variable or another pointer variable.

> A pointer can be defined to point to other pointer variables (pointers to pointers).

> The value of a pointer variable can be stored in another variable if they are compatible—that is, if they are of the same type.

> One of the most useful applications of pointers is in functions.

> If we want a called function to access a variable in the calling function, we pass the address of that variable to the called function and use the indirection operator to access the variable.

> When we need to return more than one value from a function, we must use pointers.

> If a data item is not to be changed, it is passed to the called function by value. If a data item is to be changed, its address is passed to let the called function change its value.

> A function can also return a pointer value.

> Arrays and pointers have a close relationship. The name of an array is a pointer constant to the first element of the array.

> The name of an array and the address of the first element in the array represent the same thing: an rvalue pointer.

> The name of an array is a pointer only to the first element, not the whole array.

> A pointer variable to the first element of an array can be used anywhere the name of the array is permitted, such as with an index.

> In pointer arithmetic, if `ptr` is pointing to a specific element in an array, `ptr + n` is the pointer value n elements away.

> The name of a two-dimensional array is a pointer to a one-dimensional array—the first row.

> In a multidimensional array, the following two expressions are equivalent.

    ((a + i) + j)   a[i][j]

> We can pass an array to a function in many ways. One way is to pass the name of the array as a pointer.

> A ragged array—that is, an array of pointers—can be used to save space when not all rows of the array are full.

> The memory in a computer can be divided into program memory and data memory. Data memory can be partitioned into global area, heap, and stack.

> Static allocation of memory requires that the declaration and definition of memory be fully specified at compilation time.

> Dynamic allocation of memory is done during run time through the use of predefined functions.

> C has four predefined memory allocation functions: `malloc`, `calloc`, `realloc`, and `free`.

> To read and interpret a complex declaration, we can use the right–left rule.

> In software engineering, *quality factors* refer to characteristics that a piece of software must have to become quality software.

> Quality factors are defined as operability, maintainability, and transferability.

> One of the most important points about the quality of a piece of software is that quality must be designed into the system. It cannot be added as an afterthought. To design quality into a system, we can use a tool called the quality circle.

Key Terms

array of pointers	offset	pointer variable
dynamic array	overflow	ragged array
dynamic memory allocation	pointer	right–left rule
heap memory	pointer arithmetic	rvalue
indirection operator (*)	pointer constant	stack memory
lvalue	pointer indirection	static memory allocation

Review Questions

1. Pointer constants are drawn from the set of addresses for a computer.
   a. True   **b.** False

2. Pointers are declared using the address operator as a token.
   a. True   **b.** False

3. The value of a pointer type is always an address.
   a. True   **b.** False

4. An rvalue expression can be used only to supply a value.
   a. True   **b.** False

5. Given a pointer to an array element, `ptr`, `ptr - 5` is a pointer to the value 5 elements toward the beginning of the array.
   a. True   **b.** False

6. Adding 1 to a pointer increases the address stored in it by 1 byte.
   a. True   **b.** False

7. Dynamically allocated memory can only be referred to through pointers.
   a. True   **b.** False

8. The _____ operator is used with a pointer to dereference the address contained in the pointer.
   a. address (&)
   b. assignment (=)
   c. indirection (*)
   d. pointer (^)
   e. selection (->)

9. Which of the following statements will not add 1 to a variable?
   a. `a++;`
   b. `a += 1;`
   c. `a = a + 1;`
   d. `*p = *p + 1;`
   e. `*p++;`

10. Which of the following defines a pointer variable to an integer?
    a. `int& ptr;`
    b. `int&& ptr;`
    c. `int* ptr;`
    d. `int** ptr;`
    e. `int^ ptr;`

11. Which of the following defines and initializes a pointer to the address of x?
    a. `int* ptr = *x;`
    b. `int* ptr = ^x;`
    c. `int* ptr = &x;`
    d. `int& ptr = *x;`
    e. `int& ptr = ^x;`

12. Given the following definitions:

    ```
    int x;
    int* p = &x;
    int** pp = &p;
    ```

    Which answer can access the value stored in x?
    a. `p`   **c.** `&p`   **e.** `**pp`
    b. `pp`   **d.** `*pp`

13. Given the following definitions:

    ```
    int i;
    float f;
    int* pd;
    float* pf;
    ```

    Which answer is not valid?
    a. `i = 5;`   **c.** `pd = &i;`   **e.** `pd = pf;`
    b. `f = 5;`   **d.** `pf = &f;`

14. Which of the following operators does not require an lvalue as its operand?
    a. address operator (`&total`)
    b. assignment (`x = ...`)
    c. indirection (`*ptr`)
    d. postfix increment (`x++`)
    e. prefix increment (`++x`)

15. Which of the following statements about pointers and arrays is true?
    a. The following expressions are identical when `ary` is an array: `*ary` and `&ary[0]`.
    b. The following expressions are identical when `ary` is an array: `*ary` and `*ary[0]`.
    c. The name of an array can be used with the indirection operator to reference data.
    d. The name of the array is a pointer variable.
    e. The only way to reference data in an array is with the index operator.

16. Which of the following statements about pointer arithmetic is true?

    a. Any arithmetic operator can be used to change the value of a pointer.

    b. Given a pointer `ptr`, `ptr + n` is a pointer to the value n elements away.

    c. Pointer arithmetic is a short-hand notation that changes the value that a pointer is referencing.

    d. Pointer arithmetic is valid only with pointers to arithmetic variables, such as pointer to integer.

    e. Pointer arithmetic is valid only with the name of the array.

17. Which of the following parameters is a two-dimensional array of integers?

    a. `int ary`

    b. `int ary[] [SIZE2]`

    c. `int* ary`

    d. `int* ary[] [SIZE2]`

    e. `int* ary[SIZE2]`

18. Which of the following statements about memory allocation is true?

    a. Allocated memory can be referred to only through pointers; it does not have its own identifier.

    b. `calloc` (change allocation) is used to change the allocation to memory previously allocated through `malloc`.

    c. `malloc` (memory allocation) is used to allocate blocks of memory for arrays.

    d. `realloc` (release allocation) is used to release memory when it is no longer needed.

    e. Underflow can occur only with `calloc` and `malloc`.

19. Which of the following statements about releasing memory allocation is false?

    a. It is an error to dereference a pointer to allocated memory after the memory has been released.

    b. It is an error to *free* memory with a pointer to other than the first element of an allocated array.

    c. Memory should be freed as soon as it is no longer needed.

    d. Only one call to *free* is necessary to release an entire array allocated with `calloc`.

    e. To ensure that it is released, allocated memory should be freed before the program ends.

20. Which of the following statements about ragged arrays is false?

    a. Ragged arrays are two-dimensional arrays in which the right elements of a row may be empty.

    b. Ragged arrays can be implemented using an array of pointers to one-dimensional arrays.

    c. Ragged arrays can only be used with arrays of integers.

    d. Ragged arrays implemented as an array of pointers save memory.

    e. Ragged arrays implemented as an array of pointers can be created in dynamic memory.

Exercises

21. Declare and define the following:

    a. A pointer variable `pi` pointing to an integer

    b. A pointer variable `ppi` pointing to a pointer to an integer

    c. A pointer variable `pf` pointing to a float

    d. A pointer variable `ppc` pointing to a pointer to a char

22. If a is declared as integer, which of the following statements is true and which is false?

    a. The expression `*&a` and a are the same.

    b. The expression `*&a` and `&*a` are the same.

23. Given the following declarations:

```
int x;
double d;
int* p;
double* q;
```

    Which of the following expressions are not allowed?

    a. `p = &x;`   **c.** `q = &x;`   **e.** `p = x;`

    b. `p = &d;`   **d.** `q = &d;`

24. Given the following declarations:

```
int a = 5;
int b = 7;
int* p = &a;
int* q = &b;
```

What is the value of each of the following expressions?

a. ++a
b. ++(*p)
c. − −(*q)
d. − −b

25. What is the error (if any) in each of the following expressions?

a. int a = 5;
b. int* p = 5;
c. int a; int* p = &a;
d. int a; int** q = &a;

26. Which of the following program segments is valid? Describe each error in the invalid statements.

a. int* p; scanf("%d", &p);
b. int* p; scanf("%d", &*p);
c. int* p; scanf("%d", *p);
d. int a; int* p = &a; scanf("%d", p);

27. Which of the following program segments has a logical error in it?

a. int** p; int* q; q = &p;
b. int** p; int* q; p = &q;
c. int** p; int** q; p = &q;
d. char c = 'A'; char** p; char* q; q = & c; printf("%c", *p);

28. Given the following declaration:

```
int*** p;
```

What is the type of each of the following expressions?

a. p
b. *p
c. **p
d. ***p

29. If p is a name of a variable, which of the following expressions is an lvalue and which one is an rvalue? Explain.

a. p
b. *p
c. &p
d. *p + 2

30. If p and q are pointer variable names and a is an array, which of the following expressions are not syntactically correct, because they violate the rules concerning lvalues and rvalues?

a. *p = *p + 2;
b. &p = &a[0];
c. q = &(p + 2);
d. a[5] = 5;

31. Write a function prototype statement for a function named calc that returns void and contains a reference parameter to int, x, and a reference parameter to a long double, y.

32. Write a function prototype statement for a function named spin that returns a pointer to an integer and contains a reference parameter to an int, x, and a pointer parameter to the address of a long double, py.

33. Assuming all variables are integers, and all pointers are typed appropriately, show the final values of the variables in **Figure 9-50** after the following assignments.

```
a   = ***p;

s   = **p;

t   = *p;

b   = **r;

**q = b;
```

Figure 9-50 Exercise 33

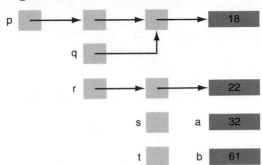

34. Assuming all variables are integer, and all pointers are typed appropriately, show the final values of the variables in **Figure 9-51** after the following assignments.

```
t   = **p;
B   = ***q;
*t  = c;
V   = r;
w   = *s;
a   = **v
*u  = *w
```

Figure 9-51 Exercise 34

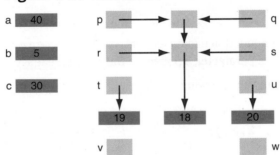

35. In the following program, show the configuration of all the variables and the output.

```
#include <stdio.h>
int main (void)
{
// Local Declarations
    int a;
    int* p;
    int** q;
// Statements
    a = 14;
    P = &a;
    q = &p;
    printf("%d\n" , a);
    printf("%d\n ", *p);
```

```
      printf("%d\n ", **q);
      printf("%p\t", p);
      printf("%p", q);
      return 0;
   } // main
```

36. Rewrite each of the following expressions by replacing the index operator ([...]) with the indirection operator (*).

    a. `tax[6]`
    b. `score[7]`
    c. `num[4]`
    d. `prices[9]`

37. Rewrite each of the following expressions by replacing the indirection operator (*) with the index operator ([...]). Each identifier refers to an array.

    a. `*(tax + 4)`
    b. `*(score + 2)`
    c. `*(number + 0)`
    d. `*prices`

38. Imagine you have the following declarations:

```
int ary[10];
int* p = &ary[3];
```

Show how you can access the sixth element of ary using the pointer p.

39. Given the following declarations:

```
float ary[200];
```

Write the function declaration for a function named fun that can manipulate a one-dimensional array of floating-point numbers, ary. Provide an additional parameter, a pointer to the last element in the array. Code a call to the function.

40. Show what would be printed from the following block:

```
{
    int num[5] ={3, 4, 6, 2, 1};
    int* p = num;
    int* q = num +2;
    int* r = &num[1];
    printf("\n%d %d", num[2], *(num +2));
    printf("\n%d %d", *p, *(p + 1));
    printf("\n%d %d", *q, *(q + 1));
    printf("\n%d %d", *r, *(r + 1));
} // Block
```

41. Show what would be printed from the following block.

```
// Function Declaration
void printOne (int*);
void printTwo (int*);
void printThree (int*);
{
// Local Declarations
    int num [5] = {3, 4, 6, 2,1};
```

```
   // Statements
      printOne (num);
      printTwo (num + 2);
      printThree (&num [2]);
      return 0;
   } // Block
   void printOne (int* x)
   {
      printf("\n%d", x[2]);
      return;
   } // printOne
   void printTwo (int* x)
   {
      printf("\n%d", x[2]);
      return;
   } // printTwo
   void printThree (int* x)
   {
      printf(M\n%d", *x);
      return;
   } // printThree
```

42. Given the following definition:

    ```
    int table [4] [5];
    ```

    Write the function declaration for a function named fun that can accept the whole array using a pointer. Write the statement that calls this function.

43. Given the following definition:

    ```
    int table [4] [5];
    ```

    Write the function declaration for a function named boredom that accepts one row of an array at a time.

44. Draw pictures to show the memory configuration for each of the following declarations:
    a. int* x [5];
    b. int (*x) [5];

45. Show what would be printed from the following block:

    ```
    {
    // Local Declarations
       int x [2] [3] = {
                          {4, 5, 2},
                          {7, 6, 9}
                       };
       int (*p) [3] = &x [1];
       int (*q) [3] = x;
    // Statements
       printf("\n%d %d %d", (*p)[0],(*p)[1],(*p)[2]);
       printf("\n%d id", *q[0], *q[1]);
    } // Block
    ```

46. Show what would be printed from the following block:

```
{
// Local Declarations
   int x [2] [3] = {
                     {4, 5, 2},
                     {7, 6, 9}
                };
// Statements
   fun (x);
   fun (x + 1);
   return 0;
} // Block
void fun (int (*p) [3])
{
   printf("\n%d %d %d", (*p) [0],(*p) [1],(*p) [2]);
   return;
}
```

47. Given the following definitions:

```
int num[26] = {23, 3, 5, 7, 4, -1, 6};
int* n = num;
int i = 2;
int j = 4;
```

Show the value of the following expressions:
a. n
b. *n
c. *n + 1
d. *(n + 1)
e. *n + j
f. *&i

48. Given the following definitions:

```
char a[20] = {'z', 'x', 'm', 's', 'e', 'h'};
char* pa = a;
int i = 2;
int j =4;
int* pi = &i;
```

Show the value of the following expressions:
a. *(pa + j)
b. *(pa + *pi)

49. Given the following definition:

```
int data[15] = {5,2,3,4,1,3,7,2,4,3,2,9,12};
```

Show the value of the following expressions:
a. data + 4
b. *(data + 4)
c. *data + 4
d. *(data + (*data + 2))

50. Given the following definitions:

```
int i = 2;
int j = 4;
int* pi = &i;
int* pj = &j;
```

Show the value of the following expressions:

a. *&j
b. *&*&j
c. *&pi
d. **&pj
e. &**&pi

51. Given the following definitions:

```
char a[20] = {'z', 'x', 'm', 's', 'e', 'h'};
int i = 2;
int j = 4;
```

Write pointer expressions that evaluate to the same value as each of the following:

a. a[0]
b. a[5]
c. The address of the element just before a [0].
d. The address of the last element in a.
e. The address of the element just after the last element in a.
f. The next element after a [3].
g. The next element after a [12].
h. The next element after a [j].

52. Given the following definitions:

```
int num[10] = {23,3,5,7,4,-1,6,12,10,-23};
int i = 2;
int j = 4;
```

Write index expressions that evaluate to the same value as each of the following:

a. *(num + 2)
b. *(num + i + j)
c. *(num + *(num + 1))
d. *(num + j)
e. *(num + i) + *(num + j)

53. Given the following definition:

```
int num[2000] = {23, 3, 5, 7, 4, -1, 6};
```

Write two pointer expressions for the address of num[0].

54. Given the following definitions:

```
int num[26] = {23, 3, 5, 7, 4, -1, 6};
int i = 2;
int j = 4;
int* n = num;
```

Write the equivalent expressions in index notation.
   a. n
   b. *n
   c. *n + 1
   d. *(n + 1)
   e. *(n + j)

55. Given the following definitions:

```
int num[26] = {23, 3, 5, 7, 4, -1, 6};
int* pn;
```

Write a test to check whether pn points beyond the end of num.

56. Given the following function for mushem and the definitions shown below

```
int mushem (int*, int*);
int i = 2;
int j = 4;
int* pi = &i;
int* pj = &j;
```

Indicate whether each of the following calls to mushem is valid:
   a. i = mushem (2, 10);
   b. j = mushem (&i, &j);
   c. i = mushem (pi, &j);
   d. j = mushem (i, j);
   e. mushem (pi, pj);

57. What is the output from the following program?

```
#include <stdio.h>
int fun (int*, int, int*);
int main (void)
{
// Local Declarations
   int a = 4;
   int b = 17;
   int c[5] = {9, 14, 3, 15, 6};
// Statements
   a = fun(&a, b, c);
   printf("2. %d %d %d %d %d %d %d\n",
          a, b, c[0], c[1], c[2], c[3], c[4]);
   return 0;
} // main
int fun (int* px, int y, int* pz)
{
// Local Declarations
   int a = 5;
   int* p;
// Statements
   printf("1. %d %d %d\n", *px, y, *pz);
```

```
        for (p = pz; p < pz + 5; ++p)
            *p = a + *p;
        return (*px + *pz + y);
    } // fun
```

58. What is the output from the following program?

```
#include <stdio.h>
int sun (int*, int, int*);
int main (void)
{
// Local Declarations
    int a = 4;
    int b = 17;
    int c[5] = {9, 14, 3, 15, 6};
    int* pc = c;
// Statements
    a = sun(pc, a, &b);
    printf("2. %d %d %d %d %d %d %d\n",
            a, b, c[0], c[1], c[2], c[3], c[4]);
    return 0;
} // main
int sun (int* px, int y, int* pz)
{
// Local Declarations
    int i = 5;
    int* p;
// Statements
    printf("1. %d %d %d\n", *px, y, *pz);
    for (p = px; p < px + 5; p++)
        *p = y + *p;
    *px = 2 * i;
    return (*pz + *px + y);
} // sun
```

Problems

59. Write a function that converts a Julian date to a month and day. A Julian date consists of a year and the day of the year relative to January 1. For example, day 41 is February 10. The month and day are to be stored in integer variables whose addresses are passed as parameters. The function is to handle leap years. If there is an error in a parameter, such as a day greater than 366, the function will return zero. Otherwise, it returns a positive number.

60. Write a function that receives a floating-point number representing the change from a purchase. The function will pass back the breakdown of the change in dollar bills, half-dollars, quarters, dimes, nickels, and pennies.

61. Write a function that receives a floating-point number and sends back the integer and fraction parts.

62. Write a function that receives two integers and passes back the greatest common divisor and the least common multiplier. The calculation of the greatest common divisor can be done using Euclid's method of repetitively dividing one number by the other and using the remainder (modulo). When the remainder is zero, the greatest common divisor has been found. For example, the greatest common divisor of 247 and 39 is 13, as in **Table 9-7**.

Table 9-7   Greatest common divisors

NUM1	NUM2	REMAINDER
247	39	13
39	(gcd) 13	0

Once you know the greatest common divisor (gcd), the least common multiplier (lcm) is determined as shown below.

$$lcm = \frac{num1 \times num2}{gcd}$$

63. We have two arrays, A and B, each containing 10 integers. Write a function that checks if every element of array A is equal to its corresponding element in array B. In other words, the function must check if A[0] is equal to B[0], A[1] is equal to B[1], and so on. The function must accept only two pointer values and return a Boolean, for true equal and false for unequal.

64. Write a function that reverses the elements of an array in place. In other words, the last element must become the first, the second from last must become the second, and so on. The function must accept only one pointer value and return void.

65. The Pascal triangle can be used to compute the coefficients of the terms in the expansion of (a + b)^n. Write a function that creates a ragged array representing the Pascal triangle. In a Pascal triangle, each element is the sum of the element directly above it and the element to the left of the element directly above it (if any). A Pascal triangle of size 7 is shown in the following.

```
1
1    1
1    2    1
1    3    3    1
1    4    6    4    1
1    5    10   10   5    1
1    6    15   20   15   6    1
```

Your function must be able to create the triangle of any size. The function should accept an integer representing the size of the triangle and return a pointer to the array it created.

66. Write a function that tests an International Standard Book Number (ISBN) to see if it is valid. The ISBN is used to define a book uniquely. It is made of 10 digits, as shown below. For an ISBN to be valid, the weighted sum of the 10 digits must be evenly divisible by 11. The 10th digit may be X, which indicates 10. (If you are not familiar with the algorithm for the weighted sum, it is explained in Chapter 8, Problem 31). The ISBN format is shown in **Figure 9-52**.

Figure 9-52   Problem 66 structure

The function must accept a pointer value (the name of the array) and return a Boolean, `true` for valid and `false` for invalid.

67. Write a function that copies a one-dimensional array of n elements into a two-dimensional array of j rows and k columns. The resulting array will be placed in the heap. The data will be inserted into the array in row order; that is, the first k items will be placed in row 0, the second k items in row 1, and so forth until all rows have been filled.

    If j and *k* are not factors of n—that is, if n ≠ j * k—the function returns a null pointer. Otherwise, it returns the pointer to the two-dimensional array. The input array and j, k, and n will be passed as parameters.

68. Given the following definition:

    ```
    int num[20];
    ```

    and using only pointer notation, write a `for` loop to read integer values from the keyboard to fill the array.

69. Given the following definition

    ```
    char a[40];
    ```

    and using only pointer notation, write a `for` loop to read characters from the keyboard to fill the array.

70. Given the following declaration and definition:

    ```
    char a[6] = {'z', 'x', 'm', 's', 'e', 'h'};
    ```

    and using only pointer notation, write a loop to rotate all values in a to the right (toward the end) by one element.

71. Write a function named addem with two call-by-address integer parameters. The function will add 2 to the first parameter and 5 to the second parameter. Test the function by calling it with the values of 17 and 25.

Projects

72. Write a program that creates the structure shown in **Figure 9-53** and then reads an integer into variable a and prints it using each pointer in turn. That is, the program must read an integer into variable a and print it using p, q, r, s, t, u, and v.

Figure 9-53   Structure for Project 72

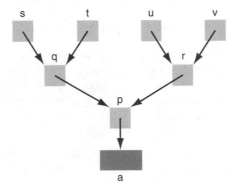

73. Write a program that creates the structure shown in **Figure 9-54**. It then reads data into a, b, and c using the pointers p, q, and r.

    After the data have been read, the program reassigns the pointers so that p points to c, q points to a, and r points to b. After making the reassignments, the program prints the variables using the pointers. For each variable, print both its contents and its address.

Figure 9-54 Data structure
for Project 73

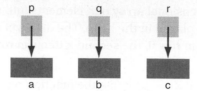

74. Write a program that creates the structure shown in **Figure 9-55** and reads data into a and b using the pointers x and y.

    The program then multiplies the value of a by b and stores the result in c using the pointers x, y, and z. Finally, it prints all three variables using the pointers x, y, and z.

Figure 9-55 Data structure for
Project 74

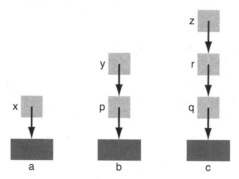

75. Write a program that reads integers from the keyboard and places them in an array. The program then will sort the array into ascending and descending order and print the sorted lists. The program must not change the original array or create any other integer arrays.

    The solution to this problem requires two pointer arrays as shown in the example in **Figure 9-56**. The first pointer array is rearranged so that it points to the data in ascending sequence. The second pointer array is rearranged so that it points to the data in descending sequence.

Figure 9-56 Sample structure for Project 75

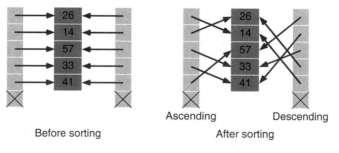

Your output should be formatted with the three arrays printed as a vertical list next to each other, as shown in **Table 9-8**.

Table 9-8   Format for Project 75

ASCENDING	ORIGINAL	DESCENDING
14	26	57
26	14	41
33	57	33
41	33	26
57	41	14

76. Write a program that creates a two-dimensional array in the heap and then analyzes it to determine the minimum, maximum, and average of each column.

The data are to be read from a file. The first two elements are the number of rows in the array and the number of columns in each row. The file data for a 12 × 8 array are shown below.

12	8						
838	758	113	515	51	627	10	419
212	86	749	767	84	60	225	543
89	183	137	566	966	978	495	311
367	54	31	145	882	736	524	505
394	102	851	67	754	653	561	96
628	188	85	143	967	406	165	403
562	834	353	920	444	803	962	318
422	327	457	945	479	983	751	894
670	259	248	757	629	306	606	990
738	516	414	262	116	825	181	134
343	22	233	536	760	979	71	201
336	61	160	5	729	644	475	993

77. Rewrite the straight insertion sort from Chapter 8 using pointer arithmetic. The data to be sorted are to be read from a file. The array is to be dynamically allocated in the heap after reading the file to determine the number of elements. While reading the data to determine the size of array you will require, print them 10 integers to a line. Use the test data shown below.

838	758	113	515	51	627	10	419	212	86
749	767	84	60	225	543	89	183	137	566
966	978	495	311	367	54	31	145	882	736
524	505	394	102	851	67	754	653	561	96
628	188	85	143	967	406	165	403	562	834
353	920	444	803	962	318	422	327	457	945
479	983	751	894	670	259	248	757	629	306
606	990	738	516	414	262	116	825	181	134
343	22	233	536	760	979	71	201	336	61

The data will be sorted as they are read into the array. *Do not fill the array and then sort the data.* After the array has been sorted, print the data again using the same format you used for the unsorted data.

78. Write a program to print out the scores, average, or grade for all students. All array functions are to receive the array as a pointer and use pointer arithmetic. The data in **Table 9-9** will be stored in a two-dimensional array.

Table 9-9 Student data for Project 78

STUDENT	QUIZ 1	QUIZ 2	QUIZ 3	QUIZ 4	QUIZ 5
1234	52	7	100	78	34
1947	45	40	88	78	55
2134	90	36	90	77	30
2877	55	50	99	78	80
3124	100	45	20	90	70
3189	22	70	100	78	77
4532	11	17	81	32	77
4602	89	50	91	78	60
5405	11	11	0	78	10
5678	20	12	45	78	34
6134	34	80	55	78	45
6999	0	98	89	78	20
7874	60	100	56	78	78
8026	70	10	66	78	56
9893	34	9	77	78	20

79. Contract bridge is a popular card game played by millions of people throughout the world. It began in the 1920s as a variation of an old English card game, whist. In bridge, the entire deck is dealt to four players named North, South, East, and West. In tournament bridge, teams of players (North–South versus East–West) compete with other players using the same hands (sets of 13 cards). Today it is common for large tournaments to use computer-generated hands. Write a program to shuffle and deal the hands for one game.

To simulate the bridge deck, use an array of 52 integers initialized from 1 to 52. To shuffle the deck, loop through the array, exchanging the current card element with a random element (use the random number generator discussed in Chapter 4). After the deck has been shuffled, print the hands in four columns using the player's position as a heading. Use the following interpretation for the cards' suits:

```
1 to 13              Clubs
14 to 26             Diamonds
27 to 39             Hearts
40 to 52             Spades
```

To determine the rank of the card, use its number (modulo 13) + 1. The interpretation of the rank follows: 1 is an ace, 2 through 10 have their value, 11 is a jack, 12 is a queen, and 13 is a king.

Strings

Learning Objectives

When you complete this chapter, you will be able to:

10.1 Use design concepts for fixed-length and variable-length strings

10.2 Describe the design implementation for C-language delimited strings

10.3 Write programs that read, write, and manipulate strings

10.4 Write programs that use arrays of strings

10.5 Implement the string functions from the string library in C programs

10.6 Write programs that parse a string into separate variables

10.1 String Concepts

It is impossible to write a well-structured and human-engineered program without using strings. Although you probably weren't aware of it, you have been using strings ever since you wrote your first C program.

Some languages such as Pascal, Ada, and C++ provide intrinsic string types, but C does not. In C, the programmer implements strings. Because strings are so important, however, functions to manipulate them have been defined in an ad hoc standard library. In this chapter we first consider how strings are defined and stored, and then we explore the standard string functions that are available in C.

In general, a string is a series of characters treated as a unit. Computer science has long recognized the importance of strings, but it has not adapted a standard for their implementation. We find, therefore, that a string created in Pascal differs from a string created in C.

Virtually all string implementations treat a string as a variable-length piece of data. Consider, for example, one of the most common of all strings, a name. Names, by their very nature, vary in length. It makes no difference if we are looking at the name of a person, a textbook, or an automobile.

Given that we have data that can vary in size, how do we accommodate them in our programs? We can store them in fixed-length objects, or we can store them in variable-length objects. This breakdown of strings is seen in **Figure 10-1**.

Figure 10-1 String taxonomy

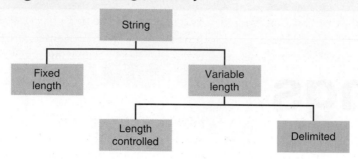

Fixed-Length Strings

When implementing a fixed-length string format, the first decision to make relates to the size of the variable. If we make it too small, we can't store all the data. If we make it too big, we waste memory.

Another problem associated with storing variable data in a fixed-length data structure is how to tell the data from the nondata. A common solution is to add nondata characters, such as spaces, at the end of the data. Of course, this means that the character selected to represent the nondata value cannot be used as data.

Variable-Length Strings

A much preferred solution is to create a structure that can expand and contract to accommodate the data. Thus, to store a person's name that consists of only one letter, we would provide only enough storage for one character. To store a person's name that consists of 30 characters, the structure would be expanded to provide storage for 30 characters.

This flexibility has a cost, however. There must be some way to tell when we get to the end of the data. Two common techniques are to use length-controlled strings and delimited strings.

A length-controlled string adds a count that specifies the number of characters in the string. This count is then used by the string manipulation functions to determine the actual length of the data.

Another technique used to identify the end of the string is the delimiter at the ends of a delimited string. You are already familiar with the concept of delimiters, although you probably don't recognize them as such. In English, each sentence, which is a variable-length string, ends with a delimiter, the period. Commas, semicolons, colons, and dashes are other common delimiters found in English.

The major disadvantage of the delimiter is that it eliminates one character from being used for data. The most common delimiter is the ASCII null character, which is the first character in the ASCII character sequence (\0). This is the technique used by C.

Figure 10-2 shows length-controlled and delimited strings in memory.

Figure 10-2 String formats

Length	Delimiter

9	C O N F U C I U S		B O O L E \0
Length-controlled string		Delimited string	

10.2 C Strings

A C string is a variable-length array of characters that is delimited by the null character. Generally, string characters are selected only from the printable character set. Nothing in C, however, prevents any character, other than the null delimiter, from being used in a string. In fact, it is quite common to use formatting characters, such as tabs, in strings.

Storing Strings

In C, a string is stored in an array of characters. It is terminated by the null character (\0). **Figure 10-3** shows how a string is stored in memory. What precedes the string and what follows it is not important. What is important is that the string is stored in an array of characters that ends with a null delimiter. Because a string is stored in an array, the name of the string is a pointer to the beginning of the string.

Figure 10-3   Storing strings

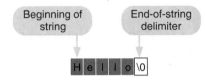

Figure 10-4 shows the difference between a character stored in memory and a one-character string stored in memory. The character requires only one memory location. The one-character string requires two memory locations: one for the data and one for the delimiter. The figure also shows how an empty string is stored. Empty strings require only the end-of-string marker.

Figure 10-4   Storing strings and characters

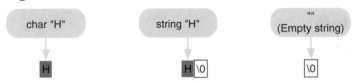

The String Delimiter

At this point, you may be wondering, "Why do we need a null character at the end of a string?" The answer is that a string is not a data type but a data structure. This means that its implementation is logical, not physical. The physical structure is the array in which the string is stored. Since the string, by its definition, is a variable-length structure, we need to identify the logical end of the data within the physical structure.

Looking at it another way, if the data are not variable in length, then we don't need the string data structure to store them. They are easily stored in an array, and the end of the data is always the last element in the array. But, if the data length is variable, then we need some other way to determine the end of the data.

The null character is used as an end-of-string marker. It is the sentinel used by the standard string functions. In other words, the null character at the end lets us treat the string as a sequence of objects (characters) with a defined object at the end that can be used as a sentinel. **Figure 10-5** shows the difference between an array of characters and a string.

Figure 10-5   Differences between strings and character arrays

Initializing Strings

We can initialize a string the same way that we initialize any storage structure by assigning a value to it when it is defined. In this case, the value is a string literal. For example, to assign "Good Day" to a string, we would code

```
char str[9] = "Good Day";
```

Since a string is stored in an array of characters, we do not need to indicate the size of the array if we initialize it when it is defined. For instance, we could define a string to store the month January, as shown below.

```
char month[ ] = "January";
```

In this case, the compiler will create an array of 8 bytes and initialize it with January and a null character. We must be careful, however, because month is an array. If we now tried to store "December" in it, we would overrun the array and destroy whatever came after the array. This example points out one of the dangers of strings: We must make them large enough to hold the longest value we will place in the variable.

C provides two more ways to initialize strings. A common method is to assign a string literal to a character pointer, as shown below. This creates a string for the literal and then stores its address in the string pointer variable, pStr. To clearly see the structure, refer to **Figure 10-10**.

```
char* pStr = "Good Day";
```

We can also initialize a string as an array of characters. This method is not used too often because it is so tedious to code. Note that in this example, we must ensure that the null character is at the end of the string.

```
char str[9] = {'G','o','o','d',' ' 'D','a','y','\0'};
```

The structures created by these three examples are shown in Figure 10-10.

Figure 10-10   Initializing strings

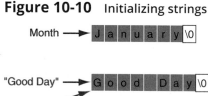

Strings and the Assignment Operator

Because the string is an array, the name of the string is a pointer constant. As a pointer constant, it is an rvalue and therefore cannot be used as the left operand of the assignment operator. This is one of the most common errors in writing a C program; fortunately, it is a compile error, so it cannot affect our program.

```
char str1[6] = "Hello";
char str2[6];
str2 = str1;      // Compile error
```

Although we could write a loop to assign characters individually, there is a better way. C provides a rich library of functions to manipulate strings, including moving one string to another. We discuss this library in the section "String Manipulation Functions."

Reading and Writing Strings

A string can be read and written. C provides several string functions for input and output. We discuss them in the following section, "String Input/Output Functions."

10.3 String Input/Output Functions

C provides two basic ways to read and write strings. First, we can read and write strings with the formatted input/output functions, `scanf/fscanf` and `printf/fprintf`. Second, we can use a special set of string-only functions, get string (`gets/fgets`) and put string (`puts/fputs`). C provides a parallel set of read functions for wide characters. They function the same except for the type.

Formatted String Input/Output

In this section, we cover the string-related portions of the formatted input and output functions.

Formatted String Input: `scanf/fscanf`

We have already discussed the basic operations of the format input functions. However, two conversion codes pertain uniquely to strings, and we discuss them here.

The String Conversion Specification

We read strings using the read-formatted function (`scanf`). The conversion code for a string is "s". The `scanf` functions then do all the work for us. First, they skip any leading whitespace. Once they find a character, they read until they find whitespace, putting each character in the array in order. When they find a trailing whitespace character, they end the string with a null character. The whitespace character is left in the input stream, and the string conversion code(s) skips whitespace. To delete the whitespace from the input stream, we use a space in the format string before the next conversion code or `FLUSH` the input stream, whichever is more appropriate.

The conversion specification strings can use only three options fields: flag, maximum field size, and size.

Flag

Like all inputs, the only flag that can be used is the asterisk (*), which discards the data read.

Maximum Field

When present, the maximum field size specifies the maximum number of characters that can be read.

Size

If no size option is specified, we read normal characters. To read wide characters, we use size l (ell). For example, to read a string, such as month, from the keyboard, we could simply write the statement shown below.

```
scanf("%s", month);
```

An address operator is not required for month, because it is already a pointer constant. In fact, it would be an error to use one. The only thing we need to worry about is to make sure that the array is large enough to store all the data. If it isn't, then we destroy whatever follows the array in memory. Therefore, we must make sure we don't exceed the length of the data. Assuming that month has been defined as

```
char month[10];
```

we can protect against the user entering too much data by using a width in the field specification. (Recall that the width specifies the *maximum* number of characters to be read.) The modified `scanf` statement is shown below.

```
scanf("%9s", month);
```

Note that we set the maximum number of characters at nine while the array size is ten. This is because `scanf` will read up to nine characters and then insert the null character. Now, if the user accidentally enters more than nine characters, the extra characters will be left in the input stream. But this can cause a problem. Assuming that the data are being entered as a separate line—that is, that there is only one piece of data on the line—we use the preprocessor-defined statement, `FLUSH`, to eliminate any extra characters that were entered. This function also flushes the newline that is left in the input stream by `scanf` when the user correctly enters data. The complete block of code to read a month is shown in **Program 10-1**.

Program 10-1 | Reading strings

```
1  {  // Read Month
2     #define FLUSH while (getchar() != '\n')
3
4     char month[10];
5     printf("Please enter a month. ");
6     scanf("%9s", month);
7     FLUSH;
8  }  // Read Month
```

The Scan Set Conversion Code ([...])

In addition to the string conversion code, we can also use a scan set conversion code to read a string. The scan set conversion specification consists of the open bracket ([ ), followed by the edit characters, and terminated by the close bracket ( ]). The characters in the scan set identify the valid characters, known as the scan set, that are to be allowed in the string. All characters except the close bracket can be included in the set.

Edited conversion reads the input stream as a string. Each character read by scanf/fscanf is compared against the scan set. If the character just read is in the scan set, it is placed in the string and the scan continues. The first character that does not match the scan set stops the read. The nonmatching character remains in the input stream for the next read operation. If the first character read is not in the scan set, the scanf/fscanf terminates and a null string is returned.

A major difference between the scan set and the string conversion codes is that the scan set does not skip leading whitespace. Leading whitespace is either put into the string being read when the scan set contains the corresponding whitespace character, or stops the conversion when it is not. Note that the edit set does not skip whitespace.

In addition to reading a character that is not in the scan set, there are two other terminating conditions. First, the read will stop if an end-of-file is detected. Second, the read will stop if a field width specification is included and the maximum number of characters has been read.

For example, let's assume we have an application that requires we read a string containing only digits, commas, periods, the minus sign, and a dollar sign; in other words, we want to read a dollar value as a string. No other characters are allowed. Let's also assume that the maximum number of characters in the resulting string is 10. The format string for this operation would be as follows:

```
scanf("%10[0123456789.,-$] ",str);
```

Note | UNIX users note that the dash (–) does not have the same meaning in the scan set that it does in UNIX.

Sometimes it is easier to specify what should not be included in the scan set rather than what is valid. For instance, suppose that we want to read a whole line. We can do this by stating that all characters except the newline (\n) are valid. To specify invalid characters, we start the scan set with the caret (^) symbol. The caret is the negation symbol and in effect says that the following characters are not allowed in the string. (If you know UNIX, this should sound familiar.) To read a line, we would code the scanf as shown below.

```
scanf("%81[^\n]", line);
```

In this example, scanf reads until it finds the newline and then stops. Note that we have again set the width of the data to prevent our string, or line, from being overrun. We would never use this code, however. As we see in the next section, an intrinsic string function does it for us.

For the last example, let's read a 15-character string that can have any character except the special characters on the top of the keyboard. In this case, we again specify what is not valid. This conversion code is shown in the following example:

```
scanf("%15[^-!@#$%^&*()_+]", str);
```

Note that the caret can be included in the scan set, as long as it is not the first character. Similarly, the closing bracket is treated as text as long as it is the first character after the opening bracket. However, if it follows the negation symbol (^), then it ends the scan set. This means that the close bracket cannot be used when the scan set is being negated. Always remember to use a width in the field specification when reading strings. The following example reads a string containing brackets and digits only.

```
scanf("%15[][0123456789]", str);
```

Formatted String Output: `printf/fprintf`

Formatted string output is provided in the `printf` and `fprintf` functions. They use the same string conversion codes that we used for string input.

C has four options of interest when we write strings using these print functions: the left-justify flag, width, precision, and size. The left-justify flag (–) and the width are almost always used together.

Justification Flag

The justification flag (–) is used to left justify the output. It has meaning only when a width is also specified, and then only if the length of the string is less than the format width. Using the justification flag results in the output being left justified, as shown below. If no flag is used, the justification is right.

```
printf("|%-30s|\n", "This is the string");
```

Output

```
|This is the string            |
```

Minimum Width

The width sets the *minimum* size of the string in the output. If it is used without a flag, the string is printed right justified as shown below.

```
printf("|%30s|\n", "This is the string");
```

Output

```
|            This is the string|
```

Precision

Strings can get quite long. Because the width is the minimum number of characters that can be printed, a long string can easily exceed the width specified, which destroys column formatting. Therefore, C also uses the precision option to set the maximum number of characters that will be written. In the following typical example, we set the maximum characters to one less than the width to ensure a space between the string and the next column. Below, the statement `%-15` tells the compiler that the string to be printed is 15. If string is less than 15 characters, the minus sign tells the blank be added to the right; otherwise, it will be added to the left.

```
printf("|%-15.14s|", "12345678901234567890");
```

Output

```
|12345678901234 |
```

> **Note** | The maximum number of characters to be printed is specified by the precision in the format string of the field specification.

Size

If no size option is specified, we write normal characters. To write wide characters, we use size l (ell).

When data are stored in secondary files, the data we need are often only a part of a file. **Program 10-2** demonstrates how to use the scan set to read part of a line and discard the rest. In the following example, the input contains numeric data, with each line containing two integers and a float. We are interested only in the second integer; the rest of each line will be discarded. As we wrote the program, it could contain any type or amount of data after the second integer. It is important to note, however, that if there are not two integers at the beginning of the line, the program fails.

Program 10-2 | Demonstrate string scan set

```
 1   /* Read only second integer.
 2      Written by:
 3      Date:
 4   */
 5   #include <stdio.h>
 6
 7   #include <stdlib.h>
 8   int main (void)
 9   {
10   // Local Declarations
11      int amount;
12      FILE* spData;
13
14   // Statements
15      if (!(spData = fopen ("P1010-03.TXT", "r")))
16      {
17         printf("\a Could not open input file.\n");
18         exit (100);
19      } // if
20      // Read and print only second integer
21      while (fscanf(spData,
22            " %*d%d%*[^\n]", &amount) != EOF)
23         printf("Second integer: %4d\n", amount);
24
25      printf("End of program \n");
26      fclose (spData);
27      return 0;
28   }  // main
```

Input
```
123 456 7.89
987 654 3.21
```

Output
```
Second integer:  456
Second integer:  654
End of program
```

As long as two numbers are at the beginning of each line, this program works just fine. It skips the first number, reads the number into *amount,* and then discards the rest of the line. Study the flags contained in the format string in statement 22 carefully. It consists of only three field specifications. The first one reads and discards an integer. The second one reads *amount.* The third one considers the rest of the line as a long string; fscanf reads until it finds a newline. Because we are not interested in these data (or the first and third parts of the line), we used the suppress flag to discard them.

A similar problem occurs when a file contains leading whitespace at the beginning of a line. In **Program 10-3**, we first determine if there is a whitespace character at the beginning of the line. If there is, we delete all leading spaces using the scan set and then read the rest of the line. Its only limitation is that the nonspace portion of the line cannot be longer than 80 characters.

Program 10-3 | Delete leading whitespace

```
 1  /* Delete leading spaces at beginning of line.
 2     Written by:
 3     Date:
 4  */
 5  #include <stdio.h>
 6
 7  #include <ctype.h>
 8  int main (void)
 9  {
10  // Local Declarations
11     char line[80];
12
13  // Statements
14     printf("Enter data: ");
15     while ((fscanf (stdin, "%*[\t\v\f ]%79[^\n]", line))
16            != EOF)
17     {
18        printf("You entered: %s\n", line);
19
20     // Discard newline and set line to null string
21        fgetc (stdin);
22        *(line) = '\0';
23        printf("Enter data: ");
24     } // while
25
26     printf("\nThank you\n");
27     return 0;
28  } // main
```

(continue)

Program 10-3   Delete leading whitespace *(continued)*

Output

```
Enter data: No whitespace here.
You entered: No whitespace here.
Enter data: Only one whitespace character.
You entered: Only one whitespace character.
Enter data: Tabs and spaces here.
You entered: Tabs and spaces here.
Enter data: Next line is only one space.
You entered: Next line is only one space.
Enter data:
You entered:
Enter data: ^d
Thank you
```

Very often, reading names requires that the names be parsed into first and last names. Parsing names presents unique problems. First, we must skip the whitespace between the parts of the name and the newline at the end of the line. The string format code (s) stops when it reads a whitespace character. Second, some names have special characters, such as a dash, in them.

In **Program 10-4** we read a file of student names and scores. As each name is read, it is printed. We read the first and last names using the string conversion code. We read the student's score as an integer. As an alternative, we could have used the scan-set conversion code, but it is simpler to use the basic string code (remember KISS).

Program 10-4 | Read student names and scores

```
1   /* Demonstrate reading names from a file.
2      Written by:
3      Date:
4   */
5   #include <stdio.h>
6   #include <stdlib.h>
7   #include <string.h>
8
9   int main (void)
10  {
11  // Local Declarations
12      char    first[80];
13      char    last[80];
14      int     score;
15      FILE*   spStuScores;
16
```

(continue)

Program 10-4   Read student names and scores *(continued)*

```
17 // Statements
18    if (!(spStuScores = fopen ("P1010-04.TXT", "r")))
19    {
20       printf("\a Could not open student file.\n"); exit (100);
21    }// if
22
23    // Read and print first name, last name, and score
24    while (fscanf(spStuScores, " %s %s %d",
25          first, last, &score) == 3)
26       printf("%s %s %3d\n", first, last, score);
27
28    printf("End of Student List\n");
29    fclose (spStuScores);
30    return 0;
31 }// main
```

Output

```
George Washington 95
Frederick Douglass 53
Mary Todd-Lincoln 91
End of Student List
```

Just a reminder that `fscanf` specifications `"%s %s %d"` is to read two strings and an integer. In addition, one significant point to note in this program—how we handle end of data. As long as we read three pieces of data, we continue looping. When the last data have been read, the scan returns 0 and the `while` statement becomes false.

String Input/Output

In addition to the formatted string functions, C has two sets of string functions that read and write strings without reformatting any data. These functions convert text-file lines to strings and strings to text-file lines. A line consists of a string of characters terminated by a newline character.

C provides two parallel sets of functions, one for characters and one for wide characters. They are virtually identical except for the type. Because wide characters are not commonly used and because the functions operate identically, we limit our discussion to the character type.

Line to String

The `gets` and `fgets` functions take a line (terminated by a newline) from the input stream and make a null-terminated string out of it. They are therefore sometimes called line-to-string input functions.

The function declarations for get string are shown below.

```
char* gets (char* strPtr);
char* fgets (char* strPtr, int size, FILE* sp);
```

Figure 10-11 shows the concept. As you can see, `gets` and `fgets` do not work the same. The `gets` function converts the return (newline character) to the end-of-string character (`\0`), while `fgets` puts it in the string and appends an end-of-string delimiter.

Figure 10-11 gets and fgets functions

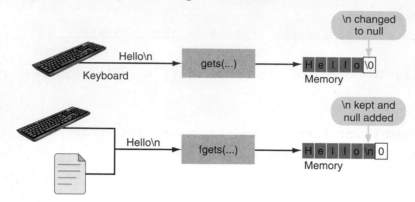

The source of data for the gets is standard input; the source of data for fgets can be a file or standard input. Both accept a string pointer and return the same pointer if the input is successful. If any input problems occur, such as detecting end-of-file before reading any data, they return NULL. If no data were read, the input area is unchanged. If an error occurs after some data have been read, the contents of the read-in area cannot be determined. The current string may or may not have a valid null character.

Note that since no size is specified in gets, it reads data until it finds a newline or until the end-of-file. If a newline character is read, it is discarded and replaced with a null character.

The fgets function requires two additional parameters: one specifying the array size that is available to receive the data, and the other a stream. It can be used with the keyboard by specifying the stdin. In addition to newline and end of file, the reading will stop when size - 1 characters have been read.

Since no length checking is possible with gets, we recommend that you never use it. Should a user enter too much data, you will destroy the data after the string input area, and your program will not run correctly. Rather, use fgets, and specify the standard input file pointer (stdin).

Now let us write a simple program that uses fgets. In **Program 10-5**, we use fgets to read a string and then print it.

Program 10-5 | Demonstrate fgets operation

```
1   /* Demonstrate the use of fgets in a program
2      Written by:
3      Date:
4   */
5
6   #include <stdio.h>
7   int main (void)
8   {
9   // Local Declarations
10     char str[81];
11
12  // Statements
13     printf("Please enter a string: ");
14     fgets (str, sizeof (str), stdin);
15     printf("Here is your string: \n\t%s", str);
```

(continue)

Program 10-5   Demonstrate fgets operation *(continued)*

```
16    return 0;
17 }  // main
```

Output

```
Please enter a string: Now is the time for all students
Here is your string:
Now is the time for all students
```

String to Line

The puts/fputs functions take a null-terminated string from memory and write it to a file or the keyboard. Thus, they are sometimes called string-to-line output functions.

Figure 10-12 shows how these functions work. All change the string to a line. The null character is replaced with a newline in puts; it is dropped in fputs. Because puts is writing to the standard output unit, usually a display, this is entirely logical. On the other hand, fputs is assumed to be writing to a file where newlines are not necessarily required. It is the programmer's responsibility to make sure the newline is present at the appropriate place.

Figure 10-12   puts and fputs operations

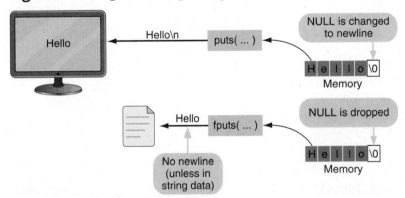

Note how the newline is handled in these functions. Then compare their use of the newline to the gets and fgets functions. While the output functions treat the newline the opposite of the input functions, they are compatible. As long as we are reading from a file and writing to a file, the newlines will be handled automatically. Care must be taken, however, when we read from the keyboard and write to a file.

The declarations for these functions are shown below.

```
int puts (const char* strPtr);
int fputs (const char* strPtr, FILE* sp);
```

The string pointed to by strPtr is written to the indicated file as explained above. If the write is successful, it returns a nonnegative integer; if any transmission errors occur, it returns EOF. Note that the absence of a null character to terminate the string is not an error; however, it will most likely cause your program to fail.

The following example demonstrates the use of these string functions.

Program 10-6 demonstrates the use of fputs with stdout. It calls fputs three times. The first time, we pass a pointer to the beginning of an array. The third time, we pass a pointer that is at the middle of the array. If you were to run this code, you would see that it does not matter where a string pointer starts. The function starts at the address in the pointer and writes until it finds a null character. Note that we had to include a newline put because `fputs` does not insert a newline. The output is shown in Program 10-6.

Program 10-6 | Demonstration of put string

```
 1  /* Demonstrate fput string
 2     Written by:
 3     Date:
 4  */
 5
 6  #include <stdio.h>
 7  int main (void)
 8  {
 9  // Local Definitions
10     char str[] = "Necessity Is the Mother of Invention.";
11     char* pStr = str;
12
13  // Statements
14     fputs(pStr, stdout);
15     fputs("\n", stdout);
16     fputs(pStr + 13, stdout);
17     return 0;
18  }  // main
```

Output
```
Necessity Is the Mother of Invention
the Mother of Invention.
```

Program 10-7 plays the role of a line-at-a-time typewriter. In other words, it accepts text, line by line, from the keyboard and writes it to a text file. The program stops when it detects an end-of-file.

Program 10-7 | Typewriter program

```
 1  /* This program creates a text file from the keyboard.
 2     Written by:
 3     Date:
 4  */
 5  #include <stdio.h>
 6
 7  #include <stdlib.h>
 8  int main (void)
```

(continue)

Program 10-7 Typewriter program *(continued)*

```
 9  {
10  // Local Declarations
11     char str[100];
12     FILE* spOut;
13
14  // Statements
15     if (!(spOut = fopen ("P1010-07.TXT", "w")))
16     {
17        printf("\aCould not open output file. \n");
18        exit (100);
19     } // if
20     while (fgets(str, sizeof (str), stdin))
21        fputs(str, spOut);
22     fclose (spOut);
23     return 0;
24  } // main
```

Note that we are reading the keyboard (stdin) using fgets (see statement 20). This requires that we specify the file name, even though we do not have to declare it or open it. By using fgets we are able to ensure that the user will not overrun our string variable area (str). But even if the user enters too much data, nothing is lost. The data are left in the input stream buffer and are read in the next loop iteration.

This little program has two problems, one stylistic and one technical. The style problem is that it contains no instructions to the user, who must therefore guess what is to be done. This leads directly to the second problem. Some systems have a problem if the user should end the program with an end-of-file but no return. Depending on the system, the last line is lost or the system may just wait for an end-of-file at the beginning of the line. This problem can be prevented by adding good user instructions and a prompt.

Program 10-8 reads text from the keyboard, line by line, and prints only the lines that start with uppercase letters. In this case, we will write to the standard output (stdout) file. This will allow us to direct the output to the printer by assigning standard output to a printer. If standard output is assigned to the monitor, then the input and output will be interleaved, as shown in the output. Note that you must press CTRL-C to end the program.

Program 10-8 | Print selected sentences

```
1   /* Echo keyboard input that begins with capital letter.
2      Written by:
3      Date written:
4   */
5   #include <ctype.h>
6
7   #include <stdio.h>
8   int main (void)
9   {
```

(continue)

Program 10-8 Print selected sentences *(continued)*

```
10 // Local Declarations
11    char strng[81];
12
13 // Statements
14    while (fgets (strng, sizeof(strng), stdin))
15       if (isupper(*strng))
16          fputs(strng, stdout);
17    return 0;
18 } // main
```

Output

```
Now is the time
Now is the time
for all good students
to come to the aid
of their school.
Great
Great
```

In this program, we use the character function, isupper, to determine which lines we want to write. In Program 10-8, the Output shows one of the entered lines spanning multiple lines. Although we are guarding against excessive input, we do not flush the line. If the user enters very long lines, they will be obvious when the program runs.

If you use this program or any variation of it to write to your printer, you will need to assign the printer to the standard output file. Refer to the documentation for your system to determine how to do this.

Program 10-9 reads a single-spaced text from a file and prints the text double spaced. In other words, it inserts a blank line after each line. In this program we direct the output to the standard output file, stdout, which is usually the monitor. To get the output to a printer, you need to redirect the output or assign stdout to the printer.

Program 10-9 | Print file double spaced

```
1  /* Write file double spaced.
2     Written by:
3     Date:
4  */
5  #include <stdio.h>
6
7  #include <stdlib.h>
8  int main (void)
9  {
10 // Local Declarations
11    char strng[81];
```

(continue)

Program 10-9   Print file double spaced *(continued)*

```
12      FILE* textln;
13
14 // Statements
15      if (!(textln = fopen("P1010-07.TXT", "r")))
16      {
17         printf("\aCan't open text data\n");
18         exit (100);
19      } // if
20      while (fgets(strng, sizeof(strng), textln))
21      {
22         fputs(strng, stdout);
23         putchar ('\n');
24      } // while
25      return 0;
26 }  // main
```

Because we are reading data from a text file, we use the `fgets` function. This function guarantees that we will not overrun our input string variable. Note how we used the `sizeof` operator to set the maximum number of characters to be read. Since `fgets` adds a newline character at the end of the data being read, we don't need to worry about adding one when we write. After writing the data string, we use a `putchar` to write the blank line.

10.4 Arrays of Strings

When we discussed arrays and pointers in Chapter 9, we introduced the concept of a ragged array. Ragged arrays are very common with strings. Consider, for example, the need to store the days of the week in their textual format. We could create a two-dimensional array of seven days by ten characters (Wednesday requires nine characters), but this wastes space.

It is much easier and more efficient to create a ragged array using an array of string pointers. Each pointer points to a day of the week. In this way each string is independent, but at the same time, they are grouped together through the array. In other words, although each string is independent, we can pass them as a group to a function by passing only the name of the array of pointers. **Program 10-10** demonstrates this structure.

Program 10-10 | Print days of the week

```
1   /* Demonstrates an array of pointers to strings.
2      Written by:
3      Date written:
4   */
5
6   #include <stdio.h>
7   int main (void)
8   {
```

(continue)

Program 10-10   Print days of the week *(continued)*

```
 9  // Local Declarations
10     char* pDays[7];
11     char** pLast;
12
13  // Statements
14     pDays[0] =   "Sunday";
15     pDays[1] =   "Monday";
16     pDays[2] =   "Tuesday";
17     pDays[3] =   "Wednesday";
18     pDays[4] =   "Thursday";
19     pDays[5] =   "Friday";
20     pDays[6] =   "Saturday";
21
22     printf("The days of the week\n");
23     pLast = pDays + 6;
24     for (char** pWalker = pDays;
25          pWalker <= pLast;
26          pWalker++)
27        printf("%s\n", *pWalker);
28     return 0;
29  } // main
```

To print the days of the week, we use a `for` loop. Since `pDays` is a pointer constant, we also need a pointer variable to use pointer arithmetic. The pointer variable must point to the strings through `pDays`, which means that it will be a pointer to a pointer, as seen in statement 11.

A point of efficiency is the way we handled the limit test in the `for` loop. We could have simply coded it as

    pWalker <= pDays + 6.

This would require, however, that the ending address be recalculated for each limit test. (A good optimizing compiler should recognize that `pDays` is a pointer constant and that the calculation needs to be done only once, but we can't be sure that such efficient code would in fact be generated.) Therefore, we calculate the ending address just once, before the `while` loop, and then we can be sure that the limit test will be efficient.

Study this code carefully. Note first that `pWalker` is a pointer to a pointer to a character. Then notice how it is used in the `for` statement. It is initialized to the first element in `pDays`, then it is incremented until it is no longer less than or equal to `pLast`. Finally, note how it is used in the `printf` statement. The `printf` syntax requires that the variable list contain the address of the string to be printed. But `pWalker` is a pointer to an address that in turn points to the string (a pointer to a pointer). Therefore, when we dereference `pWalker`, we get the pointer to the string, which is what `printf` requires. This example is diagrammed in **Figure 10-13**.

10.5 String Manipulation Functions

Because a wstring is not a standard type, we cannot use it directly with most C operators. For example, to move one string to another, we must move the individual elements of the sending string to the receiving string. We cannot simply assign one string to another. If we were to write the move, we would have to put it in a loop.

Figure 10-13 Pointers to strings

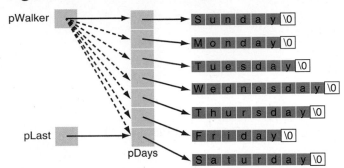

C provides a rich set of string functions. Besides making it easier for us to write programs, putting the string operations in functions provides the opportunity to make them more efficient when the operation is supported by hardware instructions. For example, computers often have a machine instruction that moves characters until a token, such as a null character, is reached. When this instruction is available, it allows a string to be moved in one instruction rather than in a loop.

In addition to the string character functions, C provides a parallel set of functions for wide characters. They are virtually identical except for the type. Because wide characters are not commonly used and because the functions operate identically, we limit our discussion to the character type. The traditional string functions have a prefix of `str`. The basic format is shown in the following.

```
int str... (parameters)
```

The string character functions are found in the string library (`string.h`).

String Length

The string length function, `strlen`, returns the length of a string, specified as the number of characters in the string excluding the null character. If the string is empty, it returns zero. The function declaration is shown below.

```
int strlen (const char* string);
```

To demonstrate the use of string length, let's write a program that reads text from the keyboard, line by line, and adds two blanks (spaces) at the beginning of each line before writing it to a file. In other words, it shifts each line two characters to the right. The code is shown in **Program 10-11**.

Program 10-11 | Add left margin

```
1   /* Typewriter program: adds two spaces to the left
2      margin and writes line to file
3      Written by:
4      Date:
5   */
6   #include <stdio.h>
7   #include <stdlib.h>
8   #include <string.h>
9
10  int main (void)
```

(continue)

Program 10-11   Add left margin *(continued)*

```
11 {
12 // Local Declarations
13    FILE* spOutFile;
14    char strng[81];
15
16 // Statements
17    if (!(spOutFile = fopen("P10-10.TXT", "w")))
18    {
19       printf("\aCould not open output file.\n");
20       exit (100);
21    } // if
22
23    while (fgets(strng, sizeof(strng), stdin))
24    {
25       fputc(' ', spOutFile);
26       fputc(' ', spOutFile);
27       fputs(strng, spOutFile);
28       if (strng[strlen(strng) - 1] != '\n')
29          fputs("\n", spOutFile);
30    } // while
31    fclose (spOutFile);
32    return  0;
33 } // main
```

To ensure that the user doesn't overrun the input area, we use the `fgets` function to read the keyboard. Some data may be left in the buffer, but we don't flush the buffer, because we want to write them to the file on the next line.

Also, since `fputs` does not add a newline when it writes the file, we need to ensure that there will be a new line at the end of each line. Therefore, in statement 28 we test the last character of the input string and if it isn't a newline, we write one.

Because we want to add characters to the beginning of the line, we must use a character operation. The function `fputc` writes one character to a designated file. To insert two characters, therefore, we use it twice, and then use `fputs` to write the line read by `fgets`.

String Copy

C has two string copy functions. The first, `strcpy`, copies the contents of one string to another. The second, `strncpy`, also copies the contents of one string to another, but it sets a maximum number of characters that can be moved. Therefore, `strncpy` is a safer function.

Basic String Copy

The string copy function, `strcpy`, copies the contents of the from string, including the null character, to the string. Its function declaration is shown below.

```
char* strcpy (char* toStr, const char* fromStr);
```

If fromStr is longer than `toStr`, the data in memory after `toStr` are destroyed. It is our responsibility to ensure that the destination string array is large enough to hold the sending string. This should not be a problem, since we control the definition of both string variables. The address of `toStr` is returned, which allows string functions to be used as arguments inside other string functions. We will demonstrate the use of these returned pointers later in the chapter.

Figure 10-14 shows two examples of string copy. In the first example, the source string is shorter than the destination variable. The result is that, after the string has been copied, the contents of the last three bytes of `s1` are unchanged; `s1` is a valid string, however.

Figure 10-14   String copy

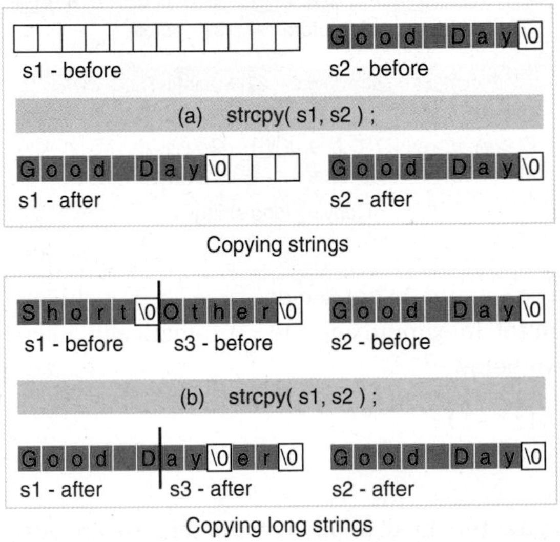

Copying strings

Copying long strings

In the second example in Figure 10-14, the destination variable, `s1`, is only 6 bytes, which is too small to hold all the data being copied from `s2` (8 bytes plus the delimiter). Furthermore, `s1` is immediately followed by another string, `s3`. Even though `s1` is too small, the entire string from `s2` is copied, partially destroying the data in `s3`. Although `s1` is a valid string, any attempt to access the data in `s3` will result in a string containing only ay.

If the source and destination strings overlap—that is, if they share common memory locations, then the results of the copy are unpredictable. In Figure 10-14, this would occur if we tried to execute the following statement:

```
strcpy((s2 + 2), s2);    // Invalid copy-overlap
```

String Copy—Length Controlled

Many of the problems associated with unequal string-array sizes can be controlled with the string-number copy function, `strncpy`. This function contains a parameter that specifies the *maximum* number of characters that can be moved at a time, as shown in its function declaration below.

```
char* strncpy (char* toStr, const char* fromStr, int size);
```

In this function, `size` specifies the maximum number of characters that can be moved. Actually, the operation is a little more complex. If the size of the from string is equal to or greater than `size`, then `size` characters are moved. If the from string is smaller than size, the entire string is copied and then null characters are inserted into the destination string until exactly `size` characters have been copied. Thus, it is more correct to think of `size` as the destination characters that must be filled.

If the sending string is longer than `size`, the copy stops after `size` bytes have been copied. In this case, the destination variable may not be a valid string; that is, it may not have a delimiter. The string number copy functions *do not* insert a delimiter if the from string is longer than `size`. On the other hand, the data following the destination variable will be intact, assuming the size was properly specified. **Figure 10-15** shows the operation of `strncpy` under these two conditions.

Figure 10-15 String-number copy

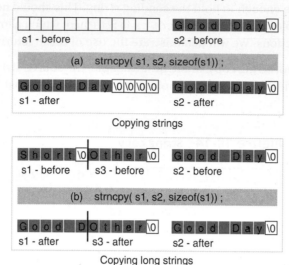

Copying strings

Copying long strings

We recommend that you always use `strncpy`; do not use `strcpy`. To prevent invalid strings, we also recommend that you move one fewer characters than the maximum and then automatically place a null character in the last position. The code for this technique is shown below.

```
strncpy(s1, s2, sizeof(s1) -1);
*(s1 + (sizeof (s1) - 1)) = '\0';
```

Because the `strncpy` places null characters in all unfilled characters, we are guaranteed that the last character in the string array is a null character. If it is not, then the copy was short. By executing the above statements, we are assured that `s1` will be a valid string, even if it doesn't have the desired contents.

A closing note: If size is zero or negative, nothing is copied. The destination string is unchanged. It is recommended to use always `strncpy` to copy one string to another.

Let's write a small program that uses the `strcpy` function. **Program 10-12** builds an array of strings in dynamic memory using the `calloc` function (see Chapter 9). It then fills the array from strings entered at the keyboard. When the array is full, it displays the strings to show that they were entered and stored correctly.

Program 10-12 | Build name array in heap

```
1   /* Build a dynamic array of names.
2      Written by:
3      Date:
4   */
5   #include <stdio.h>
6   #include <stdlib.h>
7   #include <string.h>
8
9   #define FLUSH while (getchar() != '\n')
10
11  int main (void)
```

(continue)

Program 10-12   Build name array in heap *(continued)*

```c
12 {
13 // Local Declarations
14    char input[81];
15    char** pNames;     // array of pointers to char
16
17    int size;
18    int namesIndex;
19
20 // Statements
21    printf ("How many names do you plan to input? ");
22    scanf ("%d", &size);
23    FLUSH;
24
25    // Allocate array in heap.
26    // One extra element added for loop control
27    pNames = calloc (size + 1, sizeof (char*));
28    printf("Enter names:\n");
29
30    namesIndex = 0;
31    while (namesIndex < size
32           && fgets(input, sizeof(input), stdin))
33    {
34      *(pNames + namesIndex) = (char*)
35               calloc (strlen(input) + 1, sizeof(char));
36      strcpy (*(pNames + namesIndex), input);
37      namesIndex++;
38    } // while
39
40    *(pNames + namesIndex) = NULL;
41    printf("\nYour names are: \n");
42    namesIndex = 0;
43    while (*(pNames + namesIndex))
44    {
45      printf("%3d: %s",
46             namesIndex, *(pNames + namesIndex));
47      namesIndex++;
48    } // while
49    return 0;
50 } // main
```

Output

```
How many names do you plan to input? 3
Enter names:
Tom
```

(continue)

Program 10-12   Build name array in heap *(continued)*

```
      Rico
      Huang
      Your names are:
      0:  Tom
      1:  Rico
      2:  Huang
```

This little 50-line program contains some rather difficult code. To understand it better, let's look at the array structure, shown in **Figure 10-16**.

Figure 10-16   Structure for names array

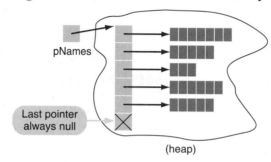

The identifier, pNames, is a pointer to an array of pointers to a character that is dynamically allocated from the heap. Then, as each name is read, space is allocated from the heap, and its pointer is placed in the next location in the pNames array. The only way to refer to the names is by dereferencing pNames. To access an individual element, we use pNames and index it to get to an individual string pointer in the array. This code is shown in statement 36. Since the first parameter in string copy is a pointer to a string, only one dereference is required.

To build the pointer array, we use a while loop with two limit tests: end-of-file and a full array. Either condition will stop the loading of the array. To print the array, however, we only need to test for a null pointer, since the pointer array is allocated with one extra element. Using an extra element is a common programming technique that makes processing arrays of pointers easier and more efficient.

String Compare

As with the string copy functions, C has two string compare functions. The first, strcmp, compares two strings until unequal characters are found or until the end of the strings is reached. The second, strncmp, compares until unequal characters are found, a specified number of characters have been tested, or until the end of a string is reached.

Both functions return an integer to indicate the results of the compare. Unfortunately, the results returned do not map well to the true–false logical values that we see in the if ... else statement, so you will need to memorize a new set of rules:

1. If the two strings are equal, the return value is *zero*. Two strings are considered equal if they are the same length and all characters in the same relative positions are equal.

2. If the first parameter is less than the second parameter, the return value is less than zero. A string, s1, is less than another string, s2, if starting from the first character, we can find a character in s1 that is less than the character in s2. Note that when the end of either string is reached, the null character is compared with the corresponding character in the other string.

3. If the first parameter is greater than the second parameter, the return value is *greater than zero*. A string, s1, is greater than string, s2, if starting from the first character, we can find a character in s2 that is greater than the corresponding character in s1. Note that when the end of either string is reached, the null character is compared with the corresponding character in the other string.

Note that the not-equal values are specified as a range. If the first parameter is less than the second parameter, the value can be any negative value. Likewise, if the first parameter is greater than the second parameter, the value can be any positive number. This differs from other situations, such as EOF, where we can rely on one given value being returned.

The string compare operation is shown in **Figure 10-17**.

Figure 10-17 String compares

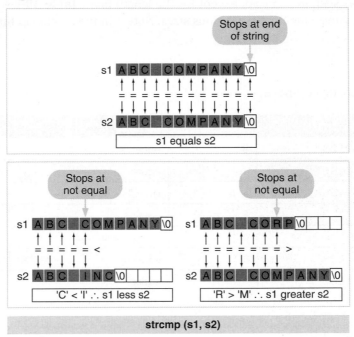

strcmp (s1, s2)

strcmp

The function declaration for the string compare function is shown below.

```
int strcmp (const char* str1, const char* str2);
```

While the string compare functions return integer values, (<=1, 0, >=1), we can code a logical expression that returns true or false by using the compare function and relational operators. For example, to compare two strings for equal, we must write the statement as shown below.

```
if (strcmp(str1, str2) == 0)
    // strings are equal else
else
    // strings are not equal
```

The following statement tests whether the first string is less than the second string.

```
if (strcmp (string1, string2) < 0)
    // string1 is less than string2
```

To test for string1 greater than string2, use the following code:

```
if (strcmp (string1, string2) > 0)
    // string1 is greater than string2
```

We can also test for greater than or equal to with the following statement:

```
if (strcmp (string1, string2) >= 0)
    // string1 is greater than or equal to string2
```

strncmp

The string number compare function, `strncmp`, tests two strings for a specified maximum number of characters (`size`). The function declarations are shown below.

```
int strncmp (const char* str1, const char* str2, int size);
```

In this function, `size` specifies the maximum number of characters to be compared in the first string. The `strncmp` compare logic is the same as seen in `strcmp`, except for the length limit. **Table 10-1** shows the results of comparing two strings using the `strncmp` function for various sizes. Note n in the `strncmp` functions indicates number of characters to be compared.

Table 10-1   Results for string compare

STRING1	STRING2	SIZE	RESULTS	RETURNS
"ABC123"	"ABC123"	8	equal	0
"ABC123"	"ABC456"	3	equal	0
"ABC123"	"ABC456"	4	string1 < string2	<0
"ABC123"	"ABC"	3	equal	0
"ABC123"	"ABC"	4	string1 > string2	>0
"ABC"	"ABC123"	3	equal	0
"ABC123"	"123ABC"	−1	equal	0

String Concatenate

The string concatenate functions append one string to the end of another. They return the address pointers to the destination string. The size of the destination string array is assumed to be large enough to hold the resulting string. If it isn't, the data at the end of the string array are destroyed. As we saw with string copy, the results are unpredictable if the strings overlap.

Basic String Concatenation

The function declaration for string concatenation, `strcat`, is shown below.

```
char* strcat (char* str1, const char* str2);
```

The function copies `str2` to the end of `str1`, beginning with `str1`'s delimiter. That is, the delimiter is replaced with the first character of `str2`. The delimiter from `str2` is copied to the resulting string to ensure that a valid string results. The length of the resulting string is the sum of the length of `str1` plus the length of `str2`. **Figure 10-18**a shows the operation.

String Concatenation—Length Controlled

The function declaration for length-controlled string concatenate function, `strncat`, is shown below.

```
char* strncat (char* str1, const char* str2, int size);
```

Figure 10-18b demonstrates the operation of the `strncat` function. If the length of `string2` is less than `size`, then the call works the same as the basic string concatenation described above. However, if the length of `string2` is greater than `size`, then only the number of characters specified by size are copied, and a null character is appended at the end.

If the value of size is zero or less than zero, then both strings are treated as null, and no characters are moved. The variable `string1` is unchanged.

Figure 10-18   String concatenation

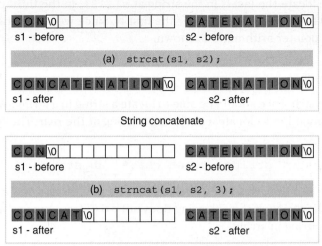

Character in String

Sometimes we need to find the location of a character in a string. Two string functions search for a character in a string. The first function is called string character `strchr`; it searches for the first occurrence of a character from the beginning of the string. The second string rear character called `strrchr`, searches for the first occurrence beginning at the rear and working toward the front.

In either case, if the character is located, the function returns a pointer to it. If the character is not in the string, the function returns a null pointer. The declarations for these functions are shown below.

```
char* strchr (const char* string, int ch);
char* strrchr (const char* string, int ch);
```

Note that, as often is the case in the library functions, the character in the ASCII functions is typed as an integer. We don't need to worry about this. The compiler will implicitly cast any character types to integer types before the call. **Figure 10-19** shows three examples of character-in-string calls.

Figure 10-19   Character in string (`strchr`)

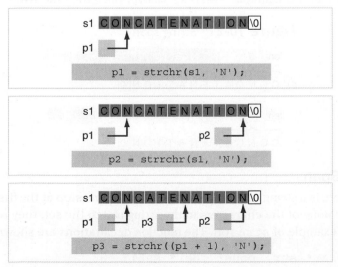

In the first example, we locate the first N at the third position in the string (s1 [2]). The pointer is then assigned to p1. In the second example, we locate the last N in the string at s1[12], In the third example, we want to locate the second N. To do this, we need to start the search after the first N. Since we saved the location of the first N, this is easily done with a pointer and pointer arithmetic as shown.

Search for a Substring

If we can locate a character in a string, we should be able to locate a string in a string. We can, but only from the beginning of the string. There is no function to locate a substring starting at the rear. The function declaration for *strstr* is shown below.

```
char* strstr (const char* string, const char* sub_string);
```

As indicated by the function declaration, this function also returns a pointer to a character. This pointer identifies the beginning of the substring in the string. If the substring does not exist, then they return a null pointer. **Figure 10-20** demonstrates the operation of string in string.

Figure 10-20   String in string

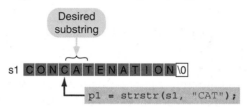

Search for Character in Set

Very often, we need to locate one of a set of characters in a string. C provides two string functions to do this. The first, strspn, locates the first character that does *not* match the string set. The second, strcspn, locates the first character that is in the set.

Basic String Span

The basic string span function, strspn, searches the string, spanning characters that are in the set and stopping at the first character that is not in the set. They return the number of characters that matched those in the set. If no characters match those in the set, they return zero. The function declaration is seen below.

```
int strspn(const char* str, const char* set);
```

An example of string span is shown in **Figure 10-21**. We use strspn to determine the number of characters that match the characters in the string set. In this example, len is set to five, since the first five characters match the set.

Figure 10-21   String span

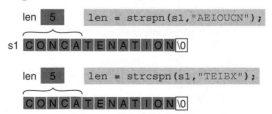

Complemented String Span

The second function, strcspn, is a string *complement* span; its functions stop at the first character that matches one of the characters in the set. If none of the characters in the string match the set, they return the length of the string. Figure 10-21 also contains an example of strcspn. The function declarations are shown below.

```
int strcspn(const char* str, const char* set);
```

String Span—Pointer

Very often, we need a pointer to a substring rather than its index location. C provides a set of functions that return pointers. They operate just like the string complement functions except that they return a pointer to the first character that matches the set. The p in the function names stands for pointer—brk is short for break. As with the complement spans, if no matching characters are found, they return null.

Similar to strcspn, the strpbrk function returns a pointer to the first character found in the set. Its function declaration is shown below.

```
char* strpbrk (const char* str, const char* set);
```

Note	Traditional C has a function called strrpbrk that returns a pointer to the last character found in the set. This function is not part of the ANSI/ISO C function library.

String Token

The string token function, strtok, is used to locate substrings, called tokens, in a string. Its most common use is to parse a string into tokens, much as a compiler parses lines of code. Depending on how it is called, it either locates the first or the next token in a string. Its function declaration statement is shown below.

```
char* strtok (char* str, const char* delimiters);
```

The first parameter is the string that is being parsed; the second parameter is a set of delimiters that will be used to parse the first string. If the first parameter contains an address, then strtok starts at that address, which is assumed to be the beginning of the string. It first skips over all leading delimiter characters. If all the characters in the string are delimiters, then it terminates and returns a null pointer. When it finds a nondelimiter character, it changes its search and skips over all characters that are not in the set; that is, it searches until it finds a delimiter. When a delimiter is found, it is changed to a null character ('\0'), which turns the token just parsed into a string.

If the first parameter is not a string, strtok assumes that it has already parsed part of the string and begins looking at the end of the previous string token for the next delimiter. When a delimiter is located, it again changes the delimiter to a null character, marking the end of the token, and returns a pointer to the new token string.

Let's look at a simple example of a string containing words separated by spaces. We begin by calling the string token with the address of the full string. It returns the address of the first character of the first string that was just parsed. The second execution of the string token function parses the second string and returns its address, and so on until the complete string has been parsed. This design is shown in **Figure 10-22**.

Figure 10-22   Parse a simple string

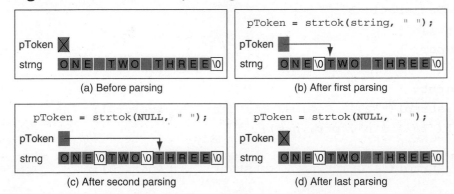

(a) Before parsing

(b) After first parsing

(c) After second parsing

(d) After last parsing

String to Number

The standard library (stdlib.h) provides several functions that convert a string to a number. The two most important are string to long and string to double. A complete list is found at the end of this section.

String to Long

The string-to-long function, strtol, can perform two tasks: (1) convert a string to a long integer; or (2) use strtoul to convert a string to an unsigned long integer. It skips leading whitespace characters and stops with the first nonnumeric character, which is considered to be the start of a trailing string. The address of the trailing string is stored in the second parameter, unless it is a null pointer. A third parameter determines the base of the string number. The function declaration is shown below.

```
long strtol (char* str, char** ptr, int base);
```

The base is determined by the following rules:

1. The base may be 0 or 2 ... 35.

2. The letters a ... z or A ... Z represent the values 10 ... 35. Only the numeric and alphabetic characters less than the base are permitted in any string.

3. If the base is 0, the format is determined by the string as follows:

   a. If the number begins **0x** or **0X,** the number is a hexadecimal constant.

   b. If the first digit is 0 and the second digit is not **x** or **X,** the number is an octal constant.

   c. If the first digit is a nonzero, the number is a decimal constant.

If the string does not begin with a valid number, zero is returned and the trailing string pointer is set to the beginning of the string. **Program 10-13** demonstrates the use of strtol.

| Program 10-13 | Demonstrate string to long |

```
1   /* Demonstrate string to long function.
2      Written by:
3      Date:
4   */
5   #include <stdio.h>
6
7   #include <stdlib.h>
8   int main (void)
9   {
10  // Local Declarations
11     long num;
12     char* ptr;
13
14  // Statements
15     num = strtol ("12345 Decimal constant: ", &ptr, 0);
16     printf ("%s %ld\n", ptr, num);
17
18     num = strtol ("11001 Binary constant:  ", &ptr, 2);
```

(continue)

Program 10-13 Demonstrate string to long *(continued)*

```
19      printf("%s %ld\n", ptr, num);
20
21      num = strtol("13572 Octal constant:     ", &ptr, 8);
22      printf("%s %ld\n", ptr, num);
23
24      num = strtol("7AbC Hex constant:       ", &ptr, 16);
25      printf("%s %ld\n", ptr, num);
26
27      num = strtol("11001 Base 0-Decimal:    ", &ptr, 0);
28      printf("%s %ld\n", ptr, num);
29
30      num = strtol("01101 Base 0-Octal:      ", &ptr, 0);
31      printf("%s %ld\n", ptr, num);
32
33      num = strtol("0x7AbC Base 0-Hex:       ", &ptr, 0);
34      printf("%s %ld\n", ptr, num);
35
36      num = strtol("Invalid input: ", &ptr, 0);
37      printf("%s %ld\n", ptr, num);
38
39      return 0;
40  } // main
```

```
Output
Decimal constant:  12345
Binary constant:   25
Octal constant:    6010
Hex constant:      31420
Base 0-Decimal:    11001
Base 0-Octal:      577
Base 0-Hex:        31420
Invalid input:  0
```

The first thing to note in this program is that the address of the character pointer must be passed to strtol. If this surprises you, go back and look at the strtol function declaration statement again. Note that the declaration of ptr has two asterisks.

Observe that the pointer is set to the first character after the last valid digit. In our example, this character was always a space. If there were no characters after the last digit, the pointer would point to the string delimiter, resulting in a null string.

String to Double

The string-to-double functions—strtod and wcstod—are similar to the string-to-long functions, except that they do not have a base. The function declaration is seen below.

```
double strtod (char* str, char** ptr);
```

The numeric string must be a floating-point in either decimal or scientific notation. The valid numeric values in the string are the digits, the plus and minus signs, and the letter e or E in the exponent. After using the longest possible sequence of digits and characters to convert the string to a number, strtod sets the pointer to the address of the next character in the string. If no characters are present, the pointer is set to the string delimiter. As with string-to-long, if the number is invalid, zero is returned and the pointer is set to the beginning of the string.

Other Number Functions

Table 10-2 lists the complete set of string-to-number functions.

Table 10-2   String-to-number functions

NUMERIC FORMAT	ASCII FUNCTION	WIDE-CHARACTER FUNCTION
Double	strtod	wcstod
Float	strtof	wcstof
long double	strtold	wcstold
long int	strtol	wcstol
long long int	strtoll	wcstoll
unsigned long int	strtoul	wcstoul
unsigned long long int	strtoull	wcstoull

String Examples

In this section, we discuss two functions that use string functions. The first uses strtok to parse an algebraic expression. The second uses string input/output functions and several string manipulation functions to compare strings.

Assume we want to parse a string containing a simple algebraic expression as shown below.

```
sum = sum + 10;
```

Each token in this simple expression is separated by whitespace. Our program will identify each token and print it out. The step-by-step parsing is shown in **Figure 10-23**. The code is shown in **Program 10-14**.

Figure 10-23   Parsing with string token

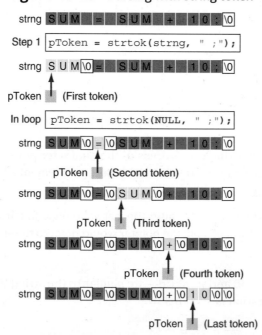

Program 10-14 | Parsing a string with string token

```c
1  /* Parse a simple algebraic expression.
2     Written by:
3     Date:
4  */
5  #include <stdio.h>
6  #include <string.h>
7
8  int main (void)
9  {
10 // Local Declarations
11    char string [16] = "sum = sum + 10;";
12    char* pToken;
13    int tokenCount;
14
15 // Statements
16    tokenCount = 0;
17    pToken = strtok (string, " ;");
18
19    while (pToken)
20    {
21       tokenCount++;
22       printf("Token %2d contains %s\n",
23               tokenCount, pToken);
24       pToken = strtok (NULL, " ;");
25    } // while
26
27    printf("End of tokens\n");
28    return 0;
29 } // main
```

Output
```
Token  1 contains sum
Token  2 contains =
Token  3 contains sum
Token  4 contains +
Token  5 contains 10
End of tokens
```

Since the first call to strtok must contain the address of the string, it is coded *before* the loop. If the string contains at least one token, the first call will return a valid address and the while loop will print it and parse out the remaining tokens. Note that the delimiter set includes the semicolon as well as the blank between tokens. The semicolon serves as the last token in the string.

Compare Packed Strings

When working with strings, we often find that two strings are logically the same but physically different to the computer. For example, consider a program that generates mailing labels. Often a name is put into a mailing list with an extra space or other character that prevents it from being matched to an existing name. One way to eliminate such errors is to compare only the letters of the names by removing everything except alphabetic characters. **Program 10-15** shows a function that compares two strings after packing the data so that only letters are left.

Program 10-15 | Compare packed string function

```
 1  /* This program packs and compares a string.
 2     Written by:
 3     Date:
 4  */
 5  #include <stdio.h>
 6  #include <string.h>
 7
 8  #define ALPHA \
 9  "ABCDEFGHIJKLMNOPQRSTUVWXYZabcdefghijklmnopqrstuvwxyz"
10
11  // Function Declarations
12  int strCmpPk (char* S1, char* S2);
13  void strPk (char* s1, char* s2);
14
15  int main (void)
16  {
17  // Local Declarations
18     int  cmpResult;
19     char s1[80];
20     char s2[80];
21
22  // Statements
23     printf("Please enter first string:\n");
24     fgets (s1, 80, stdin);
25     s1[strlen(s1) - 1] = '\0';
26
27     printf("Please enter second string:\n");
28     fgets (s2, 80, stdin);
29     s2[strlen(s2) - 1] = '\0';
30
31     cmpResult = strCmpPk (s1, s2);
```

(continue)

Program 10-15   Compare packed string function *(continued)*

```
32      if (cmpResult < 0)
33          printf ("string1 < string2\n");
34      else if (cmpResult > 0)
35          printf ("string1 > string2\n");
36      else
37          printf ("string1 == string2\n");
38
39      return 0;
40 } // main
41
42 /* =================== strCmpPk ===================
43      Packs two strings and then compares them.
44      Pre s1 and s2 contain strings
45      Post returns result of strcmp of packed strings
46 */
47 int strCmpPk (char* s1, char* s2)
48 {
49 // Local Declarations
50      char s1In [80];
51      char s1Out[81];
52      char s2In [80];
53      char s2Out[81];
54
55 // Statements
56      strncpy (s1In, s1, sizeof(s1In) - 1);
57      strncpy (s2In, s2, sizeof(s2In) - 1);
58      strPk (s1In, s1Out);
59      strPk (s2In, s2Out);
60      return (strcmp (s1Out, s2Out));
61 } // strCmpPk
62
63 /*=================== strPk===================
64    Deletes all non-alpha characters from s1 and
65    copies to s2.
66    Pre s1 is a string
67    Post packed string in s2
68    S1 destroyed
69 */
70 void strPk (char* s1, char* s2)
71 {
72 // Local Declarations
73      int strSize;
74
```

(continue)

Program 10-15   Compare packed string function *(continued)*

```
75 // Statements
76    *s2 = '\0';
77    while (*s1 != '\0')
78    {
79    // Find non-alpha character & replace
80       strSize = strspn(s1, ALPHA);
81       s1[strSize] = '\0';
82       strncat (s2, s1, 79 - strlen(s2));
83       s1 += strSize + 1;
84    } // while
85    return;
86 } //strPk
```

Output

```
Please enter first string:
a b!c 234d
Please enter second string:
abcd
string1 == string2
Please enter first string:
Abcd
Please enter second string:
aabb
string1 > string2
```

To test the string compare, we need to write a test driver. Since the test driver is throw-away code, we have coded the test logic in `main`.

Statement 8 contains a C language construct that we have not used before: the *statement continuation*. When a statement does not fit on a line, it can be continued by putting an escape character (\) immediately before the end of the line. This is consistent with the meaning of the escape character; in this case, it means escape the end of line that follows; it is not really an end of line. This allows us to continue the *define* statement on the next line.

Since we are passing addresses to strings, we need to be careful that we don't destroy the original data. The first thing we do in `strCmpPk`, therefore, is to use `strncpy` to copy the input string to a work area. After we have protected the original data, we pack the two strings to be compared and then use the `strcmp` function to determine if the reformatted data are equal.

The `strPk` function merits a little discussion. It uses a `while` loop to process the input string. Each iteration of the loop scans the valid characters, as defined in `ALPHA`, looking for invalid data. When `strPk` finds an invalid character—and there will always be at least one, the input string delimiter—it (1) replaces that character with a string delimiter, (2) concatenates the input string to the output string, and then (3) adjusts the input string pointer to one past the last scanned character. This is necessary to point it to the data beyond the string just copied.

But what if the pointer adjustment puts it beyond the end of the input data? In that case, we will have a delimiter, because we used `strncpy` to copy the data from the original input, and it pads the output string with delimiters.

Therefore, the character after the original string delimiter is another delimiter. Note that we made the output area one character larger than the input area to provide for this extra delimiter even with a full string.

At least three test cases are required to test the program. We show two of them in the result. In addition to an equal and greater-than result, you should conduct at least one less-than test case.

10.6 String/Data Conversion

A common set of applications format data by either converting a sequence of characters into corresponding data types or vice versa. Two such applications are parsing and telecommunications.

C already has an extensive set of data conversion functions created for `scanf` and `printf`. The C standard also includes two sets of memory formatting functions, one for ASCII characters and one for wide characters, that uses these same formatting functions. Rather than reading and write files, however, they "read" and "write" strings in memory.

String to Data Conversion

The string scan function is called `sscanf`. This function scans a string as though the data were coming from a file. Just like `fscanf`, it requires a format string to provide the formatting parameters for the data. All `fscanf` format codes are valid for the scan memory functions. Like `fscanf`, the scan memory functions also return the number of variables successfully formatted. If they reach the end of a string before all the format string conversion codes have been used—that is, if they attempt to "read" beyond the end of string—they return an end-of-file flag. The basic concept is shown in **Figure 10-24**.

Figure 10-24   *sscanf* operation

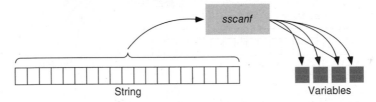

The function declaration is shown below.

```
int sscanf (char* str, const char* frmt_str, ...);
```

The first parameter specifies the string holding the data to be scanned. The ellipsis (. . .) indicates that a variable number of pointers identify the fields into which the formatted data are to be placed.

Let's demonstrate the use of `sscanf` with an example. Assume that we have a string that contains a name terminated with a semicolon, a four-digit student number, an exam score, and a character grade. Each field is separated from the rest by at least one whitespace character. A data sample is shown below.

```
Einstein, Albert; 1234 97 A
```

In this problem, we want to format the name and student number as strings, the score as an integer, and the grade as a character. We therefore construct the following format string:

```
"%49[^;] %*c %4s %d %*[^ABCDF] %c"
```

Let's examine each format code individually. First, we are expecting a string of up to 49 characters terminated by a semicolon. Note that we use the scan set with a terminating token of a semicolon. Following the scan set that reads to a semicolon is a format code that reads and discards one character. The asterisk is a flag indicating that the character is not to be stored. This code is necessary because the terminating semicolon from the string remains in the input string. We need to read and discard it.

The third format code is a simple four-character string. Any leading whitespace is discarded with the string token (). Likewise, the third field, the score, is converted to an integer format after the leading whitespace is discarded.

Parsing the grade is a little more difficult. We can have one or more whitespaces between the numeric grade and the alphabetic grade, but we must dispose of them ourselves, because the character token (%c) does not discard whitespace. Our solution is to use a scan set with the suppress flag (*) to discard all characters up to the grade. Again, we use the negation to set the terminating character. Having discarded all the leading whitespace, we can now format the grade with a character token.

Using our example above, we can code the sscanf call as shown below.

```
sscanf(strIn, "%25[^*;]%*c%4s%d%*[^ABCDF]%c", name, stuNo, &score, &grade);
```

Note that this code has six format codes but only four variables because the second and fifth fields have their formatting suppressed. You may use sscanf in a one-to-many function that splits one string into many variables.

Data to String Conversion

The string print function, sprintf, follows the rules of fprintf. Rather than sending the data to a file, however, it simply "writes" them to a string. When all data have been formatted to the string, a terminating null character is added to make the result a valid string. If an error is detected, sprintf returns any negative value, traditionally EOF. If the formatting is successful, it returns the number of characters formatted, not counting the terminating null character. The string print operation is shown in **Figure 10-25**.

Figure 10-25 sprintf operation

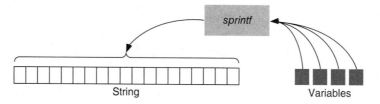

The function declaration for formatting memory strings is shown below.

```
int sprintf (char* out_string,
             const char* format_string, ...);
```

The first parameter is a pointer to a string that will contain the formatted output. The format string is the same as printf and follows all of the same rules. The ellipsis (. . .) contains the fields that correspond to the format codes in the format string.

It is our responsibility to ensure that the output string is large enough to hold all the formatted data. If it is not large enough, sprintf destroys memory contents after the output string variable. The wide-character function, swprintf, on the other hand limits the output. The additional parameter, max_out, specifies the maximum wide characters. It should be noted that sprintf is a many-to-one function. It joins many pieces of data into one string.

To demonstrate the memory formatting functions, we first format a string to variables and print them. We then format them back to a string and print the string. The data use the format described in "String to Data Conversion." The code is seen in **Program 10-16**.

As a practical example, let's write a program that, given two Internet addresses, determines all of the addresses in their range. An Internet address is a 4-byte Dotted Decimal Notation address in the form X.Y.Z.T. Each byte can have a decimal value between 0 and 255.

To determine the range, we multiply each portion of the address by 256 and add it to a counter. The second address is then subtracted from the first, which gives the number of addresses in the range.

Program 10-16 | Demonstrate memory formatting

```c
1   /* Demonstrate memory formatting.
2      Written by:
3      Date:
4   */
5
6   #include <stdio.h>
7   int main (void)
8   {
9   // Local Declarations
10     char string[80] = "Einstein, Albert; 1234 97 A";
11     char stringOut[80];
12     char name[50];
13     char id[5];
14     int score;
15     char grade;
16
17  // Statements
18     printf ("String contains: \"%s\"\n" , string);
19
20     sscanf(string, "%49[^;] %*c %4s %d %c",
21     name, id, &score, &grade);
22
23     printf("Reformatted data: \n" );
24     printf(" Name: \"%s\"\n", name);
25     printf(" id: \"%s\"\n", id);
26     printf(" score: %d\n", score);
27     printf(" grade: %c\n", grade);
28
29     sprintf(stringOut, "%s %4s %3d %c",
30     name, id, score, grade);
31     printf("New string: \"%s\n", stringOut);
32     return 0;
33  } // main
```

Output

```
String contains:  "Einstein, Albert; 1234 97 A"
Reformatted Data:
 Name: "Einstein, Albert "
 id: "1234"
 score: 97
 grade: A
New String: "Einstein, Albert 1234 97 A"
```

This program could be used by system administrators when their organization is given a range of addresses. For example, if an organization is given the range of address 193.78.64.0 to 193.78.66.255, the system administrator needs to know how many addresses are available for computers to be connected to the Internet. **Program 10-17** answers this question.

Program 10-17 | Determine Internet addresses in a range

```
1   /* Given two Internet addresses, determine the number
2      of unique addresses in their range.
3      Written by:
4      Date:
5   */
6   #include <stdio.h>
7   #include <stdlib.h>
8
9   int main (void) {
10
11  // Local Declarations
12     unsigned int    strt[4];
13     unsigned int    end[4];
14     unsigned long   add1 = 0;
15     unsigned long   add2 = 0;
16     unsigned long   range;
17
18     char addr1[15];
19     char addr2[15];
20
21  // Statements
22     printf ("Enter first address: ");
23     fgets (addr1 , sizeof (addr1), stdin);
24
25     printf ("Enter second address: ");
26     fgets (addr2 , sizeof (addr2) , stdin);
27
28     sscanf (addr1 , "%d %*c %d %*c %d %*c %d\n",
29             &strt[3], &strt[2], &strt[1], &strt[0]);
30     sscanf (addr2 , "%d %*c %d %*c %d %*c %d\n",
31             &end[3], &end[2], &end[1], &end[0]);
32
33     for (int i = 3; i >= 0; i--)
34     {
35        add1 = add1 * 256 + strt[i];
36        add2 = add2 * 256 + end[i];
37     } // for
```

(continue)

Program 10-17   Determine Internet addresses in a range *(continued)*

```
38      range = abs (add1 - add2) + 1;
39
40      printf ("First Address: %s", addr1);
41      printf ("\nSecond Address %s", addr2);
42      printf ("\nThe range: %ld", range);
43
44      return 0;
45 } // main
```

Output
```
Enter first address: 23.56.34.0
Enter second address: 23.56.32.255
First Address: 23.56.34.0
Second Address: 23.56.32.255
The range: 258
```

Programming Example: Morse Code

Morse code, patented by Samuel F. B. Morse in 1837, is the language that was used to send messages by telegraph from the middle of the nineteenth century until the advent of the modern telephone and today's computer-controlled communications systems. In Morse code, each letter in the alphabet is represented by a series of dots and dashes, as shown in **Table 10-3**.

TABLE 10-3   Morse code

LETTER	CODE	LETTER	CODE	LETTER	CODE	LETTER	CODE
A	.-	H	....	O	---	V	...-
B	-...	I	..	P	.--.	W	.--
C	-.-.	J	.----	Q	--.-	X	-..-
D	-..	K	-.-	R	.-.	Y	-.--
E	.	L	.-..	S	...	Z	--..
F	..-.	M	--	T	-		
G	--.	N	-.	U	..-		

Program 10-18 encodes (converts) a line of text to Morse code and decodes (converts) Morse code to a line of text. We use a two-dimensional array of pointers in which each row has two string pointers, one to a string containing English characters and one to a string containing the corresponding Morse code. Note that the pointers are stored in the program's memory, while the strings are stored in the heap. The array structure is shown in **Figure 10-26**.

Each column has 27 pointers. Each pointer in the first column points to a string of length one, which contains one English letter (uppercase). Each pointer in the second column points to a string of varying size, a ragged array, which contains the corresponding Morse code for the English letter.

The program is menu driven. The menu, which is shown in **Figure 10-27**, has three options: encode English to Morse code, decode Morse code to English, and quit.

Figure 10-26 Character to Morse code structure

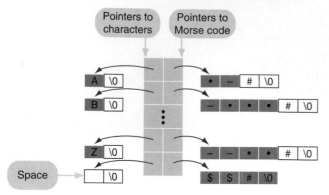

Figure 10-27 Morse code menu

MENU	
E	encode
D	decode
Q	quit
Enter option: press return key:	

The program begins by initializing the conversion table. It then displays the menu and loops until the user quits. Each loop either encodes a line of English text or decodes a line of Morse code. The only allowable characters are the alphabetic characters and spaces. When Morse code is entered, each coded character is terminated by a pound sign (#). Morse code space is represented by two dollar signs ($$). The complete design is shown in **Figure 10-28**.

Figure 10-28 Morse code program design

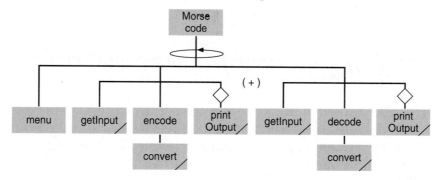

If the encode or decode function detects an error—such as an invalid character or an invalid Morse code sequence—it returns an error code, and the calling program prints an error message.

The solution, as shown in **Program 10-18**, uses three arrays. The first is the encode/decode (encDec) array. As seen in Figure 10-26, this is a two-dimensional array of pointers to English and Morse code values. The second array is an array of 81 characters to hold the input line. The third is an array of 81 characters to hold the output line. To ensure that we do not overrun the output line, we limit the input string to 16 characters when we are reading English text. When appropriate, we provide some analysis to points in the individual functions.

Program 10-18 | Morse code: main

```
1   /* This program packs and compares a string.
2      Written by:
3      Date:
4   */
5   #include <stdio.h>
6   #include <string.h>
7
```

(continue)

Program 10-18   Morse code: main *(continued)*

```
 8   #define ALPHA \
 9   "ABCDEFGHIJKLMNOPQRSTUVWXYZabcdefghijklmnopqrstuvwxyz"
10
11   // Function Declarations
12   int strCmpPk (char* S1, char* S2);
13   void strPk (char* s1, char* s2);
14
15   int main (void)
16   {
17   // Local Declarations
18      int  cmpResult;
19      char s1[80];
20      char s2[80];
21
22   // Statements
23      printf("Please enter first string:\n");
24      fgets (s1, 80, stdin);
25      s1[strlen(s1) - 1] = '\0';
26
27      printf("Please enter second string:\n");
28      fgets (s2, 80, stdin);
29      s2[strlen(s2) - 1] = '\0';
30
31      cmpResult = strCmpPk (s1, s2);
32      if (cmpResult < 0)
33         printf("string1 < string2\n");
34      else if (cmpResult > 0)
35         printf("string1 > string2\n");
36      else
37         printf("string1 == string2\n");
38
39      return 0;
40   } // main
41
42   /* ================== strCmpPk ==================
43      Packs two strings and then compares them.
44      Pre s1 and s2 contain strings
45      Post returns result of strcmp of packed strings
46   */
47   int strCmpPk (char* s1, char* s2)
48   {
49   // Local Declarations
50      char s1In [80];
```

(continue)

Program 10-18   Morse code: main *(continued)*

```
 51      char s1Out[81];
 52      char s2In [80];
 53      char s2Out[81];
 54
 55  // Statements
 56      strncpy (s1In, s1, sizeof(s1In) - 1);
 57      strncpy (s2In, s2, sizeof(s2In) - 1);
 58      strPk (s1In, s1Out);
 59      strPk (s2In, s2Out);
 60      return (strcmp (s1Out, s2Out));
 61  } // strCmpPk
 62
 63  /*==================== strPk=================
 64     Deletes all non-alpha characters from s1 and
 65     copies to s2.
 66     Pre s1 is a string
 67     Post packed string in s2
 68     S1 destroyed
 69  */
 70  void strPk (char* s1, char* s2)
 71  {
 72  // Local Declarations
 73     int strSize;
 74
 75  // Statements
 76     *s2 = '\0';
 77     while (*s1 != '\0')
 78     {
 79        // Find non-alpha character & replace
 80        strSize = strspn(s1, ALPHA);
 81        s1[strSize] = '\0';
 82        strncat (s2, s1, 79 - strlen(s2));
 83        s1 += strSize + 1;
 84     } // while
 85     return;
 86  } // StrPk
```

The function main is rather straightforward. Although it could be argued that the switch statements should be in a subfunction, we place it here because it controls the entire program. One noteworthy point is the default condition. We test for only two options, encode and decode; if it is neither, then we assume quit. We can do this because we validate the option in menu (see **Program 10-19**). At this point in the program, therefore, option can be one of only three values. We test for two and default the third.

Program 10-19 | Morse code: menu

```
1   /* ================menu==================
2       Display menu of choices; return selected character.
3       Pre nothing
4       Post returns validated option code
5   */
6   char menu (void)
7   {
8   // Local Declarations
9       char option;
10      bool validData;
11
12  // Statements
13      printf("\t\t\tM E N U \n");
14      printf("\t\tE) encode \n");
15      printf("\t\tD) decode \n");
16      printf("\t\tQ) quit \n");
17
18      do
19      {
20          printf ("\nEnter option: press return key: ");
21          option = toupper (getchar());
22          FLUSH;
23          if (option == 'E' || option == 'D'||
24              option == 'Q')
25             validData = true;
26          else
27          {
28             validData = false;
29             printf("\aEnter only one option\n");
30             printf(" \tE, D, or Q\n ");
31          } // else
32      } while (!validData);
33      return option;
34  } // menu
```

The menu function in Program 10-19 displays the options and reads the user's choice. It then validates the choice and if invalid, displays an error message and asks for the option again. Although it is always good design to validate the user input, it must be validated in the correct place. Since menu is communicating with the user, this is the logical place to do the validation. One more point: As the option is read, it is converted to uppercase. Not only does this make the validation simpler, but it also simplifies the switch statement in main. Whenever you have a single character code, convert it to uppercase or lowercase for processing in the program.

The input string is read in **Program 10-20**.

Program 10-20 | Morse code: get input

```
 1   /* ==================== getInput ====================
 2       Reads input string to be encoded or decoded.
 3       Pre inStr is a pointer to the input area
 4       Post string read into input area
 5   */
 6   void getlnput (char* inStr)
 7   {
 8   // Statements
 9       printf ("\nEnter line of text to be coded: \n" );
10       fgets (inStr, STR_LEN, stdin);
11
12       // Eliminate newline in input string
13       *(inStr-1 + strlen(inStr)) = '\0';
14
15       if (isalpha(*inStr) && strlen(inStr) > 16)
16       {
17       // Exceeds English input length
18          printf("\n***WARNING: Input length exceeded: ");
19          printf("Only 16 chars will be encoded.\a\a\n");
20          *(inStr + 16) = '\0' ;
21       } // if
22       return;
23   } // getInput
```

Note that to prevent a runaway string in getInput we use the fgets function and specify the maximum number of characters in the string area. This function creates a minor problem, however; it places the newline in the input string. We must, therefore, overlay it with a null character.

The code to print the output of this program is shown in **Program 10-21**.

Program 10-21 | Morse code: print output

```
 1   /* ================== printOutput ==================
 2       Print the input and the transformed output
 3       Pre inStr contains the input data
 4          outStr contains the transformed string
 5       Post output printed
 6   */
 7   void printOutput (char* inStr, char* outStr)
```

(continue)

Program 10-21   Morse code: print output *(continued)*

```
8  {
9  // Statements
10    printf("\nThe information entered was: \n");
11    puts(inStr);
12    printf("\nThe transformed information is: \n");
13    puts(outStr);
14    return;
15 } // printOutput
```

Program 10-22 transforms character data to Morse code.

Program 10-22 | Morse code: encode to Morse

```
1   /* ==================== encode ====================
2      Transforms character data to Morse code
3      Pre  encDec is the conversion table
4      inStr contains data to be put into Morse
5      Post data have been encoded in outSt
6      Return true if all valid characters;
7      false if invalid character found
8   */
9   bool encode (char* (*encDec)[2],
10              char* inStr, char* outStr)
11 {
12 // Local Declarations
13    char s1[2];
14    char s2[6];
15    int error = 0;
16
17 // Statements
18    outStr[0] = '\0';
19    while (*inStr != '\0' && error)
20    {
21       s1[0] = toupper(*inStr);
22       s1[1] = '\0';
23       error = !convert (encDec, s1, 0, s2);
24       strcat (outStr, s2);
25       inStr++;
26    } // while
27    return (!error);
28 } // encode
```

Note how the encode/decode table is declared in the formal parameter list in statement 9. It uses a complex type. To understand it, let's use right–left analysis.

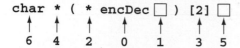

Reading this declaration, at 0 we have encDec. Moving to the right, we find the 1, which is ignored. Moving left, at 2 we find a pointer. We therefore have encDec as a pointer. Moving right to 3, we see that it is a pointer to an array of two. Moving to the left to 4, we see that it is an array of pointers.

At this point, we see that encDec is a pointer to an array of two pointers. Now, moving back to the right, we see that 5 is empty, so we go to the left and find char at 6. The final type is, therefore, a pointer to an array of two pointers to char. Referring back to Figure 10-26, we see that this is exactly what we have.

The code to decode Morse code to English is shown in **Program 10-23**.

Program 10-23 | Morse code: decode to English

```
1   /* ===================== decode =====================
2       Transforms Morse code data to character string
3       Pre encDec is the conversion table
4       inStr contains data to transform to string
5       Post data encoded and placed in outStr
6       Return true if all valid characters;
7       false if invalid character found
8   */
9   bool decode (char* (*encDec)[2],
10      char* inStr, char* outStr)
11  {
12  // Local Declarations
13      char s1[6];
14      char s2[2];
15      bool error = false;
16      int i;
17
18  // Statements
19      outStr[0] ='\0';
20      while (*inStr != '\0' && !error)
21      {
22          for (i = 0; i < 5 && *inStr != '#'; i++, inStr++)
23              s1[i] = *inStr;
24
25          s1[i] = *inStr;
26          s1[++i] = "\0';
27
```

(continue)

Program 10-23   Morse code: decode to English *(continued)*

```
28          error = !convert (encDec, s1, 1, s2);
29          strcat (outStr, s2);
30          inStr++;
31       } // while
32       return (!error);
33    } // decode
```

Program 10-24 converts characters to Morse code and Morse code to characters.

Program 10-24 | Morse code: convert codes

```
1    /* ==================== convert ====================
2       Looks up code and converts to opposite format
3       Pre encDec is a pointer decoding table
4          s1 is string being converted
5          s2 is output string
6          col is code: 0 for character to Morse
7                       1 for Morse to character
8       Post converted output s2
9    */
10   int convert (char* (*encDec)[2],
11                char* s1, int col, char* s2)
12   {
13   // Local Declarations
14      bool found = false;
15      int i;
16
17   // Statements
18      for (i = 0; i < 27 && !found; i++)
19         found = !strcmp(s1, encDec[i][col]);
20
21      if (found)
22         strcpy (s2, encDec [i - 1][(col + 1) % 2]);
23      else
24         *s2 = '\0 ' ;
25
26      return found;
27   } // convert
28   // ================= End of Program ===============
```

The `convert` function does the actual conversion. Note, however, how it is designed to handle the conversion both from English to Morse and Morse to English. The only difference between the two conversions is which pointer we want to use. We pass the column to be used for the search as a parameter. After we have located the correct string, we use the formula shown below to pick up the matching string (see statement 22).

```
(col + 1) % 2
```

If we are searching on the English letters in column 0, then the modulus of the column (0 + 1) is column 1, which contains the pointer to the matching Morse code string. Conversely, if we are searching Morse code using the pointers in column 1, then the modulus of the column (1 + 1) is column 0, which contains the pointer to the English letter.

Software Engineering

In this section, we've formalized some of the principles of good programming that we've discussed throughout the text. Although you will find little in this discussion of software engineering that relates directly to the subject of strings, all of the string functions have been written using the principles discussed in this section.

Program Design Concepts

You will study many different analysis and design tools as you advance in computer science. Because this text deals primarily with program analysis and design, we will discuss the primary tool we have used throughout the text: the structure chart.

The overriding premise of good design is that the program is modular; that is, it is well structured. This is the mark of good programming. A program's degree of good design can be measured by two principles: Its modules are independent—that is, their implementation is hidden from the user—and they have a single purpose.

Information Hiding

The principle of information hiding in program design means that the data structure and functional implementation are screened from the user. Modules are independent when their communication is only through well-defined parameters and their implementation is hidden from the user. The purpose of the function should be defined in its inputs and outputs, and the user should not need to know how it is implemented or how its data are structured.

The concept of information hiding is the basis of the object-oriented design and programming. When you study data structures, you will see another technique used for information hiding, the abstract data type.

Cohesion

The most common weakness of function design is combining related processes into one primitive function. In Chapter 4, we discussed the concept that each module (function) should do only one thing. This principle of structured programming is known as cohesion, which is a measure of how closely the processes in a function are related.

We are concerned with cohesion for three primary reasons. The first and most important is *accuracy*. The more cohesive a function is, the simpler it is. The simpler it is, the easier it is to write, and the fewer errors it will have.

This is closely related to the second reason for high cohesion, *maintainability*. If a function is easy to understand, it is easy to change. This means that we will get the job done faster and with fewer errors.

Finally, cohesive modules are more *reusable*. Reusability is also closely related to the concepts of accuracy and ease of use. Existing functions have stood the test of time and have been tempered in the heat of use. They are more likely to be error free, and they certainly are easier and faster to develop.

Cohesion is most applicable to the primitive functions in a program, those that are at the bottom of the structure chart and less applicable to the controlling functions that appear above the lowest level. This does not mean, however, that cohesion can be ignored at the higher levels. To make the point with an absurd example, you wouldn't write a program to manage your checkbook and maintain your daily calendar. Even though both of these processes are related to things you do, they are so unrelated that you wouldn't put them in the same program. The same concept applies in a program. For example, at the lower levels of your program, you shouldn't combine functions that read data with functions that print a report.

The seven levels of cohesion are shown in **Figure 10-29**.

Figure 10-29 Types of cohesion

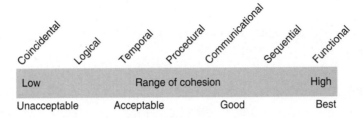

Functional Cohesion

Functional modules that contain only one process demonstrate functional cohesion. This is the highest level of cohesion and the level that we should hold up as a model. Using the example of printing a report, the report function should call three lower-level functions, one to get the data, one to format and print the report header, and one to format and print the data. This design is shown in **Figure 10-30**. The print report heading function is optional because it is called only when a page is full.

Figure 10-30 Example of functional cohesion

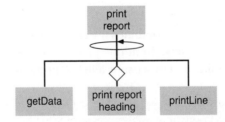

Sequential Cohesion

A sequential module contains two or more related tasks that are closely tied together, usually with the output of one flowing as input to the other. An example of sequential cohesion is shown in the calculations for a sale. The design for this function might well be:

1. Extend item prices

2. Sum items

3. Calculate sales tax

4. Calculate total

In this example, the first process multiplies the quantity purchased by the price. The extended prices are used by the process that calculates the sum of the purchased items. This sum is then used to calculate the sales tax, which is finally added to the sum to get the sale total. In each case, the output of one process was used as the input of the next process.

Although it is quite common to find the detail code for these processes combined into a single function, it does make the function more complex and less reusable. On the other hand, reusability would be a concern if the same or similar calculations were being made in different parts of one program.

Communicational Cohesion

Communicational cohesion combines processes that work on the same data. It is natural to have communicational cohesion in the higher modules in a program, but you should never find it at the primitive level. For example, consider a function that reads an inventory file, prints the current status of the parts, and then checks to see if any parts need to be ordered. The pseudocode for this process is shown in **Algorithm 10-1**.

ALGORITHM 10-1 | Process inventory pseudocode

Algorithm Process Inventory

1 while not end of file

    1.1 read a record

    1.2 print report

    1.3 check reorder point

2 end while

end Process Inventory

All three of these processes use the same data. If they are calls to lower level functions, they are acceptable. If the detail code is found in the function, however, the design is unacceptable.

The first three levels of cohesion are all considered to be good structured programming principles. Beyond this point, however, ease of understanding and implementation, maintainability, and accuracy begin to drop off rapidly. The next two levels should be used only at the higher levels of a structure chart, and then only rarely.

Procedural Cohesion

The fourth level of cohesion, procedural cohesion, combines unrelated processes that are linked by a control flow. (This differs from sequential cohesion, where data flows from one process to the next.) As an example, consider the high-level logic main line of a program that builds and processes a list. A procedural flow could look like **Algorithm 10-2**.

ALGORITHM 10-2 | Process list pseudocode

Algorithm Process List

1 open files

2 initialize work areas

3 create list

4 print menu

5 while not stop

    5.1 get users response

    5.2 if locate …

    5.3 if insert …

    5.4 if delete …

    5.5 print menu

(continue)

Algorithm 10-2   Process list pseudocode *(continued)*

    6 end while

    7 clean up

    8 close files

    end Process List

A much better approach would be to have only three function calls in `main`: initialize, process, and end. Not only is this easier to understand, but it also simplifies the communication.

Temporal Cohesion

The fifth level, temporal cohesion, is acceptable only over a limited range of processes. It combines unrelated processes that always occur together. Two temporally cohesive functions are initialization and end of job. They are acceptable because they are used only once in the program and because they are never portable. Recognize, however, that they should still contain calls to functionally cohesive primitive functions whenever practical.

Logical and Coincidental Cohesion

The last two levels are seldom found in programs today. Logical cohesion combines processes that are related only by the entity that controls them. A function that conditionally opened different sets of files based on a flag passed as a parameter would be logically cohesive. Finally, coincidental cohesion combines processes that are unrelated. Coincidental cohesion exists only in theory. We have never seen a productional program that contained coincidental cohesion.

A Final Word on Cohesion

We have discussed two design concepts in this chapter: information hiding and cohesion. Cohesion describes the relationship among processes within a function. Keep functions as highly cohesive as possible. When designing a program, pay attention to the levels of cohesion. It is much easier to design high cohesion into a program than it is to program it in.

Tips and Common Programming Errors

1. Do not confuse characters and string constants: The character constant is enclosed in single quotes, and the string constant is enclosed in double quotes.

2. Remember to allocate memory space for the string delimiter when declaring and defining an array of char to hold a string.

3. Strings are manipulated with string functions, not operators.

4. The header file `string.h` is required when using string functions.

5. The standard string functions require a delimited string. You cannot use them on an array of char that is not terminated with a delimiter.

6. Do not confuse string arrays and string pointers. In the following example, the first definition is a string (array of characters), and the second is a pointer to a character (string). Each is shown with a typical initialization statement.

```
char str[20];
strcpy (str, "Now is the time");
char* str;
str = "Now is the time";
```

7. Passing a character to a function when a string is required is another common error. This is most likely to occur with the formatted input/output functions, in which case, it is a logic error. Passing a character in place of a string when a function header is declared is a compile error.

8. Using the address operator for a parameter in the `scanf` function with a string is a coding error. The following is an invalid call and will most likely cause the program to fail:

```
scanf("%s", &string);    // Coding Error
```

9. It is a compile error to assign a string to a character, even when the character is a part of a string.

10. Using the assignment operator with strings instead of a function call is a compile error.

```
char string [20];
string = "This is an error";  // Compile Error
```

11. Because strings are built in an array structure, they may be accessed with indexes and pointers. When accessing individual bytes, it is a logic error to access beyond the end of the data structure (array).

Summary

> Strings can be fixed length or variable length.

> A variable-length string can be controlled by a length or a delimiter.

> The C language uses a null-terminated (delimited) variable-length string.

> A string constant in C is a sequence of characters enclosed in double quotes. A character constant is enclosed in single quotes.

> When string constants are used in a program, C automatically creates an array of characters, initializes it to a null-terminated string, and stores it, remembering its address.

> To store a string, we need an array of characters whose size is one more than the length of the string.

> There is a difference between an array of characters and a string. An array of characters is a derived data type (built on the type character) and is an intrinsic structure in C. A string is a data structure that uses the array as its basic type. It requires a delimiter for all of its operations.

> We can initialize a string:

   ▪ With an initializer when we define it.

   ▪ By using a string copy function.

   ▪ By reading characters into it.

> A string identifier is a pointer constant to the first element in the string.

> An array of strings is a very efficient way of storing strings of different sizes.

> The scanf and printf functions can be used to read and write strings using the %s format.

> The scan set format, %[...], can also be used in the scanf function to read a string.

> The functions gets, fgets, puts, and fputs are used for reading and writing strings. They transform a line to a string or a string to a line.

> The functions sscanf and sprintf are used for reading and writing strings from memory—that is, memory-to-memory formatting.

> The functions strcpy and strncpy are used to copy one string into another.

> The functions strcmp and strncmp are used to compare two strings.

> The function strlen is used to determine the length of a string.

> The functions strcat and strncat are used to concatenate one string to the end of the other.

> The functions strchr and strrchr are used to look for a character in a string.

> The function strstr is used to look for a substring in a string.

> The functions strspn and strcspn are used to locate the position of a set of characters in a string.

> Information hiding is the principle of programming in which the data structure and function's implementation are screened from the user.

> The cohesion principle dictates that each module must do only a single job.

> The mark of good programming is modularity.

> Program design has seven layers of cohesion; only the first three (functional, sequential, and communicational) should be used for lower-level functions. The last two (logical and coincidental) should never be used.

Key Terms

cohesion	delimiter	logical cohesion
coincidental cohesion	fixed-length string	procedural cohesion
communicational cohesion	information hiding	sequential cohesion
delimited string	length-controlled string	temporal cohesion

Review Questions

1. The two basic techniques for storing variable-length data are fixed-length strings and delimiters.
   a. True   **b.** False

2. To initialize a string when it is defined, it is necessary to put the delimiter character before the terminating double quote, as in "hello\0".
   a. True   **b.** False

3. Both the gets and fgets functions change the newline to a delimiter.
   a. True   **b.** False

4. The function that can be used to format several variables into one string in memory is string token (strtok).
   a. True   **b.** False

5. A(n) _____ is a series of characters treated as a unit.
   a. array
   b. character
   c. field
   d. record
   e. string

6. The delimiter in a C string is _____.
   a. newline
   b. defined by the programmer
   c. a del character
   d. a null character
   e. not specified in ANSI C

7. Which of the following statements about string variables is false?
   a. The assignment operator copies the value of one string variable to another.
   b. The array bracket operator is not needed if a string is defined as a pointer to character.
   c. The string name is a pointer.
   d. When a string is initialized at definition time, C automatically inserts the delimiter.
   e. When a string is read with `scanf`, it automatically inserts the delimiter.

8. Which of the following `printf` statements will not print a string? (Assume that name is properly defined and formatted.)
   a. `printf("%s", name);`
   b. `printf("%30s", name);`
   c. `printf("%-30s", name);`
   d. `printf("%30[^\0]", name);`

9. The _____ function reads a string from the standard input device.
   a. `fgets`   c. `gets`   e. `puts`
   b. `fputs`   d. `getstr`

10. The _____ string manipulation function returns the number of characters in the string excluding the null character.
    a. `strcmp`   c. `strlen`   e. `strtok`
    b. `strcpy`   d. `strsize`

11. Which of the following statements determines if the contents of string1 are the same as the contents of string2? Assume that string1 and string2 are properly defined and formatted strings.
    a. `if (string1 == string2)`
    b. `if (strcmp (string1, string2))`
    c. `if (strcmp (string1, string2) == 0)`
    d. `if (strcmp (string1, string2) < 0)`
    e. `if (strcmp (string1, string2) > 0)`

12. The _____ string manipulation function adds a string to the end of another string.
    a. `stradd`   c. `strcmp`   e. `strtok`
    b. `strcat`   d. `strcpy`

13. The _____ string manipulation function determines if a character is contained in a string.
    a. `strchr`   c. `strcmp`   e. `strtok`
    b. `strchar`   d. `strcpy`

14. The _____ function is used to format a string into variables in memory.
    a. `scanf`   c. `strfrmt`   e. `strtok`
    b. `sscanf`   d. `strscan`

15. The best level of cohesion is _____.
    a. coincidental   d. sequential
    b. communicational   e. functional
    c. procedural

Exercises

16. Find the value of `*x`, `* (x + 1)`, and `* (x +4)` for the following declaration:

    ```
    char* x = "The life is beautiful";
    ```

17. Find the value of `*y`, `* (y + 1)`, and `* (y +4)` for the following program segment:

    ```
    char x [ ] = "Life is beautiful";
    char* y = &x [3];
    ```

18. What is the error in the following program block?

    ```
    {
        char* x; scanf ("%s", x);
    }
    ```

19. What would be printed from the following program block?

```
{
    char s1[50] = "xyzt";
    char* s2 = "xyAt";
    int dif;
    dif = strcmp (s1, s2);
    printf("\n%d", dif);
}
```

20. What would be printed from the following program block?

```
{
    char s1[50] = "xyzt";
    char* s2 = "uabefgnpanm";
    char* s3;
    char* s4;
    char* s5;
    char* s6;
    s3 = s1;
    s4 = s2;
    strcat (s1, s2);
    s5 = strchr(s1, 'y');
    s6 = strrchr(s2, 'n');
    printf("\n%s", s3);
    printf("\n%s", s4);
    printf("\n%s", s5);
    printf("\n%s", s6);
}
```

21. What would be printed from the following program block?

```
{
    char s1[50] = "uabefgnpanm";
    char* s2 = "ab";
    char* s3 = "pan";
    char* s4 = "bef";
    char* s5 = "panam";
    char* s6;
    char* s7;
    char* s8;
    char* s9;
    s6 = strstr (s1, s2);
    s7 = strstr (s1, s3);
    s8 = strstr (s1, s4);
    s9 = strstr (s1, s5);
```

```
        printf("\n%s", s6);
        printf("\n%s", s7);
        printf("\n%s", s8);
        printf("\n%s", s9);
    }
```

22. What would be printed from the following program block?

```
    {
        char* s1 = "abefgnpanm";
        char* s2 = "ab";
        char* s3 = "pan";
        char* s4 = "bef";
        char* s5 = "panam";
        int d1;
        int d2;
        int d3;
        int d4;
        d1 = strspn (s1, s2);
        d2 = strspn (s1, s3);
        d3 = strcspn (s1, s4);
        d4 = strcspn (s1, s5);
        printf("\n%d", d1);
        printf("\n%d", d2);
        printf("\n%d", d3);
        printf("\n%d", d4);
    }
```

23. What would be printed from the following program block?

```
    {
        char* w = "BOOBOO";
        printf("%s\n", "DOO");
        printf("%s\n", "DICK" + 2);
        printf("%s\n", "DOOBOO" +3);
        printf("%c\n", w[4]);
        printf("%s\n", w+4);
        w++;
        w++;
        printf("%s\n",w);
        printf("%c\n", *(w+1));
    }
```

24. What would be printed from the following program block?

```
    {
        char* a[5] = {"GOOD", "BAD", "UGLY", "WICKED", "NICE"};
        printf("%s\n",    a[0]);
        printf("%s\n", *  (a + 2));
```

```
    printf("%c\n", *  (a[2] + 2));
    printf("%s\n",    a[3]);
    printf("%s\n",    a[2]);
    printf("%s\n",    a[4 ]);
    printf("%c\n", *  (a[3] +2));
    printf("%c\n", *  (*(a+4)+3));
}
```

25. What would be printed from the following program block?

```
{
    char c[ ] = "programming";
    char* p;
    int i;
    for (p = &c[5]; p >= &c [0]; p--)
        printf("%c", *p);
    printf("\n");
    for (p = c+5, I = 0; p >= c; p—,i++)
        printf("%c", *(p - i));
}
```

Problems

26. Write a function that accepts a string (a pointer to a character) and deletes the last character by moving the null character one position to the left.

27. Write a function that accepts a string (a pointer to a character) and deletes the first character.

28. Write a function that accepts a string (a pointer to a character) and deletes all the trailing spaces at the end of the string.

29. Write a function that accepts a string (a pointer to a character) and deletes all the leading spaces.

30. Write a function that returns the number of times the character is found in a string. The function has two parameters. The first parameter is a pointer to a string. The second parameter is the character to be counted.

31. Write a function that inserts a string into another string at a specified position. It returns a positive number if it is successful or zero if it has any problems, such as an insertion location greater than the length of the receiving string. The first parameter is the receiving string, the second parameter is the string to be inserted, and the third parameter is the insertion (index) position in the first string.

32. Write a function that, given a string, a width, and an empty string for output, centers the string in the output area. The function is to return 1 if the formatting is successful and 0 if any errors, such as string length greater than width, are found.

33. Write a function called newStrCpy that does the same job as strcpy. The declaration for your function is to be the same as the library function.

34. Write a function called newStrCat that does the same job as strcat. The declaration for your function is to be the same as the library function.

35. Write a function called newStrCmp that does the same job as strcmp. The declaration for your function is to be the same as the library function.

36. A string is a palindrome if it can be read forward and backward with the same meaning. Capitalization and spacing are ignored. For example, *anna* and *go dog* are palindromes. Write a function that accepts a string and returns `true` if the string is a palindrome and `false` if it is not. Test your function with the following two palindromes and at least one case that is not a palindrome:

```
Madam, I'm Adam
Able was I ere I saw Elba
```

37. Today's spelling checkers do much more than simply test for correctly spelled words. They also verify common punctuation. For example, a period must be followed by only one space. Write a program that reads a text file and removes any extra spaces after a period, comma, semicolon, or colon. Write the corrected text to a new file.

Your program is to read the data using `fgets` and parse the strings using `strtok`. Print your test data before and after they are run through your program.

Projects

38. Write a C program that converts a string representing a number in Roman numeral form to decimal form. The symbols used in the Roman numeral system and their equivalents are given below.

```
I          1
V          5
X          10
L          50
C          100
D          500
M          1000
```

For example, the following are Roman numbers: `XII (12)` `CII (102)`; `XL (40)`. The rules for converting a Roman number to a decimal number are as follows:
   a. Set the value of the decimal number to zero.
   b. Scan the string containing the Roman character from left to right. If the character is not one of the symbols in the numeral symbol set, the program must print an error message and terminate. Otherwise, continue with the following steps. (Note that there is no equivalent to zero in the Roman numerals.)

   ■ If the next character is a null character (if the current character is the last character), add the value of the current character to the decimal value.

   ■ If the value of the current character is greater than or equal to the value of the next character, add the value of the current character to the decimal value.

   ■ If the value of the current character is less than the next character, subtract the value of the current character from the decimal value.

Solve this project using parallel arrays. Do not solve it using a switch statement.

39. Write a program that "speaks" pig-latin. Words in pig-latin are taken from English. To form a word in pig-latin, the first letter of the English word beginning with a consonant is removed and added at the end of the word, adding the letters *ay* after the moved consonant. Words that begin with a vowel are simply appended with *ay*. Thus, in pig-latin, *pig-latin* is *igpay-atinlay*.

Your program will read a sentence at a time using `fgets`. It is to parse the words into strings. As words are parsed, they are to be converted to pig-latin and printed.

40. Write a program that provides antonyms to common words. An antonym is a word with the opposite meaning. For example, the antonym of *happy* is *sad*.

   The program is to use an interactive user interface. The words are to be read from a dictionary file. Use your dictionary to provide at least 30 antonyms, including at least one from each letter in the alphabet.

   Test your program by finding the antonyms for the first word, last word, and a word somewhere in the middle on both sides of the structure. Include in your test data at least three words that are not found, one less than the first word on the left side, one in the middle somewhere, and one greater than the last word on the right side.

41. The Morse code program in this chapter is a public example of a cryptographic system. We can apply the same techniques to encoding and decoding any message. For example, we can substitute the letter Z for the letter A, the letter Y for the letter B, and so forth, to create the following simple encoded message:

   ```
   NZWZN, R ZN ZWZN
   MADAM, I AM ADAM
   ```

   Write a program that encodes and decodes messages using any user supplied code. To make it more difficult to read, include spaces and the common punctuation characters in the code. The code is to be read from a text file to build the encode/decode array. The user is then given a menu of choices to encode, decode, or enter a new code from the keyboard.

   Test your program with the following code and message and with the complete alphabet entered in its encoded sequence so that it prints out in alphabetical order:

   ```
   ABCDEFGHIJKLMNOPQRSTUVWXYZ .,?'.;
   ?Q.W,EMRNTBXYUV!ICO PZA;SDLFKGJH
   ```

   Message
   ```
   WNWLSVPLM, LN GGG
   ```

42. Write a program that parses a text file into words and counts the number of occurrences of each word. Allow for up to 100 different words. After the list has been built, sort and print it.

43. Modify the program you wrote in Project 42 to eliminate common words such as *the, a, an, and, for,* and *of*. You may add other common words to the list.

Enumerated, Structure, and Union Types

Learning Objectives

When you complete this chapter, you will be able to:

11.1 Use the type definition statement in programs

11.2 Use enumerated types, including anonymous types, in programs

11.3 Create and use structures in programs

11.4 Use unions in programs

11.1 The Type Definition (`typedef`)

We have already discussed three of the six derived types: functions, arrays, and pointers. In this chapter, we discuss the three remaining derived types: enumerated, structure, and union. We also discuss a very useful construct, the type definition. The derived types are shown in **Figure 11-1**.

Figure 11-1 Derived types

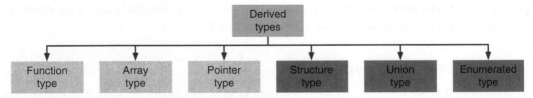

Before discussing these derived types, let's discuss a C declaration that applies to all of them—the type definition.

A type definition, `typedef`, gives a name to a data type by creating a new type that can then be used anywhere a type is permitted. The format for the type definition is shown in **Figure 11-2**.

Figure 11-2 Type-definition format

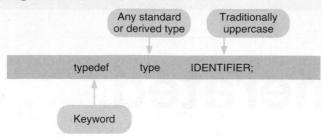

We can use the type definition with any type. For example, we can redefine `int` to `INTEGER` with the statement shown below, although we would never recommend this.

```
typedef int INTEGER;
```

Note that the `typedef` identifier is traditionally coded in uppercase. This alerts the reader that there is something unusual about the type. We saw this previously with defined constants. Simple style standards such as this make it much easier to follow a program.

One of the more common uses of the type definition is with complex declarations. To demonstrate the concept, let's see how we can declare a rather simple construct, an array of pointers to strings (a ragged array). Without a type definition, we must define the array as shown below.

```
char* stringPtrAry[20];
```

We can simplify the declaration by using a type definition to create a string type and then defining the array using the new type as shown below.

```
typedef char* STRING;
STRING stringPtrAry[20];
```

11.2 Enumerated Types

The enumerated type is a user-defined type based on the standard integer type. In an enumerated type, each integer value is given an identifier called an enumeration constant. We can thus use the enumerated constants as symbolic names, which makes our programs much more readable.

Recall that a type is a set of values and a set of operations that can be applied on those values. Each type also has an identifier or name. For example, the standard type `int` has an identifier (`int`), a set of values ($-\infty \ldots +\infty$), and a set of operations (such as add and multiply). While the system defines the names, values, and operations for standard types, we must define them for types we create. When the defined type directly translates into a standard type, as with the enumerated type, the standard types may be automatically defined.

Declaring an Enumerated Type

To declare an enumerated type, we must declare its identifier and its values. Because it is derived from the integer type, its operations are the same as for integers. The syntax for declaring an enumerated type is:

```
enum typeName {identifier list};
```

The keyword, `enum`, is followed by an identifier and a set of enumeration constants enclosed in a set of braces. The statement is terminated with a semicolon. The enumeration identifiers are also known as an enumeration list.

Each enumeration identifier is assigned an integer value. If we do not explicitly assign the values, the compiler assigns the first identifier the value 0, the second identifier the value 1, the third identifier the value 2, and so on until all of the identifiers have a value. For example, consider an enumerated type for colors as defined in the next statement. Note that for enumeration identifiers, we use uppercase alphabetic characters.

```
enum color {RED, BLUE, GREEN, WHITE};
```

The color type has four and only four possible values. The range of the values is 0 . . . 3, with the identifier red representing the value 0, blue the value 1, green the value 2, and white the value 3.

After we have declared an enumerated type, we can create variables from it just as we can create variables from the standard types. In fact, C allows the enumerated constants, or variables that hold enumerated constants, to be used anywhere that integers can be used. The following example defines three variables for our color type.

```
enum color productColor;
enum color skyColor;
enum color flagColor;
```

Operations on Enumerated Types

In this section we discuss storing values in enumerated types and manipulating them.

Assigning Values to Enumerated Types

After an enumerated variable has been declared, we can store values in it. Remember, however, that an enumerated variable can hold only declared values for the type. The following example defines a color variable and uses it in several statements.

```
enum color x;
enum color y;
enum color z;
x = BLUE;
y = WHITE;
z = PURPLE; // Error. There is no purple.
```

Similarly, once a variable has been defined and assigned a value, we can store its value in another variable of the same type. Given the previous example, the following statements are valid.

```
x = y;
z = y;
```

Comparing Enumerated Types

Enumerated types can be compared using the comparison operators. For example, given two color variables, we can compare them for equal, greater than, or less than. We can also compare them to enumeration identifiers. These comparisons are shown in the following example.

```
if (colorl == color2)
...
if (colorl == BLUE)
...
```

Another natural use of enumerated types is with the switch statement. Because enumerated types are derived from integer types, they may be used in the case expressions. For example, consider an enumerated type for the months of the year.

```
enum months {JAN,FEB,MAR,APR,MAY,JUN,JUL,AUG,SEP,OCT,NOV,DEC};
enum months dateMonth;
```

Given the months type, we can use it in a switch statement as shown in the next example.

```
switch (dateMonth)
{
case JAN: ...
        break;
case FEB: ...
        break;
...
} // switch
```

Other Operations on Enumerated Types

In general, any operation defined for integers can be used with enumerated types. We can add, subtract, multiply, and divide enumerated types. We can also pass them to standard and application functions.

Be aware, however, that the result may not be in the defined set, which may cause the program to fail. C does not ensure that the values stored in an enumerated variable are valid.

Enumeration Type Conversion

Enumerated types can be implicitly and explicitly cast. The compiler implicitly casts an enumerated type to an integer as required. However, when we implicitly cast an integer to an enumerated type we get either a warning or an error, depending on the compiler. The following example demonstrates implicit casts.

```
int    x;
enum color y;
x = BLUE;    // Valid, x contains 1
y = 2;    // Compiler warning
```

We can explicitly cast an integer to an enumerated type without problems. To assign y the value blue in the previous example, we could use the following code.

```
enum color y;
y = (enum color)2;    // Valid, y contains blue
```

Initializing Enumerated Constants

While the compiler automatically assigns values to enumerated types starting with 0, we can override it and assign our own values. For example, to set up an enumerated type for the months of the year, we could use the following declaration.

```
enum months
{JAN,FEB,MAR,APR,MAY,JUN,JUL,AUG,SEP,OCT,NOV,DEC};
enum months dateMonth;
```

While this declaration works, it could be confusing because JAN is assigned the value 0, FEB the value 1, and so forth until DEC, which is 11. To make JAN start with 1, we could use the following declaration.

```
enum months {JAN = 1, FEB, MAR, APR, MAY, JUN,
             JUL, AUG, SEP, OCT, NOV, DEC};
```

Note that we don't have to assign initializers to every value. If we omit the initializers, the compiler assigns the next value by adding 1. To initialize the months, therefore, we simply assign the value for JAN. The rest will be automatically assigned by the compiler.

C also allows us to assign duplicate values to identifiers. For example, we could assign similar colors identical values as shown in the next example.

```
enum mycolor    {RED, ROSE = 0, CRIMSON = 0, SCARLET = 0,
                 BLUE, AQUA = 1, NAVY = 1,
                 GREEN, JADE = 2, WHITE};
```

To emphasize the point, even though RED in Color (shown again below) has the same value as RED in myColor, the two types are different and cannot be used together unless one of them is cast.

```
enum color {RED, BLUE, GREEN, WHITE};
```

Anonymous Enumeration: Constants

If we create an enumerated type without a name, it is an anonymous enumerated type. Because the identifiers in enumerated types are constants, enumerated types are a convenient way to declare constants. For example, to assign names to common punctuation characters, we would use the following code.

```
enum {space = ' ', comma = ',', colon = ':', ...};
```

As another example, to declare the constants ON and OFF, we could use the following code. Anonymous enumeration cannot be used to declare a variable.

```
enum {OFF, ON};
```

The identifier OFF is a constant with a value of 0; ON is a value of 1. As an aside, we coded OFF first because we wanted it to have a connotation of false. Similarly, ON has a connotation of true.

If you have cable or satellite TV, you know that TV providers often change the numbers of the channels they offer. To help us keep track of the ones we watch most often, we wrote a program that prints out a list of our favorites. Since the channel numbers often change, using their names in an enumerated type makes it easy to update them when necessary and to follow the code. The implementation is seen in **Program 11-1**.

Program 11-1 | Print cable TV stations

```
 1   /* Print selected channels for our cable provider.
 2      Written by:
 3      Date
 4   */
 5
 6   #include <stdio.h>
 7   int main (void)
 8   {
 9   // Local Declarations
10      enum TV {fox = 802, nbc  = 804, cbs = 855,
11               abc = 811, hbo  = 815, osn = 817,
12               pbs = 831, espn = 839, cnn = 851};
13
14   // Statements
15      printf("Here are my favorite cable channels:\n");
```

(continue)

Program 11-1 Print cable TV stations *(continued)*

```
16    printf(" ABC:  \t%2d\n", abc);
17    printf(" CBS:  \t%3d\n", cbs);
18    printf(" CNN:  \t%3d\n", cnn);
19    printf(" ESPN:\t%3d\n", espn);
20    printf(" Fox:  \t%3d\n", fox);
21    printf(" HBO:  \t%3d\n", hbo);
22    printf(" PBS:  \t%3d\n", pbs);
23    printf(" NBC:  \t%3d\n", nbc);
24    printf(" OSN:  \t%3d\n", osn);
25    printf("End of my favorite channels.\n");
26    return 0;
27 } // main
```

Output
```
Here are my favorite cable channels:
    ABC:   811
    CBS:   855
    CNN:   851
    ESPN: 839
    Fox:   802
    HBO:   815
    PBS:   831
    NBC:   804
    OSN:   817
End of my favorite channels.
```

Input/Output Operations

Because enumerated types are derived types, they cannot be read and written using the formatted input/output functions. When we read an enumerated type, we must read it as an integer. When we write it, it displays as an integer. When necessary, C implicitly casts variables as described in "Enumeration Type Conversion" earlier in the chapter.

The following example shows how we would read and write two months.

```
enum months {JAN = 1, FEB, MAR, APR, MAY, JUN,
    JUL, AUG, SEP, OCT, NOV, DEC);
enum months month1;
enum months month2;
scanf ("%d %d", &month1, &month2); // Input 1-12
printf("%d %d", month1, month2); // Prints 1-12
```

Note | Don't be confused about strings and enumerated types. "Jan" is a string made of three characters; JAN, as defined in the previous code example, is an enumerated type (identifier), which has the integer value 1.

11.3 Structure

Today's modern applications require complex data structures to support them. For example, the structures needed to support the graphical user interface found in common operating systems such as Windows, macOS, and Linux are very complex. So complex, in fact, that they could not be built using the relatively primitive data types we have seen so far. A much more powerful capability is needed. This is the role of the structure.

A structure is a collection of related elements, possibly of different types, having a single name. For example, consider the file structure you have been using ever since you wrote your first program that used files. The file table is a type-defined structure, `file`.

Each element in a structure is called a field. A field is the smallest element of named data that has meaning. It has many of the characteristics of the variables you have been using in your programs. It has a type, and it exists in memory. It can be assigned values, which in turn can be accessed for selection or manipulation. A field differs from a variable primarily in that it is part of a structure.

We have studied another derived data type that can hold multiple pieces of data, the array. The difference between an array and a structure is that all elements in an array must be of the same type, while the elements in a structure can be of the same or different types.

Figure 11-3 contains two examples of structures. The first example, `fraction`, has two fields, both of which are integers. The second example, `student`, has three fields, made up of two different types.

Figure 11-3   Structure examples

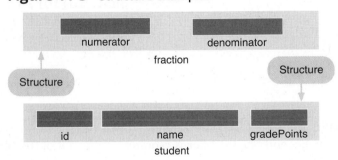

Another way to look at a structure is as a pattern or outline that can be applied to data to extract individual parts. It allows us to refer to a collection of data using a single name and, at the same time, to refer to the individual components through their names. By collecting all the attributes of an object in one structure, we simplify our programs and make them more readable.

One design caution, however. The data in a structure should all be related to one object. In Figure 11-3, the integers in the fraction both belong to the same fraction, and the data in the second example all relate to one student. Do not combine unrelated data for programming expediency. That would not be good structured programming.

Structure Type Declaration

Like all data types, structures must be declared and defined. C has two ways to declare a structure: tagged structures and type-defined structures.

Tagged Structure

The first way to define a structure is to use a tagged structure. A tagged structure can be used to define variables, parameters, and return types. The format is shown in **Figure 11-4**.

A tagged structure starts with the keyword `struct`. The second element in the declaration is the tag. The tag is the identifier for the structure, and it allows us to use it for other purposes, such as variables and parameters. If we

Figure 11-4 Tagged structure format

```
struct TAG
{

     field list

};
```
Format

```
struct STUDENT
{
    char id[10];
    char name[26];
    int  gradePts;
}; // STUDENT
```
Example

conclude the structure with a semicolon after the closing brace, no variables are defined. In this case, the structure is simply a type template with no associated storage.

Type Declaration with `typedef`

The more powerful way to declare a structure is to use a type definition, `typedef`. The `typedef` format is shown in **Figure 11-5**.

Figure 11-5 Structure declaration with `typedef`

```
typedef struct
{

     field list

} TYPE;
```
Format

```
typedef struct
{
    char id[10];
    char name[26];
    int  gradePts;
} STUDENT;
```
Example

The type-defined structure differs from the tagged declaration in two ways. First, the keyword, `typedef`, is added to the beginning of the definition. Second, an identifier is required at the end of the block; the identifier is the type definition name.

Variable Declaration

After a structure has been declared, we can declare variables using it. Generally, we declare the type in the global area of a program to make it visible to all functions. The variables, on the other hand, are usually declared in the functions, either in the header or in the local declarations section. **Figure 11-6** demonstrates the declaration of a structure type and variables that use it.

Figure 11-6 Structure declaration format and example

```
// Global Type Declarations
struct STUDENT
{
    char id[10];
    char name[26];
    int  gradePts;
};

// Local Declarations
struct STUDENT aStudent;
```

```
// Global Type Declarations
typedef struct
{
    char id[10];
    char name[26];
    int  gradePts;
} STUDENT;

// Local Declarations
STUDENT aStudent;
```

Initialization

We can initialize a structure. The rules for structure initialization are similar to the rules for array initialization. The initializers are enclosed in braces and separated by commas. They must match their corresponding types in the structure definition. Finally, when we use a nested structure (see "Nested Structures" later in this chapter), the nested initializers must be enclosed in their own set of braces.

Figure 11-7 shows two examples of structure initialization. The first example shows an initializer for each field. Note how they are mapped to the structure in sequence. The second example demonstrates what happens when not all fields are initialized. As we saw with arrays, when one or more initializers are missing, the structure elements will be assigned null values, zero for integers and floating-point numbers, and null (`'\0'`) for characters and strings.

Figure 11-7   Initializing structures

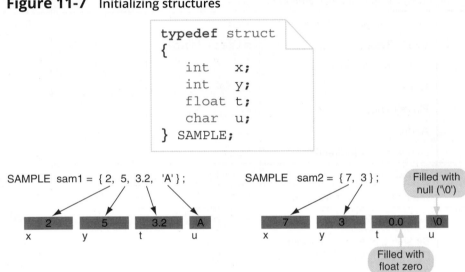

Accessing Structures

Now that we have discussed how to declare and initialize structures, it's time to see how we can use them in our programs. We will first describe how to access individual components of a structure and then examine the assignment of whole structures. After looking at how pointers are used with structures, we conclude with a program that uses structures.

Referencing Individual Fields

Each field in a structure can be accessed and manipulated using expressions and operators. Anything we can do with an individual variable can be done with a structure field. The only problem is to identify the individual fields we are interested in.

To refer to a field in a structure we need to refer to both the structure and the field. C uses a hierarchical naming convention that first uses the structure-variable identifier and then the field identifier. The **structure variable** identifier is separated from the field identifier by a dot. The dot is the direct selection operator, which is a postfix operator at precedence 16 in the precedence table shown in **Table 11-1**.

Using the structure `student` in "Type Declaration with typedef," we would refer to the individual components as shown below.

```
aStudent.id
aStudent.name
aStudent.gradePoints
```

Table 11-1 Precedence table

OPERATOR	DESCRIPTION	EXAMPLE	SIDE EFFECTS	ASSOC	PR
	Identifiers	amount	N	N/A	16
	Constants	3.14159			
	Parenthetical Expressions	(a + b)			
[ ]	Array Index	ary[i]	N	Left-Right	16
f(...)	Function Call	doIt(x, y)	Y		
.	Direct Member Selection	str.mem	N		
->	Indirect Member Selection	ptr->mem	N		
++ --	Postfix Increment • Decrement	a++	Y		
++ --	Prefix Increment • Decrement	++a	Y	Right-Left	15
sizeof	Size in Bytes	sizeof(int)	N		
~	Ones Complement	-a	N		
!	Not	!a	N		
+ -	Plus • Minus	+a	N		
&	Address	&a	N		
*	Dereference / Indirection	*ptr	N		
( )	Type Cast	(int)ptr	N	Right-Left	14
* / %	Multiply • Divide • Modulus	a * b	N	Left-Right	13
+ -	Addition • Subtraction	a + b	N	Left-Right	12
<< >>	Bit Shift Left • Bit Shift Right	a << 3	N	Left-Right	11
< <= > >=	Comparison	a < 5	N	Left-Right	10
== !=	Equal • Not Equal	a == b	N	Left-Right	9
&	Bitwise And	a & b	N	Left-Right	8
^	Bitwise Exclusive Or	a ^ b	N	Left-Right	7
|	Bitwise Or	a | b	N	Left-Right	6
&&	Logical And	a && b	N	Left-Right	5
||	Logical Or	a || b	N	Left-Right	4
? :	Conditional	a ? x : y	N	Right-Left	3
= += -= *= /= %= >>= <<= &= ^= |=	Assignment	a = 5 a %= b a &= c a |= d	Y	Right-Left	2
,	Comma	a, b, c	N	Left-Right	1

Figure 11-8 contains another example using the structure SAMPLE, defined in Figure 11-7. With this structure, we can use a selection expression to evaluate the sam2 field, u, and if it is an A, add the two integer fields and store the result in the first. This code is shown below.

```
if (sam2.u == "A")
sam2.x += sam2.y;
```

Figure 11-8 Structure direct selection operator

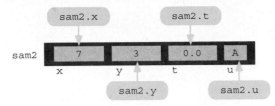

We can also read data into and write data from structure members just as we can from individual variables. For example, the value for the fields of the sample structure can be read from the keyboard and placed in sam1 using the following scanf statement. Note that the address operator is at the beginning of the variable structure identifier.

```
scanf("%d %d %f %c",
&sam1.x, &sam1.y, &sam1.t, &sam1.u);
```

Precedence of Direct Selection Operator

As we saw in the previous section, the direct selection operator (.) is a postfix expression that has a priority of 16. Let's look at several examples to see how it works.

First, let's look at examples in which all operators have a priority of 16. In this case, the expressions are evaluated using left to right associativity as shown in the following examples.

```
typedef struct
{
    int total;
    int ary[10];
} DATA;
DATA sales;
sales.total++; // interpreted as (sales.total)++
fun(sales.total); // sales.total passed to fun
fun(sales.ary[3]); // (sales.ary)[3] passed to fun
```

Now let's examine cases in which the direct selection operator is used with an operator of lesser precedence. In these cases, the direct selection is applied first.

```
++sales.total; // interpreted as ++(sales.total)
fun(&sales.total); // &(sales.total) passed to fun
```

As an example of a function that uses structures and direct selection, let's look at a program that multiplies two fractions and prints the result. The structure for this example was shown in Figure 11-3. The code is shown in **Program 11-2**.

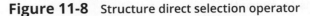

Program 11-2 | Multiply fractions

```
1   /* This program uses structures to simulate the
2       multiplication of fractions.
3       Written by:
4       Date:
5   */
6
```

(continue)

Program 11-2 Multiply fractions *(continued)*

```
 7  #include <stdio.h>
 8  // Global Declarations
 9     typedef struct
10     {
11        int numerator;
12        int denominator;
13     } FRACTION;
14
15 int main (void)
16 {
17 // Local Declarations
18     FRACTION fr1;
19     FRACTION fr2;
20     FRACTION res;
21
22 // Statements
23     printf("Key first fraction in the form of x/y: ");
24     scanf ("%d /%d", &fr1.numerator, &fr1.denominator);
25     printf("Key second fraction in the form of x/y: ");
26     scanf ("%d /%d", &fr2.numerator, &fr2.denominator);
27
28     res.numerator = fr1.numerator * fr2.numerator;
29     res.denominator = fr1.denominator * fr2.denominator;
30
31     printf("The result of %d/%d * %d/%d is %d/%d",
32     fr1.numerator, fr1.denominator,
33     fr2.numerator, fr2.denominator,
34     res.numerator, res.denominator);
35     return 0;
36 }  // main
```

Output
```
Key first fraction in the form of x/y: 2/6
Key second fraction in the form of x/y: 7/4
The result of 2/6 * 7/4 is 14/24
```

Although this is a very simple program, several points are of interest:

1. Note that we have coded the typedef in the global area before main. This is the first time that we have included statements here other than preprocessor directives. Even though this program has no subfunction, it is customary to put the typed definition statements there so that they are in scope for the entire compilation unit.

2. Note that the name of the typed definition is all UPPERCASE. This is another C style tradition. It warns the reader that there is something special about this type, in this case that it is a typed definition.

3. Now examine the `scanf` statements. Since we need a pointer for `scanf`, we must use the address operator as well as the direct selection operator. As you can see, we have not used the parentheses around the field name. The reason is that the direct selection operator (`.`) has a higher priority (16) than the address operator (15). In other words, the expression

`&fr1.numerator`

is interpreted by the compiler as

`&(fr.numerator)`

which is exactly what we need.

Operations on Structures

The structure is an entity that can be treated as a whole. However, only one operation, assignment, is allowed on the structure itself. That is, a structure can only be copied to another structure of the same type using the assignment operator.

Rather than assign individual members when we want to copy one structure to another, as we did earlier, we can simply assign one to the other. **Figure 11-9** copies `sam1` to `sam2`.

Figure 11-9 Copying a structure

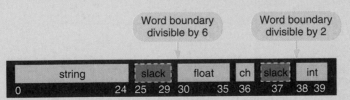

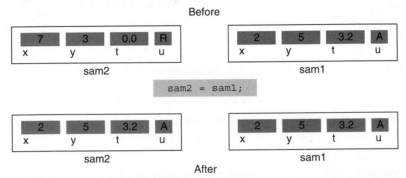

> **Note**
>
> It is interesting to examine why we cannot compare two structures. Sometimes hardware requires that certain data, such as integers and floating-point numbers, be aligned on a word boundary in memory. When we group data in a structure, the arrangement of the data may require that slack bytes be inserted to maintain these boundary requirements. For example, consider the structure shown here.
>
> In this structure we assume that a floating-point number is stored in a word that requires 6 bytes and must be on an address evenly divisible by 6, such as 24 or 30. We also assume that integers are stored in 2-byte words that require an address evenly divisible by 2. The 25-byte string at the beginning of the structure forces 5 slack bytes between the string and the float. Then the character after the float forces a slack byte to align the integer at the end of the structure.
>
> Since these extra bytes are beyond the control of the program, we cannot guarantee what their values will be. Therefore, if we were to compare two structures and their first components were equal, the inserted slack bytes could cause an erroneous compare result, either high or low, if they weren't equal. C prevents this problem by not allowing selection statements with structures. Of course, if we really need to compare structures, we can simply write a structure compare function of our own that would compare the individual fields in the structure.

Pointers to Structures

Structures, like other types, can also be accessed through pointers. In fact, this is one of the most common methods used to reference structures. For example, let's use our SAMPLE structure with pointers (**Figure 11-10**).

Figure 11-10   Pointers to structures

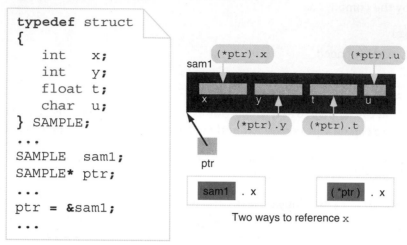

The first thing we need to do is define a pointer for the structure as shown below.

```
SAMPLE* ptr;
```

We now assign the address of sam1 to the pointer using the address operator (&) as we would with any other pointer.

```
ptr = &sam1;
```

Now we can access the structure itself and all the members using the pointer, `ptr`. The structure itself can be accessed like any object using the indirection operator (*).

```
*ptr  // Refers to whole structure
```

Because the pointer contains the address of the beginning of the structure, we no longer need to use the structure name with the direct selection operator. The pointer takes its place. The reference to each of the sample members is shown below and in Figure 11-10.

```
(*ptr).x (*ptr).y (*ptr).t (*ptr).u
```

Note the parentheses in the above expressions. They are absolutely necessary, and to omit them is a common mistake. They are needed because the precedence priority of the direct selection operator (.) is higher than the indirection operator (*). If we forget to put the parentheses, C applies the dot operator first and the asterisk operator next. In other words,

```
*ptr.x is interpreted as * (ptr.x)
```

which is wrong. The expression * (ptr.x) means that we have a completely different (and undefined) structure called `ptr` that contains a member, x, which must be a pointer. Since this is not the case, you will get a compile error. **Figure 11-11** shows how this error is interpreted.

The correct notation, `(*ptr).x`, first resolves the primary expression `(*ptr)` and then uses the pointer value to access the member, x.

Indirect Selection Operator

Fortunately, another operator— indirect selection—eliminates the problems with pointers to structures. The indirect selection operator is at the same level in the precedence table (shown in Table 11-1) as the direct selection operator.

Figure 11-11   Interpretation of invalid pointer use

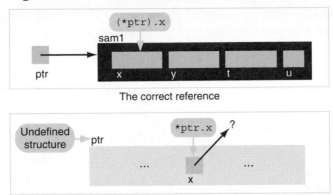

Note | (*pointerName).fieldName ⟷ pointerName–>fieldname

The token for the indirect selection operator is an arrow formed by the minus sign and the greater than symbol (–>). It is placed immediately after the pointer identifier and before the member to be referenced. We use this operator to refer to the members of our previously defined structure, sam1, in **Figure 11-12**.

Figure 11-12   Indirect selection operator

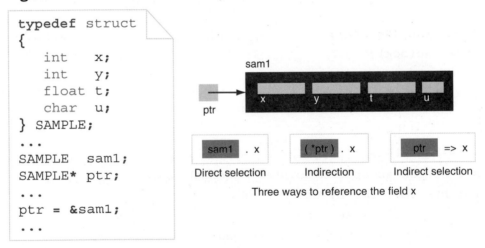

Program 11-3 simulates a digital clock that shows time. A structure is defined to represent the three components of time: hour, minute, and second. Two functions are used. The first function, called increment, simulates the passage of the time. The second function, called show, shows the time at any moment.

Program 11-3 | Clock simulation with pointers

```
1  /* This program uses a structure to simulate the time.
2     Written by:
3     Date:
4  */
5  #include <stdio.h>
```

(continue)

Program 11-3   Clock simulation with pointers *(continued)*

```
 6
 7   typedef struct
 8   {
 9       int hr;
10       int min;
11       int sec;
12   } CLOCK;
13
14   // Function Declaration
15   void increment (CLOCK* clock);
16   void show (CLOCK* clock);
17
18   int main (void)
19   {
20   // Local Declaration
21       CLOCK clock = {14, 38, 56};
22
23   // Statements
24       for(int i = 0; i < 6; ++i)
25       {
26           increment (&clock);
27           show (&clock);
28       } // for
29       return 0;
30   } // main
31
32   /* ===================increment =============
33      This function accepts a pointer to clock and
34      increments the time by one second.
35      Pre previous clock setting
36      Post clock incremented by one second.
37   */
38   void increment (CLOCK* clock)
39   {
40   // Statements
41       (clock->sec)++;
42       if (clock->sec == 60)
43       {
44           clock->sec = 0;
45           (clock->min)++;
46           if (clock->min == 60)
47           {
48               clock->min = 0;
```

(continue)

Program 11-3   Clock simulation with pointers *(continued)*

```
49              (clock->hr)++;
50                if (clock->hr == 24)
51                   clock->hr = 0;
52          } // if 60 min
53       } // if 60 sec
54    return;
55 } // increment
56
57 /*====================show================
58    Show the current time in military form.
59    Pre clock time
60    Post clock time displayed
61 */
62 void show (CLOCK* clock)
63 {
64 // Statements
65    printf("%02d:%02d:%02d\n",
66            clock->hr, clock->min, clock->sec);
67    return;
68 } // show
```

Output
```
14:38:57
14:38:58
14:38:59
14:39:00
14:39:01
14:39:02
```

Complex Structures

As mentioned earlier, structures were designed to deal with complex problems. The limitations on structures are not on the structures themselves but on the imagination of the software engineers who solve the problems. Structures within structures (nested structures), arrays within structures, and arrays of structures are all common. We deal with the first two here and arrays of structures in the next section.

Nested Structures

We can have structures as members of a structure. When a structure includes another structure, it is a nested structure. There is no limit to the number of structures that can be nested, but we seldom go beyond three.

For example, we can have a structure called stamp that stores the date and the time. The date is in turn a structure that stores the month, day, and year. The time is also a structure that stores the hour, minute, and second. This structure design is shown in **Figure 11-13**.

Figure 11-13 Nested structure

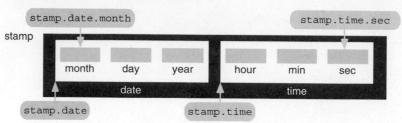

There are two concerns with nested structures: declaring them and referencing them.

Declaring Nested Structures

Although it is possible to declare a nested structure with one declaration, it is not recommended. It is far simpler and much easier to follow the structure if each structure is declared separately and then grouped in the high-level structure.

When we declare the structures separately, the most important point to remember is that nesting must be done from inside out—that is, from the lowest level to the most inclusive level. In other words, we must declare the innermost structure first, then the next level, working upward toward the outer, most inclusive structure.

Consider the time stamp structure seen in Figure 11-13. The inner two structures, date and time, must be declared before the outside structure, stamp, is declared. We show the declaration of stamp and a variable that uses it in the following example.

```
// Type Declaration
typedef struct
{
    int month;
    int day;
    int year;
} DATE;
typedef struct
{
    int hour;
    int min;
    int sec;
} TIME;
typedef struct
{
    DATE date;
    TIME time;
} STAMP;
// Variable Declaration
STAMP stamp;
```

It is possible to nest the same structure type more than once in a declaration. For example, consider a structure that contains start and end times for a job. Using the STAMP structure, we create a new declaration as shown below.

```
// Type Declaration
typedef struct
{
```

```
      ......
      STAMP startTime;
      STAMP endTime;
   } JOB;
   // Variable Declaration
   JOB job;
```

Regardless of how we declared the structure, using it will be the same. The major advantage of declaring each of the structures separately is that it allows much more flexibility in working with them. For example, with DATE declared as a separate type definition, it is possible to pass the date structure to a function without having to pass the rest of the stamp structure.

Referencing Nested Structures

To access a nested structure, we include each level from the highest (stamp) to the component being referenced. The complete set of references for stamp is shown below. The last two references are to job.

```
stamp
stamp.date
stamp.date.month
stamp.date.day
stamp.date.year
stamp.time
stamp.time.hour
stamp.time.min
stamp.time.sec
job.startTime.time.hour
job.endTime.time.hour
```

Nested Structure Initialization

Initialization follows the rules mentioned for a simple structure. Each structure must be initialized completely before proceeding to the next member. Each structure is enclosed in a set of braces. For example, to initialize stamp, first we initialize date, then time, separated by a comma. To initialize date, we provide values for month, day, and year, each separated by commas. We can then initialize the members of time. A definition and initialization for stamp are shown below.

```
STAMP stamp = {{05, 10, 1936}, {23, 45, 00}};
```

Structures Containing Arrays

Structures can have one or more arrays as members. The arrays can be accessed either through indexing or through pointers, as long as they are properly qualified with the direct selection operator.

Defining Arrays for Structures

As with nested structures, an array may be included within the structure or may be declared separately and then included. If it is declared separately, the declaration must be complete before it can be used in the structure. For example, consider the structure that contains the student name, three midterm scores, and the final exam score, as shown in **Figure 11-14**.

Referencing Arrays in Structures

Regardless of how we declared the structure, each element will have the same reference. First we refer to the structure, then to the array component. When we refer to the array, we can use either index or pointer notation. Let us look at each in turn.

Figure 11-14 Arrays in structures

```
// Global declarations
typedef struct
{
    char  name[26];
    int   midterm[3];
    int   final;
} STUDENT ;
// Local declarations
STUDENT student;
```

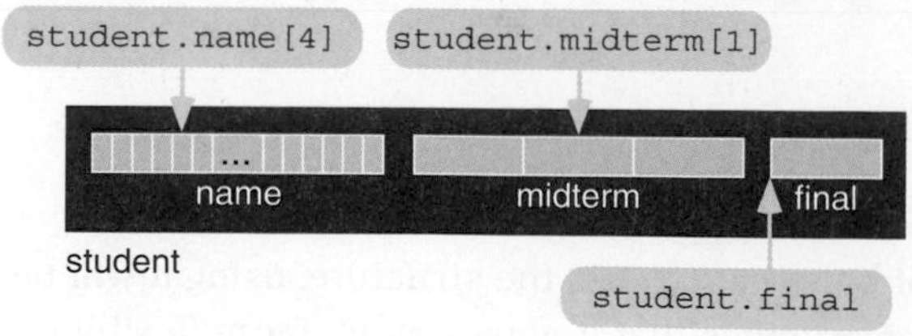

student.name[4]   student.midterm[1]

name   midterm   final

student

student.final

The index applies only to elements within an array. Therefore, it must follow the identifier of an array. Our student example has two arrays, one of characters (a string) and the other of midterm scores. Each of these arrays can be referenced with an index as shown below.

```
student
student.name
student.name[i]
student.midterm
student.midterm[j]
student.final
```

We have already seen how to refer to fields in a structure using the indirect selection operator (->). When one structure contains an array, we can use a pointer to refer directly to the array elements. For example, given a pointer to integer, pScores, we could refer to the scores in student as shown below.

```
pScores = student.midterm;
totalScores = *pScores + *(pScores + 1) + *(pScores + 2);
```

Array Initialization in Structures

The initialization of a structure containing an array is simply an extension of the rules for structure initialization to include the initialization of the array. Since the array is a separate member, its values must be included in a separate set of braces. For example, the student structure can be initialized as shown below.

```
STUDENT student = {"John Marcus", {92, 80, 70}, 87};
```

Note that the name is initialized as a string and the midterm scores are simply enclosed in a set of braces.

Structure Containing Pointers

It should not be surprising that a structure can have pointers as members. In fact, we will see that pointers are very common in structures.

The use of pointers can save memory. For example, suppose that we wanted to use the alphabetic month in our stamp structure rather than an integer month. We could add an array of nine characters to each structure element, but it would be much more memory efficient to use a 4-byte pointer if we had to store a lot of these structures. Given the months of the year defined as strings, as shown below, we could then use a pointer to the correct month.

```
char  jan[] =  "January";
char  feb[] =  "February";
...
char  dec[] =  "December";
```

To assign the month May to the structure, we would use the following statement. Note that we are copying a pointer to a string, not the string itself.

```
stamp.date.month = may;
```

The modified structure is shown in **Figure 11-15**. The structure code for the date structure is shown below. It is important to remember that declaring a structure does not allocate memory for it. Even when the structure is defined, however, there is still no memory provided for month until we allocate it using malloc or calloc.

```
typedef struct
{
    char* month;
    int day;
    int year;
} DATE;
```

Figure 11-15 Pointers in structures

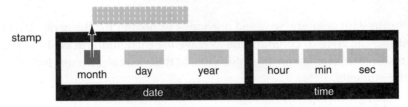

Array of Structures

In many situations, we need to create an array of structures. To name just one example, we would use an array of students to work with a group of students stored in a structure. By putting the data in an array, we can quickly and easily work with the data, to calculate averages, for instance.

Let's create an array to handle the scores for up to 50 students in a class. **Figure 11-16** shows how such an array might look.

Figure 11-16 Array of structures

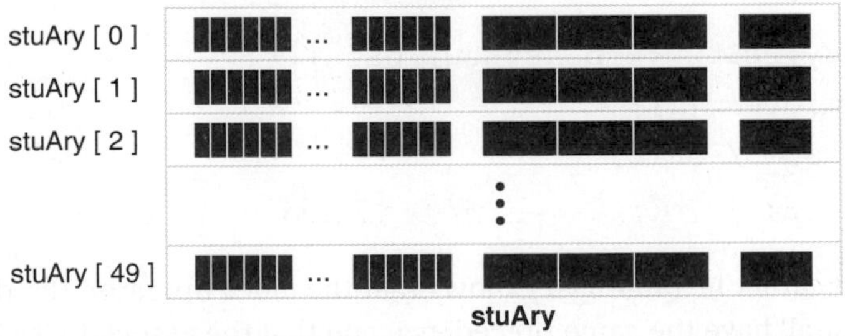

stuAry [0]	
stuAry [1]	
stuAry [2]	
stuAry [49]	

stuAry

Since a structure is a type, we can create the array just as we would create an array of integers. The code is shown below.

```
STUDENT stuAry[50];
```

Study this array carefully. Note that it is an array that contains two other arrays, name and midterm. This is not a multidimensional array. To be a multidimensional array, each level must have the same data type. In this case, each type is different: the stuAry is STUDENT, while name is character, and midterm is integer.

To access the data for one student, we refer only to the structure name with an index or a pointer as shown below.

```
stuAry[i]    *pStu
```

For example, let's write a short segment of code to compute the average for the final exam. We use a for loop since we know the number of students in the array.

```
Int    totScore = 0;
Float average;
STUDENT* pStu;
STUDENT* pLastStu;
...
pLastStu = stuAry + 49;
for (pStu = stuAry; pStu <= pLastStu; pStu++)
    totScore += pStu->final;
average = totScore / 50.0;
```

However, to access an individual element in one of the student's arrays, such as the second midterm for the fifth student, we need to use an index or pointer for each field as shown below.

```
stuAry[4].midterm[1]
```

To access students' midterms with pointers, we need one index or pointer for the array. We also need a second index or pointer for the midterms. The code to compute the average for each midterm is shown below. We use a separate array, midTermAvrg, to store the average for the midterms. In this example, we use indexes to access the midterms and pointers to access the students.

```
float midTermAvrg[3];
int sum;
STUDENT* pStu;
......
STUDENT* pLastStu;
pLastStu = stuAry + 49;
for (int i = 0; i < 3; i++)
{
    sum = 0;
    for (pStu = stuAry; pStu <= pLastStu; pStu++)
        sum += pStu->midterm[i];
    midTermAvrg[i] = sum / 50.0;
} // for i
```

The precedence table (shown earlier in Table 11-1) shows that the index operator, the direct selection operator, and the indirect selection operator all have the same precedence and that the associativity is from left to right. So we do not need parentheses to total the scores for a midterm.

Insertion Sort Revisited

To demonstrate using structures in arrays, let's sort an array of students. We will use the student structure seen in Figure 11-14. Whenever we sort a structure, we need to define the field that controls the sort. This control field is usually called a key. In our student structure, the key field is the name. **Program 11-4** shows the code.

This program follows the insertion sort design you have seen before. There are only two significant changes: First, all the array handling is done with pointers, and second, the compare logic was changed to use the strcmp function.

To test the sort, we wrote a small driver that uses an initialized array for its data. To verify that the sort works, we printed the data before and after the sort process.

Program 11-4 | Sort array of student structures

```c
1   /* This program sorts an array of student structures
2      Written by:
3      Date:
4   */
5   #include <stdio.h>
6   #include <string.h>
7
8   #include <stdbool.h>
9   #define NUM_STU 5
10
11  // Global Type Declaration
12  typedef struct
13  {
14     char name[26];
15     int midterm[3];
16     int final;
17  } STUDENT;
18
19  // Function Declarations
20  void insertionSort (STUDENT list[], int last);
21
22  int main (void)
23  {
24  // Local Declarations
25     STUDENT stuAry[NUM_STU] =
26     {
27        {"Charles, George", {85, 94, 79}, 93},
28        {"Adams, Karin", {75, 91, 89}, 89},
29        {"Nguyen, Tuan", {87, 88, 89}, 90},
30        {"Oh, Bill", {78, 96, 88}, 91},
31        {"Chavez, Maria", {83, 79, 93}, 91}
32     }; // stuAry
33
34  // Statements
35     printf("Unsorted data:\n");
36     for (STUDENT* pStuPtr = stuAry;
37          pStuPtr < stuAry + NUM_STU;
38          pStuPtr++)
39        printf("%-26s %4d %4d %4d %4d\n",
40               pStuPtr->name,
41               pStuPtr->midterm[0],
```

(continue)

Program 11-4 Sort array of student structures *(continued)*

```
42                    pStuPtr->midterm[1],
43                    pStuPtr->midterm[2],
44                    pStuPtr->final);
45      printf("\n");
46
47      insertionSort (stuAry, NUM_STU - 1);
48
49      printf("Sorted data:\n");
50      for (STUDENT* pStuPtr = stuAry;
51           pStuPtr < stuAry + NUM_STU;
52           pStuPtr++)
53        printf("%-26s %4d %4d %4d %4d\n",
54                  pStuPtr->name,
55                  pStuPtr->midterm[0],
56                  pStuPtr->midterm[1],
57                  pStuPtr->midterm[2],
58                  pStuPtr->final);
59      return 0;
60  } // main
61
62  /* ================== insertionSort ==================
63     Sort list using Insertion Sort. The list is divided
64     into sorted and unsorted lists. With each pass, the
65     first element in unsorted list is inserted into
66     sorted list.
67     Pre list must contain at least one element
68     last is index to last element in list
69     Post list has been rearranged.
70  */
71  void insertionSort (STUDENT list[], int last)
72  {
73  // Local Declarations
74     bool located;
75     STUDENT temp;
76     STUDENT* pCurrent;
77     STUDENT* pWalker;
78     STUDENT* pLast;
79
80  // Statements
81     for (pCurrent = list +1, pLast = list + last;
82          pCurrent <= pLast;
83          pCurrent++)
84       {
```

(continue)

Program 11-4   Sort array of student structures *(continued)*

```
85         located = false;
86         temp = *pCurrent;
87
88         for (pWalker = pCurrent - 1;
89              pWalker >= list && !located;)
90            if (strcmp(temp.name, pWalker->name) < 0)
91            {
92               *(pWalker + 1) = *pWalker;
93               pWalker—;
94            } // if
95            else
96               located = true;
97         *(pWalker + 1) = temp;
98      } // for pCurrent
99      return;
100 } // insertionSort
101 // ================= End of Program ===============
```

Output
```
Unsorted data:
Charles, George    85 94 79 93
Adams, Karin    75 91 89 89
Nguyen, Tuan    87 88 89 90
Oh, Bill 78 96 88 91
Chavez, Maria    83 79 93 91

Sorted data:
Adams, Karin    75 91 89 89
Charles, George    85 94 79 93
Chavez, Maria    83 79 93 91
Nguyen, Tuan    87 88 89 90
Oh, Bill 78 96 88 91
```

Structures and Functions

For structures to be fully useful, we must be able to pass them to functions and return them. A function can access the members of a structure in three ways:

1. Individual members can be passed to the function.

2. The whole structure can be passed and the function can access the members using pass by value.

3. The address of a structure or member can be passed, and the function can access the members through indirection and indirect selection operators.

Sending Individual Members

Sending individual members to a function is no different from what we have done before. To demonstrate the calling sequence, we will use a simple example to multiply two fractions. The flow is shown in **Figure 11-17**.

Figure 11-17   Passing structure members to functions

```
...
res.numerator =
   multiply(frl.numerator, fr2.numerator)
res.denominator =
   multiply(frl.d.denominator, fr2.denominator);
...
```

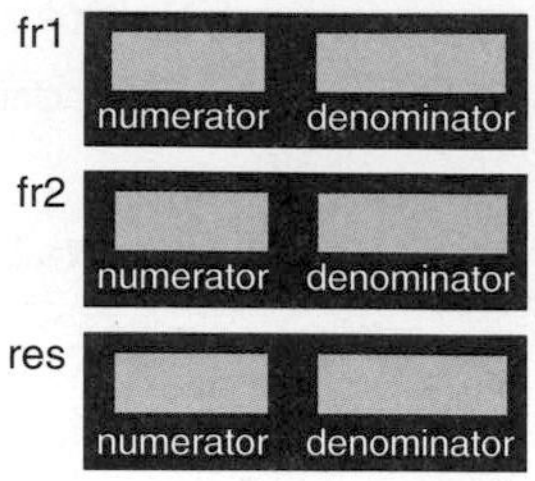

```
// ============= multiply =============
int multiply (int x, int y)
{
   return x * y;
}// multiply
```

As you can see from Figure 11-17, the only difference is that we must use the direct selection operator to refer to the individual members for the actual parameters. The called program doesn't know if the two integers are simple variables or structure members.

Sending the Whole Structure

The problem with the above solution is that the multiplication logic is split between the calling and called programs. This is not considered good structured programming. A much better solution is to pass the entire structure and let `multiply` complete its job in one call.

Passing a structure is really no different from passing individual elements. Since the structure is a type, we simply specify the type in the formal parameters of the called function. Similarly, the function can return a structure. Again, all that is necessary is to specify the structure as the `return` type in the called function.

The same pass-by-value rules apply, however; when we pass a structure to a function, C will copy the values to the local structure just as it does for variables. This may lead to some inefficiencies when large structures are used. We address this problem in the next section.

We will rework the multiply fractions program to pass structures. In this case, we have written the complete program. The design is shown in **Figure 11-18**, and the code is shown in **Program 11-5**.

Figure 11-18   Passing and returning structures

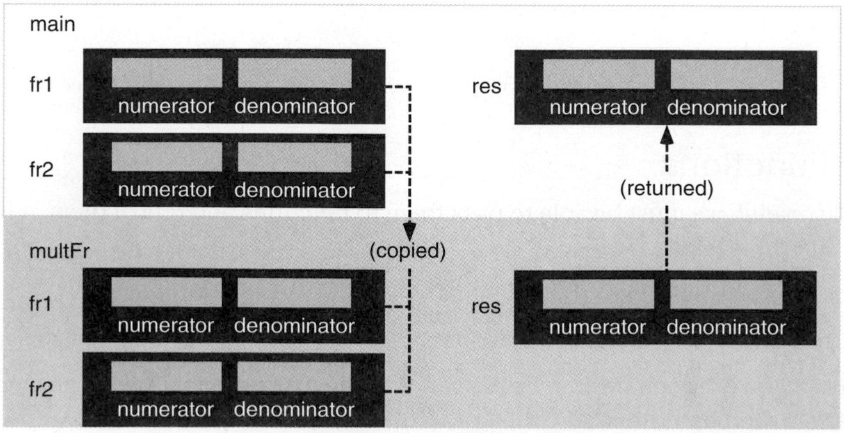

Program 11-5 | Passing and returning structures

```c
1  /* This program uses structures to multiply fractions.
2     Written by:
3     Date:
4  */
5
6  #include <stdio.h>
7  // Global Declarations
8  typedef struct
9  {
10    int numerator;
11    int denominator;
12 } FRACTION;
13
14 // Function Declarations
15 FRACTION getFr (void);
16 FRACTION multFr (FRACTION fr1, FRACTION fr2);
17 void printFr (FRACTION fr1, FRACTION fr2,
18               FRACTION result);
19
20 int main (void)
21 {
22 //Local Declarations
23    FRACTION fr1;
24    FRACTION fr2;
25    FRACTION res;
26
27 //Statements
28    fr1 = getFr ();
29    fr2 = getFr ();
30    res = multFr (fr1, fr2);
31    printFr (fr1, fr2, res);
32    return 0;
33 } // main
34
35 /*================== getFr ================
36    Get two integers from the keyboard, make & return
37    a fraction to the main program.
38    Pre nothing
39    Post returns a fraction
40 */
41 FRACTION getFr (void)
```

(continue)

Program 11-5 Passing and returning structures *(continued)*

```c
42 {
43 // Local Declarations
44    FRACTION fr;
45
46 // Statements
47    printf("Write a fraction in the form of x/y: ");
48    scanf ("%d/%d", &fr.numerator, &fr.denominator);
49    return fr;
50 }// getFraction
51
52 /* ==================== multFr ===================
53    Multiply two fractions and return the result.
54    Pre fr1 and fr2 are fractions
55    Post returns the product
56 */
57 FRACTION multFr (FRACTION fr1, FRACTION fr2)
58 {
59 // Local Declaration
60    FRACTION res;
61
62 // Statements
63    res.numerator = fr1.numerator * fr2.numerator;
64    res.denominator = fr1.denominator * fr2.denominator;
65    return res;
66 } // multFr
67
68 /* ==================== printFr ====================
69    Prints the value of the fields in three fractions.
70    Pre two original fractions and the product
71    Post fractions printed
72 */
73 void printFr (FRACTION fr1, FRACTION fr2,
74               FRACTION res)
75 {
76 // Statements
77    printf("The result of %d/%d * %d/%d is %d/%d\n",
78           fr1.numerator, fr1.denominator,
79           fr2.numerator, fr2.denominator,
80           res.numerator, res.denominator);
81    return;
82 } // printFractions
83 // ================== End of Program=================
```

(continue)

Program 11-5   Passing and returning structures *(continued)*

> **Output**
> Write a fraction in the form of x/y: 4/3
> Write a fraction in the form of x/y: 6/7
> The result of 4/3 * 6/7 is 24/21

There are five points you should study in this program:

1. The `fraction` structure is declared in global memory before `main`. This makes it visible to all the functions.

2. In `getFr`, the data are read by using the address operator and the direct selection operator. Since the direct selection operator (`.`) has a higher priority, they can be coded without parentheses.

3. In `getFr` we pass back two values in the structure without using pointers. This is another advantage of structures: We can return more than one piece of data when we put the data in a structure.

4. The structure type is passed using the `FRACTION` type definition.

5. The references to the data in `multFr` and `printFr` must use the direct selection operator to get to the individual members.

Passing Structures through Pointers

As mentioned, passing structures is still pass-by-value. For the multiply fractions program, this is the correct way to write the program. It provides the necessary data protection and data encapsulation for good structured programming while at the same time being efficient.

When the structure is very large, however, efficiency can suffer, especially with a heavily used function. Therefore, we often use pointers to pass structures. It is also common to pass structures through pointers when the structure is in dynamic memory. In these cases, all we have to pass is the pointer.

We modify the multiply fractions program once more to pass the structures using pointers. The memory flow is shown in **Figure 11-19** and the coding in **Program 11-6**.

Figure 11-19 Passing structures through pointers

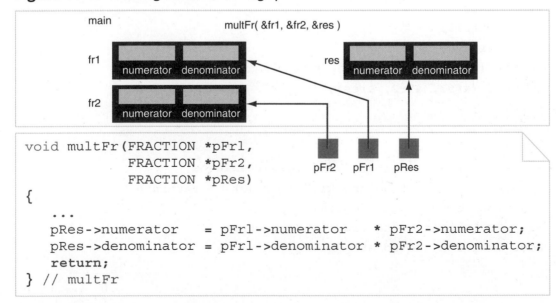

Program 11-6 | Passing structures through pointers

```
1  /* This program uses structures to multiply fractions.
2     Written by:
3     Date:
4  */
5
6  #include <stdio.h>
7  // Global Declarations
8  typedef struct
9  {
10    int numerator;
11    int denominator;
12 } FRACTION;
13
14 // Function Declarations
15 void getFr(FRACTION* pFr);
16 void multFr(FRACTION* pFr1; FRACTION* pFr2,
17            FRACTION* pRes2);
18 void printFr(FRACTION* pFr1, FRACTION* pFr2,
19             FRACTION* pRes);
20
21 int main (void)
22 {
23 // Local Declarations
24    FRACTION fr1;
25    FRACTION fr2;
26    FRACTION res;
27
28 // Statements
29    getFr (&fr1);
30    getFr (&fr2);
31    multFr (&fr1, &fr2, &res);
32    printFr (&fr1, &fr2, &res);
33    return 0;
34 } // main
35
36 /*================= getFr ====================
37    Get two integers from the keyboard, make & return a
38    fraction to the main program.
39    Pre pFr is pointer to fraction structure
40    Post fraction stored at pFr.
41 */
```

(continue)

Program 11-6 Passing structures through pointers *(continued)*

```c
42 void getFr (FRACTION* pFr)
43 {
44 // Statements
45    printf("Write a fraction in the form of x/y: ");
46    scanf ("%d/%d", &pFr->numerator,
47           &(*pFr).denominator);
48    return;
49 } // getFr
50
51 /* ===================== multFr =====================
52    Multiply two fractions and return the result.
53    Pre fr1, fr2, pRes are pointers to fractions
54    Post product stored at pRes
55 */
56 void multFr (FRACTION* pFr1, FRACTION* pFr2,
57             FRACTION* pRes)
58 {
59 // Statements
60    pRes->numerator =
61       pFr1->numerator * pFr2->numerator;
62    PRes->denominator =
63       pFr1->denominator * pFr2->denominator;
64    return;
65 } // multFr
66
67 /* ===================== printFr =====================
68    Prints the value of the fields in three fractions.
69    Pre pointers to two fractions and their product
70    Post fractions printed
71 */
72 void printFr (FRACTION* pFr1, FRACTION* pFr2,
73             FRACTION* pRes)
74 {
75 // Statements
76    printf("\nThe result of %d/%d * %d/%d is %d/%d\n",
77           pFr1->numerator, pFr1->denominator,
78           pFr2->numerator, pFr2->denominator,
79           pRes->numerator, pRes->denominator);
80    return;
81 } // printFr
82 // ================== End of Program ==================
```

In this version of the program, the structure is passed and returned as a pointer. Note the syntactical notation for reading the data in the get Fr function. We reproduce it below for your convenience.

```
scanf ("%d/%d", &pFr->numerator, &(*pFr).denominator);
```

Even though we are using pointers, we still need to pass scanf addresses. We have used two different notations in this example. (This is not good coding style, but it demonstrates both techniques in one statement.) In both cases, since we are reading a field within the structure, we need to pass the address of the individual field, not the structure. In the first example, we use the indirect selection operator (->). Because it has a higher precedence than the address operator (&), it can be coded without parentheses.

In the second example, we use the direct selection operator (.). In this case we need parentheses because the direct selection operator has a higher precedence (16) than the indirection operator (*) and the address operator (both 15). However, since the address and direct selection operator are at the same level, we need to use the parentheses only around the pointer dereference.

11.4 Unions

The union is a construct that allows memory to be shared by different types of data. This redefinition can be as simple as redeclaring an integer as four characters or as complex as redeclaring an entire structure. For example, we know that a short integer is 2 bytes and that each byte is a character. Therefore, we could process a short integer as a number or as two characters.

The union follows the same format syntax as the structure. In fact, with the exception of the keywords struct and union, the formats are the same. **Figure 11-20** shows how we declare a union that can be used as either a short integer or as two characters.

Figure 11-20 Unions

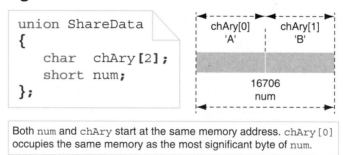

Both num and chAry start at the same memory address. chAry[0] occupies the same memory as the most significant byte of num.

Referencing Unions

The rules for referencing a union are identical to those for structures. To reference individual fields within the union, we use the direct selection (dot) operator. Each reference must be fully qualified from the beginning of the structure to the element being referenced. This includes the name of the union itself. When a union is being referenced through a pointer, the selection operator (arrow) can be used. The following are both valid references to the union shown in Figure 11-20.

```
shareData.num
shareData.chAry[0]
```

Initializers

While C permits a union to be initialized, only the first type declared in the union can be initialized when the variable is defined. The other types can only be initialized by assigning values or reading values into the union. When initializing a union, we must enclose the values in a set of braces, even if there is only one value.

Program 11-7 demonstrates unions in a program. It uses the structure in Figure 11-20 to print a variable, first as a number and then as two characters.

Program 11-7 | Demonstrate effect of union

```c
 1  /* Demonstrate union of short int and two char.
 2     Written by:
 3     Date:
 4  */
 5
 6  #include <stdio.h>
 7  // Global Declarations
 8     typedef union
 9     {
10        short num;
11        char chAry[2];
12     } SH_CH2;
13
14  int main (void)
15  {
16  // Local Declarations
17     SH_CH2 data;
18
19  // Statements
20     data.num = 16706;
21
22     printf("Short: %hd\n" , data.num);
23     printf("Ch[0]: %c\n", data.chAry[0]);
24     printf("Ch[l]: %c\n", data.chAry[1]);
25
26     return 0;
27  } // main
```

```
Output
Short: 16706
Ch[0]: A
Ch[1]: B
```

To prove to yourself that 16706 creates the characters A and B, you will need to analyze its bit pattern. Don't be surprised, however, if you get a different number on your computer. If you do, it means that you have a "little-endian" computer (described later in this section).

Unions and Structures

In a union, each piece of data starts at the same memory location and occupies at least a part of the same memory. Thus, when a union is shared by two or more different data types, only one piece of data can be in memory at one time.

Consider, for example, an address book that contains both company and individual names. When we store a company name, the name has only one field. On the other hand, when we store an individual's name, the name has at least three parts—first name, middle initial, and last name. If we want to have only one name field in our address book, we need to use a union to store the name. This design is shown in **Figure 11-21**. Note that in the figure, un is the member name to access the union structure.

Figure 11-21   A name union

```
typedef struct
{
    char first[20];
    char init;
    char last[30];
} PERSON;

typedef struct
{
    char type;
    union
    {
        char company[40];
        PERSON person;
    } un;
) NAME;
```

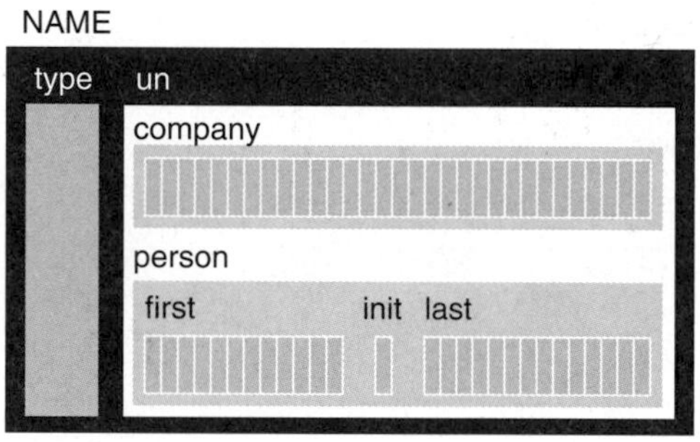

Because two different types of data can be stored in the same union, we need to know which type currently is stored. This is done with a type flag that is created when the data are stored. If the name is in the company format, the flag is C, and if it is in the person format it is a P.

When a union is defined, C reserves enough room to store the largest data object in the construct. In Figure 11-21, the size of the company name is 40 bytes and the size of the person name is 51 bytes. The size of the union structure is therefore 52 bytes (the size of the person name plus the type) regardless of what type of data are being stored. When a company name is stored, the last 11 bytes are present but unused.

Program 11-8 demonstrates the use of a union in a structure by printing each format.

Program 11-8 | Demonstrate unions in structures

```
1   /* Demonstrate use of unions in structures.
2      Written by:
3      Date:
4   */
5   #include <stdio.h>
6   #include <string.h>
7
```

(continue)

Program 11-8   Demonstrate unions in structures *(continued)*

```c
 8  // Global Structures
 9  typedef struct
10  {
11     char first[20];
12     char init;
13     char last[30];
14  } PERSON;
15
16  typedef struct
17  {
18     char type; //C—company: P-person
19     union
20     {
21        char company[40];
22        PERSON person;
23     } un;
24  } NAME;
25
26  int main (void)
27  {
28  // Local Declarations
29     NAME business = {'C', "ABC Company"};
30     NAME friend;
31     NAME names[2];
32
33  // Statements
34     friend.type = 'P';
35     strcpy (friend.un.person.first, "Martha");
36     strcpy (friend.un.person.last,"Washington");
37     friend.un.person.init = 'C';
38
39     names[0] = business;
40     names[1] = friend;
41
42     for (int i = 0; i < 2; i++)
43     switch (name s[i].type)
44     {
45        case 'C': printf("Company: %s\n",
46                        names[i].un.company);
47                 break;
48        case 'P': printf("Friend: %s %c %s\n",
49                        names[i].un.person.first,
50                        names[i].un.person.init,
```

(continue)

Program 11-8 Demonstrate unions in structures *(continued)*

```
 51                        names[i].un.person.last);
 52               break;
 53     default:  printf("Error in type\a\n");
 54               break;
 55    } // switch
 56    return 0;
 57 } // main
```

Output
```
Company: ABC Company
Friend: Martha C Washington
```

We begin by creating two union structures, one for a business and one for a friend. To initialize the business union, we used initializers. To initialize the friend union, we used string copy and assignment. Once the unions were created, we copied them to an array to demonstrate one common processing concept.

Unions are often processed with a switch statement that uses the type to determine what data format is currently being processed. Note that it is the programmer's responsibility to process the data correctly. If a business identifier is used while person data are present, the program will run but garbage will be produced.

Once the correct union type has been determined, the rest of the processing is routine. We simply print the data in the union using the appropriate identifiers for its content. Note that we provide a default statement even though there is no possibility of an error in this simple program.

> **Note**
>
> Computer hardware can be physically designed to store the most significant byte of a number at either the left end of the number (big endian) or at the right end of the number (little endian), as shown below.
>
>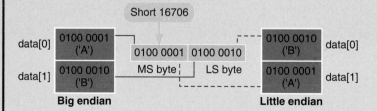
>
> If we consider memory as an array of bytes, then a computer that uses big endian stores the most significant byte—that is, the larger portion of the number (16,000 in the above example) at the beginning of the array. This is shown in the example on the left. Note that data [0] is 'A' and data [1] is 'B'.
>
> In a little-endian computer, the most significant byte is stored on the right. This example is seen on the right in the above example. This time, data [0] contains 'B' and data [1] contains 'A'. If you want to know if your computer is big or little endian, run Program 11-7 and check out the results.

Internet Addresses

As a final example of union processing, let's consider how Internet addresses are formatted and processed. We are most familiar with the Internet domain names such as www.deanza.edu. These names are easy to remember and use. The real Internet Protocol (IP) address, however, is defined as dotted decimal notation, as shown below.

```
153.18.8.105
```

The decimal–dot notation is used primarily by system administrators. To conserve transmission time and facilitate processing, however, the IP address must be converted to a 4-byte integer for transmission down the Internet.

Each portion of the IP address has a maximum value of 255. This means that it can be stored in 1 byte. To store the address in an integer, we simply convert each portion of the address to 1 byte and store it in the appropriate portion of the integer. Thus, in our example, we convert 153 to its corresponding (extended) ASCII character and store it in the first byte of the integer. Then we convert the 18 and store it in the second byte, 8 into the third byte, and finally 105 into the fourth byte. To process the integer address as both an integer and an array of four characters requires a union.

Given that the IP address is a string, we use the string token operator and a loop for the conversion. The code is shown in **Program 11-9**.

Program 11-9 | Convert IP address to `long`

```
1   /* Reformat IP string address to long integer.
2      Written by:
3      Date:
4   */
5   #include <stdio.h>
6   #include <string.h>
7   #include <stdlib.h>
8
9   // Global Structures
10  typedef union
11  {
12     unsigned char chAddr[4];
13     unsigned long numAddr;
14  } IP_ADDR;
15
16  int main (void)
17  {
18  // Local Declarations
19     IP_ADDR addr;
20     char* parser;
21     char strAddr[16] = "153.18.8.105";
22
23  // Statements
24     // Convert first address segment
25     parser = strtok (strAddr, ".");
26     addr.chAddr[3] = strtol (parser, (char**)NULL, 10);
27
28     for (int i = 2; i>=0; i--)
29     {
30     // Convert decimal dot positions 2, 3, 4
31        parser = strtok (NULL, ".");
```

(continue)

Program 11-9 Convert IP address to `long` (continued)

```
32          addr.chAddr[i] =
33             strtol (parser, (char**)NULL, 10);
34      } // for
35
36      // Now print results
37      printf ("IP decimal dot: %d.%d.%d.%d\n",
38                  addr.chAddr[3] , addr.chAddr[2],
39                  addr.chAddr[1] , addr.chAddr[0]);
40      printf ("IP binary: %lu\n", addr.numAddr);
41      return 0;
42 } // main
```

Output
```
IP decimal dot: 153.18.8.105
IP binary address: 2568095849
```

Before you study this program, you may want to review parsing concepts including the `strtok` function. They are used extensively in this program.

In statement 21, we set up an IP address using the dotted-decimal notation. It is constructed so that each portion is a decimal number (A.B.C.D). We then parse the first number and place it in the first byte of the binary address. This is necessary because the first string token format differs from the one that parses the rest of the string (see statements 25 and 31).

Within the loop, we parse the rest of the string, convert it to a decimal value, and store the address elements in the second, third, and fourth positions of the binary address. After the loop, we print the converted address, first in its character format and then as a long integer.

This program is designed to work with little-endian computers. For big-endian computers, statement 26 would use index 0, and the `for` in statement 28 would start at 1 and move up to 3. The indexes in statements 38 and 39 would also need to be reversed.

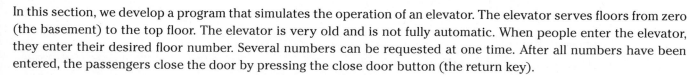

Programming Example: Elevator Application

In this section, we develop a program that simulates the operation of an elevator. The elevator serves floors from zero (the basement) to the top floor. The elevator is very old and is not fully automatic. When people enter the elevator, they enter their desired floor number. Several numbers can be requested at one time. After all numbers have been entered, the passengers close the door by pressing the close door button (the return key).

Each time the door closes, the elevator checks to see if any floors in the current direction (up or down) need to be serviced. If they do, then it services these floors first, starting with the closest one to the current floor. If no floors in the current direction need service, it checks the opposite direction, again servicing the one closest to the current floor.

Each time the elevator arrives at a floor, new passengers can get on and request their floor. The new requests are added to the ones still pending, and the elevator again evaluates which floor will be processed next.

The structure for this program is portrayed in **Figure 11-22**. The elevator is represented as a structure with two fields: the current floor and a pointer to an array of buttons. The button values are IN, meaning the floor has been requested, and OUT, meaning the floor has not been requested. After a floor has been serviced, the button is reset.

Figure 11-22 Elevator structure

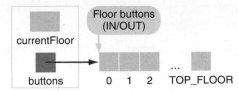

The elevator design is shown in two different ways. **Figure 11-23** is a structure chart for the program.

Figure 11-23 Elevator structure chart

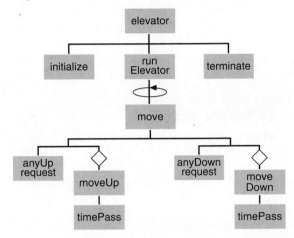

Figure 11-24 is a state diagram for the elevator. A state diagram is a design technique often used with real-time systems to show how a system moves from one state to another. For an elevator, it can be in one of three states: moving up, moving down, or stopped. Each of these states is represented by a circle in the diagram. To move from one state to another, a change must occur in the elevator environment. For example, to change from the stop state to the up state, a button must be pressed. This is reflected on the line between stop and up as `anyUp`.

Figure 11-24 Elevator state diagram

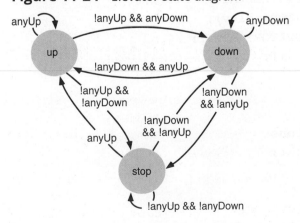

The `main` function for the elevator program is seen in **Program 11-10**. It calls three other functions: initialize (Program 11-11), run elevator (Program 11-12), and terminate (Program 11-17). Of the three, run elevator is the function of primary interest; it simulates the actual running of the elevator.

Program 11-10 | Elevator: `main`

```c
 1  /* This program simulates the operation of an elevator.
 2     Written by:
 3     Date:
 4  */
 5  #include <stdio.h>
 6  #include <stdlib.h>
 7  #include <ctype.h>
 8  #include <stdbool.h>
 9
10  #define TOP_FLOOR 10
11  #define DELAY_FACTOR 10000
12
13  // Global Type Declarations
14  typedef enum {OUT, IN} BUTTON_STATUS;
15  typedef enum {DOWN, STOP, UP} DIRECTION_STATUS;
16  typedef struct
17  {
18     int currentFloor;
19     BUTTON_STATUS* buttons;
20  } ELEVATOR;
21
22  // Function Declarations
23  void   initialize(ELEVATOR* elev);
24  void   runElevator(ELEVATOR* elev);
25  void   terminate(ELEVATOR* elev);
26  void   move(ELEVATOR* elev);
27  bool   anyUpRequest(ELEVATOR* elev);
28  bool   anyDownRequest(ELEVATOR* elev);
29  void   moveUp(ELEVATOR* elev);
30  void   moveDown(ELEVATOR* elev);
31  void   timePass(int m);
32
33  int main (void)
34  {
35  // Local Declarations
36     ELEVATOR elevator;
37
38  // Statements
39     initialize (&elevator);
40     runElevator (&elevator);
41     terminate (&elevator);
42     return 0;
43  } // main
```

Program **11-11** initializes the state of the elevator.

Program 11-11 | Elevator: initialize

```
1   /* ================= initialize ==================
2       This function dynamically allocates memory locations
3       for buttons & initializes current floor to 1 to show
4       that the elevator is parked at the first floor.
5       Pre  nothing
6       Post elevator created, all buttons reset, and
7       parked at first floor (not basement)
8   */
9   void initialize (ELEVATOR* elev)
10  {
11  // Statements
12      elev->buttons = calloc(TOP_FLOOR + 1,
13      sizeof (BUTTON_STATUS));
14
15      for (int i = 0; i <= TOP_FLOOR; i++)
16         elev->buttons [i] = OUT;
17      elev->currentFloor = 1;
18
19      return;
20  } // initialize
```

Program **11-12** simulates the operation of the elevator.

Program 11-12 | Elevator: run elevator

```
1   /* ================= runElevator ==================
2       Simulate the operation of the elevator.
3       Pre  elevator structure has been initialized
4       Post simulation is complete
5   */
6   void runElevator (ELEVATOR* elev)
7   {
8   // Local Declarations
9       char buffer [81];
10      int floor;
11      char* pStrIn;
12
13  // Statements
14      printf("\n\nThis elevator goes from basement (0) ");
```

(continue)

Program 11-12   Elevator: run elevator *(continued)*

```
15      printf("to floor %d", TOP_FLOOR);
16      printf( "\n\nType floors & press return to start");
17      printf( "\nIf no new floors, press return key.");
18      printf("\nTo quit, key EOF");
19      printf("\n\nPlease enter floors: ");
20
21      while (fgets(buffer, 81, stdin))
22      {
23         pStrIn = buffer;
24         while (*pStrIn != '\n')
25         {
26  // Locate next floor digit & convert to int
27            while (*pStrIn == ' ')
28               pStrIn++;
29            if (isdigit (*pStrIn))
30            {
31               printf("\aInvalid floor %c\n", *pStrIn);
32               pStrIn++;
33            } // if
34            else
35            {
36               sscanf (pStrIn, "%d", &floor);
37               if (floor == elev->currentFloor)
38                  printf("\n\aAlready on floor %d.",
39                         elev->currentFloor);
40               else
41                  if (floor < 0 || floor > TOP_FLOOR)
42                     printf("\n\a%d invalid floor",
43                            floor);
44                  else
45                     elev->buttons [floor] = IN;
46
47  // Synchronize sscanf & *pStrIn
48               while (isdigit (*pStrIn))
49                  pStrIn++;
50            } // else
51         } // while
52
53         move (elev);
54         printf("\n\nPlease enter floors: ");
55      } // while
56      return;
57  } // runElevator
```

The simulation is controlled by runElevator. The technique we use to prevent invalid user input is interesting. After reading the input stream, we use a pointer to parse the string after skipping whitespace. If the current character is a digit, we use sscanf to format the digit(s) as an integer. If it is not a digit, we print an error message and skip it. (Of course, in a real elevator, it is impossible to get an invalid floor.) Then, after converting the digit string to an integer, we synchronize the buffer and our pointer with a small while loop.

As we parse the integers in the input stream, we "push" their corresponding buttons in our data structure. This code is shown at statement 45 in Program 11-12.

Program 11-13 moves the elevator to a requested floor.

Program 11-13 | Elevator: move

```
1   /* ============== move ==============
2      Moves the elevator to a requested floor. It stops
3      the elevator after responding to one request.
4      Pre given elevator
5      Post elevator has been moved--while it is
6      moving, the floors are called out
7   */
8   void move (ELEVATOR* elev)
9   {
10  // Local Declarations
11     static DIRECTION_STATUS direction = STOP;
12
13     bool anyUp;
14     bool anyDown;
15
16  // Statements
17     anyUp = anyUpRequest (elev);
18     anyDown = anyDownRequest (elev);
19
20     if (direction == UP)
21     {
22        if (!anyUp && anyDown)
23           direction = DOWN;
24        else
25           if (!anyUp && !anyDown)
26              direction = STOP;
27     } // UP
28
29     else if (direction == DOWN)
30     {
31        if (!anyDown && anyUp)
32           direction = UP;
```

(continue)

Program 11-13   Elevator: move *(continued)*

```
33          else
34             if (!anyDown && !anyUp)
35                 direction = STOP;
36      }// DOWN
37
38      else if (direction == STOP)
39      {
40         if (anyUp)
41            direction = UP;
42         else
43            if (anyDown)
44                direction = DOWN;
45      } // else if stop
46
47      if (direction == UP)
48         moveUp (elev);
49      else
50         if (direction == DOWN)
51            moveDown (elev);
52         else
53            printf("\n***** NO BUTTON PRESSED ***** ");
54      return;
55 } // move
```

The move function is one of the more interesting functions in the simulation. At any given point in the operation, the elevator can be in one of three states: moving up, moving down, or stopped. We use an enumerated type to track the state.

If the elevator is moving up, we continue up as long as there are requests for higher floors. If there are none, we test for down requests. If there are any down requests, we change the state to down and proceed. If there are no up requests and no down requests, we change the state to stop. This logic is seen in statements 21 through 47 of Program 11-13. Note the use of the blocks to ensure that the if and else statements are properly paired.

Program 11-14 simulates the elevator movement as it moves up and down.

Program 11-14 | Elevator: move up and move down

```
1  /*====================moveUp====================
2     This function simulates the movement of the elevator
3     when it is going up.
4     Pre given moving up elevator
5     Post up simulation is displayed on the screen
6  */
7  void moveUp (ELEVATOR* elev)
```

(continue)

Program 11-14   Elevator: move up and move down (*continued*)

```
8  {
9  // Statements
10     printf ("\nThe door is being closed ...");
11     printf ("\nWe are going up.");
12     (elev->currentFloor)++;
13     while (elev->buttons[elev->currentFloor] != IN)
14     {
15        printf("\n");
16        timePass (2);
17        printf("\nPassing floor %d", elev->currentFloor);
18        printf("\n ");
19        timePass (2);
20        (elev->currentFloor)++;
21     } // while
22
23     elev->buttons [elev->currentFloor] = OUT;
24     printf ("\nThe door is being opened ...");
25     printf("\n");
26     printf("\n ***** FLOOR %d ***** ",
27            elev->currentFloor);
28     printf("\n");
29     timePass(4);
30     return;
31 } // moveUp
32
33 /* ==================== moveDown ====================
34    This function simulates the movement of the elevator
35    when it is going down.
36    Pre given moving down elevator
37    Post down simulation is displayed on the screen
38 */
39 void moveDown (ELEVATOR* elev)
40 {
41 // Statements
42     printf ("\nThe door is being closed ...");
43     printf("\nWe are going down");
44     (elev->currentFloor)--;
45     while (elev->buttons [elev ->currentFloor] != IN)
46     {
47        printf("\n");
48        timePass (2);
49        printf("\nPassing floor %d", elev->currentFloor);
50        printf("\n");
51        timePass (2);
```

(*continue*)

Program 11-14   Elevator: move up and move down *(continued)*

```
52            (elev->currentFloor)--;
53        } // while
54        elev->buttons [elev->currentFloor] = OUT;
55        printf ( "\nThe door is being opened ...");
56        printf("\n ");
57        printf("\n ***** FLOOR %d *****",
58                elev->currentFloor);
59        printf("\n");
60        timePass (4);
61
62        return;
63    } // moveDown
```

Both moveUp and moveDown operate similarly. They move past the current floor in the correct direction and "call out" the floors as we pass them. A timing loop is included to simulate the time it takes the elevator to reach the next floor.

Program 11-15 contains two functions: anyUpRequest checks for floors above the current position; anyDownRequest checks for floors below the current position.

Program 11-15 | Elevator: any up and any down request

```
1   /* ================= anyUpRequest ===================
2       This function checks to see if any request is for a
3       floor above the current floor.
4       Pre given elevator
5       Post return true if button above current floor
6       pushed; return false otherwise
7   */
8   bool anyUpRequest (ELEVATOR* elev)
9   {
10  // Local Declarations
11      bool isAny = false;
12
13  // Statements
14      for (int check = elev->currentFloor;
15           check <= TOP_FLOOR && !isAny;
16           check++)
17        isAny = (elev->buttons[check] == IN);
18      return isAny;
19  } // anyUpRequest
20
21  /* ================= anyDownRequest =================
22      This function checks to see if any request is for a
```

(continue)

Program 11-15   Elevator: any up and any down request *(continued)*

```
23        floor below the current floor.
24        Pre given elevator
25        Post return true if button below current floor
26        pushed; return false otherwise
27 */
28 bool anyDownRequest (ELEVATOR* elev)
29 {
30 // Local Declarations
31    bool isAny = false;
32
33 // Statements
34    for (int check = elev->currentFloor;
35         check >= 0;
36         check--)
37      isAny = isAny || (elev->buttons[check] == IN);
38    return isAny;
39 } // anyDownRequest
```

Compare the `for` loops in `anyDownRequest` and `anyUpRequest`. One is much more efficient than the other. Do you see why? In `anyUpRequest`, we stop when we find the first request for a floor above the current one. In `anyDownRequest`, we check all floors below the current one, even if the first one has been requested. This means we always examine all lower floors.

Note the logic to set `isAny` at statement 37 in Program 11-15. The current setting is or'ed with `buttons`. If either are true, the result is true. Thus, once we find a floor has been requested, `isAny` will remain set regardless of the settings of the other `buttons`. This is a common technique to analyze a series of logical values.

Program 11-16 contains a loop to simulate time passing. We use a simple `for` loop.

Program 11-16 | Elevator: `timePass`

```
1  /* ================== timePass ==================
2     This function simulates the concept of passing time by
3     executing an empty for-loop.
4     Pre time to be passed (number of moments)
5     Post time has passed
6  */
7  void timePass (int time)
8  {
9  // Statements
10    for (long i = 0; i < (time* DELAY_FACTOR); i++)
11      ;
12    return;
13 } // timepass
```

The factor in the timing loop depends on the speed of your computer. In this case, we use 10,000. On a faster computer, you need to make the factor larger. On a slower computer, you need to make it smaller.

Note how we code the null statement in the `for` loop. Putting the null statement on a line by itself makes the function more readable. If the null statement were put at the end of the `for` statement, it would be too easy to think that the next statement, the `return` in this function, were part of the `for` loop.

The termination code is shown in **Program 11-17**.

> **Program 11-17** | Elevator: terminate

```
 1   /*==================terminate==================
 2       Release the memory occupied by buttons.
 3       Pre given elevator
 4       Post elevator memory is released
 5   */
 6   void terminate (ELEVATOR* elev)
 7   {
 8   // Statements
 9       free (elev->buttons);
10       return;
11   } // terminate
12   //================End of Program================
```

Although we do not need to release memory when terminating a program, we include the logic to do so for completeness.

Software Engineering

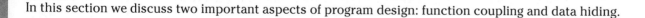

In this section we discuss two important aspects of program design: function coupling and data hiding.

Coupling

Previously, we discussed a concept known as functional cohesion, a measure of how closely related the processes are within a function. A related topic, coupling, is a measure of how tightly two functions are bound to each other. The more tightly coupled they are, the less independent they are. Because our objective is to make the modules as independent as possible, we want them to be loosely coupled.

Loose coupling is desirable for several reasons:

1. Independent—that is, loosely coupled—functions are more likely to be reusable.
2. Loosely coupled functions are less likely to create errors in related functions; conversely, the tighter the coupling, the higher the probability that an error in one function will generate an error in a related function.
3. Maintenance modifications—that is, modifications required to implement new user requirements—are easier and less apt to create errors with loosely coupled functions.

In the following sections we review five types of coupling.

Data Coupling

The first type of coupling, known as **data coupling**, passes only the minimum required data from the calling function to the called function. All required data are passed as parameters, and no extra data are passed. This is the best form of coupling and should be used whenever possible.

When you write simple functions that work on only one task, the coupling naturally tends to be data coupling. Consider the function exchange in the selection sort in algorithm. This function exchanges two integers. It receives pointers to the two integers that it will exchange and nothing else. It makes no references to any data outside the function, except through the parameter pointers. This function uses data coupling and is highly reusable.

| Note | Well-structured functions are highly cohesive and loosely coupled. |

We could have fallen into the trap of passing extra parameters by passing the function, the array, and the index locations of the two integers to be exchanged. The function would have worked just as well, but the coupling would not have been as loose. Now it requires an array of integers instead of just integers. Furthermore, we could have made the coupling even tighter had we referred to the maximum size of the array using the precompiler declaration SIZE. At this point, it is highly questionable whether the function could be used in another program.

Stamp Coupling

Functions are stamp coupled if the parameters are composite objects such as arrays or structures. Most of the functions in the selection sort use **stamp coupling** because they pass the array. (Although it could be argued that we are passing only a pointer to the array, the intent is to modify the array. We are, therefore, passing the array for the purposes of this discussion.)

You should now be arguing, "But we have to pass the array!" Yes, that is true. Stamp coupling is not bad and is often necessary. The danger with stamp coupling is that often it is just too easy to send a structure when all the data in the structure are not required. When extra data are sent, we begin to open the door for errors and undesired side effects.

Consider the time stamp described in Figure 11-15. This structure contains two nested structures, date and time. If we were to use these data, for example, to print the date in a report heading, and passed the whole structure, we would send too much data. In addition, if we were to pass the structure by address rather than by value, we risk the possibility of an error in one function accidentally changing the data in the structure and causing a second error. The correct solution is to pass only the data that are needed and then only by value when possible.

A common practice to reduce the number of parameters required for a function is to create a structure that contains all the data the function needs and pass it. This practice, sometimes referred to as bundling, is a common practice, but it is not a good practice for three reasons:

1. Maintenance is made more difficult because it is more difficult to trace data through a program.

2. Extra data can be passed. For example, a bundled structure is created for a series of related functions, but not all of them use all the data. The temptation is just too great to pass the structure even though only one or two of the members are needed.

3. The semantics of the structure are often artificial, making the program more difficult to read and understand.

Control Coupling

The next type of coupling, **control coupling**, is the passing of flags that may be used to direct the logic flow of a function. It closely resembles data coupling except that a flag is being passed rather than data.

In C, flags are often returned from a function rather than being passed as parameters, but the intent and usage are the same. For example, consider the return values from scanf. It returns either EOF, a definite flag, or the number of values successfully read, which can also be used as a flag for success. An example of a flag being passed in a function you might write is the user-selected option in the menu function of an interactive program. This flag directs the entire flow of the program. The option is a special type of flag known as a data flag. It is data entered by the user, and at the same time, it is a flag intended to direct the flow of the program.

Properly used, control coupling is a necessary and valid method of communicating between two functions. Like stamp coupling, however, it can be misused. Properly used, it communicates status: The end of the file has been reached. The search value was found.

Poor flag usage is usually an indication of poor program design, for example, when a process is divided between two or more independent functions. Flags used to communicate horizontally across several functions in the structure chart are often an indication of poor design. Action flags, as opposed to status flags, that require the receiving function to perform some special processing are also highly suspect. An example of an action flag is a flag that directs a customer's purchase not be approved rather than simply reporting that the credit limit has been exceeded or that no payment was received last month.

Global Coupling

A type of coupling known as global coupling (sometimes referred to as common coupling) uses global variables to communicate between two, or usually more, functions. With all that we have said about not using global variables, it should not come as a surprise that this is not a good coupling technique.

In fact, you should never use global coupling for several reasons. We cite only the big three:

1. Global coupling makes it virtually impossible to determine which modules are communicating with each other. When a change needs to be made to a program, therefore, it is not possible to evaluate and isolate the impact of the change. This often causes functions that were not changed to suddenly fail.

2. Global coupling tightly binds a function to the program. This means that it cannot be easily transported to another program.

3. Global coupling leads to multiple flag meanings. This problem is often made worse by using generic flag names, such as `f1`, `f2`, `...`, `f21`. (Finding 21 flags in a single program is not an exaggeration. We know of one assembly program that had even more flags. In fact, it had one flag that was used solely to indicate that another flag had been set but was now turned off; in other words, a flag that returned the status of a flag.)

The danger here should be obvious. If a flag can be used globally to communicate between two functions, it is highly probable that at some point this flag could be erroneously changed by a third function that used it for another purpose.

Content Coupling

The last type of coupling is content coupling, which occurs when one function refers directly to the data or statements in another function. Obviously, this concept breaks all the tenets of structured programming. Content coupling is very difficult, but not impossible, to use in C, but as a best practice, should never be used.

Referring to the data in another function requires that the data be made externally visible outside the function. This is impossible in C. The only thing that comes even remotely close is global variables. Because we have stressed the dangers of global variables before, we will simply state here that they should not be used for communication within one compile unit.

Data Hiding

We have previously discussed the concept of global and local variables. In the discussion, we pointed out that anything placed before `main` was said to be in the global part of the program. With the exception of data that need to be visible to functions in other compile units, no data need to be placed in this section.

One of the principles of structured programming states that the internal data structure should be hidden from the user's view. The terms data hiding and data encapsulation refer to principles that have as their objective protecting data from accidental destruction by parts of your program that don't need access to the data. In other words, if a part of your program doesn't need data to do its job, it shouldn't be able to see the data.

Do not place any variables in the global area of a program. Any variables placed in the global area of your program—that is, before `main`—can be used and changed by every part of your program. This is in direct conflict with the structured programming principles of data hiding and data encapsulation.

A Wrap-Up of Function Coupling and Data Hiding

We have described five different ways that two functions can communicate. The first three are all valid and useful, although not without some dangers. These communication techniques also provide data hiding. Data coupling is universally accepted and provides the loosest communication between two functions. Stamp and control coupling present some dangers that must be recognized. When using stamp coupling, do not pass more data than required. Keep control coupling narrow—that is, between only two functions. You should always avoid global and content coupling. They do not protect the data.

Tips and Common Programming Errors

1. Don't forget the semicolon at the end of the declaration of structures and unions. This is one of the locations where you see a semicolon after a closing brace (}) in C.

2. Because the direct selection operator has a higher precedence than the indirection operator, parentheses are required to reference a member with a pointer.

   ```
   (*ptr).mem
   ```

3. The indirect selection operator (->) is one token. Do not put a space between its symbols (between - and >).

4. To access a member in an array structure, you need the index operator. For example, the correct expression to access a member named `mem` in an array of structure named `ary` is

   ```
   ary[i].mem
   ```

5. The type name in a `typedef` comes after the closing brackets and before the semicolon:

   ```
   typedef struc
   {
   ...;...
   ...;
   } TYPE_NAME;
   ```

6. You cannot define a variable at the same time that you declare a type definition. In other words, you are not allowed to do the following:

   ```
   typedef struct
   {
   ...;
   ...;
   } TYPE_NAME variable_name; // ERROR
   ```

7. You may not use the same structure name with a tag inside a structure. The following declaration is not valid:

   ```
   typedef struct TAG_NAME
   {
   ...;...;
   ...;...
   struct TAG_NAME field_name; // ERROR
   } ID;
   ```

8. A union can store only one of its members at a time. You must always keep track of the available member. In other words, storing one data type in a union and accessing another data type is a logic error and may be a serious run-time error.

9. Although structures can be assigned to each other, it is a compile error to assign a structure of one type to a structure of a different type.

10. It is a compile error to use a structure type with only its tag; that is, without the keyword struct, as shown below.

```
struct stu
{
......
};
stu aStudent;           // Compile Error
struct stu aStudent; // Correct Code
```

11. It is a compile error to compare two structures or unions, even if they are of the same type.

12. It is a compile error to refer to a structure member without qualification, such as id rather than student.id.

13. It is a compile error to omit a level of qualification when structures are nested. For example, in **Figure 11-13**, it is an error to omit the time qualifier in the following reference.

```
stamp.time.min
```

14. It is a compile error to forget the address operator with scanf when referring to a nonstring member. The pointer is the address of the structure, not the address of the member.

15. Referencing an identifier in a union when a different type is active is a logic error and may cause the program to fail.

16. It is a compile error to initialize a union with data that do not match the type of the first member.

Summary

> An enumerated type is built on the standard type, integer.

> In an enumerated type, each identifier is given an integer value.

> A structure is a collection of related elements, possibly of different types, having a single name.

> Each element in a structure is called a field.

> One difference between an array and a structure is that while all elements in an array must be of the same type, the elements in a structure can be of the same or different types.

> We have discussed two different ways to declare and/or define a structure: tagged structure and type-defined structure.

> A structure can be initialized when it is defined. The rule for structure initialization is the same as for array initialization.

> We can access the members of a structure using the direct selection operator (.).

> Structures can be accessed through a pointer. The best way to do this is to use the indirect selection operator (->).

> The following two expressions are the same if `ptr` is a pointer to a structure:

    (*p).x   p->x

> The information in a structure can be sent to a function using one of the following methods:

  1. Sending individual members

  2. Sending the whole structure

  3. Sending a pointer to the structure

> A union is a construct that allows a portion of memory to be used by different types of data.

> In software engineering, coupling is the measure of how tightly two functions are bound to each other.

> Computer science has identified five types of coupling: data, stamp, control, global, and content.

> Functions in a well-structured program are loosely coupled.

> Avoid global coupling and never use content coupling.

> Good program design can be measured by three principles: Modules must be independent, modules must be loosely coupled, and each module must do a single job.

Key Terms

content coupling

control coupling

data coupling

data encapsulation

data hiding

enumeration constant

enumerated type

global coupling

nested structure

slack bytes

stamp coupling

structure

structure variable

tag

tagged structure

union

Review Questions

1. Variables are created with a type definition (`typedef`).
   - **a.** True
   - **b.** False

2. An integer value can be assigned to only one enumeration constant in an enumerated type.
   - **a.** True
   - **b.** False

3. A structure variable is used to declare a type containing multiple fields.
   - **a.** True
   - **b.** False

4. The indirect selection operator is used with a pointer to access individual fields in a structure.
   - **a.** True
   - **b.** False

5. The structured programming concept known as coupling describes how data are passed to functions.
   - **a.** True
   - **b.** False

6. Which of the following is not a derived type?
   - **a.** Arrays
   - **b.** Enumerated
   - **c.** Float
   - **d.** Pointers
   - **e.** Union

7. The _____ can be used to create a new type that can be used anywhere a type is permitted.
   - **a.** array
   - **b.** record type
   - **c.** structure (`struct`)
   - **d.** type definition
   - **e.** both a structure and a type definition

8. The enumerated type (`enum`) is derived from the _____ type.
   - **a.** character
   - **b.** boolean
   - **c.** floating-point
   - **d.** integer
   - **e.** structured

9. Which of the following statements about enumerated types is true?
   a. Declaring an enumerated type automatically creates a variable.
   b. Declaring an enumerated variable without a tag creates an enumerated type.
   c. Enumerated types cannot be used in a type definition.
   d. The enumerated values are automatically assigned constant values unless otherwise directed.
   e. The identifiers in an enumerated type are enumeration variables.

10. A(n) _____ is the smallest element of named data that has meaning.
    a. array
    b. field
    c. record type
    d. structure (`struct`)
    e. type

11. Which of the following statements about structures (`struct`) is true?
    a. A structure without a tag can be used as a derived type.
    b. Structures are derived types based on the integer standard type.
    c. The fields in a structure must be of the same type.
    d. C normally uses two different structure declarations: tagged and type-defined.

12. The _____ structure creates a type that can be used later to define variables.
    a. array
    b. record-typed
    c. tagged
    d. type-defined
    e. variable

13. Given a structure variable named `stu`, whose type is STU, which contains a field named major, which of the following statements correctly refers to major?

    a. `major`
    b. `stu-major`
    c. `stu.major`
    d. `STU-major`
    e. `STU.major`

14. Given a pointer, `ptr`, to a structure `stu` containing a field name, which of the following statements correctly references name?
    a. `ptr.name`
    b. `ptr->name`
    c. `ptr.stu.name`
    d. `ptr->stu->name`
    e. `ptr->stu.name`

15. A(n) _____ is a construct that allows a portion of memory to be shared by different types of data.
    a. `array`
    b. `field`
    c. `struct`
    d. `union`
    e. `variable`

16. Determine which of the following statements are true and which are false:
    a. A structure cannot have two fields with the same name.
    b. A structure cannot have two fields of the same type.
    c. A structure must have at least one field.
    d. A field in a structure can itself be a structure.

17. Determine which of the following statements are true and which are false:
    a. A union can have another union as one of the fields.
    b. A structure cannot have a union as one of its fields.
    c. A structure cannot have an array as one of its elements.
    d. When accessing the fields of a structure through a pointer p, the following two expressions are the same:

       `(*p).field_name`   `p >field_name`

Exercises

18. Declare a tagged structure for a student record consisting of five fields: student ID (integer), first name (a dynamically allocated string), last name (a dynamically allocated string), total credits completed (integer), and accumulated grade point average (floating-point). A graphic representation of the structure is shown in **Figure 11-25**.

Figure 11-25   Data for Exercise 18

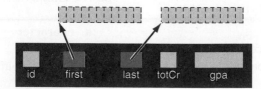

19. Declare a type-defined structure for an inventory item consisting of six fields: part number (integer), part description (a dynamically allocated string), reorder point (integer), number of items currently on hand (integer), unit measure (a string, maximum size 8), and unit price (floating-point). A graphic representation of the structure is shown in **Figure 11-26**.

Figure 11-26 Data for Exercise 19

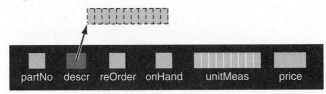

20. Declare an array of 12 elements. Each element is a structure with three fields. The first field shows the month in numeric form (1 to 12). The second field shows the name of the month (a dynamically allocated string). The third field shows the number of days in the month. Initialize the array. A graphic representation of the structure is shown in **Figure 11-27**.

Figure 11-27 Data for Exercise 20

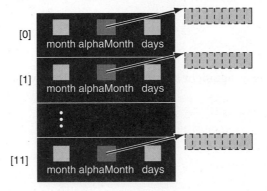

21. Declare a calendar as an array of 366 elements. Each element of the array is a structure having three fields. The first field is the name of the month (a dynamically allocated string). The second field is the day in the month (an integer). The third field is the description of activities for a particular day (a dynamically allocated string). A graphic representation of the structure is shown in **Figure 11-28**.

Figure 11-28 Data for Exercise 21

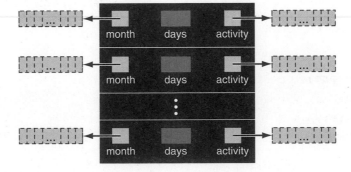

22. Assume we have declared the following structure:

```
typedef struct
{
    char x;
```

```
    char* y;
    int z[20];
} FUN;
```

Determine which of the following definitions are valid and which are invalid. If invalid, explain the error.

a. STRUCT FUN f1;

b. STRUCT FUN f5[23];

c. FUN f3;

d. FUN f4 [20];

23. Assume we have the following declaration and definitions:

```
STRUCT FUN
{
    char x;
    char* y;
    int z[20];
} ;
STRUCT FUN fn1;
STRUCT FUN fn2;
STRUCT FUN fn3 [10];
STRUCT FUN fn4 [50];
```

Determine which of the following assignment statements are valid and which are invalid. If invalid, explain the error.

a. fn1.x = "b" ;

b. fn2.y = "b";

c. fn3[4].z[5] = 234;

d. fn4[23].y = "1234";

e. fn4[23] = fn3[5];

24. Assume we have the following declaration:

```
typedef enum {ONE = 1, TWO = 2} CHOICE;
typedef union
{
    char choice1;
    int choice2;
} U_TYPE;
typedef struct
{
    float fixedBefore;
    CHOICE choice;
    U_TYPE flexible;
    float fixedAfter;
} S_TYPE;
```

Draw a schematic diagram for S_TYPE.

25. Using the declaration of S_TYPE (declared in Exercise 24), show what will be printed from the following program segment. (Assume that the S TYPE declaration is global.)

```
#include <stdio.h>
int main (void)
```

```
        {
            S_TYPE s;
            S_TYPE* ps;
            s.fixedBefore = 23.34;
            s.choice = ONE;
            s.flexible.choicel = 'B';
            s.fixedAfter = 12.45;
            ps = &s;
            printf ("\n%f", ps->fixedAfter);
            printf ("\n%d", ps->flexible.choicel);
            printf ("\n%f", s.fixedBefore);
            return 0;
        } // main
```

Problems

26. Write a function called `elapsedTime` with two parameters, the start time and the end time. Each parameter is a structure with three fields showing the hours, minutes, and seconds of a specific time (see Figure 11-13). The function is to return a time structure containing the time elapsed between the two parameters. You must handle the situation when the start time is in the previous day.

27. Write a function called `increment` that accepts a date structure with three fields. The first field contains the month (a pointer to a string). The second field is an integer showing the day in the month. The third field is an integer showing the year. The function increments the date by 1 day and returns the new date. If the date is the last day in the month, the month field must also be changed. If the month is December, the value of the year field must also be changed when the day is 31. A year is a leap year if
   a. It is evenly divisible by 4 but not by 100, or
   b. It is evenly divisible by 400.

28. Write a function called `futureDate`. The function is to use two parameters. The first parameter is a structure containing today's date (as defined in Problem 27). The second parameter is an integer showing the number of days after today. The function returns a structure showing the next date, which may be in a future year.

29. Write a function called `later` that receives two date parameters, compares the two dates, and returns `true` (1) if the first date is earlier than the second date and `false` (0) if the first date is later. Each parameter is a structure containing a date (as defined in Problem 27).

30. Write a function that accepts an integer representing money in dollars (no fractions) and returns a structure with 6 fields. The fields represent, respectively, the minimum number of $100, $50, $20, $10, $5, and $1 bills needed to total the money in the parameter.

31. Write a function that compares two fraction structures (refer back to Figure 11-3). If the fractions are equal, it returns zero. If the fraction in the first parameter is less than the fraction in the second parameter, it returns a negative number. Otherwise, it returns a positive number. Hint: Convert the fraction to a floating-point number.

32. A point in a plane can be represented by its two coordinates, x and y. Therefore, we can represent a point in a plane by a structure having two fields as shown below.

```
typedef struct
{
    int x;
    int y;
} POINT;
```

Write a function that accepts the structure representing a point and returns an integer (1, 2, 3, or 4) that indicates in which quadrant the point is located, as shown in **Figure 11-29**. Zero is positive.

Figure 11-29 Quartile coordinates for Problem 32

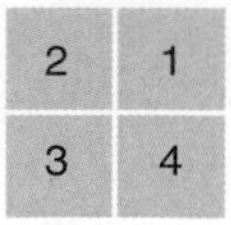

	x	y
I	positive	positive
II	negative	positive
III	negative	negative
IV	positive	negative

33. A straight line is an object connecting two points. Therefore, a line can be represented by a nested structure having two structures of the type POINT, as defined in Problem 32.

```
typedef struct
{
    POINT beg;
    POINT end;
} LINE;
```

Write a function that accepts two parameters of type `POINT` and returns a structure of type `LINE` representing the line connecting the two points.

34. Write a function that accepts a structure of type `LINE` (see Problem 33) and returns an integer (1, 2, 3), where 1 means vertical, 2 means horizontal, and 3 means oblique. A vertical line is a line whose x coordinates are the same. A horizontal line is a line whose y coordinates are the same. An oblique line is a line that is not vertical or horizontal.

35. Write a function that shuffles a deck of cards. The deck of cards is represented by an array of 52 elements. Each element in the array is a structure for one card, as shown below.

```
typedef struct
{
    char* suit; // Clubs, Diamonds, Hearts, Spades
    int value;  // Ace, 2...9, Jack, Queen, King
} CARD;
typedef CARD DECK [52];
```

The function must use a random number to ensure that each shuffle results in a different card sequence. Hint: Generate a random number in the range 0 ... 51, and then exchange the current card with the card in the random position.

36. Program 11-8 creates a union of company and person names. Write a program that reads names from the keyboard and places them into an array of names. For each entry, prompt the user to enter a code that indicates if the name is a company or person name. After all names have been entered, print the array. Your program is to contain separate functions for reading names and printing the array.

37. Modify the program in Problem 36 to add a function to sort the names after they have been entered. Person names are to be sorted on last name, first name, and middle initial.

Projects

38. Write a program to keep records and perform statistical analysis for a class of students. For each student, we need a name of up to 20 characters, an ID for four digits, four quizzes, and one examination. The student data will be stored in an array of student structures. Provide for up to 50 students.

The input is read from a text file. Each line in the file contains a student's name, four quiz scores, and one examination score in order. If a quiz or examination was not taken, the score is zero. The student's name, the quiz scores, and the examination score are all separated from each other by one or more spaces. A new line ends the data for one student. The number of lines in this file is the same as the number of students.

The output consists of a listing of the students in the order they are read from the file; no sorting is required. Print each student on a separate line with an appropriate caption for each column. After the last student, print the highest, lowest, and average score for each quiz and the examination. In determining the lowest score, do not consider zero scores. A suggested report layout is shown in **Table 11-2**.

Table 11-2   Sample output for Project 38

DATA						
NAME	ID	QUIZ 1	QUIZ 2	QUIZ 3	QUIZ 4	EXAM
Student 1	1234	23	19	22	23	89
Student 2	4321	0	23	21	18	76
...						
Student n	1717	21	22	18	19	91
STATISTICS						
Highest scores		23	25	23	25	96
Lowest scores		17	15	12	18	53
Average scores		21.3	20.1	19.8	21.1	81.3

The data for the project are shown in **Table 11-3**.

Table 11-3   Data for Project 38

NAME	ID	QUIZ 1	QUIZ 2	QUIZ 3	QUIZ 4	EXAM
Omar Ramez	1234	52	7	100	78	34
Harry Smith	2134	90	36	90	77	30
Tuan Nguyen	3124	100	45	20	90	70
Jorge Gonzales	4532	11	17	81	32	77
Amanda Trapp	5678	20	12	45	78	34
Keerthi Raj	6134	34	80	55	78	45
Sarah Black	7874	60	100	56	78	78
Bryan Devaux	8026	70	10	66	78	56
Ling Wong	9893	34	09	77	78	20
Fatmeh Asmer	1947	45	40	88	78	55
Joe Giles	2877	55	50	99	78	80
Jim Nelson	3189	82	80	100	78	77
Paula Hung	4602	89	50	91	78	60
Sou Chong	5405	11	11	0	78	10
Evelyn Gilley	6999	0	98	89	78	20

39. Rework Project 38 to report the average quiz score, total quizzes score, and total score for each student. Then assign a grade based on an absolute scale of 90% for A, 80% for B, 70% for C, and 60% for D. Any score below 60% is an F. A total of 500 points are available. Print the student data to the right of the input data. At the end of the report, print the number of students who earned each grade, A to F.

40. Write a program that uses an array of student structures to answer inquiries. Using a menu-driven user interface, provide inquiries that report a student's scores, average, or grade based on an absolute scale (90% A, 80% B, etc.). A fourth menu option provides all data for a requested student, and a fifth prints a list of student IDs and names. To create the array, load the data from Project 38.

41. Using a sort of your choice, modify Project 40 to sort the data on student ID.

42. A standard deck of playing cards consists of 52 cards as shown in **Table 11-4**. Create an array of 52 structures to match it.

Table 11-4 The order of a new deck of playing cards

SUIT	RANK
Clubs	Ace ... King
Diamonds	Ace ... King
Hearts	Ace ... King
Spades	Ace ... King

Then simulate shuffling the deck using **Algorithm 11-1**. After the cards have been shuffled, print them.

Algorithm 11-1 | Shuffle deck of cards

Algorithm shuffle

1 loop through each card in the deck

  1.1 get a random number in range 0 ... 51

  1.2 Swap current card with card at random position

2 end loop

end shuffle

43. Write a function that calculates the area of one of the geometric figures shown in **Table 11-5**. The function receives one parameter, a structure that contains the type of figure and the size of the components needed for the calculation structured as a union. The format of the structure is shown in Table 11-5. Use an enumerated type for the figure type.

Table 11-5 Geometric figure components

FIGURE TYPE		COMPONENTS	
Rectangle	length	width	
Circle	width		
Triangle	side1	side2	side3

The formulas for the figures are shown below.

RectangleArea = length × width

CircleArea = πr^2

TriangleArea = $\sqrt{t(t - side1) \times t(t - side2) \times t(t - side3)}$

Where $t = 1/2(side1 + side2 + side3)$

Then write an interactive test driver that prompts the user for the type of figure to be entered and the appropriate components. It should then call the area function and print the area before looping for the next input. Hint: Use a `switch` statement to process the different codes.

44. Modify Program 11-5 to include functions to add, subtract, divide, and compare fractions. Also change the print function to print the fraction in its simplified format—that is, to reduce the numerator and denominator by the largest common factor. Thus, the fraction

$$\frac{20}{8}$$

would be printed as

$$\frac{5}{2}$$

The compare function is to compare the functions algebraically. Thus, if the following two fractions were compared, it would return equal:

$$\frac{20}{8} \quad and \quad \frac{5}{2}$$

Then modify `main` to include a loop that allows the user to enter two fractions and an option to add, subtract, multiply, divide, or compare the fractions.

Binary Input/Output

Learning Objectives

When you complete this chapter, you will be able to:

12.1 Explain the difference between text files and binary files

12.2 Use standard library functions to work with binary files in C

12.3 Create text files from binary files and vice versa

12.1 Text versus Binary Streams

We have previously discussed text input/output, including text streams and text input and output formatting. We have also discussed some text input and output facilities. In this chapter, we discuss binary input/output. We first show the difference between a text stream and a binary stream. We then discuss the C input and output functions, which are mainly designed to be used with binary streams. We conclude with a discussion of converting text files to binary files and binary files to text files.

Data is input from a source and output to a destination: text input/output and binary input/output. For text input/output, we convert a data type to a sequence of characters. For binary input/output, we transfer data without changing their memory representations.

Some data sources and destinations are capable of only reading and writing text. For example, a keyboard and a monitor can be a destination for only text; a keyboard is not capable of handling binary input and output. On the other hand, a file can be used to read or write any type of data, both text and binary.

Text and Binary Files

Although a file records data only in a binary format, we can distinguish between a text file and a binary file.

Text Files

A text file is a file in which data are stored using only characters; a text file is written using a text stream. Noncharacter data types are converted into a sequence of characters before they are stored in the file. When data are input from a text file, they are read as a sequence of characters and converted into the correct internal formats before being stored in memory. We read and write text files using the input/output functions that convert the characters to data types, as shown in **Figure 12-1**.

Figure 12-1 Reading and writing text files

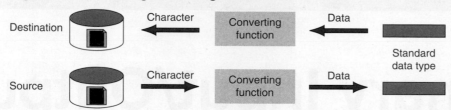

The converting functions consist of three categories: formatting, character, and string. The formatting functions, such as `scanf` and `printf`, reformat a series of input characters into standard types or reformat standard type data into characters for output. The character input and output functions, such as `getchar` and `putchar`, input or output one character at a time. The string functions, such as `fgets` and `fputs`, input and output strings of characters.

> **Note** | Formatted input/output, character input/output, and string input/output functions can be used only with text files.

Binary Files

A binary file is a collection of data stored in the internal format of the computer. Unlike text files, the data do not need to be reformatted as they are read and written; rather, the data are stored in the file in the same format that they are stored in memory. Binary files are read and written using binary streams known as block input/output functions. **Figure 12-2** depicts the operation of block read and write functions.

Figure 12-2 Block input and output

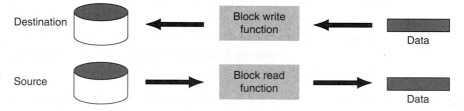

Differences between Text and Binary Files

Let's review the major differences between text files and binary files.

The major characteristics of text files are as follows:

1. All data in a text file are human-readable graphic characters.

2. Each line of data ends with a newline character.

3. There may be a special character called an end-of-file (EOF) marker at the end of the file.

Binary files, on the other hand, store data in their internal computer format. This means that an `int` in C is stored in its binary format, usually 4 bytes in a PC; a character is stored in its character format, usually 1 byte; and so forth. There are no lines in a binary file but there is an end-of-file marker.

The major characteristics of binary files are as follows:

1. Data are stored in the same format as they are stored in memory.

2. There are no lines or newline characters.

3. There may be an end-of-file marker.

Figure 12-3 shows how two data items are stored in a text file (which uses 8-bit ASCII code) and in a binary file.

Figure 12-3 Binary and text files

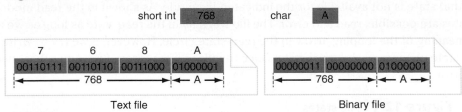

In the text file, the number 768 is stored as three numeric characters. The character A is stored as one character. At the end, there is an end-of-file marker that is not shown because its representation depends on the implementation.

In the binary file, the number 768 can be stored in 2 bytes, which assumes that the short int type has a size of 2 bytes. The character A is stored as 1 byte. At the end of the file there is an end-of-file (EOF) marker, again its format is implementation dependent.

> **Note** | Text files store data as a sequence of characters; binary files store data as they are stored in primary memory.

State of a File

An opened file is either in a read state, a write state, or an error state. If we want to read from a file, it must be in the read state. If we want to write to a file, it must be in the write state. The error state results when an error occurs when the file is opened or when it is read or written. If we try to read from a file in the write state, an error occurs. Likewise, if we try to write to a file in the read state, an error occurs. When a file is in an error state, we cannot read from it or write to it.

To open a file in the read state, we specify the read mode in the open statement. A file opened in the read state must already exist. If it doesn't, then the open fails.

A file can be opened in the write state using either the write or append mode. In write mode, the writing starts at the beginning of the file. If the file already exists, its data are lost. In append mode, the data are added at the end of the file. If the file exists, the writing begins after the existing data. If the file does not exist, a new file is created.

In addition to read, write, and append, files can be opened in the update mode. Updating allows a file to be both read and written to. Even when the file is opened for updating, however, it can still be in only one file state at a time.

To open a file for updating, we add a plus sign (+) to the basic mode. The initial state of a file opened for updating is determined by the basic mode: r+ opens the file in the read state, while w+ and a+ open the file in the write state. **Table 12-1** lists the six file modes with their features.

Table 12-1 File modes

MODE	r	w	a	r+	w+	a+
Open state	read	write	write	read	write	write
Read allowed	yes	no	no	yes	yes	yes
Write allowed	no	yes	yes	yes	yes	yes
Append allowed	no	no	yes	no	no	yes
File must exist	yes	no	no	yes	no	no
Contents of existing file lost	no	yes	no	no	yes	no

The file states and their potential error conditions are shown in **Figure 12-4**. Study this figure carefully. If a state is shaded gray, then that state is not available for the indicated file mode. As shown in the read mode (r) portion of the figure, only two states are possible, read and error. The file will stay in the read state as long as we use only read functions. That is the meaning of the looping arrow in the read-state circle. However, if we try to write when the file is in the read state, the state changes to the error state. Once the file is in an error state, any subsequent attempt to read it will result in an error.

Figure 12-4 File states

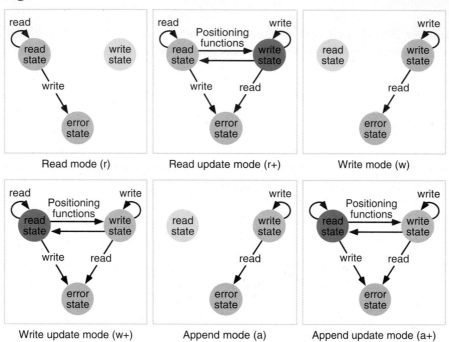

The file states and their potential error conditions are shown in Figure 12-4.

Now look at the read update mode, r+. In this mode, the file can be in either the read or the write state. To move from one to the other, we must use one of the positioning functions, which are discussed later. That is the meaning of the arrows between the read state and write state. If we try to write after a read without repositioning, the file will be in the error state. The error can be cleared by clearerr, which is discussed in the section "File Status Functions" later in the chapter.

Opening Binary Files

The basic open operation is unchanged for binary files—only the mode changes. The function declaration fopen is repeated here for convenience.

```
FILE* fopen (const char* filename, const char* mode);
```

Recall that the file name is the name used for the file by the operating system. The name we use internally in our program is a file pointer whose address is filled by the fopen return value. Here, we are most interested in the mode, which is a string that contains a code defining how the file is to be opened—for reading, writing, or both—and its format—text or binary. Text files use just the basic modes discussed above. To indicate that a file is binary, we add a binary indicator (b) to the mode. The six binary file modes are: read binary (rb), write binary (wb), append binary (ab), read and update binary (r+b), write and update binary (w+b), and append and update binary (a+b). The following are examples of open statements for binary files.

```
spReadBin = "myFile.bin", "rb");    // Read Binary
spWriteUp = "myFile.bin", "w+b");   // Write with Update
spApndBin = "myFile.bin", "ab");    // Append Binary
```

Figure 12-5 shows the basic file modes and the file state they create. The marker(s) represents the end-of-file marker.

Figure 12-5 File-opening modes

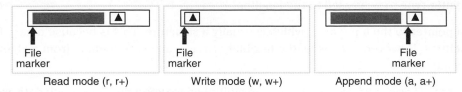

File marker	File marker	File marker
Read mode (r, r+)	Write mode (w, w+)	Append mode (a, a+)

Closing Binary Files

Just like text files, binary files must be closed when they are no longer needed. Closing destroys the file table and erases the logical file name. The close function declaration is shown here.

```
int fclose (FILE* sp);
```

12.2 Standard Library Functions for Files

C has eight categories of standard file library functions (see **Figure 12-6**). We have already discussed the first four; file open and close, character input and output, formatted input and output, and line input and output. We discuss the other four categories, which are more related to binary files, in this section.

Figure 12-6 Types of standard input/output functions

Categories of I/O funtions
- File open/close
- Character input/output
- Formatted input/output
- Line input/output
- Block input/output
- File positioning
- System file operations
- File status

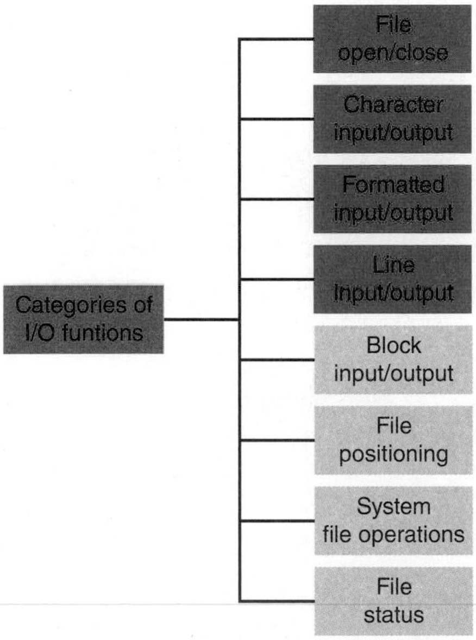

Block Input/Output Functions

The C language uses the block input and output functions to read and write data to binary files. As noted previously, when we read and write binary files, the data are transferred just as they are found in memory. There are no format conversions. This means that, with the exception of character data, we cannot "see" the data in a binary file; it looks like hieroglyphics. If you have ever accidentally opened a binary file in a text editor, you have seen these strange results. The block read function is file read (`fread`). The block write function is file write (`fwrite`).

File Read: `fread`

The function `fread`, whose declaration is shown below, reads a specified number of bytes from a binary file and places them into memory at the specified location.

```
int fread(void* pInArea, int elementSize, int count, FILE* sp);
```

The first parameter, pInArea, is a pointer to the input area in memory. Note that a generic (void) pointer is used. This allows any pointer type to be passed to the function.

File read expects a pointer to the input area, which is usually a structure. This is because binary files are most often used to store structures. However, C gives us the flexibility to read any type of data, from a character to a complex structure or even a multidimensional array.

The next two elements, elementSize and count, are multiplied to determine how much data are to be transferred. The size is normally specified using the sizeof operator, and the count is normally one when reading structures.

The last parameter is the associated stream. **Figure 12-7** illustrates a file read that reads data into an array of integers. When fread is called, it transfers the next three integers from the file to the array, inArea.

Figure 12-7   File read operation

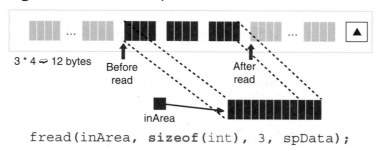

```
fread(inArea, sizeof(int), 3, spData);
```

The code to read the file is shown in **Program 12-1**.

Program 12-1 | Read file of integers

```
1    // Read a file of integers, three integers at a time.
2    {
3        ...
4    // Local Declarations
5        FILE* spIntFile;
6        int itemsRead;
7        int intAry[3];
8
9    // Statements
10       spIntFile = fopen("int_file.dat", "rb");
11       ...
12       while ((itemsRead = fread(intAry,
13              sizeof(int), 3, spIntFile)) != 0)
14       {
15       // process array
16           ...
17       } // while
18       ...
19   } // block
```

File read returns the number of items read. In Figure 12-7, it will range between 0 and 3 because we are reading three integers at a time. For example, assume that when we try to read the file, only two integers are left to be read. In this case, `fread` will return 2. If we return and try to read the file again, `fread` will then return 0.

Note that `fread` does not return end of file—it returns the number of elements read. End of file is detected in the above situation when we called `fread` with fewer than three integers left in the file. The question is, how can we tell that we are at the end of file? C provides another input/output function, `feof` to test for end of file. We discuss this function in "File Status Functions" later in this section.

Now let's look at a more common use of `fread`: reading structures (records). Assume that we have defined a structure that stores data about students. Given the type of data that will be stored, we would expect the structure to contain some string data and other data, such as integers or real numbers. One advantage of block input/output functions is that they can transfer these data one structure (record) at a time. A second advantage is that the data do not need to be formatted. **Figure 12-8** shows the operation of `fread` when a structure is being read.

Figure 12-8   Reading a structure

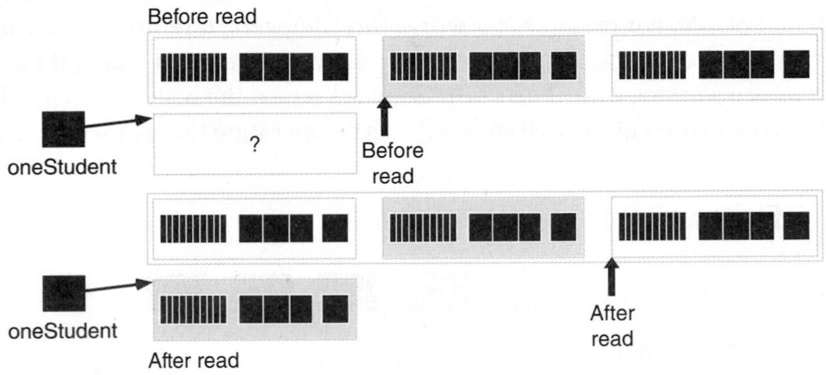

The code shown in **Program 12-2** reads the file.

Program 12-2 | Read student file

```
1    /* Reads one student's data from a file
2         Pre spStuFile is opened for reading
3         Post stu data structure filled
4            ioResults returned
5    */
6    int readStudent (STU* oneStudent, FILE* spStuFile)
7    {
8    // Local Declarations
9        int ioResults;
10
11   // Statements
12       ioResults = fread(oneStudent,
13                     sizeof(STU), 1, spStuFile);
14       return ioResults;
15   } // readStudent
```

Different organizations have different standards. One company with which we are familiar has a standard that programs shall have only one read and one write statement for each file. The standard was created to make it easier to make changes to the programs. Program 12-2 is a typical implementation of this standard. One difficulty with this type of function, however, is that it is impossible to generalize the steps that are to be taken for various input results, such as error handling and end of file. Therefore, we pass the input/output result back to the calling function for analysis and action.

File Write: `fwrite`

The function `fwrite`, whose declaration is shown below, writes a specified number of items to a binary file.

```
int fwrite (void*  pOutArea,
            int    elementSize,
            int    count,
            FILE*  sp);
```

The parameters for file write correspond exactly to the parameters for the file read function.

Functionally, `fwrite` copies `elementSize` x `count` bytes from the address specified by `pOutArea` to the file. It returns the number of items written. For example, if it writes three integers, it returns 3. We can use the return value, therefore, to test the write operation. If the number of items written is fewer than count, then an error has occurred. Depending on the device we are working with, it may be possible to repeat the write, but generally the program should be aborted when we get a write error. **Figure 12-9** shows the write operation that parallels the read in Figure 12-7.

Figure 12-9 File write operation

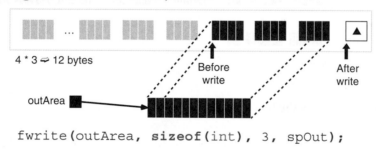

```
fwrite(outArea, sizeof(int), 3, spOut);
```

Assuming that we are writing a file of student structures, **Figure 12-10** shows the write operation. **Program 12-3** contains the code for the function that writes the data.

Figure 12-10 Writing a structure

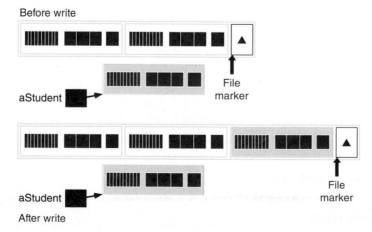

Program 12-3 | Write structured data

```
1   /* Writes one student's record to a binary file.
2      Pre aStudent has been filled
3      spOut is open for writing
4      Post aStudent written to spOut
5   */
6   void writeStudent (STU* aStudent, FILE* spOut)
7
8   {
9   // Local Declarations
10     int ioResult;
11
12  // Statements
13     ioResult = fwrite(aStudent,
14                       sizeof(STU), 1, spOut);
15     if (ioResult != 1)
16     {
17        printf("\a Error writing student file \a\n");
18        exit (100);
19     } // if
20     return;
21  } // writeStudent
```

Contrast this write structured data function with the one that we wrote to read data. Although it is not possible to generalize on the action to be taken if data are not read, it is possible to do so with write errors. If the program cannot write data, it must be aborted. Therefore, we put the error checking and action in the write function itself.

File Status Functions

C provides three functions to handle file status questions: test end of file (feof), test error (ferror), and clear error (clearerr).

Test End of File: feof

The feof function is used to check if the end of file has been reached. If the file is at the end—that is, if all data have been read—the function returns nonzero (true). If end of file has not been reached, zero (false) is returned. The function declaration is shown below. Although the C99 Standard introduced the Boolean type, most standard functions continue to use the traditional nonzero for true and zero for false return status.

```
int feof (FILE* stream);
```

In general, two different techniques can be used to detect end of file. Some languages have a look-ahead function. When look-ahead logic is being used, the system transfers the current data to the program and then reads the next data. Under this design, we can detect the end of file at the same time that we read (transfer data back to our work area) the last data from the file. The second technique, the one used by C, detects end of file when we attempt to read and there is nothing left on the file. Even if all the data have been read from the file, feof does not return true until we attempt to read beyond the last data.

Test Error: `ferror`

Test error (`ferror`) is used to check the error status of the file. Errors can be created for many reasons, ranging from bad physical media (disk or tape) to illogical operations, such as trying to read a file in the write state. The `ferror` function returns true (nonzero) if an error has occurred. It returns false (zero) if no error has occurred. The function declaration is shown below.

```
int ferror (FILE* stream);
```

Note, however, that testing for an error does not reset the error condition. After a file enters the error state (see Figure 12-4) it can only return to a read or write state by calling clear error (discussed in the next section).

Clear Error: `clearerr`

When an error occurs, the subsequent calls to `ferror` return nonzero, until the error status of the file is reset. The function `clearerr` is used for this purpose. Its function declaration is shown in the next example.

```
void clearerr (FILE* stream);
```

Note, however, that even though we have cleared the error, we have not necessarily cured the problem. We may find that the next read or write returns to the error state.

Positioning Functions

Positioning functions have two uses. First, to randomly process data in disk files (we cannot process tape files randomly), we need to position the file to read the desired data. Second, we can use the positioning functions to change a file's state. Thus, if we have been writing a file, we can change to a read state after we use one of the positioning functions. It is not necessary to change states after positioning a file, but it is allowed.

We will discuss three file position functions: rewind, tell location, and file seek.

Rewind File: `rewind`

The `rewind` function simply sets the file position indicator to the beginning of the file (see **Figure 12-11**). The function declaration is shown below.

```
void rewind(FILE* stream);
```

Figure 12-11   Rewind file

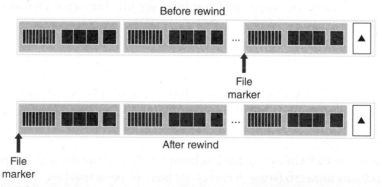

A common use of the `rewind` function is to change a work file from a write state to a read state. Often it is necessary to place data in a file temporarily for later processing. When all the data have been written and we are ready to begin reading, we rewind the file and simply start reading. Remember, however, that to read and write a file with only one open, we must open it in update mode, in this case, `w+` or `w+b`.

The same effect can be accomplished by closing the output file and opening it as input. However, rewind is a faster operation.

Current Location: `ftell`

The `ftell` function reports the current position of the file marker in the file, relative to the beginning of the file. Recall that C considers a file to be a stream of data. It measures the position in the file by the number of bytes, relative to zero, from the beginning of the file. Thus, when the file position indicator is at the beginning of the file, `ftell` returns zero. If the file position indicator is at the second byte of the file, `ftell` returns 1, representing the position 1 byte offset from the beginning of the file. The function declaration for `ftell` is shown below.

```
long int ftell (FILE* stream);
```

Note that `ftell` returns a long integer. This is necessary because many files have more than 32,767 bytes, which is the maximum integer value on many computers. The operation of `ftell` is graphically shown in **Figure 12-12**.

Figure 12-12 Current location (`ftell`) operation

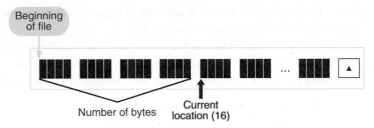

Another important factor to consider is that `ftell` returns the number of bytes from the beginning of the file. This is true even when we read or write structures. If we need to know the structure number relative to the first structure, then we must calculate it. This can be done by dividing the `ftell` return value by the size of the structure, as shown below.

```
numChar = ftell (sp);
numStruct = numChar / sizeof(STRUCTURE_TYPE);
```

In Figure 12-12, `ftell` returns 16. Because each structure is 4 bytes, the result of the calculation shown above is 4, which means that there are four structures before the current location. Another way to look at it is that the file is positioned at the fourth integer relative to zero.

If `ftell` encounters an error, it returns −1. We know of only two conditions that can cause an error. The first, using `ftell` with a device that cannot store data, such as the keyboard, is a program logic or design error. The second error occurs when the position is larger than can be represented in a long integer. Obviously, this could occur only with very large files, but files of more than a million records are common in industry.

The primary purpose of `ftell` is to provide a data address (offset) that can be used in a file seek. It is especially useful when we are dealing with text files for which we cannot calculate the position of data.

Set Position: fseek

The `fseek` function positions the file location indicator to a specified byte position in a file. It gets its name from the disk-positioning operation, seek. Seek moves the access arm on a disk to a position in the file for reading or writing. Because this is exactly the purpose of **seek file**, it is an appropriate name. Its function declaration is shown below.

```
int fseek(FILE* stream, long offset, int wherefrom);
```

The first parameter is a pointer to an open file. Because the seek is used with both reading and writing files, the file state can be either read or write. The second parameter is a signed integer that specifies the number of bytes the position indicator must move absolutely or relatively. To understand what we mean by absolutely or relatively, we must first discuss the third parameter, `wherefrom`.

C provides three named constants that can be used to specify the starting point (`wherefrom`) of the seek. They are shown below.

```
#define SEEK_SET 0
#define SEEK_CUR 1
#define SEEK_END 2
```

When `wherefrom` is `SEEK_SET` or `0`, then the offset is measured absolutely from the beginning of the file. This is the most common use of file seek. Thus, to set the file indicator to byte 100 on a file, we would code the following statement:

```
fseek(sp, 99L, SEEK_SET);
```

We can use zero in place of `SEEK_SET`. If you are puzzling over the second parameter in the above statement, remember that the file position is relative to zero and must be a long integer. Actually, the compiler is smart enough to convert an integer value to long integer, but it is more efficient if we specify the correct type, especially with literals.

Now let's look at the `wherefrom` option, `SEEK_CUR`. If `wherefrom` is `SEEK_CUR` or `1`, then the displacement is calculated relatively from the current file position. If the displacement is negative, the file's position moves back toward the beginning of the file. If it is positive, it moves forward toward the end of the file. It is an error to move beyond the beginning of the file. If we move beyond the end of the file, the file is extended, but the contents of the extended bytes are unknown. Whenever we extend the file, there is always the possibility of running out of space, which is an error. To position the file marker to the next record in a structured file, we execute the following statement:

```
fseek(sp, sizeof(STRUCTURE_TYPE), SEEK_CUR);
```

To position the student file described earlier at the structure indicated by the integer variable `stuLoc`, we use the following statement:

```
fseek(stuFile, (stuLoc - 1) * sizeof(STU), SEEK_SET);
```

It is necessary to adjust the integer location, `stuLoc`, by subtracting 1 to convert the ordinal structure number to a zero base. That is, if `stuLoc` contains 55, indicating we want to read the 55th student in the file, we position the file to the location of the 54th student relative to zero.

Finally, if `wherefrom` is `SEEK_END` or `2`, the file location indicator is positioned relative to the end of the file. If the offset is negative, the file position marker is moved backward toward the beginning of the file; if it is positive, it extends the file. This technique can be used to write a new record at the end of the file. We simply position the file at the end with a `SEEK_END` and a displacement of zero (as shown below) and then write the new record.

```
fseek(stuFile, 0L, SEEK_END);
```

The seek function returns zero if the positioning is successful. It returns nonzero if the positioning is not successful. **Figure 12-13** shows the effect of `fseek` in different situations.

Figure 12-13 File seek operation

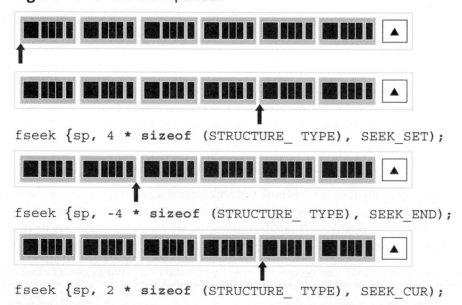

```
fseek {sp, 4 * sizeof (STRUCTURE_ TYPE), SEEK_SET);
```

```
fseek {sp, -4 * sizeof (STRUCTURE_ TYPE), SEEK_END);
```

```
fseek {sp, 2 * sizeof (STRUCTURE_ TYPE), SEEK_CUR);
```

The file seek is intended primarily for binary files. It does, however, have limited functionality with text files. We can position a text file to the beginning using `fseek` with a zero offset from the beginning of the file (`SEEK_SET`). However, `rewind` provides the same functionality and is more appropriate for text files. To position a text file at the end, we can use `fseek` with a zero offset and a `wherefrom` `SEEK_END`, as discussed earlier.

We cannot use file seek to position ourselves in the middle of a text file unless we have used `ftell` to record the location. The reasons for this have to do with control codes, newlines, vertical tabs, and other nuisances of text files. However, if we have saved a location using `ftell` and want to go back to that position, we can use `fseek`, as shown below.

```
fseek(sp, ftell_location, SEEK_SET);
```

Note that since `ftell` returns a position relative to the beginning of the file, we must use `SEEK_SET` when we reposition the file.

Let's look at a program that reads and writes binary files. Suppose, for example, that we had two copies of files with integer data. Perhaps one file represents data from one week and the other file represents data for a second week. We want to combine both files into a single file. The most efficient way to do this is to append the data from one file to the end of the other file. This logic is shown in **Program 12-4**.

> **Program 12-4** | Append two binary files

```
1    /* This program appends two binary files of integers.
2       Written by:
3       Date:
4    */
5    #include <stdio.h>
6
7    #include <stdlib.h>
8    int main (void)
9    {
10   // Local Declarations
11      FILE* sp1;
12      FILE* sp2;
13      int data;
14      long dataCount;
15      char fileID[13];
16
17   // Statements
18      printf("This program appends two files.\n" );
19      printf("Please enter file ID of the primary file: ");
20      scanf("%12s", fileID);
21      if (!(sp1 = fopen (fileID, "ab")))
22         printf("\aCan't open %s\n", fileID), exit (100);
23
24      if (!(dataCount = (ftell (sp1))))
25         printf("\a%s has no data\n", fileID), exit (101);
26      dataCount /= sizeof(int);
27
28      printf ( "Please enter file ID of the second file: ");
29      scanf("%12s", fileID);
30      if (!(sp2 = fopen (fileID, "rb")))
```

(continue)

Program 12-4 Append two binary files *(continued)*

```
31              printf("\aCan't open %s\n", fileID), exit (110);
32
33      while (fread (&data, sizeof(int), 1, sp2) == 1)
34      {
35          fwrite (&data, sizeof(int), 1, sp1);
36          dataCount++;
37      } // while
38
39      if (! feof(sp2))
40          printf("\aRead Error. No output.\n"), exit (120);
41
42      fclose (sp1);
43      fclose (sp2);
44
45      printf("Append complete: %ld records in file\n",
46              dataCount);
47      return 0;
48  } // main
```

First, note the way the files are opened in Program 12-4. Because it appends the data from the second file to the end of the first file, the first file is opened in append mode and the second file is opened in read mode. Both files are opened as binary.

Opening the first file in append mode presents a minor problem: The open is successful even if the file doesn't exist. Recall that the append mode places the file marker at the end of an existing file or, if there is no existing file, at the beginning of a new file. To ensure that an existing file was opened successfully, therefore, we use the `ftell` function in statement 24. If an existing file was opened, `dataCount` will be nonzero.

Now look at the way the external file names are handled. Under the assumption that this program will be used to append different files at different times, we asked the user to enter the file names. This technique provides maximum flexibility for generalized programs.

Statement 22 contains one of the few valid uses of multiple statements on one line—in this case, multiple expressions separated by the comma operator. Why is this statement considered valid when we have so strongly emphasized one statement per line? The answer is that we are handling an error situation that should never occur. In good human engineering style, we want to deemphasize the error logic so that it doesn't distract the reader. Therefore, we place the print error message and exit in one expression.

The heart of the program is contained in statements 33 through 37. As long as the read is successful, we keep going. When we reach the end of file, the read returns zero and the loop terminates. We now have another problem, however. We don't know if the read terminated at end of file or because of a read error. We therefore use the `feof` function to make sure we read to the end of the file.

The program concludes with a printed message that contains the number of records on the appended file. Because we didn't read all the data on the first file, however, we must calculate the number of integers in it. To do this, we used the result of the `ftell` that verified that the first file existed. Recall that `ftell` returns the number of bytes to the current location in the file—in this case, the end of the file. To get the number of integers, we simply divide by the size of one integer (see statement 26). Then, each time we write, we add 1 to the record count. This gives us the number of integers in the combined file.

System File Operations

A few functions operate on the whole file instead of the contents. These functions generally use operating system calls to perform operations such as remove a file, rename a file, or create a temporary binary file.

Remove File: `remove`

The `remove` function removes or deletes the file using its external name. The parameter is a pointer to the name of the file. Its function is shown below.

```
int remove (char* filename);
```

The `remove` function returns zero if the deletion is successful. It returns nonzero if there is an error, such as the file can't be found. For example, if we want to delete a file named `file1.dat`, we execute the following statement.

```
if (remove ("file1.dat"))
    printf("Error, file cannot be deleted");
```

Any attempt to access a file after it has been removed will result in an error.

Rename File: `rename`

When we create a new version of a file and want to keep the same name, we need to rename the old version of the file. The `rename` function declaration is shown below.

```
int rename (const char* oldFilename,
            const char* newFilename);
```

Both the old name and the new name must be given as parameters. The `rename` function returns zero if renaming is successful; it returns nonzero if there is an error.

For example, in a Microsoft Windows system, if we want to rename a student file and designate it a backup, we could use the `rename` function as shown below.

```
if (rename ("STUFILE.DAT", "STUFILE.BAK"))
    printf("Error, the file cannot be renamed");
```

Create Temporary File: `tmpfile`

The `tmpfile` function creates a new temporary output file. Although we could do the same thing with an `fopen` in the `w+b` mode, the difference with the `tmpfile` function is that the file is available only while the program is running. It will be closed and erased when the execution of the program is finished. It is a temporary file, not a permanent one. Its function declaration is

```
FILE* tmpfile (void);
```

To create a temporary file, we first define a file pointer and then open it, as shown below.

```
FILE* sp;
sp = tmpfile ();
```

Now we can write to the file as we would to any file. Because the file is opened in the `w+b` mode, if we want to read from the file we must reposition it using one of the repositioning functions such as `rewind` or `fseek`.

12.3 Converting File Type

A rather common but somewhat trivial problem is to convert a text file to a binary file and vice versa. C has no standard functions for these tasks. We must write a program to make the conversion. We describe the file conversion logic in this section.

Creating a Binary File from a Text File

To create a binary file, we usually start with data provided by the user. Since the user is providing the data, it will be in human readable form—that is, in text form. If only a small amount of initial data are required, they are often read from a keyboard. With a lot of data, however, it is easier for the user to enter the data with a text editor and then read the text file and create the binary file.

When we read the text file, we can use either the `fscanf` function to convert the data as they are being read, or the `fgets` and `sscanf` functions to read the data a line at a time and then convert the data to the proper internal format. As the data are being converted, they are placed in a structure. At the end of each line, the structure is written to the binary file. This process is repeated until the text file has been completely converted to the binary structure. The structure chart for this program is shown in **Figure 12-14**.

Figure 12-14   Create binary file structure chart

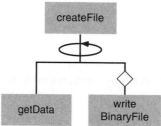

Let's assume that we want to convert student data to a binary file. The data consist of a student's name, ID, three exams, eight problems, and a final grade. In the text file version, each field is separated by one or more whitespace characters and each student's data are stored on a separate line. The create file program is shown in **Program 12-5**.

> ## Program 12-5 | Text to binary student file

```
1    /* Reads text file of student data & creates binary file.
2       Written by:
3       Date:
4    */
5    #include <stdio.h>
6    #include <stdlib.h>
7    #include <stdbool.h>
8
9    // Type Declarations
10   typedef struct stuData
11   {
12      char name[26];
13      char id[5];
14      int exams[3];
15      int problems[8];
16      char grade;
17   } STU_DATA;
18
19   // Function Declarations
20   bool getData(FILE* textFile,
```

(continue)

Program 12-5   Text to binary student file *(continued)*

```
21                    STU_DATA* aStudent);
22  void writeBinaryFile(STU_DATA* aStudent,
23                        FILE* binFile);
24
25  int main (void)
26  {
27  // Local Declarations
28     char* textFileID = "P12-stu.txt";
29     char* binFileID  = "P12-stu.bin";
30
31     STU_DATA aStudent;
32
33     FILE* textFile;
34     FILE* binFile;
35
36  // Statements
37     printf("\nBegin Student Binary File Creation\n");
38     if (!(textFile = fopen(textFileID, "r")))
39        {
40         printf("\nCannot open %s\n", textFileID);
41         exit (100);
42        } // if textFile
43     if (!(binFile = fopen(binFileID, "wb")))
44        {
45         printf("/Cannot open %s\n", binFileID);
46         exit (200);
47        } // if binFile
48
49     while (getData (textFile, &aStudent))
50        writeBinaryFile (&aStudent, binFile);
51
52     fclose(textFile);
53     fclose(binFile);
54     printf("\n\nFile creation complete\n");
55     return 0;
56  } // main
57
58  /* ==================== getData ====================
59     This function reads the text file.
60     Pre textFile is opened for reading
61     Post data read and returned
62  */
63  bool getData(FILE* textFile, STU_DATA* aStu)
64  {
```

(continue)

Program 12-5 Text to binary student file *(continued)*

```
65  // Local Declarations
66     char buffer[100];
67
68  // Statements
69     fgets(buffer, sizeof(buffer), textFile);
70     if (!feof(textFile))
71     {
72        sscanf(buffer, "%s %s %d%d%d%d%d%d%d%d%d%d%d %c",
73                aStu->name, aStu->id,
74                &aStu->exams[0],
75                &aStu->exams[1],&aStu->exams[2],
76                &aStu->problems[0], &aStu->problems[1],
77                &aStu->problems[2], &aStu->problems[3],
78                &aStu->problems[4], &aStu->problems[5],
79                &aStu->problems[6], &aStu->problems[7],
80                &aStu->grade);
81        return true;
82     } // if
83     return false;
84  } // getData
85
86  /* ================= writeBinaryFile =================
87     Write student data to a binary file.
88     Pre binFile is opened as a binary output file
89     aStudent is complete
90     Post Record written
91  */
92  void writeBinaryFile(STU_DATA* aStudent,
93     FILE* binFile)
94  {
95  // Local Declarations
96     int amtWritten;
97
98  // Statements
99   amtWritten = fwrite(aStudent,
100                      sizeof(STU_DATA), 1, binFile);
101     if (amtWritten != 1)
102     {
103        printf("Can't write student file. Exiting\n");
104        exit (201);
105     } // if
106     return;
107 } // writeBinaryFile
```

Note how we specified the external file names as strings. This makes it easy to change the file names when necessary. It also allows us to identify the file by name if the open fails.

The program starts and ends with a message that identifies what program is running and that it has successfully completed. This is a good programming technique and a standard in many organizations.

The `while` loop is controlled by the results of the `getData` function call. To understand how it works, therefore, first look at `getData`. When you need to read a lot of text data, especially if it is coming from a file, the preferred technique is to use the get string (`fgets`) function and then use the string scan (`sscanf`) function to convert it into internal binary formats. The get string function reads text data until it finds a newline character, an end of file, or the maximum number of characters has been read. It returns the address of the input string, in this case `buffer`. When end of file is detected, it returns a null pointer.

To make this function robust, we would break the `sscanf` into several calls, one for the first two strings, one for the exams, one for the problems, and one for the grade at the end. This would allow us to easily verify that the correct data were read by examining the returned value from `sscanf`.

Now that we understand that the `getData` function returns either an address or NULL, we understand how the `while` statement in `main` works. It simply loops until an end of file is detected—that is, until NULL is returned.

Creating a Text File from a Binary File

Programmers convert a binary file to a text file in two situations. The first is when we need to display the data for people to read. The second is when it is necessary to export the data to another system that can't read the binary file. This occurs, for example, if the word sizes for integers and floats are different on two different hardware systems. As long as all lines are formatted the same and they use the same character alphabet, text files are portable.

An interesting problem is to create a report of the data in the binary file. Obviously, we need to read the binary file and write the data as a text file, but there is much more to it than that. First, the report needs a name, so each page must have a title. The title should include the report date and a page number. To make the report meaningful, each column should have a column caption. Finally, the report should have an end-of-report message as the last line of the report so that the user knows that all data have been reported.

Because we put a title on the top of each page, we need to know when a page is full. This is generally done by counting the number of lines on a page, and when the count exceeds the maximum, skipping to the next page. Good structured programming requires that the heading logic be in a separate function. The design for printing the student data is shown in **Figure 12-15**.

Figure 12-15   Design for print student data

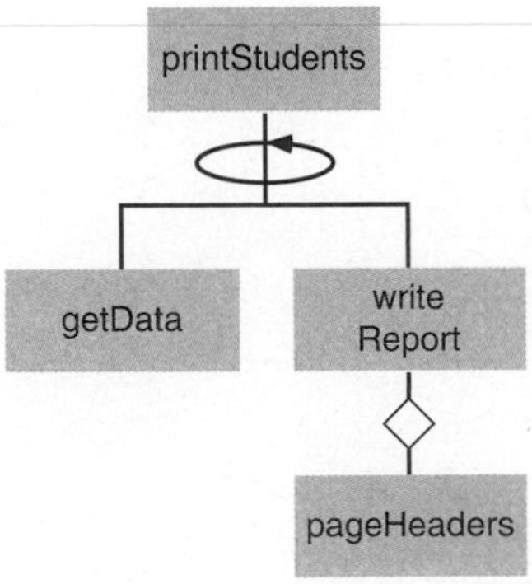

We write the data to a file so that it can be sent to the printer when we want a hard copy. You should be aware of one final point before looking at the program. In the print functions, we use a type modifier known as the static storage class (see statements 97 and 128). We discuss the concept of storage classes in Appendix E. For now, you only need to know that static keeps the contents of a variable available between calls. The first time we call a function with a static variable, the variable is initialized. After that, its value is retained between calls. This is a great C feature that reduces the need to pass parameters just to retain a local variable. The code is shown in **Program 12-6**.

Program 12-6 | Print student data

```
1   /* Reads a binary file of student data, and prints it.
2      Written by:
3      Date:
4   */
5   #include <stdio.h>
6   #include <stdlib.h>
7
8   #define MAX_LINES_PER_PAGE 50
9   #define BUFFER_SIZE 133
10  #define FORM_FEED '\f'
11
12  // Type Declarations
13  typedef struct stuData
14  {
15     char name[26];
16     char id[5];
17     int  exams[3];
18     int  problems[8];
19     char grade;
20  } STU_DATA;
21
22  // Function Declarations
23  STU_DATA getData (FILE* binFile);
24  void writeReport (STU_DATA aStudent,
25                     FILE* prtFile);
26  void pageHeaders (FILE* prtFile);
27
28  int main (void)
29  {
30  // Local Declarations
31     char stuFileID[] = "P12-stu.bin";
32     char prtFileID[] = "P12-stu.prt";
33     STU_DATA aStudent;
34     FILE* stuFile;
```

(continue)

Program 12-6 Print student data *(continued)*

```
35       FILE* prtFile;
36
37   // Statements
38       printf("\nBegin Student Report Creation\n ");
39
40       if(!(stuFile = fopen(stuFileID, "rb")))
41       {
42          printf("\nCannot open %s\n", stuFileID);
43          exit (100);
44       } // if stuFile
45       if (!(prtFile = fopen(prtFileID, "w")))
46       {
47          printf("\nCannot open %s\n", prtFileID);
48          exit (200);
49       } // if prtFile
50
51       aStudent = getData (stuFile);
52       while (!feof(stuFile))
53       {
54          writeReport (aStudent, prtFile);
55          aStudent = getData (stuFile);
56       } // while
57
58       fprintf(prtFile, "\nEnd of Report\n");
59       fclose(stuFile);
60       fclose(prtFile);
61       printf("\n\nEnd Student Report Creation\n");
62       return 0;
63   } // main
64
65   /* ==================== getData ====================
66       This function reads the student binary file.
67       Pre stuFile is opened for reading
68       Post one student record read and returned
69   */
70   STU_DATA getData (FILE* stuFile)
71   {
72   // Local Declarations
73       int ioResult;
74       STU_DATA aStu;
75
76   // Statements
77       ioResult = fread(&aStu,
```

(continue)

Program 12-6   Print student data *(continued)*

```c
 78                      sizeof(STU_DATA), 1, stuFile);
 79      if (!ioResult)
 80        if (!feof(stuFile))
 81        {
 82           printf("\n\nError reading student file\n");
 83           exit (100);
 84        } // if !feof
 85      return aStu;
 86   } // getData
 87
 88   /* ==================== writeReport =================
 89      Write student report to a text file.
 90      Pre prtFile is opened as a text output file
 91      aStudent is complete
 92      Post Report line written
 93   */
 94    void writeReport (STU_DATA aStu, FILE* prtFile)
 95    {
 96    // Local Declarations
 97       static int lineCount = MAX_LINES_PER_PAGE + 1;
 98       char buffer[BUFFER_SIZE];
 99
100    // Statements
101       if (++lineCount > MAX_LINES_PER_PAGE)
102       {
103          pageHeaders (prtFile);
104          lineCount = 1;
105       } // if
106
107       sprintf (buffer,
108          "%-25s %4s %4d%4d%4d%4d%4d%4d%4d%4d%4d%4d%4d %c\n", 109,
109          aStu.name, aStu.id,
110          aStu.exams[0], aStu.exams[1], aStu.exams[2],
111          aStu.problems[0],
112          aStu.problems[1], aStu.problems[2],
113          aStu.problems[3], aStu.problems[4], aStu.problems[5],
114          aStu.problems[6], aStu.problems[7],
115          aStu.grade);
116          fputs (buffer, prtFile);
117       return;
118    } // writeReport
119
120    /* ================= pageHeaders ==================
```

(continue)

Program 12-6   Print student data *(continued)*

```
121          Writes the page headers for the student report.
122          Pre  prtFile is opened as a text output file
123          Post Report headers and captions written
124   */
125   void pageHeaders (FILE* prtFile)
126   {
127   // Local Declarations
128        static int pageNo = 0;
129
130   // Statements
131      pageNo++;
132      fprintf(prtFile, "%c", FORM_FEED);
133      fprintf(prtFile, "%-66s Page %4d\n",
134              "Student Report ", pageNo);
135      fprintf(prtFile, "%-25s %-6s %-10s %-27s Grade\n\n",
136              "Student Name", "ID", "Exams", "Problems");
137      return;
138   }// pageHeaders
139   // ================= End of Program =================
```

Even though this program is rather simple, you should note several important points. First, we have declared the maximum number of lines per page and the print buffer size as preprocessor-defined constants. This makes it easy to change them should it be necessary. It also makes it easy to set the print logic so that it will print the header the first time through the function. This leads us to the second point to note, which is that the logic for pageHeaders will cause the first page to be blank. That is, we issue a page form feed before any data have been written. This is standard in production programs, but you may want to change it so that the first page is not wasted. In this case, you will have to call the pageHeaders function before you start the file reading to write the first headings and move the form feed write to just before statement 103.

The file is read using look-ahead logic. At statement 51, we read the first record of the file. This allows us to use the feof function to control the while loop. At the end of the loop, we read the file again. Although this loop closely resembles a posttest loop, there is one difference. If the file is empty, a posttest loop would fail. By reading the first record from the file before the loop, we ensure that we can process any file condition using the simplest possible logic.

Note the way we handle the report title and line captions in pageHeaders. Many programmers simply try to code them in the format string. This works, but it takes a lot of trial and error to get it right. Our technique simply adds the widths from the data write and uses them for the widths in the caption prints. The program may still need a little manual adjustment, but it is a much simpler approach.

Finally, note how we formatted the student output. We used sprintf to format a line of output. There is no significant advantage to using the string format function rather than the print function, but we wanted to demonstrate its use. After the data have been formatted, we use fputs to write them. Note also the way we aligned the data for readability. Because it takes several lines, we group the common data on lines by themselves. This makes it much easier to read the code. We could have used for statements to print the array data, but that would have been less efficient.

Programming Example: File Programs

This section contains two common file applications. The first uses the file position functions to randomly process the data in a file. The second merges two files.

Program 12-7 demonstrates the concept of randomly accessing data in a file. We begin by creating a binary file of integers. Each integer is the square of the data's position in the file, relative to 1. After the file has been created, we print it in sequence, starting at the beginning of the file. We then print it in a random sequence using fseek and a random number generator.

| Program 12-7 | Random file application |

```
1    /* Shows application of some functions we have studied
2       in this chapter. The program first creates a binary
3       file of integers. It then prints the file, first
4       sequentially and then randomly using rand()
5       Written by:
6       Date:
7    */
8    #include <stdio.h>
9    #include <stdlib.h>
10
11   // Function Declarations
12   void buildFile (FILE** sp);
13   void printFile (FILE* sp);
14   void randomPrint (FILE* sp);
15
16   int main (void)
17   {
18   // Local Declarations
19      FILE* fpData;
20
21   // Statements
22      buildFile (&fpData);
23      printFile (fpData);
24      randomPrint (fpData);
25      return 0;
26   } // main
```

The main function simply calls three functions in order. The first function receives a pointer to the file pointer, which is the only variable declared in main. It is necessary to use double dereferencing here because buildFile needs to pass back the file pointer to main. The other two calls do not change the file pointer, they just use it. Therefore, it can be passed to them by value.

Program 12-8 builds a binary file.

Program 12-8 | Random file: `buildFile`

```
1    /* ==================== buildFile ====================
2       Creates a disk file that we can process randomly.
3       Pre nothing
4       Post file has been built
5    */
6    void buildFile(FILE** spData)
7    {
8    // Local Declarations
9       int data;
10
11   // Statements
12      if (!(*spData = fopen("SAMPLE.DAT", "w+b")))
13      {
14         printf("\aError opening file.\n");
15         exit (100);
16      } // if open
17      for (int i = 1; i <= 10; i++)
18      {
19         data = i * i;
20         fwrite(&data, sizeof(int), 1, *spData);
21      } // for
22      return;
23      } // buildFile
```

The `buildFile` function in Program 12-8 simply creates a file with ten records. Each record consists of a single integer, which is the square of the ordinal record number relative to 1 (not 0). The file is opened with write plus so that we can first write to it and then, later in the program, read it. Note that all references to the file use the dereference operator to update the file pointer, which exists in `main`.

Program 12-9 prints the file sequentially.

Program 12-9 | Random file: sequential print

```
1    /* ==================== printFile ====================
2       Prints the file starting at the first record.
3       Pre spData is an open file
4       Post file has been printed
5    */
6    void printFile(FILE* spData)
7    {
8    // Local Declarations
9       int data;
```

(continue)

Program 12-9 Random file: sequential print *(continued)*

```
10        int recNum;
11
12    // Statements
13        recNum = 0;
14        rewind(spData);
15        fread(&data , sizeof(int), 1, spData);
16        while (!feof(spData))
17        {
18           printf("Record %2d: %3d\n", recNum++, data);
19           fread(&data, sizeof(int), 1, spData);
20        } // while
21        return;
22    } // printFile
```

```
Output
Record   0:   1
Record   1:   4
Record   2:   9
Record   3:  16
Record   4:  25
Record   5:  36
Record   6:  49
Record   7:  64
Record   8:  81
Record   9: 100
```

The printFile function in Program 12-9 simply reads the file sequentially starting at the beginning (Record 0). Study the while loop. Note that we have coded it with the first read before the loop. We use this technique so that we can detect end of file in the while statement. The while loop prints the current record and then reads the next record. When all records have been processed, the read will detect end of file, and the loop will terminate with all records processed.

Program 12-10 prints the file randomly.

Program 12-10 | Random file: randomPrint

```
1    /* ================= randomPrint ===================
2        This function randomly prints the file. Some data
3        may be printed twice, depending on the random
4        numbers generated.
5        Pre spData is an open file
```

(continue)

Program 12-10   Random file: randomPrint *(continued)*

```
 6          Post Ten records have been printed
 7     */
 8     void randomPrint (FILE* spData)
 9     {
10     // Local Declarations
11        int data;
12        int randomSeek;
13
14     // Statements
15        printf("\nFile contents in random sequence.\n");
16        for (int i = 0; i < 10; i++)
17        {
18           randomSeek = (rand() % 10);
19           fseek(spData,
20                 sizeof(int) * randomSeek, SEEK_SET);
21           fread(&data, sizeof(int), 1, spData);
22           printf("Record %3d ==> %3d\n",
23                    randomSeek, data);
24        } // for
25        return;
26     } // randomPrint
```

Output
```
File contents in random sequence.
Record 8 ==>   81
Record 8 ==>   81
Record 3 ==>   16
Record 5 ==>   36
Record 1 ==>    4
Record 7 ==>   64
Record 0 ==>    1
Record 9 ==>  100
Record 2 ==>    9
Record 6 ==>   49
```

The `randomPrint` function is the most interesting of these functions. We use a `for` loop to print ten records. Within the loop, we use a random number generator to determine which record we will read next. Because there are ten records in the file, we set the random number to modulo ten, which gives us potential record numbers from zero to nine. This corresponds exactly with the file on disk, which occupies record positions zero to nine. The function output created using our computer is shown in Program 12-10. Note that it starts by printing Record 8 twice and then prints all other records other than Record 4. Compare the output to the file print in Program 12-9.

Merge Files

In the "Block Input/Output Functions," section, we discussed the concept of combining two files by appending the data. In this section, we discuss another way to combine data: the file merge. When we merge data from two files, the result is one file with the data ordered in key sequence. This requires that we completely read two input files and create a new output file. This concept is shown in **Figure 12-16**.

Figure 12-16 File merge concept

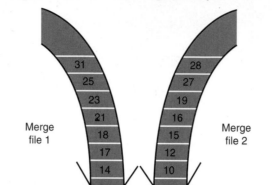

Output (merged) file

The merge files pseudocode is shown in **Algorithm 12-1**. The design is rather simple. We start by reading data from each merge file. We then (1) compare the data in the two files, (2) write the smaller to the merge output file, (3) read the next record from the file whose record was written, and (4) continue the loop.

Algorithm 12-1 │ Pseudocode for merging two files

Algorithm MergeTwoFiles

This program merges two files

1 input (File1, Rec1)

2 input (File2, Rec2)

3 HighSentinel = high-value

4 loop (not eof(File1)) OR (not eof(File2))

  1 if Rec1.Key <= Rec2.Key then

    1 output (File3, Rec1)

    2 input (File1, Rec1)

    3 if eof(File1)

      1 Rec1.Key = HighSentinel

    4 end if

  2 Else

    1 output (File3, Rec2)

(continue)

Algorithm 12-1   Pseudocode for merging two files *(continued)*

```
         2 input (File2, Rec2)
         3 if eof(File2)
            1 Rec2.Key = HighSentinel
         4 end if
       3 end if
     5 end loop
   End MergeTwoFiles
```

The difficult part of the merge design is the end-of-file logic. One of the merge files will end first, but we never know which one. To simplify the end-of-file processing, this design introduces a concept known as a sentinel. A sentinel is a guard; in our merge algorithm, the sentinel guards the end of file. The sentinel has the property that its value is larger than any possible key. For the sentinel value, we use INT_MAX, which is found in the limits.h header file. The code is seen in **Program 12-11**.

Program 12-11 | Merge two files

```c
1     /* This program merges two files
2        Written by:
3        Date:
4     */
5     #include <stdio.h>
6     #include <stdlib.h>
7
8     #include <limits.h>
9     #define READ_MODE "rb"
10    #define WRITE_MODE "wb"
11
12    int main (void)
13    {
14  // Local Declarations
15       FILE* spM1;
16       FILE* spM2;
17       FILE* spOut;
18
19       int recM1;
20       int recM2;
21       int sentinel = INT_MAX;
22       int mergeCnt = 0;
23
24       char file1ID[] ="P13Mrg1.bin";
25       char file2ID[] ="P13Mrg2.bin";
26       char fileOutID[] = "P13Mrg3.bin";
27
```

(continue)

Program 12-11 Merge two files *(continued)*

```c
28    // Statements
29       printf("Begin File Merge:\n");
30       if (!(spM1  = fopen (file1ID, READ_MODE)))
31          printf("\aError on %s\n", file1ID), exit (100);
32
33       if (!(spM2  = fopen (file2ID, READ_MODE)))
34          printf("\aError on %s\n", file2ID), exit (200);
35
36       if (!(spOut = fopen (fileOutID, WRITE_MODE)))
37          printf("\aError on %s\n", fileOutID), exit (300);
38
39       fread (&recM1, sizeof(int), 1, spM1);
40       if (feof(spM1))
41          recM1  = sentinel;
42       fread (&recM2, sizeof(int), 1, spM2);
43       if (feof(spM2))
44          recM2  = sentinel;
45
46       while (!feof(spM1) || !feof(spM2))
47       {
48          if (recM1 <= recM2)
49          {
50             fwrite (&recM1, sizeof(int), 1, spOut);
51             mergeCnt++;
52             fread (&recM1, sizeof(int), 1, spM1);
53             if (feof(spM1))
54                recM1 = sentinel;
55          } // if
56          else
57          {
58             fwrite (&recM2, sizeof(int), 1, spOut);
59             mergeCnt++;
60             fread (&recM2, sizeof(int), 1, spM2);
61             if (feof(spM2))
62                recM2 = sentinel;
63          } // else
64       } // while
65       fclose (spM1);
66       fclose (spM2);
67       fclose (spOut);
68       printf("End File Merge. %d items merged.\n",
69              mergeCnt);
70       return 0;
71    } // main
```

We have written this simple program without any subfunctions. Once again, we have used the multiple-statement error message format for the error message and exit after each open statement when a failure to open the file occurs.

Programs that involve the comparison of data from two files require that the first record from both files be read before any comparisons can be made. This is sometimes called "priming the files." The reads that prime the files are coded before the main `while` loop. Because duplicate read statements are required in the loop, you might wonder why we didn't use a `do ... while`. The reason is that the program would fail if both files were empty. As we coded it, the program works if either or both merge files are empty.

Study the logic at statements 54 and 62 carefully. These statements implement the sentinel concept. When a file reaches its end, we set the key in the record area for the file to the sentinel value. This ensures that all the data on the other file will compare low and be written to the output file.

The most difficult statement in this simple program is the `while` statement. We need to keep looping as long as either of the files is not at the end of file. The most straightforward code is as we coded it in statement 46. Another common way to code it is shown below.

```
(!(feof(spM1) && feof(spM2)))
```

Software Engineering

Any file environment requires some means of keeping the file current. Data are not static; they are constantly changing, and these changes need to be reflected in their files. The function that keeps files current is known as updating. To complete our discussion of files, we discuss some of the software engineering design considerations for file updating. For this discussion, we assume a student binary file similar to the ones we have discussed in the chapter.

Update Files

Three specific files are associated with an update program. First is the permanent data file, called the master file, which contains the most current computer data for an application.

The second file is the transaction file. It contains changes to be applied to the master file. Three basic types of changes occur in all file updates; others may also occur, depending on the application. *Add* transactions contain data about new students to be added in the master file; *delete* transactions identify students who will be deleted from the file; and *change* transactions contain revisions to specific student records in the file.

To process any of these transactions, we need a key. A key is one or more fields that uniquely identify the data in the file. For example, in the student file, the key would be student ID. In an employee file, the key would be Social Security number.

The third file needed in an update program is an error report file. An update process is very rarely error free. When an error occurs, we need to report it to the user. The error report contains a listing of all errors discovered during the update process and is presented to the user for corrective action.

File updates are of two types: batch and online. In a batch update, changes are collected over time and then all changes are applied to the file at once. In an online update, the user is directly connected to the computer and the changes are processed one at a time—often as the change occurs.

Sequential File Update

For our discussion, we will assume a batch, sequential file environment. A sequential file is a file that must be processed serially starting at the beginning. It does not have any random-processing capabilities. The sequential master file has the additional attribute that it is ordered on the key.

A sequential file update actually has two copies of the master file: the old master and the new master. This is because whenever a sequential file is changed, it must be entirely re-created—even if only one student's score on one exam is changed.

Figure 12-17 contains an environment chart for a sequential file update. In this chart, we see the four files we discussed above. We use the tape symbol for the files because it is the classic symbol for sequential files. Sequential files could just as easily be stored on a disk. Note that after the update program completes, the new master file is sent to off-line storage, where it is kept until it is needed again. When the file is to be updated, the master file is retrieved from the off-line storage and used as the old master.

Figure 12-17 Sequential file update environment

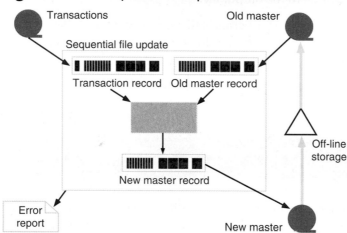

Generally, at least three copies of a master file are retained in off-line storage in case it becomes necessary to regenerate an unreadable file. This retention cycle is known as the grandparent system because three generations of the file are always available: the grandparent, the parent, and the child.

The Update Program Design

In 1981, a computer scientist named Barry Dwyer published an update algorithm in the journal *Communications of the ACM* that was so elegant that it has become a classic. We have adapted his algorithm for our discussion.

Because a sequential master file is ordered on a key and because it must be processed serially, the transaction file must also be ordered on the same key. The update process requires that we match the keys on the transaction and master file and, assuming that there are no errors, take one of the following three actions:

1. If the transaction file key is less than the master file key, add the transaction to the new master.

2. If the transaction file key is equal to the master file key, either

   a. Change the contents of the master file data if the transaction is a revise transaction, or

   b. Remove the data from the master file if the transaction is a delete.

3. If the transaction file key is greater than the master file key, write the old master file record to the new master file.

This updating process is shown in **Figure 12-18**. In the transaction file, the transaction codes are A for add, D for delete, and R for revise. The process begins by matching the keys for the first record on each file, in this case,

```
14 > 10
```

Thus, rule 3 is used, and we write the master record to the new master record. We then match 14 and 13, which results in 13 being written to the new master. In the next match, we have the following situation:

```
14 == 14
```

Figure 12-18 File updating example

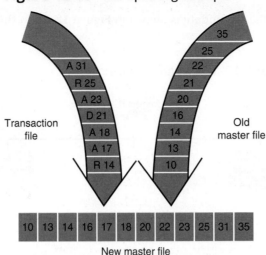

Transaction file

A 31
R 25
A 23
D 21
A 18
A 17
R 14

Old master file

35
25
22
21
20
16
14
13
10

| 10 | 13 | 14 | 16 | 17 | 18 | 20 | 22 | 23 | 25 | 31 | 35 |

New master file

Thus, according to rule 2a, we use the data in the transaction file to change the data in the master file. However, we do not write the new master file at this time. More transactions may match the master file, and we need to process them, too.

After writing 16 to the new master, we have the following situation:

```
17 < 20
```

According to rule 1, we must add 17 to the new master file. We do this by copying the transaction to the new master file, but again, we don't write it yet. This newly added record may have some revision transactions, and we need to be able to process them. For example, this capability is needed when a new student registers and adds classes on the same day. The computer has to be able to add the new student and then process the class registrations in the same batch run. We write the new master for 17 when we read transaction 18.

The processing continues until we read the delete transaction, at which time we have the following situation:

```
21 == 21
```

Because the transaction is a delete, according to rule 2b, we need to drop 21 from the new master file. To do this, we simply read the next master record and transaction record without writing the new master. The processing continues in a similar fashion until all records on both files have been processed.

Update Errors

Two general classes of errors can occur in an update program. For example the user could submit bad data, such as a grade that is not A, B, C, D, or F. For our discussion, we will assume that no data errors are present. Detecting data errors is the subject of data validation.

The second class of errors is file errors. File errors occur when the data on the transaction file are not in synchronization with the data on the master file in one of three different situations:

1. An add transaction matches a record with the same key on the master file. Master files do not allow duplicate data to be present. When the key on an add transaction matches a key on the master file, therefore, we reject the transaction as invalid and report it on the error report.

2. A revise transaction's key does not match a record on the master file. In this case, we are trying to change data that do not exist. This is also a file error and must be reported on the error report.

3. A delete transaction's key does not match a record on the master file. In this case, we are trying to delete data that do not exist, and this must also be reported as an error.

Update Structure Chart

The structure chart for the sequential file update is shown in **Figure 12-19**. In this structure chart, process contains the updating function.

Figure 12-19 Update structure chart

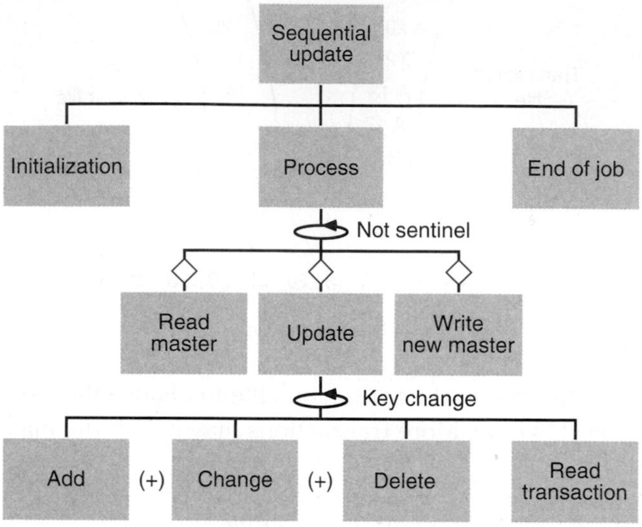

Update Logic

`Initialization` is a function that opens the files and otherwise prepares the environment for processing. `EndofJob` is a function that closes the files and displays any end of job messages. The mainline processing is done in Process.

Although it is beyond our scope to develop the complete set of update functions, it is important that you at least understand the mainline logic found in Process. Its pseudocode is shown in **Algorithm 12-2**.

Algorithm 12-2 | Pseudocode for file update

Algorithm Sequential Update

1 read first record from transaction file

2 read first record from old master file

3 select next entity to be processed

4 loop current entity not sentinel

  1 if current entity equals old master entity

    1 copy old master to new master work area

    2 read old master file

  2 end if

  3 if current entity equals transaction entity

    1 update new master work area

  4 end if

  5 if current entity equals new master entity

(continue)

Algorithm 12-2   Pseudocode for file update *(continued)*

      1 write new master file

   6 end if

   7 select next entity to be processed

 5 end loop

End Sequential Update

Let's look at the update logic in a little more detail. The first three statements contain initialization logic for Process. The driving force behind the update logic is that in each `while` loop, we process all the data for one student (entity). To determine which student we need to process next (statements 3 and 4.7), we determine the current entry by comparing the current transaction key to the current master key. The current key is the smaller.

Before we can compare the keys, however, we must read the first record in each file. This is known as "priming the files" and is seen in statements 1 and 2.

The `loop` statement in Algorithm 12-2 contains the driving logic for the entire program. It is built on a very simple principle: As long as data are present in either the transaction file or the master file, we continue to loop. When a file has been completely read, we set its key to a sentinel value. When both files are at their end, therefore, both of their keys will be sentinels. Then, when we select the next student to be processed, it will be a sentinel, which is the event that terminates the `while` loop.

Three major processing functions take place in the `while` loop. First, we determine if the student in the old master file needs to be processed. If it does, we move it to the new master output area and read the next student from the old master file. The key in the old master can match the current key in two situations: a change or delete transaction exists for the current student. This logic is seen in statement 4.1.

The second major process handles transactions that match the current student. It calls a function that determines the type of transaction being processed (add, change, or delete) and handles it accordingly. If it is an add, it moves the new student's data to the new master area. If it is a change, it updates the data in the new master area. And if it is a delete, it clears the key in the new master area so that the record will not be written. To handle multiple transactions in the update function, it reads the next transaction and continues if its key matches the current student.

The last major process writes the new master when appropriate. If the current student matches the key in the new master file area, then the record needs to be written to the file. This will be the case unless a delete transaction was processed.

Update Algorithm Summary

In this section we looked at an important algorithm, the classic sequential file update, and discussed its mainline logic flow.

The elegance of Dwyer's update algorithm, as seen in Algorithm 12-2, lies in the determination of the current student and the separation of the update process into three distinct functions: read the old master, update the current student, and write the new master. Study the concept of the current student carefully, and make sure you understand how it controls the three major processes in the loop. Then, with a little thought, you should be able to develop the other functions in the update program.

Also note that Algorithm 12-2 contains only one read transaction function. Its function is to read a valid transaction. Therefore, it contains all of the simple data validation logic to determine if the data are correct. It does not perform any file errors; they are handled in the update function. If any errors are found, the read transaction function writes the transaction to an error report and reads the next transaction. When it returns to the calling function, it has either read a valid transaction or has found the end of the file.

Tips and Common Programming Errors

1. EOF is an integer type, and its value is normally -1. Therefore, if you want to test the value of a variable to EOF, use an integer variable, not a character. In most systems, a character variable cannot store a negative number (-1 here).

2. Remember to open a file before using it.

3. You can create a file for writing; but to read a file, it must exist.

4. When you open a file for writing using w mode, you must close it and open it for reading using r mode if you want to read from it. To avoid this problem, you can open it in w+ mode.

5. An open file can be in one of the three states: read, write, or error. If you want to switch from read to write or from write to read, you must use one of the file position functions.

6. Do not open a file in w mode if you want to preserve the contents of the file. Opening a file in w mode erases the contents of the file.

7. Remember that in general you cannot print the contents of a binary file. It must be converted to a text file first.

8. Unlike other input/output functions, the first parameter of the fread and fwrite functions is a pointer to the input area, not a file pointer. The file parameter is the last (fourth) parameter.

9. The second parameter of the fread and fwrite functions is the size of the element. The third parameter is the count of elements.

10. The fread and fwrite functions return the number of elements read or written, not the number of bytes read or written.

11. Remember that feof does not look ahead. It returns true only if an attempt is made to read the end of file.

12. The second parameter in the fseek function is the number of bytes, not the number of elements.

13. When the third parameter in the fseek function is SEEK_END(2), the middle parameter should normally be a negative long integer to access a byte in the file. If it is positive, it is referring to a byte after the end of file.

14. To add an element at the end of the file, use the fseek function with the second parameter set to zero and the third parameter set to the value of SEEK_END.

15. Remember that every time you use the fread or fwrite function, it automatically advances the file position indicator toward the end of the file the number of bytes equal to the size of the element times the number of elements read or written.

16. It is good practice to close all files before terminating a program.

17. It is a compile error to refer to a file with its external file name rather than its file pointer.

18. It is a compile error to omit the file pointer when using a file function. This error most often occurs when using the file versions of the file format functions, such as fprintf.

19. It is a logic error to refer to a file before it is opened.

20. It is a logic error to open a file for reading when it doesn't exist. This is usually an error in the external file name in the open statement.

21. It is a logic error to attempt to read from a file in the write state and vice versa. This is true even when the file has been opened in the update mode.

22. Opening an output disk file will fail if the disk is full.

23. Opening an existing file in write mode deletes the data in the file. If your input file disappears, check your open modes.

24. It is a logic error to use fseek to place the file marker before the first byte of a file.

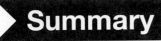

Summary

> A file is a collection of related data stored in an auxiliary storage device.

> A stored stream of 0s and 1s can be interpreted as either a text or a binary file.

> A text file is a file of characters.

> A binary file is a collection of related data stored in the internal format of the computer.

> A file is always in one of the following states: read, write, or error.

> A binary file can be opened in one of the following modes: rb, r+b, wb, w+b, ab, and a+b.

> The fread function reads the number of bytes specified by the product of the element size and the number of elements.

> The fwrite function writes the number of bytes specified by the product of the element size and the number of elements.

> The feof function checks for end of file.

> The ferror function is used to check the error status of a file.

> The clearerr function is used to clear an error.

> The rewind function sets the file position indicator to the beginning of the file.

> The ftell function tells you the current position of the file position indicator.

> The fseek function positions the file position indicator to the beginning of a specified byte.

> The remove function removes or deletes a file from the disk.

> The rename function renames a file on the disk.

> The tmpfile function creates a new temporary file.

> To be kept current, master files must be updated.

> The master file update requires four files: the old master, a new master, a transaction file, and an error report file.

> The basic master file transactions are add, revise, and delete.

Key Terms

batch update	master file	sentinel
end-of-file (EOF) marker	merge	sequential file
error report file	online update	transaction file
error state	read state	update mode
key	seek file	write state

Review Questions

1. A file can only be read if it is in the read state.
   a. True **b.** False

2. A file opened in the `r+b` mode is a binary file opened in the read state and update mode.
   a. True **b.** False

3. Binary files are read using the block input/output function `fread`.
   a. True **b.** False

4. Using `fseek` to position a file beyond the current end of file places the file in an error state.
   a. True **b.** False

5. To merge two files, you can use the merge function found in the standard input/output library.
   a. True **b.** False

6. Which of the following statements about files is true?
   a. All files must be opened before they can be used.
   b. Binary files are more portable than text files.
   c. Binary files are slower than text files.
   d. Files must be closed.
   e. Text files contain data stored in the internal format of the computer.

7. Which of the following statements about files is false?
   a. Because they are more flexible, binary files are more portable.
   b. Binary files contain data stored in the internal format of the computer.
   c. Binary files usually contain records in the form of structured data.
   d. Text files store only character data.
   e. Some text file data need to be converted to internal storage formats for processing.

8. The _____ results when a failure occurs during an open or during either a read or write operation.
   a. error state
   b. fail state
   c. read state
   d. update state
   e. write state

9. If a file in the read state is written to, then the following occurs:
   a. The file is placed in an error state regardless of the file mode.
   b. The file is placed in an error state unless it was opened in the update write mode (`w+b`).
   c. The file state is automatically switched if the file is opened for updating.
   d. The program is aborted regardless of how the file was opened.
   e. The program is aborted unless the file was opened for updating.

10. Which of the following file modes opens a file in the write state for updating?
    a. `ab` **c.** `rb` **e.** `wb`
    b. `a+b` **d.** `r+b`

11. Which of the following C functions is used to output data to a binary file?
    a. `fwrite` **c.** `write` **e.** `fprintf`
    b. `output` **d.** `writef`

12. Which of the following is a file status function?
    a. `feof` **c.** `frewind` **e.** `ftell`
    b. `freport` **d.** `fseek`

13. The _____ function may be used to position a file at the beginning.
    a. `fclose` **c.** `freport` **e.** `ftell`
    b. `feof` **d.** `fseek`

14. A _____ is one or more fields that uniquely identify the data in a file.
    a. field **c.** key **e.** transaction
    b. identifier **d.** structure

15. Which of the following statements about sequential file updating is false?
    a. Add, change, and delete transactions are used to update the file.
    b. Sequential files are often updated in an online environment.
    c. Sequential files contain structures (records) with a key to identify the data.
    d. The file must be processed starting at the beginning.
    e. The file must be entirely re-created when it is updated.

Exercises

16. Explain the difference between the following pairs of modes:

```
rb and r+b
```

```
wb and w+b
```

```
ab and a+b
```

17. Find the error(s) in the following code. (Assume the PAY_REC type has been properly declared.)

```
char* m = "wb";
char* str = "Payroll";
PAY_REC payRec;
FILE* sp;
sp = fopen (str, m);
fread(payRec, sizeof(payRec), 1, sp);
```

18. Given the following declarations and assuming that the file is open:

```
FILE* sp;
char s[20];
```

find any errors in each of the following statements:
  a. `fread(s, 20, sp);`
  b. `fread(s, 20, 1, sp);`
  c. `fread(s, 1, 20, sp);`
  d. `fread(sp, 1, 20, s);`
  e. `fread(sp, 20, 1, s);`

19. Given the following declarations and assuming that the file is open:

```
FILE* sp;
char s[20];
```

find any errors in each of the following lines:
  a. `locn = ftell(sp);`
  b. `locn = ftell(1, sp);`
  c. `fseek(0, 20L, sp);`
  d. `fseek(sp, 20L, 0);`
  e. `fseek(sp, 20L, 1);`

20. What would be printed from the following program? Draw a picture of the file with the file marker to explain your answer.

```
#include <stdio.h>
int main (void)
{
    long int pos;
    FILE* sp;
    sp = fopen ("SAMPLE.DAT", "w+b");
    for (char c = 'A'; c <= 'E'; c++)
```

```
        fwrite(&c , sizeof(char), 1, sp);
    pos = ftell (sp);
    printf("The position of the file marker is : %ld", pos);
    return 0;
} // main
```

21. What would be printed from the following program? Draw a picture of the file with the file marker to explain your answer.

```
#include <stdio.h>
int main (void)
{
    char c;
    FILE* sp;
    sp = fopen("SAMPLE.DAT", "w+b");
    for (c = 'A'; c <= 'E'; C++)
        fwrite(&c, sizeof(char), 1, sp);
    fseek(sp, 2, 0);
    fread(&c, 1, 1, sp);
    printf("\n\n%c", c);
    return 0;
} // main
```

22. What would be printed from the following program? Draw a picture of the file with the file marker to explain your answer.

```
#include <stdio.h>
int main (void)
{
    char c;
    FILE* sp;
    sp = fopen("SAMPLE.DAT", "w+b");
    for (c = 'A'; c <= 'E'; C++)
        fwrite(&c, sizeof (char), 1, sp);
    rewind(sp);
    fread(&c, 1, 1, sp);
    printf("\n\n%c", c);
    return 0;
} // main
```

23. What would be printed from the following program? Draw a picture of the file with the file marker to explain your answer.

```
#include <stdio.h>
int main (void)
{
    char c;
    long int pos;
```

```
    FILE* sp;
    sp = fopen("SAMPLE.DAT", "w+b");
    for (c = 'A'; c <= 'E'; c++)
        fwrite(&c, sizeof(char), 1, sp);
    pos = ftell (sp);
    pos--;
    pos--;
    fseek(sp, pos, 0);
    fread(&c, 1, 1, sp);
    printf("\n\n%c", c);
    return 0;
} // main
```

24. What would be printed from the following program? Draw a picture of the file with the file marker to explain your answer.

```
#include <stdio.h>
int main (void)
{
    char c;
    long int pos;
    FILE* sp;
    sp = fopen("SAMPLE.DAT", "w+b");
    for (c= 'A'; c<= 'E'; c++)
        fwrite(&c , sizeof(char), 1, sp);
    pos = ftell(sp);
    pos--;
    pos--;
    fseek(sp, -pos, 1);
    fread(&c, 1, 1, sp);
    printf("\n\n%c", c);
    return 0;
} // main
```

25. What would be printed from the following program? Draw a picture of the file with the file marker to explain your answer.

```
#include <stdio.h>
int main (void)
{
    char d;
    long int pos;
    FILE* sp;
    sp = fopen("SAMPLE.DAT", "w+b");
    for (char c = 'A'; c <= 'E'; c++)
        fwrite(&c , sizeof(char), 1, sp);
```

```c
      pos = ftell(sp);
      pos--;
      pos--;
      fseek(sp, 2, 2);
      fseek(sp, 1, 1);
      fread(&d, 1, 1, sp);
      printf("\n\n%c", d);
      return 0;
} // main
```

26. What would be printed from the following program? Draw a picture of the file with the file marker to explain your answer.

```c
#include <stdio.h>
int main (void)
{
      long int pos;
      FILE* sp;
      sp = fopen("SAMPLE.DAT", "w+b");
      for (int i = 1; i <= 5; i++)
          fwrite(&i , sizeof(int), 1, sp);
      pos = ftell(sp);
      printf("The position of the file marker is : %ld", pos);
      return 0;
} // main
```

27. What would be printed from the following program? Draw a picture of the file with the file marker to explain your answer.

```c
#include <stdio.h>
int main (void)
{
      int i;
      FILE* sp;
      sp = fopen("SAMPLE.DAT", "w+b");
      for (i = 1; i <= 5; i++)
          fwrite(&i , sizeof(int), 1, sp);
      fseek(sp, sizeof (int) * 2, 0);
      fread(&i, sizeof (int), 1, sp);
      printf("%d\n", i);
      return 0;
} // main
```

28. What would be printed from the following program? Draw a picture of the file with the file marker to explain your answer.

```c
#include <stdio.h>
int main (void)
```

```
{
    int i; FILE* sp;
    sp = fopen ("SAMPLE.DAT", "w+b");
    for (i = 1; i <= 5; i++)
        fwrite(&i, sizeof(int), 1, sp);
    fseek(sp, -sizeof(int) * 2, 1);
    fread(&i, sizeof(int), 1, sp);
    printf("%d", i);
    fclose (sp);
    return 0;
} // main
```

29. What would be printed from the following program? Draw a picture of the file with the file marker to explain your answer. Is the answer strange? Why?

```
#include <stdio.h>
int main (void)
{
    int i;
    FILE* sp;
    sp = fopen("SAMPLE.DAT", "w+b");
    for (i = 1; i <= 5; i++)
        fwrite(&i, sizeof(int), 1, sp);
    fseek(sp, 7, 0);
    fread(&i, sizeof(int), 1, sp);
    printf("%d", i);
    fclose (sp);
    return 0;
} // main
```

30. What would be printed from the following program? Draw a picture of the file with the file marker to explain your answer.

```
#include <stdio.h>
int main (void)
{
    int i;
    long int pos;
    FILE* sp;
    sp = fopen("SAMPLE.DAT", "w+b");
    for (i = 1; i <= 5; i++)
        fwrite(&i, sizeof(int), 1, sp);
    pos = ftell(sp);
    pos = 2 * sizeof(int);
    fseek(sp, pos, 0);
    fread(&i, sizeof(int), 1, sp);
```

```
    printf("%d", i);
    fclose (sp);
    return 0;
} // main
```

Problems

31. Write a function that copies the contents of a binary file of integers to a second file. The function must accept two file pointers and return an integer (zero representing a processing error and nonzero indicating successful completion).

32. Write a function that prints a specified number of records from the beginning of a file. The function is to accept two parameters. The first is a pointer to a binary file of structure type STR. The second is an integer that specifies the number of records to be printed (inclusive). The structure type is shown below:

```
typedef struct
{
    int i;
    float f;
} STR;
```

If any errors occur, such as fewer records in the file than specified, it should return zero. Otherwise, it returns nonzero.

33. Write a function that compares two files and returns equal or not equal based on the result of the comparison. The functions should receive file pointers to two opened files and compare them byte by byte.

34. Write a function that returns the number of items in a binary file.

35. Write a function that prints the last integer in a binary file of integers.

36. Write a function that physically removes all items with a specified value (data) from a binary file of structure STR. You may use a temporary file. The file may contain more than one record with the delete value. The key value removed is to be entered from the keyboard.

```
typedef struct
{
    int data;
    char c;
} STR;
```

37. Write a function that appends one binary file at the end of another. Use the structure described in Problem 36.

38. Write a function that, given a binary file, copies the odd items (items 1, 3, 5, ..., *n*) to a second binary file and the even items (items 2, 4, 6, ..., *n*) to a third binary file. After all items have been copied, print the contents of both output files.

39. Write a function that reads items from a binary file and copies them to a dynamically allocated array. The function must first find the size of the binary file to allocate the array.

40. Write a function that takes a binary file of long integers and appends a new long integer at the end that is the sum of all integers in the original file.

Projects

41. A company has two small warehouses. The list of the products in each warehouse is kept in a text file (`invFile1` and `invFile2`), with each line representing information about one product. The manager wants to have only one list showing information about all products in both warehouses. Therefore, the two text files must be combined into one single text file (`OutFile`).

Write a program that will copy information from the two text files (`invFile1` and `invFile2`) to two binary files (`BinFile1` and `BinFile2`). After creating the binary files, the program is to merge the two binary files to produce a combined binary file. After the combined binary file has been created, create a report file that can be printed. The report file is to contain page headers with an appropriate title and page numbers. The structure for the files is shown below.

```
typedef struct inv_rec
{
    char partNo[5];
    char partName[15];
    int qtyOnHand;
} INV_REC;
```

42. A company keeps a list of parts that it purchases, with a line of information for each part that gives the part's unique code, name, and three codes for three suppliers that supply that particular part. This list is kept in a binary file and is sorted in ascending order according to the supplier's code.

The company also keeps a list of its suppliers, with a line of information for each supplier, which gives the supplier's unique code, name, and address. This list is also kept in a binary file, which is sorted in ascending order according to the supplier's code.

Write a program that enables the user to enter a part's unique code and to receive a list of three suppliers. If the code is found, the program prints the names and addresses of the three suppliers. If the code is not found, it prints a message to tell the user that the code is not in the file. After each inquiry, the program gives the user the option to quit.

Each record in the part file is made up of a part's code, name, and the codes for three suppliers. The part's code is an integer; the name is a string with a maximum length of ten characters; and each supplier's code is an integer. Note that not all parts have three suppliers. For parts with less than three suppliers, a special supplier code of 0000 is used to indicate no supplier.

Each record in the supplier file is made up of a supplier's code, name, and address. The supplier's code is an integer, the name is a string with a maximum length of ten characters, and the address has a maximum length of 20 characters.

The output is to be formatted with the first line showing the data for the part and the following lines showing data for the suppliers, indented one tab.

Sample data for the files are shown in **Tables 12-2** and **12-3**. You will first need to write a file conversion program to create the binary files. We suggest that you create a text file version of each file with your text editor and then read it to create the binary version.

Table 12-2 Project 42 part file

PART CODE	PART NAME	SUPPLIER 1	SUPPLIER 2	SUPPLIER 3
1000	Pen	5010	5007	5012
1001	Pencil	5006	5008	0000
1002	Paper	5001	5000	5003
1003	Ball pen	5013	5009	5014
1004	Folder	5009	5007	5002
1005	Pointer	5012	5006	5005
1006	Mouse	5012	0000	0000
1007	Monitor	5000	5002	5007

Table 12-3 Project 42 supplier file

SUPPLIER CODE	SUPPLIER NAME	SUPPLIER ADDRESS
5000	John Marcus	2322 Glen Place
5001	Steve Chu	1435 Main Ave.
5002	David White	2345 Steve Drive
5003	Bryan Walljasper	780 Rose Mary Street
5004	Andrew Tse	P. O. Box 7600
5005	Joanne Brown	1411 Donnybrook Square
5006	Lucy Nguyen	2345 Saint Mary Road
5007	Fred West	11 Duarte Rd.
5008	Dennis Andrews	14 California Ave.
5009	Leo Washington	134234 San Rosa Place
5010	Frankie South	12234 North Justin St.
5011	Amanda Trapp	1345 Swan Lake Circle
5012	Dave Lightfoot	222 River Front Drive
5013	Danna Mayor	11 Clearview Avenue
5014	Robert Hurley	14 Blue Bay Road

43. Write a program that simulates database operations on a data file for a pet supply store that maintains a list of products. Your program should display an interactive menu as follows:

1. Add new product

2. Delete existing product

3. Update existing product

4. List all products

5. Search for a product

6. Purge deleted products

7. Display total number of records

8. Quit program

The following is a description for each menu option:

> **Add:** Prompt the user to enter product details; this operation will insert the new product record and append it at the end of the data file.

> **Delete:** Mark record to be logically deleted.

> **Update:** Prompt user to enter field to update and the value for it.

> **List:** Display all records in the data file.

> **Search:** Display full details of the record using unique product id.

> **Purge:** Remove all marked records.

> **Display:** Show total number of records, total number of records that are active, and number of records marked for deletion.

Use the data listed in **Table 12-4**.

Table 12-4 Project 43 product file

PROD_ID	PRODUCT_DESCRIPTION	QUANTITY	PRICE	CATEGORY	REC_STATUS
AD72	Dog feeding station	12	84.99	DOG	A
BC33	Feathers bird cage (12x24x18)	3	79.99	BRD	A
CA75	Enclosed cat litter station	7	39.99	CAT	A
DT12	Dog toy gift set	12	39.99	DOG	A
FM23	Fly mask	57	24.95	HOR	A
FS39	Folding saddle stand	21	39.99	HOR	A
FS42	Aquarium (55 gallon)	5	124.99	FSH	A
KH81	Wild bird food (25 lb)	1	19.99	BRD	A
LD14	Locking small dog door	0	49.99	DOG	A
LP73	Aquarium pump and filter	10	59.99	DOG	A
PF19	Automatic litter	32	74.99	FSH	A
QB92	Quilted stable blanket	2	119.99	HOR	A
SP91	Small pet carrier	6	39.99	CAT	A
UF39	Electric fence system	8	199.99	DOG	A
WB49	Insulated water bucket	22	79.99	HOR	A

Note that value 'A' for rec_status indicates that a record is visible, and 'D' indicates it is marked for deletion. When displaying any product, you must check rec_status to determine whether it is deleted or not. In addition, use fseek to locate a record and ftell to calculate total number of existing records in the data file. Create a text file using the data in Table 12-4 and then convert it to binary data file. Use the following data structure:

```
Structure
    prod_id       string [5]
    prod_name     string [35]
    category      string [4]
    Qty           Integer
    Price         floating-point
    rec_stats     Character
```

44. Your stockbroker has an online inquiry system that allows you to check the price of stocks using your personal computer. Simulate this system as described below.

Each stock is assigned a unique integral number in the range 1000–5000. They are stored on the disk so that stock 1000 is stored in location 0, stock 1001 in location 1, stock 2010 in location 1010, and so forth. To calculate the disk address for a requested stock, your program subtracts 1000 from the stock number and uses the result as the address in the file. (This is actually a simplified version of a concept known as "hashing," which you will learn when you study data structures.)

The data for each stock are described as follows:

```
Structure
    stock key              short integer
    stock name             string[21]
    stock symbol           string[6]
    current price          floating-point number
    YTD High               floating-point number
    YTD Low                floating-point number
    Price-Earnings         short integer
    Ratio
(YTD: Year to Date)
```

Using data from your favorite stock exchange provider, create a binary file of at least 20 stocks. Then write a menu-driven system that allows the user to request data on any individual stock.

In addition, provide a capability to get a report of up to 20 stocks at one time. When this option is requested, open a temporary work file, and write the requested stocks to the file. After the last stock has been entered, read the file (without closing it), and prepare the report.

CHAPTER 13

Bitwise Operators

Learning Objectives

When you complete this chapter, you will be able to:

13.1 Explain how C programming uses operators to manipulate data at the bit level

13.2 Implement logical bitwise operators in programs

13.3 Use shift bitwise operators in programs

13.4 Create and use masks to manipulate bits

13.1 Exact Size Integer Types

Although we have already covered the material typically included in a traditional first course in programming, we have not discussed all the basic capabilities of the C language. Because C contains operators that can manipulate data at the bit level, it is well suited to system programming, such as for the Internet, which requires that bits be manipulated to create addresses for subnets. C has two categories of bitwise operators that operate on data at the bit level: logical bitwise operators and shift bitwise operators. Before we discuss these operators, however, we need to introduce exact-size integer types.

The integer types, such as int and long, discussed previously, are machine dependent. In one computer, the size of int may be four bytes; in another computer it may be two bytes. While many bitwise applications work well on machine-dependent integer types, other applications need the integer size to be fixed. For example, to manipulate an Internet address, we need to define an unsigned integer of size 32 bits (4 bytes). Beginning with C99, C allows us to define integer types of sizes 8, 16, 32, and 64 bits. They are defined in the stdint.h header file. **Table 13-1** documents these types. As you will see, most of the time we use unsigned integers.

Table 13-1 Fixed-size integer types

	TYPE	DESCRIPTION
Signed	`int8_t`	8-bit signed integer
	`int16_t`	16-bit signed integer
	`int32_t`	32-bit signed integer
	`int64_t`	64-bit signed integer
Unsigned	`uint8_t`	8-bit unsigned integer
	`uint16_t`	16-bit unsigned integer
	`uint32_t`	32-bit unsigned integer
	`uint64_t`	64-bit unsigned integer

13.2 Logical Bitwise Operators

The logical operators look at data as individual bits to be manipulated. Four operators are provided to manipulate bits: bitwise *and* (&), bitwise inclusive *or* (|), bitwise exclusive *or* (^), and *one's complement* (~). The first three are binary operators; the one's complement is a unary operator.

Bitwise *and* Operator

The bitwise *and* (&—precedence 8) is a binary operator that requires two integral operands (character or integer). It does a bit-by-bit comparison between the two operands. The result of the comparison is 1 only when both bits are 1; otherwise, it is 0. **Table 13-2** shows the result of bit-by-bit comparison.

Table 13-2 *And* truth table

FIRST OPERAND BIT	SECOND OPERAND BIT	RESULT
0	0	0
0	1	0
1	0	0
1	1	1

Program 13-1 demonstrates the bitwise *and* operator.

Program 13-1 | Simple bitwise *and* demonstration

```
1   /* Demonstrate bitwise AND operator
2       Written by:
3       Date:
4   */
5   #include <stdio.h>
6   #include <stdlib.h>
7
```

(continue)

Program 13-1   Simple bitwise *and* demonstration *(continued)*

```
8   #include <stdint.h>
9   int main (void)
10  {
11  // Local Declarations
12      uint16_t num1 = 0x0257;
13      uint16_t num2 = 0xA463;
14      uint16_t res;
15
16  // Statements
17      res = num1 & num2;
18
19      printf ("Input and results in hexadecimal:\n");
20      printf ("num1: %#06X\n", num1);
21      printf ("num2: %#06X\n", num2);
22      printf ("result: %#06X\n", res);
23
24      return 0;
25  } // main
```

Output
```
Input and results in hexadecimal:
num1: 0X0257
num2: 0XA463
result: 0X0043
```

The result of an *and* operation is logically the intersection of the two values. We can verify the result by manually calculating it using binary values.

Bitwise Inclusive *or* Operator

The bitwise inclusive *or* (| —precedence 6) is a binary operator that requires two integral operands (character or integer). It does a bit-by-bit comparison between the two operands. The result of the comparison is 0 if both operands are 0; otherwise, it is 1. **Table 13-3** shows the result of bit-by-bit comparison.

Table 13-3   Inclusive *or* truth table

FIRST BIT	SECOND BIT	RESULT
0	0	0
0	1	1
1	0	1
1	1	1

Program 13-2 demonstrates the basic operation of the inclusive *or*.

> **Program 13-2** | Simple inclusive *or* demonstration

```
1   /* Demonstrate the inclusive OR operator
2      Written by:
3      Date:
4   */
5   #include <stdio.h>
6   #include <stdlib.h>
7   #include <stdint.h>
8
9   int main (void)
10  {
11  // Local Declarations
12     uint16_t num1 = 0x0257;
13     uint16_t num2 = 0xA463;
14     uint16_t res;
15
16  // Statements
17     res = num1 | num2;
18     printf ("Input and results in hexadecimal:\n");
19     printf ("num1: %#06X\n", num1);
20     printf ("num2: %#06X\n", num2);
21     printf ("res: %#06X\n", res);
22
23     return 0;
24  } // main
```

```
Output
Input and results in hexadecimal:
num1: 0X0257
num2: 0XA463
res: 0XA677
```

Bitwise Exclusive *or* Operator

The bitwise exclusive *or* (^—precedence 7) is a binary operator that requires two integral operands. It does a bit-by-bit comparison between the two operands. The result of the comparison is 1 only if one of the operands is 1 and the other is 0; it is 0 if both operands' bits are 0 or 1—that is, if they are both the same. **Table 13-4** shows the result of bit-by-bit comparison.

Table 13-4 Exclusive *or* truth table

FIRST BIT	SECOND BIT	RESULT
0	0	0
0	1	1
1	0	1
1	1	0

Program 13-3 demonstrates the basic operation of the bitwise exclusive *or*.

Program 13-3 | Simple exclusive *or* demonstration

```
1   /* This program demonstrates the use of the exclusive or
2      Written by:
3      Date:
4   */
5   #include <stdio.h>
6   #include <stdlib.h>
7   #include <stdint.h>
8
9   int main (void)
10  {
11  // Local Declarations
12     uint16_t num1 = 0x0257;
13     uint16_t num2 = 0xA463;
14     uint16_t res;
15
16  // Statements
17     res = num1 ^ num2;
18
19  // Print results in hexadecimal
20     printf ("Input and results in hexadecimal:\n");
21     printf ("num1: %#06X\n", num1);
22     printf ("num2: %#06X\n", num2);
23     printf ("res: %#06X\n", res);
24
25     return 0;
26  } // main
```

(continue)

Program 13-3 Simple exclusive *or* demonstration *(continued)*

```
Output
Input and results in hexadecimal:
num1: 0X0257
num2: 0XA463
res: 0XA634
```

One's Complement Operator

The one's complement (~—precedence 15) is a unary operator applied to an integral value (character or integer). It complements the bits in the operand; that is, it reverses the bit value. The result is 1 when the original bit is 0; it is 0 when the original bit is 1. **Table 13-5** shows the result of the one's complement.

Table 13-5 One's complement truth table

ORIGINAL BIT	RESULT
0	1
1	0

Program 13-4 demonstrates the basic operation of the one's complement.

Program 13-4 | One's complement

```c
 1   /* Demonstrate use of one's complement
 2      Written by:
 3      Date:
 4   */
 5   #include <stdio.h>
 6   #include <stdlib.h>
 7   #include <stdint.h>
 8
 9   int main (void)
10   {
11   // Local Declarations
12      uint16_t num = 0x0257;
13      uint16_t res;
14
15   // Statements
16      res = ~num;
17
```

(continue)

Program 13-4   One's complement *(continued)*

```
18  // Print results in hexadecimal
19     printf ("Input and results in hexadecimal:\n");
20     printf ("num: %#06X\n", num);
21     printf ("res: %#06X\n", res);
22
23     return 0;
24  } // main
```

Output

```
Input and results in hexadecimal:
num: 0X0257
res: 0XFDA8
```

Checksum

One bitwise manipulation application is the calculation of a checksum. A checksum is a mathematical calculation used for error detection. For example, credit card processing systems use a checksum to verify that the card number is valid. Another example involves the detection of a bad transmission through a communication channel. When the data are sent, a checksum is calculated and attached to the transmission. When the data are received, the checksum that includes the sender's checksum is recalculated. If the newly calculated checksum is not zero, an error has occurred.

The traditional Internet checksum uses a 16-bit calculation. To calculate the checksum, the following steps are used.

1. Set the checksum to 0.

2. Add 16-bit sections of data to the checksum using one's complement arithmetic. (See Appendix A.)

3. Complement the result.

We complement the result at the end because a number (T) and its complement (–T), when added, always give –0 in one's complement.

Figure 13-1 shows the calculation of a checksum for a small string, "ABCDEFGHI." Note that because the number of characters is nine, we include the null character (\0) at the end of the string to make five 16-bit values. The string is logically divided into groups of 16 bits (two characters), which are then added together using one's complement.

Figure 13-1   Checksum calculation

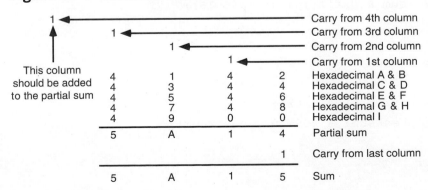

Program 13-5 demonstrates the calculation of a checksum for the sender site. To properly weigh the first character, we multiply it by 256. To get the one's complement, we add the carry bits after the sum is calculated as shown in Figure 13-1. This is done using a loop. The loop extracts the higher (left) 16 bits and adds them to the lower (right) 16 bits.

Program 13-5 | Demonstrate checksum

```
1   /* Demonstrate the calculation of a checksum using one's
2      complement arithmetic.
3      Written by:
4      Date:
5   */
6   #include <stdio.h>
7   #include <string.h>
8   #include <stdint.h>
9
10  int main (void)
11  {
12  // Local Declarations
13     uint32_t sum = 0x00000000;
14     uint16_t checksum = 0x0000;
15     char* str = "ABCDEFGHI";
16     int len;
17
18  // Statements
19     len = strlen (str);
20     if (len % 2 == 1)
21     // Make the number of characters even
22        len++;
23
24     for (int i = 0; i < len; i += 2)
25        sum = (sum + str[i] * 256 + str[i + 1]);
26
27     // Add carries into lower 16 bits
28     while (sum >> 16)
29        sum = (sum & 0xffff) + (sum >> 16);
30
31     // Complement
32     checksum = -sum;
33
34     printf ("str: % s\n", str);
35     printf ("checksum: % #06X\n", checksum);
36
37     return 0;
38  } // main
```

(continue)

Program 13-5   Demonstrate checksum *(continued)*

Output
```
str: ABCDEFGHI
checksum: 0XA5EA
```

13.3 Shift Operators

The shift operators move bits to the right or the left. When applied to unsigned numbers, these operators are implementation independent. When used with signed numbers, however, the implementation is left to the discretion of the software engineer who designs the compiler. It is often predicated on the hardware for which the compiler is being written. Therefore, shift operators must be used with caution with signed numbers.

> **Note** | Because the C standard leaves the implementation up to the compiler writer (there is no standard), code that shifts signed negative numbers may not be portable to other platforms.

Bitwise Shift-Right Operator

The bitwise shift right (>>—precedence 11) is a binary operator that requires two integral operands (character or integer). The first operand is the value to be shifted. The second operand specifies the number of bits to be shifted.

Shifting binary numbers is just like shifting decimal numbers. When bits are shifted right, the bits at the rightmost end are deleted. What is shifted in on the left, however, depends on the type and the implementation. If the type is unsigned, then the standard calls for zero bits to be shifted in. If the type is signed, however, the implementation may either shift in zeros or copies of the leftmost bit. Because the implementation is the system programmer's responsibility, any function that shifts signed negative values may not be portable. The shift-right operation is diagrammed in **Figure 13-2**.

Figure 13-2   Shift-right operation

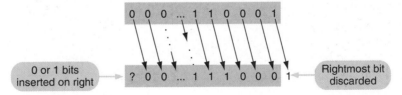

Program 13-6 demonstrates the shift-right operation. Because C does not provide any formatted conversion for binary numbers, we wrote a simple function to print a 16-bit fixed integer variable as a binary number.

> **Program 13-6** | Simple shift-right demonstration

```
1   /* Demonstrate the bitwise shift-right operator.
2      Written by:
3      Date:
4   */
5   #include <stdio.h>
6   #include <stdlib.h>
7
```

(continue)

Program 13-6 Simple shift-right demonstration *(continued)*

```c
 8  #include <stdint.h>
 9  // Function Declaration
10  void bin16 (uint16_t num, char* bitStr);
11
12  int main (void)
13  {
14  // Local Definitions
15      uint16_t num = 0x0040;
16      uint16_t res;
17      char bitStr[17] = {0};
18
19  // Statements
20      bin16(num, bitStr);
21      printf("Original value: %s (%#06x)\n",
22             bitStr, num);
23
24      res = num >> 1;
25      bin16 (res, bitStr);
26      printf("Shifted 1 right: %s (%#06x)\n",
27             bitStr, res);
28
29      res = num >> 2;
30      bin16(res, bitStr);
31      printf("Shifted 2 right: %s (%#06x)\n",
32             bitStr, res);
33
34      res = num >> 4;
35      bin16(res, bitStr);
36      printf("Shifted 4 right: %s (%#06x)\n",
37             bitStr, res);
38
39      return 0;
40  } // main
41
42  /* =====================bin16 =====================
43     Convert fixed 16-bit integer to binary digit string.
44     Pre num contains integral value to be converted
45     bitStr is pointer to variable for bit string
46     Post bit string stored in str
47  */
48  void bin16 (uint16_t num, char* bitStr)
49  {
50  // Statements
```

(continue)

Program 13-6   Simple shift-right demonstration *(continued)*

```
51      for (int i = 0; i < 16; i++)
52          bitStr[i] = (char) ((num >> 15 - i) &
53                      0X0001) + 48;
54      return;
55 } // bin16
```

Output
```
Original value: 0000000001000000 (0x0040)

Shifted 1 right: 0000000000100000 (0x0020)

Shifted 2 right: 0000000000010000 (0x0010)

Shifted 4 right: 0000000000000100 (0x0004)
```

Dividing by 2

Let's start with something we know, decimal numbers. When we shift a decimal number one position to the right and insert a 0 on the left, we are in effect dividing by 10. If we shift it two places, we are dividing by 100. If we shift it three places, we are dividing by 1000. But actually, we are dividing by a power of 10—in our examples, 10^1, 10^2, and 10^3.

Applying the same principle to binary numbers, the right-shift operator divides by a power of 2. If we shift a binary number two places to the right, we are dividing by 4 (2^2). If we shift it three places, we are dividing by 8 (2^3). **Table 13-6** shows the division pattern used with bit shifting.

Table 13-6   Divide by shift

$2^{\text{SHIFT VALUE}}$	DIVIDES BY	SHIFT OPERATOR
1	2	>> 1
2	4	>> 2
3	8	>> 3
4	16	>> 4
n	2^n	>> n

Bitwise Shift-Left Operator

The bitwise shift left (<<—precedence 11) is a binary operator that requires two integral operands (character or integer). The first operand is the value to be shifted. The second operand specifies the number of bits to be shifted.

Shifting binary numbers is just like shifting decimal numbers. If we have an eight-digit decimal number, and we shift it three places to the left, then the leftmost three digits are lost and three zero digits are added on the right. The binary shift operation is shown in **Figure 13-3**.

Figure 13-3   Shift-left operation

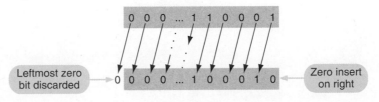

Program 13-7 demonstrates the basic operation of the shift-left operator. Again, it uses the bin16 function, which we have now included as a library.

Program 13-7 | Simple shift-left demonstration

```
 1  /* Demonstrate the bitwise shift-left operator.
 2     Written by:
 3     Date:
 4  */
 5  #include <stdio.h>
 6  #include <stdlib.h>
 7
 8  #include <stdint.h>
 9  #include "bin16.c"
10
11  int main (void)
12  {
13  // Local Definitions
14     uint16_t num = 0x0031;
15     uint16_t res;
16     char bitStr[17] = {"0"};
17
18  // Statements
19     bin16(num, bitStr);
20     printf("Original value: %s (%#06x)\n", bitStr, num);
21
22     res = num << 1;
23     bin16(res, bitStr);
24     printf("Shifted 1 left: %s (%#06x)\n", bitStr, res);
25
26     res = num << 2;
27     bin16(res, bitStr);
28     printf("Shifted 2 left: %s (%#06x)\n", bitStr, res);
29
30     res = num << 4;
31     bin16(res, bitStr);
32     printf("Shifted 4 left: %s (%#06x)\n", bitStr , res);
33
34     return 0;
35  } // main
```

(continue)

Program 13-7 Simple shift-left demonstration *(continued)*

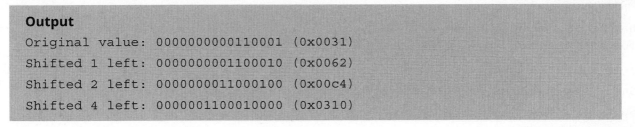

```
Output
Original value: 0000000000110001 (0x0031)
Shifted 1 left: 0000000001100010 (0x0062)
Shifted 2 left: 0000000011000100 (0x00c4)
Shifted 4 left: 0000001100010000 (0x0310)
```

Multiplying by 2

Shift left is the opposite of shift right; multiply is the opposite of divide. It is reasonable to assume, therefore, that shifting left has the effect of multiplying by a power of 2. If you examine the results of Program 13-7 closely, you will note that is exactly what happens. When we shift a binary number two places to the left, we are multiplying by 4 (2^2). If we shift it three places, we are multiplying by 8 (2^3). **Table 13-7** shows the multiplication pattern used with bit shifting.

Table 13-7 Multiply by shift

$2^{SHIFT\ VALUE}$	MULTIPLIES BY	SHIFT OPERATOR
1	2	<< 1
2	4	<< 2
3	8	<< 3
4	16	<< 4
n	2^n	<< n

Rotation

In computer science, we often need to rotate bits. For example, in security, the creation of a hash digest of a message rotates and then scrambles bits to create a hash value of data.

Rotation requires that bits be taken off one end of a value and moved to the other end. When we rotate bits left, we shift them off the left end of the value and insert them on the right. When we rotate right, we shift off the right end and insert them on the left. **Figure 13-4** demonstrates the rotation of a 16-bit integer 4 bits to the right and then 4 bits to the left.

Figure 13-4 Right and left rotation

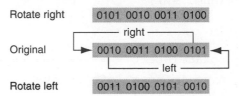

Note that the original number in hexadecimal is 0x2345. The rotated right number is 0x5234; the rotated left number is 0x3452.

Although there are no explicit operands for rotating left or right, the rotations can be coded using two shifts and an *or*. For example, to rotate the original 16-bit number in Figure 13-4, we use the following steps.

```
Original: 0 x2 3 4 5
Shift right 4 bits: 0x0234
Shift left (16 - 4) bits: 0x5000
or'd results:
0x5234
```

The rotate left operation is similar. **Program 13-8** is a test driver for the rotate left and right functions.

Program 13-8 | Rotate left and right test driver

```
 1   /* Test driver for rotate left and right.
 2       Written by:
 3       Date:
 4   */
 5   #include <stdio.h>
 6   #include <stdint.h>
 7
 8   // Function Declarations
 9   uint16_t rotate16Left(uint16_t num, int n);
10   uint16_t rotate16Right(uint16_t num, int n);
11
12   int main (void)
13   {
14   // Local Declaration
15       uint16_t num = 0X2345;
16
17   // Statements
18       printf("Original: %#06X\n", num);
19       printf("Rotated Left: %#06X\n",
20               rotate16Left(num, 4));
21       printf("Rotated Right: %#06X\n",
22               rotate16Right(num, 4));
23   } // main
24
25   /* ==================== rotate16Left ===============
26       Rotate 16 bit fixed size integer left n bits.
27       Pre num is a fixed size 16-bit integer
28       Post num rotated n bits left
29   */
```

(continue)

Program 13-8 Rotate left and right test driver *(continued)*

```
30 uint16_t rotate16Left (uint16_t num, int n)
31 {
32    return ((num << n) | (num >> 16 - n));
33 } // rotate16Left
34
35 /*================= rotate16Right ============
36    Rotate 16 bit fixed size integer right n bits.
37    Pre num is a fixed size 16-bit integer
38    Post num rotated n bits right
39 */
40 uint16_t rotate16Right (uint16_t num, int n)
41 {
42    return ((num >> n) | (num << 16 - n));
43 } // rotate16Right
```

Output
```
Original: 0X2345
Rotated Left: 0X3452
Rotated Right: 0X5234
```

13.4 Masks

In many programs, bits are used as binary flags: 0 is off, and 1 is on. To set and test the flags, we use a bit mask. A mask is a variable or constant, usually stored in a byte or short integer, that contains a bit configuration used to control the setting or testing of bits in a bitwise operation. The bits are numbered from the least significant bit (rightmost), starting at 0, as shown in **Figure 13-5**.

Figure 13-5 Bit mask in a 16-bit integer

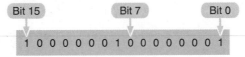

Creating Masks

Masks can be created statically or dynamically. Static masks are generally literals. For example, to create the mask in Figure 13-5, we could code the constant 0x8101. Dynamic masks are created using the bit manipulation operators: shift, *and*, *or*. In this section, we examine the basic techniques for creating dynamic masks, that is, masks that may change as the program executes.

One-Bit Masks

Given a byte flag in which bit 5 is an error flag, we need to create a mask to test it. To test bit 5, the mask must have bit 5 set to 1 and the rest of the bits to 0. This is easily done, as shown below.

```
uint8_t mask;
mask = 0x01 << 5;
00000001 << 5 00100000
```

We start with a constant binary 1. This places a one bit in the rightmost position. We then shift the one bit to the left five positions. The result is shown in the previous example.

An easier way to control the location of the bit flags is to name them. This is easily done with a defined constant, as shown in the next example.

```
#define FLAG0 0
#define FLAG1 1
...
#define FLAG5 5
mask = 0x01 << FLAG5;
```

By using named flag positions, we free ourselves from remembering their locations and at the same time make the code more readable. Of course, in an application, we would use meaningful names, such as OVERFLOW_FLAG, not FLAG1.

Two-Bit Masks

Creating a mask with two flags requires that we set 2 bits on. The easiest way to do this is to set two individual flags and then *or* them.

```
uint8_t mask;
mask = (0x01 << FLAG1) | (0x01 << FLAG5);
```

The result of the above code would set the mask as shown below.

```
00100010
```

Setting Bit Range Masks

To set a range of bits requires a loop. The following example sets bits 7 through 3.

```
uint8_t mask = 0x00;
for (i = 3; i <= 6; i++) // 01111000
    mask = mask | 0x01 << i;
```

Complement Masks

To create a mask that turns off a specific bit—that is, that complements it—we must set the bit to 0 while setting the rest of the bits in the mask to 1. This requires two statements. In the first statement, we set only the desired bit on. In the second step, we complement the mask, changing all zero bits to 1 and all one bits to 0. The code is shown below.

```
mask = 0x01 << FLAG1;
mask = ~mask;
```

Using Masks

Now that we've seen how to create masks with various bit flags set, let's look at some examples that use them.

Turning Bits Off

One of the applications of the bitwise *and* operator is turning bits off—that is, forcing selected bits to zero. For example, an Internet address uses the format x.y.z.t as we have seen before. A mask in the form /n, often called prefix, is used to find the network or subnet address to which a computer is attached. The prefix /n defines the number of leftmost contiguous 1s out of 32 bits. A prefix of /20 means that the leftmost 20 bits are 1s and the rightmost bits are 0s. This is demonstrated in the next example.

```
Computer address: 01111011010011100001100100001101
Mask:             11111111111111111111000000000000
Network address:  01111011010011100001000000000000
```

Program 13-9 determines a network address given a computer host address. To be flexible, it asks the user to enter the size of the prefix.

Program 13-9 | Determine network address

```c
1   /* Given a host address and the size of the prefix,
2      determine its network address.
3      Written by:
4      Date:
5   */
6   #include <stdio.h>
7   #include <stdlib.h>
8   #include <stdint.h>
9
10  int main (void)
11  {
12  // Local Declarations
13     unsigned int comAddr[4];
14     unsigned int mask[4];
15     unsigned int netAddr[4];
16     uint32_t comAd = 0;
17     uint32_t mask32 = 0;
18     uint32_t netAd = 0;
19     int prefix;
20
21  // Statements
22     printf ("Enter host address <x.y.z.t>: ");
23     scanf ("%d%*c%d%*c%d%*c%d",
24            &comAddr[3], &comAddr[2], &comAddr[1], &comAddr[0]);
25
26     printf ("Enter prefix: ");
27     scanf ("%d", &prefix);
28
29     // Convert address to a 32-bit computer address
30     for (int i = 3; i >= 0; i--)
31        comAd = comAd * 256 + comAddr[i];
32
33     // Create a 32-bit mask
34     for (int i = 32 - prefix; i < 32; i++)
35        mask32 = mask32 | (1 << i);
36
37     // AND to get a 32-bit Network Address
38     netAd = comAd & mask32;
39
```

(continue)

Program 13-9   Determine network address (*continued*)

```
40      // Change mask into the form x.y.z.t
41      for (int i = 0; i < 4; i++)
42      {
43         mask[i] = mask32 % 256;
44         mask32 = mask32 / 256;
45      } // for
46
47      // Change IP address into the form x.y.z.t
48      for (int i = 0; i < 4; i++)
49      {
50         netAddr[i] = netAd % 256;
51         netAd = netAd / 256;
52      } // for
53
54      // Print Addresses
55      printf ("\nAddresses:\n");
56      printf ("Computer Address: ");
57      printf ("%d.%d.%d.%d\n",
58              comAddr[3], comAddr[2], comAddr[1], comAddr[0]);
59
60      printf ("Mask: ");
61      printf ("%d.%d.%d.%d\n",
62              mask[3], mask[2], mask[1], mask[0]);
63
64      printf ("Net Address: ");
65      printf ("%d.%d.%d.%d\n",
66              netAddr[3], netAddr[2], netAddr[1], netAddr[0]);
67      return 0;
68 } // main
```

Output
```
Enter host address <x.y.z.t>: 123.45.78.12
Enter prefix: 18

Addresses:
Computer Address: 123.45.78.12
Mask: 255.255.192.0
Net Address: 123.45.64.0
```

Several parts of this program need to be studied carefully. First, note that the variable for the network address is an array of four integers. In statement 23, we read the address in dotted decimal format into the array.

The `for` loop in statement 30 converts the components of the address into a 32-bit address. Each component of the address is considered one byte in the final address. Because each byte has a value of 256 (2^8), we compute the address as follows:

$$byte[0] + byte[1] \times 256^1 + byte[2] \times 256^2 + byte[3] \times 256^3$$

After we have the dotted-decimal address converted to a 32-bit address, we must create a prefix mask by setting a 32-bit mask to /n leading 1 bits. This is done in the `for` loop in statement 34.

Finally, the network address and mask are converted back to the dotted-decimal format. Each byte is determined by taking modulo 256 of part of the network address. To get the next byte in the address, we then divide by 256. This logic is seen in the `for` loops in statement 41 and 48.

Turning Bits On

One common application of bit inclusive *or* is turning bits on—that is, forcing selected bits in a field to one. To force to one, all that we need to do is to construct a mask with the desired one bit set on. This guarantees that the result will have a one bit in that location.

A mask can be used to find the last address in a block of network addresses. The last address is used for limited broadcasts. If a computer wants to send a message to all computers inside its network, it uses this address.

To find the last address, we *or* the complement of a prefixed mask with any address in the block. Conversely, to find the first address in the network block, we *and* the mask with any address. **Program 13-10** determines the last address in a network.

Program 13-10 | Determine last address in a network

```
1   /* Determine the last address in a broadcast network.
2       Written by:
3       Date:
4   */
5   #include <stdio.h>
6   #include <math.h>
7   #include <stdint.h>
8
9   int main (void)
10  {
11  // Local Declarations
12      unsigned int comAddr[4];
13      unsigned int mask[4];
14      unsigned int broadAddr[4];
15
16      uint32_t comAd = 0;
17      uint32_t mask32 = 0;
18      uint32_t broadAd = 0;
```

(continue)

Program 13-10 Determine last address in a network *(continued)*

```
19      int prefix;
20
21  // Statements
22      printf("Enter host address <x.y.z.t>: ");
23      scanf("%d%*c%d%*c%d%*c%d",
24              &comAddr[3], &comAddr[2],
25              &comAddr[1], &comAddr[0]);
26      printf("Enter prefix: ");
27      scanf("%d", &prefix);
28
29      // Convert address to 32-bit computer address
30      for(int i = 3; i >= 0; i--)
31         comAd = comAd * 256 + comAddr[i];
32
33      // Create 32-bit prefix mask
34      for(int i = 32-prefix; i < 32; i++)
35         mask32 = mask32 | (0x0001 << i);
36
37      // And to get a 32-bit Network Address
38      broadAd = comAd | (~mask32);
39
40      // Change the mask into the form x.y.z.t
41      for (int i= 0; i < 4; i++)
42      {
43         mask[i]= mask32 % 256;
44         mask32 = mask32 / 256;
45      } // for
46
47      // Change the IP address to the form x.y.z.t
48      for (int i= 0; i < 4; i++)
49      {
50         broadAddr[i] = broadAd % 256;
51         broadAd = broadAd / 256;
52      } // for
53
54      printf("\nPrinting Addresses\n");
55      printf("Computer Address: ");
56      printf("%d.%d.%d.%d\n",
57              comAddr[3], comAddr[2],
58              comAddr[1], comAddr[0]);
59      printf("Mask:");
60      printf("%d.%d.%d.%d\n",
61              mask[3], mask[2], mask[1], mask[0]);
62
```

(continue)

Program 13-10 Determine last address in a network *(continued)*

```
63      printf("Broadcast Address: ");
64      printf("%d.%d.%d.%d\n",
65              broadAddr[3], broadAddr[2],
66              broadAddr[1], broadAddr[0]);
67      return 0;
68 } // main
```

Output
```
Enter host address <x.y.z.t>: 123.45.78.12
Enter prefix: 18

Printing Addresses
Computer Address: 123.45.78.12
Mask: 255.255.192.0
Broadcast Address: 123.45.127.255
```

Let's compare Program 13-9 and Program 13-10. In Program 13-9, we calculate the first address in a block. In Program 13-10, we calculate the last address in a block. If we subtract these addresses (in base 256) and add 1, we get the total addresses in the block. Looking at the program results, we see that the first address is 123.45.64.0 (Program 13-9) and the last address is 123.45.127.255 (Program 13-10). The difference is

```
(127-64) * 256 + (255 - 0) + 1 = 16,384
```

We have 16,384 addresses in this block. We could have found this result using the prefix (18).

$$2^{32-prefix} = 2^{32-18} = 2^{14} = 16,384$$

Flipping Bits

One of the applications of bitwise exclusive *or* is flipping bits—that is, forcing 0s to 1s and 1s to 0s, called force to change. The resulting bit is 1 when 1 bit is a 0 and the other is a 1; if both bits are 0 or both are 1, the result is 0. To force a bit to change: therefore, the forcing bit in the mask is set to 1; bits that are to be unchanged are set to 0.

For example, assume that we want to change the 5 leftmost bits of a number stored as an 8-bit integer. We create the mask with 5 one bits and 3 zero bits, as shown below. (Y indicates a changed bit.)

```
operator ^ number   XXXXXXXX
   mask   11111000
   result   YYYYYXXX
```

Dividing Polynomials

As a more advanced example of flipping bits, let's examine how we can use fixed-size integers to represent polynomials. Polynomials with coefficients of 1 or 0 are used in computer science for error detection, encoding, and other applications.

A fixed-size integer can represent a polynomial if we think of 0 and 1 as coefficients of the polynomial. For example, the bit stream 01001001 can represent a polynomial of degree 6 or $x^6 + x^3 + 1$. In this polynomial, the coefficients of x^7, x^5, x^4, x^2, and x^1 are 0 and the coefficients of x^6, x^3, and x^0 are 1. This relationship is shown in **Figure 13-6**.

Figure 13-6 Polynomial coefficients

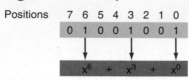

In general, a bit stream of length n can represent a polynomial of length $n - 1$. So a data type of `uint16_t` can represent a polynomial of up to degree 15.

A common polynomial operation is division. The division of one polynomial by another is shown in **Figure 13-7**.

Figure 13-7 Polynomial division

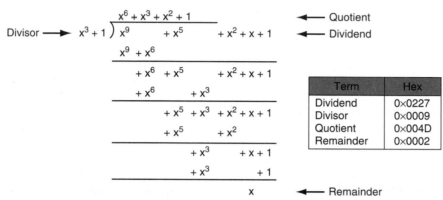

Although the division of polynomials is similar to the division of numbers we learned in elementary school, there are two differences:

1. Because we use only coefficients 0 and 1, if we have two terms of the same exponent, the result is zero ($1 + 1 = 0$). In other words, polynomial division uses modulo 2 arithmetic on the coefficients.

2. Subtraction and addition of the coefficients are actually the same (exclusive *or*) because we are interested in only coefficients 0 and 1.

Note that if we multiply the quotients by the divisor and add it with the remainder, we get the dividend. However, if we get two identical coefficients (such as x^6), we cancel them because $1 + 1 = 0$.

Program 13-11 demonstrates polynomial division.

> ## Program 13-11 | Polynomial division

```
1   /* Demonstrate polynomial division.
2      Written by:
3      Date:
4   */
5   #include <stdio.h>
6   #include <stdint.h>
7
8   // Function Declaration
9   int degree (uint16_t);
```

(continue)

Program 13-11 Polynomial division *(continued)*

```
10
11 int main (void)
12 {
13 // Local Declaration
14    uint16_t dvdn = 0X0227;
15    uint16_t dvsr = 0X0009;
16    uint16_t qtnt = 0X0000;
17    uint16_t rmdr;
18    uint16_t q;
19    int dgre;
20
21 // Statements
22    printf ("Dividend: %#06X\n", dvdn);
23    printf ("Divisor: %#06X\n", dvsr);
24
25    rmdr = dvdn;
26    while ((dgre = degree (dvdn) - degree (dvsr)) >= 0)
27    {
28       q = 1 << dgre;
29       rmdr = dvdn ^ (dvsr << degree (q));
30       qtnt = qtnt | q;
31       dvdn = rmdr;
32    } // while
33
34    printf ("Quotient : %#06X\n", qtnt);
35    printf ("Remainder: %#06X\n", rmdr);
36    return 0;
37 } // main
38
39 /* Determine degree of polynomial represented by
40    a fixed-length 16-bit variable.
41    Pre poly represents a polynomial
42    Post degree returned
43 */
44 int degree (uint16_t poly)
45 {
46 // Local Declarations
47    uint16_t mask = 0X0001;
48    uint16_t temp;
49    int pos= -1;
50
51 // Statements
```

(continue)

Program 13-11   Polynomial division *(continued)*

```
52     for (int i = 0; i <16; i++)
53     {
54         temp = poly >> i;
55         if ((temp & mask) == 1)
56             pos = i;
57     } // for
58     return pos;
59 } // degree
```

Output
```
Dividend: 0X0227
Divisor: 0X0009
Quotient : 0X004D
Remainder: 0X0002
```

We use a function to determine the degree of the polynomial. In `main` we use a `while` loop to simulate the division. The variable poly is the term in the quotient that is obtained in each step. Note that the multiplication of a term such as x^n by the division is done by shifting the divisor n bits.

Software Engineering

Previously, we looked at what makes a good function. In this section, we look at how you design good programs.

Payroll Case Study

To provide a discussion focus, we will use a payroll program. Although our example is rather simple, it contains all the elements involved in designing a program. The description of the payroll program is shown in **Figure 13-8**.

Figure 13-8   Requirements for payroll case study

Payroll Case Study
1. Requirements: 　　Given employees and their hours worked, compute net pay and record all payroll data for subsequent processing, such as W2 statements. Prepare paychecks and a payroll ledger. 　　Maintain data on a sequential payroll file.

continued

Figure 13-8   Requirements for payroll case study   (*continued*)

2. Provide for the following nonstatutory deductions:

   a. Health plan
   b. United Way
   c. Union dues

3. The payroll data are:

   a. Employee number
   b. Pay rate
   c. Union member flag
   d. United Way contribution
   e. Exemptions

4. Maintain the following year-to-date totals:

   a. Earnings
   b. FICA taxes
   c. SDI taxes
   d. Federal withholding
   e. State withholding
   f. Health plan fees
   g. United Way donations
   h. Union dues

5. Algorithms:

   a. Gross pay = (Reg hrs * Rate) + (OT hours * Rate * 1.5)
   b. FICA taxes = (Gross pay*FICA rate) if less than Max FICA
   c. SDI taxes = (Gross pay * SDI Rate) if less than Max SDI
   d. Taxable earnings = (Gross pay – (Exemptions * Exemption rate))
   e. Federal taxes = (Taxable earnings * Federal tax rate)
   f. State taxes = (Taxable earnings * State tax rate)
   g. Net pay = (Gross pay – (FICA taxes + SDI taxes + Federal taxes + State taxes + Health fee + United Way donation + Union dues))

Program Design Steps

As you know by now, a program is developed in seven steps:

1. Determine requirements.

2. Determine data structures.

3. Build structure charts.

4. Create test cases.

5. Write and unit test the programs.

6. Test system.

7. Implement system in production.

Our interest here is only in the third step: Build the structure charts. A few general comments are in order, however. The second and third steps are often reversed or done concurrently. Which one is done first is not of major consequence, as long as they are done before the fourth step.

Many programmers think that test cases should be built after the program is written. Good programmers know better. By creating test cases based on the requirements (Step 1) and your design (Steps 2 and 3), you will understand the problem better. You will even find occasions when you change your design based on what you learned creating test cases.

This does not mean that you will be finished creating test cases at Step 4; you just start there. You will develop more test cases while you are writing the program, and you will create still more as you conduct unit testing.

Structure Chart Design

A good program starts with a good design, as reflected in the structure chart. By now, you should have progressed to the point at which you are designing your programs before you start coding; that is, you are creating your structure chart first.

One tool for designing a structure chart is known as transform analysis, which is a design technique that identifies the processes in a program as input, process, and output and then organizes them around one or more processes that convert inputs to outputs. These conversion processes are known as the central transforms. Having determined the first-cut design, you repeat the process, decomposing the identified modules into subtasks using transform analysis.

This is a good design technique whenever a program reads, processes, and writes data, which covers the majority of programs. Although it is usually used in conjunction with another tool known as a data flow diagram, you can use it independently.

Recognize, however, that transform analysis is an approach to the design of a program. It is not a cookbook that leads to the same results every time. Different programmers using the same steps will arrive at different designs.

Programmers use six steps in designing a structure chart:

1. Determine program modules.
2. Classify modules.
3. Construct preliminary structure chart.
4. Decompose modules.
5. Complete structure chart.
6. Validate design.

Determine Modules

The first step in program design is to identify the processes that the program will use. This is usually done by reviewing the program specification and identifying the tasks it needs to accomplish. A review of our payroll case identifies the following tasks. (The references are to the case study description in Figure 13-8.)

1. Read hours worked (1).
2. Compute pay (1).
3. Maintain payroll master file (1).
4. Prepare paychecks (1).
5. Prepare payroll ledger (1).
6. Calculate nonstatutory deductions (2).
7. Calculate year-to-date totals (4).
8. Calculate gross pay (5).
9. Calculate taxes (5).

Remember the rule that each module should do only one thing. You might be tempted to start with a module to prepare output instead of prepare paychecks and prepare payroll ledger. And in fact, you may well end up with an intermediate module that combines the preparation of all reports. But at this point, we want to keep different things separate as much as possible. On the other hand, experience indicates that separate modules for calculating FICA taxes, SDI taxes, federal taxes, and state taxes are not necessary.

Classify Modules

In transform analysis, we look for the central transforms—that is, the module(s) that turns inputs into outputs. To identify these transforms, we classify each identified task, which now represents a module in the structure chart, as afferent, efferent, or transform. A module is an afferent module if its processing is directed toward the central transform. Another way of looking at this concept is to say that the module is a gatherer of data. An efferent module directs data away from the central processing or toward the outputs of the program. (Remember that input comes before output, and *a* comes before *e*; therefore, afferent is input and efferent is output.) A transform module is balanced; that is, it has data flowing both in and out. The concepts of afferent, efferent, and transform are shown in **Figure 13-9**.

Figure 13-9   Afferent, efferent, and transform modules

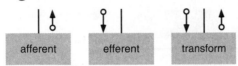

Table 13-8 classifies each of the modules identified above as afferent, efferent, or transform.

Table 13-8   Classification of payroll modules

MODULE	AFFERENT	EFFERENT	TRANSFORM
Read hours worked	✓		
Compute pay			✓
Maintain payroll master file	✓	✓	
Prepare paychecks		✓	
Prepare payroll ledger		✓	
Calculate nonstatutory deductions			✓
Calculate year-to-date totals			✓
Calculate gross pay			✓
Calculate taxes			✓

Note that "maintain payroll master file" is classified as both input and output. This is because it is a master file. We will need to read it to get the employee personnel and history data, and we will need to write the updated data after they have been calculated. Therefore, it is really two modules: one to read the master and one to write the master.

Also note that there are many transform modules. This will result in a large fan out, which is not desirable. The fan out of a module is the number of submodules emanating from it. We will need to reduce the fan out later.

Construct Structure Chart

At this point, you are ready to construct the first-cut structure chart. Transform analysis structure charts are organized with inputs on the left, transforms in the center, and outputs on the right. This organization is shown in **Figure 13-10**.

Figure 13-10 Basic structure chart organization

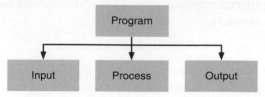

For the first-cut structure chart, place all afferent modules below the input block, all transform modules below the process block, and all efferent modules below the output block. In this process, analyze each module to determine if it needs to be called before or after the other processes at the same level. Those that need to be called first are placed on the left, and those that need to be called last are placed on the right. The resulting structure chart is shown in **Figure 13-11**.

Figure 13-11 First-cut structure chart

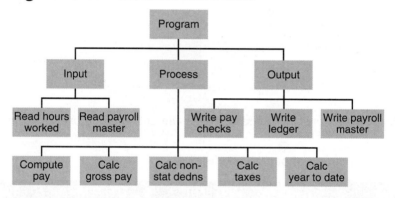

Up to this point, we have been almost algorithmic; that is, we have exercised little judgment. We now need to analyze the preliminary structure chart to see if it makes sense. This is done by asking a simple question, "What do we mean by … ?" For example, "What do we mean by compute pay?" The answer is that we must take hours worked and multiply them by the pay rate, also considering overtime and so forth. Or, to put it another way, we compute gross pay. But this is already a module in the structure chart, so these two modules are the same. We will therefore delete compute pay since it is a less specific description than calculate gross pay.

Decompose Modules

To decompose modules, we look at the cohesion of each module. For example, when we ask what we mean by calculate taxes, the answer is calculate federal taxes and calculate state taxes. Because we are dealing with two different entities (things), the cohesion of this module is communicational; it uses the gross pay and payroll data to calculate the different taxes.

When we find that a module is doing more than one thing, or that it is so complex that it is difficult to understand, then we need to consider breaking the module into submodules. This refinement of the modules, called stepwise refinement, refines the processes in a module until each module is at its most basic, primitive meaning.

Decomposition continues until the lowest levels in our structure chart are all functionally cohesive and easily understood.

Complete Structure Chart

At this point we have the nucleus of the structure chart complete, and all we have to do is add the finishing touches. These steps are almost mechanical.

1. Identify any common processes with a crosshatch in the lower right corner. In our payroll case, there are none.

2. Consider adding intermediate (middle-level) modules if necessary to reduce fan out. This step should not be done arbitrarily, however. If the modules next to each other have a common entity, then they can be combined. If they

don't, they should be left separate. For example, in the payroll case, we have combined calculate nonstatutory deductions and calculate taxes into one module called calculate deductions. We would not combine calculate gross pay with calculate nonstatutory deductions, and we would not combine calculate taxes with calculate year-to-date deductions.

3. Verify that the names are descriptive and meaningful for their processes.

4. Add loops, conditional calls, and exclusive or designators.

5. Add input/output modules, if not already present.

6. Add initialization and end of job modules.

7. Add error routines (if necessary).

8. Add data flows and flags as required.

The completed design for the payroll case study is shown in **Figure 13-12**.

Figure 13-12   Final payroll structure chart

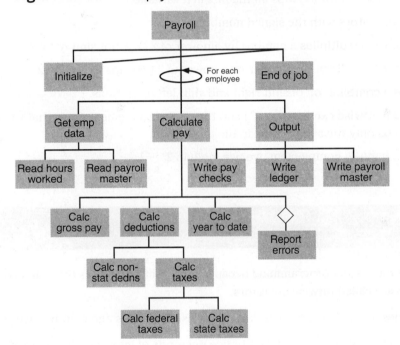

Validate the Design

At this point, you are ready to validate the design with a structured walkthrough. Before you convene with the review committee, however, you should review your design once more by repeating all the design steps, especially the functional decomposition step.

Tips and Common Programming Errors

1. We recommend that bitwise operators be used only with unsigned fixed-size operands.

2. To use fixed-size integers, we need to include the stdint.h file header file.

3. The bitwise *and* operator is only one ampersand (&), not two.

4. The bitwise inclusive *or* operator is only one bar (|), not two.

5. There are two differences between the logical *and* operator (&&) and the bitwise *and* operator (&).
   a. The result of && is a logical value (true or false). The result of & is another number.
   b. The evaluation of an expression that uses && terminates if the first operand is false. Expressions with the & operator are always completely evaluated.

6. There are two differences between the logical *or* operator (||) and the bitwise inclusive *or* operator (|).
   a. The result of the || is a logical value (true or false). The result of | is another number.
   b. The evaluation of an expression that uses the || operator terminates if the first operand is true. Expressions with the | operator are always completely evaluated.

7. There is a difference between the *not* operator (!) and the one's complement operator (~). The result of ! is a logical value (true or false). The result of ~ is another number.

8. The bitwise *and* operator (&) turns off only the corresponding bits in a data item that match 0s in the mask.

9. The bitwise *or* operator (|) turns on only the corresponding bits in a data item that match 1s in the mask.

10. The bitwise exclusive *or* operator (^) flips only the corresponding bits in a data Item that match 1s in the mask.

11. The bitwise complement operator (~) flips all the bits in a variable.

12. Avoid using the shift operators with the signed number

13. The shift-left operator (<<) multiplies a number by a power of 2 (2^n), not simply by 2.

14. The shift-right operator (>>) divides a number by a power of 2 (2^n), not simply by 2.

15. Rotating bits requires a combination of shift right and shift left operations.

16. The difference between bitwise exclusive *or* (^) and the one's complement (~) is that the ~ operator flips all the bits; the ^ operator flips only the specific bits in the mask.

17. To add w-bit numbers in one's complement, we use modulo $2^n - 1$.

Summary

> C is a proper language for system programming because it contains operators that can manipulate data at the bit level. These operators are called bitwise operators.

> There are two categories of bitwise operators: logical bitwise operators and shift bitwise operators.

> The bitwise *and* (&) is a binary operator applied to two operands of integral value. It does a bit-by-bit comparison of the two operands. The result of each comparison is 1 if both bits are 1s. It is 0 otherwise.

> The bitwise *and* operator (&) is used to turn off masked bits in an operand.

> The bitwise inclusive *or* (|) is a binary operator applied to two integral operands. It does a bit-by-bit comparison of its two operands. The result of each comparison is 0 if both bits are 0s. It is 1 otherwise.

> The bitwise inclusive *or* operator (|) is used to turn on mask bits in an operand.

> The bitwise exclusive *or* (^) is a binary operator applied to two integral operands. It does a bit-by-bit comparison of its two operands. The result of each comparison is 1 only if the two bits are different. If they are the same, the result is 0.

> The bitwise exclusive *or* operator (^) is used to flip masked bits in an operand.

> The bitwise complement operator (~) is a unary operator. It changes the value of each bit from 0 to 1 or from 1 to 0.

> The second operand in the bitwise *and*, bitwise inclusive *or*, and bitwise exclusive *or* is often called a mask.

> Bitwise shift operators are binary operators used to shift data to the right or the left. The second operand in these operators is an integer that defines the number of bits to be shifted.

> The bitwise left-shift operator (<<) shifts the bits in the first operand to the left as many bits as is defined by the second operand. This effectively multiplies a number by 2^n, where n is the number of bits to be shifted.

> The bitwise right-shift operator (>>) shifts the bits in the first operand to the right as many bits as is defined by the second operand. This effectively divides a number by 2^n, where n is the number of bits to be shifted.

> The C language has no operator to rotate bits in a data item. Rotation can be accomplished by *or*'ing a shift-left operation and a shift-right operation.

Key Terms

afferent module

bitwise operators

central transforms

efferent module

fan out

flipping bits

mask

one's complement

stepwise refinement

transform analysis

transform module

turning bits on

Review Questions

1. The result of bitwise *and*'ing of two bits is 1 if
   _____.
   a. both bits are 0s
   b. both bits are 1s
   c. bits are different

2. The result of bitwise inclusive *or*'ing of two bits is 0 if _____.
   a. both bits are 0s
   b. both bits are 1s
   c. bits are different

3. The result of bitwise exclusive *or*'ing of two bits is 1 if _____.
   a. both bits are 0
   b. both bits are 1
   c. bits are different

4. To change every bit in a variable from a 1 to a 0 or from a 0 to a 1, we need to use the_____ operator.
   a. &
   b. |
   c. ^
   d. ~

5. The _____ operator can be used to turn a masked bit on.
   a. &
   b. |
   c. ^
   d. ~

6. The _____ operator can be used to turn a masked bit off.
   a. &
   b. |
   c. ^
   d. ~

7. The _____ operator can be used to flip a masked bit.
   a. &
   b. |
   c. ^
   d. ~

8. The bitwise _____ operator is used to divide a data item by a power of 2.
   a. &
   b. |
   c. ^
   d. >>
   e. <<

9. In program design, a function that collects data that are directed toward a central transform is classified as a(n) _____ module.
   a. afferent
   b. efferent
   c. input
   d. output
   e. transform

10. To find the first address in a block of addresses, we need to use the _____ operator with the network mask.

a. &

b. |

c. ^

d. >>

e. <<

11. To find the last address in a block of addresses, we need to use the _____ operator with the complement of network mask.

a. &

b. |

c. ^

d. >>

e. <<

Exercises

12. Show the value of each of the following binary numbers in hexadecimal:

a. `11011001`

b. `11111111`

c. `1111000100011111`

d. `0000000011100001`

13. Show the value of each of the following hexadecimal numbers in binary:

a. `0x37`

b. `0xAB`

c. `0x0237`

d. `0xA234`

14. Determine the result of the following operations (operands are in binary):

a. `~11011001`

b. `~11111111`

c. `~11110001`

d. `~00000000`

15. Determine the result of the following operations (operands are in binary):

a. `11111100 & 00111111`

b. `11111111 & 10101010`

c. `00000000 & 11111001`

d. `10101010 & 11100001`

16. Determine the result of the following operations (operands are in binary):

a. `11111100 | 00111111`

b. `11111111 | 10101010`

c. `00000000 | 11111001`

d. `10101010 | 11100001`

17. Determine the result of the following operations (operands are in binary):

a. `11111100 ^ 00111111`

b. `11111111 ^ 10101010`

c. `00000000 ^ 11111001`

d. `10101010 ^ 11100001`

18. When numbers are represented in hexadecimal, we can simplify the result of the one's complement (~) operation. The result of complementing each digit is 15 minus the value of that digit (5 = ~A). Using the above shortcut rule, find the result of the following operations:

a. `~0x02A1`

b. `~0xF305`

c. `~0xE2A8`

d. `~0x0FFA`

19. When numbers are represented in hexadecimal, we can use some rules that simplify the bitwise *and* (&) operation in three cases. If one of the digits is 0, the result is 0 (0 = 5 & 0). If one of the digits is F, the result is the other digit (3 = F & 3). If two digits are the same, the result is one of them. (A = A & A). Using the above shortcut rules, find the result of the following operations:

   a. 0xC201 & 0x02AF

   b. 0xA240 & 0xF005

   c. 0xE205 & 0xE2A0

   d. 0xA531 & 0x0FF0

20. When numbers are represented in hexadecimal, we can use some rules that simplify the bitwise inclusive *or* (|) operation in three cases. If one of the digits is 0, the result is the other digit (5 = 5 | 0). If one of the digits is F, the result is F (F = F | 3). If two digits are the same, the result is one of them. (A = A | A). Using the above shortcut rules, find the result of the following operations:

   a. 0xC201 | 0x02AF

   b. 0xA240 | 0xF005

   c. 0xE205 | 0xE2A0

   d. 0xA531 | 0x0FF0

21. When numbers are represented in hexadecimal, we can use some rules that simplify the bitwise exclusive *or* (^) operation in three cases. If one of the digits is 0, the result is the other digit (5 = 5 ^ 0). If one of the digits is F, the result is 15 minus the other digit (9 = F ^ 6). If two digits are the same, the result is 0 (0 = A ^ A). Using the above shortcut rules, find the result of the following operations:

   a. 0xC201 ^ 0x02AF

   b. 0xA240 ^ 0xF005

   c. 0xE205 ^ 0xE2A0

   d. 0xA531 ^ 0x0FF0

22. Find the value of the following expressions:

   a. 0x13 << 2

   b. 0x13 >> 2

   c. 0x13A2 << 4

   d. 0xB23E >> 2

23. Show the mask and the operator that turn on the most significant bit of an 8-bit integer. (Remember, the bits are numbered from the right, starting with 0.) Give the answer in binary and hexadecimal form.

24. Show the mask and the operator that turn off the most significant bit of an 8-bit integer. (Remember, the bits are numbered from the right, starting with 0.)

25. Find the mask that complements the values of the first and third bits of an 8-bit integer. (Remember, the bits are numbered from the right, starting with zero.) What operator should be used?

26. Find the mask that when used with the & operator sets the second and fourth bits of an 8-bit integer to zero. (Remember, the bits are numbered from the right, starting with 0.)

27. Find the mask that when used with the | operator sets the second and fourth bits of an 8-bit integer to 1. (Remember, the bits are numbered from the right, starting with 0.)

28. What is the result of the following expressions if *a* is an 8-bit unsigned integer?

   a. a & ~a

   b. a | ~a

   c. a ^ ~a

   d. a & 0xFF

   e. a & 0x00

   f. a | 0xFF

   g. a | 0x00

   h. a ^ 0xFF

   i. a ^ 0x00

29. Show the binary and hexadecimal representation of the following polynomial using a 16-bit unsigned integer:
$x^{11} + x^6 + x^3 + x + 1$

30. Given two polynomials $x^4 + x^3 + 1$ and $x^6 + x^3 + x + 1$
    a. Add them using modulo 2 arithmetic for coefficients.
    b. Use 8-bit unsigned integers (in hexadecimal) to represent each polynomial and apply addition using exclusive *or* operations.
    c. Compare the results of parts a and b.

31. Given two polynomials $x^5 + x^2 + 1$ and $x^6 + x^4 + x^2 + 1$
    a. Subtract the first polynomial from the second using modulo 2 arithmetic for coefficients.
    b. Use 8-bit unsigned integers (in hexadecimal) to represent each polynomial and apply subtraction using exclusive *or* operations.
    c. Compare the results of parts a and b.

32. Given two polynomials $x^{12} + x^4 + x^3 + 1$ and $x^6 + x^3 + x + 1$
    a. Divide the first polynomial by the second using modulo 2 arithmetic for coefficients. Find the quotient and the remainder.
    b. Use 16-bit unsigned integers (in hexadecimal) to represent each polynomial and use Program 13-11 to find the quotient and the remainder.
    c. Compare the results of parts a and b.

Problems

33. Write a function that sets a specified bit in a 16-bit unsigned integer to 1. The function is to have two parameters: The first parameter is the integer to be manipulated and the second is the bit location, relative to the least significant bit, that is to be turned on. Your test program should start with 0 and turn on several bits in turn.

34. Rework Problem 33 to turn off (set to zero) the specified bit.

35. Rework Problem 33 to flip the specified bit.

36. Write a function that flips the bits in a 16-bit unsigned integer.

37. Write a function that accepts two polynomials (with 0 and 1 coefficient) in the form of two 16-bit unsigned integers and returns the result of adding the two in the form of a 16-bit unsigned integer. Use hexadecimal notations. Can the same function be used for subtracting the two polynomials? If yes, does the order of the two polynomials make a difference?

38. Write a function that returns the first (leftmost) hexadecimal digit from a 32-bit unsigned integer.

39. Rework Problem 38 to return the last (rightmost) digit.

40. Write a function that complements the first (leftmost) hexadecimal digit in a 32-bit unsigned integer. Note that the complement of a hexadecimal digit is the 15 minus that digit.

41. Rework Problem 40 to complement the last (rightmost) digit.

42. Write a function that changes the first (leftmost) hexadecimal digit in a 32-bit unsigned integer. The function is to have two parameters: The first is the integer to be manipulated, the second the replacement digit.

43. Rework Problem 42 to change the last (rightmost) digit.

Projects

44. Modify Program 13-5 for checksum calculation at the sender site to a checksum checker at the receiver site. The program receives a message of an arbitrary length and a 16-bit checksum calculated at the sender site. It then

calculates a new checksum out of both. If the new checksum is 0, it prints a message that the data is valid; otherwise, it prints a message that the data is corrupted.

a. Test your program with the string and checksum calculated in Program 13-5. The new checksum should be 0.

b. Change one of the characters in the string and test the program again. The result should be non-zero.

c. Note that the checksum itself can be corrupted during the transmission. Also check your program by changing one of the hexadecimal digits of the checksum calculated at the sender site. The result should be non-zero again.

45. There is one major problem with the traditional checksum calculation discussed in the text. If two 16-bit items are transposed in transmission, the checksum cannot catch this error. The reason is that the traditional checksum is not weighted; it treats each data item equally. In other words, the order of data item is immaterial to the calculation.

To catch transposition errors, John Fletcher created a new checksum algorithm. The Fletcher checksum was devised to weigh each data item according to its position. The algorithm uses eight bits (known as octets in telecommunication systems) and creates a 16-bit checksum. The calculation uses modulo 256 (2^8), which means the intermediate results are divided by 256 and the remainder is kept. The algorithm uses two accumulators, a and b. The first is the sum of the data; the second is a weighted sum. These two accumulators are then used to form the checksum, a being the first byte and b being the second byte. **Figure 13-13** shows the logic diagram for the Fletcher checksum.

Figure 13-13 Fletcher checksum design

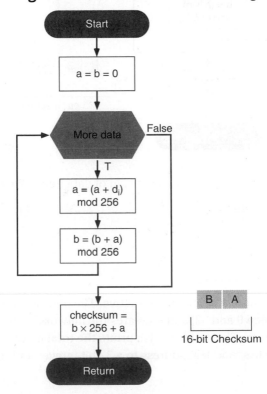

The following equations represent the calculations shown in the flowchart.

```
// Calculations in modulo 256
a = d₁ + d₂ + ... + dₙ
b = nd₁ + (n - 1)d₂ + ... + dₙ
```

If, for example, d_1 and d_2 are swapped during the transmission, the calculation of b at the receiver is different from the one done at the sender. Write a function to calculate a Fletcher checksum. Test it with an appropriate test driver.

46. The Adler checksum, designed by Mark Adler, is a 32-bit checksum. It is similar to the Fletcher checksum with three differences. First, calculation is done on two bytes at a time to produce a 32-bit checksum. Second, a is initialized to 1 instead of 0. Third, the modulus is a prime number, 65,521, which is the largest prime number less than 65,536 (2^{32}). It has been proved that a prime modulo has a better detecting capability in some combinations of data. **Figure 13-14** shows a simple, though inefficient, algorithm in flowchart form.

Figure 13-14 Adler checksum process

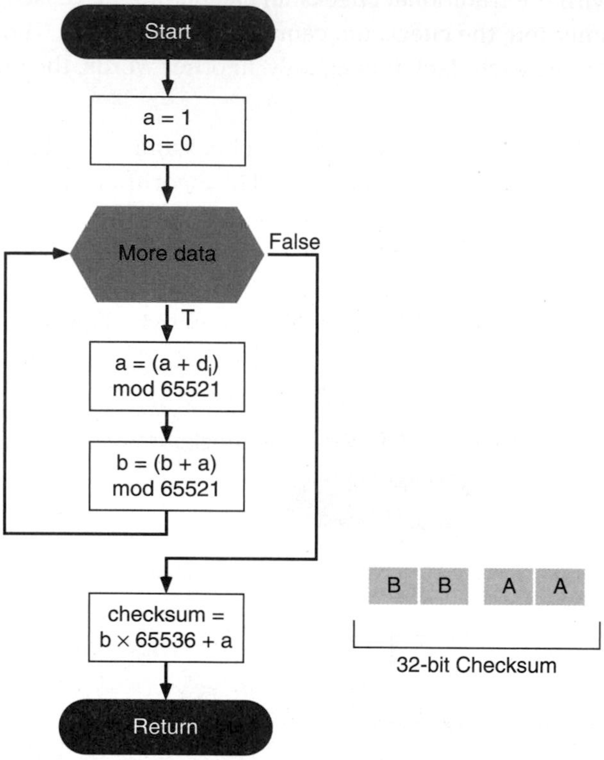

It can be proved that the accumulator b is the weighted sum of data items. We have

```
// Calculations in modulo 65521
a = d₁ + d₂ + ... + dₙ + 1
b = nd₁ + (n - 1)d₂ + ... + dₙ + n
```

Write a program to calculate an Adler checksum.

47. Combine Programs 13-9 and 13-10, and make them interactive. The new program accepts an address in the form x.y.z.t, and an integer prefix between 0 and 32, and it creates the network address (first address), broadcast address (last address), and the mask. The program also prints the total number of addresses in the block. This can be done by first changing the first and last address to a 32-bit integer and then finding the difference plus 1.

Recursion

Learning Objectives

When you complete this chapter, you will be able to:

14.1 Describe recursion and its use in programming

14.2 Distinguish between recursion and iteration

14.3 Describe the different types of recursion

14.4 Implement different sorting algorithms

14.5 Implement searching algorithms

14.6 Explain the purpose of recursive backtracking

14.1 Recursion as a Concept

Before we begin discussing recursion in depth, let's briefly consider the origins of recursion theory, which is a branch of logic theory. The notion of recursion, a problem-solving method in which the solution of a problem depends on a similar solution of other instances of the problem, was introduced by Dedekind in 1888, and was further developed in the 1930s by two well-known logicians: Alonzo Church and Kurt Gödel. Later, Alan Turing, Emil Post, and A. A. Markov wrote publications defining recursion based on Church's work, known as *Church's Thesis*.

The concept of recursion does not apply solely to the field of computer science. Rather, it is a universal concept used in many disciplines, including mathematics, linguistics, and the arts. Although recursion is often considered the most challenging topic in the foundation of programming, it is simple to implement and code. In this chapter, we will walk through recursion in depth, defining and discussing the different types of recursion with examples while showing its use and implementation in different practical scenarios.

Previously, we learned how to create a function and call it from `main` or another function. But what if we wanted to call it from its own function? To do this, we would use recursion, which in programming is a repetitive process in which a function calls itself.

Consider the following scenario. Suppose you have a stack of dollar bills that needs to be counted. You could do this in one of two ways. Method #1: Start counting the whole stack one by one. Method #2: Divide the stacks into smaller ones and then count each stack separately. Note that the process of counting is the same for each stack, and both methods will lead to the same result. The difference between the two methods in this scenario is that in the second one we have broken down the stack into smaller ones, which means we could have more than one person counting the smaller stacks using the former method of counting. The second method falls into the category of solutions that implement a recursion technique.

Another scenario that illustrates this concept is one in which someone is given a gift, such as a teddy bear. For the purpose of suspense, the teddy bear might be placed inside a small box, which is then placed inside a bigger one, and the bigger one inside an even bigger one, and so on. The person opening the gift box will find another box inside and so on, until they open the last box that has the teddy bear, as illustrated in **Figure 14-1**. As you can see, the process of opening the largest box is the same as the process of opening the next, smaller box, and the process is repeated until the last box is opened and the teddy bear is found.

Figure 14-1   Real-life example of recursion

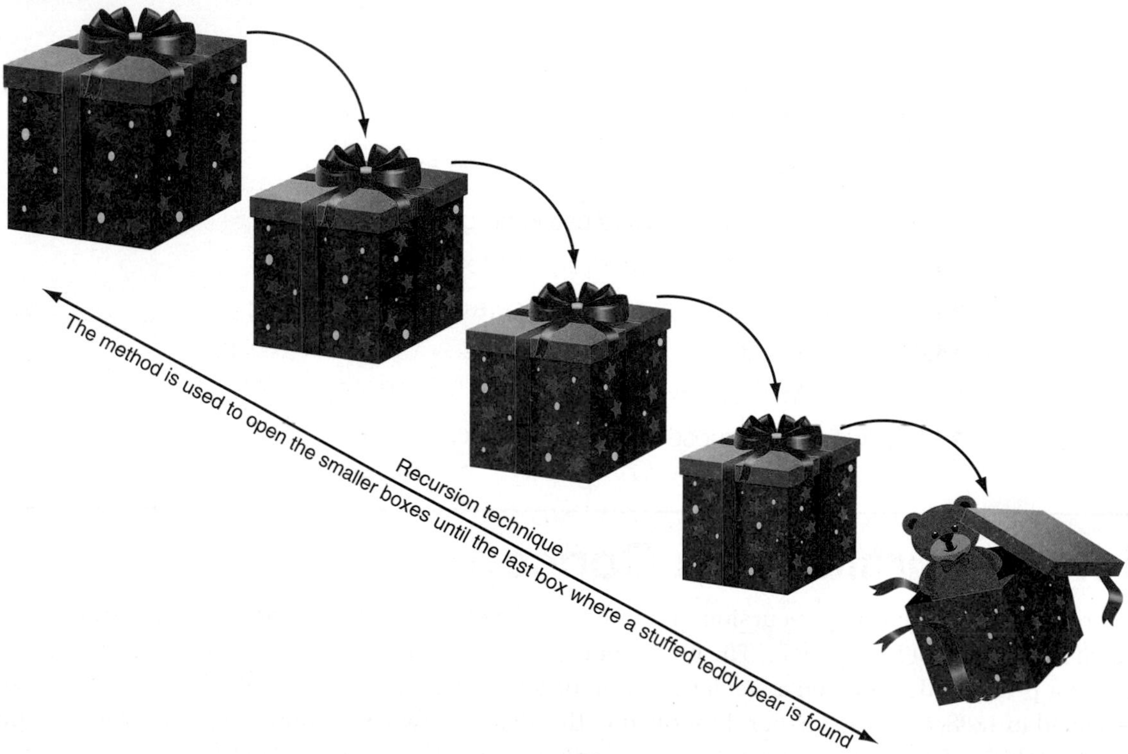

Now, let's consider a business scenario in which an organization is conducting a full audit of its accounting system. The audit process is completed for each department and its different sections until all sections and departments have been examined. This scenario is another example of recursion.

The question that comes to mind here is: Why use recursion? The two primary reasons for using recursion are simplicity and efficiency. Simplicity in this context refers to the fact that the same solution is used to solve the same problem in a straightforward matter. Efficiency results from the multiple instances in which the same solution is executed. It should be noted that not all problems lend themselves to recursion as a solution; however, in many situations, recursion is advantageous and a good fit. To gain a better understanding of when recursion is used, let's review some of the advantages and disadvantages of recursion in programming.

Advantages of recursion:

> Recursion code is simple, easy to read, and concise. A recursion function contains the general case (the statement in which the function calls itself) for solving a problem and the base case (the statement that ends execution of recursion).

> Recursion reduces debugging time due to the simplicity of the code, especially when the depth (or number of recursion calls) is low.

> Recursion code is efficient for links-lists and tree traversal; these topics are discussed later in this text.

> Recursion is an inherent solution for mathematical problems such as factorial models.

> Although recursion algorithms can be coded using iterative statements, recursive code is lean and therefore easy to implement.

Disadvantages of recursion:

> Recursion cannot be used for solving all types of problems.

> Recursion programming consumes more memory and CPU time than other iterative algorithms. In some cases, recursion can be inefficient depending on computer hardware resources.

> Although recursion code reduces debugging time, the code is difficult to trace.

> If a recursion function is missing the base case, or the base case condition is not met, the function will infinitely execute recursion until computer resources are exhausted, and the program will crash.

Now, let's delve more deeply into the topic of recursion and its relationship to mathematical models.

Factorials and the Fibonacci Sequence

Many mathematical models fall naturally into recursion programming where computational efficiency is very apparent. Two of these models are factorials and the Fibonacci sequence. In this section, we will discuss these two models to provide a foundation for the coming sections.

In mathematics, the factorial is an important function that is used to find out how many ways things can be arranged or to determine the ordered set of numbers. The well-known interpolating function of the factorial function was discovered by Daniel Bernoulli. A factorial of some positive integer n is defined as the product of all positive integers less than or equal to n, as shown in the formula below (note that factorial of n is denoted as $n!$).

$$n! = n \times (n - 1) \times (n - 2) \times (n - 3) \times \ldots \times 3 \times 2 \times 1$$

For example, four factorial is calculated as follows:

$$4! = 4 \times 3 \times 2 \times 1$$

$$4! = 24$$

Note that by convention, the factorial of zero, $0!$, is equal to 1.

Using this definition of a factorial, the permutation and combination of a number can be determined. The number of permutations of n distinct objects, or the number of different ways n distinct objects can be arranged into a sequence, is $n!$. A combination on the other hand is a unique arrangement of a possible selection of some number of elements, k, that can be chosen from a total number of n elements, where the order of the chosen elements in a sequence does not matter, and $k \leq n$. The number of possible combinations is often represented as $\binom{n}{k} = \frac{n!}{k!(n-k)!}$. It is easy to see that there only exists one combination of k elements from the set n if $k = n$.

Over time, these basic expressions were shown to arise in algebra, calculus, and probability theory. They have also proven to be most crucial in the analysis of the computational complexity of sorting algorithms. In short, a factorial is simple; it is just a product.

To better understand factorials and permutations, let's consider the following scenario. Suppose we are looking for the number of possible ways the letters in a specific word could be scrambled. Take the word *EAT* as an example. As shown in **Figure 14-2**, we see the word *EAT* is scrambled into 6 letter sequences or arrangements, which is equivalent to three factorial, 3! Similarly, in Figure 14-2, the word *READ* is permuted to 24 different arrangements, which is 4!. Now imagine you need to scramble a word of 5 letters. This mean the possible number of permutations is 5! which equates to 120.

Figure 14-2 Scrambling of the words *EAT* and *READ*

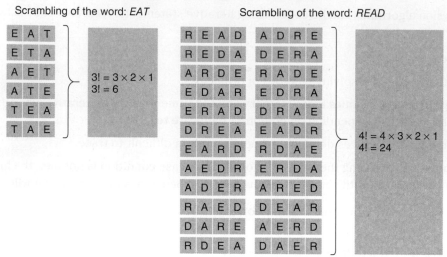

As noted earlier, recursion is the process of breaking up a problem into smaller ones. This divide-and-conquer approach is used in everyday life to solve big problems. We see this concept in action when we divide programs into several functions to simplify a problem.

Life is an expression of patterns, and mathematics is the ultimate tool for analysis of such patterns. These patterns are ubiquitous and waiting to be found. Once they are presented in the language of mathematics, their simplicity and beauty become clear. Some of these forms that exist in nature arise from patterns that occur through permutations and combinations, which at their heart incorporate factorials. One field in which these patterns show themselves is genetics. Gregor Mendel, who is considered the father of genetics, was a mathematician and biologist. He compiled enormous amounts of data from breeding and studying tens of thousands of pea plants. It can be argued that were it not for Mendel's understanding of the factorial system, he would not have developed the heredity and mutation models that he did, and modern genetics would not be where it is today.

One specific pattern found virtually everywhere in nature stems from the Fibonacci sequence, which was discovered around thirteen hundred years ago in India and later introduced to the Western world in the early thirteenth century by a man named Leonardo Fibonacci. Fibonacci is the same man who introduced the West to Arabic numerals, without which we would still be using the tedious Roman numeral system. The Fibonacci sequence is such that any term (excluding the first two terms, which are both often defined as one) is the sum of the two terms immediately preceding it. It looks like this: 1, 1, 2, 3, 5, 8, 13, 21, 34, ... and is shown in **Figure 14-3**.

Figure 14-3 Fibonacci sequence

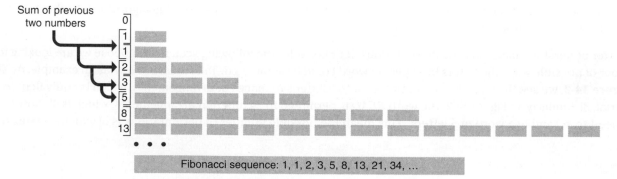

These numbers are so scattered across nature that the number of petals a flower has or the number of segments in a pine cone tends to be one of the terms from the sequence, whether it is three, five, eight, twenty-one, and so on. Even trees, often starting from one main trunk, will split into two. Then one will split leaving three total branches, then five and so on. Moreover, the Fibonacci sequence contains in it the golden ratio.

Before Fibonacci, Phidias, a famous painter, architect, and sculptor in ancient Greece, had used the golden ratio, or *phi* as it is also known. Phidias considered phi to be the ideal proportion of the total height of a human sculpture to the height of the feet to the naval. It was similarly shown in the length of the "ideal" face to its width. This ratio is approximated from the Fibonacci sequence and most accurately so when one of the larger terms is divided by the one right before it. Phi in numerical form is 1.618.... The Fibonacci spiral is a graphical model connecting arcs representing each of the Fibonacci numbers to form a spiral graph that is an approximation of the golden spiral, a logarithmic spiral of growth factor phi. The spiral growth is seen in the geometry of the calcium carbonate structure of seashells and snail shells. Nature, however, does not exist this way at random; it just happens to be that this is the most efficient design and way of packing things, like the hexagonal structure of the honeycomb in a bee hive.

In the following sections, you will see how recursion, factorials, and the Fibonacci sequence have a close relationship in terms of implementation. Next, we will discuss how to think in terms of recursion before discussing how these two mathematical models are coded.

How Does One Think in Terms of Recursion?

We learned the technique of divide and conquer to decompose a problem into smaller ones in order to solve it. In many cases, solving the various smaller problems may require different logic and algorithms, while in other cases it may be obvious that the solution for the larger problem can also be used for all of the smaller problems contained within it. As you can see in **Figure 14-4**, the recursive solution is simpler and cleaner.

Figure 14-4   Recursive vs nonrecursive solution

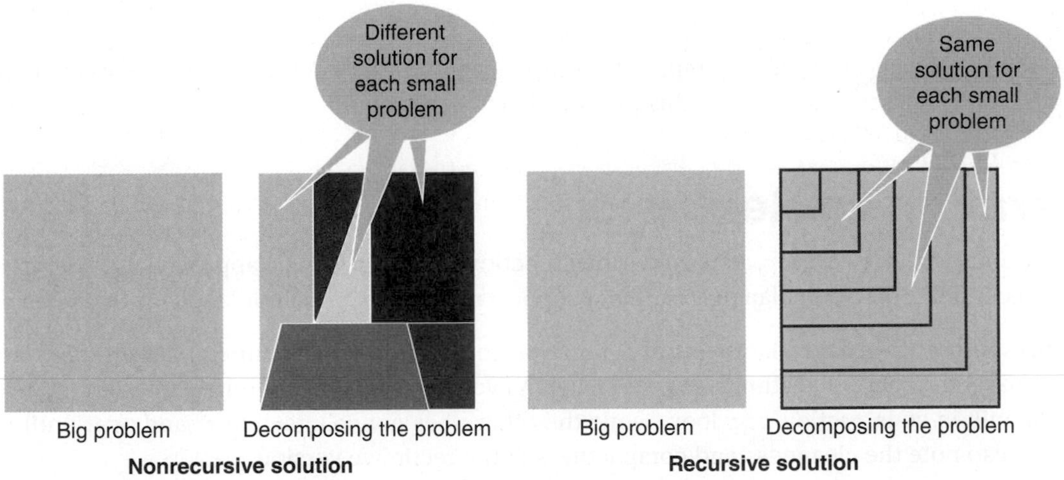

Now let's consider how to identify a problem that can be solved by using recursion. If the answer to each of the following questions is "Yes," then recursion can be used to solve the problem:

> Can you decompose the problem into smaller tasks?

> Do any of the smaller tasks require/involve multiple iterations?

> Do the steps of any of the smaller tasks require the same process to be completed? In other words, are the smaller tasks a repetition of the same process?

> Is the result of the smaller tasks needed to solve the problem?

> Is there an exception that needs to be met to complete the process?

Suppose we are asked to write an algorithm that reverses any string, such as "Hello World" to "drloW olleH," or "12345" to the reversed "54321." To determine if recursion can be used in this situation, we will need to answer the questions shown in **Table 14-1**.

Table 14-1   Determining if recursion can be used to reverse the string "Hello World" problem

QUESTION	ANSWER

1. Can you decompose the problem into smaller tasks?	**Yes**
	❯ Function #1: Get from user the desired string to be reversed.
	❯ Function #2: Reverse string using the following steps:
	   1. Extract first character of the string ("d").
	   2. Print the extracted character.
	   3. Return the remainder of the string "Hello World."

2. Do any of the smaller tasks require/involve multiple iterations?	**Yes** ❯ Function #2 is repeated until all characters in the string are extracted (string becomes null).
3. Do the steps of any of the smaller tasks require the same process to be completed? In other words, are the smaller tasks a repetition of the same process?	Yes ❯ The same steps can be used.
4. Is the result/returned value of the smaller task needed for the same task to be completed?	**Yes** ❯ The returned string can be used by function #2. ❯ "Hello World" is used by the same function.
5. Is there an exception that needs to be met to complete the process?	**Yes** ❯ There is one exception when the string is null.

Answering "Yes" to all the questions above implies that an algorithm to carry out the desired task can be accomplished with recursion. We will present the code for this problem later in this chapter.

14.2 Iteration vs Recursion

In general, programmers use two approaches to writing repetitive algorithms. One approach uses iteration (or loops); the other uses recursion. Some older languages do not support recursion. One major language that does not is COBOL.

Figure 14-5 presents a flowchart algorithm of a function to countdown a number, written using iteration, and **Figure 14-6** presents the same algorithm using recursion. As you can see, the difference between the two methods is that one uses a built-in construction `for` loop, while the other does not call itself over and over until the base case (n==0) is met. Also note the cleanness and compactness of the recursive version.

Figure 14-5   Countdown function flowchart using iteration

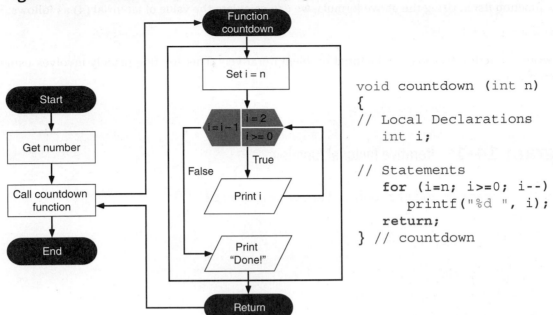

```
void countdown (int n)
{
// Local Declarations
   int i;

// Statements
   for (i=n; i>=0; i--)
      printf("%d ", i);
   return;
} // countdown
```

Figure 14-6   Countdown function flowchart using recursion

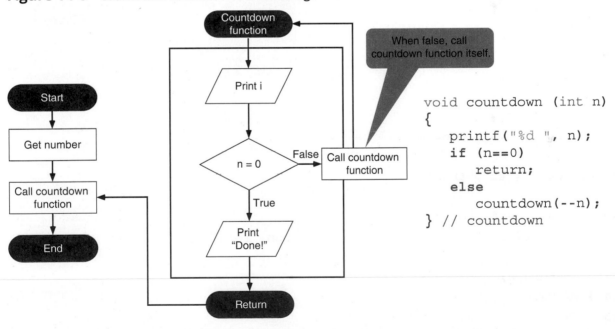

```
void countdown (int n)
{
   printf("%d ", n);
   if (n==0)
      return;
   else
      countdown(--n);
} // countdown
```

It is worth mentioning here that C is a computer language that is built with compact constructs—unlike other procedural languages. One last thing to note is that reading and understanding the recursive version is not as easy without having some background in recursion.

Iterative Definition

In order to compare the two programming techniques of iteration and recursion, let's look again at some factorial calculation examples. Recall that the factorial of a number is the product of the integer values from 1 to the number, as shown in the following formula (*n!*).

$$factorial\ (n) = \begin{bmatrix} 1 & if\ n-0 \\ n*(n-1)*(n-2)\dots3*2*1 & if\ n>0 \end{bmatrix}$$

This definition is iterative. A repetitive function is considered iterative if the definition involves only the parameter(s) and not the function itself. Using the above formula, we can calculate the value of factorial (4) as follows:

factorial (4) = 4 * 3 * 2 * 1 = 24

Now, let's write a function to solve the factorial problem iteratively. This solution usually involves using a loop, as shown in **Program 14-1**.

Program 14-1 | Iterative factorial function

```
 1  /* This program prints out a factorial series.
 2     Written by:
 3     Date:
 4  */
 5  #include <stdio.h>
 6
 7  // Function Declaration
 8  long factorial (int n);
 9  int main (void)
10  {
11  // Local Declarations
12     int num;
13     long result;
14
15  // Statements
16     printf("This program prints the factorial of a number.\n");
17     printf("Enter an integer: ");
18     scanf ("%d", &num);
19
20     result = factorial (num);
21     printf("Calculation of %d! = %ld", num, result);
22
23     return 0;
24  } // main
25
26  /* Calculate the factorial of a number using a loop.
27     There is no test that the result fits in a long integer.
28     Pre n is the number to be raised factorially.
29     Post result is returned.
30  */
31  long factorial (int n)
32  {
```

(continue)

Program 14-1   Iterative factorial function *(continued)*

```
33 // Local Declarations
34    long factN = 1;
35
36 // Statements
37    for (int i = 1; i <= n; i++)
38        factN = factN * i;
39    return factN;
40 } // factorial
```

Recursive Definition

A repetitive function is considered recursive if the function appears within the definition itself. For example, the factorial function can be defined recursively, as shown here.

$$factorial\ (n) = \left[\begin{array}{ll} 1 & \text{if } n = 0 \\ n * factorial\ (n-1) & \text{if } n > 0 \end{array}\right]$$

The decomposition of factorial (3), using the above formula, is shown in **Figure 14-7**. Study this figure carefully and note that the recursive solution for a problem is a two-way journey: first we decompose the problem from the top to the bottom, and then we solve it from the bottom to the top.

Figure 14-7   Factorial (3) recursively

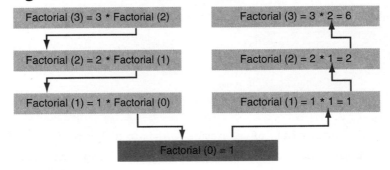

Judging from the above example, the recursive calculation looks much longer and more difficult. So why would we want to use the recursive method? We use it because, although the recursive calculation looks more difficult when using paper and pencil, it is often a much easier and more elegant solution when using computers. Additionally, it offers a conceptual simplicity to the creator and the reader.

The recursive solution for factorials is shown in **Program 14-2**. This program does not need a loop; the concept itself involves repetition.

Program 14-2 | Recursive factorial

```
 1  /* This program prints out a factorial series.
 2     Written by:
 3     Date:
 4  */
 5
 6  #include <stdio.h>
 7  //  Function Declaration
 8  long factorial (int n);
 9
10  int main (void)
11  {
12  // Local Declarations
13     int num;
14     long result;
15
16  // Statements
17     printf("This program prints factorial calculations of a number.\n");
18     printf("What factorial number would like to calculate? ");
19     scanf ("%d", &num);
20
21     result = factorial (num);
22     printf("Calculation of %d! = %ld", num, result);
23
24     return 0;
25  } // main
26
27
28  /* Calculate the factorial of a number using a loop.
29     There is no test that the result fits in a long integer.
30     Pre n is the number to be raised factorially
31     Post result is returned
32  */
33  long factorial (int n)
34  {
35  // Local Declarations
36     long factN = 1;
37
38  // Statements
```

(continue)

Program 14-2   Recursive factorial *(continued)*

```
39      if (n == 0)
40          return 1;
41      else
42          return (n * factorial (n - 1));
43 } // factorial
```

In the recursive version, we let the function factorial call itself, each time with a different set of parameters. Figure 14-7 shows the recursive execution with the parameters for each individual call.

Designing Recursive Functions

All recursive functions have two elements: each call either solves one part of the problem or reduces the size of the problem. In Program 14-2, statement 40 solves a small piece of the problem—factorial(0) is 1. Statement 42, on the other hand, reduces the size of the problem by recursively calling the factorial with n - 1. Once the solution to factorial(n - 1) is known, statement 42 provides part of the solution to the general problem by returning a value to the calling function. As we see in statement 42, the general part of the solution is the recursive call. Statement 42 calls its own function to solve the problem. We also see this in **Figure 14-8**. At each recursive call, the size of the problem is reduced from the factorial of 3 to factorial 2, to factorial 1, and finally to factorial 0.

The statement that "solves" the problem is known as the base case. *Every recursive function must have a base case.* The rest of the function is known as the general case. In our factorial example, the base case is factorial(0); the general case is n * factorial(n - 1). The general case contains the logic needed to reduce the size of the problem.

> **Note |** Note that every recursive call must either solve part of the problem or reduce the size of the problem.

In the factorial problem, once the base case has been reached, the solution begins. The program has found one part of the answer and can return that part to the next more general statement. Thus, in Program 14-2, after the program has calculated that factorial(0) is 1, it then returns value 1. That leads to solving the next general case:

factorial (1) → 1 * factorial (0) → 1 * 1 → 1

The program now returns the value of factorial(1) to the more general case, factorial(2), which we know to be:

factorial (2) → 2 * factorial (1) → 2 * 1 → 2

As the program solves each general case in turn, the program can solve the next higher general case, until it finally solves the highest and most general case, the original problem.

The following are the steps for designing a recursive function:

1. Determine the base case.

2. Determine the general case.

3. Combine the base case and general case into a function.

In combining the base and general cases into a function, we must pay careful attention to the logic. Each call must reduce the size of the problem and move it toward the base case. The base case, when reached, must terminate without a call to the recursive function; that is, it must execute a return.

Figure 14-8 Calling a recursive function

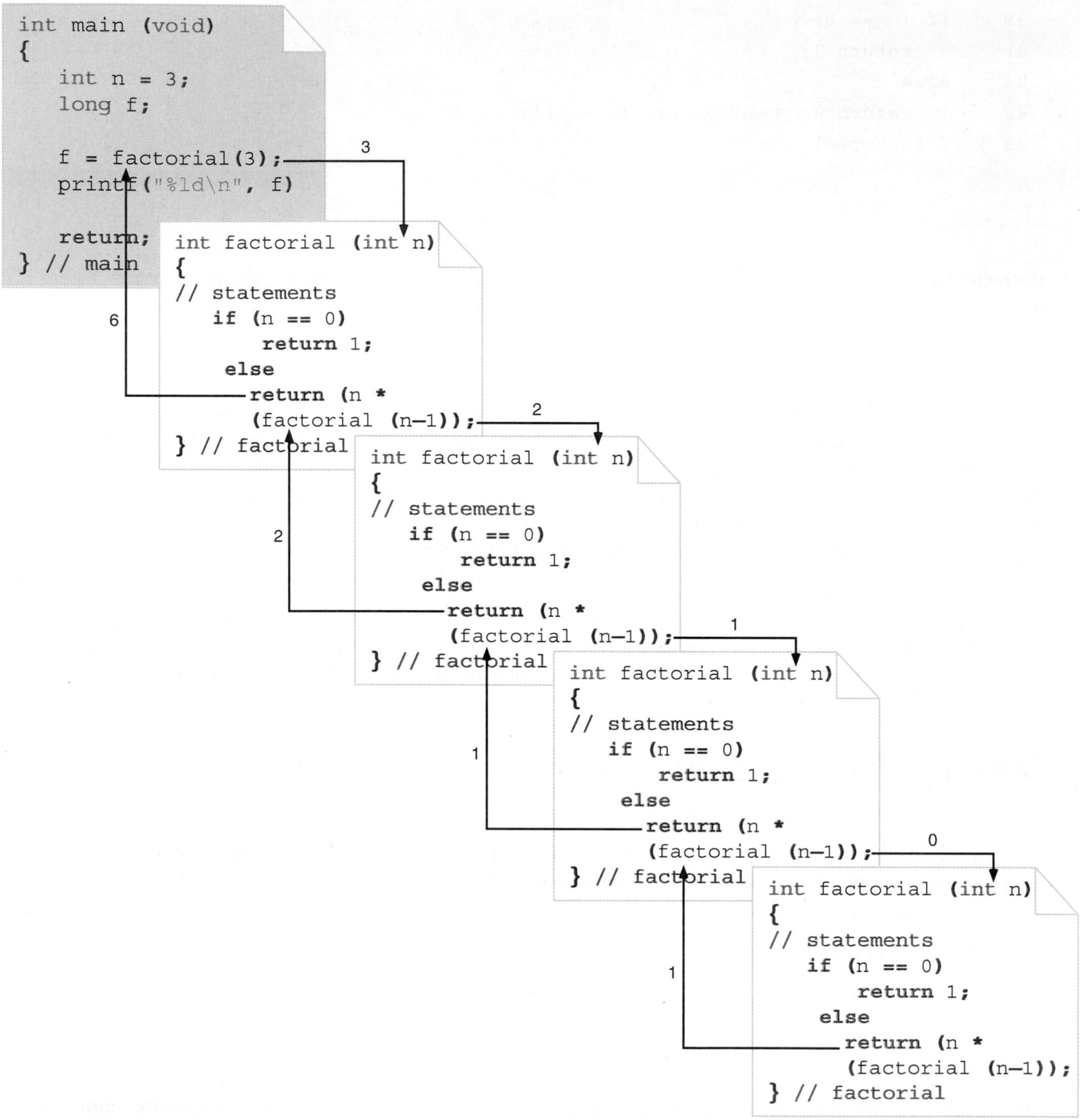

```
int main (void)
{
    int n = 3;
    long f;

    f = factorial(3);
    printf("%ld\n", f)

    return;
} // main
```

```
int factorial (int n)
{
    // statements
    if (n == 0)
        return 1;
    else
        return (n *
        (factorial (n-1));
} // factorial
```

```
int factorial (int n)
{
    // statements
    if (n == 0)
        return 1;
    else
        return (n *
        (factorial (n-1));
} // factorial
```

```
int factorial (int n)
{
    // statements
    if (n == 0)
        return 1;
    else
        return (n *
        (factorial (n-1));
} // factorial
```

```
int factorial (int n)
{
    // statements
    if (n == 0)
        return 1;
    else
        return (n *
        (factorial (n-1));
} // factorial
```

14.3 Types of Recursion

We have introduced the concept of recursion and presented one of the most common examples with the factorial function. In the following sections, we will discuss several specific types of recursion, as presented in **Figure 14-9**. We have stated before that recursion falls naturally in the field of mathematics; however, note that our discussion and definition of these types will be from the aspect of programming only, without touching on mathematical definitions and representations. If you would like to learn more about these recursion types from the computational aspect, you will need to review computational theory, computability theory, or mathematical recursive function theory—which are advanced areas of studies in mathematics.

Figure 14-9   Recursion types summary

RECURSION TYPE	RECURSION DEFINITION
Primitive	A recursion method that can be simply rewritten using iteration construct.
Single	A recursion method in which the recursive function has one reference statement to itself.
Linear	A recursive function that has only a single reference to itself; also known as single.
Multiple	A recursion method in which the recursive function has more than one reference statement to itself.
Mutual	A method in which one function A calls recursively function B, and function B calls recursively function A.
Binary	A recursion method that contains two different references to itself.
Tail	The last statement in a recursive function.
Nested	A recursion method in which a function references itself as a parameter within the function call.
Indirect	A recursion method in which recursive function A calls recursive function B, and recursive function B calls recursive function C, and recursive function C calls function A; also known as mutual recursion.
General	A recursive function that is not easily converted to an iterative function.

Primitive Recursion

Let's look at each type of recursion by presenting a full definition, flowchart, and programming example. We will begin with primitive recursion, a recursive function that can be easily written using iteration construct and the most common type of recursion. Most functional languages, such as Haskell, do not have any iteration constructs; they solely depend on recursion. Fortunately, in C, both methods are available to us to devise algorithms using the technique we prefer. Primitive recursion is a recursive function that can simply be written using loops to achieve the same task. For example, suppose we would like to write a bubble sort algorithm. We can use loops to order the array in an ascending or descending manner, and at the same time we can write it recursively. The point we are trying to emphasize here is that primitive recursion is the other way around, like generating a countdown starting from a given number with a recursive function rather than opting to write it using iteration. **Program 14-3** presents one function using recursion and another using iteration to generate a countdown.

Program 14-3 | Countdown generation

```
1   /* This program prints countdown of a number.
2      Written by:
3      Date:
4   */
5
6   #include <stdio.h>
7
8   //  Function Declaration
9   void countdownRecursion (int n);
10  void countdownIteration (int n);
11
12  int main (void)
13  {
14  //  Local Declarations
15      int num;
```

(continue)

Program 14-3   Countdown generation *(continued)*

```
16       long result;
17
18 // Statements
19     printf("Enter a number to start countdown: ");
20     scanf ("%d", &num);
21
22     printf("Countdown using recursion method:\n");
23     countdownRecursion (num);
24
25     printf("\nCountdown using iteration method:\n");
26     countdownIteration (num);
27
28     return 0;
29 } // main
30
31 /* Countdown generation using
32    recursion method
33 */
34 void countdownRecursion (int n)
35 {
36    printf("%d ", n);
37
38    if (n==0)
39       return;
40    else
41       countdownRecursion(--n);
42
43 } // countdownRecursion
44
45 /* Countdown generation using
46    iteration method
47 */
48 void countdownIteration (int n)
49 {
50 // Local Declarations
51    int i;
52
53 // Statements
54    for (i=n; i>= 0; i--)
55       printf("%d ", i);
56
57    return;
58 } // countdownIteration
```

Single Recursion

Single recursion refers to a function that has one calling statement to itself. In other words, it has no more than one reference to itself. There are many examples of this type, we already saw two examples: factorial calculations and the number countdown generation. Let's look at another simple example of a single recursion function: number summation. The sum of all consecutive numbers for a given number is presented by the following formula.

$$\sum_{i=1}^{n} x_i = x_1 + x_2 + x_3 + \cdots + x_{n-1} + x_n$$

Suppose we would like to get summation of number 6, if we apply the formula above, we get the following:

$$\sum_{i=1}^{6} x_i = 1 + 2 + 3 + 4 + 5 + 6$$

$$\sum_{1}^{6} x_i = 21.$$

Presenting this formula as a recursive function, we get **Program 14-4**. As you can see, the only reference to the function itself is in statement 35.

Program 14-4 | Summation of a number

```
 1  /* This program prints the summation of a consecutive series of numbers.
 2     Written by:
 3     Date:
 4  */
 5  #include <stdio.h>
 6
 7  // Function Declaration
 8  int Summation (int n);
 9
10  int main (void)
11  {
12  // Local Declarations
13     int num;
14     int result;
15
16  // Statements
17     printf("Enter a number to calculate its summation: ");
18     scanf ("%d", &num);
19
20     result = Summation (num);
21     printf("Sum of %d", result);
22
23     return 0;
24  } // main
25
26
```

(continue)

Program 14-4   Summation of a number *(continued)*

```
27 /* Summation calculation using
28      recursion method
29 */
30 int Summation (int n)
31 {
32     if (n == 0)
33         return n;
34     else
35         return n + Summation(n-1);
36
37 } // Summation
```

Linear Recursion

Linear recursion, also known as single recursion, refers to a recursive function that makes one call to itself only—unlike in multiple recursion. Suppose we want to write a recursive function to compute the number 3 to the power of 5 and we expect the result to be 243. This task can be written in a recursive function, as presented in **Program 14-5**. Statement 37 is the base call and statement 39 is the recursive call (only one call).

Program 14-5 | Linear recursion example

```
1  /* This program illustrates linear recursion.
2
3     Written by:
4     Date:
5  */
6  #include <stdio.h>
7
8  //  Function Declaration
9  int power (int b, int p);
10
11 int main (void)
12 {
13 // Local Declarations
14     int base;
15     int pow;
16     int res;
17
18 // Statements
19     printf("Enter a base: ");
20     scanf ("%d", &base);
```

(continue)

Program 14-5   Linear recursion example *(continued)*

```
21        printf("Enter power: ");
22        scanf ("%d", &pow);
23
24        res = power(base, pow);
25        printf("%d to the power of %d = %d\n", base, pow, res);
26
27        return 0;
28  } // main
29
30
31  // Power recursion function
32  int power (int b, int p)
33  {
34      // Statements
35
36      if (p <= 0)
37          return 1;
38      else
39          return b * power(b, p-1);
40
41  } // power
```

Output

```
Enter a base: 3
Enter power: 5
3 to the power of 5 = 243
```

Multiple Recursion

Multiple recursion is a type of recursive function that calls itself in multiple statements. Suppose you want to write a recursive function that generates odd numbers up to a specified number—for example, all odd numbers from 1 to 44. You could code this task as in **Program 14-6**. You may have noticed that the function generateOdd has two statements in which it calls itself. If the starting number is odd, statement 41 skips 2 numbers, and if it is even, the else statement 44 is executed and skips 1 number. Note two important points. First, this function has two calls to itself in two different statements. Second, if the entered starting number is even, the function calls itself once in statement 44 and then it calls itself in statement 41 and keeps on calling itself until the base case is met in statement 34.

Program 14-6 | GenerateOdd function

```
1  /* This program prints a series of odd numbers within
2     a range of two specified numbers.
3     Written by:
4     Date:
5  */
6  #include <stdio.h>
7
8  // Function Declaration
9  int generateOdd (int n1, int n2);
10
11 int main (void)
12 {
13 // Local Declarations
14     int num1, num2;
15
16 // Statements
17    printf("Enter starting number: ");
18    scanf ("%d", &num1);
19    printf("Enter ending number: ");
20    scanf ("%d", &num2);
21    generateOdd(num1, num2);
22
23    return 0;
24 } // main
25
26
27 /* Generate a series of odd numbers that do not exceed
28    the passed integer number.
29 */
30 int generateOdd (int n1, int n2)
31 {
32
33    // Statements
34    if (n1 >= n2)
35       return 0;
36    else
37    {
38       if(n1%2==1)
39       {
40          printf("%d ", n1);
41          generateOdd(n1+2, n2);
42       }
```

(continue)

Program 14-6   GenerateOdd function *(continued)*

```
43        else
44           generateOdd(n1+1, n2);
45     }
46     return 0;
47 } // generateOdd
```

Output

```
Enter starting number: 0
Enter ending number: 44
 1  3  5  7  9  11  13  15  17  19  21  23  25  27  29  31  33  35  37  39  41  43
```

The fact that the generateOdd function has two separate active calls to itself is the reason why it is considered to be multiple recursion. This should not be confused with two statements 41 and 46 in **Program 14-7**. Notice there are two references of the function to itself in generateOddorEven. However, only one call to itself will be active through the execution of the program.

Program 14-7 | GenerateOddorEven function

```
1   /* This program prints odd numbers sequence within
2      a range of two specified numbers.
3      Written by:
4      Date:
5   */
6   #include <stdio.h>
7
8   //  Function Declaration
9   void generateOddorEven (int n1, int n2);
10
11  int main (void)
12  {
13  //  Local Declarations
14     int num1, num2;
15
16  //  Statements
17     printf("Enter starting number: ");
18     scanf ("%d", &num1);
19     printf("Enter ending number: ");
20     scanf ("%d", &num2);
21     generateOddorEven(num1, num2);
22
```

(continue)

Program 14-7 GenerateOddorEven function *(continued)*

```
23        return 0;
24  }    // main
25
26
27  /* Generate a series of odd or even sequence numbers that
28     do not exceed the passed integer number.
29  */
30  void generateOddorEven (int n1, int n2)
31  {
32
33      // Statements
34      if (n1 >= n2)
35         return;
36      else
37      {
38         if(n1%2==1)
39         {
40             printf("%d ", n1);
41             generateOddorEven(n1+2, n2);
42         }
43         else
44         {
45             printf("%d ", n1);
46             generateOddorEven(n1+2, n2);
47         }
48      }
49      return;
50  } // generateOddorEven
```

Program 14-8 provides another example of multiple recursion—one in which a recursive function has two or more calls to itself in the same statement. The first thing you will see, in statement 39, is that there are two calls to the function itself (addNumbers). Next, function addNumbers contains two base cases statements: 34 and 36. Finally, both functions are being called at the same time, meaning that both are active until base case is met for each call.

Program 14-8 | Multiple recursion example

```
1   /* This program illustrates multiple recursion
2      where a function makes two calls to itself in
3      the same statement.
4      Written by:
5      Date:
6   */
```

(continue)

Program 14-8   Multiple recursion example *(continued)*

```c
7   #include <stdio.h>
8
9  //  Function Declaration
10 int addNumbers (int n);
11
12 int main (void)
13 {
14 //  Local Declarations
15     int num;
16     int res;
17
18 //  Statements
19     printf("Enter a number: ");
20     scanf ("%d", &num);
21
22     res = addNumbers(num);
23     printf("Result = %d\n", res);
24
25     return 0;
26 }   // main
27
28
29 // Multiple recursion function
30 int addNumbers (int n)
31 {
32    // Statements
33
34    if (n <= 0)
35       return 0;
36    else if (n <= 2)
37       return n;
38    else
39       return addNumbers(n-1) + addNumbers(n-2);
40
41 } // addNumbers
```

Output

```
Enter a number: 4
Result = 5
```

An illustration of this program is seen in **Figure 14-10**.

Figure 14-10   Multiple recursion illustration

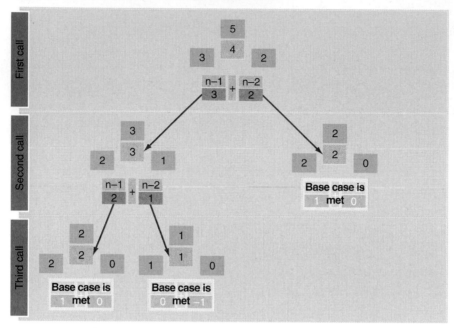

We see that the addNumbers function is called from main in statement 22 with a value 4. In statement 39, there are function calls as follows:

```
addNumbers(n-1) -> addNumbers(4-1) -> addNumbers(3)
addNumber(n-2) -> addNumber(4-2) -> addNumbers(2)
```

The result of these two calls are added and returned to the program or function. Also, we see that in the second call—addNumbers(2)—it stops and returns 2 since the base case is met, while addNumber(3) continues to call itself with addNumber(2) + addNumber(1). In the third call, the base cases for both are met to return 2 and 1, respectively.

Note that multiple recursion is not simple to trace since multiple calls in the same statement are spawned each time it is executed.

Mutual Recursion

We've come to a more complex type of recursion—mutual recursion, which occurs when two recursive functions are defined in terms of each other, as illustrated in **Figure 14-11**.

Figure 14-11 Mutual recursion illustration

```
    // printOdd Recursive function
    void printOdd(int n)◄───────────────────────────┐
    {                                                │
        printf("In Odd function = %d\n", n);         │
        if (n%2==0 || n < 0)                         │
            return;                                  │
        else                                         │
            printEven(n-1);─┐                        │
        return;             │                        │
    } // PrintEven          │                        │
                            │                        │
                            └►// printEven Recursive function
                              void printEven(int n)  │
                              {                      │
                                  printf("In Even function = %d\n", n);
                                  if (n%2==1 || n<1) │
                                      return;        │
                                  else               │
                                      printOdd(n-1);─┘
                                  return;
                              } // printEven
```

Program 14-9 shows the mutual recursion of Figure 14-11. Notice statement 34 in `printOdd` function calls recursive `printEven` function, and statement 45 in `printEven` function calls recursive `printOdd` function.

Program 14-9 | Mutual recursion example

```
 1  /* This program illustrates mutual recursion
 2      where a recursive function calls another
 3      recursive function.
 4      Written by:
 5      Date:
 6  */
 7  #include <stdio.h>
 8
 9  // Function Declaration
10  void printOdd(int n);
11  void printEven(int n);
12
13  int main (void)
14  {
15  // Local Declarations
16      int num;
17
18  // Statements
```

(continue)

Program 14-9   Mutual recursion example *(continued)*

```
19       printf("Enter a number: ");
20       scanf ("%d", &num);
21
22       printOdd(num);
23
24       return 0;
25  } // main
26
27  // printOdd Recursive function
28  void printOdd(int n)
29  {
30       printf("In Odd function = %d\n", n);
31       if (n%2==0 || n < 0)
32          return;
33       else
34          printEven(n-1);
35       return;
36  } // PrintOdd
37
38  // printEven Recursive function
39  void printEven(int n)
40  {
41       printf("In Even function = %d\n", n);
42       if (n%2==1 || n<1)
43          return;
44       else
45          printOdd(n-1);
46       return;
47  } // printEven
```

Output

```
Enter a number: 5
In Odd function = 5
In Even function = 4
In Odd function = 3
In Even function = 2
In Odd function = 1
In Even function = 0
```

Binary Recursion

Binary recursion, a form of multiple recursion, is a recursion type in which a function makes two calls to itself in the same non-base statement. **Figure 14-12** compares binary recursion and multiple recursion.

Figure 14-12   Binary and multiple recursion illustration

```
int fnBinary(int n)
{
   ...

   // base case
   if (n<=0)
      return 0;
   else
      // binary recursion - two calls
      return fnBinary(n) + fnBinary(n-1);          Two calls
                                                    itself
   ...
} // fnBinary

int fnMultiple(int n)
{
   ...

   // base case
   if (n<=0)
      return 0;
   else if (n <=2)
   // multiple recursion - two calls
      return fnMultiple(n) + fnMultiple(n-1);
   else
      // multiple recursion - three calls
      return fnMultiple(n) + fnMultiple(n-1) + fnMultiple(n-2);     Three calls
                                                                     to itself
   ...
} // fnMultiple
```

Tail Recursion

Tail recursion is a recursion type in which the reference call is the last statement in the function. In other words, the recursive call is at the end of the function, and no other statements are executed after it. **Figure 14-13** shows an illustration of tail recursion. It should be noted that many professional programmers prefer to code recursive functions as tail recursion for code readability, simplicity, and memory efficiency (it consumes fewer memory stacks).

Figure 14-13   Tail recursion illustration

```
int fnTail(int n)
{
   ...

   // base case
   if (n<=0)
      return 0;
   else
      // last statement
      return fnTail(n-1) + n;          Last call statement
                                        in the functions
} // fnTail
```

Nested Recursion

Now we look at another complex type of recursion: nested recursion. A recursive function is of the nested recursion type if one of the arguments in the function parameter is a call to itself. The most common example of nested recursion is the Wilhelm Ackermann function, which is defined as follows:

$$A(m, n) = \begin{cases} n + 1 & \text{if } m = 0 \\ A(m - 1, 1) & \text{if } m > 0 \text{ and } n = 0 \\ A(m - 1, A(m, n - 1)) & \text{if } m > 0 \text{ and } n > 0 \end{cases}$$

The Ackermann function is typically used for recursion performance measurement and optimization; however, there are not many day-to-day uses for this function outside the mathematics field. **Program 14-10** is a code representation of this function. Statement 36 shows that one of the parameters is a call to the function itself fnNested.

Program 14-10 | Nested recursion example of Ackermann function

```
1   /* This program illustrates nested recursion
2       using the Ackermann function.
3       Written by:
4       Date:
5   */
6   #include <stdio.h>
7
8   //  Function Declaration
9   int fnNested(int m, int n);
10
11  int main (void)
12  {
13  // Local Declarations
14      int m, n;
15      int res;
16
17  // Statements
18      printf("Enter a value for m: ");
19      scanf ("%d", &m);
20      printf("Enter a value for n: ");
21      scanf ("%d", &n);
22
23      res = fnNested(m, n);
24      printf("Result = %d", res);
25      return 0;
26  } // main
27
28  int fnNested(int m, int n)
29  {
```

(continue)

Program 14-10   Nested recursion example of Ackermann function *(continued)*

```
30    // base case
31    if (m == 0)
32        return n+1;
33    else if (m > 0 && n == 0)
34        return fnNested(m-1, 1);
35    else
36        return fnNested(m-1, fnNested(m, n-1));
37
38 } // fnNested
```

Output

```
Enter a value for m: 3
Enter a value for n: 5
Result = 253
```

Indirect Recursion

Simply stated, indirect recursion is a chain recursion, which means that function fnRecursion1 calls function fnRecusrion2, and function fnRecusrion3 calls function fnRecursion1, as shown in **Figure 14-14** and **Program 14-11**. A slight distinction of indirect recursion from mutual recursion is that the latter has function A calling function B and function B calling function A.

Figure 14-14   Indirect recursion illustration

```
int fnRecursion1(int n1)
{
   if (n1 < 0)
      return 0;
   else
      return (fnRecursion2(n1-1) + n1);
} // fnRecursion1

    int fnRecursion2(int n2)
    {
       if (n2 < 0)
          return 0;
       else
          return (fnRecursion3(n2-1) + n2);
    } // fnRecursion2

        int fnRecursion3(int n3)
        {
           if (n3 < 0)
              return 0;
           else
              return (fnRecursion1(n3-1) + n3);
        } // fnRecursion3
```

Program 14-11 | Indirect recursion example

```c
1   /* This program illustrates indirect recursion
2      using the Ackermann function.
3      Written by:
4      Date:
5   */
6   #include <stdio.h>
7
8   //  Function Declaration
9   int fnRecursion1(int n1);
10  int fnRecursion2(int n2);
11  int fnRecursion3(int n3);
12
13  int main (void)
14  {
15  // Local Declarations
16     int num;
17     int res;
18
19  // Statements
20     printf("Enter a number: ");
21     scanf ("%d", &num);
22
23     res = fnRecursion1(num);
24     printf("Result = %d", res);
25     return 0;
26  } // main
27
28  int fnRecursion1(int n1)
29  {
30     if (n1 < 0)
31        return 0;
32     else
33        return (fnRecursion2(n1-1) + n1);
34  } // fnRecursion1
35
36  int fnRecursion2(int n2)
37  {
38     if (n2 < 0)
39        return 0;
40     else
41        return (fnRecursion3(n2-1) + n2);
```

(continue)

Program 14-11   Indirect recursion example *(continued)*

```
42 } // fnRecursion2
43
44 int fnRecursion3(int n3)
45 {
46    if (n3 < 0)
47        return 0;
48    else
49        return (fnRecursion1(n3-1) + n3);
50 } // fnRecursion3
```

Output

```
Enter a number: 6
Result = 21
```

We have examined different types of recursion commonly used in programming. However, we need to use caution when writing recursive functions that are mutual, multiple, nested, or indirect as they may lead to circular dependencies, creating a domino effect of infinite recursions and causing you to run out of memory.

General Recursion

General recursion is a recursive function that is not easily converted to a function using iteration construct. It can also refer to a case in which the complexity of the recursion algorithm makes it difficult to translate it into a nonrecursive algorithm. Usually, most tail recursion type functions can be converted to functions employing iteration technique (loops). An example of such a general recursion type is the Ackermann function as stated below:

$$A(m, n) = \begin{cases} n + 1 & \text{if } m = 0 \\ A(m - 1, 1) & \text{if } m > 0 \text{ and } n = 0 \\ A(m - 1, 1), A(m, n - 1) & \text{if } m > 0 \text{ and } n > 0 \end{cases}$$

14.4 Recursive Sorting Algorithms

Previously, we introduced sorting algorithms such as bubble sort, insertion sort, and others using iteration constructions with `for` and `while` loops. In this section, we will revisit and compare sorting algorithms using recursion.

Selection Sort

Recall that selection works by repeatedly selecting the smallest (ascending) or largest (descending) element in the list and moving it to the beginning of the list. **Program 14-12** provides an example of a selection sort using both an iterative and recursive approach.

Program 14-12 | Selection sort using iteration and recursion

```
1  /* This program illustrates selection sort
2       using iteration and recursion methods.
3       Written by:
4       Date:
5  */
6  #include <stdio.h>
7
8  // Function Declaration
9  void printArray(int a[], int cnt);
10 void itrSelectionSort(int a[], int cnt);
11 int minPos(int a[], int i, int j);
12 void recSelectionSort(int a[], int cnt, int pos);
13
14 int main (void)
15 {
16 // Local Declarations
17    int arr1[] = { 34, 88, 5, 56, 33, 44, 77, 2, 18, 48 };
18    int arr2[] = { 34, 88, 5, 56, 33, 44, 77, 2, 18, 48 };
19
20 // Statements
21    printf("Array before sorting:\n");
22    printArray(arr1, 10);
23
24    itrSelectionSort(arr1, 10);
25    printf("\nArray after sorting using iterative selection sort:\n");
26    printArray(arr1, 10);
27
28    recSelectionSort(arr2, 10, 0);
29    printf("\nArray after sorting using recursive selection sort:\n");
30    printArray(arr2, 10);
31
32    return 0;
33 } // main
34
35 void printArray(int a[], int cnt)
36 {
37    int i;
38    for(i=0; i<cnt; i++)
39       printf("%d ", a[i]);
40
41 } // printArray
42
```

(continue)

Program 14-12   Selection sort using iteration and recursion *(continued)*

```
43 // Selection sort using iteration approach
44 void itrSelectionSort(int a[], int cnt)
45 {
46    int i, j;
47    int temp, min;
48
49    for (i=0; i<cnt-1; i++)
50    {
51       min = i;
52
53       for (j=i+1; j<cnt; j++)
54          if (a[j] < a[min])
55             min = j;
56
57       if(min !=i)
58       {
59          temp  = a[min];
60          a[min] = a[i];
61          a[i] = temp;
62       }
63    }
64 } // itrSelectionSort
65
66 // Selection sort using recursive approach
67 void recSelectionSort(int a[], int cnt, int pos)
68 {
69    int min, temp;
70
71    if (pos == cnt)
72       return;
73
74    min = minPos(a, pos, cnt-1);
75
76    if (min != pos)
77    {
78       temp  = a[min];
79       a[min] = a[pos];
80       a[pos] = temp;
81    }
82
83    recSelectionSort(a, cnt, pos + 1);
84 } // recSelectionSort
85
86 // finding minimum pos value recursively
```

(continue)

Program 14-12   Selection sort using iteration and recursion *(continued)*

```
87 int minPos(int a[], int i, int j)
88 {
89    int min;
90
91    if (i == j)
92       return i;
93
94    min = minPos(a, i + 1, j);
95
96    return ( a[i] < a[min]) ? i : min;
97 } // minPos
```

Output

```
Array before sorting:
34 88 5 56 33 44 77 2 18 48
Array after sorting using iterative selection sort:
2 5 18 33 34 44 48 56 77 88
Array after sorting using recursive selection sort:
2 5 18 33 34 44 48 56 77 88
```

Figure 14-15 shows the iteration and recursion functions of selection sort side by side.

Merge Sort

Have you asked yourself how many sort algorithms are out there? There are at least forty different sorting algorithms, with some that may vary slightly from another algorithm and some that are totally different. Some of these sorting algorithms include heap, radix, bucket, shell, shake, merge, and quick. Here, we will present merge sort, which is based on a divide-and-conquer strategy created by John Von Neumann. Merge sort works like this:

> **Step 1:** If the list contains only one item, the list is already sorted and is complete.

> **Step 2:** Keep dividing the list into two until each sublist is no longer divisible (has one item).

> **Step 3:** Merge the smaller sublist with the larger sublist or vice versa based on ascending or descending order.

Figure 14-16 illustrates the merge sort steps for a list of 5 numbers.

Figure 14-15 Selection sort using iteration and recursion

// Selection sort using Iteration	// Selection sort using recursive
``void itrSelectionSort(int a[], int cnt)
{
    int i, j;
    int temp, min;

    for (i=0; i<cnt-1; i++)
    {
        min = i;
``` | ```void recSelectionSort(int a[], int cnt,
int pos)
{
    int min, temp;
    if (pos == cnt)   ← Base case
        return;
``` |
| ```   for (j=i+1; j<cnt; j++)
            if (a[j] < a[min])
                min = j;
``` | ```   min = minPos(a, pos, cnt-1);   ← Calling a recursive
                                    function minPos
``` |
| ```   if(min !=i)
        {
            temp = a[min];
            a[min] = a[i];
            a[i]   = temp;
        }
    }
} // itrSelectionSort
``` | ```   if (i != pos)
    {
        temp = a[min];   ← Exchanging places
        a[min] = a[pos];
        a[pos] = temp;
    }

    recSelectionSort(a, cnt, pos + 1);   ← Function
                                          recSelectionSort
                                          calling itself
} // recSelectionSort
``` |

Figure 14-16 Merge sort iteration and recursion

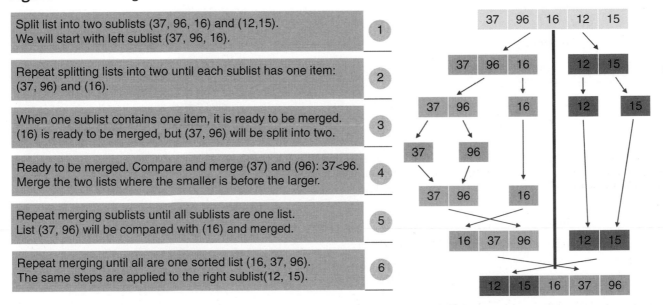

Split list into two sublists (37, 96, 16) and (12,15).
We will start with left sublist (37, 96, 16). **1**

Repeat splitting lists into two until each sublist has one item:
(37, 96) and (16). **2**

When one sublist contains one item, it is ready to be merged.
(16) is ready to be merged, but (37, 96) will be split into two. **3**

Ready to be merged. Compare and merge (37) and (96): 37<96.
Merge the two lists where the smaller is before the larger. **4**

Repeat merging sublists until all sublists are one list.
List (37, 96) will be compared with (16) and merged. **5**

Repeat merging until all are one sorted list (16, 37, 96).
The same steps are applied to the right sublist(12, 15). **6**

Now, let's translate merge sort steps into C code using recursion, as shown **Program 14-13**.

Program 14-13 | Merge sort using recursion

```
1   /* This program illustrates merge sort
2       using recursion method.
3       Written by:
4       Date:
5   */
6   #include <stdio.h>
7
8   // Function Declaration
9   void printArray(int a[], int cnt);
10  void recMergeSort(int a[],  int l, int r);
11  void mergeArray(int a[],int l1,int r1,int l2,int r2);
12
13  int main (void)
14  {
15  // Local Declarations
16      int temp[10];
17      int arr[] = { 34, 88, 5, 56, 33, 44, 77, 2, 18, 48 };
18
19  // Statements
20      printf("\nArray before sorting:\n");
21      printArray(arr, 10);
22
23      recMergeSort(arr, 0, 9);
24      printf("\nArray after sorting using recursive merge sort:\n");
25      printArray(arr, 10);
26
27      return 0;
28  } // main
29
30  // Print out array elements
31  void printArray(int a[], int cnt)
32  {
33      int i;
34      for(i=0; i<cnt; i++)
35          printf("%d ", a[i]);
36  } // printArray
37
38  // Merge sort using recursive approach
39  void recMergeSort(int a[], int l, int r)
40  {
```

(continue)

Program 14-13 Merge sort using recursion *(continued)*

```
41    int mid;
42
43    if (l>=r)
44    return;
45
46    mid = (l + r) / 2;
47
48    //sort left half of the array
49    recMergeSort(a, l, mid);
50    //sort right half of the array
51    recMergeSort(a, mid+1, r);
52    //mergeArray(a, l, mid, r);
53    mergeArray(a, l, mid, mid+1, r);
54
55 } // recMergeSort
56
57 void mergeArray(int a[],int l1,int r1,int l2,int r2)
58 {
59    int temp[10];
60    int l,r,k;
61
62    l=l1;
63    r=l2;
64    k=0;
65
66    while(l<=r1 && r<=r2)
67    {
68       if(a[l]<a[r])
69          temp[k++] = a[l++];
70       else
71          temp[k++] = a[r++];
72    }
73
74    while(l<=r1)
75       temp[k++] = a[l++];
76
77    while(r<=r2)
78       temp[k++] = a[r++];
79
80    for(l=l1,r=0; l<=r2; l++,r++)
81       a[l] = temp[r];
82 } // mergeArray
```

Quick Sort

Another popular sort algorithm, which is named for what it does, the quick sort algorithm was developed by computer scientist Tony Hoare. Like merge sort, quick sort is based on a divide-and-conquer approach, but it is more efficient with space as it does not require an extra subarray for merging. Quick sort efficiency is O(n Log n). For example, a list of 200 elements will be sorted in O(200 log 200) equaling a 460 average case scenario and an O($n2$) 40000 worst case.

Here are the quick sort algorithm steps:

1. Select a pivot value from the list (the pivot can be the first, last, or any random position in the list).

2. Partition the list using the following steps:

   a. Place two pointers—one at the left end of the list called "Left" and the other at the right end called "Right."

   b. Move the element from the left to the right until it reaches a value larger than or equal to the pivot value.

   c. Move element from the right to the left until it reaches the left bound or a value less than the pivot.

   d. Swap elements of Left and Right, and repeat steps b and c until the Right pointer crosses the Left pointer.

   e. Swap pivot with the Right pointer position.

3. Repeat Step 2 until there is either one element or zero elements in the partition.

Figure 14-17 depicts the partitioning steps outlined above. The quick sort algorithm is presented in **Program 14-14**.

Figure 14-17   Quick sort partitioning steps

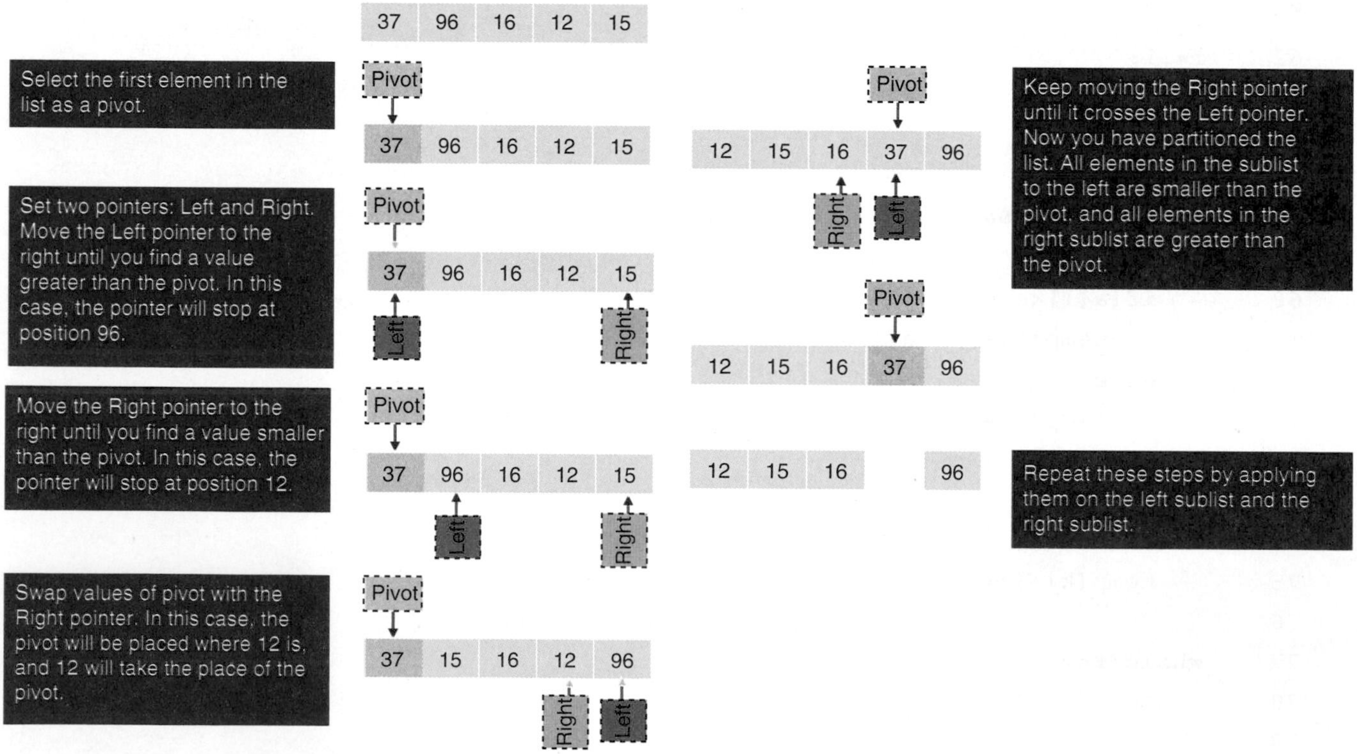

Program 14-14 | Quick sort program

```c
1   /* This program illustrates a quick sort
2      recursion method.
3      Written by:
4      Date:
5   */
6   #include <stdio.h>
7
8   // Function Declaration
9   void printArray(int a[], int cnt);
10  void recQuickSort(int a[], int left, int right);
11
12  int main (void)
13  {
14  // Local Declarations
15
16      int arr[] = { 34, 88, 5, 56, 33, 44, 77, 2, 18, 48 };
17
18  // Statements
19      printf("\nArray before sorting:\n");
20      printArray(arr, 10);
21
22      recQuickSort(arr, 0, 9);
23      printf("\nArray after sorting using recursive Quick sort:\n");
24      printArray(arr, 10);
25
26      return 0;
27  } // main
28
29  // Print out array elements
30  void printArray(int a[], int cnt)
31  {
32      int i;
33      for(i=0; i<cnt; i++)
34          printf("%d ", a[i]);
35  } // printArray
36
37  // Quick sort using recursive approach
38  void recQuickSort(int a[], int left, int right)
```

(continue)

Program 14-14 Quick sort program *(continued)*

```
39 {
40     int i, j, pivot, temp;
41
42     //Partition Array
43     if(left < right)
44     {
45        i     = left;
46        j     = right;
47       pivot = left;
48
49       while(i<j)
50       {
51          while(a[i]<=a[pivot] && i<right)
52             i++;
53
54          while(a[j]>a[pivot])
55             j--;
56
57          if(i<j)
58          {
59             temp = a[i];
60             a[i] = a[j];
61             a[j] = temp;
62          }
63       }
64
65       temp     = a[pivot];
66       a[pivot] = a[j];
67       a[j] = temp;
68
69       //Sort Left sub-array
70       recQuickSort(a, left, j-1);
71
72       //Sort Left sub-array
73       recQuickSort(a, j+1, right);
74    }
75
76 } // recQuickSort
```

14.5 Recursive Searching Algorithms

Other uses of recursion are simple and powerful as searching algorithms. In this section, we will present two searching techniques, sequential search and binary search.

Sequential Search

Sequential search is the simplest form of search algorithm, and it is very inefficient for large lists. The steps of a sequential search are as follows:

1. Compare the target element with each element in the array, starting from the first element in the array.

2. If the target and the element match, then return *True*, indicating it is found.

3. If not found, repeat steps 1 and 2 by comparing the target with the next element in the array until there are no more elements in the tree.

Program 14-15 is a recursive sequential search.

> **Program 14-15** | Sequential search function using recursion

```
1   /* Recursive Sequential Search
2      returns
3      -1 if NOT FOUND
4      position in array if FOUND
5   */
6   int recSequentialSearch(int a[], int first, int last, int target)
7   {
8       if (last < first)
9           return -1;
10      if (a[first] == target)
11          return first;
12      if (a[last] == target)
13          return last;
14      return recSequentialSearch(a, first + 1, last - 1, target);
15  } //recSequentialSearch
```

Binary Search

Binary search is a mechanism used to determine if an element is in a list or not. As you already know, the list must be ordered prior to searching. In **Program 14-16**, we have written the binary search function using iteration. The same binary search algorithm using recursion is presented in **Program 14-17**.

Program 14-16 | Binary search function using iteration

```
 1  /* ============= binarySearch ==============
 2     Search an ordered list using binary search.
 3     Pre list must contain at least one element.
 4     End is index to the largest element in list.
 5     Target is the value of the element being sought.
 6     locn is address for located target index.
 7     Post Found: locn = index to target element
 8     return 1 (found)
 9     Not Found: locn = element below or above target
10     return 0 (not found)
11  */
12  bool binarySearch (int list[], int end, int target, int* locn)
13  {
14  // Local Declarations
15     int first;
16     int mid;
17     int last;
18
19  // Statements
20     first = 0;
21     last = end;
22     while (first <= last)
23     {
24        mid = (first + last) / 2;
25        if (target > list[mid])
26           // look in upper half
27           first = mid + 1;
28        else if (target < list[mid])
29           // look in lower half
30           last = mid - 1;
31        else
32           // found equal: force exit
33           first = last + 1;
34     } // end while
35
36     *locn = mid;
37
38     return target == list[mid];
39  } // binarySearch
```

| **Program 14-17** | Binary search function using recursion |

```
1   /* ============= binarySearch =============
2      Search an ordered list using binary search.
3      The function returns
4      if Found: location
5      if Not Found: -1
6   */
7   int recBinarySearch(int list[], int first, int last, int target)
8   {
9      int mid;
10
11     if (last >= first)
12     {
13        mid = first + (last - first)/2;
14
15        if (list[mid] == target)
16           return mid;
17
18        if (list[mid] > target)
19           return recBinarySearch(list, first, mid-1, target);
20
21        return recBinarySearch(list, mid+1, last, target);
22     }
23
24     return -1;
25  } // recBinarySearch
```

14.6 Recursive Backtracking

You've probably played games such as chess and Scrabble, or tried your hand at solving crosswords, mazes, or sudoku puzzles. If so, you have likely applied a backtracking algorithm recursively without even realizing it. People tend to solve these types of puzzles by either incrementally building a solution and/or eliminating solutions that are not successful. Recursive backtracking, also known as heuristics, is exactly that. It is the idea of solving a problem by incrementally applying steps that are successful while removing steps that fail. Backtracking is a technique of searching for a solution. When applying the backtracking recursion technique, we use the following steps:

1. Explore the different choices to perform the next step.

2. For each valid choice, we apply step 1 recursively.

3. Decide what to do when no more choices are available.

To develop a better understanding of backtracking, let's look at a game of sudoku, which has the following parameters and rules:

> A sudoku board is a nine-by-nine matrix.

> Each cell of the board is also a three-by-three matrix called a mini matrix.

> Depending on the difficulty of the game, the board may have numbers prefilled in some of the cells (fewer prefilled numbers translates to a higher level of difficulty).

> The goal of the game is to fill all the empty cells with numbers from 1 to 9.

> Numbers cannot be repeated in any of the rows, columns, and mini matrices.

Figure 14-18 shows an example of a sudoku game in process.

Figure 14-18   Sudoku game example

	1	2	3	4	5	6	7	8	9
1	1			9		4		8	2
2		5	2	6	8		3		
3	8	6	4	2			9	1	
4		1			4	9	8		6
5	4	9	8	3			7		1
6	6		7		1			9	3
7		8	6		3	5	2		9
8	5		9			2	1	3	
9		3		4	9	7			8

Let's see how we could solve this game by using the backtracking technique. We will focus on the left-top matrix in the board.

1. Explore the different options for performing the next step: Fill out row 2, column 1—that is, cell (2,1). Our choices are 3, 7, or 9.

2. For each valid choice, we apply step 1 recursively:

   a. Choice 3 is not possible because a 3 already appears in another cell in the same row (2,7).

   b. Choice 7 is a viable solution; however, if we place a 7 in cell (2,1), a 9 would have to be placed in either cell (1,2) or cell (1,3), which is not possible since a 9 already appears in the same row in cell (1,4).

   c. Choice 9 is the only solution since it does not violate the rules of the game.

3. Decide what to do when no more choices are available: Place 9 in cell (2,1).

We repeat these steps until the full board is solved. Notice that our thinking to resolve this game involves searching for all possible solutions and then backtracking to a solution that is the best fit.

Here is another example of backtracking recursion. Consider a subset sum where we have a list of numbers and we need to find the subset of numbers which, when summed, equal a given number, also known as the target sum. See **Figure 14-19** for an illustration. Note that in Figure 14-19, the target sum is 20.

Figure 14-19   Subset sum example

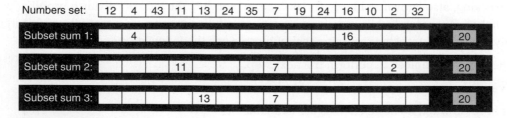

Now, let's put it into steps:

1. Start with an empty set and with the first next element in the set.

2. Sum all elements in the subset. Stop if the subset is equal to the target sum.

3. If the subset is not equal to the target sum or if all elements in the list are exhausted, then perform backtracking through the subset until a solution is found.

4. If the subset sum is less than the target sum, then repeat step 2.

5. If all elements in the set have been tried and no solution was found, and if no more backtracking is possible, then stop without a solution.

Program 14-18 is a subset sum example using the recursive `generateSubsetSum` function.

Program 14-18 | Recursive subset sum example

```
1   /* This program illustrates subset sum
2      using recursion method.
3      Written by:
4      Date:
5   */
6
7   #include <stdio.h>
8   #include <stdlib.h>
9
10  #define SIZE 14
11
12  // Function Declaration
13  void printArray(int a[], int size, int flag);
14  void generateSubsetSum(int a[], int temp[], int size,
15                         int sumTarget, int sum,
16                         int temp_size, int subsets);
17
18  int main(void)
19  {
20  // Local Declarations
21     int arr[] = {12, 4, 43, 11, 13, 24, 35,
22                  7, 19, 24, 16, 10, 2, 32};
23     int temp[SIZE];
24     int sumTarget;
25
26  // Statements
27     printf("\nElements in the list:\n");
28     printArray(arr, SIZE, 0);
29
30     printf("Enter a sum value target: ");
31     scanf("%d", &sumTarget);
32
33     generateSubsetSum(arr, temp, SIZE, sumTarget, 0, 0, 0);
34
35     return 0;
36  } // main
37
```

(continue)

Program 14-18   Recursive subset sum example *(continued)*

```
38 // Generate subset sums recursively
39 void generateSubsetSum(int a[], int temp[], int size,
40                        int target_sum, int sum,
41                        int temp_size, int subsets
42                        )
43 {
44     if(target_sum == sum)
45     {
46         // print array when subset sum is found
47         printArray(temp, temp_size, 1);
48         // keep searching for other subset sums
49         generateSubsetSum(a, temp, size, target_sum,
50                         sum - a[subsets], temp_size, subsets + 1);
51         return;
52     }
53     else
54         for(int i = subsets; i < size; i++)
55         {
56             temp[temp_size] = a[i];
57             // keep searching for other subset sums
58             generateSubsetSum(a, temp, size, target_sum,
59                         sum + a[i], temp_size + 1, i + 1);
60         }
61 } // generateSubsetSum
62
63 // Print out array elements
64 void printArray(int a[], int size, int flag)
65 {
66     if (flag == 1)
67         printf("Subset Sum: ");
68
69     for(int i=0; i<size; i++)
70         printf("%d ", a[i]);
71     printf("\n");
72 } // printArray
```

Output

```
Elements in the list:
12 4 43 11 13 24 35 7 19 24 16 10 2 32
Enter a sum value target: 20
Subset Sum: 4 16
Subset Sum: 11 7 2
Subset Sum: 13 7
```

Backtracking recursion is useful and efficient because it does not involve processing choices that are not successful.

Programming Example: Recursion

Practice makes perfect. Here we present more examples universally taught in computer programming where thinking in terms of recursion is clearly the appropriate approach for solving a problem.

Fibonacci Numbers

Let's revisit the most popular and classic example of recursion: a function that generates Fibonacci numbers, a series in which each number is the sum of the previous two numbers (see **Figure 14-20**).

Figure 14-20   Fibonacci numbers

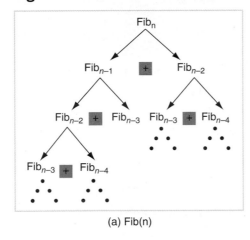 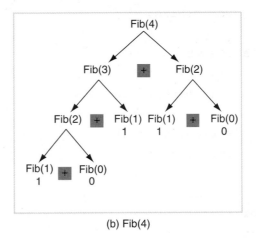

(a) Fib(n)   (b) Fib(4)

The first few numbers in the Fibonacci series are as follows:

```
0, 1, 1, 2, 3, 5, 8, 13, 21, 34
```

To start the series, however, we need to know the first two numbers. As you can see from the above series, they are 0 and 1. Since we are discussing recursion, you should recognize these two numbers as the base cases.

We can generalize the Fibonacci series as follows:

Given:

```
Fibonacci₀ = 0
Fibonacci₁ = 1
```
$$Fibonacci_0 = 0$$
$$Fibonacci_1 = 1$$

Then:

$$Fibonacci_n = Fibonacci_{n-1} + Fibonacci_{n-2}$$

Figure 14-20 shows the generalization of $Fibonacci_4$. Figure 14-20 (a) shows the components of $Fibonacci_4$ using a general notation. Figure 14-20 (b) shows the components as they would be called to generate the numbers in the series.

To determine $Fibonacci_4$ we can start at 0 and move up until we have the number, or we can start at $Fibonacci_4$ and move down to zero. The first technique is used in the iterative solution; the second is used in the recursive solution, which is shown in **Program 14-19**.

Program 14-19 | Recursive Fibonacci

```
 1  /* This program prints out a Fibonacci series.
 2     Written by:
 3     Date:
 4  */
 5  #include <stdio.h>
 6
 7  // Function Declaration
 8  long fib (long num);
 9
10  int main (void)
11  {
12  // Local Declarations
13     int seriesSize;
14
15  // Statements
16     printf("This program prints a Fibonacci series.\n");
17     printf("How many numbers do you want? ");
18     scanf ("%d", &seriesSize);
19     if (seriesSize < 2)
20     seriesSize = 2;
21
22     printf("First %d Fibonacci numbers: \n", seriesSize);
23     for (int looper =0; looper < seriesSize; looper++)
24     {
25        if (looper % 5)
26           printf(", %8ld", fib(looper));
27        else
28           printf("\n%8ld", fib(looper));
29     }
30     printf("\n");
31     return 0;
32  } // main
33
34  /* ================= fib ===================
35     Calculates the nth Fibonacci number.
36     Pre num identifies Fibonacci number.
37     Post returns nth Fibonacci number.
38  */
39  long fib (long num)
40  {
41  // Statements
```

(continue)

Program 14-19   Recursive Fibonacci *(continued)*

```
42    if (num == 0 || num == 1)
43        // Base Case
44        return num;
45
46    return (fib (num - 1) + fib (num - 2));
47 } // fib
```

Output

```
This program prints a Fibonacci series.
How many numbers do you want? 30
First 30 Fibonacci numbers:

      0,         1,         1,         2,         3
      5,         8,        13,        21,        34
     55,        89,       144,       233,       377
    610,       987,      1597,      2584,      4181
   6765,     10946,     17711,     28657,     46368
  75025,    121393,    196418,    317811,    514229
```

Compare `fib` in Program 14-19 with the solution in Figure 14-20. To determine the fourth number in the series, we call `fib` with `num` set to 4. To determine the answer requires that `fib` be called recursively eight times, as shown in Figure 14-20, which, with the original call, gives us a total of nine calls.

This sounds reasonable. How many calls does it take to determine Fibonacci$_5$? The answer is 15 (as shown in **Table 14-2**). As you can see from Table 14-2, the number of calls goes up quickly as we increase the size of the Fibonacci number we are calculating.

Table 14-2   Fibonacci run time

NUMBER	CALLS	NUMBER	CALLS
1	1	11	287
2	3	12	465
3	5	13	753
4	9	14	1,219
5	15	15	1,973
6	25	20	21,891
7	41	25	242,785
8	67	30	2,692,573
9	109	35	29,860,703
10	177	40	331,160,281

Table 14-2 leads us to the conclusion that a recursive solution to calculate Fibonacci numbers is not realistic.

You should be aware of the two major limitations of recursion. First, recursive solutions may involve extensive overhead because they use function calls. Second, each time you make a call, you use up some of your memory allocation. If the recursion is deep—that is, if the program has a large number of recursive calls—then you may run out of memory. Both the factorial and Fibonacci numbers solutions are better developed iteratively.

Does this mean that iterative solutions are always better than recursive functions? The answer is definitely no. Many algorithms are easier to implement recursively and are efficient. When you study data structures, you will study many of them. Unfortunately, most of those algorithms require data structures beyond the scope of this text.

The Towers of Hanoi

One classic recursion problem, the Towers of Hanoi, is relatively easy to follow, efficient, and uses no complex data structures. Let's look at it.

According to legend, the monks in a remote mountain monastery knew how to predict when the world would end. They had a set of three diamond needles. Stacked on the first diamond needle were 64 gold disks of decreasing size. The monks moved one disk to another needle each hour, subject to the following rules:

1. Only one disk could be moved at a time.

2. A larger disk must never be stacked above a smaller one.

3. One and only one auxiliary needle could be used for the intermediate storage of disks.

The legend said that when all 64 disks had been transferred to the destination needle, the stars would be extinguished and the world would end. Today we know that we need to have $2^{64} - 1$ moves to do this task. **Figure 14-21** shows the Towers of Hanoi with only three disks.

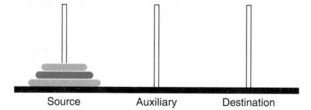

Figure 14-21 Towers of Hanoi—start position

This problem is interesting for two reasons. First, the recursive solution is much easier to code than the iterative solution would be. This is often the case with good recursive solutions. Second, its solution pattern differs from the simple examples we have been discussing. As you study the Towers of Hanoi solution, note that after each base case, we return to a decomposition of the general case for several steps. In other words, the problem is divided into several subproblems, each of which has a base case: moving one disk.

To solve this problem, we must study the moves to see if we can find a pattern. We will use only three disks because we do not want the world to end! First, imagine that we have only one disk to move. This very simple case involves only one step as shown in Case 1.

Case 1:

> Move one disk from source to destination needle.

Now imagine that we have to move two disks. First, the top disk is moved to the auxiliary needle. Then the second disk is moved to the destination. Finally, the first disk is moved to the top of the second disk on the destination. These three steps are shown in Case 2.

Case 2:

> Move one disk to auxiliary needle.

> Move one disk to destination needle.

> Move one disk from auxiliary to destination needle.

Figure 14-22 traces the steps for two disks.

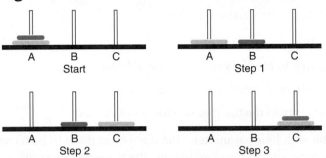

Figure 14-22   Towers of Hanoi solution for two disks

We are now ready to study the case for three disks. Its solution is shown in **Figure 14-23**.

Figure 14-23   Towers of Hanoi solution for three disks

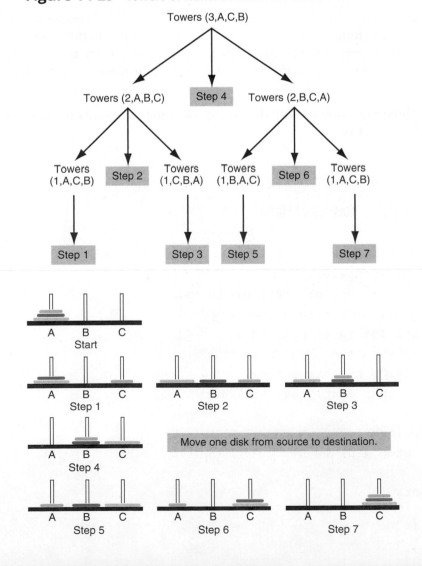

The first three steps move the top two disks from the source to the auxiliary needle. (To see how to do this, refer to Case 2.) In step 4 in Figure 14-23, we move the bottom disk to the destination. We now have one disk in place. This is an example of Case 1. It then takes three more steps to move the two disks on the auxiliary needle to the destination. These steps are shown in Case 3.

Case 3:

> Move two disks from source to auxiliary needle.

> Move one disk from source to destination needle.

> Move two disks from auxiliary to destination needle.

We are now ready to generalize the problem:

1. Move $n - 1$ disks from source to auxiliary needle. (General case)

2. Move one disk from source to destination needle. (Base case)

3. Move $n - 1$ disks from auxiliary to destination needle. (General case)

Our solution requires a function with four parameters: the number of disks to be moved, the source needle, the destination needle, and the auxiliary needle. Using pseudocode, the three moves in the generalization shown above are:

1. Call Towers (n − 1, source, auxiliary, destination)

2. Move one disk from source to destination

3. Call Towers (n − 1, auxiliary, destination, source)

Study the third step carefully. After we complete the move of the first disk, the remaining disks are on the auxiliary needle. We need to move them from the auxiliary needle to the destination. In this case, the original source needle becomes the auxiliary needle. Remember that the positions of the parameters in the called function are source, destination, and auxiliary. The calling function must remember which of the three needles is the source and which is the destination for each call.

We can now put these three calls together with the appropriate print statements to show the moves. The complete function is shown in **Program 14-20**.

Program 14-20 | Towers of Hanoi

```
1   /* Move one disk from source to destination through
2      the use of recursion.
3      Pre The tower consists of n disks—source,
4      destination, & auxiliary towers given
5      Post Steps for moves printed
6   */
7   void towers (int n, char source,
8               char dest, char auxiliary)
9   {
10  // Local Declarations
11  static int step = 0;
12
13  // Statements
```

(continue)

Program 14-20   Towers of Hanoi *(continued)*

```
14        printf("Towers (%d, %c, %c, %c)\n",
15            n, source, dest, auxiliary);
16        if (n == 1)
17            printf("\t\t\t\tStep %3d: Move from %c to %c\n",
18                    ++step, source, dest);
19        else
20        {
21            towers(n - 1, source, auxiliary, dest);
22            printf("\t\t\t\tStep %3d: Move from %c to %c\n",
23                    ++step, source, dest);
24            towers(n - 1, auxiliary, dest, source);
25        } // if ... else
26        return;
27 } // towers
```

The output from Program 14-20 is shown in **Table 14-3**.

Table 14-3   Tracing of Program 14-20: Towers of Hanoi

CALLS	OUTPUT
Towers (3, A, C, B)	
Towers (2, A, B, C)	
Towers (1, A, C, B)	
	Step 1: Move from A to C
	Step 2: Move from A to B
Towers (1, C, B, A)	
	Step 3: Move from C to B
	Step 4: Move from A to C
Towers (2, B, C, A)	
Towers (1, B, A, C)	
	Step 5: Move from B to A
	Step 6: Move from B to C
Towers (1, A, C, B)	
	Step 7: Move from A to C

Scrambling a Word

Suppose you are playing Scrabble, and you have only three tiles, with the letters E, A, and T. Obviously, you want to find all the valid words that these letters can make. You need to scramble these letters to determine all three-letter words that can be made, and then decide which ones are valid. **Program 14-21** generates all the different combinations using a recursive approach.

Program 14-21 | Word scrambler example

```
1   /* This program illustrates scrambling
2      a given word.
3      Written by:
4      Date:
5   */
6
7   #include <stdio.h>
8   #include <string.h>
9
10  // Function Declaration
11  void swap(char *s1, char *s2);
12  void recScramble(char *a, int left, int right);
13
14  // Global variable keeping count of words generated
15  int cnt = 0;
16
17  int main(void)
18  {
19  // Local Declarations
20     char str[50];
21     int len;
22
23  // Statements
24     printf("\nEnter a word: ");
25     scanf("%s", str);
26
27     printf("Scrambled word %s: \n", str);
28     len = strlen(str);
29     recScramble(str, 0, len-1);
30
31     return 0;
32  } // main
33
34  // Generate subset sums recursively
35  void recScramble(char a[], int left, int right)
36  {
37     int i;
38
39     if (left == right)
40     {
41        printf("Word %d: %s\n", ++cnt, a);
```

(continue)

Program 14-21   Word scrambler example *(continued)*

```
42     }
43     else
44     {
45         for (i = left; i <= right; i++)
46         {
47             swap((a+left), (a+i));
48             recScramble(a, left+1, right);
49             swap((a+left), (a+i)); //backtrack
50         }
51     }
52 }
53
54 void swap(char *s1, char *s2)
55 {
56     char temp;
57     temp = *s1;
58     *s1 = *s2;
59     *s2 = temp;
60 }
```

Output

```
Enter a word: EAT
Scrambled word EAT:
Word 1: EAT
Word 2: ETA
Word 3: AET
Word 4: ATE
Word 5: TAE
Word 6: TEA
```

Knapsack Problem Example

Another popular example of a problem for which the solution lends itself to thinking in terms of recursion is the knapsack problem. So, what is the knapsack problem? It is the idea of filling a knapsack with items to the maximum. In other words, you would fill it with as many items it can fit while maximizing the value of the knapsack. It should be noted that no fraction of an item can be used, which means the only choice you have is to add an item to the knapsack or leave it out. This is known as the 0/1 (pronounced *zero-one*) knapsack problem. This is a discreet version of the knapsack problem. The knapsack problem is similar to the following other types of problems:

> Shortest path: Find the shortest path between two points problem.

> Bin packing: Maximize the number of objects you can fit in a bin.

> Travel sales person: Minimize the cost of a round trip to visit a number of cities based on the cost of flights and within a given budget.

All of the above scenarios represent optimization problems in which the solution is to maximize (profit) or minimize (losses) within given constraints. **Figure 14-24** illustrates the knapsack problem. Suppose we need to pack a carryon bag for travelling. We tend to fill it with items that are most important to us for the trip without exceeding the allowed weight.

Figure 14-24   Knapsack problem illustration

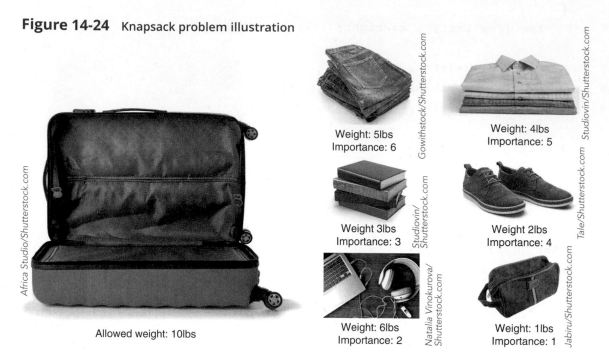

Allowed weight: 10lbs

Weight: 5lbs
Importance: 6

Weight: 4lbs
Importance: 5

Weight 3lbs
Importance: 3

Weight 2lbs
Importance: 4

Weight: 6lbs
Importance: 2

Weight: 1lbs
Importance: 1

Figure 14-25 shows a scenario in which we have three items to choose from to put in a box. Each item has an associated weight and value of significance. In this scenario, we have a box with a limited weight capacity (7lbs), and we are asked to pack any, all, or a combination of the three items: a book, a calculator, and a clock. Each item has a specific weight and monetary value, and the box size is not a limitation. What items should you put in the box to get the highest value?

Figure 14-25   Knapsack example

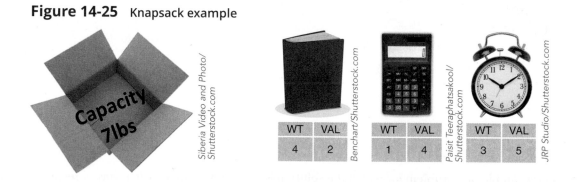

WT	VAL
4	2

WT	VAL
1	4

WT	VAL
3	5

The following is a variation of the knapsack problem called the greedy thief algorithm.

1. The greedy thief algorithm involves packing the most valuable item and moving to the next most valuable and so on, as long as you are within the weight capacity of the box.

2. The brute force algorithm involves summing the values of all combinations within the weight limit and then picking the maximum outcome.

3. Using a function based on the greedy thief algorithm but applying constraints, results in a summation of maximum value within the weight limit. This is known as the branch and bound algorithm, which involves partitioning a problem into valid solutions of the subproblems.

The following formulas are used for the branch and bound algorithm:

$\sum_{i=1}^{n} v_i \, x_i$ where n = number of items; v is the value of the item; and x is 0 or 1 (1 chosen, 0 not chosen)

$\sum_{i=1}^{n} w_i \cdot x_i \le W$ where w is the weight of the item, and W is the allowed weight capacity.

Figure 14-26 provides an example of the branch and bound algorithm.

Figure 14-26   Branch and bound algorithm illustration

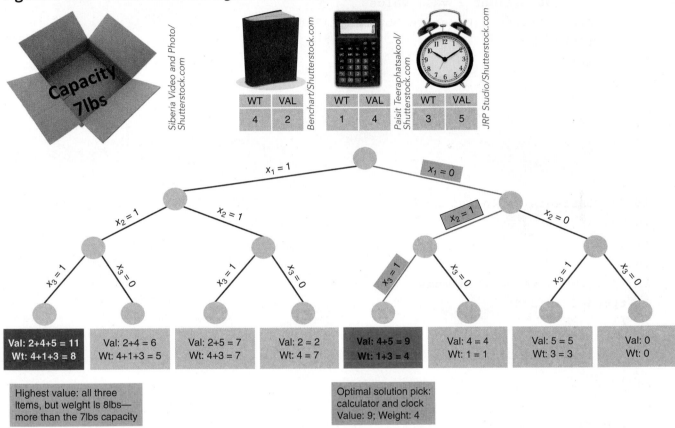

State space is a set of all solutions represented as states. To understand the state space graph, apply the following steps:

1. Start from the root.

2. Left branch, first level indicates item #1 is chosen; therefore it is 1.

3. Right branch, first level indicates item #2 is not chosen; therefore it is 0.

4. Repeat steps 2 and 3, adding a level for each item.

5. Compute all possible solutions based on formula listed above.

6. Choose the maximum (optimal) solution within the restriction formula listed above.

Note the total number of possible solutions is 2^n. In our example, we have three items, which yields 2^3. That means there are eight possible solutions. Note, that the first solution of picking all items in the box will yield the highest possible value, but it does not meet the capacity restriction of 7lbs.

Program 14-22 is the code for the knapsack problem using recursive branch and bound algorithm for the example in Figure 14-24.

Program 14-22 | Knapsack problem example

```
1   /* This program illustrates knapsack problem solution recursively
2      CNT: number of items to choose from
3      MAX: allowed capacity weight
4      ITEM: structure containing items to choose from
5          wt: weight - val: value
6      SOLN: structure to store optimal solution.
7      Written by:
8      Date:
9   */
10
11  #include <stdio.h>
12  #include <stdlib.h>
13  #include <stdbool.h>
14
15  // Constants Declarations
16  #define CNT 6
17  #define MAX 10
18
19  // structures Declarations
20  typedef struct
21  {
22      int wt;
23      int val;
24  } ITEM;
25
26  typedef struct
27  {
28      bool optimal[CNT];
29      int wt;
30      int val;
31  } SOLN;
32
33  // Function Declarations
34  void printKnapsackSolution(SOLN*);
35  void recKnapsackSolution(SOLN soln, int turn, SOLN* opt);
36
37  // Global Declarations
38  ITEM items[CNT] = { {5,6}, {4,5}, {3,3},
39                      {2,4}, {6,2}, {1,1}
40                    };
41
```

(continue)

Program 14-22   Knapsack problem example *(continued)*

```c
42 int main(void)
43 {
44 // Local Declarations
45    SOLN soln = { {0}, 0, 0 };
46
47 // Statements
48    recKnapsackSolution(soln, 0, &soln);
49    printKnapsackSolution(&soln);
50
51    return 0;
52 } // main
53
54 // Print out optimal solution
55 void printKnapsackSolution(SOLN* soln)
56 {
57    printf("Knapsack Example\n");
58    printf("================\n");
59    printf("Items to select from:\n");
60    for(int i=0; i<CNT; i++)
61       printf("Item #%d: wt=%d - value=%d\n",
62             i+1, items[i].wt, items[i].val);
63
64    printf("\n\nOptimal Solution:\n");
65    printf("-----------------\n");
66    for(int i=0; i<CNT; i++)
67       if((soln->optimal)[i])
68          printf("Item #%d: weight=%d - value=%d\n",
69                i+1, items[i].wt, items[i].val);
70
71    printf("\nTotal Weight: %d\ - Total Value: %d\n", soln->wt,
       soln->val);
72 } // printKnapsackSolution
73
74 // Recursive function to solve Knapsack problem
75 void recKnapsackSolution(SOLN soln, int turn, SOLN* opt)
76 {
77    int acc = 0;
78
79    if(turn >= CNT && soln.val > opt->val)
80       *opt = soln;
81    else
82    {
83       if(soln.wt + items[turn].wt <= MAX)
```

(continue)

Program 14-22   Knapsack problem example *(continued)*

```
84          {
85              soln.optimal[turn] = true;
86              soln.wt = soln.wt + items[turn].wt;
87              soln.val= soln.val +items[turn].val;
88
89              recKnapsackSolution(soln, turn+1, opt);
90
91              soln.optimal[turn] = false;
92              soln.wt = soln.wt - items[turn].wt;
93              soln.val= soln.val - items[turn].val;
94          }
95
96          for(int i=turn+1; i<CNT; i++)
97              acc = acc + items[i].val;
98          if(opt->val < soln.val + acc)
99              recKnapsackSolution(soln, turn+1, opt);
100     }
101 } // recKnapsackSolution
```

Output

```
Knapsack Example
================
Items to select from:
Item #1: wt=5 - value=6
Item #2: wt=4 - value=5
Item #3: wt=3 - value=3
Item #4: wt=2 - value=4
Item #5: wt=6 - value=2
Item #6: wt=1 - value=1


Optimal Solution:
-----------------
Item #1: weight=5 - value=6
Item #3: weight=3 - value=3
Item #4: weight=2 - value=4


Total Weight: 10 - Total Value: 13
```

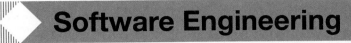

Software Engineering

Optimization is a term you will likely hear frequently in programming and other computer science disciplines. Optimization deals with efficiency and efficacy: improving the efficiency of resources (running faster with less memory, for instance) while increasing efficacy (providing more benefits with higher quality). Optimization applies to everything we do in life.

In this section, we will briefly discuss dynamic programming, which optimizes the use of recursion. Dynamic programming is a field of study that emphasizes optimization of decision-making and problem-solving. As a strategy, dynamic programming involves breaking up a problem into subproblems to derive an optimal solution. One of the key areas in computer science is optimization of recursion. Dynamic programming has two primary characteristics:

> Identifying overlapping subproblems

> Identifying optimal substructure

The first thing you might be asking yourself is where the name dynamic programming came from and who first developed it as a field of study. While working for the Department of Defense in the 1950s, a mathematician named Richard Bellman was researching decision-making optimization. When it was time to publish his work, he needed a title that was interesting, impressive, and acceptable for the times; hence, he came up with the name dynamic programming.

Let's consider the classic example presented in this chapter with Fibonacci numbers. As you saw earlier:

Given:

```
Fibonacci₀= 0
Fibonacci₁= 1
```

Then:

```
Fibonacciₙ = Fibonacciₙ₋₁ + Fibonacciₙ₋₂
```

For a given value of n = 5, the following calculations are used to generate a Fibonacci sequence of value 5:

$Fib_5 = Fib_4 + Fib_3$

and $Fib_4 = Fib_3 + Fib_2$

and $Fib_3 = Fib_2 + Fib_1$

and $Fib_2 = Fib_1 + Fib_0$

where $Fib_1 = 1$

and $Fib_0 = 0$

What we observe is that in order to solve Fib_5 we need to solve Fib_4 and Fib_3. At the same time, to solve Fib_4 we need to solve Fib_3 and Fib_2, and so we have overlapping subproblems: Fib_4, Fib_3, and Fib_2. Once any of these subproblems are solved there is no need to solve them over and over. In a plain recursive Fibonacci function, the subproblems are solved over and over again—meaning Fib_4 is solved two times, Fib_3 is solved three times, and Fib_2 is also solved three times. This can be optimized on processing time and memory resources if Fib_4, Fib_3, and Fib_2 are each solved once, and the results are stored to be used later. This would create an optimized Fibonacci function. This is an important technique when it comes to solving, for example, Fib_9 where Fib_8 is called 7 times; in an optimized recursive function, it would be called only once. This process of optimization is applicable in many recursive functions. The question here is: How do we do optimize? The answer is: by caching results, which is known as **memoization**.

Here is the original Fibonacci function as we wrote it earlier:

```
long fib (long num)
{
// Statements
   if (num == 0 || num == 1)
      // Base Case
      return num;

   return (fib (num - 1) + fib (num - 2));
} // fib
```

Using the concept of memoization, the same function would be written in the following manner:

```
long fibMemoized(int num, int result_cache[])
{
   // If results already calculated
   if (result_cache[num] >= 0)
      return result_cache[num];

   else
      result_cache[num] = fibMemoized(num - 1, result_cache) +
                                      fibMemoized(num - 2, result_cache);
   return result_cache[num];
} // fibMemoized
```

The difference between these two functions is not entirely obvious until we put them in a program that prints every time a function is called. Examine the output of **Program 14-23**.

Program 14-23 | Comparing unoptimized and optimized recursive Fibonacci functions

```
1   /* This program prints out the number of calls for
2      unoptimized and optimized Fibonacci recursive
3      functions.
4      Written by:
5      Date:
6   */
7   #include <stdio.h>
8
9   #define MAX 50
10
11  // Function Declaration
12  long fib (long num);
13  long fibMemoized(int num, int result_cache[]);
```

(continue)

Program 14-23   Comparing unoptimized and optimized recursive Fibonacci functions *(continued)*

```c
14
15 int main (void)
16 {
17 // Local Declarations
18    int looper, seriesSize;
19    int result_cache[MAX];
20
21    result_cache[0] = 0;
22    result_cache[0] = 1;
23
24 // Statements
25    printf("This program prints a Fibonacci series.\n");
26    printf("How many numbers do you want? ");
27    scanf ("%d", &seriesSize);
28    if (seriesSize < 2)
29       seriesSize = 2;
30
31 // Calling unoptimized fib function
32    printf("Unoptimized Fibonacci calls: \n", seriesSize);
33    for (looper = 0; looper < seriesSize; looper++)
34       fib(looper);
35
36 // store result_cache with -1 indicating not computed yet
37    for (looper = 2; looper <= seriesSize; looper++)
38        result_cache[looper] = -1;
39
40    printf("\n\n\n");
41
42 // Calling optimized fibMemoized function
43    printf("Optimized Fibonacci calls: \n", seriesSize);
44    for (int looper = 0; looper < seriesSize; looper++)
45       fibMemoized(looper, result_cache);
46
47    printf("\n");
48    return 0;
49 } // main
50
51 // Unoptimized Fibonacci recursive function
52 long fib (long num)
53 {
54 // Statements
```

(continue)

Program 14-23 Comparing unoptimized and optimized recursive Fibonacci functions *(continued)*

```
55      printf("calling fib(%d)\n", num);
56      if (num == 0 || num == 1)
57          // Base case
58          return num;
59
60      return (fib (num - 1) + fib (num - 2));
61  } // fib
62
63  // Optimized Fibonacci recursive function
64  long fibMemoized(int num, int result_cache[])
65  {
66      // If results already calculated
67      if (result_cache[num] >= 0)
68          return result_cache[num];
69      else
70      {
71          printf("calling fib(%d)\n", num);
72          result_cache[num] = fibMemoized(num - 1, result_cache) +
73                              fibMemoized(num - 2, result_cache);
74      }
75
76      return result_cache[num];
77  } // fibMemoized
```

Output

```
How many numbers do you want? 5
Unoptimized Fibonacci calls:
calling fib(0)
calling fib(1)                         fib(0) is called 5 times
calling fib(2)                         fib(1) is called 7 times
calling fib(1)                         fib(2) is called 4 times
calling fib(0)                         fib(3) is called 2 times
calling fib(3)                         fib(4) is called 1 time
calling fib(2)
calling fib(1)
calling fib(0)
calling fib(1)
calling fib(4)
calling fib(3)
calling fib(2)
calling fib(1)
calling fib(0)
```

(continue)

Program 14-23   Comparing unoptimized and optimized recursive Fibonacci functions *(continued)*

```
calling fib(1)
calling fib(2)
calling fib(1)
calling fib(0)



Optimized Fibonacci calls:
calling fib(2)
calling fib(3)
calling fib(4)
```

As you can see, the number of calls for an unoptimized `fib` function is much higher than it is for the optimized function `fibMemoized`.

Tips and Common Programming Errors

1. When writing recursive algorithms, always follow a divide-and-conquer strategy. First, divide your problem into smaller problems, and then tackle the smaller ones.

2. Recursive functions should comply with the following guidelines:
   a. A recursive function should always have a base case to end function execution.
   b. A recursive function should always have a general case in which some of the function parameters' values are changing (incrementing or decrementing) so the base case is met.

3. The base case should always have a return statement—either return a value or just return to end execution of the function.

4. Recursion has more overhead on memory than iteration.

5. Some recursive functions require more than one base case. In such instances, test your function for all exceptions. These exceptions are usually converted to base cases.

6. It is important to know the finite number of recursions before writing the function in order to make sure that execution of the function will not cause you to run out of memory.

7. Use dynamic programming's concept of overlapping subproblems to reduce the number of recursive calls.

8. Recursion starts with the first call to itself; therefore, the number of recursive calls is counted with the execution of the function call within itself.

9. Always test your function with a small number of recursions to make sure it is working properly and its output matches the results of your mathematical model.

10. When testing, working with a small set of numbers is easier to debug and trace.

11. Avoid using mutual recursion or nested recursion. These types of recursive functions are difficult to debug and trace.

12. A common technique for tracing recursive functions is to use manual drawings to show the function, the parameters passed, and the parameters being passed to itself.

13. The most common error in recursion is a missing base case or a base case that is not met, resulting in an infinite recursion in which the program terminates due to insufficient memory.

14. Not every function using iteration should be converted to recursion. Recursion is not necessarily more efficient than iteration.

15. Recursive functions are simpler to convert to iteration than vice versa.

16. Recursion is very useful in a situation in which branching is needed. This is applicable for data structures such as binary trees or graphs.

17. Practice makes perfect. Thinking in terms of recursion requires practice to develop a knack for writing recursive code naturally. Once you have a good grasp of recursion, writing recursive functions becomes easier.

18. In most cases, try to use tail recursion.

19. Use recursion if you can formulate your problem—as, for instance, in the summation of a series of numbers.

Summary

> Recursion is a problem-solving method in which the solution of a problem depends on a similar solution of other instances of the same problem. In programming, recursion refers to a repetitive process in which a function calls itself.

> A recursion solution is simple and efficient.

> A recursion function always contains the general case for solving a problem and the base case for an exception to end recursion.

> Recursion cannot be used for solving all types of problems.

> A factorial of some positive integer n is defined as the product of all positive integers less than or equal to n.

> The Fibonacci sequence is such that any term (excluding the first two terms, which are both often defined as one) is the sum of the two terms immediately preceding it (1, 1, 2, 3,5, 8, 13, 21, 34, ...).

> The divide-and-conquer technique involves decomposing a problem into smaller ones in order to solve it.

> Programmers use two approaches to writing repetitive algorithms: iteration (or loops) and recursion.

> A repetitive function is considered iterative if the definition involves only the parameter(s) and not the function itself.

> A repetitive function is considered recursive if the function appears within the definition itself.

> All recursive functions have two elements: each call either solves one part of the problem or it reduces the size of the problem.

> The steps for designing a recursive function are as follows:

   1. Determine the base case.

   2. Determine the general case.

   3. Combine the base case and general case into a function.

> In a recursive function, each call to itself must reduce the size of the problem and move it toward the base case.

> Primitive recursion is a recursive function that can be easily written using iteration construct.

> Single recursion refers to a function that has one calling statement to itself.

> Multiple recursion is a type of recursive function that calls itself in multiple statements.

> Linear recursion, also known as single recursion, is a recursive function that makes one call to itself.

> Mutual recursion occurs when two recursive functions are defined in terms of each other.

> Tail recursion is a recursion type in which the reference call is the last statement in the function.

> A recursive function is of the nested recursion type if one of the arguments in the function parameter is a call to itself.

> Selection works by repeatedly selecting the smallest (ascending) or largest (descending) element in the list and moving it to the beginning of the list.

> Merge sort is based on a divide-and-conquer strategy.

> Merge sort works like this:

   ■ **Step 1:** If the list contains only one item, the list is already sorted and is complete.

   ■ **Step 2:** Keep dividing the list until each sublist is no longer divisible (has one item).

   ■ **Step 3:** Merge the smaller sublist with the larger sublist or vice versa based on ascending or descending order.

> The quick sort algorithm is based on the divide-and-conquer approach, with the efficiency of $O(n \log n)$.

> Sequential search is the simplest form of search algorithm.

> Binary search is a mechanism used to determine if an element is in a list or not.

> Backtracking involves searching for a solution.

> When applying the backtracking recursion technique, we use the following steps:

   1. Explore the different choices to perform the next step.

   2. For each valid choice, we apply step 1 recursively.

   3. Decide what to do when no more choices are available.

> Dynamic programming is a field of study that emphasizes optimization of decision-making and problem-solving.

> Dynamic programming has two primary characteristics:

   ■ Identifying overlapping subproblems.

   ■ Identifying optimal substructure.

Key Terms

backtracking algorithm	Fibonacci sequence	mutual recursion
base case	general case	nested recursion
binary recursion	general recursion	optimization
branch and bound	greedy thief algorithm	primitive recursion
brute force algorithm	indirect recursion	recursion
divide and conquer	linear recursion	single recursion
dynamic programming	memoization	state space
factorial	multiple recursion	tail recursion

Review Questions

1. The general case contains the logic needed to increment the size of the solution.
   a. True   **b.** False

2. Factorial function is used to compute permutation.
   a. True   **b.** False

3. A function is recursive if it has a calling statement to a recursive function.
   a. True   **b.** False

4. Recursive function should not have loop constructs.
   a. True   **b.** False

5. A function that uses a loop construct like `for` or `while` is not considered a recursive.
   a. True   **b.** False

6. Which of the following is not a valid recursion type?
   a. Single recursion   **c.** Multiple recursion
   b. Double recursion   **d.** Mutual recursion

7. A function that has multiple calls to another recursive function is called_____ .
   a. single recursion   **d.** nested recursion
   b. double recursion   **e.** indirect recursion
   c. multiple recursion

8. Which statement is a base case in the following function?

   ```
       void printOdd(int n)
       {
   1       printf("In Odd function =
           %d\n", n);
   2       if (n%2==0 || n < 0)
   3           return;
   4       else
   5           printEven(n-1);
           return;
       } // PrintOdd
   ```

   a. Statement 1   **d.** Statement 4
   b. Statement 2   **e.** Statement 5
   c. Statement 3

9. Which statement is a general case in the following function?

   ```
       void printOdd(int n)
       {
   1       printf("In Odd function =
           %d\n", n);
   2       if (n%2==0 || n < 0)
   3           return;
   4       else
   5           printEven(n-1);
           return;
       } // PrintOdd
   ```

   a. Statement 1   **d.** Statement 4
   b. Statement 2   **e.** Statement 5
   c. Statement 3

10. What type of recursion is shown in the following function?

```
void printOdd(int n)
{
    printf("In Odd function = %d\n",
    n);
    if (n%2==0 || n < 0)
        return;
    else
            printEven(n-1);
    return;
} // PrintOdd
```

   a. Multiple recursion
   b. Mutual recursion
   c. Nested recursion
   d. Primitive recursion
   e. Double recursion

11. Which of the following is a characteristic of dynamic programming?
   a. Overlapping subprograms
   b. Divide and conquer
   c. Overlapping subproblems
   d. Divide and resolve
   e. Overlapping substructures

12. Which of the following recursion types should be avoided?
   a. Single recursion
   b. Double recursion
   c. Primitive recursion
   d. Mutual recursion
   e. Nested recursion

13. Which of the following is a disadvantage of recursive functions?
   a. Resource overhead
   b. Complexity of code
   c. Easy to convert to a function using iteration construct
   d. Always requires a base case

14. Which of the following is an advantage of recursion?
   a. Resource overhead
   b. Complexity of code
   c. Easy to convert to a function using iteration construct
   d. Always requires a base case

15. How many calls are made using a recursive function to compute the sum of a set of numbers {4, 5, 8, 12, 14, 15}?
   a. 8   **c.** 6   **e.** 4
   b. 7   **d.** 5

Exercises

16. What is the output of the following program?

```
#include <stdio.h>
#include <stdlib.h>

int main(void)
{
        print(90, 100);
}

void print(int num, int max)
{
    if(num <= max)
    {
        printf(" %d ",num);
        print(num + 1, max);
    }
    else
        return;
}
```

17. What is the output of the following program?

```c
#include <stdio.h>
#include <stdlib.h>

int main(void)
{
   print(10, 100);
}

void print(int num, int max)
{
    if(max >= num && max%5 == 0)
    {
        printf(" %d ", max);
        print(num, max - 1);
    }
    else if (max >= num)
        print(num, max - 1);
    else
        return;
}
```

18. Consider the program that follows, and complete these steps:
   a. Describe the purpose of the recursive function.
   b. Identify the base case and the general case in the function.
   c. Describe the output of the program.

```c
#include <stdio.h>
#include <stdlib.h>

int main(void)
{
    printf("output = %d", function(3421));
}

int function(int num)
{
    static int cnt;

    if(num != 0)
    {
        cnt++;
        function(num/10);
    }
    else
        return cnt;
}
```

19. Consider the function that follows, and complete these steps:

    a. Describe the purpose of the recursive function.

    b. Identify the base case and the general case in the function.

    c. Describe the output of the program.

    d. Write a test driver for the recursive function.

```
void function(char str1[], char str2[], int cnt)
{
    if (str1[cnt] == '\0')
    {
        str2[cnt]='\0';
        return;
    }
    else
        str2[cnt] = (str1[cnt]) + 1;

    function(str1, str2, cnt + 1);
}
```

20. Write pseudocode for a recursive function that prints a series of odd numbers less than a given a number.

21. Convert the following recursive function to a function using a `for` loop construct.

```
void function(char str1[], char str2[], int cnt)
{
    if (str1[cnt] == '\0')
    {
        str2[cnt]='\0';
        return;
    }
    else
        str2[cnt] = (str1[cnt]) + 1;

    function(str1, str2, cnt + 1);
}
```

22. You were asked by your colleague to help fix the following recursive function that is supposed to convert a decimal number to a binary number.

```
long convertBinary(int dec)
{
    long bin;
    long ratio;
    long factor = 1;

    if(dec >= 0)
    {
```

```
        ratio = dec % 2;
        bin = dec + ratio * factor;
        factor = factor * 10;
        convertBinary(dec/2);
    }
    return bin;
}
```

23. Devise pseudocode for a recursive function to determine the greatest common divisor of two numbers.

24. The following function returns the sum from 1 to a given number. Rewrite this function to return the sum of the numbers between two given numbers.

```
int Sum(int num)
{
    int result;
    if (num == 1)
        return (1);
    else
        result = num + Sum(num - 1);
    return (result);
}
```

25. Convert the function flowchart shown in **Figure 14-27** to a recursive function.

Figure 14-27   Flowchart for Exercise 25

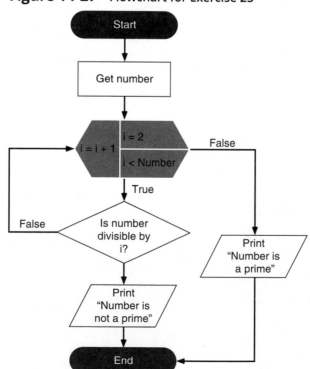

26. Consider the recursive function that follows, and complete these steps:
- **a.** Describe the purpose of the recursive function.
- **b.** Identify the base case and the general case in the function.
- **c.** Describe the output of the program.
- **d.** Write a test driver for the recursive function.

```
int function(int num)
{
    static int sum = 0;
    if(num!=0)
    {
        sum = sum + (num%10);
        function(num/10);
    }
    return sum;
}
```

Problems

27. Write a memoized version of the recursive factorial function.

28. Write a program that prompts the user to enter an integer number and then call a function that calculates the power of the entered number using recursion.

29. Convert the recursive `recMergeSort` function presented in Program 14-13 to a merge sort function using iteration, and name it `itrMergeSort`.

30. Use Program 14-14 to extract the partitioning code in the `recQuickSort` function and convert it into a function called `partitioning`.

31. Write a program using recursion that generates all prime numbers within a given range of numbers and prints out the sum of the prime numbers.

32. Write a program that reads a list of store names in an array. The program should prompt a user to search the array sequentially for a specific name and then respond whether the name is found or not. The program should use a recursive sequential function.

33. Write a recursive function that prints the Collatz sequence, which is generated based on the following rules:
- ❭ Base case: If n is 1
- ❭ General case #1: If n is even then divide by 2
- ❭ General case #2: If n is odd then multiple by 3 and add 1

34. Convert the following recursive function into an iterative function.

```
void reverse(char *str)
{
    if (*str)
    {
        reverse(str+1);
        printf("%c", *str);
    }
}
```

35. Convert the following insertionSort function into a recursive function.

```
void insertionSort(int arr[], int n)
{
    int i, j, key;

    for (i = 1; i < n; i++)
    {
        key = arr[i];
        j = i - 1;

        while (j >= 0 && arr[j] > key)
        {
            arr[j + 1] = arr[j];
            j = j - 1;
        }
        arr[j + 1] = key;
    }
}
```

36. Write a program that reads a list of numbers with a recursive function to determine if the list is ordered in ascending order, descending order, or not sorted.

Projects

37. Write a program that reads a set of names from a file into an array and then prints the array in ascending order. Your program should use a recursive function to sort the array using recBubbleSort.

38. Write a program that reads a word with six letters or less and then prints out all permutations of the word.

39. Using the program you wrote for Project 38, create a small dictionary containing 20 words, as illustrated in Table 14-4. Your program should scramble the word TEA and generate only valid words based on the provided dictionary.

Table 14-4 Dictionary Sample

WORD #	WORD	#	WORD
1	ATE	11	TEAM
2	EAT	12	TEN
3	EATEN	13	TEEN
4	EAST	14	TENSE
5	FAT	15	TEA
6	FATE	16	THE
7	MET	17	THY
8	MEET	18	WHO
9	NET	19	WHY
10	TEA	20	YET

40. Write a program using backtracking recursion that reads in a set of numbers and then produces a combination sum for all possible combinations in the set. As an example, for a(2, 6, 13) the output of the program would be:

```
Combination Sum #1: (2) = 2
Combination Sum #2: (6) = 6
Combination Sum #3: (13) = 13
Combination Sum #4: (2, 6) = 8
Combination Sum #5: (2, 13) = 15
Combination Sum #6: (6, 13) = 19
Combination Sum #7: (2, 6, 13) = 21
```

41. Write a program that provides the user with a menu of options to select from as follows:

1. Convert a decimal number to binary

2. Convert a decimal number to octal

3. Convert a decimal number to hexadecimal

4. Convert a binary number to a decimal

5. Convert an octal number to a decimal

6. Convert a hexadecimal to a decimal

0. Quit

Your program should contain only two recursive functions—one for converting from a decimal to binary, octal, and hexadecimal, and another one to convert back from binary, octal, and hexadecimal to a decimal number.

CHAPTER 15

Lists

Learning Objectives

When you complete this chapter, you will be able to:

15.1 Describe the implementation of linked lists

15.2 Implement basic operations to work with a linear list

15.3 Implement the basic concepts of stacks

15.4 Implement the basic concepts of queues

15.5 Explain the basic concepts of tree structures

15.6 Describe the basic concepts of graph structures

15.1 List Implementations

Aside from some advanced C concepts and functions that we leave for your future studies, we have covered the basics of the C language. In this chapter, we turn our attention to a concept that is pervasive throughout computer science: lists.

A list is a collection of related data. We can divide lists into two categories: linear lists and nonlinear lists. In a linear list, each element has only zero or one successor. In a nonlinear list, each element can have zero, one, or more successors. Linear lists are divided into general lists, stacks, and queues. Nonlinear lists are divided into trees and graphs. In this chapter, we define and discuss each of these types of lists briefly. **Figure 15-1** contains the breakdown of lists.

Figure 15-1   Lists

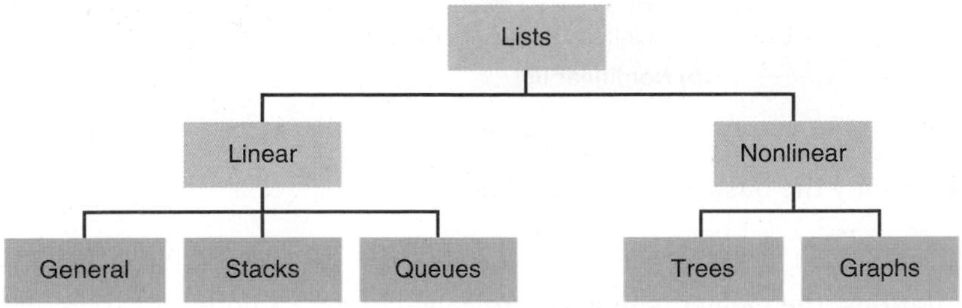

The C language does not provide any list structures or implementations. When we need lists, we must provide the structures and functions for them. Traditionally, two data types—arrays and pointers—are used for their implementation. The array implementation uses static structures that are determined during the compilation or while the program is running. The pointer implementation uses dynamically allocated structures known as linked lists.

Array Implementation

In an array, the sequentiality of a list is maintained by the order structure of elements in the array (indexes). Although searching an array for an individual element can be very efficient, addition and deletion of elements are complex and inefficient processes. For this reason arrays are seldom used, especially when the list changes frequently. In addition, array implementations of lists can become excessively large, especially when there are several successors for each element.

Linked List Implementation

A linked list is a collection of data in which each element contains the location of the next element or elements. In a linked list, each element contains two parts: data and one or more links. The data part holds the application data—the data to be processed. Links are used to chain the data together; they contain pointers that identify the next element or elements in the list. We can use a linked list to create linear and nonlinear structures.

The major advantage of a linked list over an array is that data are easily inserted and deleted. It is not necessary to shift elements of a linked list to make room for a new element or to delete an element. On the other hand, because the elements are no longer physically sequenced, we are limited to sequential searches; we cannot use a binary search. When we examine trees later in this chapter, we discuss the binary search tree, which allows for easy updates and efficient searches.

Figure 15-2(a) shows a linked list implementation of a linear list. The link in each element, except the last, points to its unique successor; the link in the last element contains a null pointer, indicating the end of the list. **Figure 15-2**(b) shows a linked list implementation of a nonlinear list. An element in a nonlinear list can have two or more links. Here each element contains two links, each to one successor. **Figure 15-2**(c) contains an example of an empty list, linear or nonlinear. We define an empty list as a pointer with a null value.

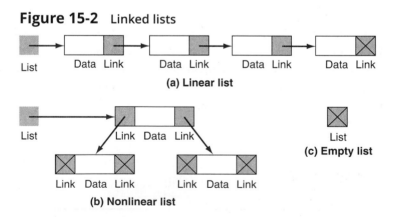

Figure 15-2 Linked lists

(a) Linear list

(b) Nonlinear list

(c) Empty list

In this section, we discuss only the basic concepts for linked lists.

Nodes

In linked list implementations, the elements in a list are called nodes. A node is a structure that has two parts: the data and one or more links. **Figure 15-3** shows two different nodes: one for a linear list and another for a nonlinear list.

Figure 15-3 Nodes

(a) Node in a linear list

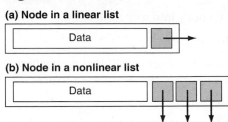

(b) Node in a nonlinear list

The nodes in a linked list are called self-referential structures. In a self-referential structure, each instance of the structure contains one or more pointers to other instances of the same structural type. In Figure 15-3, the colored boxes with arrows are the pointers that make the linked list a self-referential structure.

The data part in a node can be a single field, multiple fields, or a structure that contains several fields, but it always acts as a single field. **Figure 15-4** shows three designs for a node of a linked list. The upper-left node contains a single field, a number, and a link. The upper-right node is more common. It contains three data fields: a name, an id, and grade points (`grdPts`)—and a link. The third example is the one we recommend. The fields are defined in their own structure, which is then put into the definition of a node structure.

Figure 15-4 Linked list node structures

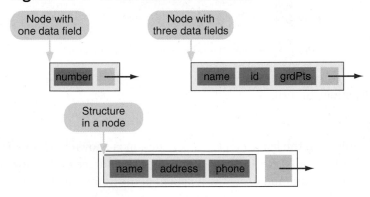

Pointers to Linked Lists

A linked list must always have a head pointer. Depending on how we use the list, we may have several other pointers as well. For example, if we are going to search a linear list, we will need an additional pointer to the location where we found the data we were looking for. Furthermore, in many structures, programming is more efficient if there is a pointer to the last node in the list as well as a head pointer.

15.2 General Linear Lists

A general linear list is a list in which operations, such as retrievals, insertions, changes, and deletions, can be done anywhere in the list, that is, at the beginning, in the middle, or at the end of the list. We use many different types of general lists in our daily lives. We use lists of employees, student lists, and lists of our favorite songs. When we process our song list, we need to be able to search for a song, add a new song, or delete one. This chapter describes how we can maintain and process general lists.

To work with a linear list, we need some basic operations that manipulate the nodes. For example, we need functions to insert a node at the beginning or end of the list, or anywhere in the middle. We also need a function to delete a node from the list. Finally, we need a function to find a requested node in the list. Given these primitive functions, we can build functions that process any linear list.

Insert a Node

We use the following four steps to insert a node into a linear list:

1. Allocate memory for the new node.

2. Determine the insertion point—that is, the position within the list where the new data are to be placed. To identify the insertion position, we need to know only the new node's logical predecessor (pPre).

3. Point the new node to its successor.

4. Point the predecessor to the new node.

As seen in step 2 above, to insert a node into a list, we need to know the location of the node that precedes the new node (pPre). This pointer can be in one of two states: It can contain the address of a node, or it can be null.

If the predecessor is null, then we are inserting into an empty list or at the beginning of the list. If it is not null, then we are inserting somewhere after the first node—that is, in the middle of the list—or at the end of the list. A list and its pointers are shown in **Figure 15-5**.

Figure 15-5 Pointer combinations for insert

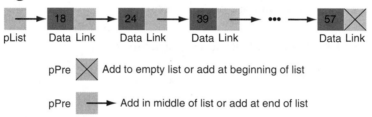

We discuss each of these situations in turn.

Insert into Empty List

When the head of the list is null, then the list is empty. This situation is shown in **Figure 15-6**. All that is necessary to insert a node into an empty list is to point the list head pointer to the address of the new node and make sure that its link field is null. We could use a constant null to set the link field of the new node, but we use the null contained in the list head pointer. The reason for this will become apparent in the next section.

Figure 15-6 Insert node into an empty list

The statements to insert a node into an empty list are shown below.

```
pNew->link = pList; // set link to NULL
pList = pNew; // point list to first node
```

Note the order of these two statements. We must first point the new node to NULL, then we can change the head pointer. If we reverse these statements, we end up with the new node pointing to itself, which would put our program into a never-ending loop when we process the list.

Insert at Beginning

We insert a node at the beginning of the list whenever it must be placed before the first node of the list. We determine that we are inserting at the beginning of the list by testing the predecessor pointer (pPre). If it is null, then there is no predecessor, which means we are at the beginning of the list.

To insert a node at the beginning of the list, we simply point the new node to the first node of the list and then set the head pointer (pList) to point to the new first node. We know the address of the new node. How can we find the address of the first node currently in the list so we can point the new node to it? The answer is simple: The first node's address is stored in the head pointer (pList).

Inserting at the beginning of the list is shown in **Figure 15-7**. If you compare the two statements in Figure 15-7 to the statements used to insert into an empty list, you will see that they are the same. This is because, logically, inserting into an empty list is the same as inserting at the beginning of a list. We can, therefore, use the same logic to cover both situations.

Figure 15-7   Insert node at beginning

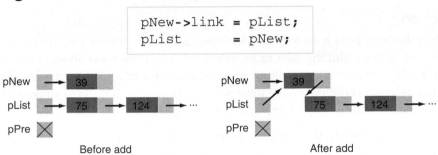

Insert in Middle

When we insert a node anywhere in the middle of the list, the predecessor (pPre) is not null. To insert a node between two nodes, we must point the new node to its successor and then point the predecessor to the new node. Again, the address of the new node's successor can be found in the predecessor's link field. The statements to insert a node in the middle of the list are shown in **Figure 15-8**.

Figure 15-8   Insert node in middle

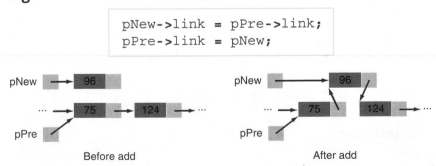

Insert at End

When we insert at the end of the list, we only need to point the predecessor to the new node. There is no successor to point to. It is necessary, however, to set the new node's link field to NULL. The statements to insert a node at the end of a list are shown below.

```
pNew->link = NULL;
pPre->link = pNew;
```

Rather than having special logic in the function for inserting at the end, however, we can take advantage of the existing linear list structure. We know that the last node in the list has a link pointer of NULL. If we use this pointer rather than a constant, then the code becomes exactly the same as the code for inserting in the middle of the list. The revised code is shown in **Figure 15-9**. Compare it to the code in Figure 15-8.

Figure 15-9 Insert node at end

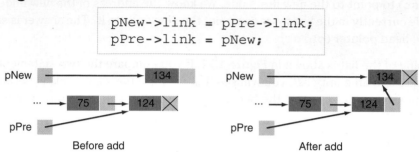

Before add   After add

Insert Node Function

Now let's write the function that puts it all together and inserts a node into the list. We are given the head pointer (pList), the predecessor (pPre), and the data to be inserted (item). We must allocate memory for the new node (malloc) and adjust the link pointers appropriately. Since we might insert a node before the beginning of the list, we also need to be able to change the contents of the head pointer. We ensure that the head pointer is always correct by returning it. The function declaration for insertNode is shown below.

```
NODE* insertNode (NODE* pList, NODE* pPre, DATA item);
```

The complete function is shown in **Program 15-1**.

Program 15-1 | Insert a node

```
1  /* ==================== insertNode ====================
2     This function inserts a single node into a linear list.
3     Pre pList is pointer to the list; may be null
4        pPre points to new node's predecessor
5        item that contains data to be inserted
6     Post returns the head pointer
7  */
8  NODE* insertNode (NODE* pList, NODE* pPre, DATA item)
9  {
10 // Local Declarations
11    NODE* pNew;
12
13 // Statements
14    if (!(pNew = (NODE*)malloc(sizeof(NODE))))
15       printf("\aMemory overflow in insert\n"),
16    exit (100);
17
18    pNew->data = item;
```

(continue)

Program 15-1   Insert a node *(continued)*

```
19      if (pPre == NULL)
20      {
21          // Inserting before first node or to empty list
22          pNew->link = pList;
23          pList = pNew;
24      } // if pPre
25      else
26      {
27          // Inserting in middle or at end
28          pNew->link = pPre->link;
29          pPre->link = pNew;
30      } // else
31      return pList;
32  } // insertNode
```

We have discussed all the logic in this function except the memory allocation. Recall that `malloc` returns either an address in the heap or null when there is no more room in the heap. Therefore, we need to test to see if memory is available.

When memory is exhausted, we have an overflow condition. The action taken depends on the application being programmed; however, the general course of action is to abort the program. We assume the general case in the algorithm; if null is returned from `malloc`, we print a message to the user and exit the program.

With the idea in mind that all code needs to be tested, how can we test the overflow logic? We could use the brute-force method—insert data until the list overflows—but that could take a long time. We tested it by inserting an array of 10,000 long double variables to the data structure. On our system, we got an overflow on the fifth node and the logic was tested.

The technique used to call `insertNode` is important, since it returns the head of the list under all circumstances. The call should assign the return value to the list head pointer. This ensures that when the head of the list changes, the change will be reflected in the calling function. A typical call to insert data into a student list is coded below. Note that the head pointer (`stuList`) is found both in the assignment and as an actual parameter.

```
stuList = insertNode (stuList, pPre, stuData);
```

Delete a Node

When we delete a node we logically remove the node from the linear list by changing various link pointers and then physically deleting it from the heap. The delete situations parallel those for insert. We can delete the first node, any node in the middle, or the end node of a list. As you will see below, these three situations reduce to only two combinations: Delete the first node, and delete any other node.

To logically delete a node, we must first locate the node itself (identified by `pCur`) and its predecessor (identified by `pPre`). We discuss location concepts shortly. After we locate the node that we want to delete, we can simply change its predecessor's link field to point to the deleted node's successor. We then recycle the node using `free`. We need to be concerned, however, about deleting the only node in a list. Deleting the only node results in an empty list, so we must be careful that in this case the head pointer is set to NULL.

Delete First Node

When we delete the first node, we must reset the head pointer to point to the first node's successor and then recycle (free) the deleted note. We can tell we are deleting the first node by testing the predecessor (pPre). If the predecessor is null, we are deleting the first node. This situation is diagrammed in **Figure 15-10**.

Figure 15-10 Delete first node

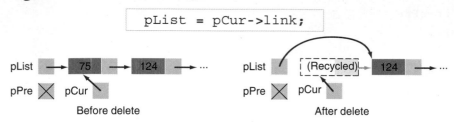

The statements to delete the first node are shown below.

```
pList = pCur->link;
free(pCur);
```

If you examine this logic carefully, you will note that it also handles the situation when we are deleting the only node in the list. If the first node is the only node, then its link field is null. Since we move its link field (a null) to the head pointer, the result is, by definition, an empty list.

General Delete Case

We call deleting any node other than the first a general case, since the same logic handles deleting a node in the middle of the list and deleting a node at the end of the list. For both of these cases, we simply point the predecessor node, identified by pPre, to the successor of the node being deleted. The node being deleted is identified by the current node pointer, pCur. Its successor is, therefore, pCur->link.

Deleting the last node is handled automatically. When the node being deleted is the last node of the list, its null pointer is moved to the predecessor's link field, making the predecessor the new logical end of the list. After the pointers have been adjusted, the current node is recycled. The delete general case statements are shown below.

```
pPre->link = pCur->link;
free (pCur);
```

The general case is shown in **Figure 15-11**.

Figure 15-11 Delete—general case

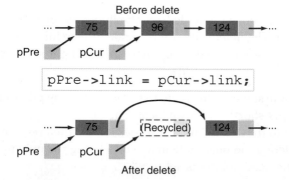

Function to Delete a Node

The complete logic to delete a node is shown in **Program 15-2**. It is given a pointer to the head of the list, the node to be deleted, and the delete node's predecessor. After deleting and recycling the node, it returns the pointer to the beginning of the list.

Program 15-2 | Delete a node

```
 1  /* ===================deleteNode ========================
 2     This function deletes a single node from the link list.
 3     Pre pList is a pointer to the head of the list
 4        pPre points to node before the delete node
 5        pCur points to the node to be deleted
 6     Post deletes and recycles pCur
 7        returns the head pointer
 8  */
 9  NODE* deleteNode (NODE* pList, NODE* pPre, NODE* pCur)
10  {
11  // Statements
12     if (pPre == NULL)
13     // Deleting first node
14        pList = pCur->link;
15     else
16     // Deleting other nodes
17        pPre->link = pCur->link;
18     free (pCur);
19     return pList;
20  } // deleteNode
```

Three points in this function merit discussion. The first and most important is that the node to be deleted must be identified before this function is called. It assumes that the predecessor and current pointers are properly set. If they aren't, then the program most likely fails. Even if it doesn't fail, the data will be wrong. (It is better that the program fail than report invalid results.)

Second, when we discussed the individual logic cases, we placed the recycle statement (free) after each delete. In the implementation, we moved it to the end of the function. When the same statements appear in both the true and false blocks of a selection statement, they should be moved out of the selection logic. This is the same concept as factoring common expressions in algebra. The result is a program that is smaller and easier to maintain.

Finally, we return the list. This is necessary because it is possible for the first node of the list to be deleted, which results in a new node being the head of the list.

Locating Data in Linear Lists

When we insert and delete data in a linear list, we must first search the list. To insert a node, we search to identify the logical predecessor of the new node in its key sequence. To delete a node, we search to identify the location of the node to be deleted and its logical predecessor.

Search Linear List

For inserts, we need to know the predecessor to the node to be inserted; for deletes, we need to know the predecessor to the node to be deleted. Also, to locate a node for processing, such as adding to a count or printing its contents, we need to know its location. Although we could write separate search functions for all three cases, the traditional solution is to write one search that satisfies all requirements. This means that our search must return both the predecessor and the current (found) locations.

Generally, lists are maintained in key sequence. A key is a field within a structure that identifies the data. Examples of keys would include a student number to identify data about students and a part number to identify data about parts. In this text, we limit our discussion of lists to key-sequenced lists, that is, lists in which each key in the list is less than or greater than the key that follows it.

To search a list on a key, we need a key field. For simple lists, the key and the data can be the same field. More complex structures require a separate key field. A generic linked-list node and key structure are seen in the following example.

```
// Global Declarations
typedef int KEY_TYPE;    // Application Dependent
typedef struct
{
KEY_TYPE key;
... // Other Data Fields
} DATA;
typedef struct nodeTag
{
DATA data;
struct nodeTag* link;
} NODE;
```

Given a target key, the search attempts to locate the requested node in the linear list. If a node in the list matches the target value, the search returns `true`; if no key matches, it returns `false`. The predecessor and current pointers are set according to the rules in **Table 15-1**.

Table 15-1   Linear list search results

CONDITION	pPRE	pCUR	RETURN
target < first node	NULL	first node	0
target == first node	NULL	first node	1
first < target < last	largest node < target	first node > target	0
target == middle node	node's predecessor	equal node	1
target == last node	last's predecessor	last node	1
target > last node	last node	NULL	1

Each of these conditions is also shown in **Figure 15-12**.

Figure 15-12   Search results

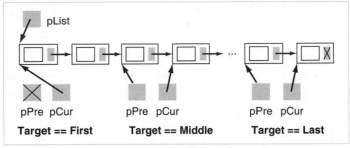

Successful searches (Return `true`)

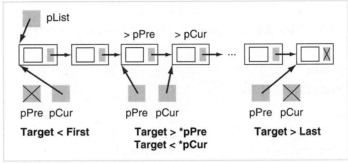

Unsuccessful searches (Return `false`)

Since the list is in key sequence, we use a modified version of the sequential search called an ordered sequential search.

We start at the beginning and search the list sequentially until the target value is no longer greater than the current node's key. At this point, the target value is either less than or equal to the current node's key while the predecessor is pointing to the node immediately before the current node. We now use the current node pointer (`pCur`) to test for equality and set the return value to `true` if the target value is equal to the list value, or `false` if it is less (it cannot be greater). Then, we terminate the search. The code for this search is shown in **Program 15-3**.

Program 15-3 | Search linear list

```
 1   /* ==================== searchList ====================
 2       Given key value, finds the location of a node
 3       Pre pList points to a head node
 4       pPre points to variable to receive pred
 5       pCur points to variable for current node
 6       Target is key being sought.
 7       Post pCur points to first node with >= key
 8       -or- null if target > key of last node
 9       pPre points to largest node < key
10       -or- null if target < key of first node
11       Function returns true if found
12       false if not found
13   */
```

(continue)

Program 15-3   Search linear list *(continued)*

```
14 bool searchList (NODE* pList, NODE** pPre,
15                      NODE** pCur, KEY_TYPE target)
16 {
17 // Local Declarations
18    bool found = false;
19
20 // Statements
21    *pPre = NULL;
22    *pCur = pList;
23
24    // start the search from beginning
25    while (*pCur != NULL && target > (*pCur)->data.key)
26    {
27       *pPre = *pCur;
28       *pCur = (*pCur)->link;
29    } // while
30
31    if (*pCur && target == (*pCur)->data.key)
32       found = true;
33    return found;
34 } // searchList
```

Examine the `while` statement at statement 25 carefully. Note that there are two tests. The first test protects us from running off the end of the list; the second test stops the loop when we find the target or, if the target doesn't exist, when we find a node larger than the target. It is important to make the null list test first. If the function is at the end of the list, then pCur is no longer valid. Testing the key first gives unpredictable results.

We can make the search slightly more efficient if we use a rear pointer. With a rear pointer, we can test the last node before the loop to make sure that the target isn't larger than its key value. If the target is larger, we simply exit the search function after setting the predecessor pointer to the last node and the current pointer to null. Once we know that the target is not greater than the last node, the loop doesn't need to test for running off the end of the list.

Traversing Linear Lists

Algorithms that traverse a list start at the first node and examine each node in succession until the last node has been processed. Several different types of functions use list traversal logic. Some examples are printing the list, counting the number of nodes in the list, totaling a numeric field in the node, or calculating the average of a field. In fact, any application that requires processing the entire list uses a **traversal**. **Figure 15-13** is a graphic representation of a linear list traversal.

Figure 15-13   Linear list traversal

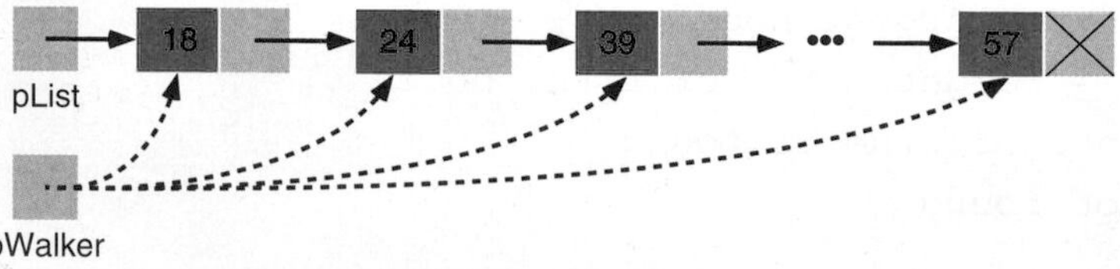

The basic logic to traverse a linear list is found in **Algorithm 15-1**. It incorporates two concepts. First, an event loop is used to guard against overrunning the end of the list. Second, after processing the current node, the looping pointer is advanced to the next element.

ALGORITHM 15-1 | List Traversal Algorithm

---

1 Set pointer to the first node in list
2 while (not end of the list)
  1 process (current node)
  2 set pointer to next node
3 end while
end traverse

Print Linear List

Program 15-4 uses the traversal logic to print a linear list.

Program 15-4 | Print linear list

```
1   /* Traverse and print a linear list.
2      Pre pList is a valid linear list
3      Post List has been printed
4   */
5   void printList (NODE* pList)
6   {
7   // Local Declarations
8
9       NODE* pWalker;
10  // Statements
11      pWalker = pList;
12      printf("List contains:\n");
13
14      while (pWalker)
15      {
16         printf("%3d ", pWalker->data.key);
17         pWalker = pWalker->link;
18      } // while
19      printf("\n");
20      return;
21  } // printList
```

Study the `while` expression in statement 14 carefully. This is the most common form of pointer evaluation for a linear list. C guarantees that the evaluation of a null pointer is `false`, and all other pointer values evaluate to `true`. This expression is, therefore, equivalent to

```
while (pWalker != NULL)
```

where `pWalker` is a pointer to current node.

The other important piece of code in the traversal is the loop update in statement 17.

```
pWalker = pWalker->link;
```

This statement advances us through the list. If we forget it, we are in a permanent loop. Since `pWalker` points to the current node, we need to change it to advance to the next node. This is done by simply assigning the link field to `pWalker`. When we finally arrive at the end of the list, the link is null, which, when assigned to `pWalker`, terminates the `while` loop.

Linear List Average

Let's write one more linear list traversal algorithm, one that averages the values in a linear list. To pass a linear list to a function, we only need to pass the value of the head pointer. Look at **Program 15-5**. The actual data structure is not shown, but the function assumes that `data.key` is an integer field.

> **Program 15-5** | Average linear list

```
1   /* This function averages the values in a linear list.
2      Pre pList is a pointer to a linear list
3      Post list average is returned
4   */
5   double averageList (NODE* pList)
6   {
7   // Local Declarations
8      NODE* pWalker;
9      int total;
10     int count;
11
12  // Statements
13     total = count = 0;
14     pWalker = pList;
15     while (pWalker)
16     {
17        total += pWalker->data.key;
18        count++;
19        pWalker = pWalker->link;
20     } // while
21     return (double)total / count;
22  }  // averageList
```

To traverse the list, we used the descriptive pointer, pWalker, which "walks" us through the list. Although we could have used pList, we advise against ever using the list pointer for any function logic. Keep it in its original state. Then, if you need to modify the function, you will still know its starting point. This is a small point, but it's the small points that make a program easy to maintain.

Building a Linear List

In the previous sections, we wrote three low-level functions for a list (insert, delete, and search) and two applications (print the list and average). It's time to put them all together in a program.

To build the list, we need to get the data, create the node, determine the insertion position in the list, and then insert the new node. The design is shown in **Figure 15-14**.

Figure 15-14   Design for inserting a node in a list

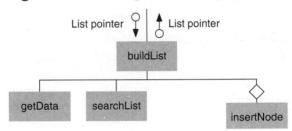

Build List

Building a key-sequenced list uses the search function to determine the insertion position. It uses the design shown in Figure 15-14. The implementation is shown in **Program 15-6**.

Program 15-6 | Implementation of `buildList`

```
1  /* ================== buildList ==================
2      This program builds a key-sequenced linear list.
3      Pre fileID is file that contains data for list
4      Post list built
5      returns pointer to head of list
6  */
7  NODE* buildList (char* fileID)
8  {
9  // Local Declarations
10     DATA data;
11     NODE* pList;
12     NODE* pPre;
13     NODE* pCur;
14     FILE* fpData;
15
16  // Statements
17     pList = NULL;
```

(continue)

Program 15-6   Implementation of `buildList` *(continued)*

```
18
19      fpData = fopen(fileID, "r");
20      if (!fpData)
21      {
22         printf("Error opening file %s\a\n", fileID);
23         exit (210);
24      } // if open fail
25
26      while (getData (fpData, &data))
27      {
28         // Determine insert position
29         searchList (pList, &pPre, &pCur, data.key);
30         pList = insertNode(pList, pPre, data);
31      } // while
32      return pList;
33 } // buildList
```

Note that in statement 29, we do not test for duplicate keys when `searchList` returns. If we want to prevent duplicates, we would test the return value and print an error message rather than insert the data when a duplicate key is detected.

Remove a Node

The design to remove a node is also simple. After reading the key to be deleted, we search for its location and its predecessor location and then call the delete node function to do the physical deletion. The design is shown in **Figure 15-15**.

Figure 15-15   Design for remove node

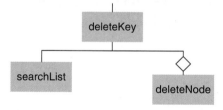

The code is shown in **Program 15-7**.

Program 15-7 | Implementation of `deleteKey`

```
1  /* ==================== deleteKey ====================
2     Delete node from a linear list.
3     Pre list is a pointer to the head of the list
4     Post node has been deleted
```

(continue)

Program 15-7   Implementation of deleteKey *(continued)*

```
 5        -or- a warning message printed if not found
 6        returns pointer to first node (pList)
 7 */
 8 NODE* deleteKey (NODE* pList)
 9 {
10 // Local Declarations
11    int key;
12    NODE* pHead;
13    NODE* pCur;
14    NODE* pPre;
15
16 // Statements
17    printf("Enter key of node to be deleted: ");
18    scanf ("%d", &key);
19
20    if (!searchList(pList, &pPre, &pCur, key))
21        printf("%d is an invalid key\a\n", key);
22    else
23        pHead = deleteNode (pList, pPre, pCur);
24
25    return pHead;
26 } // deleteKey
```

Linear List Test Driver

Now we need to test our functions. To test them, we write a test driver that builds a list, then prints it, inserts more data into it, computes its average, and finally deletes data from it. The design of our test driver is shown in **Figure 15-16**.

Figure 15-16   Link list test driver

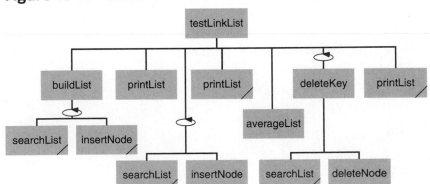

The code for the test driver is shown in **Program 15-8**.

Program 15-8 | Test driver for link list

```
 1  /* Test driver for list functions.
 2     Written by:
 3     Date:
 4  */
 5  #include <stdio.h>
 6  #include <stdlib.h>
 7  #include <stdbool.h>
 8
 9  // Global Declarations
10  typedef int KEY_TYPE;
11  typedef struct
12  {
13     KEY_TYPE key;
14  } DATA;
15  typedef struct nodeTag
16  {
17     DATA data;
18     struct nodeTag* link;
19  } NODE;
20
21  // Function Declarations
22  NODE* insertNode (NODE* pList, NODE* pPre, DATA item);
23  NODE* deleteNode (NODE* List, NODE* pPre, NODE* pCur);
24  bool searchList (NODE* pList, NODE** pPre,
25                   NODE** pCur, KEY_TYPE target);
26  void printList (NODE* pList);
27  NODE* buildList (char* fileID);
28  NODE* deleteKey (NODE* pList);
29  bool getData (FILE* fpData, DATA* pData);
30
31  double averageList (NODE* pList);
32
33  int main (void)
34  {
35  // Local Declarations
36     NODE* pList;
37     NODE* pPre;
38     NODE* pCur;
39     DATA data;
40     double avrg;
```

(continue)

Program 15-8 Test driver for link list *(continued)*

```
41     char more;
42
43 // Statements
44     printf("Begin list test driver\n\n");
45
46     // Build List
47     pList = buildList("P15-LIST.DAT");
48     if (!pList)
49     {
50        printf("Error building chosen file\a\n");
51        exit (100);
52     } // if
53     printList (pList);
54
55     printf("\nInsert data tests.\n");
56     printf("Enter key: ");
57     scanf ("%d", &data.key);
58     do
59     {
60        if (searchList (pList, &pPre, &pCur, data.key))
61           printf("Key already in list. Not inserted\n");
62        else
63           pList = insertNode(pList, pPre, data);
64        printf("Enter key <-1> to stop: ");
65        scanf ("%d", &data.key);
66     } while (data.key != -1);
67     printList (pList);
68
69     avrg = averageList(pList);
70     printf("\nData average: %.1f\n", avrg);
71
72     printf("\nDelete data tests.\n");
73     do
74     {
75        pList = deleteKey (pList);
76        printf("Delete another <Y/N>: ");
77        scanf (" %c", &more);
78     } while (more == 'Y' || more == 'y');
79
80     printList (pList);
81     printf("\nTests complete.\n");
82     return 0;
83 } // main
```

(continue)

Program 15-8   Test driver for link list *(continued)*

Output

```
Begin list test driver
List contains:
111 222 333 444 555 666 777
Insert data tests.
Enter key: 50
Enter key <-1> to stop: -1
List contains:
50 111 222 333 444 555 666 777
Data average: 394.8
Delete data tests.
Enter key of node to be deleted: 50
Delete another <Y/N>: n
List contains:
111 222 333 444 555 666 777
Tests complete.
```

While the code is rather lengthy, if you have studied each of the functions carefully, you will find this program straight-forward. Of greater interest are the test cases needed to completely validate the program. Note that for the inserts, we need to insert at the end, at the beginning, and in the middle. Likewise, for the deletes, we delete the last node, the first node, and one in the middle. We also need to try to delete a node that doesn't exist.

15.3 Stacks

A stack is a linear list in which all additions and deletions are restricted to one end, called the top. If you insert a data series into a stack and then remove it, the order of the data is reversed. Data input as {5, 10, 15, 20} is removed as {20, 15, 10, 5}. This reversing attribute is why stacks are known as the last in–first out (LIFO) data structure.

We use many different types of stacks in our daily lives. We often talk of a stack of coins or a stack of dishes. Any situation in which you can only add or remove an object at the top is a stack. If you want to remove any object other than the one at the top, you must first remove all objects above it. A graphic representation of a stack is shown in **Figure 15-17**.

Figure 15-17   Stack examples

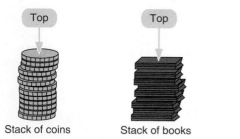

Stack of coins   Stack of books   Computer stack

Although nothing prevents us from designing a data structure that allows us to perform other operations, such as moving the item at the top of the stack to the bottom, the result would not be a stack.

Stack Structures

Several data structures can be used to implement a stack. We implement the stack as a linked list.

Data Structure

To implement the linked list stack, we need two different structures, a head node and a data node. The head structure contains metadata—that is, data about data—and a pointer to the top of the stack. The data structure contains data and a link pointer to the next node in the stack. The conceptual and physical implementations of the stack are shown in **Figure 15-18**.

Figure 15-18 Conceptual and physical stack implementations

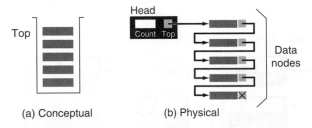

(a) Conceptual   (b) Physical

Stack Head

Generally, the head for a stack requires only two attributes: a top pointer and a count of the number of elements in the stack. These two elements are placed in a structure. Other stack attributes can be placed here also. A basic head structure is shown in **Figure 15-19**.

Figure 15-19 Stack data structure

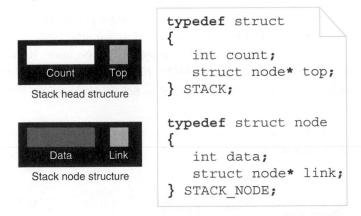

```
typedef struct
{
    int count;
    struct node* top;
} STACK;

typedef struct node
{
    int data;
    struct node* link;
} STACK_NODE;
```

Stack Data Node

The rest of the data structure is a typical linked list data node. Although the application determines the data that are stored in the stack, the stack data node looks like any linked list node. For our example, we use numbers for data. In addition to the data, the data node contains a link pointer to other data nodes, making it a self-referential structure. In a self-referential structure, each instance of the structure contains a pointer to another instance of the same structure. The stack data node is also shown in Figure 15-19.

Stack Algorithms

The basic stack operations defined in this section should be sufficient to solve basic stack problems. If an application requires additional stack operations, they can be easily added. For each operation, we describe it and then develop it in the sections that follow.

Although the implementation of a stack depends somewhat on the implementation language, it is usually implemented with a stack head structure in C. We use the design shown in Figure 15-19.

Push Stack

The push stack operation inserts an element into the stack. The first thing we need to do when we push data into a stack is find memory for the node. We must, therefore, allocate a node from dynamic memory. Once the memory is allocated, we simply assign the data to the stack node and then set the link pointer to point to the node currently indicated as the stack top. We also need to update the stack top pointer and add 1 to the stack count field. **Figure 15-20** traces a push stack operation in which a new pointer (pNew) is used to identify the data to be inserted into the stack.

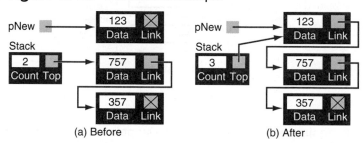

Figure 15-20 Push stack example

(a) Before   (b) After

To develop the insertion algorithm using a linked list, we need to analyze three different stack conditions: (1) insertion into an empty stack, (2) insertion into a stack with data, and (3) insertion into a stack when the available memory is exhausted.

When we insert into a stack that contains data, the new node's link pointer is set to point to the node currently at the top, and the stack's top pointer is set to point to the new node. When we insert into an empty stack, the new node's link pointer is set to null and the stack's top pointer is set to point to the new node. However, because the stack's top pointer is null, we can use it to set the new node's link pointer to null. Thus, the logic for inserting into a stack with data and the logic for inserting into an empty stack are identical. Figure 15-20 shows the before and after conditions when we push data into a stack.

As we saw with the linear list, a push can cause an overflow condition. If it does, the function simply returns a false condition. The code is shown in **Program 15-9**.

> ## Program 15-9 | Push stack

```
1   /*========================push====================
2       Inserts node into linked list stack.
3       Pre pStack is pointer to valid stack header
4       Post dataIn inserted
5       Return true if successful
6       false if overflow
7   */
```

(continue)

Program 15-9   Push stack *(continued)*

```
 8  bool push (STACK* pStack, int dataIn)
 9  {
10  // Local Declarations
11      STACK_NODE* pNew;
12      bool success;
13
14  // Statements
15      pNew = (STACK_NODE*)malloc(sizeof (STACK_NODE));
16      if (!pNew)
17          success = false;
18      else
19      {
20          pNew->data = dataIn;
21          pNew->link = pStack->top;
22          pStack->top = pNew;
23          pStack->count++;
24          success = true;
25      } // else
26      return success;
27  } // push
```

Pop Stack

The pop stack operation sends the data in the node at the top of the stack back to the calling algorithm. It then adjusts the pointers to logically delete the node. After the node has been logically deleted, it is physically deleted by recycling the memory, that is, returning it to dynamic memory. After the count is adjusted by subtracting 1, the algorithm returns the status to the caller: if the pop was successful, it returns `true`; if the stack is empty when pop is called, it returns `false`. The operations for pop stack are traced in **Figure 15-21**.

Figure 15-21   Pop stack example

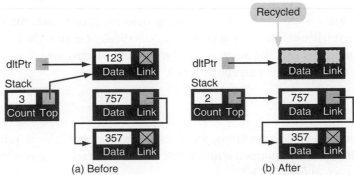

(a) Before   (b) After

The pop stack code is shown in **Program 15-10**.

Program 15-10 | Pop stack

```
 1   /* ====================pop====================
 2      Delete node from linked list stack.
 3      Pre pStackTop is pointer to valid stack
 4      Post dataOut contains deleted data
 5      Return true if successful
 6      false if underflow
 7   */
 8   bool pop (STACK* pStack, int* dataOut)
 9   {
10   // Local Declarations
11      STACK_NODE* pDlt;
12      bool success;
13
14   //Statements
15      if (pStack->top) // Test for Empty Stack
16      {
17         success = true;
18         *dataOut = pStack->top->data;
19         pDlt = pStack->top;
20         pStack->top = (pStack->top)->link;
21         pStack->count--;
22         free (pDlt);
23      } // else
24      else
25         success = false;
26      return success;
27   } // pop
```

It is interesting to follow the logic when the last node is being deleted. In this case, the result is an empty stack. No special logic is required; however, the empty stack is created automatically because the last node has a null link pointer, which when moved to top indicates that the stack is empty. A count of zero, which automatically occurs when we decrement the count, is also an indication of an empty stack.

Stack Demonstration

To demonstrate the push and pop stack algorithms, we write a program that inserts random numbers into a stack. After the numbers are inserted, they are popped and printed. When the stack is empty, the program terminates. The design for this program is shown in **Figure 15-22**.

Figure 15-22 Design for basic stack program

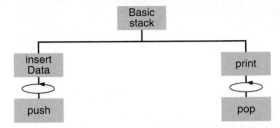

The node declarations, function declarations, and test driver are contained in **Program 15-11**.

Program 15-11 | Simple stack application program

```
 1  /* This program is a test driver to demonstrate the
 2     basic operation of the stack push and pop functions.
 3     Written by:
 4     Date:
 5  */
 6  #include <stdio.h>
 7  #include <stdlib.h>
 8
 9  #include <stdbool.h>
10  // Global Declarations
11  typedef struct node
12  {
13     int data;
14     struct node* link;
15  } STACK_NODE;
16
17  typedef struct
18  {
19     int count;
20     STACK_NODE* top;
21  } STACK;
22
23  // Function Declarations
24  void insertData (STACK* pStack);
25  void print (STACK* pStack);
26  bool push (STACK* pList, int dataIn);
27  bool pop (STACK* pList, int* dataOut);
28
29  int main (void)
30  {
```

(continue)

Program 15-11 Simple stack application program *(continued)*

```
31 // Local Declarations
32    STACK* pStack;
33
34 // Statements
35    printf("Beginning Simple Stack Program\n");
36
37    pStack = malloc(sizeof(STACK));
38    if (!pStack)
39       printf("Error allocating stack"), exit(100);
40
41    pStack->top = NULL;
42    pStack->count = 0;
43    insertData (pStack);
44    print (pStack);
45
46    printf("\nEnd Simple Stack Program\n");
47    return 0;
48 }  // main
```

Output

```
Beginning Simple Stack Program
Creating numbers: 854 763 123 532 82 632 33 426 228 90
Stack contained: 90 228 426 33 632 82 532 123 763 854
End Simple Stack Program
```

To verify that the program works correctly, we print the numbers as they are generated. This allows us to verify that the stack output was in fact correct. Note that this simple program verifies the LIFO operation of a stack.

Insert Data

The insert data function loops while creating numbers and inserting them into the stack. To create a random number, we use the random number generator and scale the return value to a three-digit range. This code is developed in **Program 15-12**.

Program 15-12 | Insert data

```
1  /*=================insertData====================
2     This program creates random numbers and
3     inserts them into a linked list stack.
4     Pre pStack is a pointer to first node
5     Post Stack has been created
6  */
```

(continue)

Program 15-12   Insert data *(continued)*

```c
7  void insertData (STACK* pStack)
8  {
9  // Local Declarations
10     int numIn;
11     bool success;
12
13 // Statements
14     printf("Creating numbers: ");
15     for (int nodeCount = 0; nodeCount < 10; nodeCount++)
16     {
17         // Generate random number
18         numIn = rand() % 999;
19         printf("%4d", numIn);
20         success = push(pStack, numIn);
21         if (!success)
22         {
23             printf("Error 101: Out of Memory\n");
24             exit (101);
25         } // if
26     } // for
27     printf("\n");
28     return;
29 } // insertData
```

Print Stack

Once the stack has been built, we print it to verify the output. The print function calls the pop function until the stack is empty. The print code is found in **Program 15-13**.

Program 15-13 | Print stack

```c
1  /* ===================== print =================
2     This function prints a singly linked stack.
3     Pre pStack is pointer to valid stack
4     Post data in stack printed
5  */
6  void print (STACK* pStack)
7  {
8  // Local Declarations
9     int* printData;
10
```

(continue)

Program 15-13   Print stack *(continued)*

```
11 // Statements
12    printf("Stack contained: ");
13    while (pop(pStack, printData))
14       printf("%4d", printData);
15    return;
16 } // print
```

15.4 Queues

A queue is a linear list in which data can be inserted only at one end, it has a pointer called the **rear**, and deleted from the other end pointer, called the **front**. These restrictions ensure that the data are processed through the queue in the order in which they are received. In other words, a queue is a **first in–first out (FIFO)** structure.

A queue is the same as a line. In fact, if you were in England, you would not get into a line, you would get into a queue. A line of people waiting for the bus at a bus station is a queue, a list of calls put on hold to be answered by a telephone operator is a queue, and a list of waiting jobs to be processed by a computer is a queue.

Figure 15-23 shows two representations of a queue: one a queue of people and the other a queue of data. Both people and data enter the queue at the rear and progress through the queue until they arrive at the front. Once they are at the front of the queue, they leave the queue and are served.

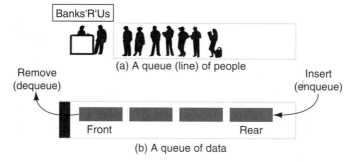

Figure 15-23   Queue concept

Banks'R'Us

(a) A queue (line) of people

Remove (dequeue)   Insert (enqueue)

Front   Rear

(b) A queue of data

Queue Operations

There are two basic queue operations. Data can be inserted at the rear and deleted from the front. Although there are many similarities between stacks and queues, one significant structural difference is that the queue implementation needs to keep track of the front and the rear of the queue, whereas the stack only needs to worry about one end: the top.

Enqueue

The queue insert operation is known as **enqueue**. After the data have been inserted into the queue, the new element becomes the rear. As we saw with stacks, the only potential problem with enqueue is running out of room for the data. If there is not enough room for another element in the queue, the queue is in an overflow state.

Figure 15-24 shows the enqueue operation.

Figure 15-24 Enqueue operation

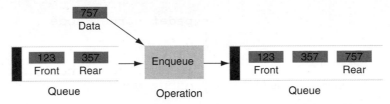

Dequeue

The queue delete operation is known as dequeue. The data at the front of the queue are returned to the user and removed from the queue. If there are no data in the queue when a dequeue is attempted, the queue is in an underflow event.

The dequeue operation is shown in **Figure 15-25**.

Figure 15-25 Dequeue operation

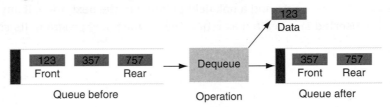

Queue Linked List Design

As with a stack, we implement our queue using a linked list.

Data Structure

We need two different structures to implement the queue: a queue head structure and a data node structure. After it is created, the queue will have one head node and zero or more data nodes, depending on its current state. **Figure 15-26** shows the conceptual and physical implementations for our queue structure.

Figure 15-26 Conceptual and physical queue implementations

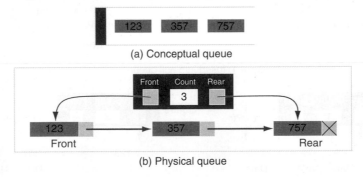

Queue Head

The queue requires two pointers and a count. These fields are stored in the queue head structure. Other queue attributes, such as the maximum number of items that were ever present in the queue and the total number of items that have been processed through the queue, can be stored in the head node if such data are relevant to an application. The queue head structure is shown in **Figure 15-27**.

Figure 15-27 Queue data structure

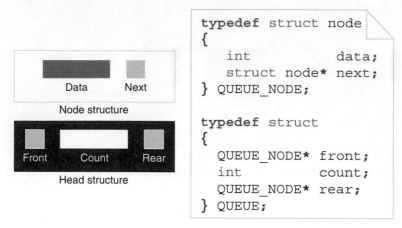

```
typedef struct node
{
    int          data;
    struct node* next;
} QUEUE_NODE;

typedef struct
{
    QUEUE_NODE* front;
    int          count;
    QUEUE_NODE* rear;
} QUEUE;
```

Queue Data Node

The queue data node contains the user data and a link field pointing to the next node, if any. These nodes are stored in dynamic memory and are inserted and deleted as requested by the using program. Its structure is also shown in Figure 15-27.

Queue Functions

The two basic functions for a queue are enqueue and dequeue.

Enqueue

The enqueue function is a little more complex than inserting data into a stack. To develop the insertion algorithm, we need to analyze two different queue conditions: insertion into an empty queue and insertion into a queue with data. These operations are shown in **Figure 15-28**.

Figure 15-28 Enqueue example

(a) Case 1: Insert into null queue

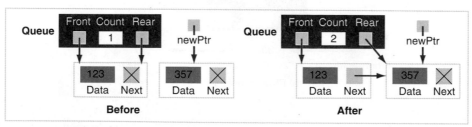

(b) Case 2: Insert into queue with data

When we insert data into an empty queue, the queue's front and rear pointers must both be set to point to the new node. When we insert data into a queue with data already in it, we must point both the link field in the last node and the rear pointer to the new node. If the insert was successful, we return a Boolean `true`; if there is no memory left for the new node, we return a Boolean `false`. The code for enqueue is shown in **Program 15-14**.

Program 15-14 | Enqueue

```
1   /* ================= enqueue =================
2      This algorithm inserts data into a queue.
3      Pre queue is valid
4      Post data have been inserted
5      Return true if successful, false if overflow
6   */
7   bool enqueue (QUEUE* queue, int dataIn)
8   {
9   // Local Declarations
10     QUEUE_NODE* newPtr;
11
12  // Statements
13     if (!(newPtr = malloc(sizeof(QUEUE_NODE))))
14        return false;
15
16     newPtr->data = dataIn;
17     newPtr->next = NULL;
18
19     if (queue->count == 0)
20        // Inserting into null queue
21        queue->front = newPtr;
22     else
23        queue->rear->next = newPtr;
24     (queue->count)++;
25     queue->rear = newPtr;
26     return true;
27  } // enqueue
```

Because we must maintain both a front and a rear pointer, we need to check to see if we are inserting into a null queue. If we are, we must set both pointers to the data just inserted. If there are already data in the queue, we need to set the next field of the node at the rear of the queue and the rear pointer to the new node. In this case the front pointer is unchanged. Because the rear pointer is updated in either case, we changed it after the if statement (see statement 25).

Dequeue

Although the dequeue function is also a little more complex than deleting data from a stack, it starts out much the same. We must first ensure that the queue contains data. If the queue is empty, we have underflow and we return false, indicating that the dequeue was not successful.

Given that there are data to be dequeued, we pass the data back through the parameter list and then set the front pointer to the next item in the queue. If we have just dequeued the last item, the queue front pointer automatically becomes a null pointer by assigning it the null pointer from the link field of the last node. However, if the queue is now empty, we must also set the rear pointer to null. These cases are shown in **Figure 15-29**.

Figure 15-29 Dequeue examples

(a) Case 1: Delete only item in queue

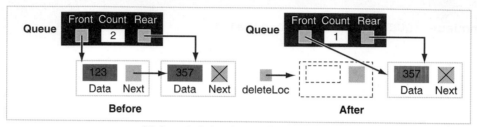

(b) Case 2: Delete item at front of queue

The dequeue implementation is shown in **Program 15-15**.

Program 15-15 | Dequeue

```
1   /* ================= dequeue =================
2      This algorithm deletes a node from the queue.
3      Pre queue is pointer to queue head structure
4      dataOut is pointer to data being deleted
5      Post Data pointer to queue front returned and
6      front element deleted and recycled.
7      Return true if successful; false if underflow
8   */
9   bool dequeue (QUEUE* queue, int* dataOut)
10  {
11  // Local Declarations
12     QUEUE_NODE* deleteLoc;
13
14  // Statements
15     if (!queue->count)
16        return false;
17
18     *dataOut = queue->front->data;
19     deleteLoc = queue->front;
20     if (queue->count == 1)
21        // Deleting only item in queue
22        queue->rear = queue->front = NULL;
```

(continue)

Program 15-15   Dequeue *(continued)*

```
23    else
24       queue->front = queue->front->next;
25    (queue->count)--;
26    free (deleteLoc);
27
28    return true;
29 } // dequeue
```

Queue Demonstration

To demonstrate a queue, we write a simple program that creates a queue of colors and then prints them. The design closely parallels the design of the stack demonstration. The node declarations, function declarations, and test driver are contained in **Program 15-16**.

Program 15-16 | Simple queue demonstration

```
1   /* This program is a test driver to demonstrate the
2      basic operation of the enqueue and dequeue functions.
3      Written by:
4      Date:
5   */
6   #include <stdio.h>
7   #include <stdlib.h>
8   #include <string.h>
9   #include <stdbool.h>
10
11  // Global Declarations
12  typedef struct node
13  {
14     int data;
15     struct node* next;
16  } QUEUE_NODE;
17
18  typedef struct
19  {
20     QUEUE_NODE* front;
21     int count;
22     QUEUE_NODE* rear;
23  } QUEUE;
24
25  // Function Declarations
```

(continue)

Program 15-16   Simple queue demonstration *(continued)*

```
26 void insertData (QUEUE* pQueue);
27 void print (QUEUE* pQueue);
28 bool enqueue (QUEUE* pList, int dataIn);
29 bool dequeue (QUEUE* pList, int* dataOut);
30
31 int main (void)
32 {
33 // Local Declarations
34 QUEUE* pQueue;
35
36 // Statements
37    printf("Beginning Simple Queue Program\n");
38
39    pQueue = malloc(sizeof(QUEUE));
40    if (!pQueue)
41       printf("Error allocating queue"), exit(100);
42
43    pQueue->front = NULL;
44    pQueue->count = 0;
45    pQueue->rear = NULL;
46
47    insertData (pQueue);
48    print (pQueue);
49
50    printf("\nEnd Simple Queue Program\n");
51    return 0;
52 } // main
```

Output

```
Beginning Simple Queue Program
Creating numbers: 854 763 123 532 82
Queue contained: 854 763 123 532 82
End Simple Queue Program
```

Insert Data

The insert data function creates a queue by inserting numbers into the queue. The code is developed in **Program 15-17**.

Program 15-17 | The insertData function

```
1   /* =================== insertData ===============
2       This program creates random number data and
3       inserts them into a linked list queue.
4       Pre pQueue is a pointer to first node
5       Post Queue created and filled
6   */
7   void insertData (QUEUE* pQueue)
8   {
9   // Local Declarations
10      int numIn;
11      bool success;
12
13  // Statements
14      printf("Creating numbers: ");
15      for (int nodeCount = 0; nodeCount < 5; nodeCount++)
16      {
17          // Generate random number
18          numIn = rand() % 999;
19          printf("%4d", numIn);
20          success = enqueue(pQueue, numIn);
21          if (!success)
22          {
23              printf("Error 101: Out of Memory\n");
24              exit (101);
25          } // if
26      } // for
27      printf("\n");
28      return;
29  } // insertData
```

Print Queue

Once the queue has been built, we print it to verify that the queue was built correctly. The print function calls the dequeue function until all items have been printed. The print code is found in **Program 15-18**.

Program 15-18 | Print queue

```
 1  /* ===================== print =================
 2     This function prints a singly linked queue.
 3     pre pQueue is pointer to valid queue
 4     post data in queue printed
 5  */
 6  void print (QUEUE* pQueue)
 7  {
 8  // Local Declarations
 9     int printData;
10
11  // Statements
12     printf("Queue contained: ");
13     while (dequeue(pQueue, &printData))
14        printf("%4d", printData);
15     return;
16  } // print
```

15.5 Trees

The study of trees in mathematics can be traced to Gustav Kirchhoff in the middle nineteenth century and several years later to Arthur Cayley, who used trees to study the structure of algebraic formulas. Cayley's work undoubtedly laid the framework for Grace Hopper's use of trees in 1951 to represent arithmetic expressions. Hopper's work bears a strong resemblance to today's binary tree formats.

Trees are used extensively in computer science to represent algebraic formulas; as an efficient method for searching large, dynamic lists, and for such diverse applications as artificial intelligence systems and encoding algorithms.

Basic Tree Concepts

A tree consists of a finite set of elements, called nodes, and a finite set of directed lines, called branches, that connect the nodes. The number of branches associated with a node is the degree of the node. When the branch is directed toward the node, it is an indegree branch; when the branch is directed away from the node, it is an outdegree branch. The sum of the indegree and outdegree branches is the degree of the node.

If the tree is not empty, the first node is called the root. The indegree of the root is, by definition, zero. With the exception of the root, all of the nodes in a tree must have an indegree of exactly one; that is, they may have only one predecessor. All nodes in the tree can have zero, one, or more branches leaving them; that is, they may have an outdegree of zero, one, or more (zero or more successors). **Figure 15-30** is a representation of a tree.

Figure 15-30 Tree

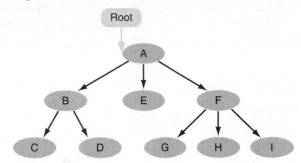

Terminology

In addition to *root*, many different terms are used to describe the attributes of a tree. A leaf is any node with an outdegree of zero, that is, a node with no successors. A node that is not a root or a leaf is known as an internal node because it is found in the middle portion of a tree.

A node is a **parent** if it has successor nodes—that is, if it has an outdegree greater than zero. Conversely, a node with a predecessor is a **child**. A child node has an indegree of one. Two or more nodes with the same parent are siblings. Fortunately, we don't have to worry about aunts, uncles, nieces, nephews, and cousins. Although some texts use the term *grandparent,* we do not. We prefer the more general term *ancestor.* An **ancestor** is any node in the path from the root to the node. A **descendant** is any node in the path below the parent node; that is, all nodes in the paths from a given node to a leaf are descendants of that node. **Figure 15-31** shows the usage of these terms.

Figure 15-31 Tree nomenclature

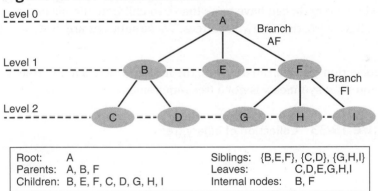

Root:	A	Siblings:	{B,E,F}, {C,D}, {G,H,I}
Parents:	A, B, F	Leaves:	C,D,E,G,H,I
Children:	B, E, F, C, D, G, H, I	Internal nodes:	B, F

Several terms drawn from mathematics or created by computer scientists are used to describe attributes of trees and their nodes. A path is a sequence of nodes in which each node is adjacent to the next one. Every node in the tree can be reached by following a unique path starting from the root. In Figure 15-31, the path from the root to the leaf I is designated as `AFI`. It includes two distinct branches, `AF` and `FI`.

The level of a node is its distance from the root. Because the root has a zero distance from itself, the root is at level 0. The children of the root are at level 1, their children are at level 2, and so forth. Note the relationship between levels and siblings in Figure 15-31. Siblings are always at the same level, but all nodes in a level are not necessarily siblings. For example, at level 2, `C` and `D` are siblings, as are `G`, `H`, and `I`. However, `D` and `G` are not siblings because they have different parents.

The height of the tree is the level of the leaf in the longest path from the root plus 1. By definition, the height of an empty tree is –1. Figure 15-31 contains nodes at three levels: 0, 1, and 2. Its height is 3. Because the tree is drawn upside down, some texts refer to the depth of a tree rather than its height.

A tree may be divided into subtrees. A subtree is any connected structure below the root. The first node in a subtree is known as the root of the subtree and is used to name the subtree. Subtrees can also be further subdivided into subtrees. In **Figure 15-32**, BCD is a subtree, as are E and FGHI. Note that by this definition, a single node is a subtree. Thus, the subtree B can be divided into two subtrees, C and D, and the subtree F contains the subtrees G, H, and I.

Figure 15-32   Subtrees

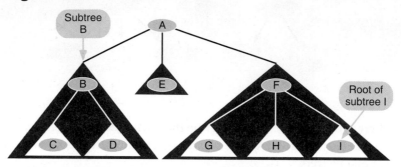

> **Note**
>
> The concept of subtrees leads us to a recursive definition of a tree:
>
> A tree is a set of nodes that either: (1) is empty or (2) has a designated node, called the root, from which hierarchically descend zero or more subtrees, which are also trees.

Binary Trees

A binary tree is a tree in which no node can have more than two children; the maximum outdegree for a node is two. In other words, a node can have zero, one, or two subtrees. These subtrees are designated as the left subtree and the right subtree.

Figure 15-33 contains a collection of eight binary trees, the first of which is a null tree, that is, a tree with no nodes. As you study this figure, note that symmetry is not a tree requirement.

Figure 15-33   Collection of binary trees

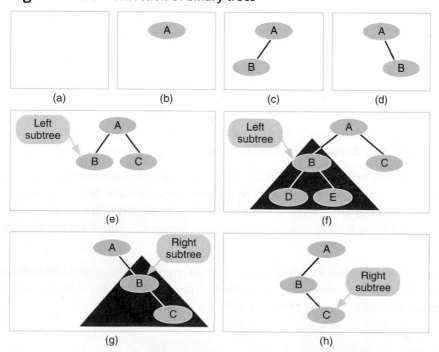

Binary Tree Data Structure

A binary tree needs two separate data structures: one for the head and one for the nodes. As with the linear list, the structure uses a simple head structure that contains a count and a root pointer.

The binary tree nodes contain the application data and two self-referential pointers to the left and right subtrees. These data structures are shown in **Figure 15-34**.

Figure 15-34   Binary tree data structure

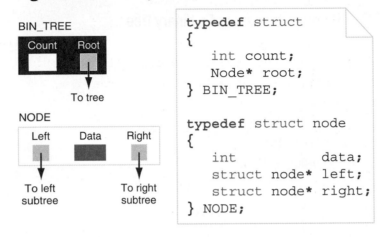

```
typedef struct
{
    int count;
    Node* root;
} BIN_TREE;

typedef struct node
{
    int          data;
    struct node* left;
    struct node* right;
} NODE;
```

Binary Tree Traversals

Given that a binary tree consists of a root, a left subtree, and a right subtree, we can define six different traversal sequences. Computer scientists have assigned three of these sequences standard names in the literature; the other three are unnamed but are easily derived. The first two standard traversals are shown in **Figure 15-35**. Note that we only discuss the preorder and inorder traversals in this text. The others will be covered in your data structures class.

Figure 15-35   Binary tree traversals

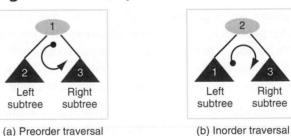

The traditional terminology for the traversals uses a designation of node (N) for the root, left (L) for the left subtree, and right (R) for the right subtree. To demonstrate the different traversal sequences for a binary tree, we use **Figure 15-36**.

Figure 15-36   Binary tree for traversals

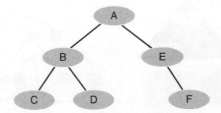

Preorder Traversal (NLR)

In the preorder traversal, the root node is processed first, followed by the left subtree and then the right subtree. It draws its name from the Latin prefix *pre*, which means to go before. Thus, the root goes before the subtrees.

Given the recursive characteristics of trees, it is only natural to implement tree traversals recursively. First we process the root, then the left subtree, and then the right subtree. The left subtree is in turn processed recursively, as is the right subtree. The code for the preorder traversal is shown in **Program 15-19**.

Program 15-19 | Preorder traversal of a binary tree

```
 1   /* Traverse a binary tree and print its data (integers).
 2          Pre  root is entry node of a tree or subtree
 3          Post each node has been printed
 4   */
 5   void preOrder (NODE* root)
 6   {
 7   // Statements
 8      if (root)
 9      {
10         printf ("%4d", root->data);
11         preOrder (root->left);
12         preOrder (root->right);
13      } // if
14      return;
15  } // preorder
```

Using the tree in Figure 15-36, the processing sequence for a preorder traversal processes this tree as follows: First we process the root A. After the root, we process the left subtree. To process the left subtree, we first process its root, B, then its left subtree and right subtree in order. When B's left and right subtrees have been processed in order, we are then ready to process A's right subtree, E. To process the subtree E, we first process the root and then the left subtree and the right subtree. Because there is no left subtree, we continue immediately with the right subtree, which completes the tree.

Figure 15-37 shows another way to visualize the traversal of the tree. Imagine that we are walking around the tree, starting on the left of the root and keeping as close to the nodes as possible. In the preorder traversal, we process the node when we meet it for the first time (on the left of the node). This is shown as a black box on the left of the node. The path is shown as a line following a route completely around the tree and back to the root.

Figure 15-37 Preorder traversal: A B C D E F

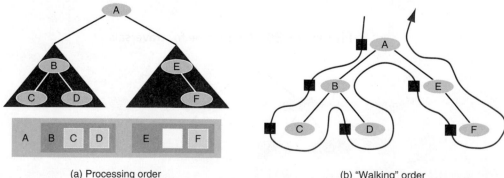

(a) Processing order   (b) "Walking" order

Figure 15-38 shows the recursive algorithmic traversal of the tree. The first call processes the root of the tree, A. It then recursively calls itself to process the root of the subtree B, as shown in Figure 15-38(b). The third call, shown in Figure 15-38(c), processes node C, which is also subtree C. At this point we call preorder with a null pointer, which results in an immediate return to subtree C to process its right subtree. Because C's right subtree is also null, we return to node B so that we can process its right tree, D, in Figure 15-38(d). After processing node D, we make two more calls, one with D's null left pointer and one with its null right pointer. Because subtree B has now been completely processed, we return to the tree root and process its right subtree, E, in Figure 15-38(e). After a call to E's null left subtree, we call E's right subtree, F, in Figure 15-38(f). Although the tree is completely processed at this point, we still have two more calls to make: one to F's null left subtree and one to its null right subtree. We can now back out of the tree, returning first to E and then to A, which concludes the traversal of the tree.

Figure 15-38 Algorithmic traversal of binary tree

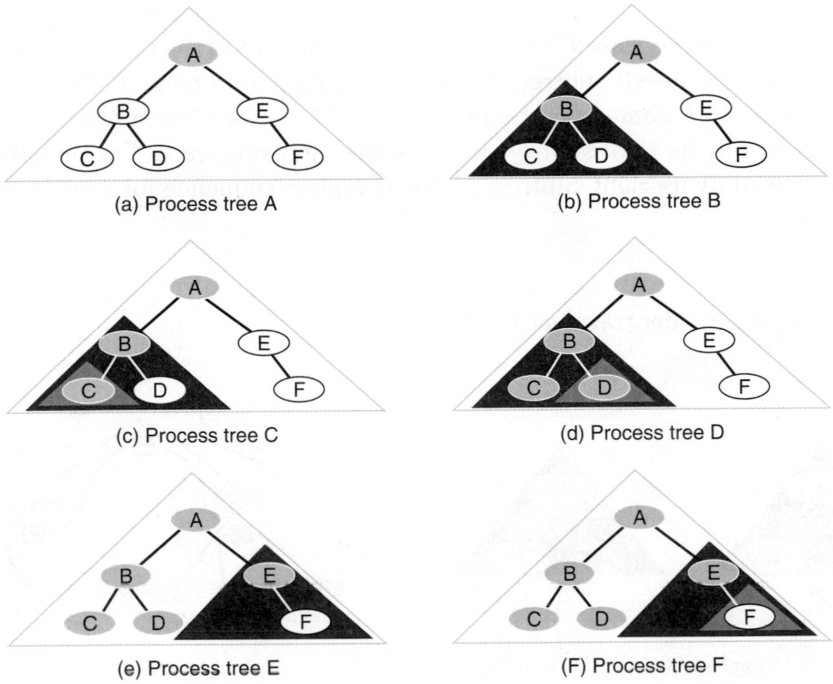

(a) Process tree A

(b) Process tree B

(c) Process tree C

(d) Process tree D

(e) Process tree E

(F) Process tree F

Inorder Traversal (LNR)

The **inorder traversal** processes the left subtree first, then the root, and finally the right subtree. The meaning of the prefix *in* is that the root is processed in between the subtrees. Once again, we implement the algorithm recursively, as shown in **Program 15-20**.

Program 15-20 | Inorder traversal of a binary tree

```
1  /* Traverse a binary tree and print its data (integers)
2     Pre root is entry node of a tree or subtree
3     Post each node has been printed
4  */
5  void inOrder (NODE* root)
6  {
7  // Statements
```

(continue)

Program 15-20   Inorder traversal of a binary tree *(continued)*

```
 8        if (root)
 9        {
10            inOrder (root->left);
11            printf("%4d", root->data);
12            inOrder (root->right);
13        } // if
14        return;
15 } // inOrder
```

Because the left subtree must be processed first, we trace from the root to the far-left leaf node before processing any nodes. After processing the far-left subtree, C, we process its parent node, B. We are now ready to process the right subtree, D. Processing D completes the processing of the root's left subtree, and we are now ready to process the root, A, followed by its right subtree. Because the right subtree, E, has no left child, we can process its root immediately followed by its right subtree, F. The complete sequence for inOrder processing is shown in **Figure 15-39**(a).

Figure 15-39   Inorder traversal: C B D A E F

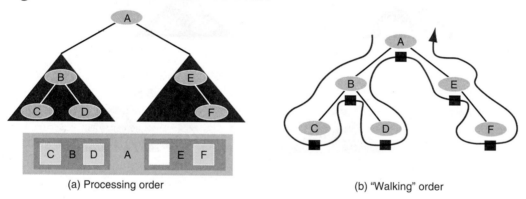

(a) Processing order   (b) "Walking" order

To walk around the tree in inOrder sequence, we follow the same path but process each node when we meet it for the second time (the bottom of the node). This processing route is shown in **Figure 15-39**(b).

Binary Search Trees

In this section, we define and discuss one of the most common binary trees: binary search trees. The binary search tree is constructed so that when the tree is traversed using an inOrder traversal, the data are in ascending sequence.

Definition

A binary search tree (BST) is a binary tree with the following properties:

> All items in the left subtree are less than the root.

> All items in the right subtree are greater than or equal to the root.

> Each subtree is itself a binary search tree.

Generally, the information represented by each node is a record rather than a single data element. When the binary search tree definition is applied to a record, the sequencing properties refer to the key of the record. **Figure 15-40** reflects the properties of a binary tree in which K is the key.

Figure 15-40   Binary search tree

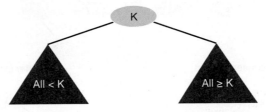

Figure 15-41 contains five binary search trees that are valid.

Figure 15-41   Valid binary search trees

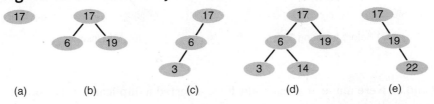

(a)   (b)   (c)   (d)   (e)

Now let's look at some binary trees that do not have the properties of a binary search tree. Examine the binary trees in **Figure 15-42**. The first tree, Figure 15-42(a), breaks the first rule: All items in the left subtree must be less than the root. The key in the left subtree (22) is greater than the key in the root (17). The second tree, Figure 15-42(b), breaks the second rule: All items in the right subtree must be greater than or equal to the root. The key in the right subtree (11) is less than the key in the root (17). Figure 15-42(c) breaks the third rule: Each subtree must be a binary search tree. In this tree, the left subtree key (6) is less than the root (17), and the right subtree key (19) is greater than the root. However, the left subtree is not a valid binary search tree because it breaks the first rule: its left subtree (11) is greater than the root (6). Figure 15-42(d) also breaks one of the three rules. Do you see which one? (*Hint:* What is the largest key in the left subtree?)

Figure 15-42   Invalid binary search trees

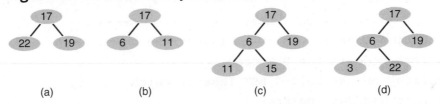

(a)   (b)   (c)   (d)

Insertion

The insert node function adds data to a binary search tree. To insert data all we need to do is follow the branches to an empty subtree and then insert the new node. In other words, all inserts take place at a leaf or at a leaflike node—a node that has at least one null subtree.

Figure 15-43 shows our binary search tree after we have inserted two nodes. We first added node 19. To locate its insertion point, we searched the tree through the path 23, 18, and 20 to a null left branch. After locating the insertion point, we inserted the new node as the left subtree of 20. We then added 38. This time we searched the tree through 23, 44, and 35 to a null right subtree and inserted the new node.

Figure 15-43 BST insertion

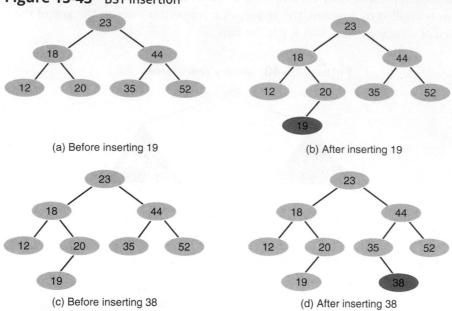

(a) Before inserting 19

(b) After inserting 19

(c) Before inserting 38

(d) After inserting 38

Insertions of both 19 and 38 were made at a leaf node. If we inserted a duplicate of the root, 23, it would become the left subtree of 35. Remember that in a binary search tree, nodes with equal values are inserted in the right subtree. The path for its insertion would therefore be 23, 44, and 35. In this case, the insertion takes place at a leaflike node. Although 35 has a right subtree, its left subtree is null. We would therefore place the new node, 23, as the left subtree of 35.

We are now ready to develop the insert algorithm. We can write an elegant algorithm that inserts the data into the tree using recursion. If the tree or subtree is empty, we simply insert the data at the root. If we are not at an empty tree, we determine which branch we need to follow and call recursively to determine whether we are at a leaf yet. The code is shown in **Program 15-21**. Note that as we saw with other dynamic structures, the BST_Insert can raise an overflow error.

Program 15-21 | Binary tree insert function

```
1   /* ==================== BST_Insert ====================
2       This function uses recursion to insert the new data
3       into a leaf node in the BST tree.
4       Pre Application has called BST_Insert, which
5       passes root and data pointer
6       Post Data have been inserted
7       Return pointer to [potentially] new root
8   */
9   NODE* BST_Insert (BST_TREE* tree,
10                     NODE* root, int dataIn)
11  {
12  // Local Declarations
13      NODE* newPtr;
14
```

(continue)

Program 15-21 Binary tree insert function *(continued)*

```c
15  // Statements
16
17     if (root)
18     {
19        // NULL tree — create new node
20        newPtr = malloc(sizeof (NODE));
21        if (!newPtr)
22           printf("Overflow in Insert\n"), exit (100);
23        newPtr->data = dataIn;
24        newPtr->left = newPtr->right = NULL;
25        return newPtr;
26     } // if
27
28     // Locate null subtree for insertion
29     if (dataIn < root->data)
30        root->left = BST_lnsert(tree, root->left,
31                                  dataIn);
32     else
33     // new data >= root data
34        root->right = BST_Insert(tree, root->right,
35                                   dataIn);
36     return root;
37  } // BST_Insert
```

This algorithm must be carefully studied to fully understand its logic. It begins with a recursive search to locate the correct insertion point in a leaf node. A leaf node is identified by a subtree pointer, either right or left, that is null. When we find a leaf pointer, we create a new node and return its address so that it can be inserted into the parent pointer (statement 25).

Because this is a recursive function, it must have a base case. Can you see it? The base case occurs when we locate a leaf and return `newPtr` in statement 25. At this point, we begin to back out of the tree.

Binary Tree Example

Let's write a program that builds a binary search tree. We build the tree by asking the user to enter numbers. Once the tree is built, we print it in both `preOrder` and `inOrder` sequence to verify the insertions. To keep the program simple, we will use integer data. The design is shown in **Figure 15-44**.

Figure 15-44 Binary tree program design

The code is shown in **Program 15-22**.

Program 15-22 | Binary tree example

```c
 1  /* Demonstrate the binary search tree insert and
 2     traversals.
 3     Written by:
 4     Date:
 5  */
 6  #include <stdio.h>
 7
 8  #include <stdlib.h>
 9  // Global Declarations
10  typedef struct node
11  {
12     int data;
13     struct node* left;
14     struct node* right;
15  } NODE;
16
17  typedef struct
18  {
19     int count;
20     NODE* root;
21  } BST_TREE;
22
23  // Function Declarations
24  void preOrder (NODE* root);
25  void inOrder (NODE* root);
26  NODE* BST_Insert (BST_TREE* tree,
27                    NODE* root, int data);
28
29  int main (void)
30  {
31  // Local Declarations
32     int numIn;
33     BST_TREE tree;
34
35  // Statements
36     printf("Please enter a series of integers.");
37     printf("\nEnter a negative number to stop\n");
38
```

(continue)

Program 15-22   Binary tree example *(continued)*

```
39      tree.count = 0;
40      tree.root = NULL;
41      do
42      {
43          printf("Enter a number: ");
44          scanf("%d", &numIn);
45          if (numIn > 0)
46          {
47              tree.root = BST_Insert
48                  (&tree, tree.root, numIn);
49              tree.count++;
50          } // if
51      } while (numIn >0);
52
53      printf("\nData in preOrder: ");
54      preOrder (tree.root);
55
56      printf("\n\nData in inOrder: ");
57      inOrder (tree.root);
58
59      printf("\n\nEnd of BST Demonstration\n");
60      return 0;
61  } // main
```

Output

```
Please enter a series of integers.
Enter a negative number to stop
Enter a number: 45
Enter a number: 54
Enter a number: 23
Enter a number: 32
Enter a number: 3
Enter a number: -1
Data in preOrder: 45 23 3 32 54
Data in inOrder: 3 23 32 45 54
End of BST Demonstration
```

15.6 Graphs

A graph is a collection of nodes, called vertices, and a collection of segments, called lines, connecting pairs of vertices. In other words, a graph consists of two sets, a set of vertices and a set of lines.

Graphs may be either directed or undirected. A directed graph (digraph) is a graph in which each line has a direction (arrow head) to its successor. A line in a directed graph is known as an arc. In a directed graph, the flow along the arcs between two vertices can follow only the indicated direction. An undirected graph is a graph in which there is no direction (arrow head) on any line, which is known as an edge. In an undirected graph, the flow between two vertices can go in either direction. **Figure 15-45** contains an example of both a directed graph (a) and an undirected graph (b).

Figure 15-45   Directed and undirected graphs

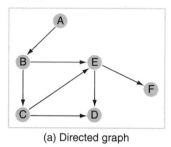
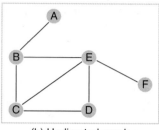

(a) Directed graph   (b) Undirected graph

A path is a sequence of vertices in which each vertex is adjacent to the next one. In Figure 15-45, {A, B, C, E} is one path and {A, B, E, F} is another. Note that both directed and undirected graphs have paths. In an undirected graph, you may travel in either direction.

Two vertices in a graph are said to be adjacent vertices (or neighbors) if there is a path of length 1 connecting them. In Figure 15-45(a), B is adjacent to A, whereas E is not adjacent to D; on the other hand, D is adjacent to E. In Figure 15-45(b), E and D are adjacent, but D and F are not.

A cycle is a path consisting of at least three vertices that starts and ends with the same vertex. In Figure 15-45(b), B, C, D, E, B is a cycle. Note, however, that the same vertices in Figure 15-45(a) do not constitute a cycle because in a digraph a path can follow only the direction of the arc, whereas in an undirected graph a path can move in either direction along the edge. A loop is a special case of a cycle in which a single arc begins and ends with the same vertex. In a loop, the end points of the line are the same. **Figure 15-46** contains a loop.

Figure 15-46   Cycles and loops

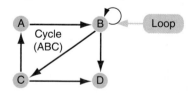

Two vertices are said to be connected if there is a path between them. A graph is said to be a **connected graph** if, ignoring direction, there is a path from any vertex to any other vertex. Furthermore, a directed graph is a **strongly connected graph** if there is a path from each vertex (node) to every other vertex in the digraph. A directed graph is a **weakly connected graph** if at least two vertices are not connected. (A connected, undirected graph would always be strongly connected, so the concept is not normally used with undirected graphs.) A graph is a disjoint graph if it is not connected. **Figure 15-47** contains a weakly connected graph (a), a strongly connected graph (b), and a disjoint graph (c).

Figure 15-47 Connected and disjoint graphs

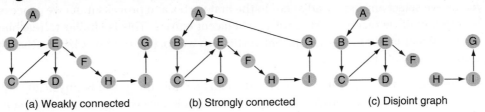

(a) Weakly connected   (b) Strongly connected   (c) Disjoint graph

The degree of a vertex is the number of lines incident to it. In Figure 15-47(a) the degree of vertex B is 3 and the degree of vertex E is 4. The outdegree of a vertex in a digraph is the number of arcs leaving the vertex; the indegree is the number of arcs entering the vertex. Again, in Figure 15-47(a) the indegree of vertex B is 1 and its outdegree is 2; in Figure 15-47(b) the indegree of vertex E is 3 and its outdegree is 1.

> **Note**
>
> One final point: a tree is a graph in which each vertex has only one predecessor; however, a graph is not a tree. We will see later in the chapter that some graphs have one or more trees in them that can be algorithmically determined.

Graph Traversal

A complete discussion of graph algorithms is beyond the scope of this text. As an example of a graph algorithm, we discuss two graph traversals. The remaining algorithms to maintain and traverse graphs are left for your data structures course.

There is always at least one application that requires that all vertices in a given graph be visited; that is, there is at least one application that requires that the graph be traversed. Because a vertex in a graph can have multiple parents, the traversal of a graph presents some problems not found in the traversal of linear lists and trees. Specifically, we must somehow ensure that we process the data in each vertex only once. However, because there are multiple paths to a vertex, we may arrive at it from more than one direction as we traverse the graph. The traditional solution to this problem is to include a visited flag at each vertex. Before the traversal we set the visited flag in each vertex to *off*. Then, as we traverse the graph, we set the visited flag to *on* to indicate that the data have been processed.

There are two standard graph traversals: depth first and breadth first. Both use the visited flag.

Depth-first Traversal

In the depth-first traversal, we process all of a vertex's descendants before we move to an adjacent vertex. This concept is most easily seen when the graph is a tree. In **Figure 15-48**, we show the tree preorder traversal-processing sequence, one of the standard depth-first traversals.

Figure 15-48 Depth-first traversal of a tree

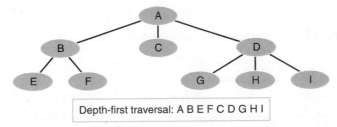

Depth-first traversal: A B E F C D G H I

In a similar manner, the depth-first traversal of a graph starts by processing the first vertex of the graph. After processing the first vertex, we select any vertex adjacent to the first vertex and process it. As we process each vertex, we select an adjacent vertex until we reach a vertex with no adjacent entries. This is similar to reaching a leaf in a tree. We then back out of the structure, processing adjacent vertices as we go. It should be obvious that this logic requires a stack (or recursion) to complete the traversal.

The order in which the adjacent vertices are processed depends on how the graph is physically stored. Because we are using a stack, however, the traversal processes adjacent vertices in descending, or last in–first out (LIFO), order.

Let's trace a depth-first traversal through the graph in **Figure 15-49**. The number in the box next to a vertex indicates the processing order. The stacks below the graph show the stack contents as we work our way down the graph and then as we back out.

Figure 15-49   Depth-first traversal of a graph

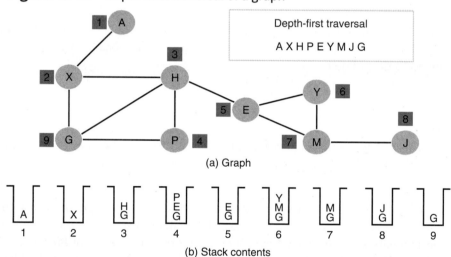

(a) Graph

(b) Stack contents

1. We begin by pushing the first vertex, A, into the stack.

2. We then loop, pop the stack, and, after processing the vertex, push all of the adjacent vertices into the stack. To process X at step 2, therefore, we pop X from the stack, process it, and then push G and H into the stack, giving the stack contents for step 3, as shown in Figure 15-49(b)—H G.

3. When the stack is empty, the traversal is complete.

Breadth-first Traversal

In the breadth-first traversal of a graph, we process all adjacent vertices of a vertex before going to the next level. We saw the breadth-first traversal earlier in the chapter. Looking at the tree in **Figure 15-50**, we see that its breadth-first traversal starts at level 0 and then processes all the vertices in level 1 before going on to process the vertices in level 2.

Figure 15-50   Breadth-first traversal of a tree

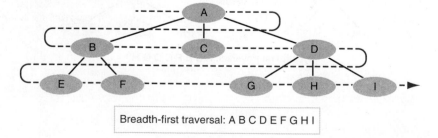

The breadth-first traversal of a graph follows the same concept. We begin by picking a starting vertex (A); after processing it, we process all of its adjacent vertices (BCD). After we process all of the first vertex's adjacent vertices, we pick its first adjacent vertex (B) and process all of its vertices, then the second adjacent vertex (C) and all of its vertices, and so forth until we are finished.

As shown in **Figure 15-51**, the breadth-first traversal uses a queue rather than a stack. As we process each vertex, we place all of its adjacent vertices in the queue. Then, to select the next vertex to be processed, we delete a vertex from the queue and process it.

Figure 15-51 Breadth-first traversal of a graph

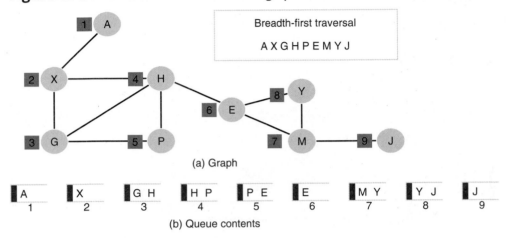

(a) Graph

(b) Queue contents

Let's trace this logic through the graph in Figure 15-51:

1. We begin by enqueuing vertex A in the queue.

2. We then loop, dequeuing the queue and processing the vertex from the front of the queue. After processing the vertex, we place all of its adjacent vertices into the queue. Thus, at step 2 in Figure 15-51(b), we dequeue vertex X, process it, and then place vertices G and H in the queue. We are then ready for step 3, in which we process vertex G.

3. When the queue is empty, the traversal is complete.

Programming Example: Tying It All Together

So far, you have seen a wide range of examples of linked lists demonstrating queues, stacks, and other structures. In addition, you have been presented with all possible operations on linked lists, including inserting a node, deleting a node, and manipulating data of a node. In this section, we will take on a programming example that ties all the concepts presented in this text and the different operations of linked lists together. In this example, we will consider a set of playing cards. Our objective is to randomly generate four hands from the deck of cards and then display the contents of each hand in sorted manner by suit and value. **Program 15-23** defines playing card structures, and **Program 15-24** builds linked list with unshuffled cards. **Program 15-25** shuffles the cards, and **Program 15-26** deals 13 cards for each hand and sorts each hand by suit only. Finally, **Program 15-27** displays each hand.

Program 15-23 | Playing cards example part 1: declaration and main functions

```c
1  /* Demonstrate playing cards operations:
2      1. Build cards deck
3      2. Shuffle deck
4      3. Deal 4 hands
5      4. Sort each hand by suit
6      5. Display each hand
7      Written by:
8      Date:
9  */
10
11 #include <stdlib.h>
12 #include <stdio.h>
13 #include <string.h>
14
15 char suit[][10]=
16 {
17     "HEARTS", "CLUBS", "DIAMONDS", "SPADES"
18 };
19
20 char face_value[][10] =
21 {
22     "TWO", "THREE", "FOUR", "FIVE",
23     "SIX", "SEVEN", "EIGHT", "NINE", "TEN",
24     "JACK", "QUEEN", "KING", "ACE"
25 };
26
27 typedef struct node
28 {
29     char face_val[10];
30     char suit[10];
31     struct node * next;
32 } card;
33
34 card * buildDeck();
35 card * shuffleDeck(card *deck);
36 card * dealHand(card *deck, int hand);
37 void sortHand(card **hand);
38 void printDeck(card *deck);
39
40 int main(void)
41 {
42 //local variables
```

(continue)

Program 15-23   Playing cards example part 1: declaration and main functions (*continued*)

```
42     card *deck=NULL;
43     card *hand1, *hand2, *hand3, *hand4;
44
45  //Statements
46     //Build and shuffle cards deck
47     deck = buildDeck();
48     deck = shuffleDeck(deck);
49     printDeck(deck);
50
51     //deal hands
52     hand1 = dealHand(deck, 0);
53     hand2 = dealHand(deck, 1);
54     hand3 = dealHand(deck, 2);
55     hand4 = dealHand(deck, 3);
56
57     //sort hands
58     sortHand(&hand1);
59     sortHand(&hand2);
60     sortHand(&hand3);
61     sortHand(&hand4);
62     //sort hands
63     printHand(hand1);
64     printHand(hand2);
65     printHand(hand3);
66     printHand(hand4);
67
68     return 0;
69  } // main
```

Program 15-24 | Playing cards example part 2: build linked list with unshuffled cards

```
1   //Build deck using defined suit and face_value arrays
2   card * buildDeck()
3   {
4      int i, j;
5      card *deck=NULL;
6      card *newCard;
7
8      for (i=0; i<13; i++)
9      {
10        for (j=0; j<4; j++)
11        {
```

(*continue*)

Program 15-24 Playing cards example part 2: build linked list with unshuffled cards *(continued)*

```
12              newCard = (card*)malloc(sizeof(card));
13              strcpy(newCard->face_val,face_value[i]);
14              strcpy(newCard->suit,suit[j]);
15
16              if (deck == NULL)
17                  deck = newCard;
18               else
19              {
20                  newCard->next = deck->next;
21                  deck->next = newCard;
22              }
23          }
24      }
25      return deck;
26 } // buildDeck
```

Program 15-25 | Playing cards example part 3: shuffle deck of cards

```
1   //shuffle deck
2   card * shuffleDeck(card * deck)
3   {
4      int i, j, pos;
5      card *newDeck = NULL;
6      card *newCard, *curr;
7      char tempStr[10], tempSuit[52][10], tempFace[52][10];
8
9      srand(time(0));
10
11     //fill temp array
12     curr = deck;
13     for(i=0; i<52; i++)
14     {
15        strcpy(tempSuit[i], curr->suit);
16        strcpy(tempFace[i], curr->face_val);
17        curr = curr->next;
18     }
19
20     //shuffle temp array
21     for(i=0; i<52; i++)
22     {
23        pos = rand()%52;
24        strcpy(tempStr, tempSuit[i]);
```

(continue)

Program 15-25   Playing cards example part 3: shuffle deck of cards *(continued)*

```
25          strcpy(tempSuit[i], tempSuit[pos]);
26          strcpy(tempSuit[pos], tempStr);
27          strcpy(tempStr, tempFace[i]);
28          strcpy(tempFace[i], tempFace[pos]);
29          strcpy(tempFace[pos], tempStr);
30      }
31
32      //re-build linked list with shuffled deck
33      for(i=0; i<52; i++)
34      {
35          newCard = (card*)malloc(sizeof(card));
36          strcpy(newCard->suit,tempSuit[i]);
37          strcpy(newCard->face_val, tempFace[i]);
38
39          if (newDeck == NULL)
40              newDeck = newCard;
41          else
42          {
43              newCard->next = newDeck->next;
44              newDeck->next = newCard;
45          }
46      }
47
48      return newDeck;
49 } // shuffleDeck
```

Program 15-26 | Playing cards example part 4: deal and sort functions

```
1  //Deal hand from deck - 13 cards
2  card * dealHand(card * deck, int hand)
3  {
4      int i;
5      card *newCard, *curr=deck, *newHand=NULL;
6
7      for(i=0; i<52; i++)
8      {
9          if(i%4==hand)
10         {
11             newCard = (card*)malloc(sizeof(card));
12             strcpy(newCard->suit,curr->suit);
13             strcpy(newCard->face_val, curr->face_val);
14             if (newHand == NULL)
```

(continue)

Program 15-26   Playing cards example part 4: deal and sort functions *(continued)*

```
15                  newHand = newCard;
16              else
17              {
18                  newCard->next = newHand->next;
19                  newHand->next = newCard;
20              }
21          }
22          curr = curr->next;
23      }
24      return newHand;
25  } // Deal hand
26
27  //Sort hand by card suit using bubble sort.
28  void sortHand(card **hand)
29  {
30      card *curr = *hand, *indx = NULL;
31      char temp[10];
32
33      if(curr == NULL)
34          return;
35      else
36      {
37          while(curr != NULL)
38          {
39              indx = curr->next;
40              while(indx != NULL)
41              {
42                  if(strcmp(curr->suit, indx->suit) > 0 )
43                  {
44
45                      strcpy(temp, curr->suit);
46                      strcpy(curr->suit, indx->suit);
47                      strcpy(indx->suit, temp);
48                      strcpy(temp, curr->face_val);
49                      strcpy(curr->face_val, indx->face_val);
50                      strcpy(indx->face_val, temp);
51                  }
52                  indx = indx->next;
53              }
54              curr = curr->next;
55          }
56      }
57
58  } //Sort hand
```

Program 15-27 | Playing cards example part 5: display deck and hand functions

```c
1   // Display full deck by hand
2   void printDeck(card *deck)
3   {
4      int i, j;
5      card *ptr;
6      ptr = deck;
7
8      if (ptr == NULL)
9         printf("Deck is empty\n");
10
11     printf("\t\tHand 1\t\t\t Hand2\t\t\t Hand 3\t\t\t Hand 4\n");
12
13     for (i=0; i<13; i++)
14     {
15        printf("Card#%2d:\t", i+1);
16        for (j=0; j<4; j++)
17        {
18           printf("%s:%s\t\t ", ptr->suit, ptr->face_val);
19           ptr = ptr->next;
20        }
21        printf("\n");
22     }
23  } //printDeck
24
25  // Display hand
26  void printHand(card *hand)
27  {
28     int i;
29     card *ptr = hand;
30
31     if ( ptr == NULL)
32        printf("Hand is empty\n");
33     for (i=0; i<13; i++)
34     {
35        printf("Card#%2d:\t", i+1);
36        printf("%s:%s\n", ptr->suit, ptr->face_val);
37        ptr = ptr->next;
38     }
39     printf("\n");
40  } // printHand
```

Software Engineering

Because linear lists are useful structures, programmers use them in many applications. Rather than rewrite their functions each time we need them, we can write functions once and put them in a library. Then, when we need to use a linear list, we simply include the library. The name given to a complete set of functions built like this is abstract data type (ADT). To present the concept, we need to define a few new terms.

Atomic and Composite Data

Data that we choose to consider as a single, nondecomposable entity are called atomic data. For example, the integer 4562 may be considered as a single integer value. Of course, you can decompose it into digits, but the decomposed digits do not have the same characteristics of the original integer; they are four one-digit integers in the range 0 to 9.

An atomic data type is a set of atomic data having identical properties. These properties distinguish one atomic data type from another. Atomic data types are defined by a set of values and a set of operations that act on the values.

For example, we can define the following atomic data types:

```
int
VALUES:  -∞, …,  -2, -1, 0, 1, 2, …, ∞
OPERATIONS: *, +, -, %, /, ++, --, <, >, …
float
VALUES:  -∞ …, 0.0, …, ∞
OPERATIONS: *, +, -, /, <, >, …
char
VALUES: \0, …, 'A', 'B' , …, 'a', 'b', …, \127
OPERATIONS: <, >, …
```

The opposite of atomic data is composite data. Composite data can be broken into subfields that have meaning. As an example of a composite data item, consider your telephone number. A telephone number actually has three different parts. First is the area code. Then, what you consider to be your phone number is actually two different data items: a prefix consisting of three digits and the number within the prefix, consisting of four digits. Years ago, these prefixes were names such as DAvenport and CYpress.

Data Structure

A data structure is a collection of elements and the relationships among them. Data structures can be nested. That is, we can have a data structure that consists of other data structures. A data structure is a combination of elements, each of which is either a data type or another data structure. Moreover, a data structure is a set of associations or relationships (structure) involving the combined elements.

For example, we can define the two structures, array and `struct`, as shown in **Table 15-2**.

Table 15-2 Two structures

ARRAY	STRUCTURE
❯ A homogeneous combination of data structures	❯ A heterogeneous combination of data structures
❯ Position association	❯ No association

Most programming languages support several data structures. In addition, modern programming languages allow programmers to create new data structures that are not available in the language they are using. In C, this is done with `struct`.

Abstract Data Type

Generally speaking, programmers' capabilities are determined by the tools in their tool kits. These tools are acquired by education and experience. Your knowledge of C is one of your tools. As you continue to study subjects such as data structures, file management, and systems analysis, your tools will increase. Abstract data types (ADT) are another tool to add to your tool kit.

The first computer programming languages had no ADTs. To read a file, programmers wrote the code to read the file device. It did not take long for it to become clear that programmers were writing the same code over and over again. So programmers created what is known today as an ADT. A programmer wrote the code to read a file and placed it in a library for all programmers to use.

This concept is found in C today. For example, the standard input/output library is an ADT. It has data structures and a set of operations that can be used to read and write data.

With an ADT, the user is not concerned with *how* the task is done but rather with *what* it can do. In other words, the ADT consists of a set of prototype definitions that allow the programmer to use the functions while hiding the implementation. This generalization of operations with unspecified implementations is known as abstraction. We abstract the essence of the process and leave the implementation details hidden.

> **Note**
>
> In the concept of abstraction:
> › We know what a data type can do.
> › How it is done is hidden.

Consider the concept of a list. At least three data structures can support a list. We can use an array, a linear list, or a file. If we place the list in an abstract data type, the user should not be aware of the structure we use. As long as data can be inserted and retrieved, it should make no difference how we store the data. **Figure 15-52** shows several structures that might be used to hold a list.

Figure 15-52 Structures for holding a list

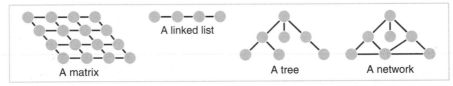

A matrix   A linked list   A tree   A network

An abstract data type is formally defined as a data declaration packaged together with the operations that are allowed on the data type. In other words, we encapsulate the data and the operations on data, and we hide their implementation from the user.

The ADT definition implies two attributes for ADTs:

1. The structures are opaque. We can use them without knowing how they are implemented.

2. The operations are opaque. We know what they do; we don't know how they do it.

We cannot overstress the importance of hiding the implementation. For example, the programmer should not have to know the data structure to use the ADT. This is a common fault in many implementations that keep the ADT from being fully portable to other applications. Fortunately, C's rich library capability gives us the tools to fully implement any ADT.

A Model for an Abstract Data Type

The ADT model is shown in **Figure 15-53**. The model is represented by the blue area with an irregular outline. Inside are two different aspects of the model: the data structure and the operational functions. Both are entirely contained in the model and are not within the user's scope. However, the data structure is available to all the ADT's operations as needed, and an operation may call on other functions to accomplish its task. In other words, the data structure and the functions are within scope of each other.

Figure 15-53 Abstract data type model

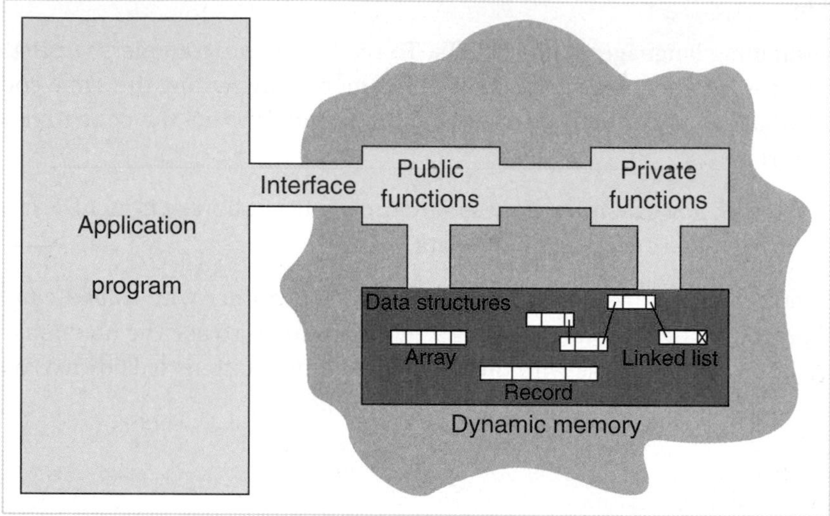

Data flows in and out of the ADT through the operation headers represented by the rectangular "interface" pathway. The interface is also the pathway for the ADT functions. For instance, a linear list ADT would have operations that we saw in this chapter, such as insert, remove, and search. In C, these operations are defined as prototype header declarations that are visible to the user. Note, however, that only the "public" functions are available to the application program; the "private" functions are totally contained with the ADT and can only be used by other functions within the ADT.

To use the ADT in our program, we need to create a user header file. When we create a header file for a linear list ADT, we give its header file a name, such as `linklist.h`. To include it in our program, we would use a preprocessor directive such as:

```
#include "linklist.h"
```

ADT Data Structure

When the list is controlled entirely by the program, it is often implemented using simple structures such as those shown in this chapter. Because the ADT must hide the implementation from the user, however, all data about the structure must be maintained inside the ADT. But just encapsulating the structure in the ADT is not sufficient. In addition, multiple versions of the structure must be able to coexist. This means that we must hide the implementation from the user while storing data about the structure in the user's program.

You have seen this concept before. When you create a file, you use the predefined structure `FILE`. Defining a file in your program creates a file structure that becomes a part of your program. We can do the same thing with the ADT. Each ADT must have a defined type that the users can define in their programs. Just like the file type, the ADT type is a pointer to a structure that contains attributes about the structure. When the ADT attribute structure is created, it is stored in the heap. The only structural element in the user's program is a pointer to the structure.

This short description of ADTs just begins to introduce the topic. When you take a data structure class, you may have the opportunity to create and use some in your programs.

Tips and Common Programming Errors

1. The link field in the last node of a linked list must have a null value.

2. Memory must be allocated for a node before you add the node to a linked list.

3. Be sure to free memory after you delete a node from a linked list.

4. You must create an empty linked list (by assigning NULL to the header pointer) before using the functions introduced in this chapter.

5. Remember that a null link means there is no pointer; therefore, you cannot use it to dereference another node (or any other object). For example, the following code creates a run-time error because when the loop terminates, the value of pCur is NULL.

```
while (pCur != NULL)
{
    ...
    pCur = pCur->link;
    // ERROR
    printf("%d", pCur->data.member_name);
} // while
```

6. It is a logic error to allocate a node in the heap and not test for overflow.

7. It is a logic error to refer to a node after its memory has been released with free.

8. It is a logic error to set the only pointer to a node to NULL before the node has been freed. The node is irretrievably lost.

9. It is a logic error to delete a node from a linked list without verifying that the node contains the target of the delete.

10. It is a logic error to fail to set the head pointer to the new node when a node is added before the first node in a linked list. The new node is irretrievably lost.

11. It is a logic error to update the link field in the predecessor to a new node before pointing the new node to its logical successor. This error results in a never-ending loop the next time the list is traversed.

12. It is a logic error to fail to set the link field in the last node to NULL. This causes the next traversal to run off the end of the list.

13. It is a potential logic error to use the node pointer in a linked list search before testing for a null pointer. In the following statement, the compares need to be reversed to prevent an invalid memory access.

```
while ((*pCur)->data.key < target
&& *pCur != NULL)
```

Summary

> Lists can be divided into linear lists and nonlinear lists.

> Linear lists can be divided into general lists, stacks, and queues.

> Nonlinear lists can be divided into trees and graphs.

> In a general linear list, data can be inserted anywhere and there are no restrictions on the operations that can be used to process the list.

> Four common operations are associated with general linear lists: insertion, deletion, retrieval, and traversal.

> When we want to insert into a general linear list, we must consider four cases:

- Adding to the empty list

- Adding at the beginning

- Adding at the middle

- Adding at the end

> When we want to delete a node from a general linear list, we must consider two cases: delete the first node or delete any other node.

> Traversing a general linear list means going through the list, item by item, and processing each item.

> A stack is a linear list in which all additions are restricted to one end, called the top. A stack is also called a LIFO list.

> The push stack operation adds an item to the top of the stack. After the push, the new item becomes the top.

> The pop stack operation removes the item at the top of the stack. After the pop, the next item, if any, becomes the top.

> A queue is a linear list in which data can be inserted at one end called the rear, and deleted from the other end, called the front.

> The enqueue operation inserts an element at the rear of the queue.

> The dequeue operation deletes the element at the front of the queue.

> A tree consists of a finite set of elements called nodes and a finite set of directed lines called branches that connect the nodes.

> A node in a tree can be a parent, a child, or both. Two or more nodes with the same parents are called siblings.

> A binary tree is a tree in which no node can have more than two children.

> In a preorder traversal of a tree, we process the left subtree first, followed by the root, and then the right subtree.

> In the `inOrder` traversal of a tree, we process the root first, followed by the left subtree and then followed by the right subtree.

> A binary search tree is a binary tree with the following properties:

- All items in the left subtree are less than the root.

- All items in the right subtree are greater than or equal to the root.

- Each subtree is itself a binary search tree.

> A graph is a collection of nodes, called vertices, and a collection of line segments, called edges or arcs, connecting a pair of nodes.

> Graphs may be directed or undirected. In a directed graph, or digraph, each line has a direction. In an undirected graph, there is no direction on the lines. A line in a directed graph is called an arc.

> There are two standard graph traversals: depth first and breadth first.

Key Terms

abstract data type (ADT)	enqueue	pop stack
ancestor	first in–first out (FIFO)	preorder traversal
arc	front	push stack
atomic data	graph	queue
binary search tree	indegree	rear
binary tree	inorder traversal	root
branches	key	self-referential structure
breadth-first traversal	key-sequenced list	stack
child	last in–first out (LIFO)	strongly connected graph
composite data	linear list	subtree
connected graph	linked list	top
data structure	links	traversal
degree	list	tree
depth-first traversal	metadata	undirected graph
dequeue	node	underflow event
descendant	nonlinear list	vertices
directed graph (digraph)	outdegree	weakly connected graph
edge	parent	

Review Questions

1. In a linked list implementation, each node must contain data and a link field.
   - **a.** True
   - **b.** False

2. In a linked list implementation, there is a need for a head pointer to identify the beginning of the list.
   - **a.** True
   - **b.** False

3. In a linked list implementation, the first step in adding a node to a list is to allocate memory for the new node.
   - **a.** True
   - **b.** False

4. The C language provides a list structure.
   - **a.** True
   - **b.** False

5. In an array, the sequentiality of a list is maintained by _____.
   - **a.** the order structure of elements
   - **b.** a pointer to the next element
   - **c.** the order of a linked list
   - **d.** a list of ordered pointers

6. _____ is an ordered collection of data in which each element contains the location of the next element or elements.
   - **a.** An array
   - **b.** A structure
   - **c.** A linked list
   - **d.** A graph

7. A stack is a _____ structure.
   - **a.** first in–last out
   - **b.** last in–first out
   - **c.** first in–first out
   - **d.** last in–last out

8. A queue is a _____ structure.
   - **a.** first in–last out
   - **b.** last in–first out
   - **c.** first in–first out
   - **d.** last in–last out

9. A general linear list is a list in which operations, such as retrievals, insertions, changes, and deletions, can be done _____.
   - **a.** anywhere in the list
   - **b.** only at the beginning
   - **c.** only at the end
   - **d.** only at the middle

10. A stack is a list in which operations, such as retrievals, insertions, changes, and deletions, can be done _____.
- **a.** anywhere in the list
- **b.** only at the top
- **c.** only at the base (bottom)
- **d.** only at the middle

11. A queue is a list in which operations, such as retrievals, insertions, changes, and deletions, can be done _____.
- **a.** only at the beginning
- **b.** only at the end
- **c.** only at the middle
- **d.** at any node in the queue

12. A _____ is a last in–first out (LIFO) data structure in which insertion and deletions are restricted to one end, called the top.
- **a.** stack
- **b.** queue
- **c.** tree
- **d.** binary tree

13. A _____ is a first in–first out (FIFO) data structure in which insertions are restricted to one end, called the rear, and deletions are restricted to another end, called the front.
- **a.** stack
- **b.** queue
- **c.** tree
- **d.** binary tree

14. To add an element to a stack, we use the _____ operation.
- **a.** pop
- **b.** push
- **c.** enqueue
- **d.** dequeue

15. To delete an element from a stack, we use the _____ operation.
- **a.** pop
- **b.** push
- **c.** enqueue
- **d.** dequeue

16. To add an element to a queue, we use the _____ operation.
- **a.** pop
- **b.** push
- **c.** enqueue
- **d.** dequeue

17. To delete an element from a queue, we use the _____ operation.
- **a.** pop
- **b.** push
- **c.** enqueue
- **d.** dequeue

18. Data that consist of a single, nondecomposable entity are known as _____.
- **a.** atomic data
- **b.** composite data
- **c.** derived data
- **d.** standard data
- **e.** structured data

19. A(n) _____ is a collection of elements and the relationship among them.
- **a.** abstract data type
- **b.** array
- **c.** data structure
- **d.** standard type
- **e.** type definition

Exercises

20. Imagine we have the general list shown in **Figure 15-54**. Show what happens if we apply the following statement to this general list:

```
pList = pList -> link;
```

Figure 15-54   Figure for Exercise 20

What is the problem with using this kind of statement? Does it justify the need for two walking pointers (pPre and pCur), which we introduced in the text?

21. Imagine we have the general list shown in **Figure 15-55**. As discussed in the "Search Linear List" section, the search function needs to be able to pass back both the location of the predecessor (pPre) and the location of the current (pCur) node based on search criteria. A typical search design is shown in Figure 15-55.

Figure 15-55   Figure for Exercise 21

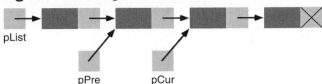

The following code to set `pPre` and `pCur` contains a common error. What is it, and how should it be corrected? (*Hint:* What are the contents of these pointers at the beginning of the search?)

```
pCur = pCur->link;
pPre = pPre->link;
```

22. Imagine we have a dummy node at the beginning of a general list. The dummy node does not carry any data. It is not the first data node; it is an empty node. **Figure 15-56** shows a general list with a dummy node. Write the code to delete the first node (the node after the dummy node) in the general list.

Figure 15-56   Figure for Exercise 22

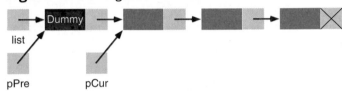

23. Write the code to delete a node in the middle of a general list with the dummy node (see Exercise 22). Compare your answer with the answer to Exercise 22. Are they the same? What do you conclude? Does the dummy node simplify the operation on a general list? How?

24. **Figure 15-57** shows an empty general list with a dummy node. Write the code to add a node to this empty general list.

Figure 15-57   Figure for Exercise 24

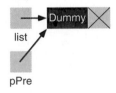

25. Write the statements to add a node in the middle of a general list with the dummy node (see Exercise 22). Compare your answer with the answer to Exercise 24. Are they the same? What do you conclude? Does the dummy node simplify the operation on a general list? How?

26. Imagine we have the two general lists shown in **Figure 15-58**. What would happen if we apply the following statement to these two lists?

```
list1 = list2;
```

Figure 15-58   Figure for Exercise 26

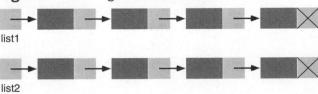

27. What would happen if we apply the following statements to the two lists in Exercise 26?

```
temp = list1;
while (temp->link != NULL)
    temp = temp->link;
temp->link = list2;
```

28. Imagine we have the general list shown in **Figure 15-59**. What would happen if we apply the following statements to this list?

```
temp = list;
while (temp->link != NULL)
    temp = temp->link;
temp->link = list;
```

Figure 15-59   Figure for Exercise 28

list

29. Imagine we have two empty stacks of integers, s1 and s2. Draw a picture of each stack after the following operations in **Algorithm 15-2**:

ALGORITHM 15-2 | Algorithm for Exercise 29

1 pushStack (s1, 3)
2 pushStack (s1, 5)
3 pushStack (s1, 7)
4 pushStack (s1, 9)
5 pushStack (s1, 11)
6 pushStack (s1, 13)
7 loop not emptyStack (s1)
    7.1 popStack (s1, x)
    7.2 pushStack (s2, x)
8 End loop
End Exercise 29

---

30. Imagine you have a stack of integers, S, and a queue of integers, Q. Draw a picture of S and Q after the following operations in **Algorithm 15-3**:

ALGORITHM 15-3 | Algorithm for Exercise 30

1 pushStack (S, 3)
2 pushStack (S, 12)
3 enqueue (Q, 5)

(continue)

Algorithm 15-3   Algorithm for Exercise 30 *(continued)*

```
 4  enqueue (Q, 8)
 5  popStack (S, x)
 6  pushStack (S, 2)
 7  enqueue (Q, x)
 8  dequeue (Q, y)
 9  pushStack (S, x)
10  pushStack (S, y)
End Exercise 30
```

31. Imagine that the contents of queue Q1 and queue Q2 are as shown. What would be the contents of Q3 after the following code is executed? The queue contents are shown front (left) to rear (right) in **Algorithm 15-4**:

ALGORITHM 15-4 | Algorithm for Exercise 31

```
1  Q3 = createQueue
2  count = 1
3  y = 0
4  loop (not empty Q1 or not empty Q2)
   4.1  dequeue (Q1, x)
   4.2  if (count > y)
        4.2.1  dequeue (Q2, y)
   4.3  end if
   4.4  if (y equal count)
        4.4.1  enqueue (Q3, x)
   4.5  end if
   4.6  count = count + 1
5  end loop
End Exercise 31
```

Q1: 42 30 41 31 19 20 25 14 10 11 12 15

Q2: 4 5 6 10 13

32. Draw all possible nonsimilar binary trees with three nodes (A, B, C).

33. Draw all possible binary search trees for the data elements 5, 9, and 12.

34. Create a binary search tree using the following data entered as a sequential set:

```
14, 23, 7, 10, 33, 56, 80, 66, 70
```

35. Create a binary search tree using the following data entered as a sequential set:

```
7, 10, 14, 23, 33, 56, 66, 70, 80
```

36. Insert 44 and 50 into the tree created in Exercise 34.

37. Insert 44 and 50 into the tree created in Exercise 35.

Problems

38. Write a program that reads a list of integers from the keyboard, creates a general list from them, and prints the result.

39. Write a function that accepts a general list, traverses it, and returns the key of the node with the minimum key value.

40. Write a function that traverses a general list and deletes all nodes whose keys are negative.

41. Write a function that traverses a general list and deletes all nodes that are after a node with a negative key.

42. Write a function that traverses a general list and deletes all nodes that are before a node with a negative key.

43. Rewrite the function `deleteNode` (see Program 15-2) using a general list with a dummy node.

44. Rewrite the function `searchList` (see Program 15-3) using a general list with a dummy node.

45. Write a function that returns a pointer to the last node in a general list.

46. Write a function that appends two general lists together.

47. Write a function that appends a general list to itself.

48. One of the applications of a stack is to backtrack—that is, to retrace its steps. As an example, imagine we want to read a list of items, and each time we read a negative number we must backtrack and print the five numbers that come before the negative number and then discard the negative number. Use a stack to solve this problem.

Read the numbers and push them into the stack (without printing them) until a negative number is read. At this point, stop reading and pop five items from the stack and print them. If there are fewer than five items in the stack, print an error message and stop the program. After printing the five items, resume reading data and placing them in the stack. When the end of the file is detected, print a message and the items remaining in the stack. Test your program with the following data:

```
1 2 3 4 5 -1 1 2 3 4 5 6 7 8 9 10 -2 11 12 -3 1 2 3 4 5
```

49. Write a function called `copyStack` that copies the contents of one stack into another. The algorithm passes two stacks, the source stack and the destination stack. The order of the stacks must be identical. (*Hint:* Use a temporary stack to preserve the order.)

50. Write a function, `catstack`, that concatenates the contents of one stack on top of another.

51. Write a function to check whether the contents of two stacks are identical. Neither stack should be changed. You need to write a function that prints the contents of a stack to verify that your function works.

52. Write a function called `copyQueue` that copies the contents of one queue to another.

53. Write a function called `stackToQueue` that creates a queue from a stack. After the queue has been created, the top of the stack should be the front of the queue and the base of the stack should be the rear of the queue. At the end of the function, the stack should be empty.

54. Given a queue of integers, write a function that calculates and prints the sum and the average of the integers in the queue without changing the contents of the queue.

55. Given a queue of integers, write a function that deletes all negative integers without changing the order of the remaining elements in the queue.

56. Write a function that calculates and passes up to the calling function the sum and average of the nodes in a tree.

57. Write a function that counts the number of leaves in a binary tree.

58. Write a function to find the smallest node in a binary search tree.

Projects

59. Write a program that reads a file and builds a key-sequenced general list. After the list is built, display it on the monitor. You may use any appropriate data structure, but it must have a key field and data. Two possibilities are a list of your favorite songs or your friends' phone numbers.

60. Write a program to read a list of students from a file and create a general list. Each entry in the general list is to have the student's name, a pointer to the next student, and a pointer to a general list of scores. You may have up to four scores for each student. The program initializes the student list by reading the students' names from the text file and creating null scores lists. After building the student list, it loops through the list, prompting the user to enter the scores for each student. The scores prompt is to include the name of the student.

61. Write a stack and queue test driver. A test driver is a program created to test functions that are to be placed in a library. Its primary purpose is to completely test functions; therefore, it has no application use. The functions to be tested are push stack, pop stack, enqueue, and dequeue. You may include other stack and queue functions as required. All data should be integers. You need two stacks and two queues in the program, as described below.

> Input stack: used to store all user input

> Input queue: used to store all user input

> Output stack: used to store data deleted from input queue

> Output queue: used to store data deleted from input stack

Use a menu-driven user interface that prompts the user to select either insert or delete. If an insert is requested, the system should prompt the user for the integer to be inserted. The data are then inserted into the input stack and input queue. If a delete is requested, the data are deleted from both structures: The data popped from the input stack are enqueued in the output queue, and the data dequeued from the input queue are pushed into the output stack.

Processing continues until the input structures are empty. At this point, print the contents of the output stack while deleting all of its data. Label this output "Output Stack," and then print all of the data in the output queue while deleting all of its data. Label this output "Output Queue." Your output should be formatted as shown below.

```
Output Stack: 18 9 13 7 5 1
Output Queue: 7 13 9 18 5 1
```

Test your program with the following operations:

```
1 input 1    5 delete      9 input 6   13 input 8
2 input 2    6 input 0    10 delete    14 delete
3 delete     7 input 5    11 input 7   15 delete
4 input 3    8 delete     12 delete    16 delete
```

Numbering Systems

Today the whole world uses the decimal number system developed by Arabian mathematicians in the eighth century. We acknowledge their contribution to numbers when we refer to our decimal system as Arabic numerals. But decimal numbers were not always commonly used. The first to use a decimal numbering system were the ancient Egyptians. The Babylonians improved on the Egyptian system by making the positions in the numbering systems meaningful. But the Babylonians also used a sexagesimal (base 60) numbering system. Whereas our decimal system has 10 values in its graphic representations, a sexagesimal system has 60. We still see remnants of the Babylonians' sexagesimal system in time, which is based on 60 minutes to an hour, and in the division of circles, which contain 360 degrees.

A.1 Computer Numbering Systems

Computer science uses several numbering systems. The computer itself uses binary (base 2). A binary system has only two values for each number position, 0 and 1. Programmers use a shorthand notation to represent binary numbers, hexadecimal (base 16). And of course, programmers also use the decimal system (base 10). Occasionally, we also encounter applications that require we use base 256. Because all these systems are used in C, we need to have a basic understanding of each to fully understand the language.

All of the numbering systems examined here are positional, meaning that the position of a symbol in relation to other symbols determines its value. Each symbol in a number has a position. In integrals and the integral portion of real numbers, the position starts from 0 and goes to $n - 1$, where n is the number of symbols in the integral part. In the fraction part of real numbers, the position starts from -1 and goes to $-m$, where m is the number of symbols in the fraction part. Each position is assigned a weight; the weights vary according to the numbering system.

Decimal Numbers (Base 10)

We all readily understand the **decimal numbers (base 10)**. In fact, we have used it so much that it is intuitive. All of our terms for indicating countable quantities are based on it, and, in fact, when we speak of other numbering systems, we tend to refer to their quantities by their decimal equivalents.

The word decimal is derived from the Latin stem deci, meaning ten. The decimal system uses 10 symbols to represent quantitative values: 0, 1, 2, 3, 4, 5, 6, 7, 8, and 9.

Decimal numbers use 10 symbols: 0, 1, 2, 3, 4, 5, 6, 7, 8, and 9.

For example, in **Figure A-1**, the decimal number 14782.721 has eight digits in positions –3 to 4.

Figure A-1   The Decimal Number 14782.721

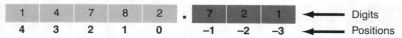

Decimal Number: 14782.721

| 1 | 4 | 7 | 8 | 2 | . | 7 | 2 | 1 | ← Digits |
| 4 | 3 | 2 | 1 | 0 | | –1 | –2 | –3 | ← Positions |

Weights

In the decimal system, each weight is 10 raised to the power of its position. The weight of the symbol at position –1 is 10^{-1} (1/10) while the weight of the symbol at position 0 is 10^0 (1) and the weight of the symbol at position 1 is 10^1 (10); and so on.

Binary Numbers (Base 2)

The **binary number** system **(base 2)** provides the basis for all computer operations. The binary system uses two symbols, 0 and 1. The word binary derives from the Latin stem bi, meaning two.

> ```
> Binary numbers use two symbols: 0 and 1.
> ```

Weights

In the binary system, each weight equals 2 raised to the power of its position. The weight of the symbol at position –1 is 2^{-1}(1/2); the weight of the symbol at position 0 is 2^0(1); the weight of the symbol at position 1 is 2^1 (2); and so on.

Binary-to-Decimal Conversion

To convert a binary number to decimal, we use the weights. We multiply each digit by its weight and add all of the weighted results. **Figure A-2** shows how we can convert binary 1001110.101 to its decimal equivalent 78. 625.

Figure A-2   Binary-to-Decimal Conversion

Binary Number: 1001110.101

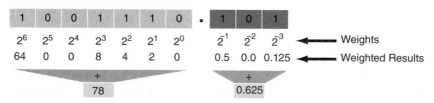

1	0	0	1	1	1	0	.	1	0	1	
2^6	2^5	2^4	2^3	2^2	2^1	2^0		2^{-1}	2^{-2}	2^{-3}	← Weights
64	0	0	8	4	2	0		0.5	0.0	0.125	← Weighted Results

+
78

+
0.625

Decimal Number: 78.625

Decimal-to-Binary Conversion

Two simple operations, divide and multiply, give us a convenient way to convert a decimal number to its binary equivalent as shown in **Figure A-3**. To convert the integral part, we divide the number by 2 and write down the remainder, which must be 0 or 1. The first remainder becomes the least significant binary digit. Now, we divide the quotient of that division by 2 and write down the new remainder in the second position. We repeat this process until the quotient becomes zero.

Figure A-3 Decimal-to-Binary Conversion

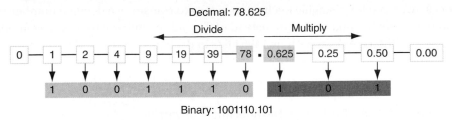

Binary: 1001110.101

To convert the fractional part, we need to multiply the fractional part by two. The integral in the product is either a 0 or a 1; it becomes the binary digit. We then multiply the fractional part of the product by two to get the next binary digit and continue until the product is zero. For example, to convert 0.625 to binary, we multiply it by 2, resulting in 1.25. We take the integral part 1 and move the fraction part (0.25) to the next step. In the next step, after we multiply the 0.25 by two, we get 0.5. The integral part is 0, which we keep. The fractional part is 0.50, which we move to the next step. However, we need to limit the process because the product may never become zero. If the resulting fraction becomes 0.0, we stop because more binary digits do not contribute to the precision of the number. If the product does not become zero, we need to make a decision as to how many digits we need at the right-hand side of the binary number and stop when we have them.

Hexadecimal Numbers (Base 16)

Another system used in this text is **hexadecimal numbers (base 16)**. The word hexadecimal is derived from the Greek word hexadec, meaning 16. The hexadecimal number system is convenient for formatting a large binary number in a shorter form. It uses 16 symbols, 0, 1, ..., 9, A, B, C, D, E, and F. The hexadecimal system uses the same first 10 symbols as the decimal system, but instead of using 10, 11, 12, 13, 14, and 15, it uses A, B, C, D, E, and F. This prevents any confusion between two adjacent symbols. Note that the hexadecimal symbols A to F can be either upper- or lowercase.

> Hexadecimal numbers use 16 symbols: 0, 1, ..., 9, A, B, C, D, E, and F.

Weights

In the hexadecimal system, each weight equals 16 raised to the power of its position. The weight of the symbol at position 0 is 16^0 (1); the weight of the symbol at position 1 is 16^1 (16); and so on.

Hexadecimal-to-Decimal Conversion

To convert a hexadecimal number to decimal, we use the weights. We multiply each digit by its weight and add all of the weighted results. **Figure A-4** shows how hexadecimal 3A73.A0C is transformed to its decimal equivalent 14963.628.

Figure A-4 Hexadecimal-to-Decimal Conversion

Hexadecimal Number: 3A73.A0C

3	A	7	3	.	A	0	C
16^3	16^2	16^1	16^0		16^{-1}	16^{-2}	16^{-3}	← Weights
12,288	2,560	112	3		0.625	0.0	0.003	← Weighted Results

+		+
14,963		0.628

Decimal Number: 14,963.628

Decimal-to-Hexadecimal Conversion

We use the same process we used for changing decimal to binary to transform a decimal number to hexadecimal. The only difference is that we divide the number by 16 instead of 2 to get the integral part and we multiply the number by 16 to get the fractional part. **Figure A-5** shows how 14963.628 in decimal is converted to hexadecimal 3A73.A0C. Note that we stop after three digits in the fractional part.

Figure A-5   Decimal-to-Hexadecimal Conversion

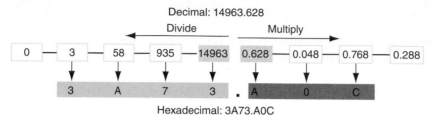

Base 256

Another numbering system that is used in computer science is **base 256**. We encounter this base normally in two situations: when we need to make a number from individual bytes and when we are dealing with Internet addresses.

In the first application, we normally have individual bytes where each byte contains an unsigned number between 0 and 255. We need to consider several of these bytes as a number. **Figure A-6** shows the situation with four bytes.

Figure A-6   Byte Conversion

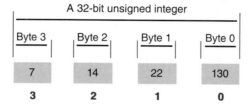

Another application is in Internet addresses. Internet addresses in version 4 use base 256 to represent an address in dotted-decimal notation. When we define an address as 131.32.7.8, we are using a base-256 number. To distinguish between the numbers, a dot is used. For example, the address 131.32.7.8 is made of four numbers 8, 7, 32, and 131 at positions 0, 1, 2, 3, respectively, as shown in **Figure A-7**.

Figure A-7   Internet Dotted-Decimal Notation

$$131 \bullet 32 \bullet 7 \bullet 8$$
$$3 \quad 2 \quad 1 \quad 0$$

Value of address as an integer: $131 \times 256^3 + 32 \times 256^2 + 7 \times 256^1 + 8 \times 256^0$

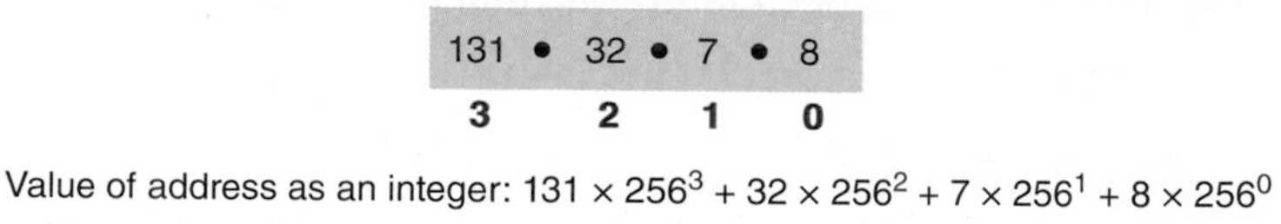

Weights

In base 256, each weight equals 256 raised to the power of its position. The weight of the symbol at position 0 is 256^0 (1); the weight of the symbol at position 1 is 256^1 (256); and so on. In base 256, each symbol can be one to three digits.

Base 256-to-Decimal Conversion

To convert a base 256 number to its decimal equivalent, we follow the same process we discussed for converting base 2 or base 16 to decimal; the weights, however, are 256^n where n is the position. Note, however, that in this case, we are normally dealing with an integral number.

Decimal-to-Base 256 Conversion

To convert a decimal number to base 256, we follow the same method we discussed for converting decimal to base 2 or base 16, but we divide the number by 256 and keep the remainder.

A Comparison

Table A-1 shows how the three systems represent the decimal numbers 0 through 15. As you can see, decimal 13 is equivalent to binary 1101, which is equivalent to hexadecimal D.

Table A-1 Comparison of Decimal, Binary, and Hexadecimal Systems

DECIMAL	BINARY	HEXADECIMAL
0	0	0
1	1	1
2	10	2
3	11	3
4	100	4
5	101	5
6	110	6
7	111	7
8	1000	8
9	1001	9
10	1010	A
11	1011	B
12	1100	C
13	1101	D
14	1110	E
15	1111	F

Other Conversions

There are other conversions such as base 2 to base 16 or base 16 to base 256. For these conversions, we use base 10 as the intermediate system. In other words, to change a number from binary to hexadecimal we first change the binary to decimal and then change the decimal to hexadecimal. We discuss some easy methods for common conversions.

Binary-to-Hexadecimal Conversion

To change a number from binary to hexadecimal, we group the binary digits from the right by fours. Then we convert each four-bit group to its hexadecimal equivalent using **Table A-1**. In **Figure A-8**, we convert binary 1010001110 to hexadecimal.

Figure A-8 Binary-to-Hexadecimal Conversion

Hexadecimal-to-Binary Conversion

To change a hexadecimal number to binary, we convert each hexadecimal digit to its equivalent binary number using **Table A-1** and concatenating the results. In **Figure A-9**, we convert hexadecimal 28E to binary.

Figure A-9 Hexadecimal-to-Binary Conversion

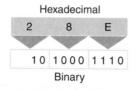

Base 256-to-Binary Conversion

To convert a base 256 number to binary, we first need to convert the number in each position to an 8-bit binary group and then concatenate the groups.

Binary-to-Base 256 Conversion

To convert from binary to base 256, we need to divide the binary number into groups of 8 bits, convert each group to decimal, and then insert separators (dots) between the decimal numbers.

A.2 Storing Integers

We have discussed how integers and real numbers are presented in different bases. Although base 16 and base 256 are used in computer science, data are stored in the computer in binary. Numbers must be changed to base 2 to be stored in the computer. All of our discussions so far have ignored the sign of the number. In computer science, we use both positive and negative numbers. We need some way to store the sign. In this section, we concentrate on how integers are stored in a computer; in the next section, we show how real numbers are stored.

Unsigned Integers

Storing **unsigned integers** is a straightforward process. The number is changed to the corresponding binary form, and the binary representation is stored. For example, an unsigned integer can be stored as a number from 0 to 15 in a 4-bit integer, as shown in **Figure A-10**.

Figure A-10 Unsigned Integers Format

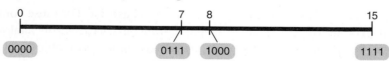

Addition of unsigned integers is very straightforward as long as there is no overflow (see the section on overflow). Subtraction of unsigned integers must be done with caution. If the result is negative, the number is not an unsigned number anymore. Normally computers promote the result to a signed integer in this case.

Signed Integers

Storing **signed integers** is different from storing unsigned integers because we must consider both positive and negative numbers. Four methods are designed to store signed integers in a computer: sign and magnitude, one's complement, two's complement, and Excess system.

Sign and Magnitude

In **sign and magnitude**, we divide the available range between the positive and negative numbers. The lower part of the range occupies the positive numbers; the upper part occupies the negative numbers. To do so, we consider the leftmost bit to represent the sign of the number and the rest of the bit to be the absolute value, the magnitude of the number. Let us see how a 4-bit integer can both hold the positive and negative numbers. **Figure A-11** shows the partition of the range between positive and negative numbers.

Figure A-11   Signed Integer Format

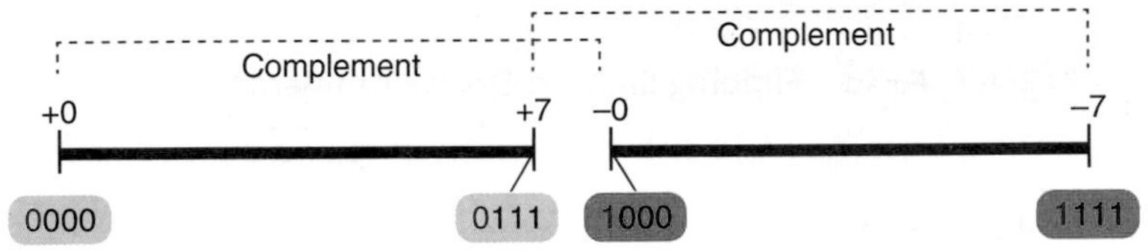

Properties

Let us summarize the sign and magnitude properties:

1. The leftmost bit contains the sign of the number; 0 for positive, 1 for negative.

2. There are two zeros in this method: $+0$ (0000) and -0 (1000).

3. To change the sign of a number, we need to flip only the first bit. We cannot use the complement operator (~) we learned in Chapter 14 because this operator will flip all bits, not just the leftmost bit.

4. Addition and subtraction are very inefficient operations. We need to do the following:

   a. Separate the sign from the magnitude.

   b. Compare two magnitudes to see if we need to add or subtract the magnitude.

   c. We have eight cases in total, four for addition and four for subtraction.

   d. Insert the sign of the result after the absolute value of the result is determined.

Applications

Properties 2, 3, and 4 make this method unsuitable for a general-purpose computer in which we need to perform mathematical operations. The sign and magnitude method, however, is used in computer science when we do not need mathematical operations. One of these areas is storing analog and digital signals.

One's Complement

One's complement is similar to sign and magnitude; however, the partition of the range between the positive and negative numbers is different. The numbers are arranged symmetrically. A positive and a negative number are symmetric with respect to the middle of the range. **Figure A-12** shows how the positive and negative numbers are distributed.

Figure A-12 One's Complement Format

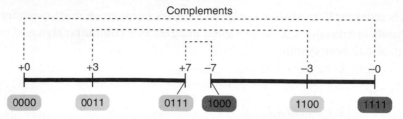

Properties

Let us summarize the one's complement properties:

> The leftmost bit contains the sign; 0 for positive, 1 for negative.

> There are two zeros in this method: +0 (0000) and −0 (1111).

> To flip the sign of a number, we flip each individual bit. We use the complement operator (~) we learned in Chapter 14 to find −A from A as shown in **Figure A-13**.

Figure A-13 Flipping Signs in One's Complement

$$-3 \longrightarrow \sim (0\ 0\ 1\ 1) \longrightarrow 1\ 1\ 0\ 0$$

$$-(-3) \longrightarrow \sim (1\ 1\ 0\ 0) \longrightarrow 0\ 0\ 1\ 1$$

The figure also shows that if we complement −A, we get back A. In one's complement, we also can find the complement of A as $-A = (2n\ -1)\ -A$. For example, -3 is stored as 15 −3 or 12, when n is 4 (number of bits in the integer).

> If we add $A\ +\ (-A)$ we get −0 (all bits are 1s). We saw this property in Chapter 14 when we used checksum.

> Addition and subtraction are very simple operations. To add $(A\ +\ B)$, we just add the numbers bit by bit. To subtract $A\ -\ B$, we just add A and the complement of B. In other words, $A\ -\ B\ =\ A+\ (-\ B)$. The only thing we need to consider about adding or subtracting is to add the carry produced at the last column to the result.

Figure A-14 shows how numbers are complemented, added, and subtracted.

Figure A-14 Add and Subtract One's Complement

Add

```
                    1                          1 1 1 1
    (+3)          0 0 1 1        (+3)          0 0 1 1
  + (+2)        + 0 0 1 0      + (—2)      +   1 1 0 1
   (+5)          0 1 0 1        (+1)          0 0 0 0
                                                    ▶ 1
                                              0 0 0 1
```

Subtract (add first with the complement of the second)

```
                  1 1                          1
    (+3)          0 0 1 1        (—3)          1 1 0 0
  — (+4)        + 1 0 1 1      — (—2)      +   0 0 1 0
   (−1)          1 1 1 0        (—1)          1 1 1 0
```

Applications

Early general-purpose computers, such as legacy hardware, used one's complement. The modern general-purpose computer does not use this method for arithmetic calculation because of the second property (existence of two 0s) and the need for keeping track of the carry from the last column. However, one's complement arithmetic has its own place in computer science. We saw the use of it in the checksum calculation in this text. We simulated the use of one's complement with unsigned numbers. To simulate adding the carry from the last column to the partial result, we used modulo $2n\ -\ 1$ in our calculations.

Two's Complement

Like one's complement, **two's complement** also shares the range between positive and negative numbers. However, the partition of the range between the positive and negative numbers is different. The symmetry is an offset. For example, the fourth number from the beginning of the range is the complement of the third number from the end. This is done for two purposes: to eliminate the negative 0 and to avoid adding the carry from the last column to the partial result. **Figure A-15** shows how the positive and negative numbers are distributed.

Note the 0 in the positive range, which means that the negative range can accommodate one more number. In the figure, the first half of the range accommodates 0 to 7; the second half accommodates –1 to –8.

Figure A-15   Two's Complement Format

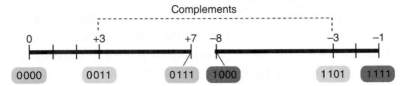

Properties

Let us summarize the two's complement properties:

1. The leftmost bit contains the sign of the number; 0 for positive, 1 for negative.

2. There is only one zero in this method: 0 (0000).

3. To change the sign of a number, we need two operations. First, we need to flip each individual bit, then we need to add 1 to the previous result as shown in **Figure A-16**.

   The figure also shows that if we complement –A, we get back A. In two's complement, we also can find the complement of A as $-A = (2n) - A$, where n is the number of bits in the integer. For example, –3 is stored as 16–3 or 13.

Figure A-16   Complementing Two's Complement

$$-3 \longrightarrow \sim (0\ 0\ 1\ 1) + 1 \longrightarrow 1\ 1\ 0\ 1$$
$$-(-3) \longrightarrow \sim (1\ 1\ 0\ 0) + 1 \longrightarrow 0\ 0\ 1\ 1$$

4. If we add $A + (-A)$ we get 0.

5. Addition and subtraction are simpler. To add $(A + B)$, we just add the numbers bit by bit. To subtract $(A - B)$, we just add A with the complement of B. We do not have to worry about the carry from the last column; we drop it. **Figure A-17** shows this feature.

Figure A-17   Adding and Subtracting Two's Complement

Add

		1			1 1
(+3)		0 0 1 1	(+3)		0 0 1 1
+ (+2)		+ 0 0 1 0	+ (−2)	+	1 1 1 0
(+5)		0 1 0 1	(+1)		0 0 0 1

Subtract (add first with the complement of the second)

		1 1			1 1
(+3)		0 0 1 1	(−3)		1 1 0 1
− (+4)		+ 1 1 0 0	− (−2)	+	0 0 1 0
(−1)		1 1 1 1	(−1)		1 1 1 1

Applications

One single zero and the simplicity of adding and subtracting have made two's complement arithmetic the best candidate for modern computers. C uses the hardware instruction set of the computers it runs on, which almost universally uses two's complement arithmetic.

Modern computers use two's complement to store signed integers.

Storing and Retrieving Two's Complement

As we said before, computers today use two's complement numbers for handling mathematical problems. However, we may wonder how an input function, such as scanf, converts a signed decimal integer to two's complement, and an output function, such as printf, converts a two's complement number to a signed decimal integer. **Figure A-18** shows two high-level algorithms that can be used by these functions.

Figure A-18 Storing and Retrieving Two's Complement

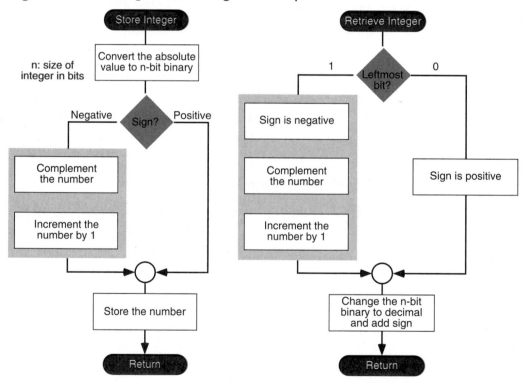

Example A-1

Let's follow the storing algorithm to see how +76 is stored in a 16-bit integer. The absolute value of the number (76) is changed to a 16-bit binary number. The sign is positive, so the number is stored in the memory.

```
Decimal number:              +76
Convert absolute value:      0000000001001100
Store value:                 0000000001001100
```

Example A-2

Let's follow the storing algorithm to see how –76 is stored in a 16-bit integer. The absolute value of the number (76) is changed to a 16-bit binary number. The sign is negative, so we need to complement the number and add 1 to it as shown below.

```
Decimal number:                -76
Convert absolute value:        0000000001001100
Complement:                    1111111110110011
Add 1:                         1111111110110100
Store value:                   1111111110110100
```

Example A-3

Let's follow the retrieving algorithm to see how a stored value in a 16-bit integer is retrieved. The process is shown below.

```
Retrieved value:               1111111111101011 (sign "-")
Complement:                    0000000000010100
Add 1:                         0000000000010101
Convert to decimal:            21
Add sign:                      -21
```

The retrieved binary value is negative, so the sign is stored to be added at the end. The number is complemented and 1 is added. The result is converted to decimal and the sign is added.

Excess

There are applications that require more numeric comparisons than arithmetic operations. In these cases, we can use a simple strategy, named **Excess** by the IEEE, to store positive and negative integers. We just add a fixed value (called the bias value) to the negative number to make them nonnegative (zero or positive) when we store the numbers. We subtract the same bias value when we retrieve the number. For example, in our hypothetical 4-bit integer, we can store numbers from –7 to 8 as shown in **Figure A-19**. In other words, we store both positive and negative numbers in an unsigned format.

Figure A-19   Excess Format

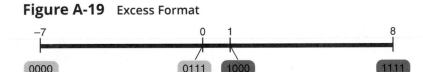

When two numbers are stored using the Excess method, we can easily compare them on the value; we do not have to worry about the sign of the numbers. When adding two numbers in the Excess system, the bias value is added twice; therefore, the bias value must be subtracted when we store the result. When subtracting two numbers, the bias value is cancelled during the subtraction; therefore, it must be added back when we store the result.

Overflow

We need to discuss a very important issue, overflow. Overflow can be the source of much confusion for a programmer. Sometimes when we print a number, we get a surprising result. Often the reason is that an overflow has occurred. Overflow occurs because integers are stored on a limited size word in the computer. For example, if the size of the integer is only 4 bits, we can either store an unsigned integer between 0 and 15 or a signed integer between −8 and +7 (using two's complement). Any number beyond this range overflows the possible values. Most of the time, the system does not issue an error or warning, it just drops the extra bit or bits that do not fit in the allocated space. This creates an invalid result, which may be positive or negative. Then when we print the results, we get a surprising number.

Overflow is better understood if we show the range of the integers that can be stored in a number in a circle. **Figure A-20** shows the range for two methods that are used in today's computers, unsigned integer and two's complement.

Figure A-20   Range of Integer Values

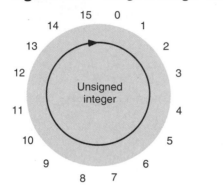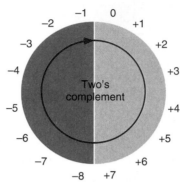

The circle for the unsigned integer shows that 15 + 1 is 0. The circle for two's complement shows that 7 + 1 is –8. If we increment an unsigned value holding the maximum possible number, we get 0. If we increment an integer value holding the maximum possible value, we get the minimum possible value. We cannot test this concept with 4-bit integers, but we can prove it with the actual size of the integer in any computer as shown in **Program A-1**.

Program A-1 | Demonstrate Overflow

```
 1 /* Demonstrate circular nature of unsigned and two's
 2    complement integer numbers.
 3    Written by:
 4    Date:
 5 */
 6 #include <stdio.h>
 7 #include <limits.h>
 8
 9 int main (void)
10 {
11 // Local Definitions
12    unsigned short x = USHRT_MAX;
13    short y = SHRT_MAX;
14
15 // Statements
16    printf("Maximum unsigned short value: %u\n", x);
```

(continue)

Program A-1   Demonstrate Overflow (*continued*)

```
17      x++;
18      printf("Maximum unsigned short value + 1: %u\n", x);
19
20      printf("Maximum short value: %d\n", y);
21      y++;
22      printf("Maximum short value + 1: %d\n", y);
23
24      return 0;
25 } // main
```

Output

```
Maximum unsigned value: 65535
Maximum unsigned value: + 1:0
Maximum short value: 32767
Maximum short value + 1: -32768
```

A.3 Storing Real Numbers

We are all familiar with scientific notation to represent a real number. In this notation, we can show a real number such as -314.625 as $-3.14625 \times 10^{+2}$. We also know that a real number is made of three pieces of information: the sign $(-)$, the precision (3.14625), and the power of ten $(+2)$. Note that we do not have to show the multiplication operator or the base of the power (10) because they are understood by the rules of scientific notation.

Computers use the scientific notation concepts to store a real number. If we write all information in binary system, 314.625 is represented as shown below with the power also in binary (4).

$$-10011.10101010 \times 2^{100}$$

Normalization

We have one problem to solve before we can store this number in the computer: the position of the binary point (the point that separates the integral part from the fractional part). We can store only binary digits, not a point. The solution is **normalization**. We normalize the number so that the point is always at a fixed position. Tradition and the standard state that the number should have only one binary digit to the left of the point. For non-zero values, the digit is a 1. To normalize the number, therefore, we shift the point to the left or to the right based on its original position. Shifting binary numbers requires multiplying or dividing the number by two for each shift. In other words, if we move the point to the left, we need to add the number of digits shifted to power; if we move the point to the right, we need to subtract the number of digits shifted from the power. The normalized version of the previous number is shown below. Note that we moved the point four positions to the right, and we added 4 to the power, making it 8 (the power is represented in binary).

$$-1.001110101010 \times 2^{1000}$$

After normalization, we are left with only the sign, the precision, and the power to store; we do not have to store the integral part of the precision or the binary point.

Fortunately, C99 provides us with help to find how real numbers are stored in the computer. We can use the %A or *%a* conversion code to print the real number in a format that represents these values. **Program A-2** displays a positive and a negative real number. Note that the values are the same except for the sign.

Program A-2 | Demonstrate Storage of Real Numbers

```
 1 /*       Demonstrate the storage of real numbers.
 2    Written by:
 3    Date:
 4 */
 5
 6 #include <stdio.h>
 7 int main (void)
 8 {
 9 //  Local Declaration
10    float x = -314.625;
11    float y = +314.625;
12
13// Statements
14    printf ("-314.625: %A\n", x);
15    printf ("+314.625: %A\n", y);
16    return 0;
17 } // main
```

Output
```
-314.625: -0X1.3AA0000000000P+8
+314.625: 0X1.3AA0000000000P+8
```

The results show the sign, the mantissa (3AA0000000000 in hexadecimal), and the power (8).

Sign, Exponent, and Mantissa

Real numbers contain three parts, which are referred to as the sign (s), exponent, and mantissa (m). We can say that the original number (N) is

$$N = (-1)^s \times 1.m \times 2^e$$

Sign

The **sign** of the number is stored using one bit (0 for plus and 1 for minus).

Exponent

The **exponent** (power of 2) defines the power. Note that the power can be negative or positive. Excess is the method used to store the exponent.

Mantissa

The **mantissa** is the binary number to the right of the binary point. It defines the precision of the number. The mantissa is stored as an unsigned integer.

IEEE Standards

The Institute of Electrical and Electronics Engineers (IEEE) has defined two standards to store numbers in memory (single precision and double precision). These formats are shown in **Figure A-21**. Note that the number inside the boxes is the number of bits for each field.

Figure A-21   IEEE Standards for Floating-Point Representation

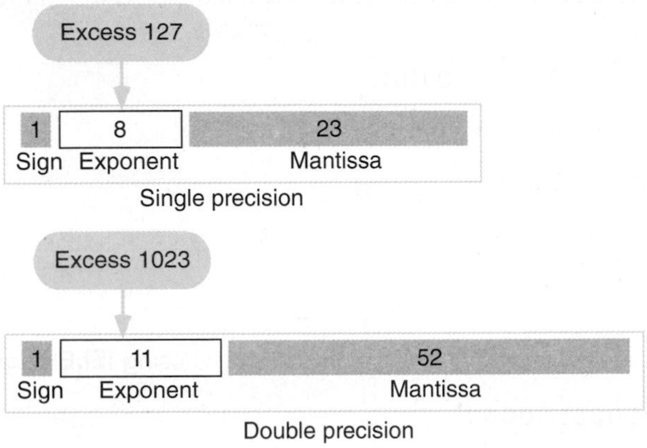

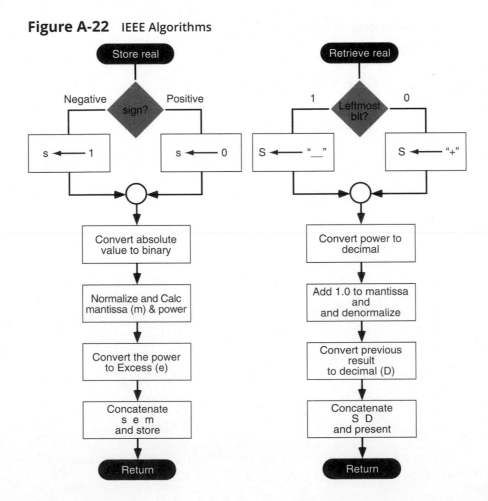

Storing and Retrieving Algorithm

Let's look at the algorithms for storing and retrieving real numbers. These algorithms, shown in **Figure A-22**, give us an insight into how the input and output functions such as *scanf* and *printf* store or retrieve real numbers.

Figure A-22   IEEE Algorithms

Example A-4

We show how the real number 123.8125 is stored in the computer using the storing algorithm in **Figure A-22** and IEEE for single precision.

1. The sign is positive; s = 0.

2. The absolute value in binary is 1111011.1101.

3. We normalize it to 1.1110111101. The value of m in IEEE single precision (23 bits) is m = 11101111010000000000000 and the power is 6.

4. The value of e in IEEE single precision is 6 +127 or 10000101.

5. When we concatenate s, e, and m, we have the value shown below:

```
0  10000101  11101111010000000000000
```

Example A-5

We show how to find the decimal value of the following 32-bit real number stored using IEEE single precision.

```
1  10000010  00011000000000000000000
```

We use the retrieve algorithm in **Figure A-22**.

1. The leftmost bit is 1; S ="–"

2. The value of next 8 bits is 130. We subtract 127 from it to get 3.

3. We add 1 and the binary point to m and shift the binary point 3 digits to the right to get 1000.11 (ignoring the trailing zeros).

4. We convert the above number to decimal to get D = 8.75.

5. We concatenate S and D to get –8.75.

APPENDIX B

Preprocessor Commands

The C compiler is made of two functional parts: a preprocessor and a translator. The preprocessor uses programmer-supplied commands to prepare the source program for compilation. The translator converts the C statements into machine code that it places in an object module. Depending on the compiler design, the preprocessor and translator can work together, or the preprocessor can create a separate version of the source program, which is then read by the translator. This is the design shown in **Figure B-1**.

Figure B-1 Compiler Components

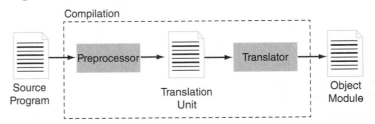

The preprocessor can be thought of as a smart editor. Like a smart editor, it inserts, includes, excludes, and replaces text based on commands supplied by the programmer. In this case, however, the commands are made a permanent part of the source program.

All **preprocessor commands** start with a pound sign (#). Some of the traditional compilers require the pound sign to be in the first column. ANSI/ISO C specifies that it can be anywhere on the line. Preprocessor commands can be placed anywhere in the source program. To distinguish a preprocessor command and a program command, the preprocessor commands are often called commands.

In this appendix, we first discuss three major tasks of a preprocessor: file inclusion, macro definition, and conditional compilation. We then briefly discuss less common commands such as line, error, and pragma.

B.1 File Inclusion

The first and most common job of a preprocessor is file inclusion, the copying of one or more files into programs. The files are usually header files that contain function and data declarations for the program, but they can contain any valid C statement.

The preprocessor command is `#nclude`, and it has two different formats. The first format is used to direct the preprocessor to include header files from the system library. In this format, the name of the header file is enclosed in pointed brackets. The second format makes the preprocessor look for the header files in the user-defined directory. In this format, the name of the file pathname is enclosed in double quotes. The two formats are shown below:

```
#include <filename.h>
#include "filepath.h"
```

Figure B-2 shows the situation of the source file before and after the preprocessor has included the header files.

Figure B-2   File Inclusion

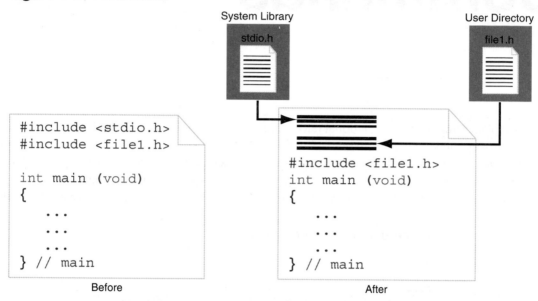

B.2 Macro Definition

The second preprocessor task is expanding **macro definition**. A macro definition command associates a name with a sequence of tokens. The name is called the `macro` name and the tokens are referred to as the `macro` body. A macro definition has the following form:

```
#define name body
```

The body is the text that is used to specify how the name is replaced in the program before it is translated. Before we discuss different applications of the macro definition, let us clarify two important issues:

1. Macros must be coded on a single line. If the macro is too long to fit on a line, we must use a continuation token. The continuation token is a backslash (\) followed immediately by a newline. If any whitespace is present between the backslash and the newline, then the backslash is not a continuation token, and the code will most likely generate an error. An example of a macro continuation is shown below:

```
#define PREND \
    printf ("Normal end of program PA5-01./n");
```

2. We need to be careful in coding the macro body. Whenever a macro call (name of the macro in the program) is encountered, the preprocessor replaces the call with the macro body. If the body is not created carefully, it may create an error or undesired result. For example, the following macro definition:

```
#define ANS = 0
```

creates a compile error when it is used as shown below:

```
...
num = ANS;
...
```

After preprocessing, the result would be

```
num == 0;  // We needed num = 0;
```

which is not what we wanted.

Coding Defined Constants

The simplest application of a macro is to define a constant. As we saw in in this text, this is one of the ways we define a constant. The following shows an example of a define command for constant definition. The name is SIZE and the body is 9. Whenever in the program **SIZE** is encountered, it is replaced with 9.

```
#define SIZE 9
```

Figure B-3 shows how we use constant definitions. As the figure shows, the replacement can happen anywhere in the code, including the declaration section.

Figure B-3   Macro Definition to Define Constants

```
...
#define ROWS 5
#define COLS 4
int main (void)
{
int ary[ROWS][COLS];
   ...
   ...
} //main
```
Before

```
...


int main (void)
{
int ary[5][4];
   ...
   ...
} //main
```
After

The body of the macro definition can be any constant value including integer, real, character, or string. However, character constants must be enclosed in single quotes and string constants in double quotes.

> A macro definition can simulate a constant definition.

Macros that Simulate Functions

The preprocessor's macro facility is very powerful. It can even be used to simulate functions. In this section we discuss using macros in place of functions, first for functions with no parameters and then for functions with parameters.

Macros to Simulate Functions without Parameters

When we simulate a function with a macro, the macro definition replaces the function definition. The macro name serves as the header and the macro body serves as the function body. The name of the macro is used in the program to replace the function call. **Figure B-4** shows how we can write a function to flush the standard input buffer.

Figure B-4 A Function for Flushing the Standard Input Buffer

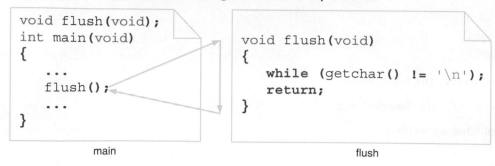

```
void flush(void);
int main(void)
{
    ...
    flush();
    ...
}
```
main

```
void flush(void)
{
    while (getchar() != '\n');
    return;
}
```
flush

While functions are called when the program is executed, macro definitions are inserted into the code during the pre-processing. The preprocessor replaces the macro name in the program with the macro body. The macro definition is simpler than the function, however, because we do not have to write the function declaration, the function header, or the return statement. It is also more efficient because the overhead associated with a function call is not required; the substituted code simply becomes statements in the program. **Figure B-5** shows how we can use a macro definition to simulate the function in **Figure B-4**.

Figure B-5 A Macro to Simulate a Function Call without Parameters

```
#define \
    while (getchar() != '\n')
int main(void)
{
    ...
    FLUSH;
    ...
}
```
Before

```
int main(void)
{
    ...
    while (getchar() != '\n');
    ...
}
```
After

Macros to Simulate Functions with Parameters

We can also use macro definitions to simulate a simple function with parameters. In this case, however, the replacement of the macro is done in two steps, as shown in **Figure B-6**.

Figure B-6 A Macro to Simulate a Function Call with Parameters

```
#define \
    PRODUCT(x, y) x * y
int main(void)
{
    ...
    p = PRODUCT(4, 5);
    ...
}
```
Before

```
int main(void)
{
    ...
    p = x * y;
    ...
}
```
After Step 1

```
int main(void)
{
    ...
    p = 4 * 5;
    ...
}
```
After Step 2

1. The body of the macro replaces the macro call with the same actual parameters used in the macro definition.

2. The actual parameters are replaced with formal parameters.

One of the advantages of using macros instead of function is type independence. We can define a PRODUCT macro that multiplies any two pairs of data type. We do not have to write separate macros for each pair. We need to give two warnings:

1. To include parameters in the macro, the opening parenthesis must be placed immediately at the end of the macro name; that is, there can be no whitespace between the macro name and the opening parenthesis of the parameter list. If there is a space, then the opening parenthesis is considered part of the token body and the macro is assumed to be simple.

2. It is a strong recommendation that the formal parameters in the body of the macro be placed inside parentheses. The reason is that the macro uses text replacement. It replaces the actual parameters with formal parameters. Let us look at the same example, but this time we pass a +1 and b +2 instead of 4 and 5:

After the first and second step, we have:

```
p = x * y;
p = a+1 * b+2; //We need (a +1) * (b+2)
```

The solution would be to include the formal parameters inside parentheses. In other words, make the parentheses part of body code. Now we have the following:

```
#define PRODUCT(x, y) (x) * (y)
```

After the first and second step, we have the correct result:

```
p = (x) * (y);       // After first step
p = (a + 1) * (b + 2); // After second step
```

Example B-1

Macros can replace many simple functions. One good example is the function we wrote in Chapter 14 to rotate a number n bits. This function can be written as a macro as shown below. Note the use of backslash to continue the definition on the next line.

```
#define ROTATE_LEFT(x, n) \
( ( (x) « (n) ) | ( (x) » (32 -x) ) )
```

Example B-2

We often need to use a power of 2 in a program. To calculate 2^x, we can easily use the shift operator in a macro as shown below:

```
#define POWER2(x) 1 << (x)
```

Example B-3

The parameter list in the macro definition can be empty. For example, most C implementations use a macro to define the getchar function from the getc function.

```
#define getchar() getc (stdin)
```

Nested Macros

It is possible to nest macros. C handles nested macros by simply rescanning a line after macro expansion. Therefore, if an expansion results in a new statement with a macro, the second macro will be properly expanded. For example, consider the macros shown below.

```
#define product(a, b) (a) * (b)
#define square(a) product(a, a)
```

The expansion of

```
x = SQUARE (5);
```

results in the following expansion:

```
PRODUCT(3, 5);
```

which after rescanning becomes

```
x = (5) * (5);
```

Undefining Macros

Once defined, a macro command cannot be redefined. Any attempt to redefine it will result in a compilation error. However, it is possible to redefine a macro by first undefining it, using the #undef command and defining it again as shown below:

```
#define SIZE 10
...
#undef SIZE
#define SIZE 20
```

Predefined Macros

The C language provides several predefined macros. **Table B-1** lists some of them. Note that these macros cannot be undefined using the undef command.

Table B-1   Predefined Macros

COMMAND	MEANING
__DATE__	Provides a string constant in the form "Mmm dd yyyy" containing the date of translation.
__FILE__	Provides a string constant containing the name of the source file.
__LINE__	Provides an integer constant containing the current statement number in the source file.
__TIME__	Provides a string constant in the form "hh:mm:ss" containing the time of the translation.
__STDC__	Provides an integer constant with value 1 if and only if the compiler confirms with ISO implementation.

Program B-1 demonstrates these macros.

Program B-1 | Demonstrate Pre-Defined Macros

```
1   /* Show the use of pre-defined macros
2      Written by:
3      Date:
4   */
5
6   #include <stdio.h>
7   int main (void)
8   {
9   // Statements
10      printf ("line %d\n", __LINE__);
11      printf ("file %s\n", __FILE__);
12      printf ("date %s\n", __DATE__);
13      printf ("time %s\n", __TIME__);
14      printf ("ISO compliance %d\n", __STDC__);
15      printf ("line %d\n", __LINE__);
16
17      return 0;
18  } // main
```

Output
```
line 10
file ApG-01.c
date May 23 2022
time 20:36:28
ISO compliance 1
line 15
```

Note that we use the __LINE__ macros two times to show that it prints the current line number.

Operators Related to Macros

C provides several operators that are directly or indirectly related to macros. We briefly discuss them here.

String Converting Operator (#)

The string converting operator (#) is a macro operation that converts a formal parameter into a string surrounded by quotes. For example, the following macro prints the name of a variable followed by its value. It can be a very helpful macro when debugging a program.

```
#define PRINT_VAL(a) printf (#a " contains: %d\n", (a))
```

When called in a program, as shown in the following example

```
PRINT_VAL (amt);
```

the preprocessor expands the macro to

```
printf ("amt" "contains: %d\n", amt);
```

Recall that the preprocessor automatically concatenates two string literals into one string. After the automatic concatenation, the statement becomes

```
printf ("amt contains: %d\n", amt);
```

Merge Operator (##)

Occasionally, it may be necessary to write macros that generate new tokens. With the merge command operator, two tokens are combined. For example, imagine we want to create A1, B3, and Z8 in our program. This can be done easily with the following macro definition:

```
#define FORM(T, N)  T##N
```

Now if we use the following code:

```
int FORM (A, 1) = 1;
float FORM (B, 3) = 1.1;
char FORM (Z, 8) = 'A';
```

we get

```
int A1 = 1;
float B3 = 1.1;
char Z8 = "A";
```

The *defined* Operator

The defined operator can be used only in a conditional compilation (see Section B.3); it cannot be used in macros. The value of defined (macro-name) is 0 if the name is not defined and 1 if it is defined. For example, after

```
#define PI 3.14
```

the value of defined (PI) is 1 and the value of ! defined (PI) is 0.

B.3 Conditional Compilation

The third use of the preprocessor commands is conditional compilation. **Conditional compilation** allows us to control the compilation process by including or excluding statements.

Two-Way Commands

The two-way command tells the preprocessor to select between two choices. This is similar to selection, which we studied in Chapter 5. The idea is shown in **Figure B-7**.

Figure B-7 Two-Way Command

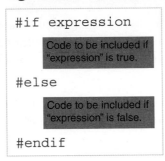

The expression is a constant value that evaluates to zero or non-zero. If the value is non-zero, it is interpreted as `true` and the code after `#if` is included. If it is zero, it is interpreted as `false` and the code after `#else` is executed.

There are two differences between this format and the one used in Chapter 5. First, the expression does not to have to be included in parentheses, although it helps readability when we use parentheses. Second, the codes cannot be included in a compound statement (braces). The commands `#else` and `#endif` serve as delimiters.

The `#if` part or the else part can be empty. However, in these cases, the alternative formats are normally used as shown in **Figure B-8**.

Figure B-8 Alternative Commands

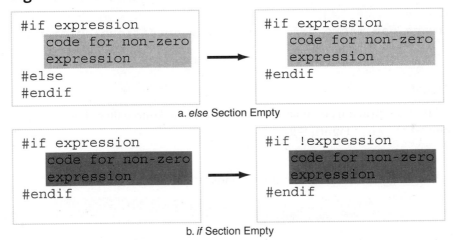

Example B-4

Let us see how a conditional command can help us in program development. Imagine we need to include a very large file in our program. However, we want to test the syntax of our program gradually, first without the included file and then with it. One way we can do this is to include the file in our program using conditional commands as shown below:

```
#if 0
    #include "large.h"
#endif
```

When we are ready to test the syntax for the entire program, we change the condition to true.

```
#if 1
    #include "large.h"
#endif
```

As we see in a later example, there are easier and better ways to do this.

Example B-5

Imagine we need to include three files in our program: file1.h, file2.h, file3.h. These files contain generalized code that are used in projects. Each file must, therefore, be able to stand alone. When combined, the result may be multiple inclusion of common macros. If the macros are duplicated, we get a compilation error because the preprocessor does not allow duplication of macros.

To prevent this error, we have a project standard: whenever we need to define a macro, we define it in a conditional command using the defined operator we discussed in "The defined Operator" in Section B.2. So, instead of

```
#define GO 0
```

we use

```
#if !defined (GO)
    #define GO 0
#endif
```

Now we are safe. Even if all three files have used the same conditional definitions, only the first one appears in the program; the rest are skipped by the preprocessor. When the first definition is encountered, GO is not defined, so the expression is true, and it becomes defined. In the second and third files, GO is already defined, so the conditional compilation expressions are false, and the define command is bypassed.

```
To be safe, always use macro definitions in a conditional command.
```

Two Abbreviations

You may have guessed that the previous commands are used often in source files. The C language provides two additional macro commands as shown in **Figure B-9**.

Figure B-9   Two Abbreviations

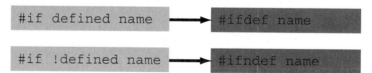

Example B-6

When we decompose a large project into different programs, it is common to create a library file that contains all of the application data types and structures. Each program in the project then includes the library file, ensuring that everyone has exactly the same data names and descriptions.

This design creates a problem, however, when multiple files are compiled together. Each file has the same library included for the data, which results in compile errors with the duplicate names. The solution is to enclose the data library file in a defined command as shown in the next example.

```
#ifndef PROG_LIB
    #define PROG_LIB
    #include "proj_lib.h"
#endif
```

Study this code carefully. The nested preprocessor commands can be executed only if a constant named PROG_LIB has not yet been defined. In this case, we define it and include the library. On the other hand, if it has been defined, the statements are skipped. This code easily and efficiently prevents the library from being included more than once.

Note that the name PROG_LIB is an internal name we use to show the include command is used. A good strategy is to use the uppercase version of the filename, without the ".h" suffix, as a defined name.

> **To prevent duplicate inclusions, always use file inclusion in a conditional command.**

In most implementations, system header files such as `stdio.h` use the above strategy to prevent multiple inclusions of that file in a source program. For example, an implementation may use

```
#ifndef STDIO
#define STDIO
    Rest of the code
#endif
```

Example B-7

Another application of conditional compilation is found in debugging. Most GUI compliers have a debugger that can be used by the programmer. If there is not such a debugger, however, we can insert `printf` statements to check the value of the program during testing. If we just include them as part of the code, however, when the program is ready for production, we must remove them. Later, when we need to change the program, we must re-insert them as needed.

A simpler solution is to insert them conditionally. We enclose the `printf` statement inside the `#if...#endif` commands to print the debug statements only when we run in the "debug" mode. For example, the following program prints the value of x only when DEBUG is true. After testing is done, we can just set the define command to false and the debug statements are not included in the code. This debug concept is demonstrated in **Program B-2**.

Program B-2 | Demonstrate Conditional Debugging

```
1  /* Use of conditional compilation for debugging
2     Written by:
3     Date:
4  */
5  // Macro to print integer values
6  #define PRINT_VAL(a) \
7      printf ("At line %d - -", __LINE__);\
8      printf (#a " contains: %d\n", (a))
9  #define DEBUG 1
10
11 #include <stdio.h>
12
13 int main (void)
```

(continue)

Program B-2   Demonstrate Conditional Debugging *(continued)*

```
14 {
15 // Declarations
16     int x;
17 // Statements
18     x = 1023;
19
20     #if DEBUG
21        PRINT_VAL (x);
22     #endif
23
24 // Later in program
25     for (int i =0; i < 2; i++)
26     {
27        x = x * x;
28        PRINT_VAL (i); PRINT_VAL(x);
29     } // for
30     return 0;
31 } // main
```

```
Output
At line 21 — x contains: 1023
At line 28 — i contains: 0
At line 28 — x contains: 1046529
At line 28 — i contains: 1
At line 28 — x contains: 6287361
```

Program B-2 Analysis

Study this program carefully; you will find it useful when you write production programs. First, study the macro definition in lines 6–8. This macro uses two of the techniques we discussed earlier in the chapter. We begin by displaying the source file line number so that we know where we are within the program. Because we have multiple debugging displays, we need to uniquely identify each one. Then we use the string conversion operator (see Section B.2) to display the variable identifier and its contents.

In the body of the program, we display the values of the variables x and i. In the debugging of a large program, we would use more displays to track the execution of the program.

Multi-Way Commands

Conditional commands can also be multi-way; selecting one of the choices among several. We saw in Chapter 5 that multi-way selection is possible with the use of else-if construct. In the preprocessor, we use the *#elif* command. **Figure B-10** shows the format of multi-way selection in the preprocessor.

For example, when we write a software application that must run at multiple locations, we need to define unique code for each location. Each installation needs unique report headings and perhaps other unique code. One way to do this is shown in **Program B-3**.

Figure B-10 Multi-Way Commands

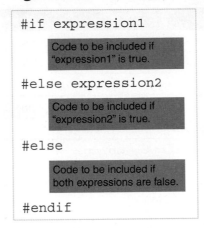

Program B-3

Program B-3 | Conditional Multi-Way Selection

```
1   #define Denver 0
2   #define Phoenix 0
3   #define SanJose 1
4   #define Seattle 0
5   ...
6   #if (Denver)
7       #include "Denver.h"
8   #elif (Phoenix)
9       #include "Phoenix.h"
10  #elif (SanJose)
11      #include "SanJose.h"
12  #else
13      #include "Seattle.h"
14  #endif
```

Program B-3 Analysis

First, we create a unique header file for each installation. Then, using conditional commands, we select which include file to use based on defined flags (or each site). In this example, we have selected San Jose, so only its code is included in the program.

Summary of Conditional Commands

Table B-2 shows the summary of commands used in this section.

Table B-2 Conditional Compilation Commands

COMMAND	MEANING
#if expression	When expression is true, the code that follows is included for compilation.
#endif	Terminates the conditional command.
#else	Specifies alternate code in two-way decision.
#elif	Specifies alternate code in multi-way decision.
#ifdef name	Abbreviation for #if defined name.
#ifndef name	Abbreviation for #if !defined name.

B.4 Other Commands

The preprocessor uses some other commands that we briefly discuss here.

Line Command

The line command, which is used in two formats, can set the line number and the filename for a program. For example,

```
#line 100
```

sets the next line of the program to 100. The line number does not show in the source code, but it can be checked by the predefined command __LINE__. The second format sets the line number and defines a name for the program. For example,

```
#line 100 "MyProgram.c"
```

sets the next line number to 100 and creates a name for the program that can be checked by the predefined macro call __FILE__.

Program B-4 demonstrates the concept.

Program B-4 | Demonstrate Line Command

```
 1   /* Demonstrate the use of line command
 2      Written by:
 3      Date:
 4   */
 5   #line 100 "myprogram.c"
 6
 7   #include <stdio.h>
 8   int main (void)
 9   {
10
11      // Statements
12      printf ("line %d\n", __LINE__) ;
13      printf ("file %s\n", __FILE__) ;
14      printf ("line %d\n", __LINE__) ;
```

(continue)

Program B-4   Demonstrate Line Command *(continued)*

```
15    return 0;
16 } // main
```

Output
```
line 106
file myprogram.c
line 108
```

Error Command

The error command is of the form

```
#error message
```

It is used to print the message detected by the preprocessor. For example, **Program B-5** demonstrates code that verifies that a program needs to define both TRUE and FALSE or neither of them and prints an appropriate message when an error is detected. Note that you may get a slightly different message format depending on your compiler.

Program B-5 | Demonstrate Error Command

```
1    /* Show the use of error command
2       Written by:
3       Date:
4    */
5
6  #define TRUE 1
7  #if defined (TRUE) && !defined (FALSE)
8     #error You need to defined FALSE too.
9  #elif defined (FALSE) && !defined (TRUE)
10    #error You need to defined TRUE too.
11 #endif
12
13 #include <stdio.h>
14 int main (void)
15 {
16    // Statements
17    printf ("Just a test \n");
18    return 0;
19 } // main
```

Output
```
Error : preprocessor error command
ApG-05.c line 8 error You need to defined FALSE too.
```

When this program is compiled, we get

```
#error You need to defined FALSE too.
```

Pragma Command

The pragma command

```
#pragma tokens
```

causes the compiler to perform implementation-defined actions. We do not discuss this command in detail because it is used only in advanced environments.

Null Command

It is interesting to mention that C language allows a null command. A command of the type

```
#
```

is considered a null command and does not generate a compilation error.

Command-Line Arguments

In all the programs we have written, `main` has been coded with no parameters. But `main` is a function, and as a function, it may have parameters. When `main` has parameters, they are known as **command-line arguments.**

Command-line arguments are parameters to `main` when the program starts. They allow the user to specify additional information when the program is invoked. For instance, if you write a program to append two files, rather than specify the names of the files as constants in the code, the user could supply them when the program starts. Thus, a UNIX user in the Korn Shell might execute the program with the command line shown below:

```
$appendFiles file1 file2
```

C.1 Defining Command-Line Arguments

As the programmer, you design the parameter lists for functions you write. When you use system functions, such as `rand`, you follow the parameter design set up by the language specification. Command-line arguments are a little like both. As the programmer, you have control over the names of the parameters, but their type and format are predefined for the language.

The function `main` can be defined either with no argument (`void`) or with two arguments: one an integer and the other an array of pointers to *char* (strings) that represent user-determined values to be passed to `main`. The number of elements in the array is stored in the first argument. The pointers to the user values are stored in the array. The two different formats are shown in **Figure C-1**.

Although the names of the arguments are your choice, traditionally they are called *argc* (argument count) and *argv* (argument vector). This data structure design, with six string pointers in the vector, is shown in **Figure C-2**.

The first argument defines the number of elements in the array identified in the second argument. The value for this argument is not entered using the keyboard; the system determines it from the arguments the user types.

The value of *argc* is determined from the user-typed values for *argvs*.

Figure C-1 Arguments to `main`

```
int main(void)
{
// Local Declarations

// Statements

} // main
```
Without command-line arguments

```
int main(int   argc,
         char *argv[])
{
// Local Declarations

// Statements

} // main
```
With command-line arguments

Figure C-2 *argc* and *argv* format

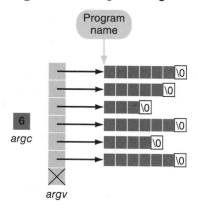

C.2 Using Command-Line Arguments

The **argc** array has several elements. The first element points to the name of the program (its filename). It is provided automatically by the program. The last element contains NULL and may be used to identify the end of the list. The rest of the elements contain pointers to the user-entered string values.

To fully demonstrate how command-line arguments work, let's write a small nonsense program. It does nothing but exercise the command-line arguments. The code is shown in **Program C-1**.

Program C-1 | Display Command-Line Arguments

```
1   /* Demonstrate the use of command-line arguments.
2      Written by:
3      Date:
4   */
5   #include <stdio.h>
6   #include <string.h>
7   #include <stdlib.h>
8
9   int main (int argc, char* argv[])
```

(continue)

Program C-1   Display Command-Line Arguments *(continued)*

```
10 {
11 // Statements
12    printf ("The number of arguments: %d\n", argc);
13    printf ("The name of the program: %s\n", argv[0]);
14
15    for (int i = 1; i < argc; i++)
16        printf ("User Value No. %d: %s\n", i, argv[i]);
17
18    return 0;
19 } // main
```

Now that we've written the program, let's run it with several different arguments. First, let's run it with no user arguments. Even when the user doesn't supply values, the program name is still supplied by the system. (For all of these runs, we assume a Windows-run line environment.)

```
C:>cmdline
The number of arguments: 1
The name of the program: CMDLINE
```

For the second run, let's add hello to the run command.

```
C:>cmdline hello
The number of arguments: 2
The name of the program: CMDLINE
User Value No. 1: hello
```

To make the exercise more interesting, let's run the program with a phrase on the command line.

```
C:>cmdline Now is the time
The number of arguments: 5
The name of the program: CMDLINE
User Value No. 1: Now
User Value No. 2: is
User Value No. 3: the
User Value No. 4: time
```

But what if our intent is to read a phrase? C looks at the user values as strings. This means that the spaces between the words separate each word into a different element. If we want an element to contain more than one word, we enclose it in quotes just like a string in code.

```
C:>cmdline "To err is human" Pope
The number of arguments: 3
The name of the program: CMDLINE
User Value No. 1: To err is human
User Value No. 2: Pope
```

The user elements cannot be numbers. If you enter a number, it is taken as a string. However, the string can be converted to a number using a standard function such as `strtod`.

Pointers to *void* and to Functions

In this appendix we discuss pointer to *void* and pointer to function.

D.1 Pointer to *void*

Because C is strongly typed, operations such as assign and compare must use compatible types or be cast to compatible types. The one exception is the ***pointer to void***, which can be assigned without a cast. In other words, a pointer to *void* is a generic pointer that can be used to represent any data type during compilation or run time. **Figure D-1** shows the idea of a pointer to *void*. Note that a pointer to *void* is not a null pointer; it is pointing to a generic data type *(void)*.

Figure D-1   Pointer to *void*

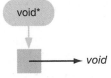

Example D-1

Let us write a simple program to demonstrate the pointer to *void* concept. It contains three variables: an integer, a floating-point number, and a *void* pointer. At different times in the program the pointer can be set to the address of the integer value or of the floating-point value. **Figure D-2** shows the situation.

Program D-1 uses a pointer to *void* that we can use to print either an integer or a real number.

Figure D-2 Pointers for **Program D-1**

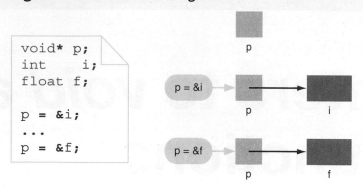

> ## Program D-1 | Demonstrate Pointer to *void*

```
1   /* Demonstrate pointer to void.
2      Written by:
3      Date:
4   */
5   #include <stdio.h>
6   int main (void)
7   {
8   // Local Declarations
9      void* p;
10     int i = 7;
11     float f = 23.5;
12
13  // Statements
14     p = &i;
15     printf ("i contains: %d\n", *((int*)p));
16
17     p = &f;
18     printf ("f contains: %f\n", *((float*)p));
19     return 0;
20  }
21  // main
```

Program D-1 Analysis

Program D-1 is trivial, but it demonstrates the point. The pointer p is declared as a *void* pointer, but it can accept the address of an integer or floating-point number. However, we must remember a very important point about pointers to *void*: a pointer to *void* cannot be dereferenced unless it is cast. In other words, we cannot use *p without casting. That is why we need to cast the pointer in the print function before we use it for printing.

A pointer to *void* cannot be dereferenced unless it is cast.

D.2 Pointer to Function

Functions in a program occupy memory. The name of the function is a pointer constant to its first byte of memory. For example, imagine that we have four functions stored in memory *main,* fun, pun, and sun. This relationship is shown graphically in **Figure D-3**. The name of each function is a pointer to its code in memory.

Figure D-3 Functions in Memory

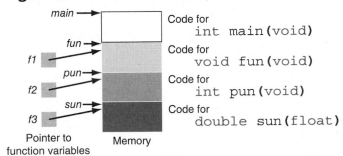

Defining Pointers to Functions

Just as with all other pointer types, we can define pointers to function variables and store the address of fun, pun, and sun in them. To declare a **pointer to function**, we code it as if it were a prototype definition, with the function pointer in parentheses. This format is shown in **Figure D-4**. The parentheses are important: without them C interprets the function return type as a pointer.

Using Pointers to Functions

Now that you've seen how to create and use pointers to functions, let's write a generic function that returns the larger of any two pieces of data. The function uses two pointers to *void* as described in the previous section. While our function needs to determine which of the two values represented by the *void* pointers is larger, it cannot directly compare them because it doesn't know what type casts to use with the *void* pointers. Only the application program knows the data types.

Figure D-4 Pointers to Functions

> *f1* is a pointer to a
> function with no parameters
> that returns *void*

```
...
// Local Declarations
void    (*f1) (void);
int     (*f2) (int, int);
double (*f3) (float);

...
// Statements

...
f1 = fun;
f2 = pun;
f3 = sun;
...
```

The solution is to write simple compare functions for each program that uses our generic function. Then, when we call the generic compare function, we use a pointer to function to pass it the specific compare function that it must use.

Example D-2

We place our generic function, which we call larger, in a header file so that it can be easily used. The Program interfaces and pointers are shown in **Figure D-5**. The code is shown in **Program D-2**.

Program D-2 | Larger Compare Function

```
1   /* Generic function to determine the larger of two
2       values referenced as void pointers.
3       Pre dataPtr1 and dataPtr2 are pointers to values
4       of an unknown type.
5       ptrToCmpFun is address of a function that
6       knows the data types.
7       Post data compared and larger value returned.
8   */
9   void* larger (void* dataPtr1, void* dataPtr2,
10  int (*ptrToCmpFun)(void*, void*))
11  {
12      if ((*ptrToCmpFun) (dataPtr1, dataPtr2) > 0)
13          return dataPtr1;
14      else
15          return dataPtr2;
16  } // larger
```

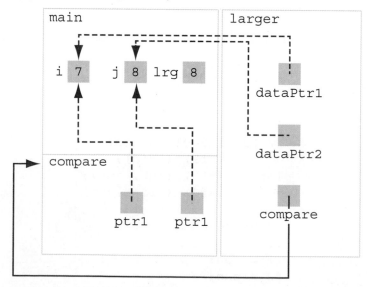

Figure D-5 Larger Compare Function

Program D-3 contains an example of how to use our generic compare program and pass it a specific compare function.

Program D-3 | Compare Two Integers

```
1   /* Demonstrate generic compare functions and pointer to
2      function.
3      Written by:
4      Date:
5   */
6   #include <stdio.h>
7   #include "ApI-05.h"
8   // Header file
9   int compare (void* ptr1, void* ptr2);
10
11  int main (void)
12  {
13  // Local Declarations
14     int i = 7;
15     int j = 8;
16     int lrg;
17
18  // Statements
19     lrg = (*(int*) larger (&i, &j, compare));
20     printf("Larger value is: %d\n", lrg);
21     return 0;
22  } // main
/*=================compare=================
   Integer specific compare function.
   Pre ptr1 and ptr2 are pointers to integer values
   Post returns +1 if ptr1 >= ptr2
   returns -1 if ptr1 < ptr2
*/
int compare (void* ptr1, void* ptr2)
{
  if (*(int*)ptr1 >= *(int*)ptr2)
     return 1;
  else
     return -1;
} // compare
```

Output

```
Larger value is: 8
```

Example D-3

Now, let's write a program that compares two real *(float)* numbers. We can use our larger function, but we need to write a new compare function. We repeat **Program D-3**, changing only the compare function and the data-specific statements in *main*. The result is shown in **Program D-4**.

Program D-4 | Compare Two Floating-Point Values

```
1   /* Demonstrate generic compare functions and pointer to
2       function.
3       Written by:
4       Date:
5   */
6   #include <stdio.h>
7   #include "Apl-02.c"
8   // Header file
9
10  int compare (void* ptr1, void* ptr2); 10
11
12  int main (void)
13  {
14  // Local Declarations
15      float i = 73.4;
16      float j = 81.7;
17      float lrg;
18
19  // Statements
20      lrg = (*(float*) larger (&i, &j, compare));
21      printf("Larger value is: %.1f\n", lrg);
22      return 0;
23  } // main
24
25  /*================compare================
26      Float specific compare function.
27      Pre ptr1 and ptr2 are pointers to float values
28      Post returns +1 if ptr1 >= ptr2
29      returns -1 if ptr1 < ptr2
30  */
31  int compare (void* ptr1, void* ptr2)
32  {
33      if (*(float*)ptr1 >= *(float*)ptr2)
34          return 1;
35      else
36          return -1;
37  } // compare
```

Output

```
Larger value is: 81.7
```

Storage Classes and Type Qualifiers

In this appendix, we discuss two attributes of data types, storage classes and type qualifiers. Storage classes specify the scope of objects. Type qualifiers specify processing limitations on objects.

E.1 Storage Classes

We define the storage class of an object using one of four specifiers: auto, register, static, and extern. Before we can discuss the storage class specifiers, however, we must describe the environment in which they are used.

Object Storage Attributes

Storage class specifiers control three attributes of an object's storage as shown in **Figure E-1**: its scope, extent, and linkage.

Figure E-1   Object storage attributes

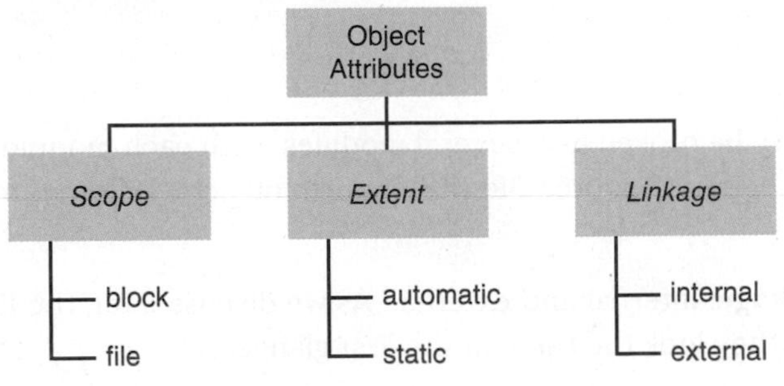

Scope

Scope defines the visibility of an object; it defines *where* an object can be referenced. In C, an object can have four levels of scope: block, file, function, and function-prototype. In this text, we do not discuss the function and function prototype scopes.

Block (Local) Scope

The body of a function is a block and a compound statement in a loop is a nested block within its function block. When the scope of an object is block, it is visible only in the block in which it is defined. An object with a block scope is sometimes referred to as a local object.

The scope of an object declared anywhere in a block has block scope. For example, a variable declared in the formal parameter list of a function has block scope. A variable declared in the initialization section of a `for` loop also has block scope, but only within the `for` statement.

File (Mai) Scope

File scope includes the entire source file for a program, including any files included in it. An object with file scope has visibility through the whole source file in which it is declared. However, objects within block scope are excluded from file scope unless specifically declared to have file scope; in other words, by default block scope hides objects from file scope. File scope generally includes all declarations outside a function and all function headers. An object with file scope is sometimes referred to as a global object.

Extent

The extent of an object defines the duration for which the computer allocates memory for it. In C, an object can have automatic, static extent, or dynamic extent. The extent of an object is also known as its storage duration.

Automatic Extent

An object with an automatic extent is created each time its declaration is encountered and is destroyed each time its block is exited. For example, a variable declared in the body of a loop is created and destroyed in each iteration. Note however, that declarations in a function are not destroyed until the function is complete; when the function calls a function, they are out of scope but not destroyed.

Static Extent

A variable with a static extent is created when the program is loaded for execution and is destroyed when the execution stops. This is true no matter how many times the declaration is encountered during the execution.

Dynamic Extent

Dynamic extent is created by the program through the *malloc* and its related library functions. We do not discuss static memory in this text.

Linkage

A large application program may be broken into several modules, with each module potentially written by a different programmer. Each module is a separate source file with its own objects. Different modules may be related when the program is link edited.

We can define two types of **linkage**: internal and external. As we discuss later, the linkage characteristic differs from scope characteristic, although they look the same at the first glance.

Internal Linkage

An object with an internal linkage is declared and visible only in one module. Other modules cannot refer to this object.

External linkage

An object with an external linkage is declared in one module but is visible in all other modules that declare it with a special keyword, `extern`, as we discuss shortly.

Storage Class Specifiers

We have defined three storage classes—scope, extent, and linkage—with potentially eight different combinations (2×2×2). If we want to use a specifier for each combination, we need a total of eight different specifiers. However, there are only four **storage class specifiers**, as shown in **Figure E-2**: auto, register, static, and extern. Three factors have contributed to this reduced set.

Figure E-2 Storage class specifiers

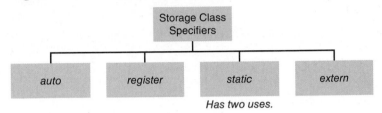

1. The scope is not defined, it is understood. The place where an object is declared defines the scope.

2. Not all combinations are logically possible.

3. One specifier, static, is used for two different purposes. The scope shows what it defines.

In the rest of the section, we discuss these specifiers only when applied to variables. The application of these specifiers to other objects, such as functions, is similar.

Auto Variables

A variable with an ***auto*** specification has the following storage characteristic:

```
Scope: block      Extent: automatic    Linkage: internal
```

In other words, the variable must be declared in a block. Each time the declaration is encountered, it is re-created. It is visible only in the source file in which it is declared. Most of the variables we have declared so far are *auto* storage class. This type of specifier is so prevalent that C allows us to omit the specifier.

Initialization

An auto variable can be initialized where it is defined or left uninitialized. If initialized, it receives the same initialization value each time it is created. If it is not initialized, its value will be undefined every time it is born. When the auto variable is not initialized, its value is unpredictable. **Program E-1** shows the use of the auto variables.

> ## Program E-1 | Demonstration of auto Variables

```
1    /* Show the use of auto variables
2       Written by:
3       Date:
4    */
5    #include <stdio.h>
6    int main (void)
7    {
```

(continue)

Program E-1   Demonstration of auto Variables *(continued)*

```
 8  //       Statements
 9  for (int i = 1; i <= 3; i++)
10  {
11      int x = 1;
12      x++;
13      printf ("Value of x in iteration %d is: %d\n",
14               i, x);
15  } // for
16  return 0;
17  } // main
```

Both i and x are auto variables. The declaration of i is encountered only once (for loop initialization), but the declaration of x is encountered three times. Each time the program encounters the declaration for x, it is initialized to 1 again.

> The keyword auto does not have to be explicitly coded. Each time a variable of block scope with no specifier is encountered, it defaults to auto.

Register Variables

A **register** storage class is the same as the auto class with only one difference. The declaration includes a recommendation to the compiler to use a central processing unit (CPU) register for the variable instead of a memory location. This is done for efficiency. The time required to access a CPU register is significantly less than the time required to access a memory location. The compiler, however, may ignore the recommendation. Registers are scarce resources, and the compiler often needs all of them for the program to run efficiently.

There is one restriction on the use of a register variable; a register variable address is not available to the user. This means that we can't use the address operator and the indirection operator with a register. It also disallows implicit conversions, such as might occur when using a register with mixed mode arithmetic.

Static Variables with Block Scope

The specifier **static** has different usages depending on its scope. When it is used with a variable that is declared in a block, static defines the extent of the variable. In other words, the variable has the following characteristic:

    Scope: block   Extent: static   Linkage: internal

A static variable in this context can be referred to only in the block within which it is defined. The extent, however, is static; the computer allocates storage for this variable only once. The linkage is internal, which means that it is not visible in other modules. Note that the specifier static must be explicitly coded in this case; it cannot be omitted.

Initialization

A `static` variable can be initialized where it is defined, or it can be left uninitialized. If initialized, it is initialized only once. If it is not initialized, its value will be initialized to zero. Note however, that it is initialized only once in the execution of the program.

> In a static variable with block scope, static defines the extent of the variable.

Program E-2 shows the use of the static variable in the block scope.

Program E-2 | `static` Variables in Block Scope

```
 1    /* Show the use of static variable with block scope
 2        Written by:
 3        Date:
 4    */
 5
 6    #include <stdio.h>
 7    int main (void)
 8    {
 9    //      Statements
10        for (int i = 1; i <= 3; i++)
11        {
12            static int x = 1;
13            x++;
14            printf ("Value of x in iteration %d is: %d\n", i, x);
15        } // for
16        return 0;
17    } // main
```

Note that the variable i is an `auto` variable. The variable x, however, is a *static* variable. It is only initialized once although the declaration is encountered three times. If we do not initialize x, it is initialized to 0 because a static value needs an initialization value.

Static Variable with File Scope

When the static specifier is used with a variable that has file scope (global scope) and we want to keep its linkage internal, it is defined with the specifier `static`. Note that the extent is still static. In other words, we have the following characteristic:

    Scope: file   Extent: static   Linkage: internal

Program E-3 shows the use of the `static` variable with file scope.

Program E-3 | `static` Variables with File Scope

```
1   /* Show the use of static variable with file scope
2      Written by:
3      Date:
4   */
5   #include <stdio.h>
6
7   // Function Declaration
8   void fun (void);
9
10  static int x = 1;
11
12  int main (void)
13  {
14  // Statements
15     for (int i = 1; i <= 3; i++)
16        x++;
17     printf ("Value of x in main is: %d\n", x);
18     fun ();
19     printf ("Value of x in main is: %d\n", x);
20
21     return 0;
22     } // main
23
24  /* ================== fun ==================
25     Increment and print global variable.
26     Pre Global variable x has been defined
27     Post x incremented and printed
28  */
29  void fun (void)
30  {
31  // Statements
32     x++;
33     printf ("Value of x in fun is: %d\n", x);
34     return;
35  } // fun
```

Output

```
Value of X in main is: 4
Value of X in fun is: 5
Value of X in main is: 5
```

The declaration of a `static` variable with file scope must be in the global area of the file (outside any function). If there is another declaration with the same identifier in the global area, we get an error message. On the other hand, if the identifier is used with another declaration *inside* a function, the new variable is an `auto` variable or `static` variable with block scope. In other words, in this case, we are defining a new variable that overrides the global variable making it not in the current scope.

External Variables

External variables are used with separate compilations. It is common, on large projects, to decompose the project into many source files. The decomposed source files are compiled separately and linked together to form one unit.

A variable declared with a storage class of `extern` has a file scope; the extent is static, but the linkage is external.

> Scope: file   Extent: static   Linkage: external

An `extern` variable must be *declared* in all source files that reference it, but it can be defined only in one of them. External variables are generally declared at the global level. The keyword `extern` is optional.

This design can create a problem: if three source files use the `extern` specifier for a variable, which one is the defining file and which are simply declaring the variable? The rules differ depending on whether the variable is initialized or not.

1. If it is not initialized, then the first declaration seen by the linkage editor is considered the definition and all other declarations reference it. **Figure E-3** contains an example of an external reference used in three programs.

2. If an initializer is used with a global definition, it is the defining declaration.

It is an error if two external variables are initialized. It is also an error to use the same identifier for external variables with incompatible types.

Figure E-3   Defining and declaring external references

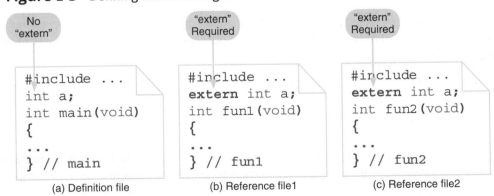

```
          No                     "extern"                "extern"
        "extern"                 Required                Required

  #include ...            #include ...            #include ...
  int a;                  extern int a;           extern int a;
  int main(void)          int fun1(void)          int fun2(void)
  {                       {                       {
  ...                     ...                     ...
  } // main               } // fun1               } // fun2

   (a) Definition file     (b) Reference file1     (c) Reference file2
```

We recommend that each external definition used in a project be placed in a common "definitions" source file. These definitions should not use the key word `extern` and should have an explicit initializer. Each source file that needs to reference an externally defined variable should use the keyword `extern` and must not use an initializer.

> The keyword extern must be explicitly used in source files that use an external variable. It is omitted in the source file that defines and initializes the variable.

We have summarized what we discussed about storage classes in **Table E-1**.

Table E-1 Summary of storage classes

CLASS	SCOPE	EXTENT	LINKAGE	KEYWORD
auto	block	automatic	internal	auto or none
register	block	automatic	internal	register
static (extent)	block	static	internal	static
static (linkage)	file	static	internal	static
extern	file	static	external	extern or none

E.2 Type Qualifiers

The **type qualifier** (**Figure E-4**) adds three special attributes to types: `const`, `volatile`, and `restrict`.

Figure E-4 Type qualifiers

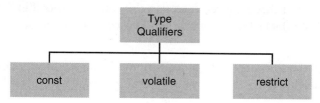

When a storage class, such as `static`, and a type qualifier are both needed, the storage class comes before the type qualifier.

Constants

The keyword for the constant type qualifier is `const`. A constant object is a read-only object; that is, it can only be used as an rvalue. A constant object must be initialized when it is declared because it cannot be changed later. A simple constant is shown below:

```
const double PI = 3.1415926;
...
PI = 3.142 ; // Invalid
```

In addition to the simple types, arrays, structures, and unions can also be defined as constant. In these cases, all their component elements are constants. For example, in the string constant shown below, none of the individual elements can be changed.

```
const char str[] = "Hello";
```

Pointers and Constants

Pointers can also be defined as constants. Depending on how they are coded, however, three different variations can occur.

1. The pointer itself is constant.
2. The object being pointed to is constant.
3. Both the pointer and its object are constants.

Case I: Pointer Constant

When the keyword `const` is associated with the identifier, that is, it is placed after the type and before the identifier, the pointer itself is a constant. This means that its contents cannot be changed after being initialized. In other words, the pointer can only point to the object that it was pointing to during initialization; it cannot point to another object. In this case, it is an error to use the pointer as an lvalue.

```
int a;
int b;
int* const ptr = &a;
ptr = &b; // Error: ptr is constant
```

Case II: Object Is Constant

When the keyword const is associated with the type, that is, it is placed before the type, then the object being referenced is a constant, but the pointer itself is not. So, while we can change the value in the pointer (address), we cannot dereference the operator as an lvalue. In other words, we cannot change the value of the variable through this pointer. Consider the following definitions:

```
int a = 5;
const int* ptr= &a;
*ptr = 21; // Error: pointing to constant
```

Case III: Both Pointer and Object Are Constant

To indicate that both the pointer and the object that it points to are constant, use the keyword const twice.

```
int a = 5;
int b = 3;
const int* const p = &a;
*p = 5; // Invalid: object of p is a
```

constant

```
p = &b; // Invalid: p is a constant
```

Volatile

The *volatile* qualifier tells the computer that an object value may be changed by entities other than this program. Normally, objects used in a program belong only to the C compiler. When the compiler owns an object, it can store and handle it in any way necessary to optimize the program. As an example, a C compiler may think that it is more efficient to remove an object from RAM memory and put it in a register.

However, sometimes objects must be shared between your program and some other facilities outside the C program, for example, some input/output routines. To tell the compiler that the object is shared, we declare it as type volatile. In this case, we are telling the compiler that this object may be referenced or changed by other entities.

The following shows how an integer or a pointer to an integer can be declared `volatile`.

```
volatile int x;
volatile int* ptr;
```

Restricted

The **restrict** qualifier, which is used only with pointers, indicates that the pointer is only the initial way to access the dereferenced data. It provides more help to the compiler for optimization. Let us look at the following program segment:

```
int* ptr;
int a = 0;
ptr = &a;
...
*ptr += 4;
...
*ptr += 5;
...
```

Here, the compiler cannot replace two statements *ptr += 4 and *ptr += 5 by one statement *ptr += 9 because it does not know if the variable a can be accessed directly or through other pointers.

Now, let us look at the same program fragment using the restrict qualifier:

```
restrict int* ptr;
int a = 0;
ptr = &a;
...
*ptr += 4;
...
*ptr += 5;
...
```

Here, the compiler can replace the two statements by one statement *ptr += 9, because it is sure that variable a cannot be accessed through any other resources.

As an application of the restrict qualifier, let us look at two functions in the C library that are used to copy bytes from one location to another:

```
void* memcpy(void* restrict destination,
const void* restrict source, size_t n);
void* memmove(void* destination,
const void* source, size_t n);
```

The memory copy function requires that the source and destination area not overlap; the memory move function does not. The restrict qualifier in the first function guarantees that there is no overlap between the source and destination area. The second function does not; the user must be sure that there is no overlap.

APPENDIX F

Understanding Complex Declarations

The declarations have become increasingly more complicated throughout this text. Sometimes the declarations are difficult to interpret, even for someone experienced in the C language.

To help you read and understand complicated declarations, we provide a rule that we call the **right-left rule**. Using this rule to interpret a declaration, you start with the identifier in the center of a declaration and read the declaration by alternatively going right and then left until you have read all entities. **Figure F-1** is a representation of the basic concept.

Figure F-1 Right-Left Rule Concept

| 6 | 4 | 2 | start here | 1 | 3 | 5 |

We will begin with some simple examples and proceed to the more complicated.

1. Consider the simple declaration

   ```
   int x;
   ```
   This is read as "x is # an integer." The pound sign (#) is just a placeholder to show that there is no entity to be considered. It is ignored when read.

   ```
   int        x          #
   ↑          ↑          ↑
   2          0          1
   ```
   Since there is nothing on the right, we simply go left.

2. Now consider the example of a pointer declaration. This example is read as "p is # a pointer # to integer."

   ```
   int    *      p    #      #
   ↑      ↑      ↑    ↑      ↑
   4      2      0    1      3
   ```
   Note that we keep going right even when there is nothing there until all the entities on the left have been exhausted.

3. In the next example, we have an equal number of entities on the right and the left.

```
int        table      [4];
 ↑           ↑          ↑
 2           0          1
```

This declaration is read as "table is an array of 4 integers."

4. Regardless of how many dimensions are in an array, it is considered as one element in the rule. Therefore, given the following declaration of a multidimensional array:

```
int        table      [4][5];
 ↑           ↑          ↑
 2           0          1
```

it is read as "table is a [4][5] array of integers."

5. The next example is quite difficult and is often misread. In this declaration, we have an array of pointers to integers. The structure is seen in **Figure F-2a**.

```
int        *        aryofPtrs      [5]        #;
 ↑         ↑            ↑            ↑          ↑
 4         2            0            1          3
```

It is read as "aryofPtrs is an array of 5 pointers to # integer."

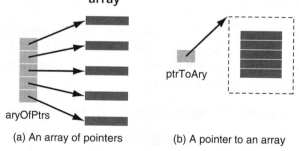

Figure F-2 Array of pointers versus pointer to array

aryOfPtrs   ptrToAry

(a) An array of pointers   (b) A pointer to an array

6. By using parentheses, we change the previous example to a pointer to an array of five integers. In this case, the pointer is to the whole array, not just one element in it. (See **Figure F-2b**.)

```
int             (*ptrtoAry #)        [5];
 ↑         ↑        ↑       ↑          ↑
 4         2        0       1          3
```

This declaration is read "ptrToAry is # a pointer to an array of 5 integers."

7. This example deals with function declarations. Here, we see a simple prototype for a function that returns an integer.

```
int        doIt       (...);
 ↑           ↑           ↑
 2           0           1
```

This declaration is read as "doIt is a function returning an integer."

8. The final example shows a function returning a pointer to an integer.

```
int        *        doIt       (int)        #;
 ↑         ↑           ↑          ↑           ↑
 4         2           0          1           3
```

This example is read "doIt is a function returning a pointer to # an integer."

GLOSSARY

A

absolute value   The magnitude of a number regardless of its sign. In C: abs.

abstract data type (ADT)   A data declaration and a set of operators that are allowed on the data, encapsulated as a type.

actual parameters   The parameters in the function-calling statements that contain the values to be passed to the function.

additive expressions   In C, the binary addition and subtraction expressions.

address list   In C, a function parameter list that consists of variable addresses.

address operator   In C, the ampersand (&).

afferent module   A module whose processing is directed toward the central transform; that is, a module that gathers data to be transmitted toward the central processing functions of a module.

Agile   A software development methodology that takes an adaptive, iterative approach to software development.

***all* inquiry**   An algorithm that determines if all data items in a list meet some criteria.

alternate flag   The data formatting flag used with real, engineering, hexadecimal, and octal conversion codes indicating that an alternative presentation should be used.

analysis phase   The phase in the waterfall development model in which the systems analyst explores different solutions to the problem.

ancestor   A node other than root that is a parent of another node in the path.

***any* inquiry**   An algorithm that determines if any data item in a list meet some criteria.

append mode   In file processing, the mode that adds to the end of a file.

application software   Computer software developed to support a specific user requirement. *See also* system software.

application-specific software   Any application software that can be used for only one purpose, such as an accounting system.

arc   A directed line in a graph.

array   A sequenced collection of elements of the same data type.

array of pointers   An array of addresses, often used to represent a sparse array.

ASCII   The American Standard Code for Information Interchange. An encoding scheme that defines control characters and graphic characters for the first 128 values in a byte. The first 128 characters in Unicode.

assembly languages   Programming languages with one-for-one correspondence between the symbolic instruction sets and the computer's machine language.

assignment expression   An expression containing the assignment operator (=) that results in the value of the expression being placed into the left operand.

Associativity   The parsing direction used to evaluate an expression when all operators have an equal priority. *See also* left-to-right associativity, right-to-left associativity, and precedence.

atomic data   Data that cannot be meaningfully subdivided.

auxiliary storage   Storage outside main memory used for permanent data storage, including external storage. Also known as secondary storage.

auxiliary storage devices   Secondary memory or storage such as hard disk, optical disks, CDs, DVDs, and tape.

B

backtracking algorithm   A method for solving problems recursively by incrementally solving the problem one part at a time, eliminating failed solutions.

base case   The statement that ends execution of a recursive function.

batch update   An update process in which transactions are gathered over time for processing as a unit. Batch update is the antonym to online update.

bidirectional communication Communication between a calling and called function in which data flows in both directions, that is, from the calling function to the called function and then from the called function to the calling function.

big-O analysis The analysis of an algorithm that measures efficiency using big-O notation rather than mathematical precision.

binary expressions Expressions containing one operator and two operands.

binary files Files that consist of a collection of data stored in the internal format of the computer. *See also* text file.

Binary recursion A recursion type in which a function contains only two calls to itself.

binary search A search algorithm in which the search value is located by repeatedly dividing the list in half.

binary search tree A binary tree in which: (1) the keys in the left subtree are all less than the root key, (2) the keys in the right subtree are greater than or equal to the root key, and (3) the subtrees are all binary search trees.

binary stream A stream in which data is represented as it is stored in the memory of a computer.

binary tree A tree in which no node can have more than two children or siblings.

bitwise operators A set of operators that operate on individual bits. The two categories of bitwise operators are logical and shift.

Blackbox testing Testing based on the system requirements rather than a knowledge of the program. *See also* whitebox testing.

block In C, a group of statements enclosed in braces { ... }.

block comment A comment that can span one or more lines. *See also* line comment.

Boolean A variable or expression that can assume only the values `true` or `false`.

branch and bound A method of partitioning a problem into valid solutions of the subproblems.

branches In computer science, subtrees (children of a tree).

breadth-first traversal A graph traversal in which nodes adjacent to the current node (siblings) are processed before their descendants.

break statement A C statement that causes a `switch` or `loop` statement to terminate.

brute force algorithm An algorithm that tries all possible solutions for a problem.

bubble sort A sort algorithm in which each pass through the data moves (bubbles) the lowest element to the beginning of the unsorted portion of the list.

buffer (1) Hardware, usually memory, used to synchronize the transfer of data to and from main memory. (2) Memory used to hold data that have been read before they are processed, or data that are waiting to be written.

C

called function In a function call, the function to which control is passed.

called module A routine that is called from another routine known as a calling module.

calling function In a function call, the function that invokes the call.

calling module A routine that calls another routine.

case label The `CASE` keyword followed by a statement.

cast A C operator that changes the type of an expression.

ceiling The smallest integral value that is larger than a floating-point value.

central processing unit (CPU) The part of a computer that contains the control components—that is, the part that interprets instructions. In a personal computer, a microchip containing a control unit and an arithmetic-logical unit.

central transforms The modules of a program that take input and convert it to output. *See also* afferent module and efferent module.

character constant A constant that defines one character enclosed in two single quotes.

character set The set of values in a computer's alphabet.

child A node in a tree or a graph that has a predecessor.

classifying function A standard C character function that classifies a character according to C's character taxonomy, such as "printable" or "alphanumeric."

client In a client/server network, the computer that provides the basic application computing; the computer residing in the user's physical area.

client/server A computer system design in which two separate computers control an application, one providing the basic application computing (the client) and the other providing auxiliary services, such as database access (the server).

close function The function that concludes the writing of a file by writing any pending data to the file and then making it unavailable for processing.

code phase The phase in the waterfall development model in which a programmer begins writing the code.

cohesion The attribute of a module that describes how closely the processes within a module are related to each other.

coincidental cohesion The cohesion level in which totally unrelated processes are combined into a module.

comma expression The last (lowest precedence) expression in C; used to combine multiple expressions into one expression statement.

comma operator In C, the operator that connects multiple statements in one expression.

comments In a C program, notes to the program reader that are ignored by the compiler.

Communicational cohesion The processes in a module that are related only in that they share the same data.

compilation The process used to convert a source program into machine language.

compiler System software that converts a source program into executable object code; traditionally associated with high-level languages.

complemented if ... else In a set of values with two symmetric sections, the operation that gives the counterpart of the current value; that is, the value in the other section. For example, the complement of a number is a number with the same value and the sign reversed. The complement of a binary digit is the other binary digit. The complement of a logical value (`true` or `false`) is the other value.

complex expression An expression that may contain more than one operator.

complex type A data type consisting of a real and an imaginary type and representing a complex number in mathematics.

composite data Data that are built on other data structures; that is, data that can be broken down into discrete atomic elements.

compound statement A sequence of statements enclosed in braces. *See also* block.

computer language Any of the syntactical languages used to write programs for computers, such as machine language, assembly language, C, COBOL, and FORTRAN.

computer system The set of computer hardware and software that make it possible to use a computer.

conditional expression In C, a shorthand form of a two-way selection.

connected graph A graph, which when direction is suppressed, has a path from any vertex to any other vertex.

constant A data value that cannot change during the execution of the program. *See also* variable.

content coupling Communication in which one function refers directly to the data or statements in another function; best practice is to never use content coupling.

continue statement In C, a statement that causes the remaining code in a loop iteration to be skipped.

control coupling The passing of flags that may be used to direct the logic flow of a function; closely resembles data coupling except that a flag is being passed rather than data.

conversion code In formatted input and output, the code in the format specification that identifies the data type.

conversion rank A data type's position in C's conversion ranking system, which is the system that determines the type of data of an expression with mixed data types.

conversion specifications The specifications that define how data are to be represented in an input or output operation.

converting functions C character functions that convert lowercase alphabetic characters to uppercase, or vice versa.

counter-controlled loop A looping technique in which the number of iterations is controlled by a count; in C, the `for` statement. *See also* event-controlled loop.

D

dangling else A code sequence in which there is no `else` statement for one of the `if` statements in a nested `if`.

data coupling   Communication between modules in which only the required data are passed; considered the best form of coupling.

data encapsulation   A programming principle that has as its objective protecting data from accidental destruction by parts of a program that don't need access to the data. *See also* data hiding.

data flow   In a structure chart, an indicator identifying data input to or output from a module.

data hiding   The principle of structured programming in which data are available to a function only if it needs them to complete its processing; data not needed are "hidden" from view. *See also* data encapsulation.

data structure   The syntactical representation of data organized to show the relationship among the individual elements; a collection of elements and the relationships among them.

De Morgan's rule   A rule used to complement a logical expression.

declaration section   In C, the association of a name with an object, such as a type, variable, structure, or function.

decomposition   The process of breaking a complex problem/program into small parts or modules.

default label   In C, the entry point to the code that is to be executed if none of the case values match the switch expression.

Definitions   In C, the process that reserves memory for named objects, such as a variable or constant.

degree   The number of lines associated with a node in a graph.

delimited string   A string terminated by a nondata character, such as the null character in C.

delimiter   The character or token that identifies the end of a structure.

demotion   An implicit type conversion in which the rank of an expression is temporarily reduced to match other elements of the expression.

dependent statement   A program statement, such as the true action in an `if` statement, whose execution is controlled by another statement.

depth-first traversal   A traversal in which all of a node's descendants are processed before any adjacent nodes (siblings).

dequeue   An operation that deletes an element from a queue.

descendant   Any node in a path from the current node to a leaf.

design phase   The phase in the waterfall development model in which the systems analyst decides how the program will look.

development software   Any computer tool used to develop software, such as, but not limited to, compilers, debuggers, and documentation tools.

directed graph (digraph)   A graph in which direction is indicated on the lines (arcs).

distributed computing environment   An environment that provides a seamless integration of computing functions between different servers and clients.

divide and conquer   The process of breaking up a big problem into smaller ones; by solving the small problems, a solution to the larger problem is found.

downward communication   Data flow from the calling function toward the called function.

dynamic array   An array that has been allocated in the heap during the execution of the program.

Dynamic memory allocation   Memory whose location is determined at run time.

dynamic programming   An algorithmic method of optimizing a solution by breaking a problem into subproblem using the divide-and-conquer strategy.

E

edge   A line, with no direction (arrow head), in an undirected graph.

efferent module   A module whose processing is directed away from the central transform; that is, a module that predominantly disposes of data by reporting or writing to a file.

end of file   An indicator that the file contains no more data.

end-of-file (EOF) marker   A flag set to indicate that a file is at the end.

enqueue   An operation that inserts an element into a queue.

enumerated type   A user-defined type based on the standard integer type.

enumeration constant   The identifier associated with a value in an enumeration declaration.

error report file   In a file-update process, a report of errors detected during the update.

error state The state of a file that occurs when a program issues an impossible command, such as a read command while the file is in a write state, or when a physical device failure occurs; one of three states that an open file may assume. *See also* read state, write state.

escape character In C, the backslash (\) character used to identify a special interpretation for the character that follows it.

event-controlled loop A loop whose termination is predicated upon the occurrence of a specified event. *See also* counter-controlled loop.

exchanging values The logic used to exchange the values in two variables.

exclusive *or* A binary logical operation in which the result is true only when one of the operands is true and the other is false.

executable program A program that can be read and loaded into memory in order to execute coded instructions.

explicit type conversion The conversion of a value from one type to another through the cast operator.

expression A sequence of operators and operands that reduces to a single value.

expression statement An expression terminated by a semicolon.

F

factorial The product of all positive integers less than or equal to *n*.

factoring The process of dividing a function into smaller functions to simplify development.

fan out An attribute of a module that describes the number of submodules it calls.

Fibonacci sequence The series of numbers in which the next number is found by adding the last two numbers.

field The smallest named unit of data that has meaning in describing information. A field may be either a variable or a constant.

field width In a field specification, the specification of the maximum input width or minimum output width for formatted data.

file A named collection of data stored on an auxiliary storage device.

file mode A designation of a file's input and/or output capability; files may be opened for reading, writing, appending, or updating.

filename The operating system name of a file on an auxiliary storage device.

first in—first out (FIFO) A data-structure-processing sequence in which data are processed in the order that they are received.

fixed-length array An array in which the number of elements are predetermined during the declaration/definition. *See also* variable-length array.

fixed-length string A string whose size is constant regardless of the number of characters stored in it.

flag modifier The input/output format specification that suppresses input or modifies output formatting.

flags Indicators used in a program to designate the presence or absence of a condition.

flipping bits Changing a bit from a 0 to a 1 or a 1 to a 0.

floating-point types Data types that declare an identifier is a number that contains both an integral and a fraction.

floor The largest integral number smaller than a floating-point value.

flowchart A program design tool in which standard graphical symbols are used to represent the logical flow of data through a function.

formal parameter list The declaration of parameters in a function header.

format control string In a formatted input/output function, the string that is used for formatting data.

frequency array An array that contains the number of occurrences of a value or of a range of values. *See also* histogram.

front When used to refer to a list, a pointer or index that identifies the first element.

function body The part of a function that contains the local definitions and statements; all of a function except the header declaration. *See also* function header.

function call An expression that involves the execution of a function.

function declaration Statement that describes a function's return type, name, and formal parameters.

function definition The implementation of a function declaration.

function header In a function definition, that part of the function that supplies the return type, function identifier, and formal parameters. *See also* function body.

functional cohesion A module in which all of the processing is related to a single task. The highest level of cohesion.

functions Named blocks of code that perform a process within a program; an executable unit of code, consisting of a header, function name, and a body, that is designed to perform a task within the program.

G

general case The statement in a recursive function in which the function calls itself; with each recursion step, it moves toward the base case.

General recursion A recursive function that is not easily converted to an iterative function.

general-purpose software Software, such as a spreadsheet, that can be used in multiple applications.

global coupling Communication between different modules using data accessible to all modules in a program; considered to be a very poor communications technique for intraprogram communication.

global declaration section The declaration and/or definition of a variable or function outside the boundaries of any function—that is, before main or between function definitions. Contrast with local declaration.

graph A nonlinear list in which each element can have zero, one, or more predecessors and zero, one, or more successors.

greedy thief algorithm An algorithm that solves a problem by selecting the parts of the solutions with the most benefits for the greedy person but which is not necessarily an optimal solution.

H

hard copy Any computer output that is printed on paper or printed to other readable mediums such as microfiche. *See also* soft copy.

hardware Any of the physical components of a computer system, such as the keyboard or a printer.

header files In C, files consisting of prototype statements and other declarations and placed in a library for shared use.

Heap memory A pool of memory that can be used to dynamically allocate space for data while the program is running.

high-level languages Portable programming languages designed to allow the programmer to concentrate on the application rather than the structure of a particular computer or operating system.

histogram A graphical representation of a frequency distribution. *See also* frequency array.

I

identifier The name of an object. In C, identifiers can consist only of digits, letters, and the underscore.

imaginary type The data type in C that can represent an imaginary number in mathematics.

implicit type conversion The automatic conversion of data from one type to another when required within a C program. *See also* explicit type conversion.

include In C, a preprocessor command that specifies a library file to be inserted into the program.

indegree In a tree or graph, the number of lines entering a node.

index The address of an element within an array. *See* subscript.

indirect recursion A recursion method in which recursive function A calls recursive function B, and recursive function C calls function A.

indirection operator (*) A pointer to the content of the variable or constant it is pointing to; a unary operator whose operand must be a pointer value.

infinite loop A loop that does not terminate.

information hiding A structured programming concept in which the data structure and the implementation of its operations are not known by the user.

initialization The process of assigning values to a variable at the beginning of a program or a function.

initializer In C, any value assigned to a constant or variable when it is defined.

inorder traversal A binary tree traversal in which the root is processed after the left subtree and before the right subtree.

input Data flowing into the computer system.

input device A device, such as a keyboard, that provides data to be read by a program.

inquiry A request for information from a program.

insertion sort A sort algorithm in which the first element from the unsorted portion of the list is inserted into its proper position relative to the data in the sorted portion of the list.

integral types Data types that can store only whole numbers.

intelligent data names The software engineering principle that requires the identifier to convey the meaning or use of an object.

J

Justification An output formatting parameter that controls the placement of a value when it is shorter than the specified output width.

justification flag A flag that determines whether the specified variable is printed left- or right-justified.

K

key One or more fields used to identify a record (structure).

key-sequenced lists Lists in which the data items are ordered based on the value of a key.

keywords The set of words in C that have a predetermined interpretation and cannot be used in the definition of an object.

KISS Abbreviation for "Keep it simple and short."

L

last in—first out (LIFO) A data-structure-processing sequence in which data are processed in the reverse order that they are received.

Latin character set The extended ASCII character set in Unicode.

Left-to-right associativity The evaluation of an expression that parses from the left to the right. *See also* right-to-left associativity.

length-controlled string A variable-length string function in which the data are identified by a structural component containing the length of the data.

limit-test expression In a loop, the expression that determines if the loop will continue or stop.

line comment A comment that spans only to the end of the current line. *See also* block comment.

linear list A list structure in which each element, except the last, has a unique successor.

Linear recursion A recursive function that has only one call to itself; linear recursion is the same as single recursion.

linear search A search technique used with a linear list in which the searching begins at the first element and continues until the value of an element equal to the value being sought is located, or until the end of the list is reached.

linked list A linear list structure in which the ordering of the elements is determined by link field contained in the structure.

linker The program that joins an object module to precompiled functions to form an executable program.

links In a list structure, the fields that identify the next element(s) in the list.

list A set of related data.

literal An unnamed constant coded in an expression.

loader The operating system function that fetches an executable program into memory for running.

local variables Variables that are defined within a function in contrast with global variables.

Logical cohesion A design attribute that describes a module in which the processing within the module is related only by the general type of processing being done; considered unacceptable design in structured programming.

logical operators The C operators (&&, | |, !) used in logical expressions.

loop body The code executed during each iteration of a loop.

loop control expression The expression in a loop statement that is used to determine if the body of the loop is to be executed.

loop update The code within a loop statement or body that changes the environment such that the loop will eventually terminate.

lvalue An expression that allows the contents of a variable to be modified.

M

machine language The instructions native to the central processor of a computer and that are executable without assembly or compilation.

main memory *See* primary storage.

maintenance phase   The phase in the waterfall development model in which the programmer fixes and enhances the program after it is in production.

mask   A variable or constant that contains a bit configuration used to control the setting of bits in a bitwise operation.

master file   A permanent file that contains the most current data for an application.

memoization   An optimization technique used to enhance the performance of a program or functions by caching the results of a function call until it is needed later.

memory constant   A C type defined using the type qualifier const.

merge   To combine two or more sequential files into one sequential file based on a common key and structure format.

metadata   Data about a list or other data structure stored within the data structure itself.

module   A part or subroutine of a program.

Multidimensional arrays   Arrays whose elements consist of one or more arrays.

Multiple recursion   A recursive function that contains more than one call to itself.

multiplicative expressions   Expressions that contain a multiply, divide, or modulus operator.

multiway selection statement   A selection statement that is capable of evaluating more than two alternatives. In C, the switch statement. *See also* two-way selection statement.

mutual recursion   A type of recursion in which two recursive functions are defined in terms of each other.

N

name   An identifier given to a variable or any other object.

negative logic   An expression that begins with the negation operator (!).

nested if statement   An if statement coded as either the true or false statement within another if.

nested recursion   A function in which one of the arguments in the function parameter is a call to itself.

nested structure   A structure within a structure.

node   In a data structure, an element that contains both data and structural elements used to process the list.

nonlinear list   A list in which each node be connected to zero, one, or more than one node.

null statement   A statement that contains only a semicolon.

O

object module   The machine language instructions output by a compiler.

offset   In pointer arithmetic, a computed value that is used to determine another index location within an array.

one-dimensional arrays   Arrays with only one level of indexing.

one's complement   The bitwise operator that reverses the value of the bits in a variable.

online update   An update process in which transactions are entered one at a time by a user who has direct access to the system.

open function   The function that locates and prepares a file for processing.

operand   An object in a statement on which an operation is performed.

operating system   The software that controls the computing environment and provides an interface to the user.

operator   The syntactical token representing an action on data (the operand). *See also* operand.

Optimization   In programming, the act of improving the efficiency of resources (running faster with less memory, for instance) while increasing efficacy (providing more benefits with higher quality).

outdegree   The number of lines leaving a node in a tree or a graph.

output device   A device to which data can be written but not read.

overflow   The condition that results when an attempt is made to insert data into a structure and there is not enough space.

P

Padding   Extra zeros or spaces added to the left or right of a data item.

padding flag   A flag that determines number of zeros or spaces added to the left or right of a data item.

parameter   A constant or variable that is defined as part of the function declaration; a value passed to a function.

parameter list   A list of values passed to a function. (Note: The values may be data or addresses.)

parameter passing   A method of sending or receiving parameters between functions

parent   A tree or graph node with an outdegree greater than 0; that is, a node with successor nodes.

pass by reference   A parameter passing technique in which the called function refers to a passed parameter using an alias name.

pass by value   A parameter passing technique in which the called function refers to a passed parameter using an alias name.

PC   An abbreviation for "personal computer" that is used primarily used to refer to a computer that runs a Microsoft operating system. *See* personal computer.

personal computer   A computer designed for individual use.

plane   The third dimension in a multidimensional array.

pointer   A constant or variable that contains an address that can be used to access data.

pointer arithmetic   Addition or subtraction in which a pointer's contents (an address) are changed by a multiple of the size of the data to which it is pointing.

pointer constant   A pointer whose contents cannot be changed.

pointer indirection   The use of a pointer to access data.

pointer variable   A variable that points to the address of another variable.

pop stack   The stack delete operation, which deletes an element from the stack.

postfix expression   An expression in which the operator follows the operand.

posttest loop   A loop in which the terminating condition is tested only after the execution of the loop statements. *See also* pretest loop.

precedence   The priority assigned to an operator or group of operators that determines the order in which operators will be evaluated in an expression.

precision   In the format string of a `print` function, the maximum number of integral digits, the number of significant digits or fractional digits in a floating-point number, or the maximum number of characters in a string.

precision modifier   The print format string modifier that specifies the number of decimal places to be printed in a floating-point value.

preorder traversal   A process in which the node in the left subtree is visited first until all nodes are done; the first node in the right subtree are each visited similarly to the left subtree.

preprocessor   The program that completes the first phase of a C compilation in which the source statements are prepared for compilation and any necessary libraries are loaded.

preprocessor commands   Commands that tell the preprocessor to look for special code libraries and make substitutions in the code.

pretest loop   A loop in which the terminating condition is tested before the execution of the loop statements. *See also* posttest loop.

primary expression   An expression consisting of only a single operator; the highest priority expression.

Primary storage   The volatile memory of a computer, which requires power to retain data; also known as main memory.

primitive recursion   A recursive function that can be simply converted to an algorithm using iteration construct.

procedural cohesion   A module design in which the processing within the module is related by control flow; considered acceptable design only at the higher levels of a program.

process-control loops   Continuous loops used to control operating equipment, such as a building air conditioning/heating system.

Program Development   The system development activity in which requirement specifications are converted into executable programs.

program documentation   Comments placed within a program to help the reader understand the purpose of the program or a portion of its implementation.

Promotion   An implicit type conversion in which the rank of an expression is temporarily increased to match other elements of the expression.

Pseudocode   English-like statements that follow a loosely defined syntax and are used to convey the design of an algorithm or function.

pseudorandom number series   A mathematical algorithm that generates a sequence of numbers.

push stack   The stack insert operation, which inserts an element into the stack.

Q

queue   A linear list in which data can be inserted only at one end, called the rear, and deleted from the other end, called the front.

R

ragged array   A two-dimensional array in which the number of elements in the rows is not equal.

random number seed   The initial number passed to a random-number generator.

random number series   An algorithm that generates a random number using a random number seed.

read mode   The attribute of a file that indicates that it is opened for input only.

read state   The state of a file in which only input operations may be performed; one of three states that an open file may assume. *See also* error state and write state.

real type   A data type representing a number with a fraction.

rear   When used to refer to a list, a pointer that identifies the last element.

record   A named collection of fields grouped together for processing.

recursion   In computer science, an algorithmic method for solving a problem using the smaller instances of it.

reserved words   The set of words in C that have a predetermined interpretation and cannot be used in the definition of an object.

return   The C statement that causes execution of a function to terminate and control to be resumed by the calling function or the operating system.

reusable code   Code that can be used by more than one process.

right–left rule   A method of reading complex declarations or definitions that starts with the identifier and alternately reads right and left until the declaration has been fully read.

right-to-left associativity   The evaluation of an expression that parses from the right to the left. *See also* left-to-right associativity.

root   The first node of a tree; the node with no predecessor.

rvalue   An expression attribute indicating that the expression can be used only to supply a value for another expression.

S

Scope   An attribute of a variable that defines whether it is visible to or hidden from statements in a program.

secondary storage   Any storage device outside main memory used for permanent data storage, including external storage.

secondary storage devices   Memory or storage such as hard disk, optical disks, CDs, DVDs, and tape.

seek file   In the processing of a disk file, the action that moves the index marker to a new position in the file; in C, the `fseek` function.

selection sort   The sort algorithm in which the smallest value in the unsorted portion of a list is selected and placed at the end of the sorted portion of the list.

selection statement   A statement that chooses between two or more alternatives. In C, the `if ... else` or `switch` statements.

self-referential structure   A linked list structure that contains a pointer back to itself.

sentinel   In an algorithm, a value that guards the end of file; it has the property that its value is larger than any possible key.

sequential cohesion   A module design in which the processing within the module flows such that the data from one process are used in the next process.

sequential file   A file structure in which data must be processed serially from the first entry in the file.

sequential search   A search technique used with a linear list in which the searching begins at the first element and continues until the value of an element equal to the value being sought is located, or until the end of the list is reached.

server   In a client/server system, the computer or software that provides auxiliary services.

side effect   A change in a variable that results from the evaluation of an expression; any input/output performed by a called function.

sign flag   The flag value (+) in the conversion code of a `print` format string that indicates that positive numbers must be printed with a plus sign.

signed   A type modifier indicating that a numeric value may be either positive or negative.

simple expression   An expression that contains only one operator.

Single recursion   A recursive function that has only one call to itself.

size modifier   The data formatting token that modifies the conversion code.

size specification   An indicator in the conversion code of a format string that modifies integer and float types.

slack bytes   Inaccessible memory locations added between fields in a structure to force a hardware-required boundary alignment.

soft copy   Computer output written to a nonpermanent display such as a monitor. *See also* hard copy.

software   The set of programs, consisting of system and application programs, that provide instructions for the computer.

source file   The file that contains program statements written by a programmer before they are converted into machine language; the input file to an assembler or compiler.

stack   A restricted linear list in which data can be inserted and deleted at only one end, called the top.

stack memory   In C, the memory management facility that is used to store local variables while they are active.

stamp coupling   A communication technique between modules in which data are passed as a structure; often results in unrequired data being passed.

standard error   The text file automatically opened by C to display error messages (`stderr.h`).

state space   A set of all possible solutions for a problem used in solution-optimization solutions.

statement   A syntactical construct in C that represents one operation in a function.

statement section   The section in a program where the executable statements are written.

static memory allocation   Memory whose location is determined by the compiler and therefore preset before run time.

stepwise refinement   A design methodology in which a system or program is developed from the top down; starting with the most inclusive, each module is decomposed and refined until the meaning of a component is intrinsically understood.

stream   In C, the flow of data between a file and the program; a sequence of bytes in time.

string   In C, a variable-length sequence of characters delimited by a null character.

string constant   A constant comprised of a sequence of characters enclosed in double quotes.

strongly connected graph   A graph in which each there is a path from every node to every other node.

structure   A collection of related elements (called fields), possibly of different types, having a single name and grouped together for processing; synonym to a record.

structure chart   A design and documentation tool that represents a program as a hierarchical flow of functions.

structure variable   A structure definition that cannot be used as a type.

stub   A temporary and incomplete function used to test function interfaces during program development.

subscript   An ordinal number that indicates the position of an element within an array. *See* index.

subtree   A tree structure with a parent.

summation   An algorithm that adds a list of data items.

`switch` statement   The C implementation of the multiway selection statement.

symbolic languages   Computer languages, one level removed from machine language, that have mnemonic identifiers for each machine instruction and have the capability of symbolic data names.

syntax   The "grammatical" rules of a language. In C, the set of keywords and formatting rules that must be followed when writing a program.

system development life cycle   A model of the steps required to develop software that begins with the need for the software and concludes with its implementation.

System software   Any software whose primary purpose is to support the operation of the computing environment. *See also* application software.

System support software   Software used for nonapplication processing, such as system utilities.

systems requirements phase   The phase in the waterfall development model in which the systems analyst identifies all functionality requirements of the proposed system to meet the user objectives.

T

tag   The identifier for a structure.

tagged structure   A structure that is given an identifier that can be used to declare variables of the structure type.

Tail recursion   A type of recursion in which the recursive call is the last statement in the function.

temporal cohesion   A module design in which processes are combined because they all need to be processed in the same time sequence.

testability   An attribute of software that measures the ease with which the software can be tested as an operational system.

text editor   Software used to create and change text files, such as a word processor or a source program editor.

text file   A file in which all data are stored as characters. *See also* binary files.

time-sharing environment   An operating system feature that allows more than one user to access a computer at the same time.

token   In C, a syntactical construct that represents an operation or a flag, such as the assignment token (=).

top   In a stack, the next element to be removed.

top-down design   A software engineering methodology that divides a big complex problem into smaller parts or modules for easier coding.

transaction file   A file containing relatively transient data that is used to change the contents of a master file.

transform analysis   An analytical process that creates a program design by classifying modules as input, process, or output.

transform module   A function in a program that takes input from the afferent modules and prepares it for processing by the efferent modules.

translation unit   In C, a temporary compilation file used to store modified source code.

translator   A generic term for any of the language conversion programs.

traversal   An algorithmic process in which each element in a structure is processed once and only once.

tree   An abstract hierarchal structure that contains a root as parent of the subtrees (children); each subtree has a parent and subtrees.

turning bits on   Forcing selected bits in a field to one.

two-dimensional array   An array in which each element contains one array. *See also* multidimensional arrays.

two-way selection statement   A selection statement that is capable of evaluating only two alternatives. In C, the `if ... else` statement. *See also* multiway selection statement.

type   A set of values and a set of operations that can be applied on these values.

type qualifier   A modifier used in the definition of an object.

U

unary expression   An expression that consists of one operator and one operand.

underflow event   An event that occurs when an attempt is made to delete data from a data structure that is empty.

undirected graph   A graph that can traverse nodes in either direction.

union   A variable structure that allows memory to be shared by different types of data.

update mode   A file process mode that specifies that the file will be both read and written.

upward communication   Data flow from the called function to the calling function.

user prompts   Monitor messages to a user that request the user input one or more values.

V

value error   An input value that does not satisfy specified criteria.

variable-length array   An array in which the number of elements can be changed during the run time. *See also* fixed-length array.

Variables   Memory storage objects whose value can be changed during the execution of a program.

vertices   Nodes in a graph.

W

waterfall model A system development life cycle in which each phase of development, such as requirement development and design, is completed before the next phase starts.

weakly connected graph A graph in which there is at least one node with no path to any other node.

while loop A sentinel-controlled, pretest loop in C.

whitebox testing Program testing in which the internal design of the program is considered. *See also* blackbox testing.

width An input conversion specification that specifies the maximum width of the input (in characters).

width modifier In a format string, a conversion code modifier that specifies the input maximum or output minimum size.

write mode The attribute of a file indicating that it is opened for output only.

write state The state of a file in which the file can only be used for output; one of three states that an open file can assume. *See also* error state and read state.

INDEX